A Cold Look at the Warm-Blooded Dinosaurs

AAAS Selected Symposia Series

Published by Westview Press
5500 Central Avenue, Boulder, Colorado

for the

American Association for the Advancement of Science
1776 Massachusetts Ave., N.W., Washington, D.C.

A Cold Look at the Warm-Blooded Dinosaurs

Edited by
Roger D. K. Thomas and Everett C. Olson

AAAS Selected Symposium 28

AAAS Selected Symposia Series

This book is based on a symposium which was held at the 1978 AAAS National Annual Meeting in Washington, D.C., February 12-17. The symposium was sponsored by the Paleontological Society and AAAS Section E (Geology and Geography) and AAAS Section G (Biological Sciences).

Published in 1980 in the United States of America by
  Westview Press, Inc.
  5500 Central Avenue
  Boulder, Colorado 80301
  Frederick A. Praeger, Publisher

Library of Congress Cataloging in Publication Data
Main entry under title:
A Cold look at the warm-blooded dinosaurs.
  (AAAS selected symposium ; 28)
  Based on a symposium held at the American Association for the Advancement of Science meeting, Feb. 12-17, 1978, and sponsored by the Paleontological Society and AAAS Section E (Geology and Geography) and AAAS Section G (Biological Sciences)
  Bibliography: p.
  Includes index.
  1. Dinosauria--Congresses. 2. Body temperature--Regulation--Congresses. I. Thomas, Roger D. K. II. Olson, Everett Claire, 1910-   III. Paleontological Society. IV. American Association for the Advancement of Science. Section on Geology and Geography. V. American Association for the Advancement of Science. Biological Sciences. VI. Series: American Association for the Advancement of Science. AAAS selected symposium ; 28.
QE862.D5C685   567.9'1   79-28160
ISBN 0-89158-464-1

Printed and bound in the United States of America

About the Book

In recent years, anatomical evidence, studies of bone microstructures, and predator/prey ratios of communities reconstructed from fossil assemblages have suggested to some scientists that dinosaurs are more like large contemporary mammals than like reptiles in their behavior patterns. This evidence has led to the revival of an old idea: that dinosaurs were warm-blooded.

This book encompasses a broad range of views, from the inference that rigorous tests show dinosaurs to have been fully endothermic (like modern mammals), to the opinion that no unequivocal evidence of homoiothermy among dinosaurs has been adduced. One conclusion does emerge: a simple dichotomy between ectothermy and endothermy does not satisfactorily represent the range of thermoregulatory adaptations effected by living vertebrates, let alone the extinct groups.

Certainly the dinosaurs were not typical reptiles in form or mode of life. While there is no general agreement as to whether they were closely convergent with the mammals or uniquely adapted in their physiology, the issue, as illustrated in this collection, is generating entirely new approaches to dinosaur paleobiology.

About the Series

The *AAAS Selected Symposia Series* was begun in 1977 to provide a means for more permanently recording and more widely disseminating some of the valuable material which is discussed at the AAAS Annual National Meetings. The volumes in this *Series* are based on symposia held at the Meetings which address topics of current and continuing significance, both within and among the sciences, and in the areas in which science and technology impact on public policy. The *Series* format is designed to provide for rapid dissemination of information, so the papers are not typeset but are reproduced directly from the camera-copy submitted by the authors, without copy editing. The papers are organized and edited by the symposium arrangers who then become the editors of the various volumes. Most papers published in this *Series* are original contributions which have not been previously published, although in some cases additional papers from other sources have been added by an editor to provide a more comprehensive view of a particular topic. Symposia may be reports of new research or reviews of established work, particularly work of an interdisciplinary nature, since the AAAS Annual Meetings typically embrace the full range of the sciences and their societal implications.

WILLIAM D. CAREY
Executive Officer
American Association for
the Advancement of Science

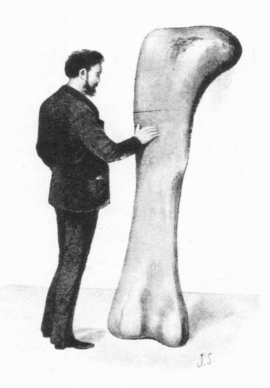

"There were giants in the Earth in those days. . ."
(Genesis 6:4)

Femur of the sauropod dinosaur, *Atlantosaurus*, contemplated
by a gentleman of the post-Darwinian period. Drawing by
J. Smit, from *Extinct Monsters*, by H. N. Hutchinson (New
York: D. Appleton & Co., 1892).

Contents

List of Figures

List of Tables

About the Editors and Authors

Roger D. K. Thomas *is an assistant professor of geology at Franklin and Marshall College, teaching courses in paleontology, evolution and historical geology. He is the Paleontological Society representative to the American Association for the Advancement of Science (Section E - Geology and Geography) and initiated and organized the symposium on which this book is based. His research interests are in functional morphology, paleoecology and the evolution of bivalved molluscs.*

Everett C. Olson *is professor emeritus of biology at the University of California, Los Angeles. A specialist in vertebrate paleontology, he has authored several books and numerous influential papers on the evolution of reptiles, vertebrate paleoecology, and the origins of mammals. He has been the president of the Society for the Study of Evolution, the Society of Vertebrate Paleontology, and is now president of the Society of Systematic Zoology.*

Robert T. Bakker *is an associate professor of paleobiology at the Johns Hopkins University. His current research focuses on data from the fossil record that bear on processes which control the direction and rate of evolution. He has published articles on bioenergetics in vertebrate evolution, energetic cost and functional morphology of locomotion in reptiles, archosaur biology, ecological diversity and species extinction, and terrestrial paleoecology and sedimentology. He has been a member of the Society of Fellows at Harvard University, and recently received the Outstanding Young Scientist Award from the Maryland Academy of Sciences (1978).*

M. E. Baur *is an associate professor of chemistry at the University of California, Los Angeles. His recent research has focused on environmental chemical factors in the origin*

*and evolution of living organisms, especially on the conse-
quences of atmospheric composition and its variation for
biological processes. A recent publication concerned a new
theory of biogenesis, involving the origin of organic mole-
cules by CO_2 reduction in early marine environments. He is
now applying quantitative models drawn from physiology and
ecology to the analysis of extinct animals.*

Pierre Béland, *a paleoecologist at the National Museum
of Natural Science in Ottawa, Canada, is a specialist in
population ecology and paleoecology. He was a post-doctoral
fellow at the Centre ORSTOM, New Caledonia, and later at
the University of Queensland. He has published articles on
the paleoecology of dinosaurs, including evidence against
endothermy in dinosaurs, and on possible terrestrial and
extraterrestrial causes of Cretaceous-Tertiary extinctions.*

Armand J. de Ricqlès *is an assistant professor at the
Laboratoire d'Anatomie Comparée, Université Paris VII,
teaching courses in ecology, zoology, and the comparative
anatomy and paleontology of vertebrates. He has undertaken
field trips in Africa in search of Permo-Triassic fossil
vertebrates and has published in both scholarly and popular
journals on the structure, functional significance and evolution of vertebrate bone. His special interests are paleo-
histology, paleobiology and herpetology.*

James O. Farlow, *a lecturer in the Department of Earth
and Space Sciences at Indiana State University, has studied
the ecology and paleobiology of vertebrates, particularly
dinosaurs and deep-sea benthopelagic fishes. He has published articles on dinosaur community trophic dynamics,
carnosaur diets and foraging behavior, and temperature regulation in* **Stegosaurus**.

Randall R. Friedl, *a graduate student in chemistry,
Harvard University, is interested in the application of
physical chemical principles to biological problems. In
particular, he has worked on the problem of size trends in
ancient animals as indications of environmental stress.*

Carl Gans, *professor of zoology at the University of
Michigan, specializes in functional morphology and evolutionary biology, particularly the functional adaptations of reptiles and amphibians. He serves as general editor of* **The
Biology of the Reptilia** *and as managing editor of* **The Journal
of Morphology**. *He is a former president of the American
Society of Zoologists, president-elect of the American Society
of Ichthyologists and Herpetologists, and is a member of*

numerous other professional organizations. A recipient of the John Simon Guggenheim Memorial Fellowship, he has been a visiting professor and researcher at numerous institutions, both in the United States and abroad.

Neil Greenberg, *currently assistant professor of zoology, University of Tennessee, has studied neuroethology, reptile ethology, and physiological and behavioral ecology. Formerly a research ethologist with the National Institute of Mental Health and at the Museum of Comparative Zoology, Harvard University, he has authored several publications on lizard behavior and temperature regulation. He was coeditor of* **Behavior and Neurology of Lizards** *(with P. D. MacLean, National Institute of Mental Health, 1978).*

James A. Hopson *is associate professor of anatomy and evolutionary biology, University of Chicago. He has spent the past year in Africa studying the fossils of mammalian reptiles and dinosaurs. His published papers concern the evolutionary transition from reptile to mammal as seen in the fossil record of mammal-like reptiles and Mesozoic mammals; the paleoneurology of reptiles; and brain evolution in dinosaurs and mammal-like reptiles. He is a coeditor of* **Paleobiology** *and a member of numerous professional societies in his field.*

Nicholas Hotton III *is a research curator in paleobiology at the Smithsonian Institution, specializing in the paleontology and functional anatomy of the lower tetrapods. His publications have been concerned with the evidence of evolution, Permo-Triassic stratigraphy and sedimentation in South Africa, diet and dentitions of extant lizards, and the function of the middle ear in reptiles, as well as various taxonomic studies. He is president of the Society of Vertebrate Paleontology.*

John H. Ostrom *is a professor of geology at Yale University and a vertebrate paleontologist. He has published on comparative anatomy, ecology, evolutionary relationships, archosaurian reptiles, bird origins and the evolution of avian flight. He was coauthor of* **Marsh's Dinosaurs: The Collections from Como Bluff** *(with J. S. McIntosh; Yale University Press, 1966). He is a former Guggenheim Fellow, a former president of the Society of Vertebrate Paleontology, and is currently an editor of the* **American** *Journal of Science and of Yale Peabody Museum publications.*

Philip J. Regal *is an associate professor of ecology and behavioral biology at the University of Minnesota, and curator*

*of herpetology for the Bell Museum of Natural History.
Recently, he has been doing field studies of lizard behavior,
vegetation patterns and ecology in Australia. His prior
research has centered on the evolution of adaptive systems
and on evolutionary processes. He has published on the
evolutionary origins of feathers, on the evolutionary significance of jaw articulation in the earliest snake fossil,
and on the functional analysis of the frog. His other research interests include biogeography, time territories and
rhythm disturbances, and temperature regulation in the
evolution of reptiles and other vertebrates.*

E. Carol Roth *is a staff fellow, National Institute of
Mental Health, and a research collaborator at the Smithsonian Institution. Her specialty is environmental physiology,
reptilian reproduction and behavior. She has published on
the evolution of the central nervous system in mammal-like
reptiles.*

Jan J. Roth *is a staff fellow at the Laboratory of Brain
Evolution and Behavior, National Institute of Mental Health
and was a postdoctoral Fellow at the Smithsonian Institution.
His previous publications have dealt with behavioral temperature regulation, reproduction in reptiles, and neuroanatomy
and evolution.*

D. A. Russell *is chief of the Paleobiology Division,
National Museum of Natural Sciences, Ottawa. His special
interest is in vertebrate paleontology. He has published
several books and papers on dinosaurs, most recently,* A
Vanished World: The Dinosaurs of Western Canada *(with*
P. Béland; *University of Ottawa Press, 1977).*

James R. Spotila, *associate professor of biology at the
State University of New York at Buffalo, is a specialist in
physiological ecology. He has published on the implications
of the body temperatures of large reptiles for dinosaur
ecology, the biophysical ecology and behavioral thermoregulation of alligators, and heat energy exchange in fishes.*

Introduction

Everett C. Olson and Roger D. K. Thomas

Dinosaurs roamed the Earth for about 135 million years, during the Mesozoic Era. A great variety of these animals evolved, including diverse and often specialized herbivores and carnivores, but the last of them became extinct, quite suddenly, at the end of the Cretaceous, 65 million years ago. While not all dinosaurs were giants, they included the largest land animals that have lived on Earth. Moreover, the smallest known dinosaurs (10 kg) were three orders of magnitude larger than the smallest mammals (10 g). Their great size, more than any other single feature, has aroused immense interest in dinosaurs, not only among geologists and paleontologists, but to an even greater extent in the general public. During the last two decades this interest has escalated to a near landslide of curiosity and controversy. Its manifestations range from books and dinosaur kits for children to continuing searches for new or more illuminating fossils, and beyond, to sophisticated analyses of the anatomy, physiology, population structures, behavior, ecology, biogeography and evolution of the long extinct monsters.

The purpose of this book is to bring together some divergent and controversial current views on the modes of life of the dinosaurs. It finds its focus in the lively debate over whether these animals were "cold-blooded" or, as some would have it, "hot-blooded". Were the dinosaurs, like living reptiles as they are usually conceived, cold-blooded creatures, active only when they could absorb heat from the external environment? Or were they, like mammals and birds, warm-blooded, generating their body heat internally? Alternatively, were these animals distinctive in their own ways, to such an extent that we have no proper model for them in our modern biota? Questions of this sort have been asked, in broad terms, for a long time. Recently, scientists in rather varied fields have begun to bring

detailed arguments and quantitative analyses to bear on
these problems.

It is no simple matter, to reconstruct the thermal
physiology of an extinct group of animals. Nevertheless,
the issue is one of considerable significance. The
bioenergetic adaptations of dinosaurs bear directly on the
evolution of endothermy in birds and indirectly on the
physiological evolution of terrestrial vertebrates in
general. Moreover, even esoteric studies of animal behavior
and physiology may yield valuable ecological insights, with
practical applications in the management of human and
natural environments. There can be no doubt, however, that
most studies of dinosaurs are undertaken almost entirely on
account of an intense urge to understand these remarkable
animals themselves. To many of us, this seems to be a
fully sufficient motivation.

Historical Background

While mythical beasts of diverse kinds have long
cultural traditions, dinosaurs, as we now know them, were
recognized comparatively recently. European , and later
American, naturalists of the 17th and 18th centuries
discovered and described enormous bones and tracks that
looked like those of improbably large birds, embedded in
solid rock. However, since the prevailing view was that the
Earth's history was short and that no species into which the
Creator had breathed life could have been lost, the
significance of these finds was uncertain. The concept of
evolutionary change was barely conceived at that time, so
such fossils generated only speculation and occasional
controversy. Early in the 19th century, the discovery of
more extensive dinosaurian remains, the development of
comparative anatomy, and the entertainment of evolutionary
hypotheses brought about a rapid advance.

The first brief reports of two major discoveries
appeared in 1822. William Buckland, professor of
mineralogy at Oxford, had found bones and teeth of a huge
carnivorous reptile, which he named <u>Megalosaurus</u>. His
specimens came from a calcareous siltstone, of Middle
Jurassic age, which accumulated in a coastal lagoon, in what
is now central England. Gideon Mantell, a surgeon and
respected geologist, obtained his specimens from freshwater,
deltaic sediments of southeastern England. This Early
Cretaceous material was more perplexing, since the teeth
clearly indicated that the animal was a herbivore, and it
was at first supposed, even by Cuvier, to have been a mammal.
By 1824, however, all agreed that <u>Iguanodon</u> was a giant,

extinct, herbivorous reptile. These discoveries, together
with earlier finds of Mesozoic marine reptiles, played a
dramatic part in establishing one of the essential
preconditions of evolutionary theories, by showing that
great faunal changes had indeed occurred.

In 1842, Richard Owen, the foremost vertebrate
paleontologist of his time, introduced the formal term
Dinosauria, the "terrible lizards", to embrace most of the
several dinosaurs that had by then been described in a
single extinct tribe of saurian reptiles. The early finds
were augmented, later in the century, by spectacular
discoveries of diverse and well-preserved dinosaur faunas
in western North America and subsequently by the discovery
of dinosaur-bearing deposits on all the continents except
Antarctica. The extraordinary variety of kinds and nearly
world wide distribution of dinosaurs soon demonstrated that
these were the dominant terrestrial animals, not only in
size, but also in the range of their adaptations, from the
Late Triassic to the end of the Mesozoic. The mammal-like
therapsid reptiles, which held sway during the latest
Paleozoic and earlier Triassic, had given way to the
dinosaurs. The Mesozoic descendants of the therapsids
survived a long and obscure evolutionary history, as tiny
primitive mammals, and did not rise to prominence again
until the beginning of the Cenozoic, after the extinction
of the dinosaurs.

Comparison of the teeth and bones of dinosaurs with
those of living animals, and later the reconstruction of
complete skeletons, led to speculation about their modes of
life, as well as their taxonomic relationships. Owen, who
entertained heterodox and obscure views on evolutionary
change, was fundamentally an idealist, strongly influenced
by Cuvier. He saw the dinosaurs as the acme of creation in
the reptilian mode, closely related to crocodiles, but
convergent in many of their adaptations with the mammals
that later replaced them in terrestrial communities.
Inferences about dinosaurian physiology and behavior can
be drawn from Owen's writings, but most of these are only
evident in retrospect. The structure of the hind limbs and
bird-like tracks recognized to be those of dinosaurs
inevitably drew comparisons with birds. T. H. Huxley,
Darwin's strongest and most articulate proponent, made such
comparisons and later represented the newly discovered
Archaeopteryx as the missing evolutionary link between
dinosaurs and birds. Later 19th century authors expanded
upon these interpretations and hints of non-reptilian
physiology crop up in their writings. On the other hand,
there was no doubt about the relationship of dinosaurs to

crocodiles, which were known to be good, cold-blooded reptiles. Most authors, until well into the 20th century, continued to regard dinosaurs as ponderous "lizards" destined for extinction, as something of an evolutionary anachronism.

By around 1850, the diversity of dinosaurs discovered and described was sufficiently great to focus interest on their classification. Several classifications appeared, among them those of T. H. Huxley and the famous combatants of American dinosaur paleontology, E. D. Cope and O. C. Marsh. Several ways of assembling the various types into three or four groups emerged. In 1877, H. G. Seeley proposed yet another classification, in which two orders, Saurischia and Ornithischia, replaced Owen's single major group, Dinosauria. These two orders were distinguished primarily on the structure of the pelvis. The Saurischia had pelves similar to those found in most other reptiles whereas the Ornithischia had bird-like pelves, as the names indicate. These groups found a natural place within the subclass Archosauria, a major subdivision of the Reptilia which also includes the primitive Thecodontia, the Crocodilia, and the flying Pterosauria. Seeley's classification has largely held up to the present day; it forms the basis for the one provided by J. H. Ostrom in this book. The two orders of dinosaurs evolved independently, from different thecodont or earliest dinosaurian ancestors, giving rise to diverse groups of animals with varied modes of life. Many instances of parallel evolution can be recognized, within and between the two dinosaur orders, the most pervasive and characteristic being the tendency to increase rapidly in size.

Apart from the tentative speculations noted above, all dinosaurs, both saurischians and ornithischians, were assumed until quite recently to have been ectotherms. It was recognized that mammals and birds had independently evolved the endothermic regulation of high body temperatures. What for Aristotle had been a higher physiological mode was now perceived as a manifestation of evolutionary "improvement". Dinosaurs, being reptiles, were type-cast as lower, cold-blooded animals. Just a decade ago, the general assumption that dinosaurs were typically ectothermic reptiles was first seriously challenged. Studies of the anatomy, behavior and ecology of dinosaurs had convinced J. H. Ostrom that these animals were much more active and sophisticated in their adaptations than had been supposed. Similar conclusions were reached, from studies of bone histology, by A. J. de Ricqlès, who went so far as to suggest that dinosaurs were endothermic. R. T. Bakker, who had reached the same conclusion, rapidly developed and extended these ideas in a series of seminal papers that have provoked both controversy and much further research. The concept of endothermic dinosaurs has also been promoted by A. J. Desmond, in his book The hot-blooded dinosaurs, which reviews the evidence and places it in a historical context. However, the issue is unresolved and the subject of much current research, as is evident from the contents of this book.

Conceptual Framework

Body temperature regulation is a physiological process, of which we have no direct fossil record. Attempts to reconstruct the thermal physiologies of dinosaurs are largely based upon evidence of the modes of acquisition, utilization and retention of energy by these animals. The interpretation of this evidence is dependent upon physiological and ecological studies of living vertebrates, which have burgeoned in recent years. Paleozoologists, using such studies and making their own analyses of living animals, are now reinterpreting fossil organisms in the light of these new data, sometimes to the dismay of physiologists whose work has been the point of departure.

It has become clear from modern physiological studies, as emphasized in several of the papers here, that the traditional simple dichotomies between cold-blooded and warm-blooded or ectothermic and endothermic animals are not altogether satisfactory. These terms, imprecise as they are usually used, refer to idealized end points of a continuum, on which lizards and small mammals lie near the opposite ends. Ostrom reproduces a number of definitions from Bligh and Johnson (1973). These have been taken as standard definitions by most of the authors here; in this area there is a fair concensus. The physiological and ecological data that bear on this problem are discussed in more detail in the paper by Greenberg.

Body size plays a central role in the thermal problems faced by terrestrial tetrapods. It is clear, both on theoretical grounds and from many experimental demonstrations, that animals of different sizes face very different problems in the attainment and maintenance of optimal body temperatures. Since most dinosaurs were large relative to other terrestrial tetrapods, this is an especially important consideration here. Several questions may be raised. Did large size impose special constraints on dinosaur physiology, behavior and ecology, or was the attainment of large size made possible by the adoption of some particular thermal

regimen? What are the advantages of homeothermy? How
critical is it that optimal temperatures be maintained
more or less continuously? Is it not preferable, all else
being equal, to reduce body temperatures whenever high
levels are not required by immediate activities?

The varied evolutionary pathways followed by divers
groups of vertebrates show that there are no simple or
absolute answers to these questions. Size is certainly a
critical factor in temperature regulation, but only one of
several. The energetic cost of maintaining a high body
temperature is great and especially so for small animals.
The cost rises in colder climates. Yet most mammals and
birds are relatively small and notably successful in cool
and cold regions. In large animals, with lower surface-to-
volume ratios, body heat tends to build up and the
dissipation of excess heat may be a more serious problem
than temperature maintenance. What then is the value of a
physiology predicated on high constant body temperature?
Why should homeothermy be so nearly ubiquitous throughout
two classes of vertebrates? Is it worth the cost? History
provides a de facto answer to this last question, in the
form of the evolutionary success of mammals and birds.
However, the pattern of evolution does not immediately show
how homeothermy is advantageous; several hypotheses have
been proposed, some of which are considered in this book.

It is possible that in directly equating evolutionary
success and a particular mode of thermal physiology we are
answering the wrong question. It is easily assumed that
birds and mammals have been successful primarily because
they are endothermic homeotherms. However, should we not
also consider the possibility that they were "trapped" by
adaptation in a physiological mode which, notwithstanding
their obvious successes, has imposed significant constraints
on their evolutionary potentials? Evolution is directed by
natural selection, acting in particular historical
circumstances. Reproductive success, not energetic
efficiency, is the direct object of selection. To the extent
that bioenergetic efficiency confers a selective
reproductive advantage on a species, in a given situation,
it is adaptive, but there is certainly no simple, general
relationship between energetics and survival. The rearing
of homeothermic young, for example, clearly is costly, but
the cost may be justified by enhanced survival and hence a
need for fewer offspring.

Largely in consequence, direct and indirect, of their
endothermic homeothermy, mammals are profligate users of
energy. Among them Homo sapiens sapiens, as a result of his

industries, his travels and his maintenance of a narrow
temperature range in the environments in which he lives and
works, is the most profligate of all. The capacity of
industrial man to manipulate his environment, in the course
of its exploitation, is orders of magnitude greater than
that of any other animal. The energy cost is high, yet
man's reproductive success, which now severely strains the
capacity of the earth to support him, is not directly
related to the level of energy use. Yet, man lies at one
extreme on a continuum from less to more complex organisms,
along which there is a general evolutionary increase in
energy demand.

Among the higher vertebrates, broad patterns of
behavior and resource exploitation are related to the
energetics of temperature regulation (Figure 1), among other
factors, of course. Reptiles, birds, and mammals have
adopted an almost continuous range of thermal physiologies,
employing ectothermic and endothermic heat in varying
proportions to maintain body temperatures that are variably
heterothermic, or homeothermic. Within this range,
individual taxa occupy more or less well defined adaptive
peaks, determined by the coordination of their physiological
and other adaptations. The study of temperature regulation
in dinosaurs and other extinct vertebrates is fundamental
to the development of a full understanding of the
evolutionary potential of vertebrate thermal physiology, as
well as its actual history.

Commentary

A principal purpose in the selection of contributors to
this volume was to assure the presentation of as many
approaches to the inference of dinosaur physiology as
possible. The relation between body size and temperature,
extensively discussed here, has been emphasized in the
published literature, but other correlates of thermal
physiology have received less attention. Individual organ
systems that are particularly important in temperature
control are the focus of some of the papers. The parietal-
pineal system is analyzed by the Roths, bone histology by
de Ricqlès. Regal and Gans discuss the blood circulatory
system, while the locomotory system of dinosaurs is analyzed
by both Ostrom and Hotton.

All these systems are, of course, interrelated by
physiological processes. This is brought out clearly in
Hopson's treatment of the brain. The relative brain sizes
of reptiles and mammals are distinctly different; most
dinosaurs fit the reptilian mode. The larger and more

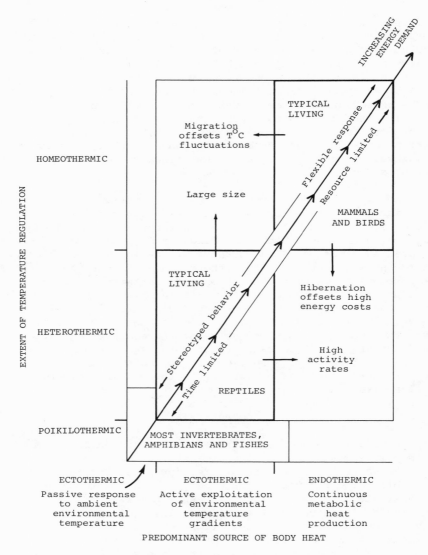

FIGURE 1. Modes of temperature regulation and sources of
body heat: schematic illustration of the characteristic
physiological ranges of major groups of animals. Ectothermy
and endothermy are conceived as end-members of a continuum,
as also are poikilothermy and homeothermy. Individual taxa
occupy more or less well defined adaptive ranges on each of
these continua. Some bioenergetic and ecological corollaries
of thermal physiology are incorporated into the diagram;
these indicate general tendencies, not absolute characteristics of all taxa within the major groups.

complex brains of mammals, which appear to be crucial to
their evolutionary success, require efficient respiration.
A continuous supply of blood to the brain is necessary,
since loss of oxygen for a relatively short time may result
in permanent damage. Thus, a fairly high level of
metabolism is required at all times, although some mammals
have evolved special mechanisms to reduce metabolic rates
in other parts of the body. Presumably, at least part of
the cost of maintaining the high body temperatures needed to
sustain this level of metabolism is compensated for by the
advantages derived from complex brain functions. The brains
of living reptiles have no such dependency on continuously
high metabolic rates. We do not know if this was true of
dinosaurs, but the reptilian rather than mammalian cast of
their brains must be considered pertinent evidence.

The physiological inferences drawn from fossils depend
upon our knowledge of the physiologies of living animals,
derived from studies such as those reviewed here by
Greenberg. We cannot put a thermometer in a dinosaur's
cloaca. Modern animals must serve as analogues, but no
really apt analogues of dinosaurs exist. Birds are directly
related to dinosaurs, but highly divergent from them, having
invaded an entirely different adaptive zone. Crocodiles
are closest in structure and phylogenetic position, but they
are semi-aquatic and, of course, not as large as most
dinosaurs. Furthermore, for practical reasons, most studies
on alligators and crocodiles have employed rather small
individuals. The Komodo Dragon, <u>Varanus komodoensis</u> is the
largest of the lizards; it provides essential data for
Hotton's study, here. It is nevertheless small compared
with dinosaurs, to which it is not at all closely related.
Most of the physiological data for living reptiles, used by
Bakker and other authors, have come from small animals, in
large part from lizards.

Investigators tend to take one of two general paths in
drawing their inferences about dinosaurs. (1) The analogy
with living organisms is used as the point of departure
for empirical projections from physiological data, back
in time to the extinct animals. (2) The characteristics of
extinct animals are assessed directly in relation to
theoretical functional models, leading to conclusions which
may be tested for consistency with our knowledge of the
physiologies of living organisms. Hotton, in his critique
of some of Bakker's interpretations, opts for the second
approach, showing how the two methodologies can lead to
different conclusions. From the second point of view, the
basic question is this: what does large size mean? From
the first, in the absence of truly appropriate analogues, the

question of size comes second to extrapolation from
physiological data, the applicability of which is often
uncertain. Many of the papers on this topic, here and
elsewhere, mix the two approaches, the emphasis depending
upon the thrust of the particular investigation.

The various writers, in seeking to answer key questions,
frequently move back and forth over different levels of
biological organization, from organ systems to individuals,
from species to populations, from assemblages to ecosystems.
Similarly, the results of physiological studies of living
animals and inferences from fossils are often intertwined.
If explicit, these shifts in focus need cause no problems,
as long as it remains clear that studies on different
organizational levels, and of modern or extinct animals,
rest on different assumptions and for the most part require
distinctive analytical methods.

The fewest difficulties arise in the area of morphology,
particularly in osteology, where similar factual data are
available for both living and extinct animals, so direct
comparisons can be made. Morphological data yield rather
specific information on feeding and locomotion. Secondary
inferences bear on some aspects of physiology, testable in
living animals and thence applicable to fossils. Erect
posture and the restriction of hind limb motion to
parasaggital planes in dinosaurs, recognized directly from
morphology, are considered by Ostrom to indicate high levels
of activity, requiring high metabolic rates and hence
presumably endothermy. Bony, porous plates arrayed on the
back of Stegosaurus and spines, cranial frills, crests and
sinuses of other dinosaurs suggest the need for dissipation
of excess body heat. Jaws and dental structures provide
evidence of diet and food gathering potential; together
with paleoenvironmental data, this may give some indication
of limits to the availability of food energy. Bone
histology, as noted by de Ricqlès, is indicative of
metabolic rates and hence of growth rates and thermal
physiology, in both adults and juveniles. Such inferences
as these provide the primary evidence as to what dinosaurs
did and how they did it.

The sediments in which fossils occur provide a second
major source of empirical data. This information extends
beyond the individual species, facilitating the ecological
interpretation of associated remains of different species
and determination of the environment of deposition. At a
single site, the types of sediments and disposition of the
bones tell much about the local environment. Roughly
contemporary sites distributed over broad areas yield data

for biogeographic studies. Successive accumultions record
the evolution of communities over time, with the changing
roles of their participating species.

The bioenergetic implications of such paleoecological
data are central to Bakker's interpretation of dinosaurs
as endotherms. Bakker argues that predator/prey ratios in
endotherm communities are and must be an order of magnitude
lower than those of ectotherm communities, reflecting the
difference in energy required for metabolic heat production.
His data show that the proportions of predator and prey
individuals found in dinosaur fossil assemblages lie within
the range of predator/prey ratios of living endotherms,
outside the range of those of undoubted ectothermic
vertebrates, living and fossil. Substantial difficulties
are involved in making such analyses, so it is not
surprising that this line of argument is more controversial
than any other current approach to dinosaur paleobiology.
Disparate critical assessments of this topic are provided
here by Farlow, Béland and Russell, Hotton, and of course
by Bakker himself.

There is disagreement both over the theoretical basis
for this argument and over the relevance of the available
data. The validity of fossil samples as estimators of
relative numbers of different kinds of once-living dinosaurs
is crucial to Bakker's case. Yet, fossil preservation is
selective and collecting practices introduce further bias.
Are these errors so large as to vitiate the results?
Opinion varies widely on the significance of the raw data,
on the values of correction factors, on body weights, and
on the exclusion of samples considered to be unrepresenta-
tive. Even if it is accepted that dinosaur predator/prey
biomass ratios were comparable with those of later endotherms, the presumption that dinosaurs were themselves
endotherms rests on further controversial ecological and
physiological assumptions. The relations of several
variables with body size are particularly at issue, here.

In order to reduce the complexities involved in the
analysis of a problem in which numerous ecological and
physiological variables interact, some authors have
constructed simplified models, based on a small number of
supposedly critical factors. These models yield scenarios
with which empirical data can be compared.

Béland and Russell have examined dinosaur predator/prey
relationships in this way, reaching conclusions very
different from those of Bakker. The utility of such models
depends on the closeness of their approach to reality,

which is often hard to assess. At the very least, they
have considerable heuristic value, yielding clear-cut
conclusions that can be tested by comparison with other
kinds of data. Other models, such as that developed by
Baur and Friedl for the ecological energetics of therapsids
and dinosaurs, are intrinsically complex. Here, acceptance
of an extended framework of simplifying assumptions and
extrapolations from the physiologies of living to those
extinct organisms is necessary, if the final conclusions are
to be accepted.

The paleogeographic distributions of dinosaurs depend
on a variety of factors, including the disposition of
continents, topography, and local habitats, as well as the
depositional environments in which characteristic assemblages
have been preserved. Mesozoic climates, especially those of
the Jurassic, were warmer and more equable than those of the
present day. Nevertheless, climatic gradients certainly
controlled dinosaur distributions and climatic conditions
must have had substantial consequences for dinosaur
energetics and temperature regulation, as noted by Spotila.
Whether they were endotherms or ectotherms, large dinosaurs
surely faced severe problems of heat dissipation if they
lived in the tropics. Modern elephants have evolved some
elaborate mechanisms to aid in solving this problem. On
the other hand, it seems unlikely that even very large
terrestrial ectotherms could have survived under cold
subarctic or arctic conditions. Among living animals, some
endotherms hibernate in seasonally cold climates, while some
ectotherms aestivate under hot, dry conditions. It is
usually assumed that dinosaurs were too large to find
adequate cover for hibernation, but Hotton argues that
Triassic dinosaurs were tolerant of drought conditions and
Thulborn (1978) claims evidence of actual aestivation in
Fabrosaurus.

Dinosaur remains have been found in regions that appear,
from geophysical evidence of paleogeography, to have been at
high northern latitudes when the animals were alive.
Although it was certainly warmer then than it is now at
comparable latitudes, it has been suggested that the long
arctic winter night would not have allowed sufficient plant
productivity for the maintenance of dinosaurs, whether they
were endothermic or ectothermic. Hotton suggests that some
dinosaurs, like many living birds, were seasonal migrants.
The concept of herds of these enormous animals traveling
north and south, season by season, is rather awe-inspiring.
Such speculations are attractive and not implausible, but,
involving extrapolation far from direct evidence of bones
and sedimentary rocks, they are not obviously amenable to

rigorous test.

It has been usual to assume that the dinosaurs constituted an ecologically and behaviorally homogeneous group, clustered closely around some physiological norm. Today, the most varied vertebrates, successful in the widest range of environments, are endotherms and nearly all homeotherms. Bakker argues by analogy that dinosaurs, since they enjoyed similar evolutionary success, were likewise all endothermic homeotherms. Formerly, the poikilothermic-ectothermic stereotype of small lizards and snakes was extended to all reptiles, including dinosaurs, more or less without question. However, it is now recognized that different species, even in fairly closely related and anatomically similar groups of reptiles, may differ widely in their thermal adaptations to particular life habits and environments. Some authors have suggested that a diverse group such as the dinosaurs would, over its broad environmental range, have exhibited a wide range of physiological adaptations. Furthermore it now seems clear, notwithstanding earlier ideas, that different thermal regimens have been acquired quite readily in the course of vertebrate evolution. It is not impossible or even improbable that some dinosaurs were endothermic-homeotherms, some ectothermic homeotherms, and still others heterotherms. The degree of constraint exerted by general reptilian physiology on the possible range of dinosaur thermal adaptations remains to be established.

All the studies in this book bear upon the course of dinosaur evolution, and particularly upon the evolution of dinosaur bioenergetics and behavior. We know certain things. The dinosaurs did evolve to occupy diverse habitats, both as carnivores and herbivores. They did evolve to large sizes; although some were relatively small, none occupied niches available only to very small animals. They did not become adapted to aquatic life, even to the extent that phytosaurs and crocodiles did. One type of dinosaur, it now appears, did give rise to the birds, which are almost exclusively endothermic homeotherms. How much can these evolutionary patterns, compared and contrasted with those of other well known adaptive radiations, tell us about the fundamental physiological basis of dinosaur activities? Bakker is convinced that dinosaurs <u>must</u> have been tachymetabolic homeotherms, to have maintained their absolute dominance of the large-vertebrate adaptive zone in the face of competition from contemporary mammals. To most authors this argument is at best suggestive, but Regal and Gans see it as an example of bare-faced mammalian chauvinism!

The evolutionary consequences of possible physiological adaptations of the therapsids, so-called mammal-like reptiles, and the dinosaurs are further assessed by Baur and Friedl and by Hotton. They seek to explain contrasting patterns of evolutionary size change and the timing of adaptive radiations in herbivorous and carnivorous therapsids, as well as in dinosaurs. Many variables and inferences are involved, relating such characteristics of the animals as their mobility, foraging capacities, mechanisms for temperature regulation and water conservation, and so on, with the availability of food resources and environmental conditions of temperature, rainfall and perhaps even the partial pressure of atmospheric oxygen. In our present state of knowledge, such studies are ambitious, even speculative, but they are intellectually stimulating and truly reflect the general problems of identifying causal factors in evolution.

The studies in this book give some indication of the variety of kinds of data and inference that can be brought to bear on the problems of dinosaur bioenergetics. By the same token, it is clear that a full understanding of dinosaur population structures, ecology, behavior, biogeography and evolution is critically dependent upon a resolution of the complex problems of dinosaur thermal physiology. No such resolution of the controversy over whether dinosaurs were scaled-up, cold-blooded reptiles or warm-blooded surrogate "mammals" is reached here, although the weight of current opinion lies between these extremes. This book will have served its purpose if it helps to clarify the issues and points the way to new lines of research in this active and exciting field.

1

The Evidence for
Endothermy in Dinosaurs

John H. Ostrom

Abstract

Several different and seemingly independent lines of
evidence have been represented, by various authors, as
indicative of internal temperature regulation and high
exercise metabolism in dinosaurs. These convergent conclusions are based on evidence of posture and gait, inferred
haemodynamics and activity levels, feeding adaptations, bone
histology, inferred trophic dynamics of dinosaurian
communities, and the geographic and latitudinal distribution
of dinosaurs. These arguments are reviewed and evaluated.
Critics of the hypothesis that dinosaurs were endothermic
have correctly pointed out that much of the supposed
evidence can be explained in other ways. However, these
other explanations do not disprove the hypothesis of warm-
bloodedness and/or endothermy; they are simply alternative,
also viable explanations of the several lines of evidence.
The range of anatomical varieties among the animals called
dinosaurs is very great. It follows that they may have
differed just as much in their modes of temperature
regulation and metabolism. It is rarely mentioned that not
all of the evidence for endothermy applies to all kinds of
dinosaurs. In fact, only one dinosaurian group - the
Theropoda - is susceptible to all the kinds of evidence that
have been marshalled by advocates of endothermy. The
probability that birds are direct descendants of theropods
adds an intriguing dimension to the subject. At the moment,
the collective evidence is highly suggestive, but as yet
still inconclusive.

Introduction

The abundance of dinosaurian remains in Mesozoic strata
around the world is clear evidence that these animals
dominated the lands of the earth for a period of close to
140 million years. There is no general concensus as to why
that was so - especially in view of the fact that primitive

mammals co-existed with them throughout their reign and also
were widespread, but never important until the demise of the
dinosaurs approximately 65 million years ago.

It is evident from the fossil record that the dinosaurs
were very diverse, with many different kinds occupying a
wide range of ecological niches. From their first appearance in the last half of the Triassic some 200 million years
ago, they quickly diversified into a wide variety of anatomical types that clearly reflect great differences in life
styles and habitat preferences. Included were carnivores
and herbivores, bipeds and quadrupeds, terrestrial and possibly amphibious forms, ranging from 2 to 3 kg chicken-sized
animals up to 60 and 80 ton monsters. Most dinosaurs were
large, weighing in excess of 500 kg, while many weighed
more than 5 tons!

The undeniable success of the dinosaurs, both in terms
of their long-term dominance of the land areas of the world,
and of their great diversity and apparently large population
numbers, has been compared to the success of the mammals
during the Cenozoic (Bakker 1968, 1971, 1972). This,
together with certain anatomical evidence, has led to the
hypothesis that dinosaurs were competitively superior to
their mammalian contemporaries, being physiologically more
like modern mammals and birds than like living reptiles.
That is to say that they were possibly endothermic and
capable of mammal-like or bird-like levels of high exercise
metabolism (Wieland 1942; Bakker 1968, 1971, 1972; Dodson
1974; Ostrom 1970, 1974; Ricqlès 1974). Not surprisingly,
these speculations precipitated a rash of contrary interpretations (Feduccia 1973,1974; Bennett and Dalzell 1973;
Bennett 1974; Thulborn 1973) and still further counter
arguments (Bakker 1974, 1975b; Halstead 1976).

The purpose of this paper is to review and evaluate the
various kinds of evidence that have been cited as being
indicative of endothermy or mammal-like thermoregulatory
physiology in dinosaurs.

Terminology

Before reviewing the evidence, it is necessary to define
a few terms that are critical for any further discussion of
the problem. The definitions that follow are those given
by Bligh and Johnson (1973), unless otherwise noted (" - ")
or emended.

Bradymetabolism. The low levels of basal metabolism of
reptiles and other nonavian, nonmammalian animals relative

to those of birds and mammals of the same body size and at
the same tissue temperature.

Cold-blooded. The thermal state of an animal in which
core temperature remains close to ambient temperature "as it
rises and falls". (The existence of only a small temperature gradient between the organism and its environment
results from the low rate of metabolic heat production
(bradymetabolism) of cold-blooded animals relative to the
high rate of heat production (tachymetabolism) of warm-
blooded animals.) Synonym: Poikilothermic.

Core temperature. The mean temperature of the tissues
at a depth below that which is affected directly by a change
in the temperature gradient through peripheral tissues.
Synonym: Deep body temperature.

Ectothermy. The pattern of thermoregulation in which
the body temperature depends on the behaviorally and
autonomically regulated uptake of heat from the environment.

Endothermy. The pattern of thermoregulation in which
the body temperature depends on a high (tachymetabolic) and
controlled rate of heat production.

Heliothermy. The regulation of the core temperature of
an ectothermic animal by behavioral variation in exposure
to solar radiation.

Heterothermy. The pattern of temperature regulation
in a tachymetabolic species in which the variation in core
temperature, either "daily" or seasonally, exceeds that
which defines homeothermy.

Homeothermy. The pattern of temperature regulation in
a tachymetabolic species in which the cyclic variation in
core temperature, either "daily" or seasonally, is maintained within arbitrarily defined limits ($\pm$ 2° C) despite
much larger variations in ambient temperature.

Poikilothermy. "The wide variation of body temperature
of a species such that core temperature varies as a" proportional function of ambient temperature.

Tachymetabolism. The high level of basal metabolism of
birds and mammals relative to those of reptiles and other
nonavian, nonmammalian animals of the same body weight and
at the same tissue temperature. (This relatively high level
of basal metabolism in mammals and birds is a precondition
for the relative stability of core temperature during

Body Temperature—Ambient Temperature Relationships

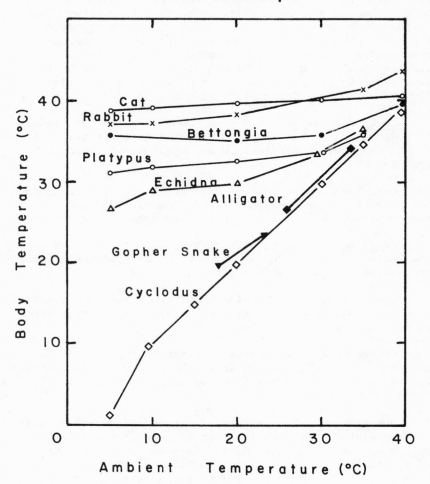

Figure 1. Comparison of the impact of environmental temperatures on the body temperatures of ectotherms (the lizard Cyclodus, the gopher snake and the alligator), vs. endotherms (the near-homeothermic monotremes, Echidna and the duck-billed platypus Ornithorhynchus; the marsupial Bettongia; and the placentals Lupus and Felis). Data from Johansen (1962), Benedict (1932), and Colbert, Cowles and Bogert (1946).

exposure to cold and of endothermic homeothermy and heterothermy.

Temperature conformer. An organism, the core temperature of which varies as a proportional function of ambient temperature; an animal without effective temperature regulation by autonomic or behavioral means. Synonym: Poikilotherm.

Temperature regulator. An organism, the core temperature of which is regulated to some extent by autonomic and/or behavioral processes. (Both homeothermic and heterothermic animals are classified as temperature regulators, having different degrees of thermostability which are defined arbitrarily.)

Warm-blooded. The thermal state of an animal which maintains its core temperature considerably higher than that of the environment when subjected to a low ambient temperature. Synonym: Tachymetabolic.

The Question

Traditionally all dinosaurs have been classified as reptiles; for that reason they have generally been assumed to have been reptile-like in their physiology and mode of temperature regulation (Colbert 1958, 1961; Swinton 1970). Living reptiles are "cold-blooded" and dependent on external heat sources - the sun, atmosphere or substrate - to elevate their body temperatures to optimum levels for activity. They lack internal temperature regulating mechanisms, in contrast with "warm-blooded" mammals and birds that are capable of adjusting their body temperatures by internal metabolic processes independent of external environmental temperatures. Body temperatures of ectotherms vary directly with the environmental temperature, whereas those of endotherms are maintained at nearly uniform high levels even at cold ambient temperatures (see Figure 1). The higher and more uniform body temperatures of mammals and birds are related to their higher metabolic rates. This is in contrast with the generally lower and more variable operating temperatures of reptiles and other lower vertebrates with their lower metabolic rates (see Figure 2). In general, until ectotherms have warmed up to optimum operating levels, they are relatively inactive or torpid, in contrast to non-hibernating endotherms that are always at optimum temperature and metabolic levels for maximum activity.

Quite incorrectly, there has been a chauvinistic tendency in some quarters to view "cold-blooded" reptiles as

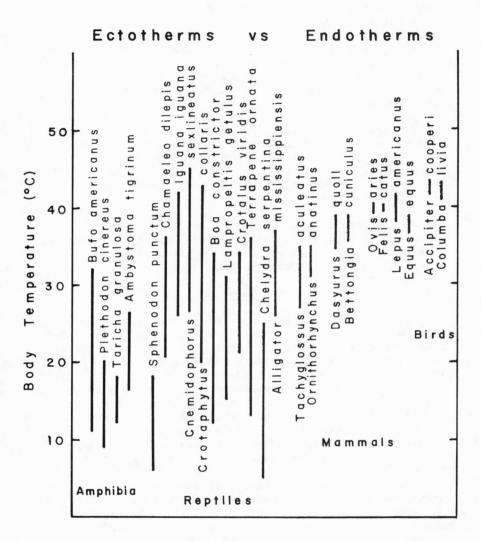

Figure 2. Comparison of active body temperature variation
ranges between ectotherms (amphibians and reptiles) and
endotherms (mammals and birds). Note that some ectotherms
experience temperatures as high, or higher than those of
some endotherms, but their body temperatures fluctuate
more widely. Data from Brattstrom (1963, 1965), Prosser
and Brown (1962), and Welty (1962).

inferior to "warm-blooded" mammals and birds. Ectothermy,
however, is a highly successful strategy among modern
reptiles and amphibians; it is not evident that the more
expensive tachymetabolic regime of endotherms is a better
one. Despite the "higher" and more complex organization of
endotherms, they are vastly outnumbered by ectotherms and
poikilotherms. Nevertheless, it has been suggested that
some or all dinosaurs - even though classified as reptiles -
may not have been either poikilothermic or ectothermic, but
rather that they were endotherms. That, according to some,
is the reason for their success.

In the absence of direct means of measuring dinosaurian
body temperatures and their fluctuations, metabolic rates
and scope, O_2 consumption, and exercise levels, we are
forced to rely on indirect evidence that may pertain to
these matters, combined with judiciously drawn analogies
with modern species. Obviously, dinosaur analogues among
modern animals must be viewed with extreme caution. The
question is this: can we determine anything about physiological thermoregulation in any of the dinosaurs?

Dramatis Personae

Although dinosaurs probably need no introduction to
most readers, it seems appropriate to include at least a
brief summary of the principals in this drama. Everyone has
his own favored classification; most of those published in
recent years conform to the one below on most major points,
although they may differ in minor details. The age and
provenance of each taxon is given, together with the common
name or a brief description of the animals. The formal
roster of dinosaurs is as follows:

Class REPTILIA
Subclass ARCHOSAURIA
Order SAURISCHIA - Mid-Triassic to Late Cretaceous.
        (All continents except Antarctica)
  Suborder THEROPODA - (Bipedal carnivores) - Mid-Triassic
        to Late Cretaceous. (Same distribution)
    Infraorder COELOSAURIA - (Small, lightly built
        carnivores) - Mid-Triassic to Late Cretaceous.
        (Same distribution)
      Family COELURIDAE - Early Jurassic to Early Cretaceous.
        (Same distribution)
      Family COMPSOGNATHIDAE - Late Jurassic (Europe)
      Family DROMAEOSAURIDAE - Early to Late Cretaceous.
        (North America and Asia)
      Family ORNITHOMIMIDAE - Early to Late Cretaceous.
        (Europe, Asia and North America). Ostrich mimics.

Family OVIRAPTORIDAE - Late Cretaceous. (Asia)
Family PODOKESAURIDAE - Mid- to Late Triassic.
   (All continents except Antarctica and Australia)
Family SEGISAURIDAE - Late Triassic. (North America)
Infraorder CARNOSAURIA (Large, heavily-built carnivores)
   Early Jurassic to Late Cretaceous.
   (All continents except Antarctica and Australia)
Family MEGALOSAURIDAE - Early Jurassic to Early
   Cretaceous. (Same distribution)
Family THEREZINOSAURIDAE - Late Cretaceous. (Asia)
Family TYRANNOSAURIDAE - Late Cretaceous. (All
   continents except Europe, Antarctica and Australia)
Suborder SAUROPODOMORPHA (Medium to extremely large
   herbivores) - Mid-Triassic to Late Cretaceous.
   (All continents except Antarctica and Australia)
Infraorder PROSAUROPODA (Semi-bipedal herbivores)
   Mid- to Late Triassic. (Same distribution)
Family ANCHISAURIDAE - Mid- to Late Triassic.
   (Same distribution)
Family MELANOROSAURIDAE - Mid- to Late Triassic.
   (Africa, Asia and Europe)
Family PLATEOSAURIDAE - Mid- to Late Triassic.
   (South America, Asia and Europe)
Infraorder SAUROPODA (Gigantic, quadrupedal,
   Brontosaurus-like herbivores) - Mid-Jurassic to
   Late Cretaceous. (All continents except
   Antarctica and Australia).
Family BRACHIOSAURIDAE - Mid-Jurassic to Late
   Cretaceous. (Same distribution)
Family TITANOSAURIDAE - Mid-Jurassic to Late
   Cretaceous. (Same distribution)

Order ORNITHISCHIA - Mid-Triassic to Late Cretaceous.
   (All continents except Antarctica and Australia)
   (All herbivores)
Suborder ORNITHOPODA (Small to large, bipedal herbivores)
   Mid-Triassic to Late Cretaceous.
   (Same distribution)
Family HADROSAURIDAE - Late Cretaceous. (Asia, North
   America and Europe) (The duck-bills)
Family HETERODONTOSAURIDAE - Mid- to Late Triassic.
   (Africa and South America)
Family HYPSILOPHODONTIDAE - Late Triassic to Late
   Cretaceous. (Africa, Asia, North America, Europe)
Family IGUANODONTIDAE - Late Jurassic to Late
   Cretaceous. (All continents except Australia,
   Antarctica and South America)
Family PACHYCEPHALOSAURIDAE - Late Cretaceous.
   (North America and Asia) (The "bone-heads")
Family PSITTACOSAURIDAE - Late Cretaceous. (Asia)

Suborder STEGOSAURIA - Late Jurassic to Early Cretaceous.
   (Europe, Asia, Africa and North America)
   (The plated dinosaurs)
   Family SCELIDOSAURIDAE - Early Jurassic to Early
      Cretaceous. (Europe)
   Family STEGOSAURIDAE - Late Jurassic to Early
      Cretaceous. (Europe, Asia, Africa, North America)
Suborder ANKYLOSAURIA - Early to Late Cretaceous.
   (Europe, Asia, Africa, North and South America)
   (The armored dinosaurs)
   Family ANKYLOSAURIDAE - Late Cretaceous.
      (Asia and North America)
   Family NODOSAURIDAE - Early and Late Cretaceous.
      (Europe, North America, Africa? and South America?)
Suborder CERATOPSIA - Late Cretaceous. (Asia and North
   America) (The horned or frilled dinosaurs)
   Family CERATOPSIDAE - Late Cretaceous. (North America)
   Family PROTOCERATOPSIDAE - Late Cretaceous. (Asia)

These are the 'players' - not in their order of appearance,
or importance.

The two orders of dinosaurs are considered by most to
have had separate and independent origins among primitive
Early Triassic archosaurs, the pseudosuchian thecodonts.

The Evidence

Several different and seemingly unrelated kinds of
evidence have been cited as indicative of warm-bloodedness,
and even endothermy in dinosaurs (Bakker 1971, 1972;
Currey 1962; Enlow and Brown 1957; Ostrom 1970, 1974;
Ricqlès 1969, 1974). The evidence can be categorized as
anatomical, histological, ecological, zoogeographic and
phylogenetic. The variety of these different lines of
evidence may be as significant as the individual items
themselves.

Posture and Gait

The majority, but not all, of the dinosaurs were characterized by upright or erect posture. The limbs were held
in nearly vertical, parasagittal positions beneath the
shoulder and hip sockets, rather than projecting out to the
sides in a sprawling posture, as in virtually all living
ectotherms. Limb-movement in a fore-and-aft, nearly
vertical plane is clearly established for both the fore and
hind limbs of most dinosaurs by the shapes of the humeri and
femora and by the design of the glenoid and acetabular
sockets. Where the head of the femur projects nearly at

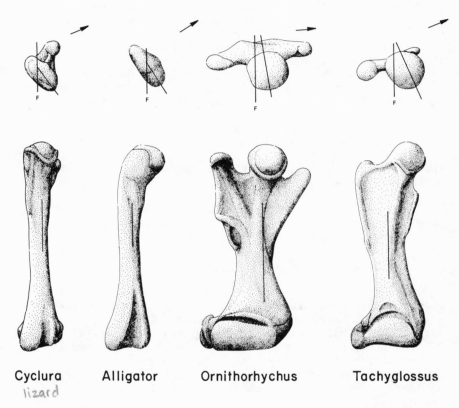

Cyclura   Alligator   Ornithorhychus   Tachyglossus
lizard

Figure 3. Right femora of selected Recent higher vertebrates viewed proximally (above) and in the plane of flexion-extension (below). In the latter, flexion of the distal limb elements is away from the viewer. All are drawn to unit length; the vertical lines equal 2 cm. The proximal views are drawn so that the plane of flexion-extension at the knee

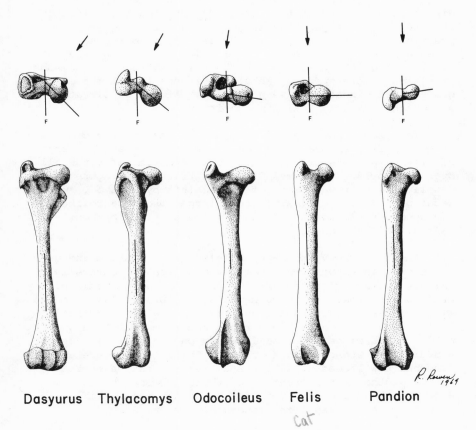

Dasyurus   Thylacomys   Odocoileus   Felis   Pandion

Cat

has a vertical trace (line F). The additional line extending to the right in each proximal view indicates the
approximate axis of the femoral head, relative to the plane
of flexion. The arrows point forward. From Ostrom (1970).
Reprinted with permission from the <u>Proceedings of the North
American Paleontological Convention, Volume 1</u>.

right angles to the shaft and in the plane formed by the
distal condyles, as in the deer, cat or osprey (Figure 3),
we know from direct observation that leg excursion is in a
near-vertical, parasagittal plane. Similarly, we know from
observation of living animals that femora with heads only
slightly offset and at a distinct angle to the plane of the
distal condyles, as in the lizard <u>Cyclura</u> and the <u>Alligator</u>
(Figure 3), are never held in an upright, parasagittal
position. Several examples of dinosaurian femora that in
life could only have been articulated in an upright, mammal-
like or bird-like position are shown in Figure 4. With some
exceptions (ceratopsians, ankylosaurs) the fore limbs of
quadrupedal dinosaurs have a form that similarly dictates
an upright, parasagittal limb position.

That such erect posture was maintained by many dinosaurs
is verified by the narrow breadth (relative to stride length)
of all known dinosaur trackways, from hundreds of sites all
over the world. The famed Glen Rose trackways (Figure 5)
display the narrow breadth of tracks left by both a
carnivorous theropod (left) and a large, brontosaur-like
sauropod, providing unequivocal evidence of the upright
carriage of both animals.

Among modern vertebrate animals, erect posture and gait
occur <u>only</u> in endotherms - mammals and birds. Conversely,
all ectotherms are sprawlers and incapable of maintaining a
true upright posture. Some mammals do "sprawl" (aquatic
kinds like seals, walruses, dugongs and whales), but no
living ectotherm can achieve truly erect, mammal-like or
bird-like carriage. Crocodilians do on occasion rise up in
a semi-erect stance, and species of <u>Chamaeleo</u> achieve a
somewhat bow-legged upright stance (an adaptation to the
narrow widths of the branches of their arboreal habitat).
However, these are rare and distinctly non-mammal-like
exceptions among reptilian locomotory adaptations.

The correlation of upright posture and endothermy, as
against sprawling posture and ectothermy, among living
tetrapods suggests that upright dinosaurs may have been
endothermic. But, as some critics have correctly pointed
out, no cause-and-effect relationship between posture and
physiology has been established. However, the correlation
between posture and endothermy or ectothermy is virtually
absolute and surely is not merely coincidental. It may be
that a metabolic regime subject to ectothermic temperature
regulation imposes a major physiological obstacle that makes
erect posture and locomotion impossible. It is true that
many mammals and birds are able to stand erect at rest at
very low metabolic expense, but erect posture has been

perfected in these forms and is well beyond any possible
"threshold" that might exist between semi-erect and fully
erect carriage. We do not know whether erect posture could
be achieved by an ectotherm, or whether the externally
affected physiology of an ectotherm is so unstable that
evolution from the primitive sprawling condition to an erect
carriage simply could not take place.

Some critics have complained that too much has been made
of the erect posture of dinosaurs, but no alternative explanation of the observed correlation has been offered. Furthermore, it is a striking fact that at least two separate and
distantly related dinosaur groups, theropods and ornithopods,
independently achieved fully bipedal posture, while a third
group, the prosauropods, was at least partly bipedal. In
the case of the theropods, this was obligatory bipedality;
in the ornithopods, the bipedal stance appears to have been
habitual, if not obligatory. I suggest that it is no
coincidence that the only living bipeds are endotherms. This
strengthens, but does not prove, the argument that posture
is controlled by physiological factors - and the key factors
here may be tachymetabolism and endothermy.

Haemodynamics

The upright posture of many dinosaurs provides another
line of indirect evidence that these animals may have been
endothermic. Skeletal reconstructions allow determination
of the vertical distance between the brain and the position
of the heart. Hence, one can calculate the systemic blood
pressure necessary to overcome the hydrostatic pressure of
that fluid column and perfuse the elevated brain (Hohnke
1973). The greater the heart-brain vertical distance, the
greater the required systemic pressure. In the case of
Brachiosaurus, with the head and neck upright, the vertical
heart-brain distance approximated 6 m, thus requiring a
systemic systolic pressure of more than 500 mm of Hg,
assuming a minimum cerebral perfusion pressure of 60 mm Hg
(Hohnke 1973; Seymour 1976)(see Figure 6).

High tissue metabolism requires high blood pressure and
rapid circulation in the systemic circuit to provide adequate
exchange of metabolites. This is especially true of tachymetabolic species. Rapid circulation within the pulmonary
circuit is required for the same reason, but systolic
pressure here must be comparatively low, in order to prevent
fluid loss (edema) or hemorrhaging across the gas exchange
membranes of the lungs. Seymour (1976) notes these requirements, assumes that the same was probably true for dinosaurs,
and concludes that at least the large forms must have had

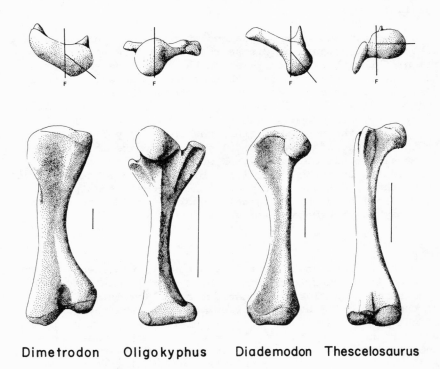

Dimetrodon   Oligokyphus   Diademodon Thescelosaurus

Figure 4.   Right femora of selected Paleozoic and Mesozoic
tetrapods, including a primitive (Dimetrodon) and advanced
(Oligokyphus and Diademodon) mammal-like reptiles and various
dinosaurs. Views and symbols as in Figure 3, except that
the vertical lines adjacent to the dinosaurian femora equal

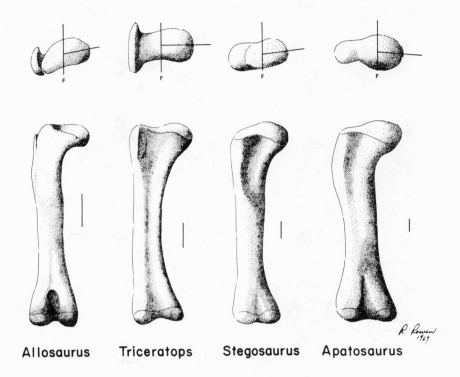

Allosaurus   **Triceratops**   **Stegosaurus**   **Apatosaurus**

10 cm here. Notice the sharply offset femoral heads, especially in the ornithopod <u>Thescelosaurus</u> and the theropod <u>Allosaurus</u>. From Ostrom (1970). Reprinted with permission from the <u>Proceedings of the North American Paleontological Convention</u>, Volume 1.

Figure 5. Trackways left by a large four-legged Brontosaurus-like dinosaur (on the right) and a large bipedal
Tyrannosaurus-like carnivore (on the left). Notice the
narrow breadth of both trackways, compared with the lengths
of the strides - proof of upright carriage in both animals.
The locality is at the Paluxy River near Glen Rose, Texas,
60 miles southwest of Fort Worth. By permission of the
American Museum of Natural History, New York.

fully divided four-chambered hearts, capable of producing large pressure differentials between the pulmonary and systemic tracts.

Several authors (Russell 1965; Bakker 1968; Swinton 1970) have theorized that dinosaurs might have had four-chambered hearts, like crocodilians, but without any evidence other than the fact that crocodiles (and birds) are believed to be the closest living relatives of the dinosaurs. It is true that crocodilians have a four-chambered heart, but the systemic and pulmonary circuits develop only moderate pressure differentials of 15 to 20 mm Hg (White 1969), about the same or slightly less than the systolic differential in *Iguana* (White 1968), which has a three-chambered heart!

The importance of all this lies in the certainty that upright posture with large vertical heart-brain separation requires a double pump, fully divided four-chambered heart, with complete separation of the pulmonary and systemic circuits. These are probably also essential requirements for endothermy. The fully divided four-chambered heart is a hallmark of both birds and mammals, where systemic and pulmonary blood pressure are very different. It is very likely that it is this common trait that has permitted tachymetabolic regimes to evolve only in birds and mammals, among all living organisms. As Seymour correctly notes, this does not prove that dinosaurs were endothermic, but it does establish that many (although not all) of them must have possessed a heart and circulatory system capable of maintaining an endothermic (tachymetabolic) regime.

White (1976) notes that non-crocodilian reptile hearts permit functional separation of cardiac sub-chambers, so that differential pressures within the systemic and pulmonary circuits may result from time-sequenced events within the single ventricle and flow through discrete channels. Nevertheless, it is impressive that high systemic blood pressures (in excess of 80 mm Hg) do not occur in living ectotherms, while all ectotherms have a very short heart-brain vertical separation, as well as sprawling posture. Conceivably, the low systemic pressure imposed by the required low pressure of the confluent pulmonary circulation may be the critical factor that limits living ectotherms to low sprawling posture and low head-heart vertical distances, as well as being ectothermic and bradymetabolic.

Activity Levels

Certain features of the skeletal anatomy of the legs, shoulders, and pelvis in some dinosaurs (theropods,

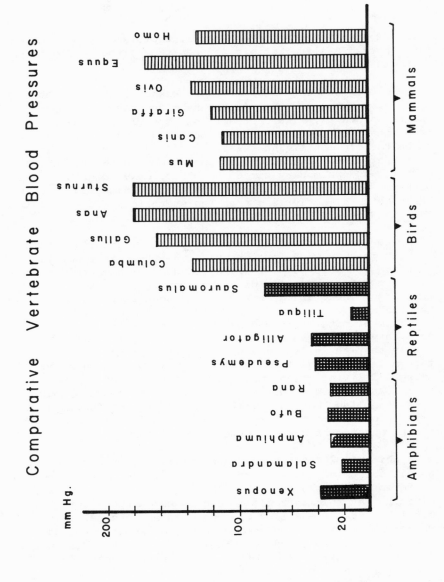

Comparative Vertebrate Blood Pressures

Estimated Dinosaurian Blood Pressures

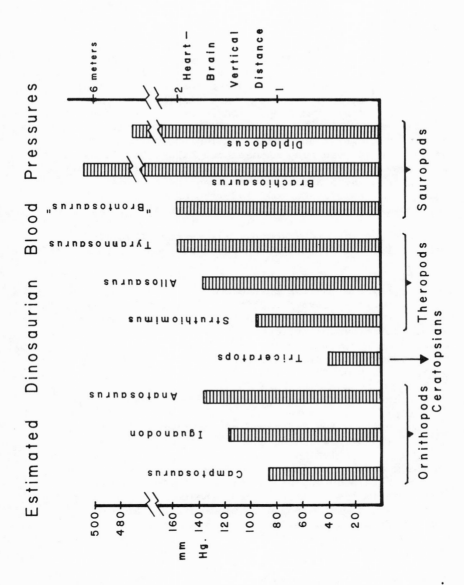

Figure 6. Comparison of systemic blood pressures in various living ectotherms and endotherms, with estimated blood pressures for some well-known kinds of dinosaurs. Dinosaur blood pressures were estimated as equivalent (at least) to the hydrostatic pressure of fluid columns equal in length to the vertical distances between the heart and the brain, as measured in the various mounted skeletons. Data from Prosser and Brown (1962), Welty (1962), and White (1976).

ornithopods and ceratopsians) have been interpreted as being
indicative of high running speeds and high levels of activity
(Bakker 1968, 1971, 1972, 1974), comparable to those of
cursorial mammals and birds. Specific features cited are
elongated limbs, limb proportions, limb joint morphology and
the capacity for acute flexion (limb joint angulation) at the
elbow, knee, wrist and ankle. All of these features are
present in fast-running mammals and birds, but it is claimed
that they are absent in modern lizards and crocodilians.
The inferred high activity and cursoriality have led some
(Bakker 1971, 1972; Desmond 1975) to conclude that an
endothermic regime was employed by these dinosaurs.

Earlier workers (Osborn 1917; Swinton 1936, 1970;
Colbert 1958, 1961) noted that some of these characteristics
and the bird-like form of some dinosaurs are suggestive of
cursorial ability and high activity, but none concluded that
they employed bird-like physiological thermoregulation.
In fact, Colbert (1958) explicitly described them to be like
modern reptiles, with their body temperatures varying in
direct relation to environmental temperature, causing fluctuations in their metabolic rates. This view was based on the
presumption that, since dinosaurs were reptiles, their
general behavior was basically reptilian.

Modern lizards and crocodilians can be very active,
and surprisingly fleet-of-foot - even without "mammal-like"
or "bird-like" limb features, or endothermy. Bennett and
Dalzell (1973) criticized Bakker's (1971) biomechanical
analysis of "galloping" dinosaurs (ceratopsians), chiefly
on their assessment that the dinosaurian scapula was not
free to rotate during protraction, as it does in mammals.
They also implied that the great shear forces developed in
a fast-running (as opposed to slow-moving) large dinosaur
could not have been tolerated by ceratopsian limb
construction. Bakker (1974), of course, does not agree.

From my own analysis of the ceratopsian shoulder
girdle and forelimb, I agree with Bennett and Dalzell
that the scapula could not possibly have swung in the
same fashion that it does in present day cursorial mammals.
Thus, ceratopsians could not have galloped in the same
way that horses, gazelles, or even rhinos gallop. As
for the significance of limb joint morphology in theropods
and ornithopods, this is clearly correlated with bipedal
(and therefore, erect) posture, which required near-vertical
parasagittal excursion of the hindlimbs. Obviously, this
could also have facilitated high speed, but it does not
prove long-term high levels of activity, or endothermy.

On a very different tangent, high activity levels
require greater motor and sensory control, and, as
Feduccia (1973, 1974) observed, this should be reflected in
increased brain size and complexity. But dinosaurs are
notorious for thier puny brains. Drawing on Jerison's
(1969) work, which described dinosaur brains as typically
reptilian in size (relative to body size) and conservatively
evolved, Feduccia concludes that the required motor and
sensory controls cannot be deduced from dinosaur endocasts.
Russell (1969, 1972), however, reported that brain size
in some of the small theropods was much larger relatively
than is true of Alligator, and Hopson (1977) has concluded
that brain sizes in all adequately known coelurosaurs and
carnosaurs, as well as in most ornithopods, were greater
that those of living crocodilians. Thus, those dinosaurian
kinds at least, may have possessed the motor and sensory
control centers necessary for high and complex activity.
Hopson concludes that

> "except for coelurosaurs, the range of
> behaviors that existed in dinosaurs, as
> inferred from trackways and skeletal
> morphology, may not have lain much outside
> the range observed in living ectotherms".

Although not explicitly aimed at the claims of high
running speeds as evidence for an endothermic metabolic
regime in dinosaurs, Alexander's (1976) estimate of dinosaur
speeds, based upon fossil trackways, does challenge these
hypothesized activity levels. Russell and Beland (1976) have
properly responded that inferences from fossil "trackway
evidence so far obtained are not yet adequate for general-
ization on dinosaurian metabolism". The admirable analysis
by Alexander deserves a much more realistic conclusion
than his

> "This does not necessarily mean that large
> dinosaurs never ran, but it seems to conform
> better with the traditional image of lumber-
> ing dinosaurs than with that of the lively
> runners shown in some recent restorations."

The restorations referred to are those of Protoceratops
(Bakker 1968) and medium-sized ornithopods (Galton 1970),
all of which are much smaller than an average-sized race
horse.

Alexander's analysis of four trackway sites should be
viewed as interesting, but of little or no relevance to the
question of dinosaurian running velocities (or activity
levels), for the simple reason that running, or even fast
walking, is not the usual mode of tetrapod (or bipedal)

locomotion. Animals walk most of the time, walk briskly or
trot some of the time, and run or gallop only under unusual
circumstances. From the point of view of energetics alone,
it is doubtful if the cumulative traverses of any individual
animal include more than 5 to 10% at velocities above that of
a walking pace. Therefore, the statistically insignificant
number of trackway sites of Alexander's study tells us only
that these particular dinosaurs walked at human-like speeds,
or slightly better (1.0 to 3.6 m/sec). Man is capable of a
four-minute mile (6.9 m/sec) or four miles an hour (1.6 m/sec)
on a brisk walk. We can come to no firm conclusion about
maximum running speeds of dinosaurs from the limited data
used by Alexander.

Group Activity

     If dinosaurs were mammal-like or bird-like in their
physiology, we might suppose that they had mammal or bird-
like behavioral patterns as well. There is some evidence
that this may have been so. In addition to the anatomical
evidence cited above, further insight into dinosaur behavior
comes from fossil footprint sites that preserve evidence of
group activity, such as multiple trackways. Bird (1944) was
the first to suggest that such multiple trackways indicated
herding behavior in dinosaurs, although von Huene (1928) had
previously suggested migratory herding behavior to explain
the many skeletons of the prosauropod Plateosaurus found at
Trossingen, in West Germany. The footprints reported by
Bird, in Bandera County, Texas, west of San Antonio, clearly
record the passage of at least 23 sauropod like animals,
walking together in a group. Bakker (1968) later pointed out
that Bird's "herd" apparently was structured - the young
individuals had been at the center of the herd, surrounded by
the adults. In 1972, I reported on another impressive
footprint site at Holyoke, Massachusetts, where a surprisingly high percentage (70%) of the trackways are preserved with
near-parallel bearings. These and other similar occurrences
are strong evidence of group behavior.

     While we normally associate herding or group behavior
with various mammals and birds, rather than with reptiles,
recent studies by Rand (1968), Brattstrom (1974) and
Burghardt (1977) document relatively complex social behavior
in a variety of ectotherms. The parallel trackways mentioned
above could be the result of truly gregarious animals aware
of the presence and behavior of others of their own kind -
and whose passage was stimulated by the actions of the group.
All this suggests a relatively high degree of neural organization, which in turn, by analogy with modern birds and
mammals, suggests but does not prove that these dinosaurs

may have been endothermic.

Feeding Adaptations

If some dinosaurs were tachymetabolic and capable of high, long-term exercise metabolism, then we must presume that, like modern mammals and birds, they required large volumes of food, at a much higher intake rate per unit of body weight than is required by comparably-sized ectotherms. We might expect to find some evidence of this in dinosaurian anatomy. In fact, some such evidence does exist.

The bipedal herbivores, the ornithopods - and especially the hadrosaurs or duck-bills - featured specialized grinding dentitions, composed of hundreds of teeth arranged in large batteries with extensive and continuous grinding surfaces. These grinding surfaces are comparable to those of modern elephants, although not as large. They were maintained by a never-ending supply of replacement teeth that erupted in such a way that no gaps ever developed in the grinding surfaces. There can be no doubt that this dental system was ideally adapted for processing large volumes of tough vegetation (Ostrom 1961, 1964) (see Figure 7).

The horned dinosaurs or ceratopsians (with the exception of the most primitive kind, Protoceratops) had similar dental batteries, also composed of hundreds of teeth and with a comparable replacement mechanism that insured uninterrupted integrity of the occlusal surfaces. Here, however, the batteries formed continuous shearing blades for slicing large quantities of fibrous plant matter (Ostrom 1966).

The largest of all dinosaurs, the sauropods, might be expected to show the most extensive specializations for processing large volumes of food, but this is not so. Their mouths are very small relative to the size of the animals, and the teeth seem poorly designed for chewing or preparing large amounts of food. Similarly, the miniscule teeth of stegosaurs and ankylosaurs provide no evidence of any capacity for enhanced food preparation in the mouth. The absence of grinding dentitions, however, cannot be taken as proof that these forms did not ingest large volumes of food (Bakker 1971), although there is no positive evidence that they did so. Their large sizes might alone be construed as evidence of the intake of a large food volume, but these animals might have been very long-lived and slow-growing, as compared with living reptiles.

Another peculiarity of some dinosaurs is the evidence that the nasal passages by-passed the mouth cavity. In

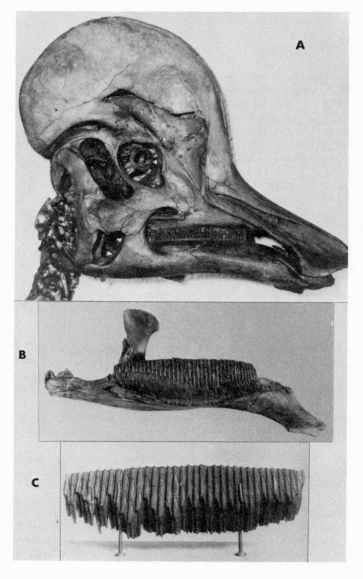

Figure 7. Skull, lower jaw and dental battery of a duck-billed dinosaur (Corythosaurus casuarius) to illustrate the highly specialized food-processing equipment of these ornithopod dinosaurs. As can be seen in C, the dental battery is composed of dozens of tightly compacted teeth forming one continuous grinding surface (upper edge).
B and C, lingual or medial views, by the author. A, by permission of the American Museum of Natural History, New York.

living non-crocodilian reptiles, the mouth constitutes a
major part of the respiratory tract, channeling air between
the internal nares in the front of the mouth and the trachea
at the rear. In many sauropods, the nostrils were placed
high on the head above the eyes, indicating that the nasal
passages descended straight down to the trachea at the back
of the mouth cavity. In many duck-billed dinosaurs, the
nasal passages ascended into a hollow crest on top of the
skull (see Figure 7A) and then descended to the trachea,
by-passing the mouth. The armored dinosaurs (ankylosaurs)
featured a secondary bony palate, with the internal nares
positioned far to the back of the mouth, as in mammals.
These conditions appear to have separated the mouth cavity
from the breathing passages, much as the secondary palate of
mammals does, completely separating breathing and feeding
activities. This may mean that food preparation could have
been carried on in the mouth without interruption for breathing - or vice versa. High food intake and high respiratory
rates are both important to endotherms.

It is reasonable to infer that these dental specializations and modifications of the nasal tracts are evidence of
large food-volume intake. Whether this large volume of food
was a requisite of endothermy and high metabolic rates, or
simply a consequence of the large body sizes of the animals
involved, cannot be determined. We simply do not know.

Predator-Prey Ratios

A continuation of this line of reasoning - that endothermic animals require greater food intake than comparably-
sized ectotherms - has led to the examination of the relative
abundance of remains of predaceous and potential prey
dinosaurs in several richly fossiliferous Late Cretaceous
strata (Bakker 1972, 1974, 1975a, 1975b). Since direct
observation of food intake by any dinosaur is now obviously
impossible, Bakker reasoned that the ratio of predaceous
dinosaurs to co-existing potential prey animals should
reflect the food requirements of the predators. From
observations of modern animal communities, it is evident that
a given number of prey animals can support a much smaller
number of endothermic predators than ectothermic predators of
similar size. Or as Bakker (1972, p. 82) has expressed it:

> "Because endothermic carnivores require prey
> at a rate an order of magnitude higher than
> that of ectotherms, the predator standing crop
> [total predator biomass] to prey standing crop
> ratio in an ectothermic predator/prey complex
> should be an order of magnitude higher than
> in an endothermic complex."

Census data of modern mammalian communities (Dasmann and Mossman 1962; Schaller 1967) indicate that mammalian predator/prey standing crop ratios range from less than 1% to something more than 6%. Comparable census data for modern reptilian communities are not available, but observations of an ectothermic predator, Varanus komodoensis (Auffenberg 1971), have led Bakker (1972) to infer a consumption rate equal to the predator's own body weight every 60 days, as contrasted with mammalian predator consumption rates equal to their own body weights every 6.6 days for wild dogs (Lycaon pictis), 7.7 to 9.1 days for the lion (Panthera leo), and 10 days for the cheetah (Acionyx jubatus) (Wright 1960; Schaller 1968). Ignoring the size differences between the Komodo dragon (50 kg), cheetah (50 to 60 kg) and lion (180 to 227 kg), these data translate into a consumption rate for mammalian predators approximately ten times that for Varanus komodoensis. This suggests that ectothermic predator/prey standing crop ratios may range as high as 60%.

A census (Russell 1967) of all the dinosaur specimens that have been collected from Late Cretaceous rocks in Alberta reveal low predator/prey standing crop ratios from 3 to 5% (Bakker 1972, 1974, 1975a, 1975b). These low values have been interpreted by Bakker as proof of endothermy in dinosaurs. Of course, that conclusion is dependent on the assumption that the predator populations were resource-limited, and that the prey populations were limited by predation, rather than by resources. Even if these two assumptions held true, which cannot be established, the predator/prey ratios of fossil communities are subject to substantial indeterminate errors (Charig 1976). As every geologist and paleontologist knows, all fossil collections are the residual end-products of several kinds of destructive filtering processes, including destruction before burial, non-random preservation, differential representation of habitats, and discovery and collecting biases. There is no way to correct, with any degree of confidence, for the effects of these errors on the collected samples. It is impossible to know what is missing.

Bakker (1972, 1975a) is aware of some of these sources of error and has attempted to correct for collecting bias. Thulborn (1973), Farlow (1976) and Tracy (1976) have pointed out certain weaknesses in Bakker's assumptions about ingest-ion rates, and Halstead (1976) notes that the low predator/ prey ratios of dinosaurs might be the direct result of their large size. However, it is well-documented that the food requirements per unit weight decrease with increasing body size, which would result in a higher predator/prey ratio, rather than the low ratio obtained by Bakker.

It is clear that the unknowns, and the unverifiable correction factors, render this approach to dinosaur trophic dynamics imprecise at the very best. The low predator/prey ratios of the Oldman Formation and other formations may reflect the original compositions of these dinosaur communities, and these ratios may be the result of high metabolic regimes and endothermy - in the predators. It must be emphasized that these ratios provide no information at all about the physiology of any of the prey animals - the other 95% of the Oldman dinosaur fauna. This point, more than any other, underscores the impropriety of viewing the dinosaurs as though they were all characterized by identical physiological parameters. As noted above, they were extremely diverse anatomically, and they were possibly just as diverse in their physiological regimes. The vast majority of dinosaurs were herbivores and the predator/prey ratios are of no value in assessing the likelihood that any of them were endothermic.

Bone Histology

A completely different line of evidence that may be related to dinosaurian physiology is found in the microscopic structure of bone. Compact bone in many living ectotherms contains few primary vascular channels - the sites of blood vessels. Such bone is termed primary vascular bone. In contrast, the compact bone of many mammals and birds commonly contains large numbers of vascular channels that are secondary (reconstructed) in origin. These are termed Haversian canals. The occurrence of such densely vascularized secondary Haversian bone in mammals and birds has been attributed to their high metabolic, endothermic physiologies, with their consequent demands for calcium and phosphorus flux from bone mineral reservoirs (Enlow and Brown 1957; Enlow 1962; Bakker 1972; Ricqlès 1974, 1976).

Dinosaurian bone has been shown to exhibit very similar densely vascularized secondary Haversian construction (Enlow and Brown 1957, 1958; Currey 1962). This was interpreted by Currey as evidence of possible physiological specialization ("homeothermy") in dinosaurs. Others (Ricqlès 1972, 1974, 1976; Bakker 1972, 1974, 1975a) see this condition as strong evidence of endothermy in dinosaurs. That interpretation may be correct, but the evidence is not conclusive. Enlow and Brown, Ricqlès, Currey, and most recently Bouvier (1977) have pointed out that the presence or absence of secondary Haversian bone is not consistent among living endotherms and ectotherms. Secondary Haversian bone is present in some ectotherms (turtles and crocodilians), but absent in many small endotherms (both mammals and birds). Since the

correlation between endothermy and secondary Haversian bone
is not absolute, we must conclude that rather than being an
index of endothermy, Haversian bone must be related to some
other factor, such as growth rates, body size, or increased
mechanical strength (Ricqlès 1974, 1976; Halstead 1976;
Bouvier 1977).

Dinosaur Zoogeography

Occasionally, the geographic distribution of dinosaur
specimens is mentioned as evidence that they were probably
not ectothermic (Bakker 1975a). The reasoning here is that
their distribution apparently extended to much higher
latitudes than we might expect of cold-blooded (or heliothermic) animals. Emphasis has been given to those discovery
sites that are now located at high latitudes, such as the
Early Cretaceous dinosaur foot print locality in Spitzbergen
(Lapparent 1962; Heintz 1963) and that where dinosaur bones
were discovered in northern Yukon Territory, Canada (Rouse
and Srivastava 1972; Russell 1973). The latter site is
practically on the Arctic Circle and Spitzbergen is within
a dozen degrees of the North Pole - environs now totally
hostile to terrestrial ectotherms.

Geophysical and tectonic evidence (Cox, Doell and
Dalrymple 1963, 1964; Vine and Matthews 1963; Vine 1966;
Isacks, Oliver and Sykes 1968) has firmly established that
the continents are not fixed but have drifted over the
earth's surface throughout geologic time (Dietz 1961; Hess
1962), in consequence of relative movements by sea-floor
spreading and subduction of rigid crustal plates. In many
cases, past positions of continent-bearing plates can be
reconstructed from paleomagnetic, tectonic and paleontologic
data; in most instances the land masses occupied very
different latitudes in past times. Precise reconstruction of
the Cretaceous geography of the tectonically complex Arctic
Ocean - North Atlantic Ocean area is uncertain, but it
appears that Spitzbergen was then situated further from the
North Pole than it is today. The Yukon site, however, now at
$66°$ north latitude, was much closer to the Late Cretaceous
North Pole - perhaps as far as $80°$ north paleolatitude. At
present, this represents the most extreme northerly occurrence (in terms of paleolatitude) of dinosaur remains yet
found. I will come back to these two sites later. The above
paleogeographic interpretations are based on the reconstructions by Briden et al (1974) and Smith et al (1973).

It is clear that the present latitudinal distribution of
dinosaur sites does not record the actual paleolatitudinal
spread of dinosaurs during the Mesozoic. In fact, as

Figures 8 and 9 show, almost all known dinosaur localities were originally situated within 40 to 50 degrees of the paleo-equator, corresponding to today's tropical to low temperate zones - the region now inhabited by the vast majority of terrestrial ectotherms. Addition of the paleo-positions of the Spitzbergen and Yukon localities increases the dinosaurian paleolatitudinal spread by approximately 25°, from about 110° to perhaps 135°. That compares with a composite latitudinal spread of 120° for modern reptiles. This might be considered important evidence for endothermy in dinosaurs (Ostrom 1970) except for the fact that Mesozoic climates were significantly warmer and more equable than those of today (Dorf 1970; Axelrod and Bailey 1968), as determined from paleobotanical evidence.

Oxygen isotope determinations (Urey et al 1951; Epstein et al 1951) provide other indications that paleotemperatures of shallow marine water, as determined from the calcareous shells of various organisms, were approximately 15^oC warmer than at present (Lowenstam and Epstein 1959), apparently at nearly all middle and high latitudes. It was estimated that the Cretaceous north polar water was no colder than 10° to 15^oC. Work by Spaeth et al (1971) showed that oxygen isotope paleotemperature determinations based on belemnites are not as reliable as had been supposed, but other studies of oxygen and carbon isotopes in the tests of both benthonic and planktonic foraminifera (Emiliani 1954; Douglas and Savin 1973; Shackleton and Kennett 1975) have confirmed the earlier conclusions. Early Cenozoic and Late Mesozoic sea water temperatures, both at the surface and on the bottom, were some 10 to 15^oC warmer than at present.

Further confirmation of this general picture is found in fossil plant remains from the Yukon dinosaur site and from other Late Cretaceous strata much closer to the Cretaceous North Pole (Russell 1973). These data, which indicate climatic conditions like those of today at latitudes 40° to 50°, clearly belie any suggestion that cold polar climatic conditions existed at high latitudes in Mesozoic times. Whatever the cause, greater solar radiation, increased heat absorption by more extensive oceanic areas, greenhouse effect, or more efficient heat distribution by ocean currents to ice-free polar regions, it is evident that high latitude climates were much warmer and less seasonal than now, especially during the Jurassic and the Cretaceous.

As the latitude-temperature graph (Figure 10) shows, given a mean annual temperature 15^oC higher than that of today, Mesozoic ectotherms should have been dispersed over 160° of latitudinal spread, as compared with 120° for today's

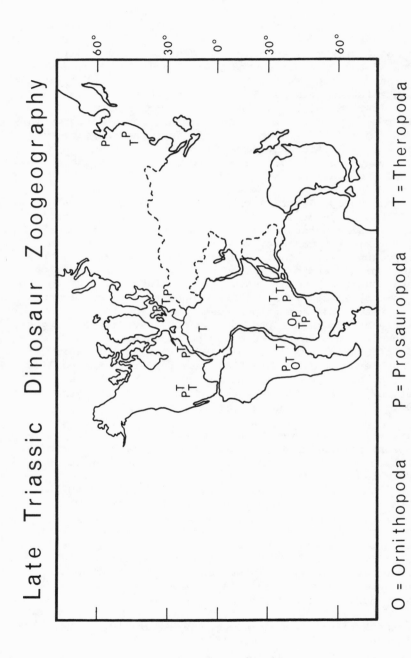

Figure 8. Location of known Late Triassic (above) and Late Jurassic (below) dinosaur sites, to show paleolatitudinal spread. Paleogeographic reconstruction of continental positions is from Smith and Briden (1977).

Late Jurassic Dinosaur Zoogeography

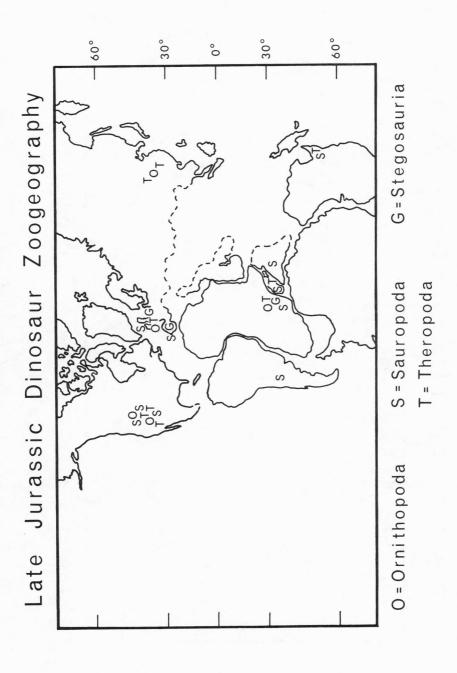

O = Ornithopoda   S = Sauropoda   G = Stegosauria

T = Theropoda

Late Cretaceous Dinosaur Zoogeography

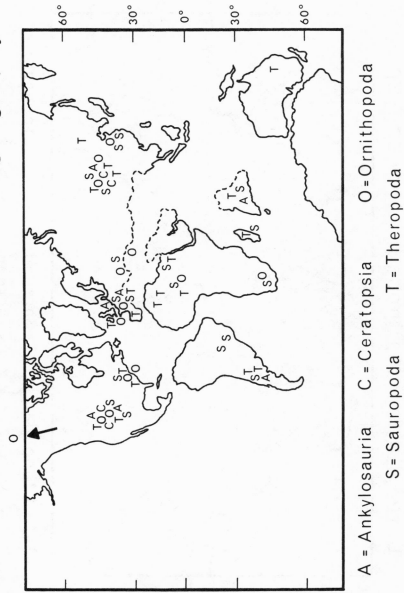

A = Ankylosauria   C = Ceratopsia   O = Ornithopoda

S = Sauropoda   T = Theropoda

Latitudinal Ranges of Dinosaurs and Living Reptiles

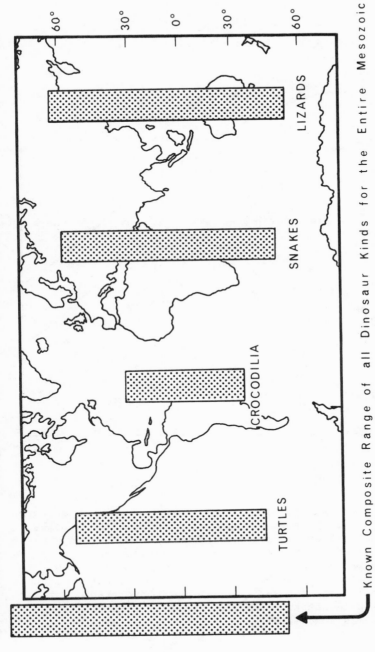

60°

30°

0°

30°

60°

LIZARDS

SNAKES

CROCODILIA

TURTLES

Known Composite Range of all Dinosaur Kinds for the Entire Mesozoic

Figure 9. Location of known Late Cretaceous dinosaur sites, with a comparison of the composite paleolatitudinal spread of all dinosaurs with that of living reptiles. Paleogeographic reconstruction of continental positions is from Smith and Briden (1977).

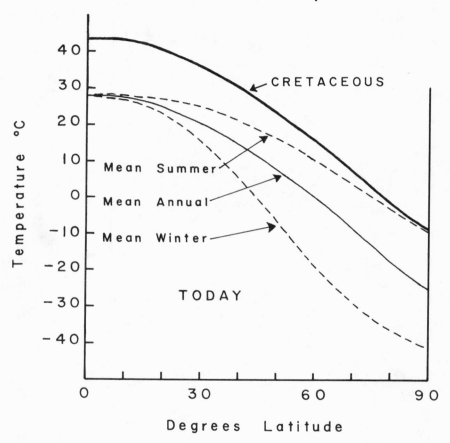

Latitude – Temperature Relationships

CRETACEOUS

Mean Summer

Mean Annual

Mean Winter

TODAY

Temperature °C

Degrees Latitude

Figure 10. The relationship between mean annual temperature and latitude: 28 °C at the equator and -25 °C at the poles. The hypothetical Cretaceous mean annual temperature curve is plotted 15 °C higher to show what paleotemperatures <u>might</u> have prevailed at particular paleolatitudes. The actual situation was probably not this simple, but note that a mean annual temperature of 28 °C could have existed at Cretaceous paleolatitudes of 42°, the present-day latitude of Boston, Massachusetts.

reptiles. That exceeds the known paleolatitudinal spread of dinosaurs, including the Yukon site. My conclusion is that paleoclimatic data, combined with the paleolatitudinal spread of known dinosaur localities, do not in fact show an unusual latitudinal dispersion of dinosaurs and therefore neither support nor refute the hypothesis that any dinosaurs were warm-blooded or endothermic.

Bird Origins

A final, very different line of evidence that may bear on the question of dinosaur endothermy exists in the rare specimens of Archaeopteryx, the oldest known bird, from the Late Jurassic Solnhofen Limestone of West Germany (Figure 11). In virtually all features of the skeleton (save one, a wishbone), Archaeopteryx is remarkably similar to various small theropod dinosaurs (Ostrom 1973, 1975a, 1975b, 1976). In fact, had these specimens been preserved without clear impressions of feathers, they would have been identified as small theropods. That is exactly what happened in the case of the most recently recognized specimen (Mayr 1973). My studies of all five presently known specimens have led me to conclude that Archaeopteryx is very close to, and directly descended from Mid-Jurassic theropod dinosaurs. Modern birds are probably the direct descendants of theropod dinosaurs.

Today's birds, of course, are endothermic and are characterized by high temperature, metabolic and activity levels. They are also feathered. Archaeopteryx, with its feather covering, also appears to have been an endotherm. The insulative properties of its feathers strongly suggest that this creature did not rely on basking to elevate its body temperature, and was therefore most probably endothermic. That raises the obvious question: were the very similar and probably very closely-related small theropods also endothermic? Did they also have high metabolic rates?

Even though modern birds are feathered and endothermic, the presence of feathers in Archaeopteryx does not necessarily mean that Archaeopteryx or its ancestors were endothermic. Cowles (1946) and Regal (1975) postulated that the feathers originated as heat shields, shade producers, rather than as insulation to minimize heat loss. It could well be that Archaeopteryx was able to occupy a small animal niche in warm or tropical environs because it had such a heat shield. But then, small creatures of the Mesozoic were surely better able to retreat to shady spots than were their ponderous contemporaries. So why did "shades" evolve in small animals rather than in giants?

Figure 11. The Berlin specimen of <u>Archaeopteryx</u>. By author.

Once again, the evidence is not conclusive, but I see it as being strongly suggestive that <u>Archaeopteryx</u> was endothermic and that at least some of the theropods approached the birds in their physiology and thermoregulation.

Reflections

In pondering the pros and cons of endothermy among the dinosaurs, it is important to keep several other questions in mind. Why adopt endothermy at all? Despite the fact that endothermy has evolved independently at least twice (mammals and birds), the adaptive value of thermoregulation at a body temperature significantly higher than that of the environment is not clear, because it is achieved at great expense. The usual explanation offered, that it permits higher levels of sustained activity, is not necessarily correct. Heinrich (1977) and many others have noted that numerous poikilotherms are capable of sustained high levels of activity.

Most air-breathing animals, including both ectotherms and endotherms, generate enough heat to reach body temperatures that may exceed ambient temperatures by several degrees centigrade when they are active. Their enzyme systems have evolved to tolerate and even capitalize upon these elevated temperatures <u>during</u> <u>such</u> <u>critical</u> <u>activities</u>; this almost certainly is the key factor behind the evolution of the high optimum body temperatures of all endotherms. But, ectotherms return to ambient temperature levels during periods of inactivity, whereas nearly all endotherms cool only to normal body temperatures that may still be well above ambient levels. What is the selective advantage of maintaining an expensive high body temperature during periods of relative inactivity? The advantages of heterothermy, characteristic of a variety of mammals and birds, are obvious, but the advantages of endothermy as maintained by most mammals and birds are not. The most frequently cited explanation is that it permits the animal to be instantly ready for activity <u>at all times</u>. However, this does not answer the related question: does that return fully compensate for the added costs? Under what circumstances is continuous alertness so essential? Were the huge dinosaurs able to pay this bill?

A final question to keep in mind is: how valid are the analogies we have used? The single most important <u>fact</u> that applies to the interpretation of <u>all</u> fossil evidence is that direct observation of the habits and activities of the organisms under study is not possible. We are forced to reconstruct the <u>possible</u> natures of extinct organisms by means of analogy with living species. Analogy

means: similarity without identity - resemblance only.
Nevertheless, analogy is the most important tool we have,
and carefully applied, it permits us to make general
inferences about the probable nature of extinct organisms.
It goes without saying, though, that any inferences drawn
are only as valid as the analogue chosen. With these matters
in mind, what can we conclude about the nature of
dinosaurian physiology and thermoregulation?

Conclusions

All of the several lines of evidence reviewed above
are susceptible to alternative explanations. Of course,
these alternatives do not disprove the hypothesis of
dinosaur endothermy. Erect posture and gait may well be
required to support large size, rather than a locomotory
advance made possible by a tachymetabolic regime. That
some small forms were also erect, or that other large
and presumed ectotherms (therapsids) were sprawlers, does
not invalidate this alternative explanation. Similarly,
the fact that some mammals "sprawl" does not eliminate
the possibility that sprawling is imposed by ectothermy.
Upright posture and gait may still be products of endothermy.

The inferred high activity levels of some dinosaurs
seem to provide particularly attractive evidence in
favor of dinosaurian endothermy, but high and sustained
activity levels do not require endothermy. The relatively
small brain size of most dinosaurs is seen as evidence
against mammal-like or bird-like levels of activity
(Feduccia 1973; Hopson 1977), but larger brains in
theropods and ornithopods (Russell 1969, 1972; Hopson
1977) might support other skeletal evidence of high activity
in these forms. Again, endothermy may be involved, but
the evidence does not prove it.

The specialized feeding adaptations of some dinosaurs
(ornithopods, ceratopsians and perhaps sauropods) may
have been responses to the great absolute volumes of
food required by animals of very large size, but this
argument is weakened by the absence of similar feeding
specializations in other comparably-sized dinosaurs
(stegosaurs, ankylosaurs and prosauropods). Could the
former have been endothermic and the latter ectothermic?
The presumed huge volumes of food that would be required
by the largest varieties is strong evidence against endothermy. Predator/prey ratios hold significance only for
the carnivores - and the data available may not provide
reliable evidence even for them.

Until the functional significance of secondary Haversian bone is understood in modern vertebrates, its presence in most dinosaurs cannot be evaluated. The fact that it apparently occurs most commonly in large animals (reptiles as well as mammals and birds) suggests that secondary Haversian bone is correlated with large size, rather than being directly related to warm-bloodedness or tachymetabolism.

Considering the 10° to 15°C warmer and less seasonal climates of the later Mesozoic, and the redistribution of dinosaur carcasses by plate movements since their heyday, the present zoogeographic distribution of dinosaur remains does not weigh on either side of this question.

The evolutionary relationship between Archaeopteryx and the theropods seems reasonably secure, but we cannot be certain of the physiological state of Archaeopteryx. In modern birds, feathers serve as insulation to minimize heat loss in endotherms. But, feathers in Archaeopteryx and its ancestors might have functioned to keep heat out in ectothermic animals. The evidence is ambiguous and susceptible to alternative explanations.

The most promising evidence for endothermy may lie in the combination of erect posture and large heart-brain vertical distances. These indicate the almost certain existance of a double-pump, four-chambered heart, with fully separated systemic and pulmonary circulation in dinosaurs. This seems to be a primary requisite of a tachymetabolic thermoregulating animal, explicable only in such a setting. Such circulation obviously is not required in bradymetabolic or ectothermic animals. No other explanation for its development in dinosaurs (and elsewhere) comes to mind.

In summary, notice that only three of the above lines of evidence (posture and gait, dental specializations, and bone histology) are factual, based on direct observation; three others are inferences, interpretations only (high blood pressure and a double-pump heart, high activity-levels, and the theropod origin of birds); and two are ambiguous or of unverified accuracy (predator/prey ratios and geographic distribution). The significance (relative to endothermy) of the first three is uncertain; interpretations of the remainder are untestable and therefore of doubtful value.

These several lines of evidence are extremely interesting and highly suggestive, but they are far from conclusive, even when taken collectively. Endothermy in any kind of dinosaur has not yet been proved. But, neither has it been

disproved. Personally, I believe that some dinosaurs -
especially the theropods, to which all lines of evidence seem
to apply, were probably endothermic. By this, I mean
tachymetabolic. The vast majority, however, I suspect were
ectothermic "homeotherms", as first suggested by Colbert,
Cowles and Bogert (1946, 1947). That is, they were "warm-
blooded" by virtue of their ectothermic response to a warm
and equable environment, and "homeothermic" by virtue of the
thermal inertia imposed by their uncommonly large body
sizes (Spotila et al 1973; McNab and Auffenberg 1976). That
conclusion is supported by the intriguing hypothesis (Farlow,
Thompson and Rosner 1976) that the staggered and highly
vascularized bony plates along the back of Stegosaurus were
"forced convection heat-loss fins" designed for shedding
excess heat.

2

Predator/Prey Biomass Ratios, Community Food Webs and Dinosaur Physiology

James O. Farlow

Abstract

Recent studies have suggested that reconstructed predator/prey biomass ratios can be used to interpret the physiology of fossil vertebrates. On the basis of such arguments, dinosaurs have been interpreted as endotherms. However, several complicating factors suggest that this conclusion may be premature.

It is difficult to satisfactorily characterize the predator/prey ratios of ectothermic as opposed to endothermic predator/prey systems, even for living animals. In particular, we do not know how low this ratio can get for large ectothermic predators and their prey. Furthermore, it is possible that there is some convergence of ectothermic and endothermic metabolic rates at large sizes. If so, predator/prey ratios might not provide sufficient resolution to distinguish ectotherms from endotherms for dinosaur-sized animals, particularly for fossil faunas, where biases of preservation and collecting, and errors in weight estimates, might distort predator/prey ratios from their true values.

Differences in community structure and function between dinosaurs (or other fossil reptiles) and mammals, or between dinosaurs and other groups of fossil reptiles (sphenacodonts, therapsids, and thecodonts), could also complicate interpretation of predator/prey biomass ratios. If large carnivorous dinosaurs preyed upon a relatively narrower range of large-vertebrate prey species than mammalian or other reptilian carnivores, or if competition from other predators significantly reduced the amount of large-vertebrate prey available to these large theropods, a large carnivorous dinosaur / large-vertebrate biomass ratio as reconstructed for a fossil community might be

55

substantially less than the effective predator/prey ratio
needed to determine large theropod physiology. Further
complications emerge if large carnivorous dinosaurs were,
to a greater extent than modern mammalian (or other ancient
reptilian) predators, secondary or higher-order carnivores,
or if large theropod juveniles were more vulnerable to
predation than the young of other kinds of carnivores. To
the extent that large theropods were similar to modern
mammalian predators in their ecology and behavior, these
problems will be lessened, at least in comparisons of
dinosaurian and mammalian predator/prey ratios. However,
we do not know just how similar to mammals dinosaurs were
in their natural history, and we may well never know.
This should generate some caution in interpretations of
the physiological meaning of predator/prey biomass ratios.

Introduction

In an original and extremely interesting paper, Bakker
(1972) called the attention of paleontologists to the possibility that data on the relative abundance of herbivores and
carnivores in modern and ancient communities might be used to
interpret the physiology of extinct animals, notably dinosaurs. Bakker believes that, by determining predator/prey
biomass ratios for fossil communities, the paleoecologist can
establish whether the animals of those communities were endotherms or ectotherms. Although some have disputed this claim
(Thulborn 1973), or at least expressed reservations about it
(Charig 1976; Farlow 1976a, Tracy 1976), Bakker nevertheless
contends that his approach provides a definitive method for
assessing the metabolic status of fossil vertebrates (Bakker
1974, 1975a, b).

In this paper I will examine some of the assumptions and
difficulties involved in the determination and interpretation
of predator/prey biomass ratios, particularly as applied to
dinosaur communities. First, however, I should explicitly
state what I mean when I talk about endothermy and ectothermy.
Endothermy is "the pattern of thermoregulation in which body
temperature depends on a high (tachymetabolic) and controlled
rate of heat generation" (Bligh and Johnson 1973). Ectothermic animals, on the other hand, have a much lower (bradymetabolic) rate of heat production, and rely primarily on
external sources of heat to maintain body warmth. These two
contrasting physiological states are endpoints of a range of
complex metabolic strategies. It is quite possible, perhaps
even probable, that the various groups of dinosaurs occupied
different positions along this continuum (Hopson 1977). I
will not go into these complexities here. Bakker asserts

explicitly that dinosaurs, as a group, were at or very close
to the continuous, automatic, endotherm endpoint of the
spectrum.   I will address the question, whether or not the
evidence of predator/prey ratios supports this contention.

Energy Budgets and Predator/Prey
Biomass Ratios
in Modern Animal Communities

The potential significance of predator/prey biomass
ratios stems from the different food requirements and bioenergetic strategies of endotherms and ectotherms of comparable size.   For example, in the Hubbard Brook Experimental
Forest in New Hampshire, shrews and salamanders are the most
important vertebrate consumers of forest floor invertebrates.
The shrew population consumes about six times as much energy
per year as does the salamander population, although the peak
midsummer biomass of salamanders is about ten times that of
shrews (Gosz et al. 1978).

Porter and Tracy (1974) estimated that a 50-gram mink
would need about 16 times as much food per day as a 50-gram
garter snake, if both animals were living in South Carolina.
In Michigan, however, the mink would require 26 times as much
food, the difference reflecting the climatic regimes in the
two regions.   Similarly a 3-gram Uta stansburiana lizard
ingests about 0.11 kcal (multiply by 4.184 to convert to
kilojoules) of food each day (Turner et al. 1976), and a 3.5-
gram Lacerta vivipara lizard eats about 0.30 kcal/day,
(Avery 1971), while a shrew of comparable weight will eat
around 5-8 kcal of food a day (Morrison et al. 1957; Buckner
1964; Barrett 1969).   Finally, a 45-kg crocodile will consume
about 440 kcal/day, but a 42-kg cougar eats about 2140 kcal/
day, in captivity (Cott 1961; Farlow 1976c; Altman and
Dittmer 1968).

Not only do endotherms eat more than ectotherms of
similar size; they expend the energy they ingest differently
as well.   An animal cannot utilize all the energy it ingests;
although part of it is assimilated, the remaining fraction,
which can be large in animals feeding on relatively indigestible material (such as herbivores and detritivores), is
egested as feces.   The energy that is assimilated is burned
in respiration or channeled into production as growth and
reproduction.   In order to maintain high body temperatures
through a rapid metabolic rate, endotherms use a larger
fraction of their assimilated energy in respiration than
ectotherms, which can put more energy into production (Table
1).   This does not mean, however, that the production/

Table 1. Bioenergetic Ratios for Small Animals from the Hubbard Brook Experimental Forest, New Hampshire.

Group	Assimilation/ Ingestion	Respiration/ Ingestion	Respiration/ Assimilation	Production/ Ingestion	Production/ Assimilation
Caterpillars	0.14	0.09	0.62	0.05	0.38
Salamanders	0.81	0.32	0.40	0.49	0.60
Birds	0.70	0.69	0.98	0.01	0.02
Shrews	0.90	0.89	0.98	0,01	0.02
Mice	0.83	0.81	0.98	0.02	0.02
Chipmunks	0.82	0.81	0.98	0.02	0.02

Data from Gosz et al. (1978).

assimilation ratio will necessarily exceed the respiration/ assimilation ratio in ectotherms; note the values for cater- pillars in Table 1, and the relative magnitude of respiration and production in arthropods reported by Menhinick (1967) and Moulder and Reichle (1972).

In a community where the populations of prey and predator species maintain a constant size the annual productivity should equal the biomass of animals dying each year. If the predators are consuming all or nearly all of this mortality, then the ratio of predator productivity/prey productivity should approximate the production/ingestion ratio for the predator. Since the assimilation/ingestion ratio seems to be fairly uniform and high for predators from a wide range of taxa, both ectothermic and endothermic, the production/inges- tion ratio will reveal the same trends indicated by the pro- duction/assimilation ratio (note, however, that this will not necessarily hold for herbivores or detritivores).

Populations of small, short-lived animals turn over more rapidly than populations of large, long-lived animals. The rate at which population biomass turns over is given by the productivity/biomass (P/B) ratio, which for our purposes will be defined as the ratio of annual productivity to average annual or seasonal population biomass. Invertebrates and small vertebrates can have P/B ratios well in excess of 1.00 (Van Hook 1971; Tranter 1976; Mann 1976; Wiegert and Evans 1967; Bobek 1971; Hansson 1971; Varley 1970, Burton and Likens 1975a, b; Barbault 1971). Deer-sized mammals have P/B ratios of around 0.20-0.50, and elephants have ratios of about 0.05 (Farlow 1976a, c; Coe et al. 1976). In general, the P/B ratio decreases with increasing life-span.

Bakker (1975) argued that the P/B ratio is about the same for predator and prey species of comparable size. This is probably true for large vertebrates (except where the prey's anti-predator strategy involves saturating the environ- ment with so many offspring that the predators can kill only a small fraction of them), but not necessarily so for small animals, particularly invertebrates. At any rate, if the predators and prey have similar P/B ratios, then the predator productivity/prey productivity ratio should be close to the predator biomass/prey biomass ratio. Then if, as noted earlier, the predators are consuming most or all of the pro- ductivity of their prey species, the predator/prey produc- tivity or biomass ratios should approximate the predator's production/ingestion or production/assimilation ratios. All of these ratios should be lower for endothermic predators than for ectothermic predators.

Table 2. Predator/Prey Biomass Ratios for Some Modern
          Large-Mammal Communities.

Locality	Predator/Prey Ratio (%)
Serengeti Ecological Unit, Africa	0.36
Ngorongoro Crater, Africa	0.92
Lake Manyara Park, Africa	0.57
Nairobi Park, Africa	0.77
Kruger Park, Africa	1.01
Mkomazi Reserve, Africa	1.6
Gir Forest, India	0.22
Jaldapara Sanctuary, India	1.47
Wilpattu Park, Ceylon	0.51
Afobaka Dam Region, Central America	0.85
North-Central United States	0.58
Isle Royale, Lake Superior	0.22
Idaho Primitive Area, North America	0.18
Algonquin Park, North America	0.39

Note: Data from Farlow (1976). Biomass estimates will vary,
       depending on which author's census and weight
       estimates are used. (Coe et al. 1976).

As Bakker (1975) notes, predator/prey ratios in fossil assemblages can reflect either the standing crop biomass ratio or the productivity ratio, or some combination of both, depending on the type of mortality represented by the sample. For large-vertebrate faunas in which predator and prey are of comparable size, the two ratios may be similar, and, as argued above, should be lower for endotherms than ectotherms for two reasons. 1) A given unit of endothermic biomass requires more food per unit time than a similar unit of ectothermic biomass. 2) An endotherm, having ingested a given amount of food, channels less of the energy assimilated from that food into production (which may ultimately be represented as carcasses in the fossil assemblage) than does an ectotherm.

Before interpreting predator/prey biomass ratios of fossil communities, we would ideally like to be able to compare these ratios for living ectothermic and endothermic predators of various sizes. It is one thing to say that the ratio will be lower for endotherms than for ectotherms, but it would obviously be better if we could quantify this difference. In particular, how high can the ratio get for endotherms, and how low for ectotherms? Is the difference between ectotherms and endotherms the same at all animal sizes, or does it change with changing size?

Tables 2 to 5 present predator/prey biomass ratios for a variety of animal communities. Immediately a problem emerges: there are no published predator/prey data for large ectothermic predators. This is largely because, in terrestrial situations at least, such animals are generally a novelty (except on some islands); mammals constitute the predominant large carnivores (and herbivores, too, for that matter) of the modern world. Thus we are forced to compare large mammals with fishes and invertebrates.

However, this can lead to difficulties in interpretation. Population biomass turns over more rapidly for small animals than large ones; populations with high P/B ratios produce more potential food per unit time than similarly-sized populations with lower P/B ratios. Thus populations with higher turnover rates should be able to support a greater biomass of predators. This may be one reason why the Arizona mammal/bird community seems to have a higher predator/prey ratio than the communities of large mammals (Tables 2 and 3). Similarly, this may be why fish communities sometimes show such high ratios of piscivores to non-piscivores (Table 4), although in this case the issue is clouded by the fact that piscivorous fishes eat other foods besides fishes, and that relative abundance in dry-season pools may not reflect

Table 3.   Density and Biomass of Endothermic Vertebrates on
            Saint Rita Range Reserve (3 km^2), Southern Arizona
            (Density data from Leopold 1933).

	Species	Number	Biomass (kg)
PREDATORS	Coyote	1	15.9
	Horned Owl	2	2.4
	Redtail Hawk	2	1.8
	Hognose/Spotted Skunks	15	23.1
	Roadrunner	20	5.9
PREY	Blacktail Jackrabbit	10	22.7
	Allen's Jackrabbit	45	184.1
	Cottontail	25	30.7
	Scaled Quail	25	4.6
	Gambel Quail	75	12.5
	Kangaroo Rats	1,280	115.2
	Woodrats	6,400	1094.4
	Ground Squirrels, Mice and other Rodents	17,948	735.9
	Cattle[1]	25	--

Predator/Prey Biomass Ratio = 2.23%

Mammal weights were estimated from Burt and Grossenheider
(1964); Craighead and Craighead (1956), Sprunt and Zim
(1961), Ohmart and Lasiewski (1971).

[1] I assume that coyote predation on cattle, or scavenging
   of carcasses, was rare.

Table 4. Piscivore/Non-Piscivore Biomass Ratios in Tropical
Freshwater Fish Communities.

Locality	Piscivore/Non-Piscivore Ratio (%)
1) Dry Season water holding pit, Kapuas River System, Borneo	312.5
2) Temporary oxbow/riverside lakes, Isla los Sapos, middle Parana River, Argentina	8.1 - 133.3
3) Residual pools, Sokoto River, Nigeria	135.1
4) Open water, Lake George, Uganda	27.5
5) Archipelago region, southeastern part of Lake Chad	∿ 38

Data from Lowe-McConnell (1975).

Table 5. Predator/Prey Biomass Ratios in Some Ectothermic Communities.

Community	Predator/Prey Ratio (%)	Predator/(Predator & Prey) Ratio (%)	Source
1) Coral reef, Eniwetok Atoll (Prey species include coral polyps, crustaceans, sea urchins, anemones, annelids, holothurians, molluscs and fishes; predator species include annelids, crabs, molluscs, starfishes and fishes. Biomass = dry weight, excluding dead skeletal material associated with protoplasm).	8.33	7.69	Odum and Odum (1955)
2) Herb stratum of sericea lespedeza stand, South Carolina (Prey include herbivorous and nectivorous insects; predators = spiders and ants).	∼ 18	∼15	Menhinick (1967)
3) Grassland arthropod community, Tennessee	15.4	13.3	Van Hook (1971)
4) Forest-floor arthropod community, Tennessee	37.2	27.1	Moulder and Reichle (1972)

year-round conditions.

The arthropod communities listed in Table 5 deserve
special consideration, because Bakker (1974, 1975) has cited
them among his standards for ectothermic predator/prey
ratios. In earlier papers, Bakker presented simple carni-
vore/herbivore biomass ratios. More recently, he has tried
to account for cannibalism and predation by one carnivore
species on another, computing the predator/prey ratio as
carnivore biomass/ (carnivore plus non-carnivore biomass).
Where carnivore biomass is relatively small, the difference
between the two ratios is negligible, but where carnivore
biomass is large, the revised ratio can be substantially
lower as shown by Table 5.

However the predator/prey ratio is computed, it is
substantially higher in the ectothermic communities listed in
Table 5 than in the endothermic communities. Unfortunately,
some of the complicating factors noted for the fish communities are probably operating here as well. Menhinick's (1967)
study considered energy flow exclusively in the herb stratum
of the plant community. The spiders and predaceous ants
obtained some of their prey below this level, from animals of
the litter and soil; thus the ratios from his work in Table 5
are too high, perhaps by a fairly large factor.

The predators in Van Hook's (1971) community were
lycosid spiders. During the 36 weeks when arthropods were
active in this grassland ecosystem, _Lycosa_ biomass averaged
46.01 mg dry weight/m^2, and the _Lycosa_/insect prey biomass
ratio was 14.3% (12.5% if _Lycosa_ is scored as both predator
and prey). However, the ratio of _Lycosa_ productivity/insect
productivity was only 7.05% (6.59%). The difference reflects
the extremely rapid turnover of acridid grasshoppers relative
to the spiders. Something similar may account for the even
higher predator/prey ratio reported by Moulder and Reichle
(1972).

In none of these studies of terrestrial arthropod
communities was the impact of vertebrate predation considered.
Spiders and other invertebrate carnivores may have been taking only part of prey productivity, the rest going to birds,
small mammals, reptiles, and amphibians. If so, this would
raise the effective predator/prey ratio, and to some extent
cancel out the difficulty in interpretation introduced by
contrasting predator and prey P/B ratios.

It follows that there is at present no really
satisfactory way to characterize predator/prey biomass ratios
for endotherms and ectotherms of comparable size in living

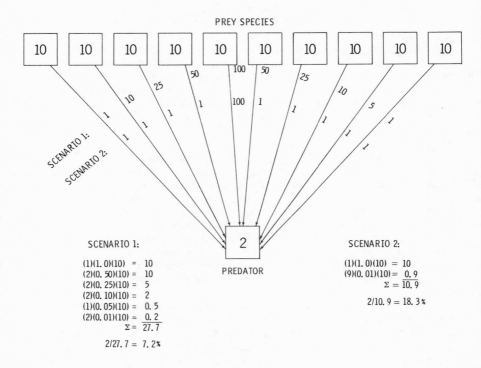

Figure 1.   The effect of predator dietary selectivity on the
            computation of the effective predator/prey bio-
            mass ratio.   There are 10 biomass units of each of
            the prey species, and 2 biomass units of the
            predator.   The numbers beside each line are the
            percentage of that species' productivity that is
            consumed by the predator.   All prey species have
            the same productivity/biomass ratio.   For each
            prey species, the effective biomass supporting
            the predator is the total biomass multiplied by
            the percentage of productivity consumed by the
            predator.   The total effective prey biomass and
            the effective predator/prey biomass ratio are
            computed for each scenario.

animal communities, where it is at least potentially possible
to measure and manipulate the factors affecting the ratio.
This is particularly true for animals of large size. On the
basis of the data that are available, for modern communities
of large mammals, the ratio may reach about 2%; where there
is a significant size discrepancy in favor of the predator,
the ratio may be higher. The ratio appears to be consistently higher in ectothermic communities, but some or most of
this difference is not directly related to metabolic rate;
rather, it seems to reflect different life-history strategies
of predator and prey. Thus comparing the predator/prey ratio
in mammalian communities with that in invertebrate or fish
communities may be like comparing "apples and oranges" due to
pronounced differences in the basic biology of mammalian as
opposed to fish or invertebrate predator and prey species.
However, large lizards, snakes, crocodilians, and perhaps
even some sharks (e.g. Carcharodon and its kin), may be
similar enough to mammalian predators in their basic biology
and kinds and/or life-history strategies of their prey to
make comparison of their biomass relative to that of their
prey, to mammalian predator/prey ratios, more meaningful.
Thus some of the complexities noted above could probably be
sorted out if we had data on the predator/prey biomass ratio,
and the factors affecting it, for living large ectothermic
predators.

Predator Diets, Community Food Webs, and Predator/Prey Biomass Ratios

Predator/prey biomass ratios will tell us nothing about
physiology if predator populations are not regulated by the
amount of food produced by their prey species. What factors
might keep predator populations below the level at which food
supplies became limiting? Assuming that for large vertebrates
these are generally not environmental calamities (violent
storms, fires, floods, etc.), such factors might include
suitable nesting or denning sites, cannibalism, or predation
by one species on another (Fox 1975). The importance of any
one or a combination of these factors in a given situation is
hard to establish, even in living communities. If they were
sufficient to keep the predator population well below the
level that prey productivity could otherwise support, we
might incorrectly conclude that a population of predators was
endothermic, or at some intermediate point between pure
endothermy and ectothermy.

We run into a similar problem in trying to determine the
predator/prey biomass ratio for a community in which we do not
know the actual feeding habits of the predator. Consider the
scenarios presented in Figure 1. In this community there are

two biomass units of an animal whose morphology identifies it as a predator, and ten biomass units of each of ten species of potential prey animals. In the absence of information on the diet of the predator, we might reasonably assume it capable of killing and eating all of the prey species, in which case we would assign a predator/prey biomass ratio of 2% to the community.

But, suppose that it became possible to determine the predator's diet, and we learned that, while it did feed upon all the available prey species, it concentrated on one or a few, taking the others only occasionally. One way of expressing the importance of any prey species to a predator is by the proportion of the prey species' productivity consumed by the predator. Let us assume, to make the calculations easier, that the P/B ratio is the same for all ten prey species in Figure 1. This means that the percentage of the productivity of each prey species that is eaten by the predator will be the same as the percentage of that species' biomass that is supporting the predator.

In the first scenario, the predator consumes 100% of the productivity of one prey species and progressively smaller amounts of the productivity of the other species. As a result, the predator population is taking 27.7% of the available prey productivity. Since there is a total of 100 biomass units of prey, and we are assuming similar P/B ratios for all the prey species, the effective prey biomass supporting the predator population is 27.7 units, not 100 units. The predator/prey biomass ratio that we would need to know in order to assess the predator's metabolic rate would be 2/27.7, or 7.2%. In the second scenario, the predator relies heavily on only one of the prey species. In this extreme case, the effective predator/prey ratio becomes 18.3%. The problem would be even worse if there were some species that the predator did not eat at all.

Thus, if we lack any direct knowledge about the quantitative composition of the diet of a predator as is inevitable with fossil forms, it is likely on the basis of this factor that we would over-estimate the importance of potential prey species in its diet. This might cause us mistakenly to conclude, on the basis of predator/prey ratios, that the predator was an endotherm. The more diverse the prey fauna, and the more restricted the predator's diet, the more likely it is that such a mistake could be made. This could occur either where the predator was limited below the carrying capacity of prey productivity by some factor other than food (otherwise, the predator population would presumably increase until it was consuming a large part of the

productivity of all the prey species), or where large proportions of the total prey productivity were unavailable to the
food-limited predator population for some reason(s). For
example, substantial fractions of total prey productivity
might be consumed by predator species that we had failed to
consider in our analysis.

The kinds of problems I have discussed so far apply
directly to the reconstruction of dinosaur communities. Consider Figure 2, a simplified food web reconstructed for a
Late Cretaceous, North American, terrestrial fauna, such as
that of the Oldman Formation (Béland and Russell 1978).
There are four or five major groups of herbivores: invertebrates (probably mainly arthropods), small vertebrates, small
ornithischian dinosaurs, large ornithischians, and possibly
ornithomimids. Similarly, there are five or six carnivorous
groups: invertebrates, small vertebrates, crocodiles and
large lizards, small theropod dinosaurs, tyrannosaurs, and
again possibly ornithomimids (assuming that this last group
was omnivorous).

In modern large-mammal communities, the chief predators
of large herbivores are large carnivores. (Note, however,
that disease, parasites, and starvation may be more lethal
than predators in many communities.) The smaller carnivores
are unable to attack adult herbivores successfully, and there
is a substantial degree of parental care of the calves that
protects them to at least some extent from predators that
would not attack an adult. At the same time, parental care
allows carnivore cubs to eat large prey that they could not
themselves kill, either directly as food is brought to them
or as they are led to kills by adults, or indirectly via
maternal milk. The key point here is that parental care may
both protect juveniles (whether herbivores or carnivores)
from the attacks of many predators, and permit cubs of predaceous species to exploit the same prey resources as their
parents.

There is a distinct possibility that juvenile dinosaurs
received parental care. Some living reptilian species show
rather sophisticated social behavior (Burghardt 1977), including parental care, and if brain size is any clue, the
same may have been true of many dinosaurs (Hopson 1977).
Trackways provide some indication of dinosaur sociality
(Ostrom 1972). Thus, juvenile dinosaurs may have received at
least some protection against predators from their elders.
Furthermore, it is possible that some carnivorous dinosaurs
were to some extent social hunters (Farlow 1976b), and that
adult theropods provided their young with a certain amount of
food.

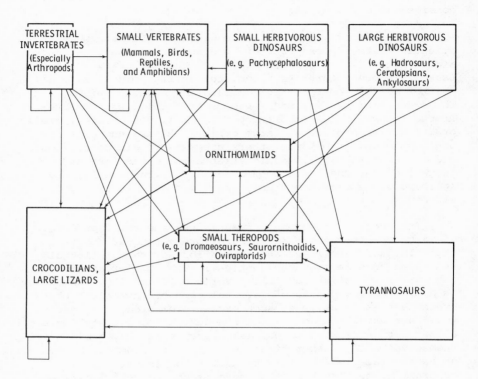

Figure 2.   A reconstruction of the possible food web for the
terrestrial fauna of the Late Cretaceous Oldman
Formation of western Canada.

However, none of these hypotheses can at present be proved, and the possibility remains that a dinosaur was more or less on its own from the time it entered the world until the day it died. If so, it may have had to run a predatory gauntlet worse than that faced by its living mammalian counterparts. As an egg, it might have been eaten by small vertebrates, large lizards, ornithomimids, small theropods, juvenile tyrannosaurs, or perhaps even the larger carnivorous invertebrates. As a hatchling, it would have continued to face most of these enemies. Only as it matured would it become progressively immune to the smaller predators, in the end being vulnerable only to large tyrannosaurs and perhaps group-hunting small theropods (Farlow 1976b) and the largest crocodilians.

Now let us consider things from the specific point of view of a tyrannosaur. Assuming the absence of nest guarding and parental care, a tyrannosaur in the egg or hatchling stage would have been as vulnerable to predation as any other dinosaur. As a maturing adult, however, it would have been free from the gastronomic designs of any predator except perhaps another tyrannosaur.

Like the young of modern crocodilians and large carnivorous lizards, the tyrannosaur cub, if it foraged on its own, probably subsisted on large invertebrates and small vertebrates (Farlow 1976b), taking the eggs and young of other dinosaurs (or even tyrannosaurs) as well and eating any carrion it stumbled upon. As it matured, it would have taken more of the larger prey species, until, as an adult, it probably fed mainly on adult and sub-adult large dinosaurs, larger individuals of small herbivorous dinosaurs, ornithomimids, small theropods, and crocodilians, and perhaps cannibalistically on its own kind.

Having constructed an elaborate Late Cretaceous scenario, let us consider its significance for our interpretation of dinosaur predator/prey biomass ratios. We have already noted, in general terms, two major areas of concern: the possible complexity of the community food web, and the need to know how much of what kinds of prey a predator eats (ate) when constructing a predator/prey ratio for that predator. The Late Cretaceous predator/prey biomass ratios with which I am familiar are based on large herbivorous dinosaurs and tyrannosaurs (Bakker 1972; Farlow 1976a; Béland and Russell 1978). These ratios are based on the assumption that tyrannosaurs alone ate large herbivorous dinosaurs (note that when I refer to large or small herbivorous dinosaurs, I am talking about the size of the adults of that species; thus a large individual of a "small" herbivorous species could be

bigger than a very young "large" herbivore), and that tyrannosaurs ate nothing but large herbivorous dinosaurs (perhaps
with occasional cannibalism for variety). If tyrannosaur
social behavior was sufficiently mammal-like or bird-like,
this may have been largely true, but we cannot presume that
this was definitely the case. Several kinds of predators
(crocodiles, small theropods, large lizards, etc.) may have
eaten large ornithischians (particularly young individuals),
and tyrannosaurs may have eaten many kinds of prey besides
large ornithischians. Therefore, an unknown fraction of the
productivity of the large herbivorous dinosaurs could have
been consumed by predators other than tyrannosaurs, and the
tyrannosaur population could have been tapping the productivity of prey other than large herbivores. While these two
factors would have opposite effects on the computation of a
tyrannosaur/supposed tyrannosaur-prey biomass ratio, there is
no reason to suppose that they would cancel one another out
exactly. Thus a tyrannosaur/large ornithischian ratio (or
even a tyrannosaur/(large ornithischian plus tyrannosaur)
ratio) might tell us rather little about the biomass necessary to support a unit of tyrannosaur biomass. Even if
tyrannosaurs did feed primarily on large ornithischians, that
tells us little about how much of any one ornithischian
species these reptiles ate. The effective predator/prey biomass ratio might have been much higher than a ratio that does
not take tyrannosaur dietary composition into account (cf.
Figure 1), and large fractions of prey productivity could
have been consumed by other predators.

     If tyrannosaurs fed to a large extent on other
carnivores and were also cannibalistic, still another complication emerges. Tracy (1976) noted that garter snakes in
Michigan feed heavily on anurans, particularly Rana pipiens.
In the communities in question, the frogs are primary carnivores; their biomass, relative to that of their herbivore
prey, is about 16.7%. The garter snake/frog biomass ratio is
a little less than 10%. If, in the absence of information on
snake diets, we assumed them to be feeding on the herbivores,
we would calculate a carnivore/herbivore ratio of (0.167)
(0.10), or roughly 1.7%, and mistakenly conclude that our
snakes were endotherms. To the extent that tyrannosaurs were
secondary carnivores (and ate small theropods, ornithomimids,
crocodilians, etc.), the tyrannosaur/herbivore ratio might
also lead to a spurious conclusion about tyrannosaur
endothermy.

     If the tyrannosaurs were not food-limited, these problems
become more acute. If young tyrannosaurs received little
parental care, and were taken by other predators as eggs and
small juveniles, then these top predators may themselves

have been limited to some extent by predation. Perhaps the predator community as a whole was food-limited, but due to secondary or higher order carnivory the population of any given predator species was kept below the carrying capacity of herbivore productivity. Tyrannosaurs might also have been limited by the availability of suitable nesting sites.

The most important point here is that Late Cretaceous terrestrial vertebrate communities may have had structural and functional attributes different from those of modern large-mammal communities. An ecological "uniformitarianism" that tries to fit Mesozoic reptilian communities into a conceptual framework based on modern mammalian biology may obscure differences that are of direct relevance to the interpretation of dinosaur physiology.

Possible Convergence of Ectotherm and Endotherm Feeding Rates at Large Body Sizes

Up until now, I have assumed that there is a clear-cut difference between the metabolic rates, and thus the food requirements, of ectotherms and endotherms. That is, I have assumed that an endothermic predator will have a feeding rate that will, on the average, be a constant multiple of that of an ectothermic carnivore of comparable size, whether the predators in question weigh 10 grams or 10,000 kilograms. However, physiological data for living vertebrates suggest that this may not be the case. In their review of reptilian metabolic rates, Bennett and Dawson (1976) presented the following equations relating metabolic rate to weight (note that I have modified these and some later equations from the forms presented by the authors to forms expressing metabolic rate in kcal/day and weight in kilograms; oxygen consumption was converted to heat production by assuming that 1 liter of oxygen consumed liberates 4.8 kcal of heat):

A) Lizards at 30°C: kcal/day = $8.54 \ W^{0.83}$ (W in kg)
B) Lizards at 37°C: kcal/day = $14.09 \ W^{0.82}$ (W in kg)
C) Composite data for reptiles of various groups at 30°C: kcal/day = $6.54 \ W^{0.77}$ (W in kg)

Kleiber (1961) and Lasiewski and Dawson (1967) presented similar equations for eutherian mammals and non-passerine birds, respectively:

D) Mammals: kcal/day = 67.6 $W^{0.756}$ (W in kg)
E) Birds: kcal/day = 78.3 $W^{0.723}$ (W in kg)

One is immediately struck by the fact that the exponents
relating body weight and metabolic rate in the two lizard
equations (but not the composite reptile equation) are substantially greater than those for birds and mammals.

In an earlier paper (Farlow 1976a), I tabulated
estimates of the feeding rates of carnivorous birds, mammals,
reptiles, and amphibians in captivity and in the wild, using
these data to construct empirical equations relating feeding
rate to weight in carnivorous endotherms and ectotherms:

F) Endotherms: kcal/day = 219.19 $W^{0.692}$ (W in kg)
G) Ectotherms: kcal/day = 16.09 $W^{0.820}$ (W in kg)

Again, the exponent in the ectotherm equation was much
greater than that for endotherms. Similarly, Turner et. al.
(1976) related daily assimilated energy in lizards to weight
by the equation:

H) Lizards: kcal/day = 20.46 $W^{0.81}$ (W in kg)

However, any similarity between their equation and mine is at
least partly explained by the fact that we were using some of
the same studies for data.

Several factors need to be considered in the interpretation of these equations. In experimental metabolism chambers,
animal size may differentially affect the amount of physical
activity sustained within the chambers. That is, smaller
animals may be more restless and active than larger animals.
If all weights across the weight range of that particular
group were not equally represented, such that smaller animals
were over-represented, the weight exponent of metabolic rate
would then be artifactually low (A. F. Bennett, pers. comm.).
Similarly, turtles seem to have a lower metabolic rate than
other reptiles (perhaps because the shell is to some extent
physiologically inert); thus a composite reptilian graph
(such as the one presented above) with many large turtles
represented would also yield an atypically low exponent
(A. F. Bennett, pers. comm.).

One could similarly argue that the data on which I based

my empirical feeding rate equations are too crude to allow
definitive determination of the weight exponent. However,
this is true for the data of both the ectotherm and endotherm
equations. This being the case, the fact that my feeding
rate equations show a larger weight exponent for ectotherms
than endotherms, just as was found in the equations based on
oxygen consumption and heat production, seems significant.
Furthermore, the physiological basis of weight exponents of
metabolism is uncertain. Therefore we cannot state any a
priori expectation as to whether these exponents should or
should not be the same for ectotherms and endotherms (A. F.
Bennett, pers. comm.).

The metabolic and feeding rate equations for endotherms
are based on observations which include data for animals as
large or larger than dinosaurs, so it seems reasonable to use
them to predict dinosaur metabolic and feeding rates. However, none of the ectotherm data are for animals anywhere
near the weight of a large dinosaur. In my feeding rate
equation, for example, the largest animal represented was a
45-kg crocodile. Extrapolating to weights well beyond those
of the data base may give spurious results. However, if the
ectotherm equations do apply for very large animals, there
would be a convergence of the metabolic rates and food requirements of endotherms and ectotherms at large sizes.
Table 6 illustrates this, showing the ratios between endotherm and ectotherm metabolic and feeding rates indicated by
the above equations for animals ranging in size from 1g to
10,000 kg. In every case there is at least some convergence
at the larger sizes; in most cases there is considerable
convergence.

Thus, even if our predators were food-limited, the
maximum sustainable predator/prey biomass ratio for a
dinosaur-sized predator might differ by only 3-6 times between an endotherm and an ectotherm, rather than the order of
magnitude difference that Bakker (1972) has suggested. Considering also the complexities introduced if the predators
were not food-limited, and the fact that we do not know the
actual diets of these animals, the possibility of confusing
ectotherms with endotherms on the basis of predator/prey
ratios emerges, at least for communities of large animals.
As noted above, studies of the trophic ecology of large
living ectothermic predators might reduce these difficulties.
In particular, it would be interesting to know whether or not
the ectothermic predator/prey ratio ever gets as low as it
does for large mammalian predators, and if it does, whether
or not this reflects the food requirements and bioenergetic
strategies of the predators.

Table 6. The Ratio of Predicted Endotherm/Ectotherm Metabolic and Feeding Rates at Various Weights.

Equations (All Weights (W) are in Kilograms):

A) Lizards at 30°C: kcal/day = $8.54\ W^{0.83}$

B) Lizards at 37°C: kcal/day = $14.09\ W^{0.82}$

C) "Composite" Reptiles at 30°C: kcal/day = $6.54\ W^{0.77}$

D) Eutherian Mammals: kcal/day = $67.6\ W^{0.756}$

E) Non-passerine Birds: kcal/day = $78.3\ W^{0.723}$

F) Endothermic Carnivores: kcal/day = $219.19\ W^{0.692}$

G) Ectothermic Carnivores: kcal/day = $16.09\ W^{0.820}$

Weight	Eutherians/Lizards at 30°C (D ÷ A)	Eutherians/Lizards at 37°C (D ÷ B)	Eutherians/"Composite" Reptiles at 30°C (D ÷ C)	Non-passerines/Lizards at 30°C (E ÷ A)	Non-passerines/Lizards at 37°C (E ÷ B)	Non-passerines/"Composite" Reptiles at 30°C (E ÷ C)	Carnivorous Endotherms/Carnivorous Ectotherms (F ÷ G)
1 g	13.2	7.5	11.4	19.2	10.9	16.6	33.0
1,000 kg	4.8	3.1	9.4	4.4	2.8	8.7	5.6
10,000 kg	4.0	2.7	9.1	3.4	2.3	7.8	4.2

Reconstructing Predator/Prey
Biomass Ratios
for Fossil Communities

One of the prime difficulties in reconstructing fossil communities is accounting for the vagaries of fossil preservation that may have changed the relative abundance of the various species in the death assemblage, relative to their original abundance in the living community. The paleoecologist endeavors to distinguish between taxa that lived in the area where the sediments that comprise the rock unit were deposited and those whose carcasses were carried there by stream action. Once this is established, it is necessary to determine whether or not the various autochthonous forms are represented in their original relative abundances. In many cases, this will not be so. The remains of small and delicately built animals are very vulnerable to a variety of biotic and abiotic agents of destruction; consequently they are under-represented in most fossil assemblages. In addition, forms that were more aquatic in their habits may be over-represented relative to forms that stayed away from the water. In order to account and correct for such biases, the paleoecologist examines the mode of formation of the fossil assemblage and the rock in which it is entombed. Understanding the nature of the biases, however, does not often make it possible to correct for them in more than a qualitative fashion. Thus, while I may be able to say that species A is probably under-represented in the fossil sample relative to species B, I am not able to say by what amount species A is under-represented.

There is always an element of uncertainty as to how closely a fossil assemblage reflects the composition of the community from which it was derived, no matter how slight taphonomic distortion appears to have been. This problem is exacerbated by conscious and unconscious collecting biases. If collectors took only the best specimens they found, or if they selectively took certain taxa, the assemblage represented in museum collections will be that much more different from the composition of the living fauna.

If one goes beyond a simple census and tries to reconstruct relative biomasses, still another problem must be considered. One now needs to know the average weights of members of the various taxa. Published estimates of dinosaur weights have been made in two ways; from the cross-sectional areas of limb bones (Bakker 1972) and by determination of the volumes of scale models (Bakker 1975a, b; Béland and Russell 1978; Colbert 1962). Any suitable equation for predicting weight from skeletal measurements would be extremely complex.

It must take into account both static stresses on the bones
(as the animal stands motionless) and dynamic compressional
and shearing stresses (as the animal moves about). Furthermore, even if such an equation could be derived for one group
of animals, another group, with a different body form, might
require an entirely different equation. Thus an equation
suitable for cats might not work for deer, and a general
equation for terrestrial mammals might not be applicable to
dinosaurs. It therefore seems unlikely that simple measurements of limb cross-sectional areas could provide accurate
estimates of dinosaur weights.

The second method begins with the careful construction
of a scale model of the dinosaur in question. The volume of
the full-sized animal can then be calculated by multiplying
the model volume by the cube of the scale factor relating
the model's linear dimensions to those of the full-sized
animal. Finally, volume is converted to weight by multiplying volume by an appropriate estimate of the specific gravity
of the living animal (Colbert 1962). (It would be helpful to
have specific gravity measurements for a range of large
living reptiles and mammals. Colbert used the value 0.89,
based on a young, 280-g alligator, in his dinosaur volume-to-
weight conversions; an 864-g Heloderma lizard had a specific
gravity of 0.81. While it seems likely that there should be
a relatively narrow range for this value in large terrestrial
vertebrates, I would still feel more comfortable knowing what
that range is). Even here, there are problems. One's interpretation of the animal's habitus (e.g. whether the creature
was a sleek, cursorial animal or a bulky, lumbering form) may
affect one's reconstruction of the muscles. In addition,
large fat deposits and various external wattles, or loose
skin folds, are unlikely to leave any traces on the animal's
bones. Resultant errors in the model volume could be considerably magnified when extrapolated to the full-sized animal,
the more so as the size difference between the model and the
full-sized animal increases. It would be interesting to see
estimates of weights for living animals made from models in
this way. Comparison of such estimates with known weights of
the species in question would provide a partial test of the
accuracy of the method. To my knowledge, this has not been
done. Even so, this method seems to provide reasonably satisfactory, rough estimates of dinosaur weights.

There is still another complication to be considered.
An animal population includes individuals ranging in size
from small neonates to large adults. Weight estimates used
to determine population biomass must take this into account.
Bakker (ms.) has tackled this problem by modifying his weight
estimates according to the size-frequency distributions of

individuals in his fossil samples. How accurately fossil
size-frequency distributions reflect those of the original,
living populations is uncertain. However, juvenile/adult
ratios in living large mammals seem to be roughly similar for
carnivores and herbivores (Farlow 1976; Bakker 1975b), as
well as for tyrannosaurs and hadrosaurs in at least one
fossil fauna (Béland and Russell 1978). Therefore, the
possible departure of size distributions in fossil assemblages from those of living populations may be the same for
predator and prey taxa, minimizing the problem with respect
to predator/prey biomass ratios.

The problems I have discussed in this section are
illustrated in Table 7, which compares estimates of dinosaur
weights and relative abundance for one of the richest dinosaur faunas, from the Oldman Formation. Russell (1967, 1970)
presented a census of Oldman dinosaurs that comprised 134
hadrosaurs, 77 ceratopsians, 35 ankylosaurs, and 22 tyrannosaurs. However, he went on to state his belief that field
parties had under-collected the most common taxa, and
suggested that the number of hadrosaur specimens in museum
collections should be doubled to take this bias into account.
Bakker (1972) used this correction factor, and increased the
number of ceratopsians by 50% for the same reason; I used
Bakker's figures in my study (Farlow 1976a), although I used
a smaller weight for tyrannosaurs taken from Bakker (1975).
Béland and Russell (1978), in another look at the Oldman
fauna, have now decided that Russell's (1967, 1970) bias does
not exist.

As a result of the various census and weight estimates,
the reported predator/prey biomass ratios for the Oldman
large dinosaurs range from as low as 2% to as high as 6%.
The difference between 2% and 6% may not seem great, given
the differences in census figures and dinosaur weights that
the authors used. Indeed, viewed in this way, the agreement
among these studies is impressive. However, when one considers the possibility of convergence of endotherm and ectotherm feeding rates at large sizes (Table 6), and its consequent effects on predator/prey biomass ratios for large,
food-limited predators, a threefold difference in estimates
for the Oldman predator/prey ratio becomes more significant,
I would not be surprised if other workers produced a similar,
or even greater, range of predator/prey ratios for any
particular fossil fauna.

Predator/Prey Biomass Ratios
in Fossil Vertebrate Assemblages

In his most recent compilation, Bakker (ms.) reported a

Table 7. A Comparison of Predator/Prey Ratios Presented by Different Authors for the Oldman Formation.

	Bakker (1972)		Farlow (1976a)		Béland and Russell (1978)	
	Number	Individual Weight	Number	Individual Weight	Number	Individual Weight
1) Hadrosaurids	268	5556 kg	268	5556	127	2200
2) Ceratopsids	115	4273 kg	115.5	4273	69	2000
3) Ankylosaurians	35	3662 kg	35	3662	37	2000
4) Tyrannosaurids a) Albertosaurus b) Daspletosaurus	a) 16 b) 6	3044 kg 3556 kg	22	2000	21	1500
5) Tyrannosaur/Herbivore Biomass Ratio	3.3%		2.1%		6.4%	
6) Tyrannosaur/(Herbivore + Tyrannosaur) Biomass Ratio	3.2%[1]		2.0%		6.0%	

[1] Bakker (ms.) estimates this ratio as 3.5%

mean predator/prey biomass ratio of 3.4% in 32 fossil mammals assemblages (Table 8). He also reported a mean predator/prey ratio of 0.8% for five modern mammalian communities. (Bakker suggested that the higher ratio for fossil mammals is due to either a greater relative abundance or a higher production efficiency (predator productivity/prey productivity) of mammalian carnivores in the past than at present. However, it could also reflect some preservation bias in favor of carnivores as opposed to herbivores). For communities in which the top predators, sphenacodont reptiles, were undoubtedly ectotherms, the mean ratio was about 45%. Thecodonts and therapsids, which Bakker suggests may have been physiologically similar to living tenrecs, had ratios of 11.2% and 10.7%, respectively. Among dinosaurs, the mean predator/prey ratio was 2.1%. Because there was no statistically significant relationship between predator/prey ratio and mean predator weight in any of these groups, Bakker concluded that the convergence of ectotherm and endotherm feeding rates at large sizes does not exist.

Given the great variability of the predator/prey ratio and the relatively narrow weight range within any of these groups, the lack of a significant correlation is not surprising. On the other hand, if we hypothesize that all the reptilian groups were ectothermic, then across the entire range of reptilian data, the predator/prey ratio should converge towards mammalian values at larger sizes. This is, in fact, what does seem to happen (Table 8). There is a significant negative correlation between the logarithms (base 10) of mean predator weight and predator/prey ratio ($r = -0.71$, $p = 0.00001$). Thus, the possibility that all the fossil reptiles represented by these data were physiologically similar to living reptiles cannot be excluded.

The main point of this paper, however, is that predator/prey biomass ratios, in both living and especially fossil communities, should not be taken at face value as indicators of predator physiology. A host of complicating factors (predator and prey P/B ratios, the quantitative composition of predator diets, the possibility of competition with predators other than those considered, predation by one carnivore species on another, cannibalism) unrelated to physiology must also be taken into account.

It may be argued that these difficulties arise in the study of all animal communities, and that there is no proof that they are any worse for ectotherms. I have used this argument myself (Farlow 1976a). However, this may be as much a testimony to our ignorance as a reason for ignoring these factors when looking at fossil vertebrate communities "across

Table 8. Mean Predator Weight and the Predator/Prey Biomass Ratio in Faunas of Various Fossil Vertebrate Groups (Data from Bakker (ms.); Suspected Predator Traps Excluded).

Group	Number of Faunas	Mean Predator Weight (kg)	Range	Mean Predator/Prey Ratio (%)	Range
Mammals [1]	37	31.4	1.8 – 113.0	3.0	0.3 – 8.6
Sphenacodonts	12	43.6	20.6 – 104.8	44.7	25.8 – 67.5
Therapsids	5	81.9	12.9 – 200.0	10.7	9.0 – 12.0
Thecodonts	5	103.1	24.7 – 190.0	11.2	5.5 – 18.9
Dinosaurs	11	1258.5	77.0 – 2870.0	2.1	0.6 – 5.0

[1] Includes data from 5 modern communities.

the board." The point of the Oldman community food web scenario presented earlier is that dinosaur communities may have "worked" differently from modern large-mammal communities. Similar scenarios could be presented for communities dominated by sphenacodonts, therapsids, or thecodonts. For example, Olsen (1971) reconstructed a Permian food web, the top predator of which was the sphenacodont <u>Dimetrodon</u>. To what extent did <u>Dimetrodon</u> feed on large vertebrates (as opposed to small vertebrates and invertebrates)? How many of the potential prey species did it eat, and in what proportions of its diet? To what extent did it compete with smaller carnivores for large-vertebrate prey, and to what extent was <u>Dimetrodon</u> itself (during the egg, hatchling, and cub stages) on the menu of these other predators? We cannot say with assurance that the extent to which these situations occurred was the same for sphenacodonts in their communities as for tyrannosaurs and predatory thecodonts, therapsids, and mammals in their respective communities. For this reason, it is difficult to say to what extent differences in predator/prey biomass ratios reflect differences in predator metabolic rate as opposed to differences in food web structure and function.

Dinosaurs, and particularly theropods, may well have been endotherms, but the evidence of predator/prey biomass ratios is not, in my opinion, conclusive. There are too many complex factors affecting predator/prey ratios to allow us to isolate one of these, the physiology of the predators, as the key element involved in determining the values of such ratios. Until we better understand the various influences on predator/prey ratios in living animals, particularly large ectotherms (e.g. large snakes and carnivorous lizards, crocodilians, and sharks), it will be premature to try to ascribe much physiological meaning to the predator/prey biomass ratio in dinosaur communities.

Acknowledgments

I wish to thank A. F. Bennett for helpful discussions of reptilian physiology. Pierre Béland, C. Richard Tracy, Everett C. Olson, and Roger D. K. Thomas provided useful comments and criticisms of the manuscript.

Dinosaur Metabolism and Predator/Prey Ratios in the Fossil Record

3

Pierre Béland and D. A. Russell

Abstract

The relationship between weight and ingestion in living tetrapods implies, in the size range of dinosaurs, that predator-prey ratios in endothermic and ectothermic systems should not differ by more than a factor of four. In theory, interchangeable use of secondary productivity and standing crop estimates from fossil assemblages can lead to erroneous appraisals of food resources available to predators. In reality, predator-prey ratios in fossil assemblages are not always controlled, in a simple manner, by the energetic requirements of predators. These ratios may be altered by predator efficiency, location of prey when most exposed to predation, size of prey and demographic structure of populations. Similar predator-prey ratios in some dinosaur and mammal assemblages suggest that increasing predator efficiency has paralleled energetic requirements since Jurassic time. On the balance, trophic evidence does not support endothermy in large dinosaurs.

Introduction

We have found that an evening spent in an African big-game reserve is an awesome experience. Visual images are vague and unreliable, and one is immersed in the sounds of a powerful animate engine processing and transmitting the diurnal productivity of green plants. It is all too apparent that a human visitor (9×10^4 kcal) can quickly become an integral part of the flow of biologic energy surrounding him. Can one conclude, as has Robert T. Bakker in an original and stimulating series of publications, that levels of energy flow would have been comparable in Cretaceous terrestrial vertebrate communities? Or must one posit a quieter Mesozoic world, inhabited by dense concentrations of giant ectothermic reptiles?

Bakker (1972, 1975a, 1975b) suggested that energy in

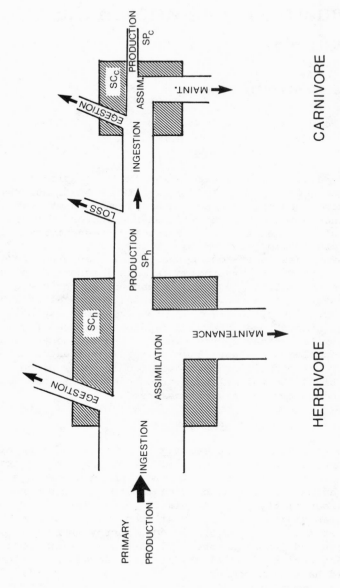

FIGURE 1. Energy flow through a simple herbivore-carnivore community.

communities dominated by endothermic vertebrates should flow an order of magnitude more rapidly than in communities dominated by ectothermic vertebrates. Using predator-prey (carnivore-herbivore) ratios in fossil assemblages as a measure of metabolism, he inferred that the ratios in dinosaur communities were within the range exhibited by fossil mammal communities. He concluded that the physiological basis underlying dinosaur food chains was the same as in mammal food chains.

We propose to evaluate the usefulness of predator-prey ratios in inferring the physiology of Jurassic and Cretaceous dinosaurs. In the first part of this paper, we examine the magnitude of the expected difference in energy flow (as reflected in predator-prey ratios) between populations of endothermic and ectothermic vertebrates. We consider simple hypothetical communities, with animals of various sizes representative of real fossil faunas, in order to demonstrate the effects of body size on the difference between predator-prey ratios in endothermic and ectothermic systems. In the second part, the reconstructed energetics of real fossil communities, recording either standing crops or secondary productivities, are discussed in the light of predator-prey interactions in modern ecosystems. We suggest that the expected differences between endothermic and ectothermic communities may be distorted in local communities near the sites of deposition, and that factors other than the energetic requirements of carnivores may alter predator-prey ratios in fossil assemblages.

Energy Flow Models

Let us imagine a simple one carnivore (C) - one herbivore (H) community in a stable state. The aggregate weights of the individuals in each population, or standing crops (SC_H, SC_C), are constant. The annual increments added to these populations through growth and births, which define their productivities (SP_H, SP_C), are also constant. It follows that the aggregate weights of individuals dying annually equal the productivities of these populations. Thus the maximum amount of food energy available annually for the carnivores is equal to the productivity of the prey (SP_H). Ecological efficiency, SP_C/SP_H (Ricklefs 1973, p. 655), may be used as an index of energy flow through this system.

Food ingested by an animal (or a population) is either assimilated, or egested unused (Figure 1). Most of the energy derived from assimilated food goes to maintenance, which includes basal metabolism, the cost of digesting food and excreting wastes, general activity, and the cost of

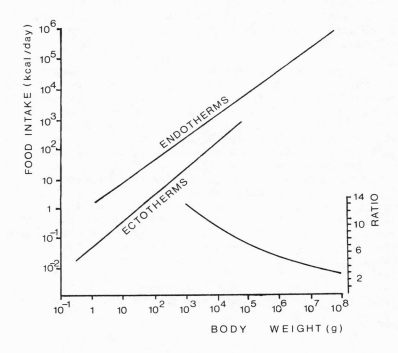

FIGURE 2. Individual daily food intakes of endothermic and
ectothermic carnivores are plotted on left ordinate. Lines are
$\log_{10}$Intake = (0.69244 ± 0.01194) $\log_{10}$W + 0.26412 for endotherms and $\log_{10}$Intake = (0.81977 ± 0.03145) $\log_{10}$W − 1.2534 for
ectotherms (after Farlow 1976a). The difference between the
slopes is significant (d = 3.8, p<.001). Ratio of intakes
for endothermic and ectothermic carnivores of the same body
weights are plotted on right ordinate.

maintaining body temperature (Davis and Golley 1963). The
remainder is stored in the population, either in the form of
tissue growth or offspring, and represents production available to other trophic levels. How does the relative
importance of the various pathways differ between endotherms
and ectotherms?

Basal metabolism, within the range of ambient temperatures normally experienced, is the first obvious difference;
although related to weight in both mammals and reptiles, it
indicates lower maintenance costs in the latter (Davis and
Golley 1963, Bennett and Dawson 1976). However, basal
metabolism is difficult to measure (Crompton et al. 1978),
and wild animals are seldom if ever under basal conditions.
Temperature regulation, which is related to body weight, is
also a maintenance cost. To what extent internal metabolic
mechanisms (in mammals) are more expensive than behavioural
responses (in reptiles) is not generally known. The costs
of digesting food and excreting wastes depend on diet, being
different for proteins than for fats or carbohydrates (Davis
and Golley 1963). Activity levels depend on size, trophic
position, behavioural traits, competition pressure and other
aspects of the niche. Thus, differences in body weight,
behaviour and diet render generalizations on maintenance
costs uncertain. Finally, the efficiency of assimilation
which determines how much energy is egested, is quite
variable in mammals as well as in reptiles, but definite
trends related to body size or trophic level are by no means
obvious (Davis and Golley 1963, p. 81; Bennett and Dawson
1976, p. 170).

In summary, it would seem premature to attempt, over a
wide range of body sizes and ecological niches, to evaluate
the relative importance of the various pathways (Figure 1)
which in turn determine the overall ecological efficiency of
endotherms and ectotherms. However, it is possible, in a
crude way, to relate input to the system — herbivore ingestion — to the output of carnivore productivity without
considering all intermediate steps.

Farlow (1976a) illustrated how the intake of food in
carnivores is related to body weight (Figure 2). The
relationships are statistically significant for endotherms
(birds and mammals) as well as for ectotherms (reptiles and
amphibians), and the difference in the slope of the lines is
also significant (d = 3.8, p<.001). Note that the ratio of
endothermic intake to ectothermic intake for animals of
similar sizes diminishes with increasing body weight.
Because sufficient data are unavailable for ectothermic
herbivores, we assume that for a given body size, the

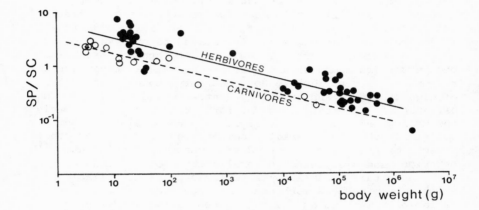

FIGURE 3.   Adult weight versus annual productivity over standing crop in tetrapods.   Closed circles : herbivorous mammals,
open circles :   carnivorous mammals and reptiles.   The upper
line for herbivores is $\log_{10}$ SP/SC = -0.29005 $\log_{10}$ W + 0.86239
(r^2 = 0.89, n = 60; data from Farlow 1976c and Hirst 1975).
The lower line for carnivores fitted by eye, parallel to the
upper one; the Y axis intercept is 0.5 (data primarily from
Farlow 1976c).

endothermic/ectothermic ratio in carnivore intake will also
apply in the case of herbivores. This may be supported by
the fact that endothermic herbivore and carnivore intakes
plot essentially on the same line (Farlow 1976a, Figures 1
and 2).

Furthermore, there is a relationship between the standing crop of a natural population, its secondary productivity
and the average weight of the animals (Farlow 1976a). The
upper line in Figure 3 describes in a statistically satisfactory manner the relationship in herbivorous mammals. In the
absence of adequate information on ectothermic herbivores, we
assume, as did Farlow (1976a), that this line is applicable
to all herbivores. We have drawn the lower line, parallel to
the upper one, which appears to be a good fit for the points
representing mammalian and reptilian carnivores. Although
there are few points, it suggests a similar trend for
decreasing SP/SC with increasing body weight in carnivores,
and simultaneously accords with their generally lower SP/SC
ratios (Bakker 1975b, Farlow 1976a).

Returning to our hypothetical one carnivore - one herbivore communities, we will derive ecological efficiencies
(SP_C/SP_H) according to both a mammalian and a reptilian
model. We will than examine the magnitude of the difference
between these efficiencies. Table 1 summarizes the calculations for three hypothetical communities where animals have
quite different body weights. In the first, herbivores weigh
45 kg and carnivores 27 kg; in the second herbivores weigh
2000 kg and carnivores 1500 kg; and in the third, herbivores
weigh 8200 kg and carnivores 1200 kg. The weights have been
chosen to approximate weights of average animals in the
Oligocene Brule mammal assemblage, the late Cretaceous Oldman
dinosaur assemblage, and the Jurassic sauropod-dominated
assemblage from Tendaguru, Tanzania (Table 2).

In the endothermic alternative for each model, the
number of herbivores is arbitrarily set at 1 individual
(Table 1). From the calorific value of this standing crop
of herbivores (SC_H) and from the weight-specific (SP/SC)
ratio described in Figure 3, we derive the productivity of
the herbivore population (SP_H). This in our ideal stable
system now represents the number of carcasses produced
annually for the carnivores to crop. Many authors have noted
that predators never fully ingest a carcass. For larger
mammalian predators, the wastage factor is between 20% and
40% (see references cited by Farlow 1976a, pp. 846-847).
This is due to several factors, including behavioural atti-
tudes, the little attention paid to energy-poor parts of the
carcass, and anatomical considerations such as jaw anatomy

TABLE 1. COMPARISON OF ECOLOGICAL EFFICIENCIES OF THREE HYPOTHETICAL ENDOTHERMIC AND ECTOTHERMIC SYSTEMS.

		BODY WT g	DAILY INTAKE (kcal) Indiv.	DAILY INTAKE (kcal) Popn	RELATIVE SC No.	RELATIVE SC kcal	SP/SC	ANNUAL SP kcal	ECOLOGICAL EFFICIENCY SP_C/SP_H	ECOLOGICAL EFFICIENCY RATIO (EER)
Oligocene Model, Brule Formation, South Dakota										
endo	H	4.5×10^4	–	–	1	6.75×10^4	.326	2.20×10^4		
	C	2.7×10^4	2151	45	0.0210	8.50×10^2	.164	1.39×10^2	.0063	6.0
ecto	H	4.5×10^4	–	–	8.4145	5.68×10^5	.326	1.85×10^5		
	C	2.7×10^4	239	253	1.0586	4.29×10^4	.164	7.03×10^3	.0380	
Cretaceous Model, Oldman Formation, Alberta										
endo	H	2×10^6	–	–	1	3×10^6	.108	3.25×10^5		
	C	1.5×10^6	34729	668	0.0192	4.33×10^4	.051	2.21×10^3	.0068	3.6
ecto	H	2×10^6	–	–	5.1905	1.56×10^7	.108	1.69×10^6		
	C	1.5×10^6	6450	2311	0.3583	8.06×10^5	.051	4.12×10^4	.0244	
Jurassic Model, Upper Saurian Beds, Tanzania										
endo	H	8.2×10^6	–	–	1	1.23×10^7	.072	8.85×10^5		
	C	1.2×10^6	29757	1818	0.0611	1.10×10^5	.055	6.00×10^3	.0068	3.7
ecto	H	8.2×10^6	–	–	4.3369	5.33×10^7	.072	3.84×10^6		
	C	1.2×10^6	5372	5258	0.9787	1.76×10^6	.055	9.61×10^4	.0250	

The body weights of the hypothetical herbivores (H) and carnivores (C) in each model are chosen equal to the average weights of the actual animals from the appropriate formations. In each case we consider an ectothermic alternative to an endothermic system with one herbivore. Assuming that primary productivity is the same for each alternative, the ectothermic herbivore numbers correspond to the endothermic/ectothermic ratios in Figure 2. Carnivore numbers are obtained from the ratio between their individual daily intake (Figure 2) and the daily intake of the population, which is (annual SP from herbivore population /365 days) × 0.75 for endotherms or 0.50 for ectotherms. The calorific value of the standing crop is obtained by assuming 1.5 kcal/g; secondary productivities are derived from the SP/SC ratios in Figure 3.

and dental occlusion. We assume here that a "mammalian" predator would crop 75% of SP_H. In natural populations, this would be an over-estimate for any one predator feeding on one prey, as many carcasses are diverted to other pathways in a complex food web. Converting this cropping to daily intake, the maximum number of carnivores sustainable (SC_C) is obtained by considering the actual daily needs of one carnivore. Finally, SP_C is derived from the appropriate carnivore SP/SC ratio in Figure 3. The ecological efficiencies SP_C/SP_H of the endothermic alternatives are 0.0063 in the Oligocene model, 0.0068 in the Cretaceous model and 0.0068 in the Jurassic model.

The same method is used to derive the ecological efficiencies of the ectothermic (reptilian) alternatives, for which herbivore numbers are determined in the following manner. It is assumed, in our hypothetical communities, that the available primary productivity would support a relatively larger standing crop of ectothermic herbivores with lower individual food intakes. Thus the ectothermic herbivore numbers are to the endothermic herbivore numbers in inverse proportion to the ratio of their weight-specific intakes. The intakes are computed from the trends in Figure 2, assuming that they hold for very large animals.

For ectothermic (reptilian) carnivores, we assume a higher wastage factor (50%) than for mammalian carnivores (75%). Carnivorous reptiles have poorer dental occlusions and relatively weaker bites than mammals (Crompton and Parker 1978). A reptilian predator would thus leave more meat on the carcass or ingest bones as well, thus expending more energy for processing and excreting materials with low energy content. The ecological efficiencies of the ectothermic alternatives are found to be SP_C/SP_H = 0.0380, 0.0244 and 0.0250 for the Oligocene, Cretaceous and Jurassic models respectively.

We can now assess the validity of the hypothesis that ecological efficiency (SP_C/SP_H) "in an ectothermic predator-prey complex should be an order of magnitude higher than in an endothermic complex" (Bakker 1972, p. 82). The ratios of 6.0 for the Oligocene model, 3.6 for the Cretaceous model and 3.7 for the Jurassic model fall substantially short of that prediction. Re-examining the calculations which yield the ecological efficiencies (SP_C/SP_H), one finds that the ecological efficiency ratio (EER) is a simple function of the relative intakes of endothermic and ectothermic carnivores and the utilization made of carcasses:

TABLE 2. NUMBERS AND WEIGHTS OF SPECIMENS OF LARGE
VERTEBRATES FROM BRULE FORMATION OF SOUTH DAKOTA, OLDMAN
FORMATION OF ALBERTA, AND UPPER SAURIAN BEDS OF TANZANIA.

	Number of Specimens	Individual Weight kg
Oligocene mammals, Brule Formation[a]		
Herbivores (34.3 × 10^6 kcal)[b]		
Bathygenus, Leptauchenia,		
Merycoidodon gracilis	47	10
Agrichoerus	12	15
Perchoerus	3	20
Poebrotherium	18	25
M. culbertsoni, Mesohippus	372	30
Colodon	4	50
Hyracodon	30	70
Bathriodon	4	100
Archaeotherium	11	350
Caeonopus	10	400
Carnivores (1.7 × 10^6 kcal)		
Daphaenus, Dinictis	28	20
Haplophoneus	5	30
Hyaenodon	8	50
Cretaceous dinosaurs, Oldman Formation[c]		
Herbivores (737.1 × 10^6 kcal)		
Hadrosaurids	127	2200
Ankylosaurians	37	2000
Ceratopsids	69	2000
Carnivores (47.3 × 10^6 kcal)		
Tyrannosaurids	21	1500
Jurassic dinosaurs, Upper Saurian Beds[d]		
Herbivores (320.6 × 10^6 kcal)		
Stegosaurs : *Kentrosaurus*	2	1400
Sauropods : *Dicraeosaurus*	5	3300
Tornieria	5	6400
Barosaurus	7	8300
Brachiosaurus	7	14900
Carnivores (3.6 × 10^6 kcal)		
Ceratosaurus	2	1200

[a] Taxa weighing less than 10 kg are excluded. Numbers after
Clark et al. 1967; weights after Bakker 1972.   [b] Caloric
value of combined weights, assuming 1.5 kcal/g.   [c] From
Béland and Russell 1978.   [d] Articulated specimens excluding
those from Basal Sands, from P. Béland, J.S. McIntosh and
D.A. Russell, ms in preparation. Weights according to one-
half sum of squared radii of the humerus and femur in quadrupeds, and one-half squared radius of femur in bipeds.

$$EER = U \left(\frac{I_{endothermic}}{I_{ectothermic}} \right)$$

where I values are the weight specific daily intakes from Figure 2 and U is the relative utilization of carcasses made by reptilian versus mammalian carnivores (in Table 1, U = (0.50/0.75) = 0.67). One can thus directly predict EER for carnivores of any body size feeding on a given herbivore productivity. Table 3 lists predicted EER for various dinosaurian faunas with carnivores of different body weights, according to various utilization ratios. It is apparent that the expected ratio between endothermic and ectothermic ecological efficiencies would never approach an order of magnitude for animals in the weight ranges of these carnivorous dinosaurs.

A similar exercise could be carried out for herbivorous dinosaurs, if plant primary productivity (PP) and herbivore secondary productivity (SP_H) were known. This is not possible due to the absence of estimates of primary productivity in terrestrial Mesozoic plant communities, and limited information on secondary productivity in large, living ectothermic herbivores. However, we have suggested above that the convergence of intake in large endothermic and ectothermic carnivores probably also applies in the case of large herbivores. Therefore, we suspect that little measurable difference would exist between the ecological efficiencies of herbivorous endotherms and ectotherms of sauropod size utilizing a given primary productivity.

TABLE 3. ECOLOGICAL EFFICIENCY RATIO (EER) BETWEEN ENDOTHERMIC AND ECTOTHERMIC ALTERNATIVES FOR THREE DINOSAUR FAUNAS, ASSUMING VARIOUS CARCASS UTILIZATION RATIOS (U).

Fauna	Carnivore Body Wt kg[a]	U = 0.50	U = 0.67	U = 0.80	U = 1.0
Tendaguru	1200	2.8	3.7	4.4	5.5
Oldman	1500	2.7	3.6	4.3	5.4
Hell Creek	3800	2.4	3.2	3.8	4.8

[a] See Table 2; weight of *Tyrannosaurus*, from terminal Cretaceous Hell Creek Formation of Montana, is calculated as for Tendaguru specimens.

Natural Populations and the Fossil Record

In comparing predator-prey ratios from various fossil assemblages, Bakker (1972, 1975b) has used productivity ratios (SP_C/SP_H) interchangeably with standing crop ratios (SC_C/SC_H), emphasizing their approximate equivalence for animals of similar sizes. That this is generally not true may be verified as follows. If (SP_C/SP_H) = (SC_C/SC_H), then ($SP_C/SC_C = SP_H/SC_H$), or the productivity/standing crop ratios of the carnivore and herbivore are equal. These last para-meters are plotted in Figure 3; assuming that the equations describing the lines therein are valid approximations, carni-vore and herbivore SP/SC — and therefore SP/SP and SC/SC — would be equivalent only where the herbivore is about 10 times heavier than the carnivore. Interchanging SP and SC ratios would in general be misleading. For example, assume that the apparent rate of energy flow toward predators in a fossil assemblage is to be compared with that of an endo-thermic community composed of animals of similar sizes. Taking the Cretaceous model in Table 1, the EER obtained by comparing SP_C/SP_H from the ectothermic alternative (0.0516) erroneously to SC_C/SC_H from the endothermic alternative (0.0068) is 7.3 instead of 3.6. It is therefore essential to compare only assemblages which both sample either standing crops or secondary productivities.

If predator-prey ratios derived from fossil assemblages are used as indicators of energy flow from herbivores to carnivores, one must assume that the relative abundance of predator and prey species are controlled by the energetic requirements of predators, and that the sedimentary record accurately reflects these abundances near sites of deposition. Other factors of a biological order could nevertheless distort predator-prey abundances in the fossil record sufficiently to obscure energy flow to predators.

Although long term accumulations may approximately record equilibrium conditions, fossil concentrations representing sudden events (Lawton 1977, Voorhies 1969) may record populations that are displaced from stable demographic structures. Predator-prey ratios would accordingly be mis-leading. For example, when prey are increasing in numbers, predators may exhibit non-linear functional responses whereby more prey are killed than fully utilized, without correspond-ing increases in SP_C. Only when such trends continue, will predators increase their productivity (Ricklefs 1973, pp. 548-556); a natural example of this may be provided by the lions of Kruger National Park (Pienaar 1969).

It has been suggested that territoriality may have

evolved as a means of dampening oscillations in predator populations. Thus, predator numbers may usually be regulated at levels corresponding to the lower part of the range of densities of their prey. This implies that predator populations are generally somewhat below carrying capacity, so that in unbiased samples they would be represented by numbers lower than those predicted from energy flow in our hypothetical systems.

In some fossil vertebrate assemblages, remains of predators occur in spectacular abundance. For example, the Early Permian assemblages from Texas and New Mexico, may have resulted from systems wherein relatively large carnivores occurred at the summit of a sequence of progressively smaller, but highly productive aquatic organisms (Charig 1976). In other cases, such as the La Brea tar pits of California, unusually attractive prey concentrations may have overwhelmed territorial behaviour in carnivores, resulting in high levels of carnivore conflict and mortality (Mech 1977). It should be noted that territoriality exists among modern crocodilians (Neill 1971) in which brain-body weight ratios are comparable to those postulated for large theropods (Hopson 1977). Such carnivore dominated assemblages are obviously of dubious worth in determining energy flow in terrestrial vertebrate communities.

The Oligocene mammal assemblage from the Brule Formation, South Dakota, and the Cretaceous dinosaur assemblage from Dinosaur Provincial Park, Alberta, have been considered as sufficiently free from primary biological bias to be used as evidence of energy flow to carnivores (Bakker 1972, Farlow 1976a). It is instructive to estimate the total energetic needs of these carnivores, according to both endothermic and ectothermic models, assuming that the fossil assemblages represent, alternatively, SC or SP. These values can then be compared with the total available secondary productivity of herbivores, as indicated by the fossil samples, in order to discern whether SC, SP or some other factor(s) controlled the relative abundance of carnivorous and herbivorous vertebrates (Table 4).

The Brule assemblage contains a higher proportion of endothermic (mammalian) carnivores than allowed if the fossil record represents   either SC or SP. This is true of several other fossil mammal assemblages (Bakker 1972, 1975a, 1975b; Farlow 1976a). Because the SP/SC of carnivores are lower than those of herbivores (Figure 3), if the fossil record usually measured secondary productivity it could be expected that fewer carnivores, on the average, would be represented in the fossil record than occur in living vertebrate

TABLE 4. COMPARISON OF ENERGETICS OF THREE REAL FOSSIL
ASSEMBLAGES, ASSUMING EITHER ENDOTHERMIC OR ECTOTHERMIC
CARNIVORES.

	Observed Assemblage Represents SC	Observed Assemblage Represents SP
Brule : Oligocene mammals		
carnivore SC	1.7	10.5
endothermic needs	31.7	196.6
ectothermic needs	3.5	22.2
herbivore SP	10.1	34.3
Oldman : Cretaceous dinosaurs		
carnivore SC	47.3	924.2
endothermic needs	266.2	5206.9
ectothermic needs	49.4	967.1
herbivore SP	78.6	737.1
Tendaguru : Jurassic dinosaurs		
carnivore SC	3.6	66.0
endothermic needs	21.7	398.3
ectothermic needs	3.9	71.9
herbivore SP	19.3	320.6

Two sets of calculations are given, assuming that the observed assemblages (roman numerals, data from Table 2) represent either standing crops (SC) or secondary productivities (SP). Other figures (italics) are estimated through the equations in Figures 2 and 3, and summing the values obtained for all weight categories. In a viable system, herbivore SP must somewhat exceed carnivore needs because of wastage (see text). Units are in 10^6 kcal.

communities. The reverse is, however, true and one is left
with the impression that the fossil bone accumulations cited
above may more accurately record locally high predator death
rates and perhaps locally dense predator populations in the
vicinity of the site of deposition.

A bias in favour of carnivore preservation could readily
occur near depositional sites. In east Africa, large herbivores must regularly visit streams and water holes to offset
water losses incurred through respiration, metabolism and
thermoregulation. According to Wright (1960) the "great
majority" of predators are concentrated near these critical
areas, where they prey on game drawn from many square kilometers of surrounding country. Predator abundance is therefore greatest near areas where sedimentation can be rapid
enough to produce a fossil record. These and similar factors
may at least partly account for predator-prey ratios in
fossil mammal assemblages which are often several times
larger than those predicted according to the energetic needs
of mammalian predators.

Reptiles also incur water losses due to respiration,
metabolism and thermoregulation (Bennett and Dawson 1976;
Cloudsley-Thompson and Butt 1977), although in ectothermic
dinosaurs dehydration would probably not have been as rapid
as in mammals because of lower metabolic rates and surface-
volume ratios. Following the standing crop model (Table 4),
ectothermic tyrannosaurids are not over-represented in the
Oldman assemblage from the Cretaceous of Alberta, Canada. In
this case, perhaps either because the herbivores needed to
drink less frequently, or because water was more generally
available in the Oldman environment, tyrannosaur populations
were apparently evenly distributed through prey populations
(Béland and Russell 1978). Thus, if Brule predators were
concentrated near water-holes, and the fossil assemblage
reflects local standing crops, tyrannosaur and mammal
predator-prey ratios may be similar in these two examples in
spite of different metabolic needs.

Articulated specimens of large carnivores occur less
frequently, relative to those of large herbivores, in the
Upper Saurian Beds (Jurassic) at Tendaguru, Tanzania than in
the Cretaceous Oldman assemblage (Tables 2 and 4). This may
have been a consequence of the great discrepancy in size
between the predators and their prey. Modern predators tend
to avoid attacking prey animals which are many times heavier
and more powerful, although this is overcome to some extent
by group foraging (Farlow 1976b). The enormous sauropods
evidently herded, may have protected their young in the centre
of herds (Bakker 1968, Ostrom 1972, Alexander 1976), and must

have been relatively immune to predator attack. If predators
were limited to cropping sick, injured or senile animals,
prey populations would tend to assume an older, less productive structure. Furthermore, a direct relationship
apparently exists between the live weight of a terrestrial
vertebrate and the proportion of indigestible skeletal
material in its body (Farlow 1976a, White 1953, R.E. Morlan,
pers. comm.). It seems probable that, in a mammalian system
composed of lion-sized carnivores and elephant-sized herbivores predator-prey ratios would be lower than in systems
where both components are of similar proportions. These
factors may have been more important in determining
differences between Tendaguru and Oldman predator-prey ratios
than differences in the energetic requirements of Jurassic
and Cretaceous predators.

One might reasonably expect Oligocene mammals to have
been endothermic, and large Jurassic and Cretaceous theropods
to have been generally similar to each other in their metabolic requirements. However, Table 4 suggests, irrespective
of what one assumes the fossil record records (SC or SP),
that mammalian Oligocene carnivores were ectotherms as were
Cretaceous tyrannosaurs. On the other hand, the relative
abundance of carnivorous theropods from the Jurassic
assemblage accords better with endothermic needs. These
discrepancies are sufficiently great, in our opinion, to cast
doubt on the utility of carnivore-herbivore ratios in fossil
assemblages in drawing inferences on energy flow in extinct
vertebrate communities, at least according to existing
models.

Conclusions

Evidence drawn from living vertebrates indicates that
the rates of food intake in mammals and reptiles converge
with increasing body weight. Furthermore, within the size
range of dinosaurs, the ecological efficiency ratio between
endotherms and ectotherms is of the order of four, rather
than an order of magnitude as predicted by Bakker. In obtain-
ing these ratios, we have assumed that large reptilian carnivores, for several reasons, do not utilize carcasses of prey
animals as efficiently as do large mammalian carnivores.
Higher ingestive and digestive efficiencies in the latter may
at least partly offset the energetic demands of a higher
metabolic rate. Similarly, if Jurassic theropods were less
efficient as predators than Cretaceous tyrannosaurs, this
would tend to alter predator-prey ratios in the direction of
an endothermic (mammalian) model. It is further apparent
that standing crop and secondary productivity ratios are not
sufficiently alike to be used interchangeably in estimating

predator-prey ratios. Irrespective of whether the record preserves standing crop or secondary productivity, available herbivore secondary productivity can only support ectothermic mammalian predators in the Brule assemblage. A high degree of caution is therefore indicated in using predator-prey ratios in fossil assemblages as indicators of the energetic needs of predators.

We are not certain which biological factors were most effective in controlling predator-prey abundances adjacent to depositional sites where vertebrate remains were entering the fossil record. The standing crop and secondary productivity of carnivorous and herbivorous animals were certainly two important factors. However, the local abundance of predators may have been affected by other physiological and ecological factors. Among these are the efficiency of ingestion and assimilation of the predators, the need of prey species for water and their consequent exposure to predation, the reduction in the proportion of digestible tissues in larger prey animals, and the influence of the demographic structure of prey populations upon secondary productivity. The effects of these factors, in our opinion, appear to swamp differences in ecological efficiencies between endothermic and ectothermic vertebrates in terrestrial communities, producing generally similar predator-prey ratios in the fossil record. A corollary is that as the metabolic needs of predators have increased through geologic time, so has their efficiency. The phenomenon has probably occurred in other components of terrestrial ecosystems as well.

Thus there would appear to be no paleoecological basis for modifying the traditional view that large dinosaurs were ectotherms. A simple comparison of predator-prey ratios in fossil assemblages may not reveal fundamental differences in rates of energy flow in ancient communities. Other factors, including those noted above, are at least as important as secondary productivity, in their cumulative effects on predator-prey ratios, and are probably equally amenable to semi-quantitative analysis. In order to enhance our understanding of the fossil record in relation to the development of community dynamics among terrestrial vertebrates, we must seek to better understand these effects. Statistically useful collections of dinosaurs are difficult and expensive to collect. However, information derived from the remains of other fossil organisms and from living communities are more easily obtained, which may bear significantly upon the estimation of energy flow in dinosaur communities.

The combination of lower metabolic rate and longer life-span result in a slower flow of energy in large animals,

whatever the evolutionary status of their physiologies. Many
of the Jurassic and Cretaceous dinosaurs attained sizes
similar to or greater than those of African elephants.   In
those ranges, the endothermy-ectothermy dichotomy becomes
obscure.   Thus, the African elephant is apparently not
strictly homeothermic, its body temperature showing a linear
relationship with ambient temperature (Elder and Rogers 1975).
This largest of terrestrial vertebrates is remarkable not
only for its size, but for the small proportion (32.6%) of
energy ingested that is used for maintenance (Laws et al.
1975).

   To visualize a world populated by dinosaurs, one must
collate images of biological situations beyond our normal
range of experience: of crocodiles balancing their energy
budgets by basking in the sun; of dense populations of large
tortoises on Aldabra atoll; and perhaps also of a herd of
ponderous but partly heterothermic elephants dozing under
acacia trees at noon.

Tissue Structures of Dinosaur Bone

4

Functional Significance and Possible Relation to Dinosaur Physiology

Armand J. de Ricqlès

Abstract

The microscopic, histological structures found in dinosaur bone have been described in several publications ranging from mid-nineteenth century reports to the results of current research. A review of this literature indicates that there is general agreement about <u>facts</u>; the available data are reasonably concordant and well established. The functional interpretation of these data is quite another matter. The tissue patterns of dinosaur bone can only be understood, in terms of function, by comparison with the bone structures of living vertebrates, whose physiologies are known directly. From such comparisons, dinosaurian bone structures indicate rapid, continuous, sustained growth, as well as protracted individual longevity. The functional analysis of dinosaur bone histology does not prove endothermy, although it is more in accord with this than any other physiological interpretation. All other things being equal, metabolic rates grossly similar to those of large mammals are inferred to have provided an essential physiological basis for the growth patterns of dinosaur bone, although other possibilities are discussed. The histological data may not necessarily indicate metabolic rates as high as those of large living endotherms, from which dinosaurs are certainly distinguished by several peculiarities of their ecological strategies. At present, it seems likely, on the balance of evidence, that the dinosaurs developed a thermal physiology that was uniquely their own. Operating between "typical" reptilian and mammalian metabolic rates, large dinosaurs probably enjoyed <u>at the very least</u> incipient endothermy, coupled with passive homoiothermy based on their size in adulthood. The resurrection of Cowles' term "heterothermy" for this physiological adaptation would emphasize its unique character and possibly reconcile divergent views of temperature regulation among the dinosaurs.

Introduction

The establishment of sophisticated, precisely controlled metabolic and thermal physiologies is a major theme
of vertebrate evolution. It has long been recognized that
the fossil record includes indirect evidence of the
evolution of thermal physiology, but only in recent years
has its interpretation attracted general attention. Now,
epitomized in the controversy over "the hot-blooded
dinosaurs", this problem has captured the interest and
imagination of a wide audience.

Some scientists, aside from being perturbed by the
journalistic tenor of this debate, have asserted that it is
pointless, since we do not and cannot know the answers, and
because the question has no more significance than that
relating to the sex of angels. It seems clear to me that
this view is not warranted. Firstly, our understanding of
the evolution of thermal physiology among fossil vertebrates
has far reaching consequences for the study of comparative
physiology, evolutionary biology and paleontology. Moreover, the range of recent research stimulated by this
question confirms its heuristic value (Dodson 1974).
Secondly, the epistemological value of the problem is no
less important. New paleontological methods and concepts
will have to be devised, as we venture from relatively well-
established comparative anatomy into paleophysiology
(Ricqlès 1974). We have a long way to go, from a range of
subjective opinions such that the issue is "moot", to a
situation where objective, scientifically reliable
demonstrations could be generally accepted. Adequate tools
and concepts must be developed to achieve this goal.

In the establishment of new knowledge, there is
frequently a conflict of interest between the needs of
scientific research and those of the general public. It is
controversy, not consensus, that leads to scientific
progress. On the other hand, the layman expects, from
teachers, from museums, and from the media, a realistic
and fair synthesis, not the uncertainties of the current
intellectual vogue. The layman has a right to an accurate
and reliable account, in which he can have confidence, of
a subject like dinosaur physiology. In this context, the
popularization of the current thinking and debates on this
topic of a small, specialized research community has been,
at best, untimely. Public controversy on such a popular
subject is liable to foster lack of confidence in the
methods of science, especially if the debate is carried on
in journalistic rather than scientific terms. Furthermore,
public knowledge changes slowly, with considerable inertia.

The scientist has a social responsibility not to bring new ideas to this domain until they have been rigorously tested and become well established.

Whether or not the dinosaurs were hot-blooded, it is time to cool the debate and focus once again on the research! A final resolution of the issue is not yet possible and the methods by which it may be reached are not yet fully developed. If we take this as a starting point, it may be possible to reach a minimal consensus which will provide a firm basis for further progress.

Dinosaur bone histology: an historical review

Histology is the study of tissues, integrated structures ranging from a few cells to a scale of centimeters. Most important bone tissue structures range in size from about 5 μm to 500 μm. They may be studied with a lens or with an electron microscope, but most routine work on fossil material is performed on thin-sections, of the petrographic type. Good three-dimensional integration of the structures is often much more important than extreme magnification. Polarized light is often very helpful, showing up the spatial organization of fibrous components of the tissues.

The terminology used in the histological description of dinosaur bone has been explained in detail elsewhere (e.g. Enlow and Brown 1956; Enlow 1966, 1969; Ricqlès 1974, 1975, 1976a). Here, only the principal terms and concepts need be recalled. Woven or fibrous bone is a primary tissue, commonly added to the surface of a bone, under the membraneous periosteum, during growth. Lamellar bone may also be deposited in centrifugal layers beneath the periosteum, forming general lamellae of surface bone. More often, however, lamellar bone is added in centripetal layers to the walls of tunnels, surrounding the vascular canals within primary compact bone. This forms primary osteons, which are a major component of densely vascularized compact bone tissues, such as are found among dinosaurs. These lamellar primary osteons, together with the fibrous woven bone in which they are buried, constitute a mixed type of primary bone, known as the fibro-lamellar complex, illustrated in Figure 1. Bone with this general structure can form a variety of distinctive patterns, characterized for example as laminar, reticular, or plexiform bone, depending on the number, orientation and spatial organization of the primary osteons. In contrast with these structures, primary osteons may be buried directly in

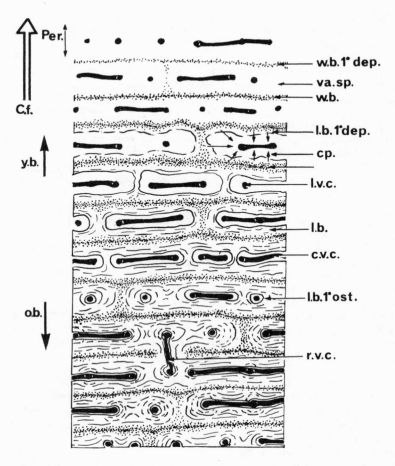

Figure 1. Deposition of fibro-lamellar primary bone.
Diagrammatic illustration of primary bone deposition (here
forming laminar cortex) as seen in a transverse section of
a shaft. This pattern of bone deposition is common in the
long bones of half-grown dinosaurs. Key: c.f., centrifugal
direction of overall bone deposition; c.p. centripetal
direction of lamellar bone deposition around vascular canals,
forming primary osteons; c.v.c., circular vascular canal;
l.b., lamellar bone; l.b.1°dep., first deposition of
lamellar (centripetal) bone; l.v.c., longitudinal vascular
canal; l.b.1°ost., lamellar bone of primary osteon; Per.,
periosteum; o.b., older bone (deeper in the cortex);
r.v.c., radial vascular canal; va.sp., vascular and
connective spaces still empty of hard tissue; w.b.1°dep.,
first deposition of woven (fibrous) periosteal bone; y.b.,
younger bone (in superficial position).

lamellar sub-periosteal bone, forming the so-called
lamellar-zonal pattern. This structure, which is less
densely vascularized than the fibro-lamellar complex, is
seldom found in dinosaur bones.

Remodeling by resorption and renewed deposition
produces secondary bone. These processes are presumed to
be involved in the turnover of calcium and phosphorus in
metabolism (Amprino 1967), while remodeling plays a direct
and fundamental part in the growth of long bones (Figure 2).
In compact bone these processes give rise to Haversian
systems (=secondary osteons), while more or less complex
brecciated trabeculae develop in cancellous bone. Haversian
systems form in contact with existing vascular canals, in
either primary or secondary bone. Thus, several generations
of Haversian systems can replace one another in massive,
compact bone, producing the familiar dense Haversian bone
typical of man's adult skeleton (Figure 3).

The fossilization of bone generally involves molecule
by molecule replacement of the bone minerals, without
changing the tissue structures. Hence these structures are
commonly preserved in dinosaur bone, which makes paleo-
histology possible! Dinosaur specimens were among the first
fossil bones to be examined histologically, soon after
Owen's recognition of the Dinosauria as a coherent
taxonomic group. As early as 1849, Queckett suggested the
possible use of sections of fossil bone in the identification of taxa. Amongst thin sections depicted in his
well-known catalogue (Queckett 1855), Haversian bone can be
recognized in Iguanodon.

Casual observations and illustrations of dinosaurian
bone structures may be found in several early works on these
animals. Mantell (1850a, b) comments on the bone tissue of
Pelorosaurus and shows osteons in the dorsal spine of
Hylaeosaurus. Owen (1859a) used bone structures as evidence
of an aquatic or marine mode of life for sauropods, which
he considered to be gigantic marine animals akin to
crocodiles, not dinosaurs (see Owen 1842). Owen's picture
of a Cetiosaurus vertebra (1859a, Plate IX, fig. 2) shows
that a good part of the bone consists of dense laminar or
plexiform tissue. His functional interpretation of sauropod
bone structures was discussed and rejected by Hatcher (1903),
but remains as the basis for the persistent interpretation
of the sauropods as aquatic or semi-aquatic animals (Coombs
1975).

These early accounts can hardly be regarded as
histological studies. Most authors report "Haversian" and

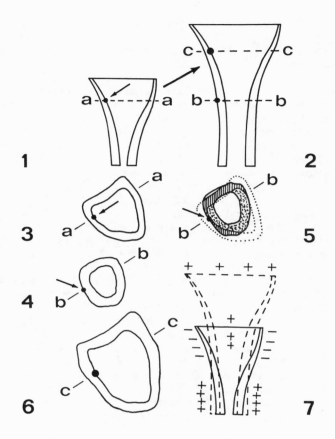

Figure 2. <u>Growth remodeling in a long bone</u>. As the flaring
end of a long bone grows, level <u>aa</u> in the younger bone (1)
becomes level <u>bb</u> in the older, larger bone (2). Thus, the
actual shape of section <u>aa</u> (3) is remodeled as <u>bb</u> (4). These
sections are "homologous". The actual structure of section
<u>bb</u> is shown in (5). Note that the cementing lines in the
cortex have nothing to do with cyclical growth in this
instance. Relative to the overall shape of the bone,
section <u>cc</u> in (2) is "analogous" to section <u>aa</u>. The shape
of the cross-section <u>cc</u> (6) is identical to that of <u>aa</u>, but
it is larger. As growth proceeds, exterior bone surfaces
sequentially experience deposition (+), erosion (-) and
further deposition (+), shown by the superimposition of
successive growth stages in (7). Modified from a figure
by D. H. Enlow, <u>Principles of Bone Remodeling</u> (Charles C.
Thomas, Publisher, 1963).

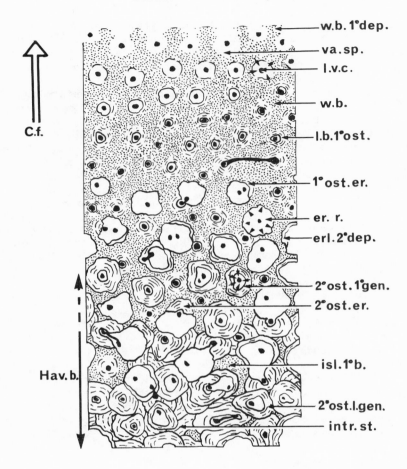

Figure 3. <u>Haversian substitution</u>. Primary bone (here a fibro-lamellar tissue with parallel longitudinal canals) is resorbed and reconstituted as secondary dense Haversian bone. Diagrammatic. Key as for Figure 1, and: <u>er.r.</u>, erosion room; <u>erl.2ᴼdep.</u>, early secondary (centripetal) deposition in an erosion room; <u>Hav.b.</u>, Haversian bone; <u>intr.st.</u>, interstitial system (remnants of older osteons); <u>isl.1ᴼb.</u>, island of primary bone; <u>1ᴼost.er.</u>, primary osteon experiencing erosion; <u>2ᴼost.er.</u>, secondary osteon experiencing erosion; <u>2ᴼost.1ᴼgen.</u>, first generation of secondary osteon (=Haversian system); <u>2ᴼost.1.gen.</u>, later generation of secondary osteon (=Haversian system).

other structures, without further details. They were more
interested in the mechanical and ecological implications of
the occurrence of cancellous or compact bone, of "solid" or
"hollow" bone shafts, than in the details of microstructure.

Modern, systematic studies of dinosaur bone histology
were initiated by Seitz (1907). His masterful "Comparative
studies on the microscopical bone structures among fossil
and living reptiles", with its meticulously objective and
well illustrated descriptions, still deserves careful
attention. Another milestone in this field was set by
Gross (1934), who drew heavily on then recent advances in
the understanding of the fibrillar organization of bone,
due especially to Weidenreich (1930). Gross emphasized the
histogenetic and functional differences between primary and
secondary osteons, a fundamental point recognized in the
nineteenth century and by Seitz, but often overlooked, even
today. At about the same time, Nopcsa and Heidsieck (1933)
published the only available study of the ontogeny of
dinosaur bone structures. They were able to demonstrate
conclusively, on histological grounds, that some ornithopod
"genera" were in fact juveniles of other taxa. However,
Nopcsa's untimely death prevented him from completing the
thorough histological study of fossil reptiles that he had
evidently planned (Nopcsa and Heidsieck 1933, 1934).

Several authors have reported incidental observations
of dinosaur bone histology. These reports are useful,
providing information on a wide range of genera. We may
note the work of Petersen (1930), Eggeling (1939) who relies
heavily on Gross (1934), Lapparent (1947, 1960), and
Halstead and Mercer (1968). Illustrations of the bone
histology of Allosaurus fragilis have recently been published, without comment, by Madsen (1976, Plate 24, figs.
A-E). These figures unquestionably show laminar bone in
the shaft of a fibula and fibro-lamellar bone with parallel
vascular canals in a young femur.

Detailed modern treatments of dinosaur bone histology
are provided by Enlow and Brown (1956-58), who rely heavily
on the work of Seitz and Gross, and by Enlow (1969) who
adds many new data and an important discussion of functional
interpretations. Papers by Currey (1962) and Ricqlès
(1968a, b) give new accounts of bone structures among
prosauropods and sauropods, with further discussion of the
functional interpretation of these structures. These
studies all helped to kindle the present debate on the
nature of dinosaurian physiology.

Most of the dinosaurian histological patterns illustrated or clearly described in the literature are summarized
in Table 1, which is not complete, but which does give a
fair indication of the data available. It is clear that at
least a good part of the skeleton of large, adult dinosaurs
is frequently transformed into dense Haversian bone. This
occurs in the cortex of bone shafts, in flat bones and ribs.
Quite different in form, the brecciated trabeculae of the
cancellous bone are also of secondary origin. They likewise
record a complex history of bone erosion and reconstruction.

However, many skeletal parts are not Haversian in
structure. Even among large, mature individuals, primary
bone tissues occur, with little evidence of any Haversian
reconstruction. The extent of Haversian replacement varies
considerably, not only from bone to bone, but also within
individual bones, which may consist partly of secondary
Haversian material and partly of primary bone. The extent
of Haversian reconstruction increases during ontogeny. It
varies substantially from one species to another, but it
does not vary significantly among individuals of a given
species, at the same growth stage. However, our knowledge
of the precise anatomical distribution of primary and
Haversian bone is not yet adequate for any dinosaur.

At first glance, the structures of primary compact
bone appear to be varied and complicated. However, in
dinosaurs, these primary tissues are nearly always variations
of the fibro-lamellar complex (Ricqlès 1974, 1975). They
are very richly vascularized, with a large number of primary
vascular canals, each surrounded by a primary osteon, all
embedded in a matrix of fibrous periosteal bone. In
carnosaurs and prosauropods, this primary bone may exhibit a
laminar pattern (sensu Gross 1934; Currey 1962; Ricqlès
1974, 1975). Here, longitudinal and circular vascular canals
are arranged in a regular mesh composed of these two elements.
The primary bone of sauropods shows the same arrangement, or
the very similar plexiform pattern (Enlow and Brown 1956;
Ricqlès 1968). In the latter case, radial vascular canals
are added to the pattern, forming a regular mesh with three
elements. These patterns also occur in the compact bone of
ornithischian dinosaurs. In addition, both a simpler
pattern, consisting of closely packed, parallel longitudinal
canals, and a reticular pattern of irregular branches and
anastomoses, occur in this group. The laminar and plexiform
variations of the fibro-lamellar complex are especially well
developed in the shafts of large bones, where there is a
large, regular accumulation of compact bone.

A clear and consistent account of dinosaur bone histology seems to emerge from the data compiled here. This picture is generally confirmed by a factor analysis of these data (Bonis et al. 1972), as well as by further unpublished results accumulated by the present author. However, this should by no means be taken to indicate that adequate descriptive information is now available. The caution previously urged remains appropriate: "It is difficult, for a given species, let alone for a large and heterogeneous group, to describe bone structure by a single term. For instance, it is dangerous to refer to the bone structure of a whole animal as being "plexiform" or "Haversian", as long as numerous parts of the skeleton have not been studied. In the case of dinosaurs, examination of the histological diversity in different parts of one bone is sufficient to show up the limitations of most of the available descriptive data" (Ricqlès 1968a).

Functional interpretation of the histological data

The methodological problem

The quality of preservation of dinosaur bone tissues generally permits their precise structural description. Thus, no special difficulties arise in the comparison of dinosaur histological patterns with those of living animals. In this connection, it is notable that unique tissue structures, lacking counterparts among living animals, have not been found in dinosaurs.

With respect to function, it would seem that any interpretation of dinosaur tissue structures should adhere strictly to the Principle of Uniformity. This approach is widely, often implicitly, accepted in paleobiology, but it does, in fact, raise some problems. The basic uniformitarian assumption required here might be stated as follows: "Bone tissues which are characteristically associated with specific processes among living animals should be interpreted as having played identical roles among dinosaurs". This seems clear enough, but, since dinosaurs were not anatomically or presumably physiologically identical with any living animals, even very similar bone tissues surely did not have exactly the same morphogenetic significance. Moreover, it is impossible to assess the amount of distortion, however slight, introduced here by the uniformitarian assumption.

Comparison of fossil bone tissues with those of living animals also depends upon the implicit assumption of uniformity in the physical environment. It is widely

believed that the Mesozoic world was not grossly different
from that of the present day, with respect to gravity,
atmospheric composition and pressure, solar energy influx,
mean surface and atmospheric temperatures, and so on, as
assumed by Spotila et al. (1973), for instance. Nevertheless, the uniformitarian assumption is still hypothetical
and it should be made explicit in relation to physiological
comparisons. It is historically interesting that Owen (1842,
p. 202-204), in the paper in which he conceived of the
Dinosauria, argued in just the opposite sense. Impressed by
the striking "mammalian" and "avian" characteristics of
dinosaurs and pterosaurs, he stressed the approach of these
animals to his hypothetical vertebrate archetype. Hence, he
did not consider the possibility that they were endothermic,
but rather speculated about the kind of physical environment
that could have led to the development of such characters
in reptiles. Cope (1870) also speculated on the consequences of changes in the proportions of atmospheric oxygen
and carbon dioxide for dinosaurs and other terrestrial
organisms, in explicitly evolutionary terms.

We may continue to take it as a first premise that
paleohistological interpretations can be made on the basis
that similar histological characteristics, of living and
fossil animals, reflect similar functions. More sophisticated analysis, at a later stage, should make it possible to
determine the extent to which this assumption is valid.

Primary bone tissues and their significance

It is still not generally recognized that there is a
direct relationship between the tissue structure of primary,
periosteal bone and its rate of deposition. Since the
pioneer work of Amprino (1947), this correlation has been
stressed repeatedly (Enlow 1966, 1969; Ricqlès 1974, 1976b).
It is striking that this relationship is maintained at all
levels of integration: between different parts of a given
bone, between different bones of one skeleton, and among
different species.

The generally accepted (but not always verified)
correlation between primary bone structure and adult animal
size is merely a secondary consequence of the relationship
between bone histology and growth rate (Ricqlès 1977). The
histogenetic basis for this relationship has been
demonstrated several times (e.g. Pritchard 1956; Ricqlès
1974, 1977). Here, it will suffice to recall the observed
correspondences. Lamellar or pseudo-lamellar, parallel-
fibered bone, with few vascular canals, is indicative of
slow deposition. Likewise, numerous bone tissues grouped

TABLE 1.   Documentation of Histological Patterns in
Dinosaur Bone, from published literature.

Key: L, long bones of limbs (mainly cortex of diaphysis);
R, ribs; F; flat bones; T, ossified muscles, tendons
or ligaments; V, vertebrae; W, unidentified or
miscellaneous elements.
l, laminar fibro-lamellar primary bone; x, plexiform
fibro-lamellar primary bone; p, primary bone with
parallel (longitudinal) canals; r, reticular fibro-
lamellar primary bone; i, incomplete Haversian bone;
d, dense Haversian bone; m, lamellar or miscellaneous
bone tissues.

References: (1) Broili 1922; (2) Campbell 1966; (3) Currey
1962; (4) Eggeling 1938; (5) Enlow and Brown 1957;
(6) Gross 1934; (7) Halstead and Mercer 1968;
(8), (9) Lapparent 1947, 1960; (10) Madsen 1976;
(11) Moodie 1928; (12) Nopcsa 1933; (13) Ostrom 1969;
(14) Petersen 1930; (15), (16), (17), (18) Ricqles
1968a, 1968b, 1975, 1976; (19) Seitz 1907.

Genera, according to original authors	Anatomical data						Histological data							References
	L	R	F	T	V	W	l	x	p	r	i	d	m	
PROSAUROPODA														
Plateosurus	+						+	+			+			5, 6, 19
Euskelosaurus	+						+					+		16, 17, 18
"Prosauropods"	+			+			+				+			3
SAUROPODA														
Cetiosaurus	+						+	+			+	+		7
Haplocanthosaurus		+									+	+		19
Brachiosaurus	+							+			+	+	+	4, 5, 6
Bothriospondylus	+							+	+		+	+		15,16, 17,18
Pelorosaurus	+											+		4, 14
Camarasaurus	+	+					+	+			+	+		19
"Morosaurus"	+	+						+			+	+	+	19
Rabbachisaurus	+											+		9
Brontosaurus		+										+		19
Diplodocus	+	+							+		+	+		5, 19
Hypselosaurus	+											+		8
"Sauropod"	+			+								+		9
COELUROSAURIA														
Procompsognathus		+										+		12
Coelophysis	+											+		12

TABLE 1 (continued).

Genera, according to original authors	L	R	F	T	V	W	l	x	p	r	i	d	m	References
COELUROSAURIA														
"Struthiomimus"	+								+			+		12
Ornithomimus	+											+		12
"Coelurosaur"	+											+		12
CARNOSAURIA														
?Zanclodon	+							+					+	19
Megalosaurus	+	+							+		+	+		5, 12, 19
Ceratosaurus	+											+		12
Allosaurus	+	+					+		+		+	+	+	5,10,12,19
Dryptosaurus			+									+		5, 19
Gorgosaurus	+											+		12
Tyrannosaurus	+											+		12
Spinosaurus	+											+		12
Deinonychus			+	+			+	+					+	13
ORNITHOPODA														
Hypsilophodon	+											+		12
Dysalotosaurus	+								+					12
Iguanodon	+	+							+		+	+		5,6,12,19
Camptosaurus	+											+		12
"Mochlodon"	+								+	+				2
Rhabdodon	+	+			+							+		8,12,17
"Trachodon"	+	+	+	+					+		+	+		1,5,11,12,19
Hypacrosaurus	+								+		+	+		12
Orthomerus	+											+		12
Tetragonosaurus	+								+					12
STEGOSAURIA														
Scelidosaurus	+											+		12
Kentrurosaurus	+											+		12
Stegosaurus	+	+							+		+	+	+	5, 19
ANKYLOSAURIA														
Struthiosaurus	+											+		12
Ankylosaurus	+		+									+	+	11, 12
CERATOPSIA														
Psittacosaurus	+											+		12
Protoceratops	+											+		12
Brachyceratops	+											+		12
Leptoceratops	+											+		12
Monoclonius	+											+		12
Triceratops	+	+										+	+	5, 12, 19

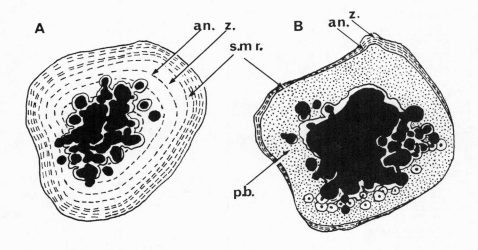

Figure 4. Growth lines. Diagrammatic sections showing
"typical" growth line patterns seen in bones of ectotherms
(A) and endotherms (B). Note decrease in growth rates
following sexual maturity. Key: an., annual slow down or
cessation of growth; z., zone: annual period of active
growth; s.mr., sexual maturity; p.b., primary fibro-lamellar
bone rapidly deposited during pre-adult ontogeny.

under the lamellar-zonal pattern are all the products of more or less slow deposition. Conversely, the fibro-lamellar pattern is always linked to more or less rapid bone deposition and high growth rates. Even the laminar, plexiform and reticulate sub-categories of fibro-lamellar bone indicate more precise differences in the rate of continuous deposition of massive, new bone. This is not to say, of course, that rate of deposition is the only factor that governs periosteal bone structure; many other factors are involved (Ricqlès 1975, 1976, 1977). In conclusion, we note:

1) Among living animals, fibro-lamellar periosteal bone tissues are linked to the rapid, continuous deposition of massive amounts of dense primary bone. This growth pattern is typical of large birds and most medium to large sized land mammals.

2) The prevalence of the same fibro-lamellar tissue structures in dinosaur bones (see Table 1), even among the smaller taxa, strongly suggests at least that dinosaurs had the same growth rates as these living endotherms. These tissues also indicate that dinosaur bone growth was not only rapid, but continuous rather than cyclical, a topic that will be taken up in the next section.

In these respects, dinosaurs differ from most other living and extinct reptiles and amphibians, in which, apart from therapsids and pterosaurs, lamellar-zonal primary bone predominates.

Are there "growth lines" in dinosaur bone?

Following the pioneer work of Peabody (1961), it has become accepted that the occurrence of growth lines in the bones of fossil vertebrates provides an important clue to their thermal physiologies. The widespread occurrence of growth lines is said to be diagnostic of ectothermy, while the absence of such lines suggests, although it does not prove, endothermy (Figure 4). In recent years, numerous studies concerned mainly with the use of growth lines in age determination have somewhat changed the picture. Hence, the value of this histological characteristic in reconstructing the thermal physiologies of extinct animals should be critically reevaluated.

First, some preliminary problems must be noted.
(a) Supposed "growth lines" may have little or nothing to do with regular, age-related, sequential growth, if, for instance, they should turn out to be "tide marks" or "resorption lines" (Figure 5), related to bone remodeling

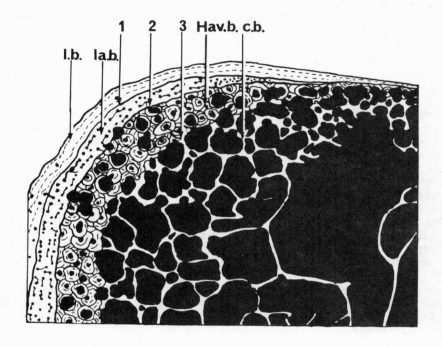

Figure 5. "False growth lines". The general stratification
of the cortex, shown diagrammatically here, is a result of
complex growth remodeling processes. Note that these
"growth lines" (1, 2, 3) are outwardly migrating "strand-
lines" of remodeling processes. They are quite unrelated
to changing rates of deposition of primary bone and cut
across distinct strata of pre-existing tissues. Compare
with Figure 4. Key as for Figures 1, 2, and c.b.,
cancellous (secondary) bone of the spongiosa; la.b.,
laminar (primary) bone of the cortex; l.b., lamellar
(primary) bone of the cortex.

(Enlow 1963). (b) Apparently good, cyclical growth lines may bear no regular relationship to age. Such is the case, for example, with the concentric imprints left by intervertebral ligaments on the vertebral centra of many tetrapods.
(c) Cyclical growth lines may be regularly related to age, but yet not be annual. Various periodic events may be recorded in hard tissues, so an a priori annual interpretation of the cycles is not warranted.

Clearly, extreme caution should be exercised in the physiological interpretation of apparently cyclic patterns of bone deposition, especially those observed only in fossil material. Current research demonstrates the existence of true annual growth lines, which can be used with confidence to determine the ages of the animals, in a number of living species (Castanet et al. 1977; Castanet 1978; Pascal 1978). However, such reliable results have been obtained only by linking critical studies of bone histology to detailed ecological observations. Broad conclusions on the thermal physiologies of extinct tetrapods cannot be drawn from casual observations of bone "growth rings", especially without detailed, comparative histological studies.

In some recent popular accounts, Halstead (1975; Halstead and Middleton 1972, p. 28), who argues that dinosaurs were passive mass homeotherms and not true endotherms, claims that bone growth lines can be used to determine the ages of individual dinosaurs. To my knowledge, this claim is based only upon a similar, tentative suggestion made in a general essay by Jepsen (1964). The only evidence presented by Jepsen is a photograph of a broken surface of a bone from the "frill" of a ceratopsian dinosaur. This photograph is supposed to show about 120 successive layers, which Jepsen called osteochrons, interpreting them as annual cycles of periosteal bone deposition. The photograph is not sufficiently enlarged (x4) for positive identification of the layers, but it seems clear that Jepsen's "osteochrons" consist simply of laminar primary bone seen under low magnification. I have often seen this kind of stratification myself, even with the naked eye, on broken surfaces of sauropod bones, especially from partly grown individuals. When this structure is examined in thin section, laminar or plexiform bone is observed, with a pattern of vascular canals which accounts for the apparent stratification. I have previously discussed these ordinary laminae of laminar and plexiform bone in some detail (Ricqlès 1968a, 1975), concluding that they have no annual or other regular periodic significance.

I have also recently investigated materials similar
to that described by Jepsen (1964). These unpublished
studies have not yet revealed structures like that described
by Jepsen; all the bone from ceratopsian "frills" is of the
dense Haversian type. It seems likely that Jepsen's
specimen exhibits a pattern of primary vascularization,
presumably having come from an immature individual. My
material does not show any structures comparable to the
annual growth layers that have been recognized among living
vertebrates. In short, there is very little basis for the
claim that dinosaur ages can be determined from annual
growth lines.

The only observations known to me of possible growth
lines in dinosaur bone are as follows: (a) In the outermost
cortex of the tibia of a large Brachiosaurus, Gross (1934,
figs. 14, 15) shows "lamellar" periosteal bone tissue that
might exhibit growth lines. In such a large, presumably old
animal, it is not surprising that the outermost thin sheet
of cortex would have been slowly deposited and hence
lamellar. However, even here, clear cyclic repetitions are
not obvious. (b) Some illustrations of Seitz (1907) might
show growth lines in Morosaurus (Pl. IX, fig. 49),
Allosaurus (Pl. X, figs. 53-55) and Stegosaurus (Pl. XI, fig.
64). (c) Bone shafts of young Allosaurus illustrated by
Madsen (1976, fig. 24A-E) show linear discontinuities within
a fibro-lamellar cortex. However, the spacing of these
lines is much more suggestive of temporary variations in
growth rate, possibly linked to sequential bone remodeling
during growth (Enlow 1963), than of regular, periodic
depositional rhythms. (d) On a polished section of a
vertebral centrum from an adult iguanodontid dinosaur, in
the Peabody Museum collections at Yale University, about 6-8
"cycles" can be discerned with the naked eye[*]. These
rhythms involve both the cortex and the central cancellous
bone. If they are indeed annual, these cycles imply an
extraordinarily high growth rate for this dinosaur.

On the basis of all the available observations, it is
clear that typical annual growth lines, such as those seen
in large crocodile bones, are remarkably inconspicuous in
dinosaur bones, if they occur at all. In this respect,
dinosaurs again stand in marked contrast with the majority
of reptiles. Bone growth lines are conspicuous in
cotylosaurs, mesosaurs, pelycosaurs, chelonians, crocodilians and in the Squamata (Enlow 1969; Ricqlès 1974;
Castanet et al. 1977). They are much less well developed,

---

[*] I thank J. O. Farlow for bringing this material to my
   attention.

or absent, in therapsids, some thecodonts, pterosaurs and dinosaurs.

Given these observations, we can consider the functional significance of bone growth lines, in relation to growth and remodeling processes, and hence to thermal physiology. The presence of growth lines suggests ectothermy, whereas their absence suggests endothermy, but neither condition is absolutely diagnostic, since growth lines have been recognized in the bone of both living ectotherms and endotherms.

Annual growth lines occur among mammals in keratinous structures derived from the skin, in teeth, and even in bone, as has been well established by the important work of Klevezal and Kleinenberg (1967). However, it must be emphasized that the bone growth lines of living ectotherms and mammals are quite dissimilar. The occurrence of growth lines in mammalian bone is very restricted and systematically consistent. They are well developed, especially in the lower jaws, in small species such as insectivores (Morris 1970), lagomorphs (Ohtaishi et al. 1976), and small felids (Pascal 1978). Growth lines are also quite common in several different bones of aquatic pinnipeds and cetaceans. In the great majority of mammals, the primary fibro-lamellar bone of the cortex (mesosteal bone of Russian workers) is devoid of growth lines. This tissue, which forms the bulk of the compact portion of long-bone shafts, is the product of the rapid, continuous growth during early life. Only the thin, outermost sheets of lamellar bone, slowly accumulated in adulthood, are likely to show any sign of annual layering. Records of growth rings in bird bones are scarce (Van Soest and Van Utrecht 1971) but their distribution seems to be comparable with that observed among the bones of mammals rather than reptiles.

Periodic growth lines in the bone of mammals thus seem to be restricted to species or individual bones and tissues with the lowest growth rates. This is in marked contrast to the situation in typical ectotherms, where growth lines occur extensively throughout the skeleton, are not restricted to the outermost cortex, and are especially well developed in bones with the highest growth rates (Peabody 1961; Ricqlès 1974, 1975, 1978). In conclusion, we note:

(1) Cyclical bone growth lines occur among both ectotherms and endotherms, so their occurrence <u>alone</u> does not provide a reliable, absolute criterion for either pattern of thermal physiology. However, diagnostic differences do exist in their mode of occurrence and distribution in the two groups.

(2)   Growth lines are well developed throughout the cortex in many bones of most ectotherms, even those living in the tropics. They are especially prominent in the most rapidly deposited bone.

(3)   Where they do occur in mammals, growth lines are often restricted to the lower jaw and outermost lamellar cortex of long bones. They are best developed in small species and in bones or tissues with the lowest growth rates.

(4)   The general absence of growth lines, comparable with those of living ectotherms, in dinosaur bone is <u>at least</u> indicative of continuous rather than cyclic bone growth. This pattern is much more similar to those observed among living endotherms than it is to those of typical ectotherms.

Haversian bone and the controversy over its significance

Recent arguments about the significance of the Haversian bone in dinosaurs have incorporated considerable over-simplification and even misinterpretation. A review of some of the results of extensive studies made by biologists on the Haversian bone of living animals may help to clarify these problems. No general explanation of the biological significance of Haversian replacement, that would account for all the known facts to everyone's satisfaction, is at hand. It is generally recognized that the process is a complex one, with many determining factors. Several individual "explanations" for Haversian substitution have been proposed. These will be briefly summarized here, before their relevance to the interpretation of dinosaur bone is assessed. More detailed accounts of these problems, fully documented from the extensive histological literature, may be found in my previous papers (Ricqlès 1976b, 1977a, b).

(1)   "Dense Haversian bone is related to age".   This assertion is well documented; older animals generally have more extensive Haversian bone. All other things being equal, it is obvious that a longer life provides more opportunity for Haversian replacement to occur. However, it does not follow that no Haversian substitution is found in young bones, nor that all old bone is densely Haversian in structure.

(2)   "Dense Haversian bone is related to size". It is a fact that dense Haversian bone is most frequently encountered among moderate or large sized species. Conversely, very small species, whether ectotherms or endotherms, generally lack dense Haversian bone. However, large species usually

live longer, so it is difficult to separate the effects of
age and size. Salamanders and some other long-lived small
animals do not have dense Haversian bone, but it may appear
after only a few years of life in some fairly small mammals
(cats, many birds).

(3) "Dense Haversian bone is related to patterns of
primary bone growth and remodeling, especially in relation
to fibrous insertions of tendons and ligaments". Some
Haversian replacement seems unquestionably to be linked to
these factors, but they cannot alone explain the general,
systematic and individual, anatomical segregation of all
dense Haversian tissue. Furthermore, the nature of the
supposed causal relationship between fibrous insertions and
Haversian remodeling remains unclear.

(4) "Dense Haversian bone is related to the bio-
mechanical adaptation of bone tissues to physical strain".
This has been suspected for more than a century. However,
micro-hardness tests and other experiments have shown that
dense Haversian bone is mechanically weaker than the primary
bone it replaces. Also, dense Haversian bone frequently
first appears in skeletons that are already large. Finally,
Haversian replacement throughout the skeleton is much more
extensive in perimedullar bone, which is submitted only to
low mechanical stresses, than in the highly stressed outer
cortex. These observations are not consistent with the idea
that all Haversian replacement occurs in adaptive response
to mechanical strain.

(5) "Dense Haversian bone serves to repair microcracks
and/or prevent the development of mechanical fatigue in
strained bone". These are interesting ideas, currently being
studied. They would link Haversian replacement more subtly
to the mechanical function of bone than would a direct,
adaptive response to strain. However, the comments noted
under (3) and (4) above apply here, also.

(6) "Dense Haversian bone develops in response to
cellular necrosis and/or microvascular accidents, as the
means for tissue replacement". Again, the comments noted
under (3) and (5) above apply here.

(7) "Dense Haversian bone is related to the histological type of primary bone initially laid down". Since
Haversian substitution occurs by erosion and replacement
along vascular canals already present, the histological
pattern of primary bone would seem to determine the pattern
of replacement. Where dense Haversian cortical bone occurs,
it is indeed likely to have replaced a dense fibro-lamellar

primary bone, rather than lamellar-zonal bone. However, it does not follow that fibro-lamellar bone is always replaced by dense Haversian bone. In the case of lamellar-zonal bone, all the vascular canals "available" may be replaced, but the result is only a scattered and not a dense Haversian tissue. These relationships between primary and secondary bone are linked to factors (1) and (2) above, and (9) below.

(8) "Dense Haversian bone is related to turnover of the organic constituents of bone". To my knowledge, this intriguing idea has so far been little explored. The cells of all the soft tissues in the body are subject to more or less rapid replacement, so it is not unlikely that a similar process could affect the organic component of bone, also. The organic phase of bone (mainly collagen) might be expected to suffer some kind of biochemical denaturation over time, requiring its replacement by new, fresh organic material. Some evidence of subtle biochemical or biophysical change over time in the organic matrix of bone supports this hypothesis, which is consistent with relations (1), (5) and (6), above. Alternatively, organic compounds (amino acids?) freed by such resorption could be made available for use elsewhere in the body. This possibility is in accord with (9), below.

(9) "Dense Haversian bone is related to turnover of the mineral phase of bone". This interpretation, proposed by Amprino (e.g. 1967), has been extensively debated. It must, at least, be admitted that, since Haversian bone itself constitutes evidence of active exchange between bone and body fluids, the mineral phase of the skeleton is involved in phosphorus and calcium homeostasis. Again it is clear, however, that this interpretation alone does not explain all the aspects of Haversian replacement.

Several points emerge from this review. First, it is important to recognize that these proposed roles (and others) of Haversian replacement are not mutually exclusive. The only interpretations of the available data that are surely untenable, although they are very common, are those which attribute the phenomenon to a single causal factor. Second, it must be kept in mind that dense Haversian bone is only one component in the remodeling process. The continual resorption and redeposition that plays such an essential part in bone growth among the higher vertebrates is always more extensive in cancellous, spongy bone than in the compact bone of the cortex. However, it is just where such intensive remodeling involves the compact bone that dense Haversian tissue is produced. Among living animals, this tissue is found only in those that are endothermic.

In dinosaurs, as in living animals, Haversian bone is assumed to have had a complex physiological role. The interpretation of dense Haversian bone as evidence for high metabolic rates, and hence endothermy, in dinosaurs, does not rest on the assumption that its development is related only to the rate of turnover of bone mineral material, as some have supposed. Indeed, it is likely that most of the processes which may contribute to Haversian replacement, including responses to individual age and growth, bio-mechanical demands, the functions of bone blood vessels, and the replacement of bone cells, would be accelerated by higher rates of metabolism. Just such an acceleration seems to be indicated by dinosaur bone structures, with their abundant intensive Haversian replacement (see Table 1), which stands in marked contrast with the bone tissues of most other fossil and living reptiles. The only assumption made here is that, all other things being equal, bone/body fluid exchange and other processes involved in Haversian replacement would be more rapid in animals with higher metabolic rates than in those with less active metabolism. With no evidence to the contrary, this seems entirely reasonable.

Resorption and reconstruction of bone occurs in all tetrapods, over the animals' life spans; Haversian replace-ment is only one aspect of this process. Hence, a high rate of metabolism cannot be inferred from the mere occurrence of remodeled bone, but is rather reflected by the rate and extent of bone replacement. For instance, a 50-year old turtle and a 5-year old dog might show the same amount of Haversian reconstruction, but the physiological significance of these tissues would be very different, particularly in regard to metabolic rate.

Some authors (e.g. McNab 1978) have argued that secondary osteons are not reliable indicators of high metabolic rates, since, if this was so, they would be especially abundant in small, metabolically very active mammals and passerine birds. This is certainly not the case (see also Bouvier 1977; and data in Enlow and Brown 1956-58). However, this argument does not take the effects of absolute size into account. Secondary osteons of most vertebrates are about 200-300 μm in external diameter, regardless of animal size. Dense Haversian replacement is not to be expected in most of the compact bone of small species, however active their metabolism, since there is simply no room for such structures in the cortex. A simi-lar argument applies to the vascularization of primary bone, here, which also limits the extent of Haversian replacement, as noted under (7) above. On the other hand,

the cancellous bone of these small, metabolically active
animals shows ample evidence of intensive resorption and
remodeling. Bone replacement of this kind is much more
extensive in small mammals and birds than in adult amphibians
and reptiles of similar weights. Hence, the lack of dense
Haversian bone in very small endotherms does not discount a
relationship between rates of metabolism and overall bone/
body fluid exchange.

Recently, Bouvier (1977) has tried to refute Bakker's
(1972) use of dense Haversian bone as evidence for endothermy in dinosaurs. She argues that since some endotherms
(small living mammals and birds) lack dense Haversian bone,
while some ectotherms (or presumed ectotherms, primarily
large fossil reptiles and amphibians) exhibit more or less
Haversian replacement, this bone structure has nothing to do
with temperature regulation. This argument is formally
correct in regard to temperature regulation in the strictest
sense. Bouvier is probably right in suggesting that Bakker
(1972) has oversimplified the argument, but she too over-
simplifies in implying that there is no correlation between
Haversian replacement and overall thermal physiology. I
regard this firm negative conclusion as being unwarranted by
the evidence. Moreover, Bakker's use of data from Enlow and
Brown (1956-58) is not as selective as Bouvier suggests.
These authors (1957, p. 200-203) themselves* observed:

> "The bone tissues of ... dinosaurs ... are
> distinctive among all recent and fossil
> reptiles. In structure, the bone ... is
> similar to, if not identical with, the bone
> tissue of many living mammals, including
> man. In general appearance, dinosaur
> bone tissues differ from most other reptiles
> and living or extinct amphibians. The
> difference is entirely one of relative
> intensity of secondary tissue replacement...
> Unlike the other groups, the primary osteons
> of the compacta, in addition to endosteal

---

* Some authors have attributed the first inference of
dinosaur endothermy from histological data to Enlow and
Brown. This conclusion is implicit in parts of their work,
but it is never explicitly stated. Professor Enlow informs
me (oral communication, 1977) that he has, of course,
considered the conclusion that the similar bone tissues of
dinosaurs and mammals reflect common physiological processes
and metabolic rates. However, since such an interpretation
was inconsistent with the then generally accepted view of
dinosaurs as reptiles, he did not pursue this issue further.

canals, also become replaced by secondary
osteons. The resulting appearance of the
mature bone is, therefore, entirely
different from other reptilian groups...
in dinosaurs, but not in most other
reptiles, all of the canals experience
reconstruction."

In his recent essay on the origin of mammalian endothermy, McNab (1978) has introduced an alternative possibility for the physiological significance of dense Haversian
bone. He suggests that Haversian reconstruction is linked
to homeothermy rather than endothermy. This is an
interesting idea, but McNab does not explain any physiological basis for such a relationship. I contend that
intensive bone remodeling, including Haversian reconstruction,
seems more likely to be linked to the higher rate of cellular
metabolism associated with the maintenance of endothermy
than with constant, high body temperature itself. Certainly,
the presumption of a relationship between rates of metabolism
and bone remodeling needs to be tested by quantitative
experiments on living animals, which will be undertaken in
the future.

In summary, notwithstanding the contentions of some
recent critics, the hypothesized relationship between rates
of metabolism and the overall intensity of bone remodeling
is well substantiated by the available comparative data.
This in turn points to high levels of metabolism, and hence
probable endothermy, among dinosaurs. For the moment, we
can conservatively conclude that:

(1) Dense Haversian replacement in large, adult
dinosaurs points to long individual life spans, at least
comparable with those of large living land mammals (several
decades), but not necessarily longer.

(2) Dense Haversian bone in dinosaurs indicates rates
of bone/body fluid exchange at least close to those of large,
living mammals. Extensively remodelled trabeculae of
dinosaur cancellous bone lead to the same conclusion.

The effects of body size

The consequences of absolute size for animal form and
physiology are pervasive. The functional integration of
dinosaur gaits, bone histology and thermal physiology is
surely closely linked to the range of sizes of these animals.
It is well established that, in living vertebrates, body
size and shape play a major physiological role, as the size-

dependent surface/volume ratio determines the relationship between metabolic rate and body temperature (e.g. Whittow 1971-73; McNab 1974, 1978). In consideration of the significance of this factor for the thermal physiology of dinosaurs, most authors have based their arguments, implicitly or explicitly, on the largest species, especially adult sauropods. The fact is that many dinosaurs were much smaller, while even very large animals had small offspring. Mass homeothermy would have been of little value to these individuals. Nevertheless, it is usually assumed that dinosaurs shared a common basic thermal physiology.

The histological evidence indicates high or very high rates of continuous rather than cyclical growth in young and subadult dinosaurs, comparable with growth patterns of large living mammals. These observations can be interpreted in two ways. (1) Extremely rapid, continuous growth occurred in ectotherms that were "active" for sustained periods of time (McNab 1978; Crompton et al., 1978). Note here that the benefits of mass homeothermy would not have been available until large size was attained and that this pattern of development has no known counterpart among living tetrapods. (2) Young dinosaurs were endothermic, their active cellular metabolism facilitating rapid, continuous growth comparable with that of large living endotherms. The available histological and anatomical data are in no way inconsistent with this possibility. The major problem in this case, as pointed out by Thulborn (1973), is that heat loss would appear to have been very great at small sizes. However, our knowledge of the soft parts and behavior of young dinosaurs is inadequate to determine whether or not this is an insuperable difficulty (Ricqlès 1974).

Comparative data clearly indicate a strong correlation between the histology of primary compact bone and animal size. However, this is only an indirect relationship, based on the direct relation between bone histology and growth rate (Ricqlès 1975, 1976a). Bone types associated with rapid growth are generally, but not invariably, found in large animals, which must grow quickly to reach adult size within reasonable longevities. In long-lived, moderately large species which grow more slowly, such as man, primary bone tissues adapted to slow growth are developed. Smaller species may show bone tissues related to either high or low growth rates, depending on their particular life histories; in this range, no general relationship between bone histology and size is recognized (see also Enlow and Brown 1956-58). It may be that the high rate of metabolism associated with endothermy is a prerequisite for the sustained high growth rates that are required to attain very large body sizes quickly; among living tetrapods, this growth pattern occurs only in endotherms. In short, the histological similarities between dinosaurs and endothermic mammals and birds cannot be explained simply on the basis of the large sizes of some adult dinosaurs.

Recently, McNab (1976, p. 349; 1978) has argued that endothermy sets an upper limit to the sizes of terrestrial mammals, where adequate dissipation of metabolic heat becomes impossible. If this is so, it has not proved to be a severe constraint. Taxonomically diverse land mammals have independently evolved to extremely large sizes, larger, indeed, than any certainly ectothermic terrestrial reptile, living or fossil. Baluchitherium and many fossil elephants, dinotheres and titanotheres reached body sizes well within the range of those of sauropods, in fact larger than those of most non-sauropod dinosaurs. We have been taken in by the "Dinosaur Image", which, partly on account of the elongated neck and tail of the sauropods, overemphasizes their sizes, relative to those of later mammals. Following McNab's (1978) reasoning, it is not endothermic mammals, but rather ectothermic reptiles that should have repeatedly adopted the very large land animal niches. They have notably failed to do so, with the obvious exceptions of therapsids and dinosaurs, the two groups whose thermal physiologies are in question! In my view, there is little justification for the argument that some dinosaurs evolved to very large body sizes simply because their lower, ectothermic rates of heat production permitted it. Rather, endothermy, which actively promotes sustained high rates of growth, and hence the attainment of large size, in mammals, probably had similar consequences for most dinosaurs and allowed some sauropods to become even larger.

Certainly, given the size dependence of surface/volume ratios and warm, equable Mesozoic climates, it seems less likely that the young of large, endothermic dinosaur species suffered the excessive heat losses cited by Thulborn (1973) than that the adults would have been in danger of overheating (cf. McNab and Auffenberg 1976; McNab 1978). In this connection, the large neck and tail surfaces of sauropods, the "frills" of ceratopsians, the elongated neural spines of Spinosaurus and Ouranosaurus, and many other specialized adaptations may have served the purpose of heat dissipation (Wheeler 1978). This possibility has been tested by experiments on models and shown to be physically highly plausible for the dorsal plates of Stegosaurus (Farlow et al.1976).

The scaling consequences of size also bear on the important and controversial issue of dinosaur posture and gait. Some authors simply explain the parasagittal limb

excursion of dinosaurs as being mechanically essential to the
support of large, heavy animals on land. Others see the
constant, parasagittal excursion of the limbs, which among
living animals is seen only in endotherms, as good
anatomical evidence for high activity and endothermy in
dinosaurs (Bakker 1972). Of course, not all living
endotherms employ a parasagittal limb excursion; there are
endothermic sprawlers and swimmers. Hence, it does not
follow that fossil taxa which lacked parasagittal limbs could
not have been endotherms (Ricqlès 1974).

The explanation of the fully parasagittal limbs of
dinosaurs solely in terms of weight-bearing at large body
sizes fails to take the historical process, the evolution of
this adaptation into account (see also Dodson 1974). Small,
light dinosaurs, occurring from the Middle Triassic to the
Late Cretaceous, were fully parasagittal, long-legged
animals, which would not have required this anatomical
arrangement to support their weights alone. Furthermore, the
earliest dinosaurs, and some of their thecodont prede-
cessors, were small, light but already highly bipedal
animals, with parasagittal limb excursions. Clearly, the
early evolution of this adaptation had little or nothing to
do with weight-bearing at large body sizes.

It is evident that an upright gait was a prerequisite
for the later adoption of large body sizes by dinosaurs,
but the evolutionary record of the early archosaurs shows
that large size cannot have been the direct causal factor in
the origin of upright posture and a parasagittal limb
excursion. Among alternative explanations of this development, the early acquisition, by some primitive archosaurs, of
high activity levels based on relatively high rates of
metabolism seems entirely plausible. It is striking that
other lineages of land reptiles, including some rather
large, heavy animals, have consistently failed to acquire
upright posture and true parasagittal limb excursion.
Admittedly, some living ectotherms temporarily employ an
almost parasagittal limb excursion in short bursts of speed,
which often depend mainly upon anaerobic metabolism
(Bennett and Dawson 1976; Bennett 1978), but such activity
necessarily occupies a very small fraction of their active
lives. As a physiological strategy, low basal metabolism
linked to ectothermy obviously has its own adaptive advantages. It is possible not only that this level of metabolism
cannot support constant active locomotion, but also that such
constant activity is counterproductive in the successful
exploitation of this physiology. If so, constant erect
posture and fully parasagittal limb excursion, which are
unknown among living ectothermic tetrapods, may be neither

necessary nor desirable for such animals.

In summary, we note that various consequences of large size have been cited to "account for" anatomical and histological similarities between dinosaurs and large mammals, discounting their other possible physiological implications. However, size itself explains nothing. Rather, we need to understand the physiological processes which relate the ontogeny and evolution of large dinosaur sizes to functional adaptation at the cellular, histological, anatomical and ecological levels.

Discussion: integration of histological and other evidence bearing on dinosaur thermal physiology

Three main features of dinosaur bone histology convey significant information about the physiology of these animals. We have noted the widespread occurrence of densely vascularized fibro-lamellar primary bone, the general absence of cyclic growth lines, and the extensive reconstitution of both cancellous and compact bone, including the formation of dense Haversian systems. These characteristics are indicative of high rates of continuous growth and intensive bone/body fluid exchange in dinosaurs.

Each of these characteristics can be used separately as a histological index of endothermy/ectothermy, by analysis of bone constructional processes and from their distribution among living vertebrates. Each leads to the same conclusion, which confirms their significance. These characteristics, which occur together in dinosaur bone, are comparable with structures observed in large mammals and birds and quite unlike those found in other groups of living and fossil reptiles. Among the living endotherms in which these structures occur, they develop in response to high rates of metabolism. The most parsimonious interpretation of these data is to infer a similar relationship in dinosaurs.

Some have argued that bone histology does not provide an absolute and clear-cut indication of thermal physiology. This is true and to be expected. Like all highly integrated biological structures, bone tissues are the products of varied processes. Since they serve more than one function, their structures reflect compromises among conflicting requirements and are not subject to explanation by any single causal factor. This point must be emphasized, since much misunderstanding of this subject has arisen from attempts to explain dinosaur and other bone structures in terms of single efficient causes, often related to the research specializations of individual scientists. Many of the arguments made are valid but incomplete, while some are simply wrong, since the great structural variety of bone tissues is the product of numerous causal factors with interrelated effects. (Ricqlès 1975, 1976b, 1977a, b). I have never claimed, although it has been ascribed to me, that dense Haversian bone is a simple causal consequence of endothermy, nor that the supposed absolute dichotomy between ectotherms and endotherms is "the explanation" of the distribution of bone tissue types among the vertebrates. These are oversimplifications which should not be allowed to obscure our understanding of these complex phenomena. I am convinced, however, that growth rates and levels of metabolism are importantly involved in the differentiation of bone tissues and their taxonomic distribution.

To whatever extent physiology is reflected by bone histology, no known structural detail contradicts the conclusion that dinosaurs were extremely mammal-like. In this regard, at least, the dinosaurs had reached an essentially mammalian or avian level of functional organization. At the same time, some other, non-histological, characteristics reflect a more conservative, more typically reptilian condition. These are now taken into account.

First, it should be noted that the ontogenetic pattern of growth suggested by dinosaur bone histology does not exactly match that of large, living endotherms. In most mammals, early life features extremely rapid, nearly continuous growth. With the attainment of sexual maturity and adult size, growth slows down and then stops, in terms of linear proportions, although not necessarily in weight. This growth pattern is also observed in birds; it appears to be characteristic of nearly all living endotherms. In contrast, it is well-known that ectotherms may continue to grow as long as they live, although their growth rates are certainly dramatically reduced after they reach sexual maturity; they become ever larger and more powerful with increasing age. As we have seen above, these distinctive growth curves of endotherms and ectotherms are linked to diagnostic patterns of primary bone deposition. Dinosaurs are peculiar in that, while bone histology indicates high juvenile growth rates, comparable with those of large endotherms, nothing suggests an abrupt cessation of growth at a terminal adult size. Rather, it appears that large sauropod dinosaurs, in particular, retained the "indefinite", life-long growth pattern of typical reptiles. The bone growth patterns of dinosaurs are thus identical neither with those of living endotherms nor ectotherms. This strongly suggests that dinosaurs were physiologically unique, that their growth processes were probably intermediate between those associated with endothermy and ectothermy among living animals.

Second, it must be kept in mind that even if growth occurred at similar rates in dinosaurs and large living mammals, as strongly suggested by the histological data, it does not necessarily follow that both groups employed the same "life-history strategies". As is well known, a large part of the metabolic burden of early growth in mammals is assumed by the parental generation. Viviparity, thermal protection and lactation enable the offspring to sustain extremely high initial growth rates, supported by the activities of adults which can be much more precisely adapted to exploit the resources of their environments. Birds achieve similar results in very different ways, by their particular reproductive adaptations. Thus, in most, if not all, living endotherms the parents provide a large part of the early metabolic needs of their young.

There is no evidence of a similar relationship among dinosaurs. The eggs that have been discovered are remarkably small relative to the sizes of their progenitors. Bonaparte (in preparation) suggests that hatchling sauropods were about 30 cm long, while Case (1978) estimates maximum weights of 0.65 kg for Protoceratops and 4.3 kg for Hypselosaurus hatchlings. The metabolic burden assumed by the female dinosaur in producing egg yolk represents a tiny investment in each of its offspring, compared with that made by living endotherms. Clearly, this is a much more typically "reptilian" mode of development than extreme protagonists of dinosaur endothermy would anticipate, but it cannot be escaped!

It follows that rapid gains in size and weight were necessary in early dinosaur ontogeny, especially among sauropods. Presumably the hatchlings had to fend for themselves from the start, as among living reptiles (Burghardt 1977) and nidifugal birds. By and large, this points to metabolic rates somewhat lower than those of most living endotherms, but yet much higher than that of any living ectotherm. Any factor that enabled young dinosaurs to grow rapidly, reducing the toll of predation and physical hazards of the environment, would have been strongly favored by natural selection. Notwithstanding Thulborn's (1973) assumption to the contrary, endothermy may have been advantageous to young dinosaurs in that it made such high growth rates possible.

    As size increased in the larger species, it is likely
that metabolic rates declined, until they may have reached
a level where it would be difficult to say whether body
temperature was maintained internally or externally. Large
adults may thus have reached a state of mass homeothermy,
coupled with incipient endothermy at relatively low,
inexpensive metabolic rates. At the largest sizes, such a
physiology would differ little from that of the ectothermic
model. This may have been the situation in adult sauropods,
stegosaurs and ankylosaurs, since various arguments have
been raised against the existence of very active cellular
metabolism in adulthood among these animals (Hopson 1976).
A similar conclusion has been reached by Halstead (1975).
However, rather smaller species, such as coelurosaurs,
carnosaurs, ornithopods and ceratopsians had higher brain/
body weight ratios (Hopson 1977) and exhibit obvious
anatomical adaptations to active life styles. In these
animals, the endothermy associated with high growth rates in
juvenile development may have retained its importance
throughout adulthood.

    On the basis of these and other published considerations
I am led to postulate a uniquely integrated set of
ecological, anatomical and physiological adaptations for the
dinosaurs. In several fundamental characteristics, these
animals appear to have been somewhat intermediate between
what are usually considered to be typical reptilian and
mammalian conditions. In other respects, they either
retained typically reptilian characters or were far advanced
towards an avian or mammalian grade.

Counterpoint. Perhaps the strongest argument against the
histological evidence for dinosaur endothermy, pointed out to
me in several discussions*, turns not on histology itself,
but on logic. Even if bone histology demonstrates rapid,
continuous growth and intensive bone/body fluid exchange in
dinosaurs and therapsids, it does not necessarily follow that
these processes are characteristic only of endotherms.
Endothermic metabolism is not an essential corollary of
these processes, so to infer it from the histological data is
to argue a non sequitur (see also Ricqlès 1974, p. 60). The
alternative, of course, is that dinosaurs and therapsids
could have been "active ectotherms" (Crompton et al. 1978;
McNab 1978). This argument deserves careful attention. That
dinosaurs, pterosaurs and therapsids were at the very least

_____

* I thank Professors A. W. Crompton, Melvin Glimcher,
  Carl Gans, and Philip Regal for fruitful discussions
  of this topic.

active ectotherms is a minimal assessment on which, I believe, all will now agree. That they could have been endotherms (perhaps incipient endotherms) seems to me to be not only possible but even likely, on the basis both of the evidence and uniformitarian inferences presented above and of the following general considerations.

The phylogenetic argument. Among living tetrapods, endothermy and ectothermy constitute distinct, contrasting physiological regimes, which have very far-reaching consequences for the whole array of morphological, functional and behavioral adaptations of the animals. Today, there is indeed a notable "physiological gap" between these two basic strategies. McNab (1976, p. 378) recognizes this gap, asking why mammals have not selected basal metabolic rates at one half of their actual values, with twice as much insulation. Indeed, the most primitive (?) living metatherians and eutherians are distinctly endothermic, despite rather low levels of metabolism (Crompton et al. 1978). Even the egg-laying monotremes are clearly endothermic, with basal metabolic rates higher than those of any living reptiles. Rates of resting and activity metabolism and hence rates of consumption of food and oxygen are generally quite distinct between endotherms and ectotherms (for data, inter alia Bennett 1972b, 1978; Bennett and Dawson 1976; McNab 1974; Whittow 1971-73).

Nevertheless, endotherms obviously evolved from ectotherms. This occurred at least twice among tetrapods, once among the synapsids and once among the archosaurs, since it is inconceivable that these groups shared a common endothermic ancestor (Ricqlès 1978). In our search for the origins of endothermy, we must look back at the ancestries of the earliest fossil archosaurs and synapsids that were unquestionably endothermic. On the basis of overall morphological similarities with modern mammals, it seems quite clear that all post-Triassic mammals were definitely endothermic. Likewise, among the archosaurs, a similar conclusion may be reached for the Upper Jurassic Archaeopteryx. Further back in each group, we find therapsids among the synapsids and dinosaurs and pterosaurs among the archosaurs, which were (not coincidentally?) the dominant elements of terrestrial faunas in Permo-Triassic and Mesozoic times.

Whatever their precise relationships with descendant mammals and birds were, it is quite clear that therapsids and dinosaurs constitute transitional morphological grades, between a typical reptilian condition and the advanced synapsid and archosaur conditions that would subsequently be

expressed in living mammals and birds. This view is not
new; it was proposed as soon as dinosaurs were integrated
into a general scheme of tetrapod evolution (Huxley 1868,
1870). It seems entirely reasonable that the physiological
transition from ectothermy to endothermy, which has not been
retained among living animals, should be sought in these
morphologically transitional groups. This reasoning does
not establish that all therapsids and dinosaurs were either
full endotherms or merely active ectotherms. Rather, it
strongly suggests that at least some of these transitional
forms developed endothermy, probably linked to characteristic intermediate metabolic rates and anatomical adaptations.

The minimalist's argument. The extremely interesting results
of recent research have made known the existence of an
exceedingly wide range of behavioral and physiological
adaptations among living reptiles (e.g. Burghardt 1977). It
is now apparent that some reptiles with typically ectothermic
physiologies nevertheless give some indication of the kind
of adaptations that presumably preceded and later gave rise
to true endothermy. In their elegant field studies of the
Komodo dragon, McNab and Auffenberg (1976) have documented
the high metabolic rates maintained by this large, active
varanid. This animal is able to raise its core body
temperature somewhat by intense exercise metabolism
(Bartholomew and Tucker 1964; Templeton 1970), while its
muscles "are a potentially important source of heat, even at
night" (McNab and Auffenberg 1976). As Bakker (1974) has
stressed, it is important that levels of resting and
exercise metabolism should not be confused here. Varanids
retain the "normal" resting metabolism of reptiles (Bennett
1972, p. 273), but yet in exercise metabolism they rely
significantly on aerobiosis and are able to pay the small
resulting oxygen debt back quickly (Bennett 1972, 1973a, b).
Their levels of cellular activity and other physiological
adaptations enable them to produce much more heat than most
other reptiles, sustaining active behavior for long periods
of time. Elevated body temperatures are also maintained,
rather differently, by large marine turtles (Frair et al.
1972) and by the well known "endothermic" brooding python.

These instances of increased rates of metabolism and
incipient endothermy among otherwise typical reptiles
demonstrate the metabolic levels that can be reached by
animals which retain fundamentally ectothermic physiologies
and related adaptations. Since both anatomical and
histological data point to considerably more mammal-like or
bird-like metabolic rates and processes in dinosaurs, it
seems likely that dinosaurs were physiologically at least as

"advanced", and probably much more so, than the most active living ectotherms. Such metabolic rates would appear to constitute endothermy (tachymetabolism, Bligh and Johnson 1973), whatever system of thermal regulation was employed and whatever "intermediate" level of basal metabolism was reached. This conclusion and several others presented in this paper are in some ways similar to those reached by Strelnikov (1959). In his generally overlooked but important paper, Strelnikov anticipated nearly all the arguments raised in the recent controversy over the "hot-blooded dinosaurs", concluding that these animals probably enjoyed an intermediate physiological condition of "endothermic heterothermy".

Assessment. In the final analysis, it seems clear to me that the nature of temperature regulation and metabolic physiology of the dinosaurs, which have been extinct for 65 million years and have no exact living counterparts, remains beyond the reach of demonstrative evidence. I refer here to the fact that there are two general categories of scientific evidence, based on different methodologies and affording different levels of confidence. Demonstrative evidence constitutes the basis for proof in mathematics, while accumulative evidence is the main source of knowledge of the historical sciences. Evidence for the evolution of life on earth clearly falls in the second category. Each line of evidence which bears on the thermal physiology of fossil vertebrates does not, in itself, provide a proof of any hypothesis, but rather yields at best a strong inference. It is only the accumulation of many such strong inferences that provides, if they are concordant, a body of evidence which may be taken to establish the validity of a theory beyond any reasonable doubt.

It should be clear that, in the preceding discussion, I have tried not to go beyond those minimal conclusions that seem to be well established by the available histological and other data. I am aware that, in consequence, this essay may seem to represent a substantial retreat from my earlier views (Ricqlès 1974, 1976a). I have set out here to develop a position which may be acceptable to those who remain more convinced that dinosaurs were fundamentally reptilian than that they might have been endothermic. I wish to stress, however, that these more limited conclusions do not extend as far as does my personal assessment of this issue.

Conclusions: towards a minimal consensus?

To sum up, I wish to propose a "minimal package" which may be largely acceptable both to those who are convinced of

dinosaur endothermy and to those who see these animals as
ectotherms. The establishment of such common ground may
provide a basis for further progress, unless it is
vehemently rejected by proponents of more extreme positions!

1. Dinosaurs, whether they are a monophyletic or
polyphyletic assemblage (Charig 1976), constitute a fairly
well delineated "structural grade" (Ricqlès 1974), with a
common overall integration of form and function.

2. It is quite unlikely that there were large, fundamental differences in physiology, within such a coherent
assemblage, some dinosaurs being ecto-poikilothermic and
others endo-homeothermic. The integration of structure,
function and ecology shared by these animals surely had a
common physiological basis.

3. Whatever the common pattern of dinosaur physiology,
divergent variations on this theme surely evolved in
different lineages, in relation to adaptive differences in
size, bulk, gait, habits and so on. Adult coelurosaurs and
sauropods were surely not geared to exactly the same
metabolic rates. Nevertheless, wide differences among taxa
and within individual ontogenies were surely based upon a
common physiological "Bauplan", as is the case among living
reptiles, birds and mammals.

4. A minimal assessment of the physiology of adult
dinosaurs ranging in weight from 100 kilograms to 50 metric
tonnes recognizes that they were passive or mass homeotherms.
The levels of activity and behavior patterns that could have
been supported by this kind of physiology, which has no real
counterpart among living ectotherms, have not been fully
explored. They may well have been convergent with the
characteristics of true endotherms, at least in large, adult
individuals. It should now be generally agreeable that
large, adult dinosaurs were at least "warm-blooded" animals,
with body temperatures that fluctuated little, if at all,
under equable climates.

5. In adult dinosaurs weighing less than 30-40
kilograms and in the hatchlings and juveniles of larger
species, body mass could not have played a significant part
in maintaining constant elevated body temperatures. It
follows that any evidence of high levels of metabolic
activity observed in such small or young dinosaurs cannot be
ascribed to the benefits of mass homeothermy and must have
some other physiological basis.

6. If dinosaurs were endothermic (tachymetabolic), anatomical adaptations designed as "radiators" should occur, especially in adults and large species.

7. At very large body sizes, the characteristics which distinguish endotherms and ectotherms tend to converge (cf. McNab 1978). Even the logical distinction between endothermy and ectothermy breaks down, as most of the animal's body heat must be produced endogenously, even at low metabolic rates. Hence, very large adult dinosaurs were not exactly comparable with more typical (smaller) ectotherms or endotherms. It may well be appropriate to consider large dinosaurs as having been heterothermic, in the sense of Cowles (1962). This emphasizes their uniquely intermediate thermal physiology and may help to limit disagreement over terminology, enabling us to focus on the actual observations and their interpretation.

8. Physiological categories such as endothermy and ectothermy do not constitute satisfactory taxonomic characters. Clear-cut distinctions are even harder to establish here than in the case of morphological character- istics (Charig 1976; Ricqlès 1974). Moreover, physiology is known only indirectly for extinct animals. Physiological inferences may play an important part in the interpretation of suites of morphological characteristics used to delineate taxa, but physiological categories should not themselves be used as key characters in systematics. It makes no more sense to call a brontosaur a "bird" than it does to delight in the song of a tiny "dinosaur" on its nest in a nearby tree!

Acknowledgments

I wish to thank Professor John Ostrom (Yale University) and the editors for their kind invitation to submit a manuscript for this volume. My special thanks are due to Dr. Roger D. K. Thomas for his extremely kind and effective editing, including the extensive revision of the original English manuscript.

Physiological and Behavioral Thermoregulation in Living Reptiles

5

Neil Greenberg

Abstract

The physiological and behavioral thermoregulatory strategies of living reptiles are useful as reference points for assessing the possible modes of temperature regulation among dinosaurs. Because of the many life history and bioenergetic variables that influence the development of a particular thermoregulatory strategy it is difficult to characterize any particular organism with a single term. Reptiles, birds and mammals all exhibit elements of both ectothermic (behavioral) and endothermic (physiological) thermoregulation. Poikilothermic (variable temperature) and homeothermic (constant temperature) organisms can be viewed as representing points of a continuum of bioenergetic economy related to time and energy budgets, ecological constraints, including availability of sources of energy in the habitat, and the evolutionary constraints on an animal's exploitation of energetic resources.

Introduction

The thermoregulatory adaptations of living reptiles provide useful reference points for consideration of possible modes of temperature regulation among dinosaurs. Recent advances in our knowledge of the range of physiological and behavioral responses of reptiles to diverse energetic needs has brought new potency to this perspective.

Organisms control the exchange of energy with their environments by means of modifications of behavior, physiology and morphology, all of which are subject to natural selection. The complexities of thermal ecology and the diversity of thermoregulatory strategies support the view that there is no clear division between alternative categories often used to characterize a species. To emphasize this point, I will describe exceptions to as well as typical examples of reptilian thermal behavior and physiology, since we are interested in

the range of possibilities. I will also draw attention to
comparable strategies of mammals and birds, to emphasize the
occurrence of common adaptive responses to similar ecological
problems. Behavior is of special interest because of its
critical importance in the thermoregulation of living reptiles and because the behavioral responses of animals under
stress or unusual conditions may indicate directions in which
they are capable of evolving as they cope with changing environments. It is behavior that first manifests the attempt
of an organism to maintain the integrity or stability of its
lifestyle when it is confronted with a unique ecological
challenge (Mayr 1970, p.353). For example, the studies of
Bogert (1959) on different species of lizards of the genus
Sceloporus indicate that, despite their occurrence in many
kinds of habitats with considerable climatic variation, they
can, by means of their behavior, maintain very similar average body temperatures. Selection may subsequently favor
physiological responses that support and eventually replace
the more time-consuming behavioral patterns.

I will describe thermal adaptations exemplified in
several extant species. But, since theories, like organisms,
grow and live and die in a complex environment, I will also
refer to some of the ideas that surround the ways in which we
think about thermoregulation. First I will consider the
adaptive value and significance of thermoregulation, then
define and provide some examples of basic thermoregulatory
strategies. Finally I will describe several of the ideas
about the consequences of large body size and some possible
dinosaurian strategies for dealing with these.

Why Thermoregulate?

At the outset, it is important to ask why a given temperature, or range of temperatures, should be sought by a
particular animal. It is not clear why any particular temperature, much less the high, physiologically dangerous temperatures many animals "prefer", has come to characterize an
individual species. Many physiological and behavioral functions are known to progress most effectively or efficiently
at a "preferred temperature", but different preferred temperatures characterize different groups of animals.

Sometimes, activity level is regarded as a principal
factor in determining body temperature levels. But, as Heinrich (1977) recently pointed out, high-temperature set points
are not necessarily a requirement for high activity rates.
Similar functions can be conducted at comparable rates under
very different conditions because of differences in biochemical reaction rates and the nature of the interactions and

bonds between enzymes and substrates (Hochachka 1973). Among
many reptiles that are active at night (Regal 1978), some are
known to maintain higher temperatures by day, lying in the
sun or under warm tree-bark (Bustard 1967), perhaps to accomplish a specific metabolic function such as digestion. We
cannot, however, assume that steady maintenance of an elevated temperature is necessarily adaptive, even in reptiles
known to regulate to high body temperatures. Wilhoft (1958)
has shown that maintaining a lizard at a constant "preferred"
temperature level can have deleterious, even fatal, effects.
Regal (1967) reports that many lizards have a daily rhythm of
temperature preferences such that they voluntarily choose reduced temperatures even when warmer temperature levels are
equally available. The important point is that within the
class Reptilia, as in the other terrestrial vertebrate
classes, there is a considerable diversity of thermal needs
and adaptations (Regal and Gans, this volume), so that generalizations predicated on only one or a few species are
likely to be misleading.

We might suspect, as Heinrich (1977) does, that adaptations for the maintenance of elevated body temperatures in
many reptiles may have evolved after thermally specialized
enzyme systems had become established in animals that possessed consistently high body temperatures. Thermal responses may have evolved as climates changed in order to
maintain favorable operating temperatures for these specialized enzymes. At a consistent body temperature, selection
for stability of biochemical function over a wider range of
temperatures might be reduced, resulting in thermal specialization. Consistent operating temperatures may have been
available in a stable climate, or they may have developed as
a consequence of increasing activity levels at which heat
generated by the muscles could not be rapidly dissipated.
They might also have resulted from an increase in body size,
such that an altered surface-mass ratio favored thermal
equilibrium with the habitat. Enlarging body size is an
effective way of becoming independent of environmental thermal fluctuations, although there are other good reasons for
increasing size (see Gould 1966; Stanley 1973).

If body size can evolve in response to thermoregulatory
needs, a climatic cooling trend could lead to selection for
enlarged body size simply to maintain body temperature at a
consistent level. Subsequent warming trends would leave
these enlarged animals warmer than their ancestors. Any reduction in body size or a climatic cooling trend would com-
pel such animals to regain an optimal temperature balance by
changes in behavior or by generating additional metabolic
heat. But descendants of animals with thermally specialized

enzyme systems may have to continue to provide at least some
of the more conservative of these systems with optimal operating temperatures. Digestive efficiency, for example, may be
sensitive to temperature; species of lizards as well as the
boa constrictor have been shown by Regal (1966) to exhibit
thermophilic responses after eating.

Mechanics of Thermoregulation

A useful approach to thermoregulation is to look at it
in terms of its energetics. A simple equation reflecting the
energetic events over the whole spectrum of an organism's
activities (Bartholomew 1972) can be represented as:

ENERGY IN + ENERGY GENERATED = ENERGY OUT + ENERGY STORED

The physical elements of energy transfer between an organism and its environment are fairly well known (Fig. 1) and
all of these elements can be influenced profoundly by morphology, physiology and behavior. ENERGY IN may be by means
of radiation (from the sun or other warm body), conduction
(contact), or convection (energy conveyed by circulation of
air or water); ENERGY OUT is by radiation, conduction, convection, and evaporation; ENERGY GENERATED is by metabolism
(fueled by food); and ENERGY STORED is in the form of high
energy chemical bonds (available for metabolism) and growth.

Thermoregulatory Strategies

It is often useful to think of the thermal relations of
a species in terms of several intersecting gradients and
balanced alternatives, the end points of which represent pure
cases that rarely, if ever, exist in nature. Such end point
terms are often used to characterize a species, but unfortunately, there is no single term that can encompass all of
the traits of an organism with respect to its thermal biology.
Ignoring this, we are vulnerable to typological thinking at
odds with the facts of variation (Mayr 1963). It is important to define key terms in order to avoid the kinds of ster-
ile controversies that have accompanied their incompletely
understood use in the past (see Ostrum, this volume).

The continuum from poikilothermy to homeothermy reflects
the relative constancy of body temperature. Poikilothermic
animals have body temperatures that vary with the temperature
of the environment, while homeotherms possess a more constant
body temperature level which may be quite different from the
ambient temperature. Poikilotherms are often termed "conformers" while homeotherms that maintain a relatively constant temperature in a thermally fluctuating environment are

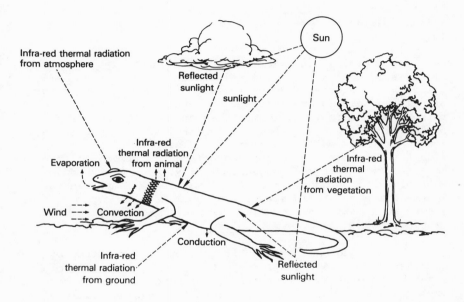

Figure 1. Energy flow between a lizard and the environment (adapted from Gates 1968).

"regulators". Regulators that utilize ectothermy do so by
behavioral means such as microhabitat selection, posturing
and orienting relative to a heat source. All reptiles regulate to some extent, but some function effectively over wide
body temperature ranges (eurythermic species) while others
function over narrow ranges (stenothermic species). Recent
work indicates that the evolution of more or less "precision"
in thermoregulation is substantially influenced by the "cost"
of thermoregulation. For example, where spots of sun for
basking are rare and may be a limiting resource, a species
will become active over a greater range (Huey and Slatkin
1976).

The exploitation of external heat sources (ectothermy)
by means of behavior and the utilization of internal (metabolic) heat sources (endothermy) are not mutually exclusive.
All living animals are more or less endothermic, but to retain heat in a cool environment, an animal must have a way
of reducing the conductance of heat from inside to outside
across its body wall. In mammals and birds, this is done
with fur, feathers or subcutaneous fat. In theory, if thermal conduction was reduced sufficiently, even a very modest
metabolic heat production could elevate body temperatures.
The relative metabolic activity of animals is sometimes
viewed as a point on a gradient from high to low rates, or
tachymetabolism to bradymetabolism.

The considerable expense in time or fuel required by
ectothermy and endothermy, respectively, may be partly mode-
rated by heterothermy, the ability of some animals to more-
or-less suspend thermoregulation. Although classically used
in connection with endothermy, ectotherms also may relax
their behavioral responses and it may, therefore, be fair to
refer to ectothermic as well as endothermic heterotherms.
Regional heterothermy refers to suspension of regulation in
some parts of the body but not in others.

Behavioral Thermoregulation

Terrestrial vertebrates that live in habitats with variable temperatures exhibit several alternative behavior patterns, employed partly, if not entirely, as an adaptive
response to ecological costs such as predator pressure, prey
abundance and the availability of structural or microclimatic
elements (Huey and Slatkin 1976). Reptilian behavioral thermoregulation is accomplished by the selection of microhabitats with thermally distinct microclimates. Subsequent
orienting and posturing then act in concert with physiological processes, "fine-tuning" the rate of flow of heat between
the animal and its environment. The thermoregulatory

ethogram (Fig. 2) developed by Heath (1965) for the horned
lizard Phrynosoma is useful in illustrating the interrelated-
ness of behavioral and thermal phenomena.

   Aggregation. Under unfavorable climatic conditions,
some snakes or lizards aggregate (e.g., Myres and Eels 1968
for Boa constrictor; Weintraub 1968 for Sceloporus orcutti)
perhaps in part to conserve heat. However, this frequently
appears to be merely the result of microhabitat selection
where favorable sites are limited. The red-sided garter
snake (Thamnophis sirtalis parietalis) can be induced to
aggregate in the laboratory by exposure to cold (Aleksiuk
1977), a phenomenon related to its behavior in hibernation
(Aleksiuk 1976). In reptile aggregations, the alteration of
surface to mass ratio may be of thermal significance no matter how it is motivated, but the behavior is not generally
regarded as very effective as it is found in nature
(Cloudsley-Thompson 1971). In mammals, "huddling" is regarded as a special case of apparently thermotactic behavior that
is of special importance to neonates and various small adults
(Barnett and Mount 1967).

   Fossorial behavior. The occupation of burrows can have
a significant thermoregulatory value and has been observed in
young crocodiles (Pooley 1969), various tortoises (Woodbury
and Hardy 1940), and many species of snakes and lizards. The
relative thermal stability of a burrow can be important in
helping a reptile avoid high daytime temperatures or low
temperatures at night. Komodo monitors, Varanus komodoensis,
sometimes use burrows at night to shelter them from radiant
heat loss to the open sky (McNab and Auffenberg 1976). The
lizard Dipsosaurus will utilize microclimatic differences
within a burrow to elevate body temperature before emergence,
eliminating the need for an exposed morning basking period
(McGinnis and Dickson 1967). Fossorial behavior is often
combined with aggregation; some territorial reptiles that are
mutually intolerant during the day may aggregate in burrows
during adverse weather or at night (Regal 1967; Curry-Lindahl
1956). Some reptiles excavate their own burrows, while
others appropriate them from other animals. Many sand-
dwelling snakes and lizards possess specialized morphological
adaptations to this mode of life (Norris and Kavanau 1966;
Pough 1969).

   Heliothermy. Basking in the sun is the most conspicuous,
if not the most common, means of raising body temperature in
reptiles. Terrestrial tortoises and snakes bask in the sun,
but this behavior is most highly developed among diurnal lizards. The high altitude lizards Lacerta agilis exigue in the
Caucasus (Strel'nikov 1944) and Liolaemus of the Altiplano in

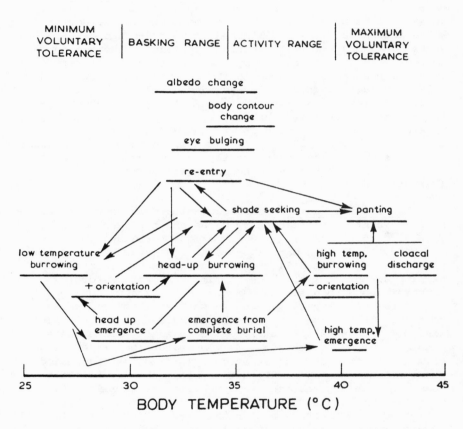

Figure 2. Thermoregulatory ethogram for the horned lizard, Phrynosoma (from Heath, 1965). Reprinted with permission from University of California Publications in Zoology, Volume 64, No. 3.

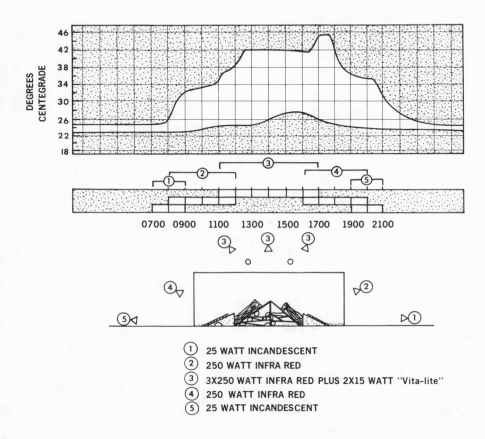

Figure 3. Photothermal regimen in an experimental habitat for studying thermoregulation in the blue spiny lizard, Sceloporus cyanogenys. The upper portion indicates the range of temperatures available to a lizard at any time of day. The lower portion diagrams the timing and position of the light and heat sources that comprise a simulated sun arc with twilight transitions (from Greenberg 1976). Reprinted with permission from Behavior, LIX, 1-2.

Peru (Pearson 1954) have been reported to acquire an elevation in body temperature almost 30°C above that of the surrounding air. Pearson and Bradford (1976) measured the body temperature of a <u>Liolaemus</u> by radiotelemetry and observed that it maintained an average body temperature 6.2°C warmer than the average shade temperature. They calculated that 20Kcl of heat is needed to maintain such a differential for one day, 350 times the lizard's own metabolic heat production and about double that of a mouse. Lizards that maintain relatively precise body temperatures also have well developed shade seeking behavior and spend much time shuttling between different microhabitats.

The effectiveness of this strategy is augmented by varying the orientation of the animal relative to the sun, so that its body can intercept the maximum possible radiant energy. Additionally, many lizards alter their profiles by spreading their ribs so as to enlarge their surface areas (Heath 1965). Further refinements in basking involved altering contact with the substratum (DeWitt 1971) or selecting a surface such as bark or moss that will insulate the animal from an underlying substrate that would otherwise act as a heat sink.

<u>Thermoregulation in the blue spiny lizard</u>. The thermoregulatory behavior of the blue spiny lizard, <u>Sceloporus cyanogenys</u>, which I have studied in detail, exemplified some of these patterns. This species was studied in a large habitat in which I tried to duplicate many critical elements of its natural environment. By using banks of ultra-violet and incandescent lights of varying kinds, I duplicated the arc the sun follows during the day and provided heat (Fig. 3). The first light on and the last light off were dim in simulation of dawn and dusk. The temperatures of the animals were obtained by the use of miniature radio transmitters implanted within their bodies. As I watched from behind a one-way window and recorded their temperatures, a fairly good picture of their thermal behavior emerged (Greenberg 1976).

After morning arousal, apparently cued by the dim light of dawn, individuals cautiously approached an inclined rock partly covered with bark that faced the "rising sun". The animals went to the bark preferentially and were thus able to utilize its insulating properties to protect themselves from the relatively cool rock beneath. They faced away from the light with their backs exposed to it and enlarged their frontal profile by spreading their ribs out sideways. As radiant heat warmed the rock, a lizard might move over to also obtain heat by conduction from beneath. On some occasions, a dominant lizard displaced a subordinate from the bark to the

adjacent rock. If the rock was still cool, the displaced
lizard would continue to bask with its torso flattened to almost wafer thinness, but elevated on its legs to minimize
contact with the cool rock and consequent heat loss by conduction. Once they have raised their body temperatures to
near the maximum they will voluntarily tolerate (Fig. 4),
blue spiny lizards leave their basking sites and take up
perches from which they may survey the feeding areas. When
basking, blue spiny lizards, like most iguanids, also have
their legs out at sprawling right angles to the body, while
perching lizards have them drawn in underneath, suggesting a
greater readiness for rapid action (Fig. 5). Perching can be
distinguished functionally as well as posturally from basking, and the assumption that all exposed lizards are basking
cannot be supported by observations on this species.

     Basking lizards are less likely to feed than perching
lizards, even when they sight prey. Employing a "sit-and-
wait" strategy (Regal 1978), perching lizards are alert for
any sign of movement. They will detect and rapidly attack
almost any small prey-like movement such as that of crickets
or mealworms. The perching and feeding behavior of this
species occurs over such a wide range of temperatures (Fig.
6) that it can be considered eurythermic as opposed to the
narrow activity ranges of stenothermic species. In contrast
with the "sit-and-wait" predation associated with perching,
active foraging by this species occurred only at relatively
elevated temperatures (Fig. 6). It is ecologically significant that this behavior resulted in the acquisition of a
class of prey that would not have been available to sit-and-
wait perching predators.

Physiological Thermoregulation

     So far I have indicated some of the ways in which rep-
tiles can behaviorally exploit the energetic equation. The
effectiveness and flexibility of utilizing behavioral responses in thermoregulation are further indicated by the fact
that they are also used by some mammals and birds. In these
principally endothermic animals, thermal behavior may be
quite highly refined (Weiss and Laties 1961; Dawson and Hudson 1970; Roberts, Mooney and Martin 1974).

     Physiological mechanisms for thermoregulation consist of
adjustments in metabolic levels and alterations in heat exchange between the organism and its environment or even within different parts of the body. Metabolic responses that
elevate body temperature involve modulating available oxida-
tive energy and can be quite energetically expensive. On the
other hand, relatively non-energetic physiological mechanisms

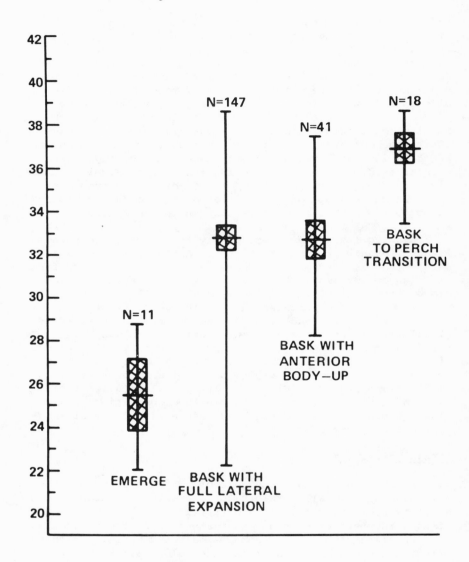

Figure 4. Body temperatures of blue spiny lizards,
<u>Sceloporus cyanogenys</u>, at the time of morning emergence,
during two basking postures and at the time of the transition from basking to perching postures (adapted from
Greenberg, 1976, with permission from <u>Behavior</u>, LIX, 1-2).

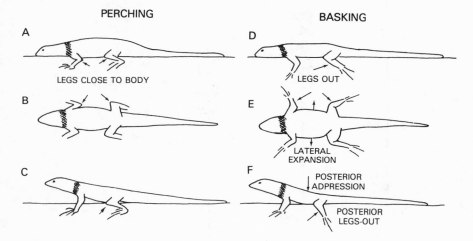

Figure 5. Perching and basking postures of the lizard
Sceloporus cyanogenys. During perching, two postures are
commonly observed when a lizard is trying to be inconspicuous (A) or survey its surroundings (C). The closeness of
the legs to the body (B) may facilitate faster predatory or
escape responses. Basking postures are (D) full enlargement
of the frontal profile with all four legs out or (F) limited
profile enlargement due to adpression of the posterior torso
with only the rear legs out. (Adapted from Greenberg, 1978,
with permission from Behavior, LIX, 1-2.)

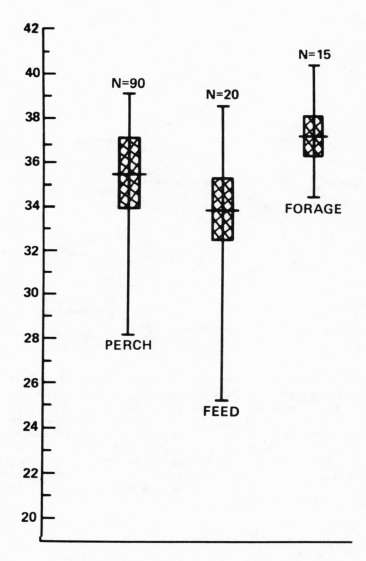

Figure 6. Body temperatures of the lizard Sceloporus cyanogenys during perching, feeding and foraging (adapted from Greenberg, 1976, with permission from Behavior, LIX, 1-2).

such as color change, evaporative cooling and vasomotor adjustments can both alter heat exchange with the environment and contribute to a strategic selective distribution of body heat (regional heterothermy).

In some cases, where the energetic quality of food is low, mammals have evolved lower basal metabolic rates. McNab (1969) has reported that fruit and meat eating bats have higher metabolic rates than insectivorous species. Similarly, birds that feed on flying insects have lower metabolic rates than those that feed on the more nutritious insect larvae.

Temporal heterothermy. When a seasonal or daily shortage of fuel is a predictable element in a regulator's ecology, and migration is not feasible, it may evolve a heterothermic strategy. Endotherms may temporarily abandon their active lifestyle and, in a sense, become more reptile-like by adopting periodic torpor--setting their thermostats down or even becoming conformers.

Daily torpor has been documented in various small birds, bats, and rodents that have limited feeding periods but high energy needs because of their small sizes (unfavorable surface to mass ratios) and high activity. For example, when weather or nightfall compels some hummingbirds to stop feeding, they must also drastically reduce their body temperatures because of their limited energy reserves. To achieve this, the metabolic rate is reduced to reptilian levels (Bartholomew 1972; Lasiewski 1963).

Many bats become essentially thermal conformers when they are inactive and cannot obtain food (Hock 1951), but at least some of these (Myotis) will remain active if provided with sufficient food (Stones and Wiebers 1967). Several small rodents such as the California pocket mouse, Perognathus californicus, and the pygmy mouse, Baiomys taylori, will change their periods of daily torpor in proportion to the quantity of food and moisture available in a feedback system that maintains a balance between energy supply and energy expenditure (Hudson 1965; Bartholomew 1972).

Muscle physiology. The principal means of heat production in birds and mammals involves the almost imperceptible oscillation of muscles known as body tone. Tone is regulated by neural mechanisms that control heat production and that can, at an extreme, produce overt shivering.

Many reptiles, like most amphibians, maintain some tone by summing many small graded muscular contractions stimulated by small nerves with many endings. Mammals do not utilize such a graded contractile mechanism in their skeletal postural muscles, but rather maintain tone by summing the "all-or-none" twitches of many motor units. This difference in physiology, and changes in posture from a typical reptilian sprawl to more erect stances facilitating the pursuit of prey, were related by Heath (1968) to changes in musculature and neural organization that led to higher endogenous heat production. Bennet and Dawson (1976) plotted weight-specific metabolic rates for mammals, birds and lizards at $37^{\circ}C$ and found that resting metabolic levels of 1-gram lizards were 9% and 13% and 1-kg lizards were 18% and 20% of the value for birds and mammals, respectively. This difference is in part attributed to differences in the number of mitochondria, but not their specific activity.

Exercise may generate heat (by similar biochemical pathways to tone or shivering) sufficient to raise the body temperature of a reptile or fish, as well as a bird or man. The total heat production of tone, shivering, and exercise is dependent on the mass of available tissue (McNab 1970). Brooding pythons have long been known to coil about their eggs and produce heat by rhythmic muscular contractions (Hutchison, Dowling and Vinegar 1966). In such reptiles, exercise endothermy can generate body temperatures comparable to those of some mammals, but they cannot sustain it any more than mammals or birds can exercise indefinitely.

Important differences in muscle physiology between taxa may be partly determined by innervation and muscle type. The contractile properties of reptilian muscle and the mechanism for tonus are intermediate between those of amphibians and mammals. The amphibian, reptilian and mammalian systems of muscle tonic and phasic physiology have been related to the terrestrial struggle with the force of gravity and an increase in mobility (Zhukov 1965; Heath 1968). Differences in muscle energetics among vertebrate classes, however, may reflect adaptive responses to the requirements of the environment that imply serious difficulties in extrapolating from well-known muscle physiologies to the energetics of unfamiliar forms. Muscle speed varies among animals as they effect different balances between power output and the economy of maintaining tension (Hill 1956). A study of the energetics of tortoise muscle indicates an efficiency greater than either man or frog--an efficiency that could permit a reduction in the need for food and oxygen, with concomitant reduction in heart and lung size (Woledge 1968).

Color change. The association of color with temperature has long been recognized. Norris (1967) has observed that many desert iguanids darken when they emerge into the sun and

then lighten as their body temperatures rise. Such visible
color changes reflect alterations in the skin's albedo (re-
flectivity to sunlight). The melanophores that control
changes in body color may be influenced directly by light,
temperature, a combination of nervous and hormonal mechanisms,
or only by hormones. An animal's excitatory state may also
be important. The evolution of thermoregulatory color adaptation appears to have been influenced by the need for cryptic
background color matching, the thermal qualities of the habitat and the feasibility of alternate thermoregulatory strategies. In habitats where cool refuges are readily available,
thermoregulatory control over pigment cells is reduced
(Harris 1964).

Evaporative cooling. Some groups of reptiles can reduce
their heat load by evaporative cooling. In contrast with
mammals, the thermal benefit gained is not great, but it may
be critical when an animal is under stress and just a few
degrees from heat paralysis. Many reptiles gape when hot and
increase their respiratory rates in what appears to be the
functional equivalent of panting. Cooling may be augmented
by vascular changes within the buccal cavity. In this way,
the desert iguana, Dipsosaurus, is capable of dissipating an
amount of heat about equal to its metabolic production
(Templeton 1960).

Other evaporative cooling techniques recorded among reptiles are salivation in turtles and the discharge of fluid
from the cloaca in some turtles and lizards. One report suggests that the enlarged bladder of turtles may function in
emergency thermoregulation (Cloudsley-Thompson 1971). Some
birds that can afford the water loss exploit evaporative
cooling by urinating on their unfeathered legs (Kahl 1963).

Cardiovascular adjustment. Thermal cardiovascular adjustments are worth emphasizing because of their implications
for the possibility of homeothermy in very large reptiles.
Many lizards that are excellent behavioral thermoregulators
have developed cardiovascular responses that accelerate the
rate at which body temperature rises in response to appropriate behavior and retard the rate at which they lose heat
in unfavorable thermal situations.

The marine iguana, Amblyrhynchus, lives on the Galapagos
Islands where it can attain a body temperature of 37°C by
basking, but it feeds on algae in the cool ocean. To extend
the time over which it can function near its preferred temperature in a thermally hostile environment, it adjusts its
heart rate and cutaneous blood flow to retard heat loss. Its
heart rate during cooling is about half its heart rate during

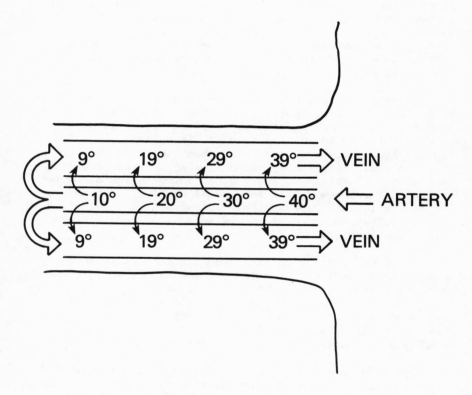

Figure 7.   Counter-current heat exchange between vessels in a hypothetical extremity.   Arterial blood leaving the torso (to the right) warms up the blood in adjacent veins as it returns from the extremity.

heating (Bartholomew and Lasiewski 1965; Morgareidge and White 1969).

Cardiovascular adjustments are achieved in two related ways. Vasomotor adjustments and vascular shunts can result in selective distribution of blood to various parts of the body, so as to modify the distribution of heat within the body (regional heterothermy); and they can alter the conductance of the body wall (Scholander 1955).

At a constant external temperature, the differential that can be maintained between an animal's body and the external environment depends upon the ratio of metabolic heat generation to thermal conductance. Increased conductance allows heat to be transferred in and out of the body rapidly, while decreased conductance reduces the rate of equilibration with external temperatures.

Mammals and birds decrease conductance by means of fur, feathers, and subcutaneous fat. Among species regularly exposed to heat stress, insulation is dispensed with, or they may even have special patches of high conductance bare skin that can be turned into radiators by cardiovascular adjustment. Most reptiles store fat within the body cavity, but at least one, the leatherback turtle, <u>Dermochelys</u>, possesses a subcutaneous layer of fat (Greer, Lazell and Wright 1973).

<u>Regional heterothermy</u>. Many birds and mammals minimize heat loss under cold stress by reducing blood flow to those parts of the body with high surface-mass ratios, such as limbs and ears, that would otherwise drain the body of heat. This phenomenon has been called regional or peripheral heterothermy.

In regional heterothermy, steep temperature gradients may be maintained between different parts of the body. One of the more remarkable mechanisms utilized for establishing regional heterothermy involves counter-current exchange of heat (Fig. 7). Claude Bernard first recognized, during the nineteenth century, that heat can be retained in a particular part of the body by its transfer across the thin walls between out-flowing and adjacent thin-walled in-flowing blood vessels. This mechanism is elaborately developed in various vertebrates whose extremities are often subjected to severe thermal stress. The so-called <u>rete mirabile</u> ("wonderful net") consists of a complex of small arteries and veins with great counter-current exchange capacity. Where it serves as an adaptation to cold habitats it is found in the extremities, near where they join the trunk of the animal (Scholander 1957). It permits the temperatures of the extremities to

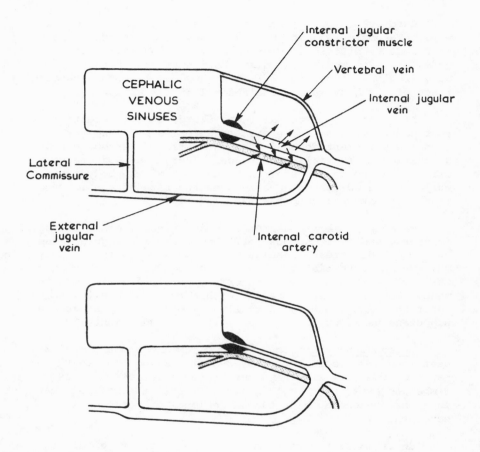

Figure 8.   Cephalic venous shunt in the head of the
horned lizard, <u>Phrynosoma</u>.   The upper figure illustrates
heat exchange between the internal jugular vein and the
internal carotid artery and neck tissue (small arrows).
When the internal jugular constrictor muscle is contracted
(lower figure) the vein is closed and blood returning from
cephalic venous sinuses is shunted to the external jugular
vein.   Adapted with permission from J. E. Heath, <u>Physio-</u>
<u>logical Zoology</u>, Vol. 39, pp. 30-35.

fall to low levels while the body is protected from the heat drain that would otherwise attend unrestricted flow of warm blood into the exposed limbs (Irving 1966). Brattstrom (1968) has reported that the Australian monitor Varanus varius can, when cooling, shunt blood from its legs and tail to its body core. While the appendages fall to ambient levels in 15 minutes, the core takes up to 7 hours to reach the same levels. The large leatherback turtle, Dermochelys, can maintain a deep body temperature as much as 18°C above the water temperature, probably by its normal metabolic activity and the slow loss of heat through its bulk to the surrounding water (Friar, Ackman and Mrosovsky 1972). This turtle also possesses adaptations necessary for homeotherms in thermally fluctuating environments: an insulating layer of subepidermal fat and counter-current heat exchangers in its flippers, near their junction with the body (Greer, Lazell and Wright 1973).

Regional heterothermy has been reported in lizards and snakes that are capable of maintaining a difference between their head and body temperatures (e.g., Heath 1964; Webb and Heatwole 1971). During morning warming, the horned lizard, Phrynosoma, will have a head temperature up to 5°C warmer than its body, as vascular adjustments effectively reduce heat exchange between the head and the body. At elevated temperatures, another vascular adjustment directs blood flow through a different route, allowing the body to function as a heatsink and reduce cephalic temperatures (Heath 1964). A similar mechanism is probably utilized by the earless lizard, Holbrookia (Bogert 1959).

Vascular adjustments involving cephalic sinuses that contribute to head-body temperature differences in reptiles have been described by Bruner (1907) and Heath (1966) (Fig. 8). Webb, Johnson and Firth (1972) have systematically investigated the head and body temperatures of ten species of lizards (geckos, a skink, and an agamid). In the species they examined, a gradient of up to 4°C could be maintained, the degree of control over head-body difference being correlated with the habitat occupied. They envision that under normal conditions warm blood is retained in the cephalic sinuses to keep the brain near its optimum temperature. At higher temperatures, increasing heat loads cause the lizards to readjust their circulation so that cooler blood from the body courses through the head. In conjunction with vascular adjustments, the benefits of evaporative cooling are sometimes restricted to the head, preferentially protecting sensitive neural tissue from heat stress (Crawford 1972). A similar mechanism operates in various mammals, such as dogs (Baker and Chapman 1977), sheep (Baker and Hayward 1968), and cats (Baker 1972).

Consequences of Large Body Size

What are the prospects for the operation of non-energetic physiological mechanisms in large reptiles? Using an ideal-ized mathematical model for the distribution of body temper-atures, Spotila et al (1973) suggested that a reptile at least 100 cm in diameter would have a relatively constant body temperature in a diurnally fluctuating environment, sim-ply because of the thermal inertia (heat storage capacity/thermal conductance) of its mass. In tropical and subtropic-al habitats such as those occupied by dinosaurs during the Mesozoic, body temperatures would be both stable and compar-able with those of modern mammalians.

The ratio of metabolic rate to thermal conductance has been determined by McNab from field data obtained by Auffen-berg for the largest living lizard--the Komodo monitor (McNab and Auffenberg 1976). They observed that large reptiles are more like large mammals than they had anticipated, because the large reptiles had lower conductances than expected. Al-though small reptiles generally have smaller temperature dif-ferentials (between their bodies and the environment) than do mammals of the same size, the differentials in reptiles and mammals are similar at weights greater than 100 kg. They interpret these data as support for the idea that herbivorous dinosaurs evolved to large sizes as a means of providing thermal stability; and that the dinosaurs that preyed upon them consequently also grew larger. At large sizes or with increased rates of metabolism, especially with a low con-ductance body wall, they might well have had severe diffi-culties with overheating.

Thermal Paleophysiology

At large body sizes, behavioral mechanisms for regulat-ing body temperature, being largely surface dependent, lose their effectiveness, and the dissipation of excess heat may present other severe problems. Consequently, it would not be surprising if giant extinct reptiles had evolved specialized morphological adaptations for thermoregulation. The familiar dermal bony plates that ranged along the back and tail of Stegosaurus (Fig. 9) may well have functioned as fins to dis-sipate heat by forced convection. Farlow, Thompson and Ros-ner (1976) demonstrated that the size, shape and arrangement of these dorsal plates closely approached a mechanical para-digm for convective heat transfer (Rudwick 1964). Their study of the plates indicates that they were richly vascular, so that, given vasomotor control of bloodflow between the plates and the body, Stegosaurus could have had considerable control over their operating in heat exchange.

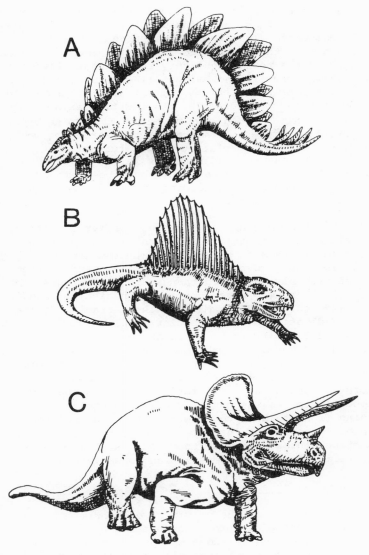

Figure 9. <u>A</u>. The large dorsal dermal plates of
<u>Stegosaurus</u> could theoretically function as forced con-
vection cooling fins (Farlow <u>et al</u> 1976). <u>B</u>. The long
neural spines supporting the sail of <u>Dimetrodon</u> provide
evidence of rich vascularization, suggesting a thermoregulatory function (Romer 1927). <u>C</u>. Grooves on the
horn-cores of Ceratopsian dinosaurs such as <u>Triceratops</u>
indicates vascularized horns and frills that might have
functioned in thermoregulation. (Greenberg and Hotten,
unpublished observations).

Some late Paleozoic pelycosaurs (primitive so-called "mammal-like" reptiles, not dinosaurs) such as <u>Dimetrodon</u> (Fig. 9) possessed elongated neural spines. These spines supported a sail that increased the surface-mass ratio and thus enlarged the thermoregulatory radiative interface (Romer 1927, 1940). Bramwell and Fellget (1963) calculated that the sail accounts for more than 60% of the lateral projected area of a 250 kg <u>Dimetrodon grandis</u>. By adopting an appropriate posture, the animal could have accelerated warming by more than 250%, from a presumed minimum temperature for voluntary activity of 26°C to a preferred temperature of 32°C. As in the case of <u>Stegosaurus</u>, adjustments in the blood supply to the sail and postural changes could have been employed by <u>Dimetrodon</u> to modulate the absorption and dissipation of heat by radiation and convection.

Another thermoregulatory strategy of large reptiles may have utilized cranial frills and horns in conjunction with vascular adjustments to dissipate heat from the head (Fig. 9). Ceratopsian dinosaurs possessed elaborate cranial ornamentation that probably reflected changes in jaw musculature (Ostrom 1966) and may have functioned in display behavior (Farlow and Dodson 1975). Many of these cranial devices have surfaces indicating a rich vascular supply, suggesting that they had the capacity to function as heat dissipating organs (Greenberg and Hotten, unpublished observations), in a manner similar to that of the horns of goats and possibly other bovids (Taylor 1966). Under heat stress, blood vessels in the horns of these mammals dilate, moderating the temperature of blood flowing to the brain by allowing cooler venous blood returning from the horn to draw heat from the adjacent carotid rete. When Taylor insulated vasodilated horns of sheep, brain temperatures rose 0.4° to 0.6°C. At low temperatures, vasoconstriction of horn vessels can conserve heat.

Evolution of Endothermy

The perception of the origin of endothermy as a pivotal factor in the entrance into a new adapative zone loses some of its edge when we adopt the perspective of adaptive energetics. All metabolizing cells generate some heat. More than sufficient heat may be generated for an animal to maintain an elevated body temperature depending on its rate of heat loss to the environment as retarded or facilitated by climate, and the organism's size and thermal conductance. When physical factors and their physiological control are considered in concert with metabolic efficiency (less efficient = more energy converted to heat rather than work), and variations in purely quantitative aspects of heat production and conservation, many of the simple distinctions between thermoregulatory strategies associated with specific animals evaporates. While the physiological mechanisms by which living reptiles and mammals maintain body tone and generate metabolic heat may be quite different, the rudiments of mammalian physiological thermoregulation are present in reptiles, and from an energetic or ecological point of view there is no clear distinction between animals characterized as ectotherms and those labelled as endotherms.

Recalling that there are several variables in the bioenergetic equation, each of which may be modified by specific morphological, physiological and behavioral adaptations, an integrative approach is called for. To deal with the multiplicity of approaches, King (1974) suggests that only a rigorous consideration of time and energy budgets can relate the many facets of an animal's life history to suggest useful hypotheses about the evolution of adaptive strategies.

As an understanding of the thermal relations of living and extinct groups emerges, the issue moves to another level. We must ask: "What selection pressures have led to the evolution of a particular thermoregulatory strategy, and along what channels in the epigenetic landscape have various strategies been directed by selection?"

Assuming the availability of sufficient fuel for metabolism, the obvious advantage of endothermy is the independence of body temperature from fluctuations in climate. Many of the physiological mechanisms assumed to be corollaries of endothermy are quite well developed among the reptiles and are of considerable advantage to them, allowing them to reduce the effects of climatic fluctuations while permitting the organism the energetic efficiency of ectothermy. Adaptations that permit a reduction in time invested in behavioral thermoregulation may have other advantages. From studies of four species of lizards, Avery (1976) observed that annual food consumption increases relatively more than the overall annual expenditure of metabolic energy at lower latitudes, yielding additional energy to be used to sustain a higher reproductive rate. Further, a reduction in the time required for behavioral thermoregulation allows additional time for interactive and "plastic" behavior, partly reflected in the inverse relationship of the complexity of social behavior with latitude.

The endothermocentric fallacy. Active heat seeking in reptiles was little appreciated before the important study of Cowles and Bogert (1944) on the thermal requirements of desert reptiles. It was here that the long established thesis of reptiles as fundamentally "cold-blooded" animals met

the clearest statement of its antithesis: "The most successful reptiles are those which, by means of their habits, are
able to approach a state comparable to that attained by
homeothermic animals." Perhaps there is a human impulse that
encourages us to see something of ourselves latent in other
successful organisms as well as something of them in us.

    This attitude embodies a kind of chauvinism that I have
called the "endothermocentric fallacy", and reflects an
Aristotelian view of the perfectability of species (Greenberg
1976). It has been (and remains) enormously stimulating to
research. Numerous deductive studies have been undertaken
and their results fitted into this conceptual framework without testing its central assumptions. As well-adapted reptiles
and reptiles on the way to becoming mammals confront one another in a welter of semantic and conceptual differences, a
more parsimonious view of the issue with unexpected heuristic
richness is emerging. The adaptive perspective engendered by
the dialog in which we are now engaged indicates that we are
entering a healthy stage of synthesis.

Acknowledgments

    This report was prepared during my tenure as a Research
Ethologist at the Laboratory of Brain Evolution and Behavior,
National Institute of Mental Health, with a concurrent
Associateship at the Museum of Comparative Zoology, Harvard
University. Research reported on blue spiny lizards was conducted at Rutgers University and supported by NSF grant GB-
6827 to D. C. Wilhoft. I thank Drs. J. Eisenberg, B. McNab,
and E. C. Frederick for their conversation and encouragement.
Drs. R. D. K. Thomas, P. J. Regal and J. E. Heath read the
manuscript and I am grateful for their many thoughtful
comments.

6

The Revolution in
Thermal Physiology
Implications for Dinosaurs

Philip J. Regal and Carl Gans

"The thicker and warmer the blood is, the more it
makes for strength". "Best of all are those animals
whose blood is hot and also thick and clear; they
stand well both for courage and for intelligence.
Consequently, too, the upper parts of the body have
this pre-eminence over the lower parts; the male
over the female; and the right side of the body over
the left". (Aristotle 1968, pp. 119-120, 647b,
648a).

"Of all the animals, man has the largest brain for
his size; and men have a larger brain than women.
In both cases the largeness is due to there being a
great deal of heat and blood in the region around
the heart and the lung. This too explains why man
is the only animal that stands upright." "The size
of the brain . . . is to secure ventilation".
(Aristotle 1968, pp. 155, 653a-b).

Introduction

The last 15 years have seen a revolution in the way
zoologists view warm-bloodedness. The new information
raises some issues of direct relevance for those
paleontologists who seek to understand living organisms
well enough to make reasonable guesses about the biology
of those that are extinct. This essay notes some of
these issues and raises questions about statements that
have appeared in advocacy of the position that the dinosaurs
were warm-blooded. First let us characterize some terms
and issues.

Both animals that employ endothermic temperature
regulation (hereafter, endothermy) and those that are
ectothermic, shuttling from thermal source to thermal

sink, may have body temperatures that are more or less
substantially different from those of the environmental
background. Temperature regulation is not equivalent to
heat production or to elevated body temperature. Regulation
implies a more constant body temperature than would occur
if a block of some inert material were exposed to the
elements in the particular habitat.

The critical point is that physiologically or
behaviorally, the organism modifies heat loading and/or
heat loss; thus, it avoids over-cooling or over-heating.
Every organism produces at least some metabolic heat and
could be called "endothermic", so the concept becomes
meaningless unless we focus upon those species in which
heat production is sufficiently high to represent an
obvious part of the overall strategy of temperature
regulation. Mere heat production by dinosaurs would not
constitute endothermic temperature regulation.

Here, we do not intend to review the physical
evidence that has been advanced to support the hypothesis
that dinosaurs were endothermic. That evidence has been
reviewed by others at least well enough to make clear for
present purposes that a strong burden of proof remains
with the advocates (cf. Bouvier 1977; Charig 1976; Farlow
1976; Tracy 1976). Rather, we intend to focus upon the
context of comparative physiology and physiological
ecology against which much of the physical evidence has
been weighed. We state at the outset that we do not know
whether any or all of the dinosaurs were ectothermic or
endothermic. We do care about the soundness of the
evidence, assumptions, and logic that are being used.

We will address particular assumptions made by the
advocates of endothermy in dinosaurs. Prominent among
these are:

1. The attitude that endothermic temperature regulation
is a necessarily superior trait. As only one example,
Bakker (1975a p. 61) notes, "The total energy
budget per year of a population of endothermic birds
or mammals is from ten to 30 times higher than the
energy budget of an ectothermic population of the
same size and adult body weight. The price is
nonetheless justified". Of course, the price is
justified in the particular context of birds and
mammals or they would not survive! But is it generally
true? Bakker continues, "One is forced to conclude
that dinosaurs were competitively superior to mammals
as large land vertebrates. And that would be baffling

if dinosaurs were cold-blooded."

2. Coupled to the above attitude is the assumption
that cold-bloodedness prevents high levels of locomotor
activity. This usually derives from the commonplace
view that all modern reptiles are inactive, and is
based on an array of putative and sometimes conflicting
physiological reasons for the supposed correlation
between activity levels and thermal physiology. For
example, "Muscles must be constantly in tone just to
stop the skeleton [of an erect animal] from collapsing;
the greater the weight of the animal the greater the
exertion. A lizard has relatively little to worry
about since it spends very little of its life standing,
rather it saves energy by collapsing on the ground.
It has to, it does not have the energy to remain
standing. It is forced to spend anything up to 90%
of its 'active' life lying motionless!" (Desmond
1977, p. 81).

3. Then there is the attitude that endothermy might
be expected to be characteristic of whole classes or
orders of organisms, as it is now in the Mammalia
and Aves. More specifically, the assumption that,
if endothermy were demonstrated for some dinosaurs,
it could reasonably be assumed that all the other
dinosaurs would also have been endothermic regulators.
In this connection we refer to Bakker and Galton's
proposal that all dinosaurs can be assumed to have
been endothermic and that (largely on this basis)
zoologists should reclassify the amniote vertebrates:
"The key advancements of endothermy and high exercise
metabolism are justification for removing dinosaurs
from the Reptilia and placing them with birds in a
new class, the Dinosauria" (Bakker and Galton 1974,
p. 168).

Let us then review some of the attributes of endothermy
in the biological world, most specifically its distribution
and energetic corollaries. Next, it may be useful to
consider the association of endothermy with such aspects
as size, activity rate and feathers, repeatedly mentioned
in this connection.

Endothermy is Widespread Among Organisms

Formerly, the only animals that were well known to
produce their own body heat for temperature regulation
through a very high metabolic rate were birds, mammals,
and the bees in their hives. It may have seemed legitimate

then to view warm-bloodedness as the terminal state in an
evolutionary progression -- as a feature of "higher", or
"advanced", creatures and as a feature that perhaps
actually causes superiority.

The issue of progress in evolution has, of course, a
long and involved history in paleontology (e.g. Bowler
1976) and is debated even today. Our use of terms such
as "higher" and "lower" creatures, and "superiority" is
not intended to endorse them, any more than we subscribe
to Aristotle's views, cited above. However, we do think
that it is important to focus on this aspect of the warm-
blooded dinosaur controversy. The belief, whether or not
well justified, that dinosaurs may have been not merely
awe-inspiring, but in fact "superior forms of life" often
seems to us to be at the root of the search to find in
them some "superior" physiological trait" also essential
to the "superior" forms of today. Possibly this would
explain why some investigators are comfortable in drawing
conclusions from evidence that other scientists regard as
quite weak.

Recently, endothermy of one sort or another[1] has
been described in multiple species of "lower" organisms.
In many cases, such occurrence of endothermy had been
suggested much earlier, but the possibilities were not
taken seriously. There may have been two major reasons
for this: First, any organism with intense metabolic
activity will generate heat. This heat production may or
may not be regulated by some control system. The heat
production in a decomposing pile of manure is literally
"endothermy" but is best not thought of as thermoregulation
(we are indebted to J. Heath for this example). Physiologists properly insist on a distinction between temperature
regulation and heat production or even elevated body
temperature. So, there is a difference between high heat
production and thermoregulation. Second, laymen and even
many scientists have had a tendency (beginning very
conspicuously with Aristotle, but rooted more generally
in Greek teleology) to retain the method of ranking
species as "higher" or "lower" on a scala naturae (see
also Greenberg, 1976). This view may have made it seem
highly improbable that "lower" forms would possess a
trait "distinctive" of "higher" forms such as ourselves,
our dogs and the birds (whose songs and graceful movements
bring much pleasure). However, recent work shows that
many "lower" creatures do not only generate heat incident
to activity, but actually regulate their body temperatures
by endothermy much as do birds and mammals. Endothermy
can no longer be viewed as difficult to evolve nor as an

exclusive capacity possessed only by the "highest forms"
in an "evolutionary progression". The new information
also reveals that endothermy in plants, insects, fishes,
and reptiles is not usually characteristic of classes or
even orders. Even within a genus some species may be
endothermic and some ectothermic.

Endothermic temperature regulation was clearly
demonstrated first in certain moths (Adams and Heath
1964). An extensive literature on endothermy in insects,
including various bees, dragonflies and beetles, has
since developed (see references in Heinrich 1974b, 1977;
May 1976; Bartholomew and Casey 1977; Bartholomew and
Heinrich 1978; Heinrich and Casey 1978). Again, while
the high heat production per se of certain insects had
been more or less well known for many years previously,
heat production cannot necessarily be viewed as temperature
regulation. Apparently, within orders or even smaller
taxonomic groupings of insects a variety of thermoregulatory
strategies seems to be the pattern. For example, large
dragonfly "flyers" are generally endothermic, while
similar "percher" species are ectothermic.

High heat production of the spadix of certain plants
has been on record at least since Lamarck's account of
it (Brattstrom, 1972). Recent work shows that the eastern
skunk cabbage, Symplocarpus foetidus, actually regulates
its "body" temperature. Observations show that the
Symplocarpus increases its metabolic rate in the cold,
enough to offset heat loss (Knutson 1974). Knutson
(1974) gives reasons to believe that the endothermy of
the eastern skunk cabbage is atypical for the family
Araceae.

Among vertebrates, earlier reports (sometimes discounted) of endothermy during incubation have been confirmed for
certain snakes of the genus Python (Hutchison et al.
1966; Vinegar et al. 1970; van Mierop and Barnard 1976).
Vinegar et al. (1970) studied heat production during
brooding of eggs by Chondropython viridis and four species
of Python, and concluded that two of the species lacked
endothermy. Evidence has also accumulated for endothermy
in the large leatherback turtle Dermochelys coriacea
(Mrosovsky and Pritchard 1971; Frair et al. 1972; Greer
et al 1973; Neill et al. 1974). Even certain fishes
appear to maintain warm bodies in colder water by the
utilization of countercurrent mechanisms. They do this
despite the long held belief that because water is an
excellent heat sink, heat loss through the gills and
body wall should make endothermy extremely unlikely

(Carey 1973; Carey and Lawson 1973; Carey and Teal 1969a, b; Graham 1975). However, only some of many sharks and tunas are endothermic.

The discovery of the wide phylogenetic distribution of endothermy raises some new and provocative questions. If endothermy provides competitive superiority and yet is not difficult to evolve, then why are not all animals warm-blooded? A more realistic phrasing of this idea would be: If endothermy is a superior trait, should not the warm-blooded taxa of fishes, snakes, turtles, and insects have become the most dominant and the most diverse? In fact, each of these groups only contains a relatively small fraction of endothermic taxa.

This apparent paradox presumably reflects not so much intrinsic physiological barriers to the evolution of endotherms, but rather economic considerations. In our own society, many technologies are uncommon, not because they are difficult to design, but rather because of their high cost. In thinking about plants and animals, it is also useful to think in economic terms and to consider the ratio of costs to benefits that a certain feature may bring to the life of an organism. In the case of endothermy, it is clear that energetic costs are much higher for a bird or a mammal than for a modern reptile. The endothermic metabolic rate of a resting mammal is five to ten times higher than that of an ectotherm with an equally high body temperature. Just to live, the mammal must consequently consume five to ten times more calories per unit time than must an ectotherm of equivalent mass. This high cost will increase even more with physical activity or in response to temperature stress, so that a mammal may each day use 30 times the energy of a comparably sized lizard (Bennett and Nagy 1977).

High metabolic rates may involve other and non-energetic costs; thus, they can cause increased water loss problems in dry habitats. In short, endothermy has multiple costs and is only likely to arise when it produces equivalent or greater benefits.

Simplification or Complication of the Dinosaur-Endothermy Hypothesis?

A first reaction to learning that endothermy is widespread can be that this makes it now even easier to imagine that the dinosaurs had mammalian-avian physiologies. In one respect, this is true. It is no longer preposterous to imagine that "lower", non-mammalian or non-avian creatures might be endothermic.   So why not dinosaurs?

Some laymen particularly are apt to assume that this justifies the assumption that dinosaurs were warm-blooded. However, our position is that "Why not?" is not a reason to conclude that dinosaurs were endothermic.   Why not trilobites?   Why not labyrinthodonts?   Why not ammonites? "Why not?" alone has no more predictive value than has the wish or the hope that a thing is true.

The physiological ecologist may still see dinosaur endothermy as a non-parsimonious hypothesis, not because endothermy is considered to be a rare evolutionary "break-through" that defines "higher" animals, but because endothermy is an energetically expensive activity that has evolved in at least 13 distinct lineages and yet seems to be characteristic only of two: the classes Mammalia and Aves.

It is not clear why endothermy is characteristic of birds and mammals.   Conceivably the large brains shown by both classes and the power of flight in birds may have allowed mammals and birds to exploit resources so effectively as to offset the costs of tachymetabolism in a wide range of situations.

For the moment, however, the main point is that endothermy is expensive.   We would not a priori predict it to be characteristic of any group of organisms.   The new evidence simplifies the suggestion that some dinosaurs could have been endothermic.   It raises difficulties for the suggestion that all dinosaurs were endothermic.

Bakker and Galton's (1974) position was (in part) that all dinosaurs were certainly endothermic and hence that we should reclassify them on the basis of their alleged physiology.   Even if their premise were sound, the conclusion would seem less well justified than an effort to reclassify the eastern skunk cabbage, which is known to be endothermic.   In our opinion, the evidence only supports Ostrom's (1970) original suggestion that dinosaurs cannot, with any certainty, be used as paleo-climatic indicators.

The remainder of this essay will explore in greater detail some of the probable reasons why only some animals are endothermic and the implications of this line of thought for dinosaurs.

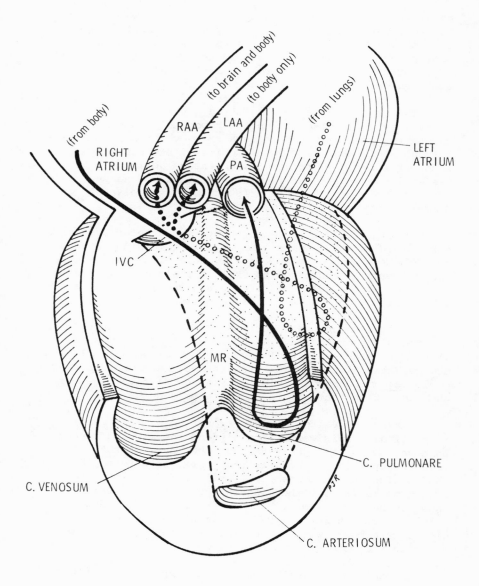

Figure 1.   MODEL OF BLOOD FLOW THROUGH THE TYPE "A" HEART
OF LIZARDS, SNAKES AND TURTLES.   The ventral and posterior
portions of the ventricle are cut away.

The heart fills during ventricular diastole with
deoxygenated blood from the body, pooling (not indicated)
in the cavum pulmonare (CP) and also crossing the muscular
ridge (MR) and pooling in the cavum venosum (CV).   At the
same time oxygenated blood from the lungs pools in the
cavum arteriosum (CA).   Mixing between the dorsal chamber
(CA) and the ventral chambers (CP and CV) via the interventricular canal (IVC) is prevented by the atrioventricular
valves, which are not shown here.
During ventricular systole, the deoxygenated blood
exits from the ventricle into the pulmonary artery (PA)
prior to any ejection into the aortae (owing to the
relatively low resistance of the pulmonary circuit);
then the oxygenated blood in the CA is forced through the
IVC and into the right and left aortic arches (RAA and
LAA).   (After discharge of most deoxygenated blood from
the CV, mixing between the CP and CV is restricted when
the muscular ridge presses against the ventral wall of
the ventricle, which is here shown cut away.   Thus the
muscular ridge prevents oxygenated blood from the CA from
entering the low resistance pulmonary circuit and directs
this blood immediately to the systemic aortic arches.
The atrioventricular valves are shifted away from the IVC
and seal off the atria from the ventricular chambers
during this phase.)
The degree of equality of the distribution of cardiac
output between systemic and pulmonary circuits is dependent
upon the relative resistance of the circuits.   High
pulmonary vascular resistance during the apneic phase of
respiration (turtles) or during diving produces a shunt.
Such a shunt around the pulmonary circuit may also be
effective during basking (see text).   After White (1959).

Endothermy Might Be Limiting for Modern Reptiles!

In his brief on behalf of dinosaur endothermy, Desmond (1977 p. 293) has asked rhetorically "Where is the beauty of the orthodox dinosaur? Retarded, handicapped and about as aesthetic as its frozen Museum relic, it scarcely conjures up that Golden Age when giants reigned". In essence, the same point is made by other advocates: Modern reptiles are slow or sluggish, so dinosaurs could not have "dominated" the earth nor the early mammals, if they had reptilian, cold-blooded physiologies.

In our opinion, this view mistakes correlation for cause and effect. First of all, certain reptiles, especially some teiid and most varanid lizards, are quite active when abroad, even though they are not being chased or rushing after prey. However, the number of such species is but a fraction of all reptiles (cf. Regal 1978). The low activity levels of many other reptiles are unlikely to be due to their ectothermy. Rather, both activity level and ectothermy are probably in large part linked to the particular types of hearts that have evolved in the Crocodilia, Testudines, and Lepidosauria. These are very complex hearts that may place various costs on any sort of intense and sustained activity, either locomotion or tachymetabolic endothermy (see Regal 1978, for extensive references).

In fishes, the heart has a simple function: it receives deoxygenated blood and pumps it into the gills; here blood is oxygenated and thence passes directly to the body tissues. In insects, the heart is also a simple pump, but the tissues receive atmospheric oxygen directly through the tracheal system.

The circulatory system is very different in reptiles, birds and mammals. These amniotes largely have a skin of low permeability and most gas exchange takes place through a special internal organ, the lung. The heart pumps blood to the lung, but the blood does not thence pass directly to the body. Instead, it passes through the heart a second time and is only then delivered to the body tissues. Thus, the amniote heart is a double pump. Its efficiency obviously depends on how well the two streams -- oxygenated and deoxygenated blood -- are kept apart. Separation is assured in birds and mammals because septa physically divide the two circulations. In other amniotes, the arrangements that separate the two circulations are quite complicated (Figures 1 and 2). Physiological studies over the last few years have begun

to reveal their mechanism. Anatomically, the double pump
is "in-complete". Physiologically speaking, studies show
that the oxygenated and deoxygenated bloodstreams mix or
remain separate to a varying degree depending on conditions
that are still only partially understood.

Our use of the usual term "incomplete" should not be
taken to support the older interpretation that reptilian
hearts are "unfinished" or transitional stages in evolution.
Their anatomies and mechanisms are now known to be complicated and the details not in accord with such an interpretation. In particular, the "A" system (Figure 1)
of turtles and lepidosaurians (lizards, snakes and
amphisbaenians) is best viewed as an independently evolved
unique solution to the problem of controlling the distribution of the bloodstreams. In principle, the type "B"
heart of crocodilians (Figure 2) could easily evolve into
a complete double pump by the simple loss of the left
aortic arch, though certain functions would be sacrificed
(see figure captions). This was probably the sequence in
birds and perhaps in many dinosaurs as well. However,
the type A heart is much more complex in its circulatory
physiology. For instance, the interventricular canal is
a critical route for the oxygenated blood and cannot
simply be closed without killing the animal. Most hypothetical schemes for the evolution of a complete double
pump from the type "A" heart may require serendipitous
and complex rearrangements of the vessels within a given
individual, i.e. major "mutations", whereby the offspring
of one individual has a functioning heart that differs in
its flow patterns from those in its parent (cf. Holmes
1975). Other schemes require complex hypothetical flow
patterns of problematical adaptive value. Such scenarios
cannot be ruled out, of course, but neither is there any
apparent need for such speculation. There is no compelling
evidence that complete double pumps have evolved from the
type "A" heart, rather than from a more primitive system.
Certainly, an A to B or complete double pump transition
has not occurred in any members of the Testudines or
Lepidosauria.

Both the "A" and the "B" systems offer certain
advantages. The lungs can be bypassed or blood shunted
preferentially to them. Tucker, White, and their co-
workers have demonstrated that this potential is functionally
important in the temperature regulation of ectotherms
(and in the diving of some species). Other advantages of
these systems also remain to be described (White, personal
communication).

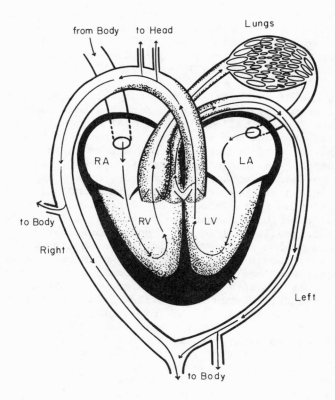

Figure 2.   MODEL OF BLOOD FLOW THROUGH THE TYPE "B" HEART
OF CROCODILIANS.

Note particularly that the left aortic arch originates
in the right ventricle (RV) along with the pulmonary
artery.   In this position, we would suppose that it
normally receives deoxygenated blood.   However, studies
on anesthetized Caiman show that this left arch fills
with oxygenated blood from the left ventricle (LV) across
the Foramen of Panizza through which the right and left
arches communicate (White, 1956).   So there is relatively
complete separation of the systemic and pulmonary flows
under resting conditions.   Blood pressure studies of
Alligator suggest that deoxygenated blood is shunted
through the left arch during diving (White, 1970).   Much
remains to be learned, but for now it seems safe to say
that this heart is not merely primitive but is specialized
for diving and perhaps for an ectothermic physiology.
Like the type "A" heart, the "B" heart may have valuable
adaptive features, but may not be efficient at separating
oxygenated and deoxygenated blood at high pressures and
flow rates.

An anatomically "incomplete" heart does not of itself prevent reptiles from being quite active. Even among those that characteristically sit motionless are species that are quick and agile in escape or pursuit of prey. Reptiles do use glycolysis and have a large anaerobic metabolic capacity. However, when a reptile engages in intense activity, it will accumulate an oxygen debt, fatigue, and the rates of repayment will be slow, as shown by the work of Moberly, Bennett, and their co-workers (see Bennett and Dawson 1976 for references). Such limited aerobic capacity and large anaerobic capacity match well the observation that most reptiles are either sit-and-wait predators or have foraging strategies that involve slow or intermittent movement. Such foraging strategies maintain metabolic reserve for escape, pursuit of prey and mates, and territorial defense. (Also, relatively immobile behavior is largely compatible with basking, avoids the attention of predators and does not frighten prey).

So the reputed slowness of reptiles may result from a complex of causes with an interplay between the oxygen support system and appropriate foraging strategies. Physiology and behavior are also matched to a mode of life history that requires a far lower resource base than that required by endotherms. The advocates' contention that reptiles are usually slow and inactive, because cold-bloodedness imposes a lack of strength, energy or power output, overlooks these possibilities. Further, the contention has a very questionable physiological basis. Any readers who have seen the strike of a rattlesnake or who have been seized by even a medium-sized python or crocodile and lived to tell about it will quickly grasp the point. We should remember that reptiles are quite successful and, even today, their species outnumber those of mammals.

Tachymetabolic endothermy for a reptile would involve increases in the metabolic rate at least equivalent to that for intense locomotor activity. This means that a switch to endothermy by a modern reptile would quite possibly leave it without metabolic reserve to escape predators or to chase prey. This may not be a serious problem for a brooding python, hidden away inside a tree cavity, but it would involve constraints on many other ways of life. Thus, were modern reptiles to evolve mammalian resting metabolic rates, the total cost of endothermy might involve not only a 5- to 30-fold increase in food requirements, but also a substantial reduction in metabolic reserve, because they lack the complete double-pump hearts of birds and mammals.

Perhaps the above explains why endothermy is so rare among living reptiles and why ectothermy in this particular group often coincides with immobility or slow, deliberate behavior. This is quite different from saying that ectothermy causes slowness.

What is the significance of these new studies for the controversy over endothermy in dinosaurs? Dinosaurs may well have had hearts like their near relatives, the birds, because the simple loss of the left systemic arch in the crocodilian heart would essentially result in an avian double pump (see also Seymour, 1976). A complete double pump would leave dinosaurs "free to evolve" either tachymetabolism or high locomotor activity levels. We certainly agree with Ostrom (1970) that it is unsafe to use the discovery of dinosaur bones as paleoclimatic indicators. We believe that the cardiovascular arrangement in the crocodilians, in birds and probably in dinosaurs makes it reasonable to speculate that endothermy may have been more frequent among dinosaurs than it is today among living reptiles. However, this is in no way evidence that all dinosaurs would have been endothermic. In fact, the analysis underscores again that low activity and ectothermy need not be linked as closely as they often appear to be in living reptiles. Dinosaurs probably did not have a type A heart. Even if they were shown to have been highly active, it would still not require the assumption that they had "overcome" the alleged limitations of cold-bloodedness.

Endothermy Has a High Cost

Endothermy carries a high energetic cost for all creatures, even those with efficient cardiovascular systems. As a result, we would not expect endothermy to become characteristic of every group in which it evolved. Where endothermy is characteristic of a group or widespread within a group, there is usually some special circumstance. We have already mentioned that the large brains of both birds and mammals and bird flight, may allow both groups to forage with exceptional efficiency. Large flying insects, heavily wing-loaded, are generally endothermic. The benefits of temperature stability may be particularly great for them as we will discuss. Relevant here is only that some kinds of flight are a fast and economical means of long-distance travel that promises easy access to objects in three-dimensional space. Consequently, it might be relatively easy for flying animals to meet the costs of endothermy. Furthermore, one may note in passing that bees and moths are highly specialized for feeding on plants that provide rich energy sources in their flowers and indeed have complex adaptations that selectively attract the pollinating bees and moths.

Certainly, an active animal might accomplish endothermic regulation during episodes of activity by conserving the heat of activity. Conservation would require effective heat retention mechanisms, such as epidermal insulation, or vascular adaptations such as countercurrent blood flow systems. This seems to be the case for many insects. The added cost of endothermy might then be small or negligible during such short-term episodes of activity. However, there are at least two complicating factors that prevent us from concluding that endothermy is free for these animals. The overall cost of the activity producing the heat must be accounted for in considering the energy budget. The individual animal must find enough food to pay for the high activity. Furthermore, the availability of mechanisms for conservation of heat during short-term intervals may involve maintenance of elevated temperatures, even during episodes of rest, increasing tissue metabolism and overall energy requirements. Thus, it might be technically correct in some discussions, but will be misleading in most, to think of endothermy as being "free". Any endotherm has a high energy requirement relative to an equivalent, but less active ectotherm.

Dinosaurs, with few exceptions, had typically reptilian-sized brains (Hopson 1977), did not fly, and were not, as a group, locked into any now obvious coevolutionary relationships which would give them special access to rich energy sources. Of course, one could claim that their large size and/or "postural advances" were alone enough to cause an increase in foraging effectiveness by at least an order of magnitude. It is hard to know if this would be the case, and we are unprepared to make such a claim. The point is that endothermy is expensive, though the benefits may be substantial. Its demonstration requires that one identify those situations in which the costs are outweighed by the benefits. Obviously, this is not always the case.

Endothermy and Activity Levels

Typically, birds and mammals are active animals and are also endothermic. Ostrom (1970) and Bakker (1972) interpreted the postures of dinosaurs as indicating high activity and began to argue that high activity must in

turn indicate endothermy. How general is the coincidence
between high activity and endothermy that we see in birds
and mammals? Even if plants, such as the endothermic
skunk cabbage, are set aside, endothermic brooding bumblebees and pythons are obvious exceptions. If we were
simply to look at these creatures and guess that they are
ectothermic because they are sedentary, we would be
wrong.

On the other hand, some ectothermic animals are very
active. Obvious examples are the various fishes commonly
kept as pets in aquaria; also, unfortunately, houseflies
and mosquitoes. Even some few species of lizards are
quite active. In a standard laboratory test situation
for spontaneous locomotor activity, a teiid lizard,
Ameiva crysolaema, was as active as a small mammal (Regal
1978). We might look at these creatures and guess that,
because they are active, they are endothermic; we would
be wrong.

This is, of course, not to say that there is no
relationship between activity and endothermy. Obviously
there often is. For example, the larger insects with
sustained flight patterns are usually or always endothermic,
while less active species of the same size may be ectothermic
(Heinrich 1974b; May 1976). Temperature stability may be
particularly beneficial for continually active animals by
minimizing fatigue, because repayment of oxygen debts may
be at an optimum at given temperature levels (Regal 1975,
1978). Also, maintenance of a high temperature level may
facilitate heat dumping and thus temperature regulation
(Heinrich 1977). But dinosaurs did not fly, and even if
they were in other ways continually and intensively
active, the bulk alone of the giants should have allowed
them the beneficial, though not essential, thermal stability
using only environmental heat (Spotila et al. 1973; McNab
and Auffenberg 1976; McNab 1978). It is true that a
large dinosaur would generate considerable heat when
active, but would this heat constitute the essential
source for regulation? It might as easily constitute an
excessive heat load for an animal that was normally
thermally stable due to its bulk and to an effective
circulatory system. Again, measurements would be needed
to resolve the various possibilities.

Two conclusions are apparent. First, the argument
that high activity requires endothermy is belied by
counterexamples alone. It is superfluous to discuss the
array of physiological reasons that were advanced to
explain the putative association. Second, it is clear

that endothermy can evolve for many reasons. The evolution
of endothermy in mammals has had much recent discussion
(Crompton et al. 1978; Hammel 1976;, Heinrich 1977;
Hopson 1973; McNab 1978; Regal 1978). While many of us
have focussed on the question of why endothermy is so
often linked to high activity, one must remember that
this is only one context in which endothermy is adaptive,
and not invariably at that.

Size and Endothermy

     Let us first note that we are not discussing the
separate question of why dinosaurs apparently monopolized
the "niches" for giant land animals in their time. It is
not clear that there are "niches" for giant animals, that
are constantly available to be filled. Where are the
modern counterparts of the giants of the Mesozoic? Also,
it is not clear that only another endothermic animal
could keep a mammal from "invading its niche" and excluding
it. We agree that this could well be the case for most
contemporary mammals versus reptiles; but these cannot be
used to establish a general case. If reptiles with
complete double-pump hearts and low metabolic rates
existed today, they might well have advantages over
tachymetabolic mammals, particularly at large-body sizes
and in warm, mild climates where thermal stability could
be achieved simply and cheaply. The question of gigantism
is a long-standing and complex problem that is not simply
answerable today, certainly not by claiming that dinosaurs
had mammalian physiology. We do wish to consider consequences of the association of endothermy and large size.

     A large body will lose and gain heat more slowly per
unit mass than will a small one. So, on a per gram
basis, it will cost less for a large endotherm to maintain
a constant body temperature than it will cost a small
one. This is in part why elephants have lower metabolic
rates per gram than do mice.

     Thus, it might seem that because the costs of endothermy
would be relatively low for large dinosaurs, the cost/benefit
ratio would favor the evolution of endothermy. However,
as with many other common-sense arguments that have been
introduced into the warm-blooded dinosaur controversy,
this one too becomes complex upon close examination. We
agree that heat conservation is a simpler problem for a
large animal than for a small one, yet this does not
eliminate other ecological considerations.

     As McNab (1971, 1978) has recently stressed, per

gram costs must be multiplied by the animal's weight to
have any significance at the ecological level. An elephant,
even with its low metabolic rate per gram, is no bargain
as a pet, because it will cost somewhat more to feed an
elephant than to feed a mouse. The point is that the
costs of endothermy to the individual increase with size
even though the energy required per gram may decrease. A
large endotherm must find more food than must a small
one. This may or may not be easy; large size does not
guarantee success.

Any superiority of size must be relative. Even with
no interspecific competition to "keep them small", mammals
(from foxes to elephants) often evolve small sizes on
islands (Sondaar 1977; Heaney 1978, for reviews). Climates
on islands are generally milder than on continents. So,
perhaps it is the resource base that favors smaller
sizes. For that matter, most mammals, birds and other
endotherms are small. The average endotherm is smaller
than man and clearly smaller than the average dinosaur.
If, as has been claimed, endothermy allowed gigantism in
dinosaurs, then where are the giant endotherms today? It
may be that the food supply today does not allow gigantism.
It may be that endothermy actually represents an adaptation
for small size (McNab 1978). It may be because of heat-
dumping restrictions in large endotherms. No one knows.

Large animals, and large endotherms in particular,
can only live when food can be obtained and processed at
high rates. Of course, not all food is edible by a
particular species. Not all species of plants are rich
food sources for given species of herbivores, because
plants vary in their chemical defenses and nutritional
value (Freeland and Janzen 1974). As the size of an
herbivore increases, its problems of finding enough
suitable food imbedded in a matrix of unsuitable plant
species may also increase. As the metabolic rate increases,
the problem of sufficient food also increases. As the
biomass of herbivore increases, so does the selective
advantage for any plant to become unpalatable.

Certainly, large mammals not only have unusual food
requirements, but also heat-dumping problems, although
the cost of size in this respect has not been thoroughly
studied. The large, flapping ears of elephants may serve
as heat dissipating organs. Yet despite this, elephants
under heat stress are stated sometimes to have to resort
to using their trunks to suck water out of their stomachs
and then spray it over their own bodies. An extraordinary
arterial temperature of 112.6° F was noted in an African

elephant moving up an escarpment one night; this was despite an apparent (remarkable) effectiveness of the ears as cooling organs. The temperature of the blood returning to the body from the ears was at the same time reduced to 95.7°F (Douglas-Hamilton 1975).

Design for a Dinosaur

If we were to design a large dinosaur, we would include the following features:

1. A complete double-pump heart to give it a high aerobic capacity for escape, territorial defense, etc. (assuming that large size did not modify these needs).

2. A low resting metabolic rate to allow the maintenance of the small-brained individual, and of an adequate population, on even a limited resource base.

3. Augmentation of the thermal stability resulting from large body size (McNab and Auffenberg 1976; Spotila et al. 1973). Thermal stability at an elevated level might be advantageous, for instance, in allowing continual rapid digestion. In cooler climates, stability could be achieved by control of vasodilation and vasoconstriction to allow the efficient uptake of solar radiation and a reduction of heat loss from the surfaces away from the sun (Morgareidge and White 1969). Houses are large and yet, with efficient design, solar heating may be possible even in cooler climates.

4. Tolerance of thermal instability could be advantageous in warm climates. Heat storage and large body size would permit survival away from shade or bodies of water, particularly if the nocturnal temperatures were low enough to discharge sensible heat gained during the day (see Taylor 1970a, b). A variable temperature may sometimes reduce the cost of survival.

Note that we would actually prefer ectothermy in the design of very large animals, especially, but not necessarily exclusively, in equitable and in tropical climates.

Archaeopteryx

After examining some recently revealed and all previously known specimens of Archaeopteryx, Ostrom (e.g. 1976) placed this earliest bird close to the dinosaurs. This could lead one to assume, with some advocates of dinosaur endothermy, the following:

1. Because it had feathers, Archaeopteryx must have been endothermic.
2. Because Archaeopteryx was essentially a dinosaur, the presumed endothermy strengthens the argument that dinosaurs were endothermic.

The new perspective on thermal physiology affects primarily the second point. Endothermy is now known to be widespread, yet is only characteristic in two major groups, the birds and mammals. (It should be kept in mind that, by the interpretation of some physiologists, among primitive mammals several are "almost poikilothermic" (Dawson 1973). At least we can agree that thermoregulatory characteristics vary considerably through the mammals.). So, given that one species in a group is endothermic, there is no reason to predict that closely related species must also be endothermic.

We should also comment on the first point. Some of the advocates have argued that because Archaeopteryx had feathers, its ancestors must have been endothermic, because feathers could only have evolved to conserve heat (Ostrom 1974; also Desmond 1977, p. 212, "Indeed, looked at logically, it could not have been otherwise. Why would a cold-blooded creature that was dependent upon the external temperature develop feathers?"). However, feathers have two demonstrated thermal functions in living birds: (a) they conserve heat, and (b) they may shield the bird from the sun. Experiments also suggest that enlarged scales in some reptiles and feather-like structures on some cacti apparently have the principal function of heat-shielding (Regal 1975). Ectotherms, as well as endotherms, face problems of overheating in many situations. The body feathers in Archaeopteryx could as well have protected the animal from the sun (though we are not advocating this particular conclusion). One could argue that feathers might also have evolved in connection with some "non-physiological" role, for instance in social behavior. Mere observation of feathers or similar structures does not indicate their principal function. Measurements are required. It would be wrong to assume that the feathered cactus, Mammalaria plumosa, is endothermic.

It has been claimed that feathers could only prevent an ectotherm from basking. Again, not so: it has been shown experimentally that some birds bask by merely raising the feathers (Ohmart and Lasiewski 1971). Further, an ectotherm may only "need" to bask in certain climates, and not all living ectotherms do (Regal 1975).

The main point made in this section is that if Archaeopteryx were indeed essentially a therapod dinosaur, that was unquestionably endothermic, we still could not use this as anything more than a vague suspicion that endothermy existed in some other dinosaurs.

Conclusion

It does not seem that endothermic creatures invariably come to replace their ectothermic relatives in the course of evolution. This calls into serious question the ancient belief and its modern versions that endothermy is an inherently "superior" trait. Endothermy is today seen as an energetically expensive physiological adaptation that is widespread among plants and animals, although seldom characteristic of whole classes and orders. Where endothermy is widespread in a large group, special circumstances apply: large brains, flight, specializations for pollination. None of these circumstances obviously pertain to dinosaurs. On this basis, we would not a priori and in the absence of strong physical evidence to the contrary expect endothermy to be found in more than a few species of dinosaurs.

Dinosaurs are awe-inspiring for good reason: there is nothing like them living today. The debate over dinosaur endothermy does not do justice to this fact. It may even distract us from what might otherwise be an obvious premise: to explain an unparalleled situation, one might well contemplate unparalleled causes. To broaden the discussion, we shall propose one. Terrestrial vertebrates with low resting metabolic rates and complete double-pump, high-pressure hearts do not exist today; yet such creatures might have extraordinary abilities to be active and grow rapidly on a limited food supply. This would be particularly true if the climate or large body size allowed relative thermal stability. It could explain how terrestrial animals could reach such gigantic sizes and yet circumvent heat-dumping problems. It could explain how some of the herbivorous dinosaurs could move large quantities of food into their gizzards and feed giant bodies with relatively tiny heads.

Our purpose, however, is not to advocate a particular view. Rather, our position is to underscore that physiological ecology is today making rapid advances. The comparative and mechanistic context in which endothermy may be discussed has broadened considerably in the last few years. Discussions of the temperature relations of Recent and fossil vertebrates hence have to proceed within this new framework.

Acknowledgments

We thank G. A. Bartholomew, A. d'A. Bellairs, W. Bemis, A. F. Bennett, B. D. Clark, L. Garrick, H. T. Hammel, B. Heinrich, M. Kottler, B. McNab, J. H. Ostrom, T. Scanlon and F. N. White, for comments and suggestions regarding this manuscript. Preparation was aided by NSF DEB 77-02605.

----

1. Note that we use "endotherm" and "tachymetabolism" more broadly than some mammalian physiologists, who find it convenient for their discussions to restrict both terms to common species, particularly to those with high basal metabolic rates (e.g., Bligh and Johnson 1973). As our comparative knowledge rapidly increases, and it becomes clear that a variety of thermal strategies have evolved, the restricted usage compounds difficulties in communication. "Non-endotherms" must be "ectotherms" by their definition. The consequence of a restricted definition of endothermy is a contradictory and even absurd classification in which not only moths but even certain mammals that raise their body temperatures by internal heat production must be called ectotherms due to their low metabolic rates when they are inactive. Hence, we here use the terms endotherm and ectotherm in the simple sense originally intended by Cowles (1940, 1962; and Cowles and Bogert 1947) to designate whether the principal source of heat contributing to regulated body temperature in active animals is internal or external. We use tachymetabolism literally: to describe an elevated metabolism. This semantic problem over a definition of "true" endothermy is in any event scarcely relevant to the substance of the dinosaur controversy and should not become a red herring. We would be impressed by good evidence for any sort of endothermy in dinosaurs and not just endothermy with high metabolic rates in sedentary individuals, such as skunk cabbages, brooding bumblebees and pythons, mammals and birds.

The Parietal-Pineal Complex Among Paleovertebrates

7

Evidence for Temperature Regulation

Jan J. Roth and E. Carol Roth

Abstract

Vertebrates respond to their environments following
the perception and integration of stimuli by sensory organs. The epiphyseal complex, which includes a pineal body
and a third eye, functions as an environmental sensor. The
presence of all or parts of the epiphyseal complex in modern
and fossil vertebrates may indicate the importance of this
system in the evolution of vertebrate adaptation to the
environment. The prototype pineal system is recorded in
fossil vertebrates by the existence of a parietal foramen,
which indicates the presence of a parietal or third eye. A
pineal body is indicated by sculpturing of the intracranial
roof. These cranial openings and impressions are used to
determine the presence of the parietal eye and pineal body
(an E-2 condition) or their absence (an E-0 condition). A
pineal body or impression alone represents an E-1 condition.
Loss of the parietal eye appears to have occurred gradually
among mammal-like reptiles and quite suddenly among ancestral
dinosaurs (thecodonts). The pineal body in fossil reptiles
was usually retained (E-1) after parietal eye loss and,
judging from modern vertebrates, developed a secretory
capacity among the ancestors of mammals and birds. However,
dinosaurs appear to have lost the entire epiphyseal complex;
like modern members of the subclass Archosauria (Crocodilia),
they exhibit the E-0 condition.

Current research indicates that temperature regulation
is a major function of pineal systems in both ectotherms and
endotherms. Therefore, it is reasonable to suggest that
possession, partial loss, or absence of pineal systems among
fossil reptiles provides an indication of thermoregulatory
mechanisms. Among modern vertebrates, an E-2 complex occurs
exclusively among ectotherms. The E-1 and E-0 conditions
occur among both ectotherms and endotherms. These correlations lead us to suggest that fossil reptiles with E-2 pineal
systems were probably ectothermic. Transitional stages

toward retention of the pineal body alone (E-1) may represent animals evolving toward endothermy (coelurosaurs and mammal-like therapsids). Body temperature and metabolic rate are low among modern E-0 vertebrates, especially in heterothermic edentates. We speculate that Mesozoic E-0 reptiles (most dinosaurs) must have employed a similar means of temperature regulation. Like modern E-0 vertebrates, dinosaurs may have had homeothermic but low body temperatures and, because of their size, have been specialists in inertial environmental homeothermy under the equable climates of the Mesozoic.

Introduction

The refinement of sensory systems and their perception of environmental stimuli has been a major theme in over 400 million years of vertebrate evolution. Experimental adaptations have either been retained or lost, as they contributed to or detracted from species fitness in changing environments. In general, progressive sensory improvements have opened the way to successful adaptation in ever more inconstant habitats. Among primitive vertebrates, environmental temperature extremes appear to have been monitored in part by a third eye which resided in the parietal foramen. This foramen is a characteristic feature of the skull of most primitive fossil vertebrates; its occurrence can be traced from the Ordovician fishes to present day lizards. The long history of this structure attests to its fundamental importance.

Over 20 years ago, Edinger (1955) successfully rejected the widespread opinion that the fossil record could not reveal the condition or even the presence of third, or more properly, parietal eyes. It may now be possible to attribute a function to parietal eyes in vertebrate evolution. An expanding literature on reptilian parietal-pineal systems strongly suggests that thermoregulation may be an important function of these structures.

The intracranial pineal body, or epiphysis, may occur as a solitary structure or in combination with the parietal eye located on the dorsal surface of the skull. In some vertebrates there is no evidence of an epiphysis. We refer to these three morphological conditions as 1) epiphysis absent: E-0; 2) epiphysis only: E-1; 3) epiphysis with parietal organ: E-2. The E-2 condition evidently represents the primitive form of the parietal-pineal complex; its morphology is duplicated among some very early fossil vertebrates. In terms of its gross morphology, the ancient complex conforms to the E-2 complex of living lizards. In this

paper we review the morphology of the epiphyseal complex and
the involvement of parietal eyes and pineal bodies in
thermoregulation among reptiles, birds and mammals, to
suggest a commonality of function in fossil and living
vertebrates.

Parietal-Pineal System:
an Hypothesis for its Evolutionary Significance

The foramen in which the parietal eye lies is a common
feature of vertebrate skull morphology. Among living
vertebrates, parietal eyes are relatively uncommon, being
found in certain families of lizards (Gundy et al. 1975;
Gundy and Wurst 1976a), Sphenodon (Dendy 1899, 1911), and
lampreys (Studnicka 1905). The Stirnorgan, observed in
three families of anuran amphibians (Ralph 1975b), apparently
completes the distribution of median, eye-like photoreceptors
among modern vertebrates. In contrast, the intracranial
counterpart of the parietal eye, the pineal body, appears to
be nearly ubiquitous among extant quadrupeds, being absent
only in edentates, dugongs and crocodilians.

The parietal eye, pineal body, and associated brain
structures are collectively termed the parietal-pineal,
epiphyseal, or E-2 complex (Fig. 1). This complex has been
simplified to the extent that the parietal eye is not
present in mammals, birds and snakes, in which photoreceptive
pineal cells have lost their outer segments and taken on
secretory functions. Fossil skulls, however, suggest that
ancient pineal systems included a parietal eye in reptiles
ancestral to birds and mammals, among ancestral amphibians,
and fishes. Thus the E-2 complex of living vertebrates is
derived from brain structures ranging back to jawless fishes
of the Ordovician. The temporal and phylogenetic antiquity
of the E-2 complex calls for an assessment of parietal eye
and pineal function in relation to evolutionary history.
Steyn (1961), Brink (1963), and Olson (1976) have explored
pineal function in fossil vertebrates. Olson has made
important comparisons, noting that the initial evolution of
a large parietal eye, inferred from foramina, appears to be
an important adaptation to terrestrial life among certain
large, slow-moving herbivorous animals.

A unique function has not been recognized for the pineal
body; like the pituitary, the pineal may have many functions
(Hamasaki and Eder 1977). Research on mammals (Reiter 1977),
birds (Binkley et al. 1971; Ralph 1975a), and reptiles
(Levey 1973; Stebbins 1970; Underwood 1977) has consistently

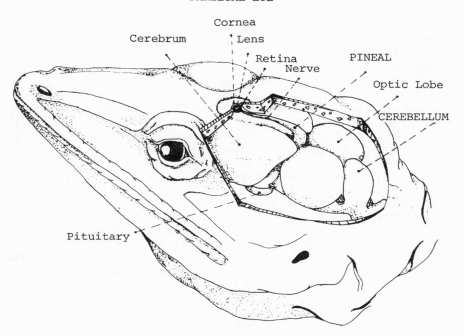

Figure 1: Parietal eye and pineal body relationships with
           the cranial roof and other brain structures in
           the lizard, <u>Anolis</u> <u>carolinensis</u>. The proximity
           of the pineal body to the intracranial roof
           results in a cranial indentation in reptiles with
           parietal eyes (E-2). The pineal body proper may
           also create intracranial sculpturing in animals
           without parietal eyes (E-1).

demonstrated an involvement of the pineal in reproduction and in the control of circadian rhythms.

Temperature regulation has been suggested as an additional function of the complex (Stebbins and Eakin 1958; Stebbins 1960; Ralph, Firth and Turner 1979), but the subtlety of thermopineal effects and a lack of comparative experiments have prevented widespread acceptance of such a role for pineal structures. Comparative studies are currently being undertaken, specifically to evaluate the influences of this complex upon both ectothermic and endothermic temperature regulation. The interpretations presented in this paper are based on our acceptance of a thermoregulatory role. However, it is difficult to evaluate fully the function of this complex in thermoregulation until further evidence, especially for mammals, becomes available.

The following scheme may be useful in interpreting the evolution and function of third eyes and pineal bodies. Among living animals, the E-2 complex occurs exclusively in ectotherms, whereas a secretory pineal body alone (E-1) occurs in both endotherms and ectotherms. In E-1 pineal systems associated with endothermy, secretory pinealocytes are present, whereas in those associated with ectothermy photoreceptors with complete outer segments occur. It is not possible to determine cellular characteristics from fossil material. However, we suggest that fossil vertebrates with E-1 pineal systems whose descendants are endothermic were transitional endotherms at the time when the parietal eye was being lost. Those vertebrates with E-1 systems whose descendants are ectothermic are presumed to have had pineal photoreceptors and to have remained ectothermic after the parietal eye was lost. Although snakes and turtles may have secretory pineals and are ectothermic, some species are capable of maintaining body temperature above ambient by means of activity or body size. In the analysis of fossil material, possession of the entire complex (E-2) is suggestive of an ectothermic physiology, while absence of the parietal eye (E-1) may be indicative of either endothermy or ectothermy. A transitional evolutionary phase between ectothermy and endothermy is possible if the pineal body is retained. Loss of both the parietal eye and pineal body (E-0) indicates that these vertebrates utilized some other means of temperature control. The modes of thermoregulation employed by modern vertebrates lacking a parietal-pineal complex altogether are based upon low metabolic rates, torpor, and low or labile body temperatures.

The evidence which bears on such an evolutionary scenario will now be considered in some detail.

Morphology of the Parietal-Pineal Complex

The brain is the site of integration for physiological and behavioral functions in vertebrates. As a consequence, various structures and areas of the brain exhibit relative hypertrophy depending on their particular contributions to individual adaptation (e.g. large optic lobes in flying vertebrates).

Central nervous system structures of subavian vertebrates are arranged more linearly than those of birds and mammals. This boxcar organization is generally represented (caudal to rostral) by the spinal cord, the hindbrain (medulla and cerebellum), the midbrain (pons and optic lobes), and the forebrain (diencephalon, cerebrum, and olfactory bulbs).

The epiphyseal complex in subavian vertebrates forms as an evagination from the roof of the diencephalon, usually with a superficial exposure above the level of the cerebrum and cerebellum. The pineal in primates is a deep brain structure as a result of neocortical expansion; however, this is an uncommon position in most living and fossil vertebrates. It is unfortunate that the primate pineal is often taken as the morphological norm, since it is not typical among vertebrate pineals.

Pineal

The pineal system of most sub-mammalian vertebrates varies in complexity and may occur with accessory structures derived embryologically from it or functionally linked to it. In living vertebrates, the pineal system in its most complete form may be regarded as a series of evaginations of the forebrain, in sequence, the paraphysis, dorsal sac, parapineal, and pineal bodies (Stebbins and Eakin 1958). The pineal complexes of ectothermic lampreys, fishes, amphibians and certain reptiles contain photoreceptive cells. Sometimes the complex includes, on the dorsal surface of the head, an extracranial parietal eye, which is a highly complex photoreceptor with a lens, retina and nerve (Eakin 1973). In most fishes and amphibians, as well as in some reptiles, there is no parietal eye, but since the intra-cranial pineal structures may also contain rod-like photoreceptor cells (Collin 1971), the pineal complex may yet have a photoreceptive capacity. In some forms that do

not possess an extracranial photoreceptor, the pineal is
located directly under a translucent area of the cranial roof
(Reiter 1977) or under a thin sheet of cartilage which may
serve to transmit light (Gundy and Wurst 1976a). In other
forms, the pineal may have a forward extension which
maximizes exposure of photoreceptive cells to vertical light
sources (Gundy and Wurst 1976b; our observations).

Comparative morphology of pineal photosensory cells
shows changes that reflect an evolutionary reduction in
direct photosensitive capacity. Histological studies
(Reiter 1977) have shown that the neurosensory elements of
photoreceptive pineal cells are structurally similar to the
neuroepithelial sensory cells of the retinas of lateral eyes.
In more advanced forms, the photoreceptor cells lose their
outer segments and become more secretory in appearance
(Reiter 1977). The pineal bodies of snakes, perhaps turtles,
birds, and mammals are primarily secretory rather than
directly photosensitive.

Parietal Eye

The third or parietal eye varies in complexity from a
simple sac-like vesicle to a structure with all the components of lateral eyes except an iris sphincter and orbital
musculature. The well developed parietal eye (as in
Sphenodon and certain lacertilians) contains a lens, a retina
with rods and cones, a fluid-filled space corresponding to
the humors of the lateral eyes, and a nerve that transmits
impulses to the brain (Eakin 1973; Engbertson and Lent 1976).
The skin immediately overlying the parietal eye is clear and
devoid of pigment, thus resembling a cornea. In some
individuals of the genus Sceloporus, the parietal eye has
failed to become extracranial and the skin over the entire
cranium is uniformly pigmented (Stebbins and Eakin 1958;
Roth and Roth, unpublished).

The parietal eye is derived embryologically from a
dorsal evagination of the diencephalic roof of the brain, or
as a bud from the tip of the pineal primordium (Eakin 1973).
Controversy exists over the origins of the pineal and
parietal anlagen. The general conclusion based on findings
of Eakin (1964) is that the origin of the parietal eye is
species dependent, arising in many reptiles from a separate
anterior diencephalic diverticulum (Gladstone and Wakeley
1940), by constriction from the pineal anlage (Sceloporus,
Eakin 1964), or from a bilaterally paired diverticulum that
may or may not fuse (the left usually giving rise to the

parietal eye, Dendy 1911).

Ontogeny of the Parietal Foramen

Recently we have studied the ontogeny of the parietal
eye and foramen in the lizard Anolis carolinensis. As it
develops, the parietal eye primordium migrates anteriorly
and assumes a position in the cranial roof. In adult
lizards, the parietal eye rests in a foramen, which is
usually located in the frontal-parietal suture (Fig. 1).
The foramen in hatchling lizards of the genus Anolis is
more properly termed a fontanelle, because nearly the entire
parietal and a portion of the frontal bones are unossified.
Bone deposition is rapid during the first year of life and
the fontanelle gradually decreases in size, finally assuming
a small triangular shape as the animal reaches reproductive
maturity (44-45 mm Snout-Vent Length, SVL). Bone deposition
continues as the animal grows until the shape of the parietal
foramen closely approximates the shape of the parietal eye
(>50 mm SVL). The foramen may close entirely in some species
(Edinger 1955); in A. carolinensis closure can occur in
individuals which are larger (>55 mm SVL) and presumably old
(our observations). Although parietal foramen closure is
not rare in large lizard species such as Iguana iguana
(Edinger 1955; our observations) it is observed infrequently
among small lizards. This may be because small species
never, or only rarely, reach old age--a stage of life during
which complete ossification most commonly occurs. The early
pattern of foramen ossification in Anolis appears to be
typical for small lizard species, but may not be representative of all extant parietal-eyed lacertilians. For example,
the foramen in Crotaphytus collaris, Iguana iguana, and some
varanids may enclose the parietal eye earlier in life.
Also, buttressing by bone around the foramen and eye may
form a small cone which is more prominent in large and
presumably older individuals. The morphology of parietal
foramina shows many similarities in form between living
reptiles and fossil vertebrates (Fig. 2).

In fossils, cranial impressions and parietal foramina
indicate that pineal structures existed in many early
vertebrates. A pineal groove may be observed on the ventral
surface of the cranial vault in well preserved skulls,
particularly those skulls of forms with parietal eyes (our
observations; Camp 1942). Arthrodires, ostracoderms,
amphibians, and primitive reptiles all possessed parietal
foramina; they may have been paired in Devonian fishes
(Edinger 1956). In a number of primitive reptiles the
parietal foramen was much larger in relation to the size of
the brain than in any extant form (Edinger 1955). The

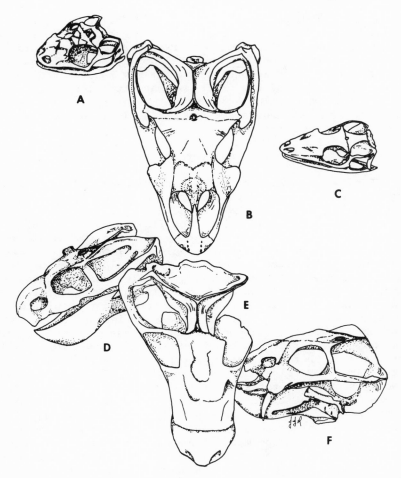

Figure 2: Parietal foramen morphology in modern (A,B,C) and
fossil (D,E,F) reptiles. The parietal foramen in
<u>Sceloporus</u> <u>magister</u> (A) is enclosed within a raised
bony platform similar to the cone-shaped foramina
of the mammal-like dicynodonts (D,F). While raised
parietal foramina (A) are more common among medium
rather than large or small lizards, buttressing of
the parietal foramen often occurs in larger lizards
(<u>Cyclura</u> <u>cornuta</u>, B) and in mammal-like therapsid
therocephalians (<u>Notosollasia</u>, E). The parietal
foramen in small lizards (<u>Anolis</u> <u>carolinensis</u>, C)
generally reflects a morphological condition common
among early stem reptiles (e.g. captorhinomorphs)
in which neither raising nor buttressing elevates
the parietal foramen above the plane of the skull
table.

structure of the parietal foramen in fossil forms such as
mammal-like reptiles varies from a simple opening in advanced
theriodonts to an elaborate bony ramification approaching a
cone in the dicynodont Aulacocephalodon. The significance
of this buttressing is uncertain. It may have served to
protect the parietal eye or it may have functioned to
enhance the exposure of the eye. At any rate, it is certain
that this buttressing raised the parietal eye above the
plane of the parietal table.

Thermal Physiology

Definitions which once adequately described the thermoregulatory mechanisms employed by animals (Adolph 1951;
Cowles and Bogert 1944) have been largely outdated by recent
research. Templeton (1970), Bligh (1973), Heath (1968,
1970) and Swan (1974) have recently reviewed the ethology
and physiology of thermoregulation among reptiles, mammals
and other vertebrates. Greenberg (this volume) reviews
behavioral thermoregulation among reptiles and presents a
discussion of thermoregulatory definitions; Whittow (1966)
and Cowles (1962) also define those terms most popular in
current usage. Taken together, these reviews point up an
important deficit. Categorical definitions of thermoregulation may depict extremes but they do not adequately describe
the range of thermoregulatory mechanisms exploited by
vertebrates. For instance, most students of thermoregulation
readily separate ectotherms from endotherms based upon the
source of heat utilized to raise or lower body temperature.
Unfortunately, distinct suites of physiological and behavioral responses are often assumed to be linked firmly to
ectothermic or endothermic patterns of temperature regulation
when, in fact, both ectotherms and endotherms use common
physiological and behavioral strategies to maintain thermal
homeostasis.

Behavioral and physiological thermoregulation are not
finite ends of a categorical spectrum ranging from ectotherms
to endotherms. Ectotherms employ endothermic strategies
during daily bouts of activity, or become transient endotherms seasonally during incubation periods (Hutchison et
al. 1966). Conversely, endotherms depend on behavioral
strategies utilized by ectotherms to avoid environmental
temperature extremes. Mammals and birds, which generate
heat internally and regulate its dissipation through the
peripheral integument, often compromise thermal homeostasis
during periods of torpor, allowing body temperature to
approximate ambient conditions (Bligh 1973; Withers 1977).
The behavioral regulation of heat transfer between the
organism and its environment may be more important, moment

to moment, even among endotherms, than is generally realized. Endotherms may control thermal homeostasis behaviorally during most activities (Hafez 1964), only resorting to autonomic controls (sweating, panting, hair-erection, gular flutter) when thermal homeostasis is challenged (Bligh 1973). In fact, if temperature control centers in the hypothalamus (pre-optic area) are lesioned (Lipton 1968; Carlisle 1969), body temperature remains normal in cold challenged rats since behavioral regulation compensates for physiological failure; Van Zoeren and Stricker (1977) contend that the degree of behavioral and physiological deficits in thermoregulatory ability depends on the location of hypothalamic lesions.

Reptiles which regulate body temperature by precise exposure to appropriate environmental temperatures primarily do so behaviorally (Templeton 1970; Bogert 1959). Most reptiles lose or gain heat across a thermal gradient by movement, changes in posture and orientation, conduction, convection, and radiation (Schmidt-Nielsen 1964; Bogert 1959), thereby maintaining body temperatures within a range characteristic of each species (Brattstrom 1965). Body temperature regulation in active lizards is precise (Dewitt 1967; Schall 1977) and may be narrow enough to be comparable to endothermic regulation around a single set-point (Templeton 1970). In addition, reptiles do not lack the ability to alter their body temperatures by physiologic or autonomic processes. Like mammals and birds, reptiles respond physiologically to changes in temperature. For example, they show different rates of heating and cooling (Bartholomew and Tucker 1963); utilize vascular shunts which serve to regulate head-body temperature differences (Heath 1964); alter heart rate in response to ambient temperature (Heath 1966); pant when stressed with high temperature (Richards 1970; Heatwole et al. 1973; Dawson and Bartholomew 1958); and flush the body periphery (shell) with blood during periods of heat transfer between the animal and the environment (Weathers and Morgareidge 1971; Weathers 1970; Schall 1977).

Metabolic heat production may also play an integral part in thermoregulation among reptiles, but its contribution to thermal homeostasis is still unclear (Bennett and Dawson 1976; Bennett and Licht 1972). Some reptiles, such as turtles (Frair et al. 1972; Mrosovsky and Pritchard 1971) and varanids (McNab and Auffenberg 1976) maintain fairly constant, above ambient body temperatures because of their large size or activity. Pythons approach endothermy when incubating their eggs in that they can keep body temperature above the ambient level by muscular contraction (Hutchison et al. 1966), but they are transient endotherms in that body temperatures eventually fall with continued exposure to cool environments. All these observations clearly support Heath's (1968) suggestion that "among higher taxa there are no purely poikilostatic or homeostatic animals". The inability of reptiles to remain homeothermic when challenged by cold is perhaps the most distinctive feature separating modern endotherms from ectotherms (McNab 1978). Of course, as Hotton (this volume) and others have suggested, even this difference could be eliminated in sufficiently large reptiles, as long as they did not experience extreme, long-term changes in environmental temperature.

The mean body temperature within the range selected by active animals is known as the preferred (laboratory) or eccritic (free-living) temperature characteristic of a species (Licht et al. 1966). The selection of appropriate species-specific eccritic temperatures among reptiles (Brattstrom 1965) and the maintainance of a constant body temperature around a specific set-point in birds and mammals require precise temperature sense and control. Lizards may regulate body temperature within a range containing many eccritic temperatures that are characteristic of different activities (Regal 1966; Kitchell 1969; Schall 1977). Lizards generally leave warm or cool places when body temperature approaches an upper or lower limit. Barbour and Crawford (1977) suggest that lizards may allow body temperature to fluctuate at random within their thermal ranges, regulating activity only at the upper and lower limits, to avoid some of the energetic costs of thermoregulation (Huey and Slatkin 1976). Although these limits may be several degrees apart in lizards and virtually at a single point in mammals, the mechanisms of body temperature control in ectotherms and endotherms may be related.

The hypothalamus, located above the pituitary and below the third ventricle, is currently believed to be the major thermoregulatory control center in mammals. The regulation of body temperature near a set-point is apparently controlled primarily by the hypothalamus, and secondarily by other cerebral structures (Cooper 1966; Jürgens 1974; South et al. 1972; Satinoff 1974). While the reviews just cited primarily deal with endotherms, Rodbard et al. (1950), Heath et al. (1968), and Hammel et al. (1967) have recognized areas in the reptilian hypothalamus containing neurons sensitive to heat and cold, comparable to those found in mammals. They suggest that a behavioral hypothalamic thermostat in reptiles may have been an evolutionary precursor of the endothermic thermostat.

The regulation of body temperature in reptiles, birds and mammals shows many striking similarities (Hammel et al. 1967). This has led to the suggestion that certain reptiles (e.g. Crotaphytus collaris) have "developed the early analogue of the posterior thermoregulatory center. If this could be demonstrated by electrical studies or bioamine responses of the midbrain, the collared lizard could be considered as lacking only an insulating coat to be able to achieve homeothermy" (Swan 1974). In view of the many common thermoregulatory mechanisms and behaviors utilized by both ectotherms and endotherms, Satinoff (1978) suggests that "ectotherms can be considered as endothermic systems in transition". Analytical determinations of hypothalamic temperature control in reptiles are still needed; however, studies illustrating the influence of other central nervous system structures upon reptilian thermoregulation may have an important bearing on any discussion concerning the evolution of a behavioral thermostat.

Current studies in which both ectotherms and endotherms are subjected to thermal challenge clearly indicate that both the parietal eye and the pineal body influence precise temperature regulation, by controlling the high and low limits within which a species regulates its body temperature. Imprecise discrimination of high or low hypothalamic set-points results in an alteration of the mean eccritic temperature, which usually shifts to higher levels in response to surgical manipulation of the parietal-pineal complex. Thus, the involvement of this complex in thermo-regulation among modern ectotherms and endotherms, together with the antiquity of the complex among fossil vertebrates, suggests that these neural structures may provide a model that will shed light on the evolution of thermoregulation among the vertebrates.

The Parietal-Pineal Complex and Evidence for Its Role in Ectotherm Temperature Regulation

Although third eyes were first described nearly 150 years ago (Brandt, Edwards and Duges 1829, cited in Gundy and Wurst 1976b) as "special glandular" spots on the heads of certain reptiles, their function was not apparent until Stebbins (1958, 1960, 1970, 1973) initiated a series of fundamental studies. Eakin (1973) reviews this and other information which clearly links parietal eye and pineal function with photoreceptivity and temperature regulation among reptiles. A similar thermoregulatory function for the pineal among birds and mammals suggests that the evolution of endothermy may have involved sequential improvements in the basic behavioral thermoregulatory machinery of ectotherms.

By examining the response behavior of free-living, but
surgically parietalectomized western fence lizards
(Sceloporus occidentalis), Stebbins and Eakin (1958) suggested
the possibility that third eyes serve to regulate exposure
to environmental light, and thus temperature. The authors
compared the behavior and physiology of sham-operated and
parietalectomized lizards, demonstrating an accentuation of
exposure to full sunlight, an increase in locomotor movement,
a change in activity with time of day, and an increase in
thyroid epithelial cell height with a corresponding reduction
in follicular colloid among parietal-eyeless animals.
Subsequent studies have recorded more active thyroids in
both sexes of S. occidentalis (Stebbins and Cohen 1973).
Some of the effects cited above (i.e., (i) changes in
activity or its intensity; (ii) alterations in reproductive
cycles; and (iii) greater exposure to bright light) have
also been recorded in Xantusia vigilis (Glaser 1958; LaPointe
1966; Stebbins 1970), Sceloporus virgatus (Stebbins 1963)
and Callisaurus draconoides (Packard and Packard 1972).

Stebbins proposed that all the responses to parietal
eye removal noted above amounted to actions taken by the
lizards to remain thermally homeostatic when active, or were
secondary effects produced by imperfect behavioral temperature selection. However, only doubtfully significant
differences in body temperature between parietal-eyeless and
control animals were observed in early experiments (Stebbins
1960), an outcome probably attributable to limitations of
the method of recording temperature using manual fast-reading
thermometers. Since temperature is an intrinsic characteristic of environmental light, the increase in photic
exposure observed in studies of several species of lizards
might be expected to bring about statistically demonstrable
alterations in body temperature.

Hutchison and Kosh (1974), using multipoint temperature
recorders, measured body temperature in female Anolis
carolinensis housed within thermal gradients. They reported
that parietalectomized animals maintained body temperatures
2-5°C higher than control animals, throughout the day
and night except for the period 0800-0900 hrs. The
importance of these results is twofold: (i) they provide
a dramatic demonstration of an effect on body temperature
after parietal eye removal, confirming Stebbins' and
Eakin's predictions; (ii) these data suggest that the
parietal eye controls thermal behavior at night even in the
absence of light. The latter response implies that, in

ectotherms, environmental light may serve only as a taxic
stimulus that is correlated with environmental temperature.

Roth and Ralph (1976b) further explored the effects of
thermal and photic stimuli upon the behavior of surgically
parietalectomized A. carolinensis. Although dark thermal
stimuli were moderately more attractive to parietalectomized
animals than to controls, both groups avoided a light source
without heat. The latter effect was significantly more
pronounced among parietalectomized animals. Initial attrac-
tion of all experimental groups to a cool light source,
followed by gradual and finally complete avoidance of that
light source, supports the suggestion that environmental
light may serve as a taxic stimulus in lizards exploiting
the thermal characteristics of light. Because photothermal
gradients with fixed heat/light sources are steep and narrow,
they encourage permanent occupation of thermal locations by
dominant animals, forcing subordinate animals to accept
suboptimal positions. Roth and Ralph (1976a) provided a
unique environmental photothermal chamber with a moving
heat/light source in which to test the thermal responses of
surgically parietalectomized female A. carolinensis. Body
temperature was measured continuously over a four-day
preoperative and four-day postoperative period, a procedure
that generated 3,264 data points for each parietalectomized,
sham-parietalectomized, and intact animal. The results
confirmed those of Hutchison and Kosh (1974); parietal eye
removal initiates hyperthermic behavior in animals freely
selecting appropriate temperatures in a thermally variable
environment and significantly increases body temperature
(2.10°C in parietalectomized animals) (Fig. 3). Similar
results were simultaneously published for the lizard S.
magister (Engbretson and Hutchison 1976).

Suspecting that the parietal eye might be a fine tuning
thermostat and that the pineal body proper might serve as a
coarse tuning thermostat influencing set-points of the
hypothalamus, Roth and Ralph (unpublished) pinealectomized
female A. carolinensis and recorded body temperatures under
conditions already described. Pinealectomy also resulted in
an immediate hyperthermic response (1.75°C increase in body
temperature) comparable to that observed after parietalectomy.
Subsequent studies indicate that injection of the pineal
hormone melatonin in pinealectomized S. undulatus just
before the dark phase of a photoperiod (14L:10D), tends to
reverse hyperthermic behavior, and animals select cool
nighttime refuges with temperatures statistically identical
to those of intact controls.

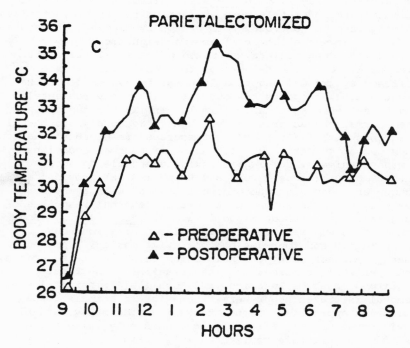

Figure 3: Body temperature in parietalectomized female <u>Anolis</u>
<u>carolinensis</u> before (preoperative) and after (post-
operative) surgical removal of the parietal eye.
Each point represents 8,160 data points condensed
around 15 minute intervals for one 24 hour cycle.

Temperature Regulation and the Pineal in Endotherms

Some elegant studies and a variety of anecdotal observations combine to suggest that pineal bodies may play a role in temperature regulation in endotherms as well as ectotherms. However, the paucity of data bearing on the relationship between the pineal gland and body temperature control among endotherms leaves much to be desired.

Gaston and Menaker (1968) have reported that the circadian rhythm of activity was lost in sparrows after pinealectomy, an effect similar to activity changes recorded among lizards (Stebbins 1963; Glaser 1958). Likewise, Binkley et al. (1971) have reported a loss of the circadian rhythm in the temperature regulation of pinealectomized sparrows in continuous darkness. Body temperature did not drop to the normal daily minimum characteristic of control birds, and pinealectomy raised the temperature. These results suggest that a hyperthermic nighttime response comparable to that of parietalectomized lizards (Hutchison and Kosh 1974) also occurs in birds. More recently, John et al. (1978) have shown that the circadian rhythm of body temperature is not abolished by pinealectomy in pigeons, but that compared with intact and sham-operated birds this operation does initiate higher body temperatures during both light and dark phases. In addition, subcutaneous implantation of melatonin pellets nullifies or reverses the hyperthermic effect of pinealectomy. Binkley (1974) observed that melatonin injected into sparrows results in a lowering of cloacal temperature. Cogburn et al. (1976) have recently reported dark phase thermoregulatory dysfunction in pinealectomized chickens.

Among mammals, melatonin may affect mechanisms that lower body temperature in mice (Arutyunyun et al. 1964), and may promote the deposition of brown fat (a readily accessible source of metabolic heat used during periods of rapid arousal) in hibernating mammals (Girardier 1977). Experimentally, nothing more is known of thermopineal effects among mammals.

Mammals with atrophic or small pineals (e.g. elephants, hyrax, sirens, rhinoceros) and certain vertebrates lacking pineal bodies altogether (crocodilians, edentates, dugongs) tend to inhabit warm or tropical regions. These groups of vertebrates may represent natural experiments. Stebbins and Eakin (1958), Stebbins (1963) and Roth and Ralph (1976a) have suggested that one function of the pineal in all vertebrates may be to prevent metabolic excess. If the pineal acts as a brake, then it might be predicted that endotherms in cold environments would possess large pineals, functioning to prevent metabolic machinery from producing heat at a pace which would debilitate energy reserves. In contrast to animals inhabiting lower latitudes, polar sea lions, seals, and walruses have the largest pineals known in mammals (Tilney and Warren 1919; Cuello and Tramezzani 1969). Lemmings also have large and temperature-sensitive pineal bodies (Quay 1978).

As another natural experiment, we can compare body temperatures between mammals with and without pineal bodies. The naturally occurring evolutionary loss of pineal bodies among vertebrates appears to coincide with lower body temperatures or reduced metabolic rates, compared with animals with well-developed pineal bodies (Table 1). This trend appears to be contradictory to the results of surgical pinealectomy, which generally leads to loss of temperature rhythms and hyperthermia. Evidently, surgical pinealectomy has different consequences from evolutionary pineal loss in terms of subsequent thermoregulatory ability. However, it is reasonable that interference with thermoregulatory mechanisms might produce either a dramatic increase or a decrease in body temperature, whereas natural pineal loss may reflect selection for inertial homeothermy near ambient temperatures. Thus some animals (e.g. elephant, rhinoceros) living in the tropics have small pineals; while others living in thermally hospitable climates or microhabitats (edentates, dugongs) lack pineals altogether. Conversely, if the pineal serves to prevent metabolic excess during cold challenge, selection for a greater influence of pineal function upon thermoregulation (larger pineals) should be observed as distance from the equator increases. Simply stated, tropical animals or animals not thermally challenged by cool temperatures should exhibit small, or nonexistent pineal bodies; at higher latitudes animals should exhibit more complex, larger pineals. In a general way, this seems to be the case (Table 1). Of course, the examples cited represent extreme cases and any explanation must have exceptions. Body temperature, pineal size and geographic distribution are strongly suggestive of thermopineal re-lationships; however, single factors rarely explain natural events adequately. Ralph (1975a) presents an excellent discussion of the pineal gland in relation to the geographic distribution of animals.

Paleoclimates and the Aquatic-Terrestrial Thermal Barrier

The existence of broad patterns of climatic change over geologic time have been established on the basis of the

distributions of climatically limited faunas and floras,
from evidence of glaciations, and from isotopically determined
paleotemperatures. Estimates of pre-Permian isotopic temperatures are not available, due to the general lack of suitably
preserved materials. However, widespread cool climates are
indicated for the late Paleozoic by the evidence of extensive
southern hemisphere glaciations. Few data are available for
the Triassic, but there is general agreement, based on
faunal, floral, and isotopic data that Jurassic climates
were much more equable than those that preceeded them. More
extensive cooler climates became established in the Cretaceous,
initiating a broad decline in equability that would continue
up until the Pleistocene glaciation. The values for most
isotopic paleotemperatures are based on marine fossils and
sediments, but a similar broad pattern for terrestrial
environments is shown for ancient lakes (Fig. 4) by Keith
and Weber (1964).

    In any discussion dealing with the evolution of thermal
physiology, it is important to emphasize that the mechanisms
of body temperature regulation are flexible. The adaptive
thermal repertoire of any species has evolved in response to
natural selection exerted by particular, gradually changing
thermal conditions of the environment. Under such conditions,
both ectothermy and endothermy are successful body temperature
regulating strategies, which meet the specific demands of
each species' unique circumstances. It is probable that
vertebrates were faced by variable thermal conditions during
their first emergence onto the land. Windley (1977) has
noted that the relative, plate tectonic movements of continents
have affected the evolution of life by changing ecologically
determinative factors, such as:

> (i) ocean circulation
> (ii) nutrient supply
> (iii) climatic changes
> (iv) habitat exploitability
> (v) submergence and emergence of land masses

All of these, in concert, can be regarded as environmental
regulators of evolution and its fossil record. If a change
of latitude results from continental drift, a fauna may be
transported from a stable climate to one with fluctuating
thermal environments. Tolerance of temperature variation is
probably as important a factor in vertebrate evolution as
food supply (Windley 1977).

Table 1.   Mammalian Body Temperatures and Pineal Size

Species	Core Body Temperature	Ref.	Absent	Small	Pineal Average	Large
Pholidota						
Pangolin	low (unknown)	4	-			
Edentata						
Armadillo	26.6-32.2°C	1	-			
Anteater	29-32.5°C	8, 2	-			
Sloth	32°C	3	-			
Sirenia						
Dugong	low (unknown)	4	-			
Monotremata						
Platypus	32°C	5		--+		
Echnida	32.2°C	5		++		
Marsupialia						
Oppossum	30-35°C, 32°C	2,6		-+		
Insectivora						
Shrew	38.8°C	7			++	
Hedgehog	30-35°C (Heterothermic)	6		-+		
Chiroptera						
Bat	32-38°C (Heterothermic)	7		++		
Primatia						
Man	37.0°C	7			+	
Proboscidea						
Elephant	20-30°C	4		--+		
Hyracoidea						
Hyrax	low and labile	4		--+		
Cetacea						
Whale	unknown			----+		
Lagomorpha						
Rabbit	39.0°C	7				++
Rodentia						
Mouse	37.0°C	7			+	
Rat	37.5°C	7			+	
Carnivora						
Dog	38.5°C	7			+	
Perissodactyla						
Horse	39.0°C	7				++
Rhinoceros	unknown			+		
Artiodactyla						
Sheep	39.0°C	7				++
Cow	38.5°C	7				++
Pinnipedia						
Walrus	39.0°C	2				++++
Weddel Seal	39.5°C	2				++++

Table 1:   Core temperature and pineal size appear to be
            correlated in that animals without pineals have
            very low or heterothermic body temperatures,
            while large pineals occur in animals with body
            temperatures near or above the mammalian average
            (37°C). Mammals with small pineals tend to have
            low body temperatures, but may be heterothermic
            or near the average mean. A system for accurately
            quantifying pineal size has not been developed;
            consequently, it is only possible to recognize the
            presence or absence of pineal bodies and broad
            size categories. Small or average size categories
            depend to some extent on the subjective interpre-
            tation of size differences. The number of +'s to
            the right of center in each box indicates a
            relatively larger pineal; the number of -'s to
            the left of center indicates a relatively smaller
            pineal; - indicates that the pineal body is absent.
            Body temperature information from (1) Block (1974);
            (2) Altman and Dittmer (1973); (3) Meritt (1974);
            (4) Ralph (1975); (5) Augee (1976); (6) Crompton,
            et al. (1978); and (7) Swan (1974).

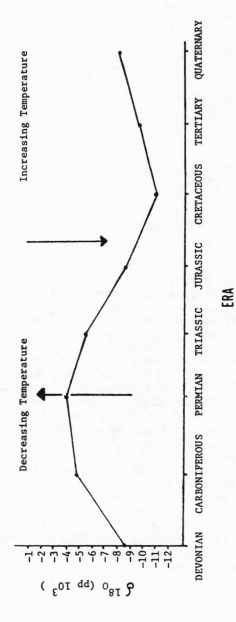

Figure 4. Paleotemperature records recorded from selected Paleozoic and Mesozoic limestones and fossils from fresh water lakes (after Keith and Weber 1964).

It is very likely that primitive fishes, amphibians, and reptiles were exposed to thermal variability in their environments and some may have developed precise behavioral thermal control. Emergence from aquatic habitats and invasion of terrestrial ecosystems occurred throughout the upper Devonian, Carboniferous and Permian as the vertebrates expanded from marshy areas into extensive terrestrial plant communities (Romer 1966; Young 1962). In these environments the atmosphere may have been warm and humid; consequently, it is often assumed that the transition from an aquatic to a terrestrial existence involved gradual change from one thermally stable environment to another (Eaton 1960). Although many Paleozoic aquatic and amphibious vertebrates appear to have lived under warm climates, thermal stresses were certainly rigorous at higher latitudes. Bowen (1966) has presented data suggesting that oceanic temperatures during the late Paleozoic were warmer than those of the present day, but that terrestrial temperatures were quite variable. Vertebrates attempting to invade terrestrial environments required and employed precise behavioral temperature control in response to these variable temperatures. This is not to imply that early reptiles, amphibians and fishes had efficient endogenous temperature control, but rather that they behaviorally selected optimal thermal surroundings in response to daily and seasonal changes in temperature, much as do modern ectotherms. Temperature regulation may even have been a prerequisite for invasion of shallow bodies of water. As in the present day large, deep bodies of water were more thermally stable than smaller, shallower waters, during the late Paleozoic. The magnitude of thermal differences may not have been as great as at present, but a thermal spectrum must have existed. Today, the annual range in oceanic temperature is no more than 10°C in any locality. Rivers are more thermally stable (11°C range) than lakes, which may have a temperature range from $4^{\circ}-20^{\circ}$C (Wilber 1964). Small, shallow bodies of water may have a thermal range of $0^{\circ}-42^{\circ}$C (Young and Zimmerman 1956), while the range in terrestrial environments may be as great as $60^{\circ}-70^{\circ}$C.

In the course of their evolution, the ancestors of terrestrial vertebrates migrated from the oceans to rivers and thence to lakes and marshes. Behavioral, physiological and morphological adaptations to environmental temperatures must have been pronounced as vertebrates responded to thermal pressures. The transition from an aquatic to a terrestrial existence implies adequate thermoregulatory abilities prior to total emergence. Precise behavioral thermoregulation was undoubtedly perfected as fossil vertebrates evolved through the hierarchy of aquatic thermal barriers discussed above. Behavioral adaptations first developed in aquatic environments ensured adequate thermoregulatory survival in more complex and variable terrestrial thermal situations. An appreciation of the thermoregulatory function of the epiphyseal complex is important for understanding the evolution of precise behavioral temperature regulation. It is possible to predict that the occurrence of the E-2 complex is frequent in lineages evolving through the aquatic thermal hierarchy and increasingly frequent in groups that were just crossing the aquatic-terrestrial thermal barrier.

Systematic Occurrence of Parietal and Pineal Structures

Modern Forms

Lacertilia. The occurrence of parietal eyes or their homologues in modern vertebrates is restricted to lampreys, (Eakin 1973), three families of frogs (Ralph 1975b), 11 families of lizards (Gundy 1974; Gundy and Wurst 1976a), and Sphenodon (Dendy 1911). In general, visual examination of the extracranial surface is sufficient to verify existence of the parietal eye; because of their embryological associ-ation, where the parietal eye is present the presence of the pineal body can be inferred. Among lizards, the parietal eye occurs in 11 of 18 families and in 96% of the genera within those families (Gundy and Wurst 1976a). Parietal-eyeless lizards occur primarily among the Gekkonidae and the Teiidae; these families, collectively, account for 92% of parietal-eyeless genera. The distribution and ecology of naturally occurring parietal-eyed and eyeless lizards suggests the possibility that the epiphyseal complex has a photothermal function. Gundy (1974) and Gundy et al. (1975) have computed the centers of distribution of parietal-eyed and eyeless species of lizards. They report that low latitudes are primarily occupied by parietal-eyeless forms while higher latitudes and altitudes are occupied by species with parietal eyes. Thus, the parietal eye appears to confer a selective advantage on species occupying thermally variable, seasonal habitats.

The only conspicuously diurnal lizards among parietal-eyeless families, the Teiidae, have eccritic temperatures near $40^{o}C$ (Brattstrom 1965). Recently, Schall (1977) measured eccritic temperatures between 39.9 and $40.4^{o}C$ in various teiid species. Individual behavior patterns (basking, active movement, quiescence in shade) are characterized by eccritic temperatures ranging from a low $38.1^{o}C$ (basking) to a high 42.0°C (in shade). Although it is tempting to suggest that evolutionary parietal eye loss in diurnal animals results in high or variable eccritic temperatures comparable to those induced by parietalectomy, this explanation is at variance with the thermal ecologies of other species without parietal eyes. The majority of parietal-eyeless lizards are weakly diurnal, fossorial, crepuscular, or nocturnal, and have mean eccritic temperatures below 35°C (Brattstrom 1965). Apparently, evolutionary loss of either the parietal eye or the pineal body is associated with lower body temperatures and is not equivalent to either surgical parietalectomy or pinealectomy which result in hyperthermia.

Serpentes. With the exception of a parietal eye-like structure observed in an embryo viper (Hanitsch 1888; cited in Stebbins and Eakin 1958), third eyes have not been reported in modern snakes (the "embryo viper" Anguis fragilis has since been placed in the lizard family Anguidae). In contrast, secretory pineal bodies comparable to those of birds and mammals are present in all snakes examined. Snakes are apparently derived from varanid lizards (Porter 1972; Romer 1966) and are thought to have lost the parietal eye as a consequence of their ancestral fossorial existence. However, a fossorial mode of life does not appear to lead to parietal eye loss, since many burrowing lizards (Scincidae) have retained parietal eyes (Gundy and Wurst 1976b). Third eyes have not been demonstrated in any living snake and all snakes examined have histologically similar pineals. No correlation has been established among pineal type, habitat, and thermoregulatory ability in this group. As a result, a thermopineal relationship remains to be evaluated in the suborder Serpentes.

Rhynchocephalia. Sphenodon, a lizard-like reptile which is the last living remnant of a once successful group, has remained relatively unchanged since the Jurassic. As part of a primitive suite of characters which include a diapsid skull with two temporal openings, Sphenodon has retained a E-2 complex similar to those of lizards. Stebbins (1958) shielded the parietal eye of two individuals with aluminum foil and observed their behavior in a thermal gradient. Thermal behavior was not affected in either animal. Stebbins concluded that either the parietal eye had no effect on temperature regulation and photic exposure in this species, or that an effect took longer than two months to appear. Sphenodon is unique among reptiles in that it is nocturnal and its thermal range of activity lies between 6.2°C and 18.0°C (Bogert 1953). It is possible that the epiphyseal complex was not appropriately challenged by the

Table 2.   Parietal Foramen and Pineal Body Occurence

Subclass	Order	E-2	E-1	E-0	Not E-2	Total Genera in Order	Fossil Record (After Romer 1966) ← Ca → ← P → ← T → ← J → ← C →
ANAPSIDA	Cotylosauria	18	1	0	-	57	
ANAPSIDA	Chelonia	0	8	0	-	203	
LEPIDOSAURIA	Eosuchia	6	2	0	-	14	
LEPIDOSAURIA	Squamata	48	7	0	-	917	
LEPIDOSAURIA	Rhynchocephalia	5	1	0	-	27	
ARCHOSAURIA	Thecodontia	2	0	0	7*	45	
ARCHOSAURIA	Crocodilia	0	0	6	-	132	
ARCHOSAURIA	Saurischia	0	1	15	-	244	
ARCHOSAURIA	Ornithischia	0	0	9	-	111	
ARCHOSAURIA	Pterosauria	0	1	0	6*	24	
SYNAPTOSAURIA	Araeoscelidia	1	1	0	-	16	
SYNAPTOSAURIA	Sauropterygia	11	2	0	-	71	
SYNAPTOSAURIA	Placodontia	7	0	0	-	9	
SYNAPSIDA	Pelycosauria	15	0	0	-	45	
SYNAPSIDA	Therapsida	118	10	0	-	298	

Parietal foramen occurrence in Paleozoic and
Mesozoic Reptilia. Numbers refer to the number
of genera with or without a parietal eye or pineal
body in each order. Possession of a parietal eye
indicates that a pineal body is present. Endocranial casts indicate presence or absence of a pineal
body when the parietal eye is not present. The
number of genera examined does not equal the total
number of genera in each order because descriptions
of many fossil genera are based upon incomplete
skeletons without skulls or fragmentary skull parts
without parietal bones. Horizontal bars indicate
the relative appearance and disappearance of orders
within the Reptilia during the following periods:
Ca = Carboniferous; P = Permian; T = Triassic;
J = Jurassic; and C = Cretaceous.
*Endocasts are not available for certain members of
these two orders to corroborate either an E-1 or E-0
epiphyseal condition. Absence of a parietal foramen
indicates that these genera are not E-2 representatives.

range of temperatures used in Stebbins' experiments. It
would be desirable to further explore effects of parietalectomy
and pinealectomy upon thermal behavior in free-living animals.

Fossil Forms

The occurrence of the epiphyseal complex among fossil
vertebrates is indicated by the presence of either a parietal
foramen (Edinger 1955) or an intracranial pineal impression
(Camp 1942). The parietal eye invariably occupied a foramen
penetrating the cranial roof, while pineal body impressions
appeared on the intracranial surface of skulls in which the
brain approximately filled the cranial cavity and had a
large diencephalic exposure. The documentation of parietal
foramen and pineal occurrence relies upon endocranial casts
made from fossil skulls and upon published information.
Unfortunately, illustrations in the early literature do not
always record parietal foramina even where they are present,
or the parietal foramen is sometimes discussed but not
illustrated. In these cases, we sought additional descriptions for verification of parietal foramen occurrence.
Because many species are described on the basis of skeletal
parts without skulls, or are based on skulls that may be
fragmented, crushed or incomplete, our survey only includes
genera which are well represented in the fossil record.
Table 2 indicates that the E-2 complex was common among
extinct reptiles. An extensive survey suggests that the E-2
complex occurred most frequently in certain ancient fish,
amphibians, stem reptiles and mammal-like reptiles. The
parietal foramen appears to be restricted to groups which
occupied the land and was ubiquitous in groups during the
Carboniferous and Permian when terrestrial ecosystems were
expanding. Most noteworthy is the occurrence of parietal
foramina and pineals among those groups whose descendants
became endothermic (mammals and birds); and E-2 absence
among groups which have been reported to have been endothermic
but became extinct at the end of the Cretaceous (dinosaurs).

Anapsida

Cotylosauria. The order Cotylosauria includes the
captorhinomorphs and the procolophonids. Although such
well-known animals as Seymouria and Diadectes were once
included among the cotylosaurs, the presence of amphibian
larvae in seymouriamorphs and the morphology of diadecto-
morphs indicate that these genera should be recognized as
advanced labyrinthodont amphibians (Olson 1971).

Cotylosaurs form the basic assemblage from which the entire reptilian, avian and mammalian radiations diverged. The morphology of these stem reptiles represents a basic pattern with primitive characteristics from which the advanced types can all be derived. The parietal eye (pineal opening) is generally regarded as a primitive character, since nearly all early reptiles, including all genera of cotylosaurs, possessed an E-2 complex. Based upon various morphological (skeletal) comparisons and the possession of an E-2 complex which, among living vertebrates is restricted to ectotherms, it seems likely that cotylosaurs were ectothermic (Ricqlès 1974). It is also important to note that these first terrestrial ectotherms were adapting to a complex thermal environment. As a consequence, virtually every genus possessed a behavioral temperature control mechanism (E-2 complex) inherited from aquatic ancestors that was capable of monitoring environmental temperatures.

The E-2 complex was not present in all earlier amphibians. It is found most frequently among those forms which gave rise to the cotylosaurs (rhachitomide and anthracosaur amphibians). The presence of a temperature regulatory E-2 system among ancestral cotylosaurs, but not other groups, may reflect an adaptive advantage which permitted early cotylosaurs to emerge and radiate into thermally variable terrestrial ecosystems.

Chelonia. The order Chelonia is an ancient group whose morphology (except for minor changes like the loss of teeth among recent turtles) has altered little since the Permian. Parietal foramina do not occur in any recent or fossil chelonid (Zangerl 1960; Gaffney 1977); however, pineal bodies appear to be present in modern genera. The loss of the parietal foramen must have occurred early in the evolution of turtles, for it is already absent in the genus Triassochelys, from the early Triassic (Romer 1966). Owens and Ralph (1978) report that the pineal body of the sea turtle Chelonia mydas may be 2-5 times larger than the largest mammalian pineal (weddell seal). Large pineals in some turtles, according to our hypothesis, would seem to imply adaptation to temperature variability. However, most turtles, with the exception of the desert tortoises, remain near water or are aquatic; thus, partially avoiding terrestrial temperature extremes. Primitive fossil turtles appear to have been primarily aquatic. Due to extensive cartilaginous deposits overlying the pineal region, nothing can be deduced about the size or presence of the pineal in fossil marine turtles.

Synapsida

Mammal-like Reptiles (Pelycosauria and Therapsida).
The earliest mammal-like reptiles had their origins in the
late Carboniferous (Olson 1974; Romer 1966), descending from
some undefined ancestor among the captorhinomorph cotylosaurs.
Thus, evolution in the direction of the mammals began long
before the emergence of typical lizards, dinosaurs and
birds. Olson (1976), Russell (1965), Brink (1963), and
Edinger (1955) have noted the size and occurrence of the
parietal foramen among pelycosaurs and therapsids, correlating
these data with possible paleohabitats. Their interpretations
are based upon Stebbins' (1958) demonstration that the
parietal eye may serve to control body temperature. Olson
(1976) has noted that the parietal eye appears to have been
larger in big, slow-moving, ponderous, herbivores than in
more active predators and certain semiaquatic or aquatic
reptiles. Although large size certainly suggests that an
organ is functionally important, and hence the object of
selection for greater size, it is difficult to prove that a
small structure is any less functional than a large one.
Olson concludes that "it appears possible that the large
parietal foramen was originally associated with terrestrial-
ism among the primitive pelycosaurs and that it was lost in
aquatic descendants of the very early terrestrial ophiacodonts,
but retained and emphasized in some of their terrestrial
descendants....Under any interpretation of relationships and
phylogeny, the initial evolution of the large parietal
foramen of pelycosaurs appears to have been an adaptation to
terrestrial life." (Olson 1976, p.22).

Among mammal-like reptiles, the parietal eye is found
in all pelycosaur genera and almost all therapsids. The
therapsids lacking a parietal eye may prove to be the most
informative, for it is in these genera that the majority of
structural changes which characterize mammals were acquired
(e.g., dentary-squamosal jaw articulation, secondary palate,
phalangeal formula, loss of post-orbital bar, and mammalian
tooth structure). Some cynodonts, particularly ictidosaurs
and tritylodonts, are very nearly mammalian, having both an
articular-quadrate and a dentary-squamosal jaw articulation.
The acquisition of mammalian characteristics coincided with
the loss of the third eye in advanced cynodonts and bauriamorphs. The mammal-like appearance of these animals has
provoked an interesting controversy, for they can be considered as either reptiles or mammals. Tartarinov (1967)
and Brink (1956) have suggested that advanced cynodonts also
possessed such typical physiological and behavioral mammalian
attributes as a furry insulation, endothermy, vibrissae and

maternal care of the young. The occurrence of a very tiny
specimen of Thrinaxodon, associated in the same matrix with
an adult female specimen, suggests that maternal care may
have been exercised among certain advanced mammal-like
reptiles (Brink 1955).

    Among the synapsids, the parietal eye decreases in size
and disappears primarily in those advanced members of the
cynodont lineage which were rapidly crossing the reptilian-
mammalian threshold, as well as in one peculiar dicynodont,
Kombuisia frerensis (Hotton 1974). Endocranial casts or
intracranial descriptions of various pelycosaurs (Olson
1944; Romer 1958), theriodonts (Anthony 1961; Hopson 1964;
Gregory 1951), and anomodonts (Edinger 1955; Olson 1962;
Camp 1956), as well as the presence of pineal bodies in most
modern mammals, indicate that the loss of the parietal eye
in synapsid reptiles was not accompanied by a concomitant
loss of the pineal body (Table 2). Perhaps the most likely
explanation for the loss of the parietal eye but retention
of the pineal body is related to the acquisition of a mammalian
thermal physiology among progressive synapsids. It seems
reasonable that acquisition of a mammalian habitus would
include perfection of thermoregulatory machinery. One might
presume that the role of the parietal eye in behavioral
thermoregulation was bypassed as the pineal body assumed a
more important endocrine role in temperature regulation
during the establishment of endothermic control.

    What we propose may not appear to be entirely consistent
with Ricqlès' (1974) demonstration that herbivorous anomodonts
(dinocephalians, dicynodonts) and some carnivorous theriodonts
(bauriamorphs, cynodonts), which retain parietal eyes,
exhibit a fibro-lamellar bone pattern that is associated
with endothermy in mammals. However, it seems reasonable
that there would have been no abrupt transition from ectothermy
to endothermy, but rather that parietal eye loss and sophis-
tication of the endocrine and neural apparatus controlling
the pineal occurred gradually as an endothermic physiology
became established. Endothermic bone patterns could have
preceded parietal eye loss among theriodonts. Endothermy
among anomodonts is not consistent with the presence of
large E-2 systems in all genera except Kombuisia. In fact,
this group would appear to be ectothermic. Bouvier (1977)
contested the idea that there are distinctive, exclusive
bone types characteristic of ectothermic or endothermic
physiology. Instead, there is an array of vertebrate histological patterns, such that ectotherms and endotherms exhibit
very similar Haversian patterns and lamellar systems.

Ricqlès (1974) notes this potential histologic variability among ectotherms living in homeostatic thermal environments and in endotherms which experience periods of torpidity or which undergo annual bouts of hibernation. Consequently, Haversian bone and secondary Haversian resubstitution may not accurately reflect metabolic activity for all animals. Advanced anomodonts may simply be ectotherms (as indicated by retention of a complete well-developed E-2 system) which were homeothermic as a consequence of precise behavioral temperature regulation, controlled by the parietal eye and pineal body.

Briefly, the distribution of E-2 systems among synapsids suggests that some advanced theriodonts (e.g. ictidiosaurs, tritylodonts) had acquired an endothermic physiology, reflected by loss of the parietal eye and retention of the pineal body. The presumed gradual evolution of endothermy would allow that more primitive therapsids were incipient endotherms, as reflected by histological bone preparations (Ricqlès 1974). Conversely, the majority of anomodonts retained and enlarged their E-2 systems, suggesting that the herbivore radiation consisted of ectothermic homeotherms.

Apparently the taxonomic separation of therapsids into theriodonts and anomodonts also includes gross differences in parietal foramen morphology (Fig. 5) and selection for two different, successful methods of body temperature regulation. More active and predaceous theriodonts acquired internal temperature control, based in part on neuroendocrine regulation by secretory pineal bodies. Less active herbivorous anomodonts adopted precise behavioral temperature regulation, employing the large parietal eye.

Small body size, in addition to parietal eye loss and pineal body retention, may be an adaptation exploited by incipient endotherms responding to environmental selective pressures. For example, as advanced therapsids lost the parietal eye and acquired mammalian characteristics, many also became smaller (Crompton 1968). Small body size may have been a prerequisite for the development of endothermy (Hopson 1973). A size decrease may (i) facilitate exploitation of niches containing greater food resources at lower trophic levels; (ii) increase metabolic rate as body size decreases (Pearson 1948); and (iii) result in exploitation of nanoclimates in which a facultative endotherm may remain homeothermic if it has the capacity for precise body temperature regulation.

Figure 5: An advanced herbivorous dicynodont, <u>Eocyclops</u>, and
a carnivorous gorgonopsian, <u>Lycaenops</u>, from the
late Upper Permian. The contrast in parietal eyes
and foramina between the two genera generally
reflects the systematic separation of herbivorous
anomodonts and carnivorous theriodonts. Large,
cone-shaped and raised parietal foramina are common
in anomodonts, while small, buttressed or inconspicuous foramina are usually, but not always,
present among theriodonts. Therapsids and
anomodonts appear to have inherited a similar
body form from pelycosaurs. Differences in
activity levels may be indicated by skeletal
morphology. Therapsids were probably more active
than anomodonts as is illustrated by a less bulky
shape and rotation of the legs to a position
almost beneath the body.

Archosauria

Thecodontia. The thecodont radiation consists of four suborders containing primitive, sprawling reptiles (Proterosuchia, Phytosauria, Aetosauria) and small bipedal forms (Pseudosuchia) probably ancestral to dinosaurs (Charig 1972). Only proterosuchians and phytosaurs are reported to have had parietal eyes or pineal bodies (Von Huene 1911, 1914; Camp 1930; Gregory 1962). The peculiar endocasts of phytosaurs are broadly similar to those of crocodiles (Fig. 6), except for an elaborate dome-shaped structure that has been identified as the place for a pineal body, anterior to the cerebellum and behind the cerebrum. A newly prepared endocast (our preparation) taken from a skull already described (Chatterjee 1978) indicates that a parietal foramen was superimposed upon the dome-shaped pineal. Parietal foramina are never located directly over the pineal body in other vertebrates; they usually occupy a more forward position over the posterior cerebrum. In addition, the location and shape of the pineal cast strongly suggests that it did not enclose a pineal at all, but is more similar to the cartilaginous riders (tips of the supraoccipital) reported in both recent and fossil turtles (Zangerl 1960). The presence of deep pits overlying the "pineal" in young phytosaurs (Camp 1930) suggests the possibility that these pits and cartilaginous riders have been misinterpreted as parts of an epiphyseal complex. Crocodiles do not have pineals or parietal eyes, and it seems unlikely that their phytosaurian equivalents retained either structure. In this context, only the proterosuchians exhibit parietal foramina among the thecodonts.

Thecodonts first appeared at the Permian-Triassic boundary (Hughes 1963; Romer 1966), when climates were beginning to ameliorate. The phytosaurs lived in thermally stable aquatic habitats, and it is not unreasonable to suggest that the terrestrial thecodonts were adapting to warming environmental temperatures. In this context, pineal systems, which functioned to prevent metabolic excesses in cooler Permian climates, would not have been retained as successful temperature regulating adaptations in the gradually warming climates of the Triassic. Retention of the E-2 system appears to confer little selective advantage during ameliorating climates; therefore, other adaptations may assume à greater importance. Bipedalism may have been an important factor in the success of ancestral dinosaurs, permitting greater mobility and activity in animals which, because of size, environment, or mobility, became inertial homeotherms. The absence of the parietal eye in all

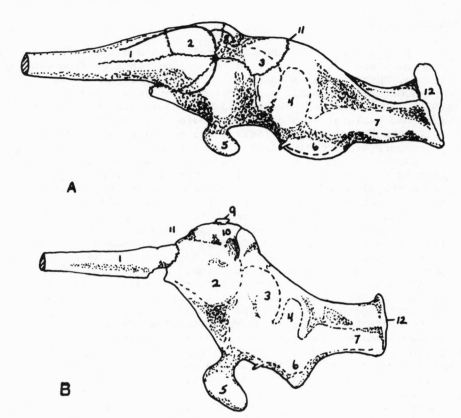

Figure 6: A comparison of the endocasts of (A) Alligator
mississippensis and (B) Parasuchus hislopi (ISI
R 44, Chatterjee 1978). Structure 9 is part of
an extracranial parietal pit which is usually not
contiguous with the intracranial space. In some
preparations, the thin parietal roof is broken;
thus, creating a supposed parietal eye (foramen)
lying over a structure which has been interpreted
as a pineal body. A similar structure among
modern and fossil turtles has been shown to be
the cartilaginous anterior portion of the supraoccipital bone. This report considers the parietal
eye and pineal body to be absent in Parasuchus and
other phytosaurs as they are in the Crocodilia.
(1) olfactory tract; (2) cerebrum; (3) optic lobe;
(4) cerebellum; (5) pituitary; (6) pons; (7) spinal
cord; (8) paraphysis; (9) supposed parietal eye;
(10) supposed pineal body; (11) sutures; (12)
foramen magnum.

thecodonts except proterosuchians, and the probable absence of the pineal body in all other thecodonts, may be a reflection of important changes affecting the thermal physiology of dinosaurs.

Saurischia and Ornithischia (Dinosaurs). These two orders of distinct but ancestrally related dinosaurs have been defined as reptiles with bipedal ancestors having specializations (antorbital fenestrae) not found in lepidosaurian diapsid reptiles (Olson 1971). One such specialization is loss of the parietal eye in all five suborders (Theropoda, Sauropodamorpha, Stegosauria, Ceratopsia, and Ankylosauria) and the loss of pineal bodies among all groups except some small coelurosaurian theropods. Although parietal foramina have been reported in ceratopsians (Gillmore 1919) and sauropods (Von Huene 1926; Holland 1906, 1924) and pineal bodies are often figured for carnosaurs (Lull, in Swinton 1958), these structures are currently regarded as fenestral openings or cranial sinuses (Holland 1906). Supposed pineal bodies may be membraneous extensions of dura mater (Osborn 1912) or cartilaginous deposits (Zangerl 1960). In any case, the pineal body among dinosaurs is considered to be an unduly emphasized feature "with no opening or indentation corresponding to it in the roof of the dinosaur skull" (Swinton 1958).

With the exception of one small coelurosaur examined, a locus for pineal bodies is not demonstrable within the cranial space of any dinosaur (Table 2). Although dinosaurs had small brains which only filled, conservatively, 50% of the cranial space (Jerrison 1973), major divisions of the brain are generally recognizable. The pituitary was especially large (Edinger 1942) and it seems probable that any brain structure of functional significance (especially in the forebrain, given its proximity to the cranial roof) would have left an intracranial impression. Thus, it seems safe to assume that the pineal was absent in dinosaurs, unless it was small enough not to leave any record of its presence. If it is accepted that the pineal was absent in dinosaurs, they may be compared with living animals such as edentates and dugongs which lack a pineal. These mammals have low body temperatures for endotherms and exhibit reduced metabolic rates. Monotremes have small pineal bodies, low body temperatures (ca. 32°C), and cannot acclimatize well to temperature extremes (Augee 1976). Body temperature also may have been low in dinosaurs if they had poor central nervous system control of responses to thermal extremes of the environment. However, paleotemperatures were generally warmer and less seasonal during the Mesozoic than either

during the Permian or during the late Cretaceous and early
Cenozoic (Windley 1977).

It seems likely that an early trend toward inertial
homeothermy among ectothermic thecodonts, established in
response to warming Triassic climates, would have been
perpetuated by their dinosaur descendants in even more
equable environments. As Hotton suggests (this volume),
dinosaurs need not have been endothermic if they could
achieve the same effect (homeothermy) by evolving large
size, rather than coping with the physiological demands of
precise endothermy.

It is significant that Ostrom (1975, 1978) finds the
origin of birds among small coelurosaurian dinosaurs. The
only pineal-like structure observed among dinosaurs occurs
in the coelurosaur, Dromiceiomimus (Russell 1972). This
observation and the fact that most modern birds have well-
developed secretory pineal bodies, lends support to Ostrom's
conclusions. As was discussed earlier, the pineal appears to
be involved in body temperature regulation in birds, and it
seems probable that this relationship goes back at least to
small theropods.

If small size is an important feature in the evolution
of endothermy (Hopson 1973), the therapsid-mammalian lineage
and the small thecodont-coelurosaur-bird lineage converged
upon this adaptive strategy, in contrast with the evolutionary
size increase of most dinosaurs. If dinosaurs were endothermic, why, with the exception of coelurosaurs like
Compsognathus (Hotton, this volume), did they not achieve
any significant radiation into small size categories? This
question is especially important for dinosaurs living in
warm climates if, as Tracy (1977) suggests, the thermal
environment is a limiting factor that prevents exceptionally
small size among endotherms challenged by cool temperatures
below the zone of thermoneutrality.

As noted by others (Bennet and Dalzell 1973; Crompton
et al, 1978; Dodson 1974; Farlow 1976; Feduccia 1973; McNab
1978), dinosaurs do not seem to have been endotherms on the
same level as modern birds and mammals. Investigators who
regard dinosaurs as equivalent endotherms may exaggerate
characteristics that appear to be correlated with endothermy.
Predator-prey ratios, posture and growth-processes are
measures of body temperature stability and not necessarily
body temperature control. Thus, proof of endothermy depends
upon observable evidence of a temperature controlling organ.
All other evidence is largely inferential. Active inertial

homeotherms may have a constant body temperature, but they cannot be expected to accommodate chronic temperature changes. The extinction of all dinosaurs at the end of the Cretaceous may be related to the likelihood that most dinosaurs were inertial homeotherms that could not survive chronic temperature changes. Although ordinary community evolution may have participated in dinosaurian extinctions (Van Valen and Sloan 1977), it seems more likely that a feeble response to long-term temperature change by essentially ectothermic reptiles resulted in permanent removal of dinosaurs from the late Cretaceous landscape.

Pterosauria. Pterosaurs are flying reptiles of the Jurassic and Cretaceous with unknown ancestors among primitive archosaurs. The group ranges from very large forms such as the Texas pterosaur, with an estimated wingspan of 15.5 m (Lawson 1975), to sparrow-sized species like Rhamphorhynchus. One of the small pterosaurs (Parapsicethalus, Newton 1888) has a pineal-like structure, appearing between the cerebrum and cerebellum. The retention of pineals in some small primitive pterosaurs suggests that these reptiles were endothermic. Endothermy among pterosaurs appears to be confirmed by fossil impressions suggesting that the body was covered by furry insulation (Sordus pilosus) (Sharov 1971). Small size among ancestral pterosaurs (Romer 1966) is consistent with the notion that small size is an evolutionary prerequisite in the development of endothermy.

Lepidosauria

Fossil lepidosaurs include the Eosuchia, Squamata and Rhynchocephalia. The Permo-Triassic eosuchians include a mixture of such typical parietal-eyed forms as Youngina and parietal-eyeless forms like Prolacerta. A well-developed epiphyseal complex is present in many, but not all, rhynchocephalians, including Sphenodon. It persists in most primitive Lacertilia (Kuehneosaurus), including some families (Anguidae; e.g. Glyptosaurus) containing living parietal-eyeless genera. Mosasaurs, large Upper Cretaceous marine lizards related to the varanids, apparently originated from small semiaquatic lizards similar to Algialosaurs (Romer 1966). Mosasaurs are unique among fossil reptiles in having partial encasement of the pineal body by a bony portion of the intra-parietal roof, behind the parietal eye. In general, parietal eyes are present neither among larger members of the Rhynchocephalia (Scaphonyx) nor among such aquatic eosuchians as Thalattosaurus and Champsosaurus. The E-2 complex is well-developed among primitive Late Carboniferous

(Petrolacosaurus, Reisz 1977), and Late Permian-Early
Triassic younginid eosuchians, but it is variably distributed
among later lepidosaurs which evolved from the Eosuchia in
the Middle and Late Triassic.

These data can be interpreted in terms of adaptive
responses to the gradual upward shift in paleotemperatures
which began in the Late Permian and continued into the
Mesozoic. The selective value of precise ectothermy, or
incipient endothermy, would have been greater in the Permian
(cool and seasonal) than during the upward shift of Triassic
temperatures. Due to the rapidity of heat exchange between
small vertebrates and the environment, precise body temperature regulation may be necessary, even in warm climates, for
small ectotherms and endotherms. Large ectothermic and
endothermic vertebrates become homeothermic (Hotton, this
volume) as a consequence of size, activity and metabolic
regulation. They may respond primarily to selection pressure
for more efficient heat loss rather than heat generation in
warm climates. This scheme seems adequate to explain the
loss of parietal eyes (and sometimes pineal bodies) among
medium-sized, large or aquatic Triassic reptiles, including
dinosaurs. It also explains the retention of an E-2 complex
among reptiles which, because of their small size, were
obligate behavioral thermoregulators (lizards and small
rhynchocephalians, Homoeosaurus).

Mosasaurs appear to contradict the hypothesis that
elimination of the E-2 complex occurs among vertebrates in
response to warm climates or thermally hospitable environments. No explanation is immediately apparent. Mosasaurs
appear to have originated in the Early Cretaceous from
small, obligate behavioral thermoregulators and flourished
until the end of the Cretaceous. Since climates became
generally cooler during this period, it is plausible that
the E-2 complex functioned in marine mosasaurs to monitor
increasing seasonal temperature variation.

Synaptosauria

Edinger's (1955) excellent discussion of the E-2
complex among synaptosaurs brings out many of the problems
associated with assessment of the evolution of the complex.
For example, primitive Triassic araeoscelids, Jurassic
nothosaurs and Triassic plesiosaurs all possessed a well-
developed complex. The parietal eye is absent in the Upper
Cretaceous plesiosaur Hydrotherosaurus (Welles 1943). It
has often been assumed that parietal eyes (foramina) are
relatively larger in more primitive than in more advanced

reptiles (von Huene 1933). Exactly the reverse occurs among synaptosaurs; the early nothosaurs have small parietal foramina compared to their descendants. The evolution and function of the E-2 complex in this group remains to be evaluated on the basis of additional material now available. The results will be most interesting, since the Synaptosauria are aquatic reptiles with well-developed pineal systems.

Summary and Discussion

Although parts of the preceding discussion are admittedly speculative, it is hoped that this attempt to link and interpret the variety of vertebrate adaptations and the somewhat fragmentary evidence provided by the fossil record will contribute to a better understanding of the evolutionary process. The argument developed here is that the parietal eye and pineal body have played an important role in the evolutionary success of vertebrates, as they occupied and adapted to thermally variable terrestrial environments. This conclusion is based on studies which have been collated in this paper to suggest that:

1. Morphological variation in epiphyseal systems is assigned to three categories, E-0, E-1, and E-2.

2. The most primitive epiphyseal system, including both a parietal eye and a pineal organ, is the E-2 complex.

3. The antiquity of the E-2 complex, in concert with the almost ubiquitous presence of the pineal body among living vertebrates, indicates that these structures must have played an important part in vertebrate evolution.

4. The parietal eye and the pineal body are central nervous system components involved in both ectothermic behavioral thermoregulation and endothermic temperature control.

5. An inverse relationship exists between dependence on environmental sources of heat and the complexity of the epiphyseal system. E-0 systems are confined to animals which maintain lower core body temperatures than related E-1 or E-2 animals. E-2 systems are found exclusively among ectotherms. E-1 systems are found among both ectotherms and endotherms; however, secretory E-1 systems occur primarily among endotherms and are largest in polar animals.

6. An evolutionary reduction of the E-2 complex occurred in most vertebrates, except for many small reptiles, under the gradually warming and less seasonal climates of

the early Mesozoic.

7. The third eye was lost (E-1) in therapsid reptiles only in taxa which were in the process of acquiring mammalian morphological and presumably also physiological characteristics.

8. Both the parietal eye and the pineal body were lost (E-0) in the early Mesozoic evolution of the dinosaurs.

9. These considerations lead us to conclude that E-2 systems represent ectothermic animals in the fossil record, and also that E-1 systems represent endothermic animals if the E-1 system evolved from an E-2 system, where other morphological evidence supports the acquisition of an endothermic physiology (some therapsids). E-0 systems are not diagnostic of either ectothermy or endothermy; they are characteristic of animals with low or labile body temperatures.

In this context, we have examined the occurrence of the parietal eye and the pineal body among fossil vertebrates of the Permian and Triassic periods. It is possible to document three major vertebrate sequences in which the extracranial parietal eye has been progressively lost. The first sequence occurred in the Devonian fish assemblage, the second in the Permo-Triassic reptilian assemblage, and the third is continuing among extant lizards. The Permo-Triassic events are most interesting, for it is during this time that loss of the parietal eye occurred among the mammal-like reptiles and early thecodonts (ancestral to dinosaurs). All mammal-like reptiles have a third eye except for bauriamorphs, some advanced cynodonts, and one dicynodont. In contrast, only a few early thecodonts and none of the dinosaurs retained third eyes. The pineal body is present in all cynodonts, but except for one small coelurosaur, cranial impressions of pineal bodies are not evident among dinosaurs. If pineal bodies were present among dinosaurs, they were undoubtedly small. Loss of the parietal eye, but retention of the pineal body among some advanced mammal-like reptiles, in contrast with what appears to be loss of the entire epiphyseal complex in dinosaurs, probably reflects different thermoregulatory adaptations. It is reasonable to conclude that the adaptation of advanced mammal-like cynodonts (ictidosaurs and tritylodonts) to seasonal climates included incipient or competent endothermy, facilitated by small size, and marked by internalization of temperature regulation by the pineal body as the parietal eye was lost.

In contrast to the mammal-like reptiles of the Permian, late Triassic dinosaurs were faced with warmer, not cooler climates. In a warm environment, large ectotherms maintain body temperatures comparable to those of large endotherms. Consequently, both may be homeothermic, the ectotherms as a result of the environment and their size, the endotherms as a result of internal regulation and size. Homeothermy, however it is maintained, makes it very difficult to infer thermoregulatory adaptations (ectothermy and endothermy) using temperature dependent activities or morphology.

Based upon the evidence provided in this paper, the tentative conclusion is presented that some mammal-like reptiles lost the parietal eye and retained the pineal as precise endothermy was perfected in response to cool environmental temperatures. In contrast, loss of the entire E-2 complex among dinosaurs in response to gradually warming climates indicates that these reptiles probably retained the ectothermic strategy of ancestral thecodonts, becoming large-size specialists in environmental homeothermy. Some small dinosaurs (certain coelurosaurs) apparently retained the pineal, as have their avian descendants; these small dinosaurs may have been endothermic.

Finally, small size may be important in the evolution of competent endothermy, since metabolic rate increases as size decreases, irrespective of thermoregulatory strategy. Thus, endothermy may be facilitated in part, if the size of a lineage decreases over time. Small size may also be an important endothermic adaptation in warm climates since a greater surface-to-volume ratio facilitates heat loss. Apparently, adult Mesozoic dinosaurs weighing as little as five kilograms were rare; a few of them weighed less than one hundred kilograms. If most dinosaurs were active endotherms, as has been proposed, the lack of any significant radiation of dinosaurs into small size categories is very surprising, particularly since successful small size specialists have evolved among all extant endotherms.

It has become clear that the variety of thermoregulatory adaptations employed by vertebrates is such that a group of animals can no longer be satisfactorily defined as being ectothermic, homeothermic or endothermic. Although it is generally agreed that mammals and birds generate their own heat from within, both groups have representatives which may regulate body heat behaviorally, or have body temperatures which drift with environmental temperature (torpidity). Both of these features are characteristic of ectothermic vertebrates. On the other hand, many ectotherms which do not generate or conserve enough body heat to be competent endotherms, can control body temperature behaviorally, often with enough precision to be considered homeothermic when they are actively regulating. Some ectotherms can, in fact, produce body heat during activity or by muscular contraction, such that they may be considered transient endotherms.

Should we wonder then, that a controversy exists over the possibility of internal temperature regulation in an extinct group of vertebrates, the dinosaurs? The controversy is perhaps more volatile because dinosaurs are reptiles, and in all living reptiles, thermal homeostasis is maintained primarily by ectothermic regulation. The dinosaurs were unique vertebrates, separated from living reptiles not only by time and morphology, but also quite probably by their physiologies. They undoubtedly employed varied thermo-regulatory strategies among their members, large and small, as do living birds and mammals. In other words, dinosaurs may have been ectothermic or endothermic in varying degrees. Some species may have employed behavioral thermoregulation during some periods and purely physiological reponses on other occasions. To define dinosaurs as endothermic or as ectothermic is as difficult as assigning any living vertebrate to one of these categories. Vertebrates, and especially reptiles, cannot be easily placed in one thermal category or another; rather, each species represents a particular adaptation to the thermal requirements of its environment. In this context, both ectothermic and endo-thermic responses may be highly successful adaptations to the dictates of different environmental conditions and individual physiological requirements.

The parietal eye and pineal body appear to have functioned as sensory systems for monitoring environmental thermal extremes. The sensory capacity of the parietal eye and pineal body may have guided the taxic responses of early ectothermic vertebrates to appropriate environmental temperatures. With the involution of photoreceptive cells and development of secretory capacity, pineal bodies assumed a more dominant role in thermoregulation as endothermy became established and the parietal eye was lost. Loss of the parietal eye in mammal-like reptiles occurred as they crossed the reptilian-mammalian boundary; it is likely that endothermy was established in synchrony with these events. The presence of all or parts of the epiphyseal complex in modern vertebrates underscores the contribution of this system to successful adaptation by almost all vertebrates, in the course of their evolution.

Acknowledgments

People from various areas of interest have contributed to the synthesis of information presented in this paper. We would especially like to recognize the leading influence of Dr. Alfred Romer for kindling our interest in Paleontology. Dr. Tilly Edinger's conviction that the pineal foramen should be recognized as a structure of scientific merit is acknowledged. Dr. Everett Olson and especially Dr. Nicholas Hotton have encouraged our recent interests with their unique insight and stimulating discussions. Our appreciation of brain function has been encouraged by Dr. Paul D. MacLean. We would like to thank Dr. Charles Ralph and Dr. Richard E. Jones for introducing us to the excitement of pineal and reptilian research. We are indebted to Dr. Roger Thomas.

Ms. Jane Bupp deserves special recognition and our gratitude for her efforts in preparing drafts of this manuscript. We also would like to recognize the dedicated help of Ms. Barbara Coulson and the assistance of Ms. Deborah Lonsdale and Ms. Susan Snyder.

8

Constraints of Body Size and Environment on the Temperature Regulation of Dinosaurs

James R. Spotila

Abstract

Large dinosaurs would have been selected for low metabolic rates because gigantism as a thermoregulatory strategy precludes the development of an elevated metabolism. Theoretical and experimental evidence is presented demonstrating that there are both qualitative and quantitative differences in the mechanisms of heat exchange between large and small ectotherms and their environments. The ability of animals to thermoregulate at a high constant body temperature depends upon the constraints imposed on them by their body sizes and physical characteristics, as well as the conditions of the external environment. Thus there may be more similarities between the thermoregulatory capacities of large reptiles and mammals than between large and small members of either class alone. Metabolic requirements are reduced for all large animals, so we expect to see a convergence of heat production and insulative capacities as the sizes of animals increase. Large dinosaurs were probably very active, with complex behavior patterns and social interactions. Such a life style is entirely compatible with their thermoregulatory status as ectothermic homeotherms.

Introduction

The thermoregulatory capacities of large reptiles have interested physiologists, ecologists and paleontologists for many years (for a review see Dawson 1975). They are of special interest in relation to recent discussions about the physiology and ecology of dinosaurs. Claims that dinosaurs were "warm-blooded", that is endothermic homeotherms (Bakker 1971, 1972, 1974; Ricqlès 1972), have given rise to counterclaims that they were "cold-blooded", that is ectothermic (Feduccia 1973, 1974; Bennett and Dalzell 1973; Thulbom 1973, Tracy 1976). This controversy and its relevance to dinosaur

extinction have been reviewed by Cloudley-Thompson and Butt
(1977). Perhaps the most reasonable approach to the physiological ecology of dinosaurs is that of Dodson (1974) who
suggested that we consider dinosaurs as neither mammals nor
reptiles but as dinosaurs.

Since physiological experiments on dinosaurs are no
longer possible it is difficult to determine whether or not
these large reptiles were endothermic homeotherms, ectothermic homeotherms or ectothermic poikilotherms. If they were
endothermic homeotherms, they would have had constant high
body temperatures and high metabolic rates. As ectothermic
homeotherms they would have gained most of their body heat
from the environment but still have had constant high body
temperatures. Ectothermic poikilotherms gain most of their
body heat from the environment and have variable body temperatures. My colleagues and I (Spotila et al. 1973) have
suggested that dinosaurs could have been ectothermic homeotherms. Large dinosaurs, living in warm Mesozoic climates,
more equable than those of the present day, would have had
high constant body temperatures simply because they were
large and the climate was warm. If that was the case, they
could have been active animals with complex behavior patterns and social organizations while retaining a typically
reptilian physiology. The evidence cited by Farlow and
Dodson (1975) for courtship and agonistic behavior among
ceratopsian dinosaurs supports the belief that dinosaurs
exhibited a complex level of social behavior. But this does
not imply that these animals were endothermic. Burghardt
(1977) has demonstrated that present day reptiles show
diverse and complex types of social behavior and we know
that in general these animals are ectotherms. Speculation
on the topic of dinosaur physiology will probably continue
for some time. Its primary value may be to stimulate additional research into the biophysical interactions between
large animals and their environments.

Large vertebrates such as elephants, crocodiles, sea
turtles, giant tortoises, rhinoceroses and others, are conspicuous residents of many ecosystems. We might expect that
there would be differences between the physiologies of these
animals and those of smaller vertebrates such as mice, rabbits, lizards, frogs, and others due to differences in size
alone. Body size should be important because of the fundamental role of animal - environment heat energy exchange
in determining the capacity of these organisms to regulate
their body temperatures. Physical characteristics of the
environment such as temperature, intensity and duration of
solar radiation, wind speed and relative humidity interact
with animal properties such as size, shape, quality and

quantity of insulation, and metabolic rate in determining
the abilities of animals to adapt to environmental heat
loads. Spotila et al. (1973) demonstrated the importance
of large body size in the thermal ecology of large reptiles.
Spotila and Gates (1975) discussed the roles of body size
and insulation in the thermoregulation of homeotherms.

During the past few years, my students and I have been
studying the mechanisms by which heat energy is exchanged
between large vertebrate ectotherms and their environments.
The purpose of these studies has been to determine the effect of body size and physical characteristics on the temperature regulation of these animals. In this paper I
present theoretical and experimental evidence that there
are both qualitative and quantitative differences in the
mechanisms of heat exchange between large and small ectotherms and their environments. The importance of these
differences in the thermoregulation of large reptiles is
discussed. Finally, the evolution of homeothermy is discussed in light of the constraints imposed on animals by
their body sizes and physical characteristics as well as
those of the environment.

Body Size and Heat Production

In general, as body size increases the demand placed on
an animal's physiology by its environment decreases. It is
well known that metabolic rate per unit body weight (or surface area) decreases as body size increases in both mammals
and birds (Schmidt-Nielsen 1975, p. 237). The same is true
for reptiles and other ectotherms. While the mechanisms
responsible for this phenomenon are not completely understood, we do know that environmental heat load, the size of
an animal, and its insulative properties place specific constraints upon an animal's net heat production. As body size
changes net heat production must change if the same body
temperature is to be maintained in a given climate. By net
heat production we mean heat generated by metabolism (M)
minus heat lost by evaporative water loss (E), per unit
surface area. We lump both respiratory and cutaneous water
loss into one term and signify net heat production as
(M - E). For the purposes of our theoretical calculations
we assume that all heat loss due to evaporation occurs
directly from the body core. Separating evaporative water
loss into respiratory and cutaneous portions increases the
complexity of our calculations but does not increase their
accuracy or sensitivity.

We can investigate this interaction for ectotherms by
conducting a mathematical analysis of heat exchange between

these animals and the environment. In 1975 David Gates and I developed a mathematical model to predict net heat production (M - E) for an animal of a given size, at a given temperature in a given environment (Spotila and Gates 1975). We derived this model using an energy budget equation (Porter and Gates 1969) that is based on the physics of heat transfer and known physical and physiological properties of animals. While originally developed for endotherms this model is readily adapted to a consideration of ectotherms.

Mathematical Model

The basic mathematical model of environment - animal energy exchange is based on the physics of heat transfer and known physical and physiological properties of animals. For a full discussion of animal - heat energy budget equations, see the papers by Birkebak (1966), Bartlett and Gates (1967), Porter and Gates (1969), Heller and Gates (1971), Spotila et al. (1972, 1973), and Bakken (1976).

According to the first law of thermodynamics, for any animal under steady-state conditions, energy gained and energy generated by the animal must equal the energy flow out of the animal. We describe the animal's energy budget by the following equation:

Energy gain = Energy loss

Absorbed + Generated =
Q_{abs} M

Reradiation + Convection   + Evaporation   (1)
$\varepsilon \sigma T_r^4$ $k\dfrac{V^{0.6}}{D_o^{0.4}}(T_r - T_a)$ E

where Q_{abs} = energy absorbed from the environment as radiation (cal cm^{-2} min^{-1})

M = heat generated by metabolism (cal cm^{-2} min^{-1})

ε = emissivity (0.97)

σ = Stefan-Boltzmann constant (8.13 x 10^{-11} cal cm^{-2} min^{-1} $°K^{-4}$)

T_r = surface temperature ($°K$ for reradiation, $°C$ for convection term)

k = constant {1.95 x 10^{-3} cal cm^{-2} min^{-1} $°C^{-1}$
     (s cm^{-1})}

V = wind speed (cm s^{-1})

D_o = outside body diameter, including insulation (cm)

T_a = air temperature ($°C$)

E = evaporative water loss from respiratory tract +
     skin (cal cm^{-2} min^{-1})

As a general case, we assume that we are dealing with
a simple ectotherm that exchanges energy with its environment primarily by radiation, convection, and evaporation.
For a discussion of the convection term see Spotila et al.
(1972) and Spotila and Gates (1975). In this first approximation model, to reduce the complexity of calculations, we
assume that the animal is cylindrical in shape, with no
appendages. Including appendages in the analysis would
result in increased heat flow to the body core. The magnitude of this effect is small (Spotila et al. 1973) and
does not alter the results of our calculations. We assume
that the belly of the animal is off the ground so we neglect
conduction to the substrate. The ratio of length to diameter is 4. Insulation consists of a layer of fat, the
thickness of the layer defined as C • D, where D is core
diameter with no fat and C is a constant proportion of D
for all sizes of D in a given set. Insulation (I) can be
defined by the expression

$$I = \frac{C \cdot D}{K} \qquad (2)$$

where K is the conductivity of insulation (cal cm^{-1} min^{-1}
$°C^{-1}$). Animal fat has a conductivity of 0.0294 cal cm^{-1}
min^{-1} $°C^{-1}$, Porter and Gates (1969). Now, since surface
temperature is related to body temperature (T_b) by

$$T_r = T_b - I(M - E) \qquad (3)$$

we can substitute for T_r in equation 1 and obtain

$$Q_{abs} + M = \varepsilon\sigma \left\{ T_b - \frac{C \cdot D}{K} (M - E) \right\}^4 +$$

$$k \frac{V^{0.6}}{D_o^{0.4}} \left\{ T_b - \frac{C \cdot D}{K} (M - E) - T_a \right\} + E \qquad (4)$$

We solve this equation for the term (M - E), the net heat
production within the animal. This is a measure of the
animal's physiological thermoregulatory activity. Using
this equation we can predict the effect of the independent
environmental variables, such as radiation, air temperature,
and wind speed, on dependent physiological variables of the
animal: body temperature, metabolic rate, and water loss.
The interaction among these variables will be influenced by
the size of the animal and the thickness and conductivity
of its insulation. Changes in mass flow rates of blood to
external tissues and local differences in insulation can
greatly affect heat-flow patterns within the animal. We
cannot deal with these specialized adaptations using our
general model. Such considerations require the use of more
detailed models like those described by Bakken and Gates
(1975) and Bakken (1976).

Predictions

    The net heat production (M - E) required to maintain a
specific body temperature changes as the size of an ectotherm increases (Fig. 1). In a cold climate (Q_{abs} =
0.4 cal cm^{-2} min^{-1}), a small ectotherm would need a net
heat production of 0.8 cal cm^{-2} min^{-1} in order to maintain
a constant body temperature of 37° C. This is almost twice
the heat production of a shrew and is beyond the metabolic
capabilities of the biochemical systems of all known animals. A large ectotherm (100 cm body diameter) would need
a net heat production of less than 0.1 cal cm^{-2} min^{-1} to
maintain the same body temperature. This is similar to the
metabolic heat production of elephants. In a hot climate
(Q_{abs} = 1.0 cal cm^{-2} min^{-1}), a small ectotherm would need
a net heat loss of at least -0.8 cal cm^{-2} min^{-1} in order to
maintain a body temperature of 10° C or less. Again the
large ectotherm would have a much reduced heat loss requirement (-0.12 to -0.15 cal cm^{-2} min^{-1}). All sizes of ectotherms could easily maintain a high body temperature in a
warm climate. Their main problem would be to prevent overheating.

    From their study of the temperature regulation of tor-
toises Cloudsley-Thompson and Butt (1977) suggest that overheating would have been a problem for dinosaurs. There is
a very real possibility that overheating would be a problem
for any large animal in a warm climate. The lower portion
of Figure 1 suggests that, in a warm climate, ectotherms
must maintain a negative heat balance even at a body temperature of 40° C. We found the same to be true of homeotherms (Spotila and Gates 1975). Any net positive heat

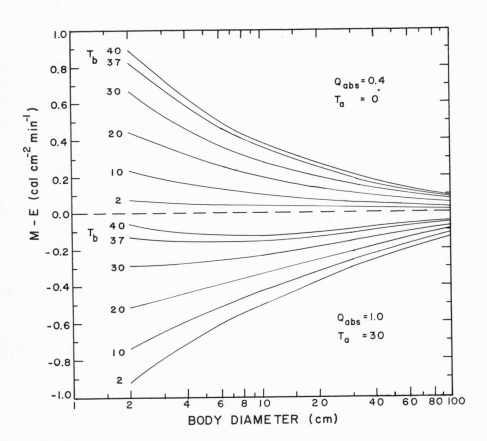

Figure 1. Net heat production (M - E) required of ectotherms as a function of body size, body temperature and climate. Insulation (fat) thickness was a constant 10% of body
diameter. D is body diameter without fat. Air temperatures
(T_a) are in °C, wind speed is 100 cm s^{-1} and radiation
absorbed (Q_{abs}) is in cal cm^{-2} min^{-1}. Upper portion of
figure (Q_{abs} - 0.4, T_a = 0) is for an animal exposed to a
cloudy sky at night, a cold condition. Lower portion of
figure is for an animal with an absorptivity of 0.8 exposed
to a clear sunny sky, a hot condition. These values are
based on Figure 1 of Spotila et al (1972). Calculations
were done with the mathematical model of Spotila and Gates
(1975), see text for equations.

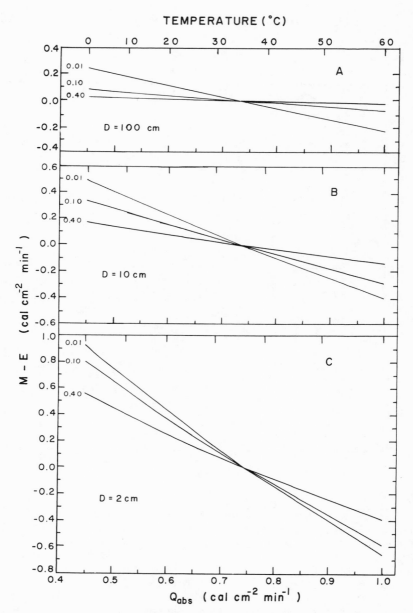

TEMPERATURE (°C)

Figure 2. Constraints of body size, insulation and climate on the net heat production requirements (M - E) of ectotherms for fixed T_b = 38 °C. Each line represents a different fractional insulation thickness (C) for a given body size (diameter = D, before insulation is added). Wind speed is 100 cm s^{-1}. Combinations of T_a and Q_{abs} are for blackbody conditions. For example blackbody radiation for T_a = 30 °C is 0.68 cal cm^{-2} min^{-1}. Calculations were done as described for Figure 1.

production would place a large animal in heat stress. Selective pressure should favor minimal metabolic rates.
Small animals would be less affected because they could dump
heat during the cooler nightime periods. A small animal
could have a positive (M - E) production and avoid hot daytime conditions by selecting cool microclimates. A large
animal would have more difficulty in avoiding the heat of
the day and could not tolerate a high metabolic rate. The
main advantage that large ectotherms would have over small
ones under these circumstances is that their bulk would dam-
pen out diurnal fluctuations in heat flow and insure a constant body temperature while small ectotherms would cool
faster at night and become inactive.

The curves for body temperatures of 37 - 40° C in the
upper portion of Figure 1 bear a striking resemblance to
the curve relating weight specific metabolism to weight for
mammals in Schmidt-Nielsen (1975) and the curves for reptiles in Pough (1973). We produced similar theoretical
curves for endothermic homeotherms in our previous study
(Spotila and Gates 1975). This should not be surprising,
since all animals are subject to the same laws of heat
transfer and all encounter similar constraints on net heat
production due to the interaction of body size, insulation
and environmental heat load. Finally, if we look at the
100 cm diameter body size in Figure 1 we see that large ectotherms could maintain high body temperatures, in both hot
and cold climates, with relatively small changes in net heat
production.

This reduction in the net heat production requirements
for large ectotherms in a variety of climates is seen in
Figure 2A. A large ectotherm with an insulation thickness
of 0.10, or 10% of its body diameter, could maintain a body
temperature of 38° C in both cold and hot climates with
little change in (M - E). A smaller animal (Fig. 2B) with
the same proportion of insulation would have a greater
(M - E) requirement. Its environment would demand a high
metabolic rate under cold conditions and high evaporative
water loss rate under hot conditions. A very small ectotherm (Fig. 2C) with D = 2 cm cannot maintain a body temperature of 38° C except under very limited conditions because its environment places demands on it that cannot be
met by its internal heat production or cooling facilities.

An increase in insulation reduces the (M - E) requirement for all sizes of animals. An increase in thickness of
fat from C = 0.01 (1.0%) to C = 0.40 (40%) can compensate
for a reduction in size from D = 100 cm to D = 10 cm, or
from D = 10 cm to D = 2 cm.

The importance of these calculations is that they help
us to visualize the role of the environment - body size
interaction in determining the metabolic heat requirements
of animals. The central thermoregulatory problem for an
animal is that its internal environment is coupled to the
external environment. Its physiological responses must
change as the outside world places new demands on it in the
form of changes in climatic conditions. In order to be a
homeotherm an animal must be "isolated" from its environment. This can be done by increasing body size or adding
insulation. As an animal becomes more and more "isolated"
from its environment, in terms of heat exchange, its body
temperature becomes more stable. No animal has achieved
complete "isolation" so all animals are affected to one degree or another by heat exchange with their environments.

Body Size and Heat Exchange

Theoretical arguments (Porter and Gates 1969) suggest
that large reptiles should be tightly coupled to the radiant (solar and thermal) environment and loosely coupled to
the convective environment, while small reptiles should be
tightly coupled to the convective environment. Thus we
expect both quantitative and qualitative differences in
animal - environment heat transfer when large and small reptiles are compared.

We have approached this question experimentally by
studying the alligator, Alligator mississippiensis, a reptile that grows to a length of 6 m and a weight of several
hundred kilograms. We modified a walk-in environmental
room to provide a microclimate simulation chamber, characterized by high visible radiation flux, stable wind flow,
and controlled air and floor temperatures. We used this
chamber to reproduce microclimates that alligators or other
reptiles would encounter in the course of their normal activities, for example, conditions on a hot summer day, a
cool night, and an overcast day. We placed alligators
(0.3 - 2 m long) individually in the chamber and subjected
them to a specific microclimate until body temperatures
reached equilibrium with the environmental heat load. We
then established a new set of environmental conditions and
conducted another test. We subjected each of 10 animals to
a minimum of 6 different microclimates. By monitoring alligator body temperatures with surgically implanted thermo-
couples together with environmental variables such as visible and thermal radiation flux, wind speed, air and substrate
temperatures, etc. we were able to quantify the roles of
convection, conduction and radiation in the exchange of heat
between these animals and their environments.

Most of these experiments were conducted by Kenneth
Terpin; experimental details and results are reported in
Terpin (1976), Spotila et al. (1977), Terpin et al. (1978)
and Terpin, Foley and Spotila (manuscript in review).

When exposed to simulated daylight conditions large
alligators (1 - 2 m long, mid-body diameter > 10 cm) reached
equilibrium body temperatures 6 - 7° above ambient while
small ones (0.3 - 1 m long, mid-body diameter < 10 cm) had
temperatures 2 - 3°C above ambient. Large and small alligators absorbed and emitted radiation at the same rates but
the larger individuals cooled less by convection to the air
and conduction to the substrate (Fig. 3). A 20 cm diameter
alligator (length = 170 cm) loses 42% less heat per unit
surface area than does a 5 cm diameter alligator (length =
43 cm). The small alligator loses 4 times more heat per
unit surface area via conduction than does the large animal. In the large animal conduction and convection are of
a similar magnitude, while in the small alligator conduction is more than twice as large as convection.

These findings support the prediction that large alligators are tightly coupled to the radiation environment.
Muth (1977) reported that Callisaurus, a small lizard, is
tightly coupled to the convective environment. The small
alligators tested in this study represent a transition
series. They are much more affected by radiation and less
by convection and conduction than Muth's lizards, but more
affected by convection and conduction than our largest (1 -
2 m long) alligators.

We would expect other terrestrial reptiles to respond
to their physical environments in a similar manner. McNab
and Auffenberg (1976) found that large Komodo dragons,
Varanus komodoensis, often have appreciable positive temperature differentials with their environment. Because of
their thermal inertia and relatively low thermal conductance, these lizards do not come to thermal equilibrium
overnight. Mackay (1964) reported similar results for a
170 kg Galapagos tortoise (Geochelone). His data also indicate that the temperature of the shell is coupled to the
radiant rather than the convective environment.

Two important conclusions can be drawn from the results
of these laboratory and field experiments. First, there are
quantitative and qualitative differences between the mechanisms by which large and small reptiles exchange heat with
their environments. The larger the animal, the more it will
be affected by radiation and the less it will be tied to
convection and conduction. Second, the increased heat

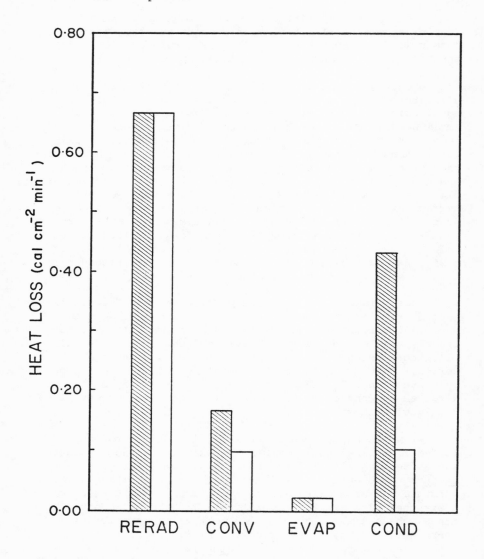

Figure 3. Heat loss computed for alligators with body temperatures of 28° C exposed to air and substrate temperatures of 20° C with a wind speed of 150 cm s^{-1} . These conditions represent the beginning of a typical cooling curve experiment. RERAD = reradiation, CONV = convection, EVAP = evaporative water loss and COND = conduction. Open columns represent a large alligator (Diameter = 20 cm., total length = 170 cm) and slashed marked columns represent a small alligator (diameter = 5 cm., total length = 43 cm.).

storage capacity (thermal inertia) of large animals dampens out short term fluctuations in body temperature and produces stable internal temperatures in diurnally varying thermal environments, as predicted by Spotila et al. (1973). Simply on the basis of the physics of heat transfer and heat storage capacity, large body size can account for most of the temperature differentials seen between present day large reptiles and their environments. The implications for dinosaur thermoregulation are clear. Large dinosaurs would have been inertial homeotherms. Their large body sizes would have "isolated" them from their thermal environments, because they exchanged heat with their surroundings at lower rates and by different mechanisms than do small reptiles. Their heat storage capacities would have dampened out diurnal variations in environmental heat flux. They would have been able to maintain stable body temperatures in seasonally equable climates.

These conclusions lead us to ask some additional questions. First, dinosaurs would have been homeothermic, but at what body temperature? Second, what would be the effect of a high "mammal-like" metabolic rate on body temperature? Third, how would changes in skin color have affected body temperature? We attempt to answer these questions by some additional theoretical calculations.

Metabolism, Skin Color and Body Temperature

Using a time dependent heat transfer model (Spotila et al. 1973), we compared the effects of high (mammalian level) metabolic rates and low (reptilian level) metabolic rates on the body temperatures of large ectotherms in a warm climate. In addition, we predicted the effect of changes in skin color on the body temperatures of such animals.

The model assumes that the animal is a cylinder with an isothermal body core surrounded by insulation. For mathematical convenience in treating heat flow through the insulation, the cylinder is divided into several layers. The effects of heating and cooling are considered to be equally distributed over the animal's surface, while heat transfer between the body core and surface is treated as occurring radially and symmetrically. This reduces the problem to one dimension. We compute the temperatures of each layer and the body core by solving a series of difference equations in an iterative fashion using Newton's method. Richard Kubb used a computer system to do the calculations discussed below. Robert Foley helped during this phase and in the experiments discussed above.

Table 1. Body temperatures of large dinosaur-sized animals calculated using the time dependent heat transfer model of Spotila et al. (1973). Ambient temperature ranged from $20°$ to $35°C$ and Q_{abs} from 0.6 to 0.8 cal cm^{-2} min^{-1} over a 24 hour cycle for the white animal, 0.9 for the pink, 1.0 for the grey and 1.1 for the black animal. All heat production values are scaled to body size according to Schmidt-Nielsen (1975), except for the M-E=0 and elephant values.

Body Temperatures (°C)

Colors	D. dorsalis Zero M - E		D. dorsalis M - E [1]		D. dorsalis M.R. [2]		Varanus gouldii M.R. [2]		Small Mammal M - E [3]		Elephant M - E [4]	
	Range	X̄	Range	X̄	Range	X̄	Range	X̄	Range	X̄	Range	X̄
White	30.1-30.8	30.4	30.1-30.8	30.4	30.4-31.1	30.7	30.8-31.4	31.1	38.1-38.9	38.5	37.2-37.9	37.5
Pink	32.5-33.5	33.0	32.5-33.5	33.0	32.9-33.9	33.4	33.3-34.2	33.7	39.2-40.1	39.6	38.3-39.3	38.8
Grey	34.9-36.1	35.5	34.9-36.2	35.5	35.3-36.6	35.9	35.7-36.9	36.3	43.2-44.5	43.8	39.9-41.2	40.5
Black	37.2-38.7	37.9	37.2-38.8	38.0	37.7-39.2	38.4	38.2-39.5	38.8	47.5-49.8	48.6	44.6-46.1	45.3

[1] M – E values were taken from Porter and Gates (1969)

[2] Metabolic rate (M.R.) values were taken from Bennett (1972)

[3] Small mammal M – E values were estimated from values given for rabbits and sheep by Porter and Gates (1969)

[4] Elephant M – E values were estimated from metabolic rates for elephants given by Brody (1945) and evaporative water loss rates for camels by Schmidt-Nielsen (1964)

Both metabolic rate and skin color could have had important effects on the body temperatures of large dinosaur-like creatures (Table 1). With zero net heat production, a dinosaur with a body diameter of 1 m, living in a subtropical climate, could have had a mean body temperature ranging from 30.4 to 37.9°C, depending on its color. Daily variation in body temperature would have been less than $\pm$ 1°C. Behavioral and physiological adaptations could easily have provided a fine tuning mechanism to allow even more precise temperature control. There is nothing that would prevent such a dinosaur from having been a very active animal, with a complex behavioral repertoire and diverse social interactions. A high, constant body temperature can be maintained in large animals without a high metabolic rate.

If we take metabolic rates and net heat production (M - E) values reported for lizards (Dipsosaurus dorsalis) and scale them according to the body size vs metabolic rate equation of Schmidt-Nielsen (1975, p. 237) we can project the heat production of dinosaur-sized lizards (body diameter of 1 m). White dinosaurs with lizard metabolic rates would have mean body temperatures of 30.4 to 30.7°C, while black ones would have body temperatures as high as 38.4°C. If we take the metabolic rates for a 750 g varanid lizard and scale them to values for dinosaur-sized animals we find that body temperatures now range from 31.1°C for a white varanid dinosaur to 38.8°C for a black one. The largest living lizard is the Komodo dragon, Varanus komodoensis. Our confidence in these calculations is bolstered by the field observations of McNab and Auffenberg (1976), who reported that large Komodo dragons (3.2 to 48 kg) had body temperatures of 36 to 40°C while active in their natural habitat. Small mammal (M - E) values scaled to dinosaur body size correspond to body temperatures of 38.5 to 48.6°C. This implies that a dinosaur with a high metabolic rate would have been under severe heat stress. Small mammals avoid this problem by being active at dawn and dusk and during the night and by remaining in burrows or being active only under heavy vegetation during the day, thus avoiding solar heating. Large dinosaurs could surely not have avoided heat stress in these ways since their large size would have made it difficult for them to avoid the sun during the day and their heat exchange would have been dominated by radiant heating and cooling (see above).

It is possible that the regression equation for heat production vs body size overestimates values for large mammals. We can circumvent this problem by applying metabolic rates determined directly for elephants, not using the scaling equation. To estimate (M - E) for an elephant we used metabolic rates determined by Brody (1945) for the Indian elephant (Elephas maximus), and estimated evaporative water loss from values reported for other large mammals such as camels by Schmidt-Nielsen (1964). This approach predicts lower body temperatures, more in line with body temperatures measured for elephants by Benedict (1936), Brattstrom et al. (1963), Hiley (1975) and ourselves (unpublished data). A pink elephant would have a body temperature of 38.8°C while a grey individual would be at 40.5°C. A black elephant would experience severe heat stress with a predicted body temperature of 45.3°C. Real elephants are usually grey with body temperatures of 36.0 - 38.2°C. This is 2°C lower than predicted by our calculations but within reason for a model that approximates an elephant as a cylinder! In addition, these animals may use accessory structures or specialized behavior to continuously dump body heat and avoid overheating. Their ears, especially the large ears of the African species (Loxodonta africana), probably dissipate large amounts of heat, acting as effective radiators and convectors. African elephants often wallow in the mud and spray water over themselves during the heat of the day (Sikes 1971; Hiley 1975). Further laboratory and field experiments are needed to determine quantitatively how these animals maintain their thermal balance when exposed to high external heat loads. In particular, careful measurement of net heat production and heat exchange in the natural habitat should receive primary consideration.

Changes in skin color would have enabled dinosaurs to change their body temperatures. A change from white to black could cause a 7 or 8°C increase in body temperature, according to our model. Changes in (M - E) would also cause large changes in body temperature. In particular, a high metabolic rate would place a large animal at or beyond the upper limit of its temperature tolerance.

There may be more similarities between the thermoregulatory capacities and strategies of large reptiles and large mammals than between large and small members of either class considered alone. While the large difference in metabolic rates between small mammals, such as mice and rats, and small reptiles, such as lizards, make it appropriate to generalize and label such groups as homeotherms and poikilotherms, this is not the case for large animals. All large animals are relatively "isolated" from the environment and have very low net heat production requirements. They see a different operative environmental temperature (Bakken 1976) from that experienced by small animals. The constraints imposed on an animal by its body size - energy exchange -

environment interaction determine the energetic cost of
homeothermy and the range of conditions over which it can
be maintained. Tracy (1977) has discussed this concept for
the specialized case of very small animals, pointing out
that the minimum size of a mammalian homeotherm is a function of its thermal environment. Metabolic requirements are
reduced for all large animals (Fig. 1), so we expect to see
a convergence of levels of heat production and insulative
capacities with increasing body size. Thus, in warm climates both large reptiles and mammals are bare skinned. In
cold climates large mammals (i.e. mastodons, mammoths, bears,
etc.) have large amounts of fur. Our calculations suggest
that large dinosaurs also could have lived in cold climates,
if they had fur coats or very large quantities of subcutaneous fat under thick skin for insulation, since the net
heat production requirements imposed upon them by such an
environment would not have exceeded the metabolic capabilities expected for large reptiles. Without a fur coat, large
dinosaurs could have lived in sub-temperate environments
without undue thermal stress. Under present day conditions,
there is no climatic reason why large dinosaurs could not
range into Canada in mid-summer if they migrated to Mexico
for the winter. The fact that large mammals like elephants
have metabolic rates somewhat above those expected for reptiles of a similar size does not mean that such metabolic
rates are necessary for survival. They may in fact be
anachronistic, remnants of mammalian evolutionary histories.
For large animals, natural selection should favor a reduction in metabolic rate, especially in warm climates where
elevated metabolic rates would in fact be detrimental.

Evolution of Homeothermy

Maintenance of a constant, relatively high body temperature is of obvious selective advantage. The evolutionary success of mammals and birds in many environments is
due in large part to their endothermic homeothermy. A combination of high metabolic rate, high quality insulation
and precise neural control enables mammals, in general, to
regulate at body temperatures between 35° and $39^\circ C$, while
birds regulate between 38° and $42^\circ C$. The resultant stability of the internal milieu allows them to employ higher
levels of activity, over longer periods of time and under
more varied environmental conditions, than can present day
poikilotherms. The selective pressures that have led to the
maintenance of homeothermy at a high body temperature have
been discussed by Heath (1968), Stevens (1973) and Heinrich (1977). We can now reconsider the evolution of homeothermy from an energy exchange viewpoint.

STRATEGIES OF THERMOREGULATION

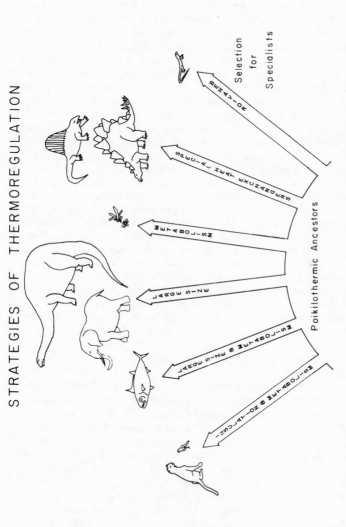

Figure 4. Evolution of homeothermy. Many animals have become partial or complete homeotherms with high body temperatures through selection for large body size, insulation, high metabolic rate, etc. Such specialization allows an animal to occupy a particular thermal niche. These thermal niches include a constant, high body temperature as one of their dimensions. Animals not to scale. Drawing by Christina Weinheimer.

Several kinds of animals have high body temperatures
when they are active. Some, such as flying insects, have
high metabolic rates while active, others rely on behavior,
like lizards basking in the sun. In the past, it has been
common to describe animals by clichés, such as "active, warm
blooded mammals" or "slow, sluggish reptiles". This type
of labelling reflects mammalian chauvinism and has been
counterproductive to the advance of our understanding of the
ecology and evolution of these animals. A sphinx moth is
very good at being a sphinx moth and a desert horned lizard
is very well adapted to its particular thermal niche. A
sparrow would not survive as a sphinx moth and a kangaroo
rat cannot successfully compete in the thermal environment
of an active horned lizard. Each of these animals is adapted to a particular thermal niche or climate space. One
thermal niche is no better or worse than another: value
judgments are inappropriate.

We can best visualize pathways in the development of
homeothermy not as proceeding sequentially from one evolutionary level to the next, but rather as divergent courses,
in which a common problem has been resolved in different
ways (Fig. 4). Several strategies are available to animals
undergoing selection for constant, high body temperatures.
Small lizards have become behavior specialists, flying insects are metabolism specialists and large dinosaurs, tunas
and elephants are body size specialists. Some animals have
added specialized accessory heat exchangers on their external surfaces, as apparently did Dimetrodon with its sail
(Bramwell and Fellgett 1973; Rodbard 1949) and Stegosaurus
with plates on its back (Farlow et al. 1976). Finally,
small mammals and birds have combined insulation and metabolism specialties such that they maintain high, homeothermic body temperatures over long periods of time. Each of
these strategies is effective in a particular thermal niche.
The fact that large dinosaurs and reptiles such as Dimetrodon are extinct implies either that their thermal niches
disappeared or that they have been replaced in those niches
by other taxonomic groups. Large mammals have filled some
of the large dinosaur niches, but the Dimetrodon niche
appears to have been lost. The thermal niches of smaller
dinosaurs and therapsid reptiles have been occupied and perhaps extended by their descendants, the birds and mammals.

The classic distinctions between poikilotherm and
homeotherm, endotherm and ectotherm are still useful in dis-
cussing the mechanisms by which animals control their body
temperatures. But, it is no more accurate or informative
to call all mammals endothermic homeotherms than it is to

label all reptiles as ectothermic poikilotherms. It is more useful to determine their thermal niches and group animals that employ the same thermoregulatory strategy together regardless of their taxonomic status. There are probably more thermoregulatory similarities between large ectothermic homeotherms, such as large dinosaurs and large mammals (body size specialists), than between elephants and small endothermic homeotherms such as rabbits and mice (insulation - metabolism specialists). Small ectotherms (behavior specialists) such as desert lizards are just as distinct, in terms of their thermal niche, from dinosaurs as they are from rats and elephants.

The plethora of thermoregulatory strategies seen among living and extinct animals have evolved within the constraints imposed on animals by their body sizes and the physical characteristics of their environments. Large body size insures constancy of body temperature and favors selection for a low metabolic rate. Small size demands a high metabolic rate if there is selection for an elevated body temperature. Alternatively, if the metabolic rate remains low, selection favors the development of behavioral mechanisms that insure the maintenance of a high body temperature during activity. We can best appreciate the mechanisms involved in dinosaur thermoregulation if we keep in mind the primary role of energy exchange between the animal and its environment in defining the thermoregulatory strategies of these animals. Most/many dinosaurs could have been very active and probably exhibited complex behavior patterns. Adults of large species would have been selected for low metabolic rates, while small dinosaurs would have undergone selection for either elevated metabolic rate and improved insulation, or improved behavioral thermoregulation. Thus, gigantism as a thermoregulatory strategy precludes the development of a high metabolic rate. Our best estimate remains that large dinosaurs were ectothermic homeotherms.

Acknowledgments

Special thanks to Richard Kubb, Robert Foley, Christina Weinheimer, Kenneth Terpin and Pamela Caron for their help during this study. George S. Bakken and C. Richard Tracy read an early draft of this paper and contributed several important suggestions. J. J. Spotila, M. N. Spotila, L. D. Spotila, J. A. MacMahon, J. A. Sealander and D. M. Gates made this investigation possible. Support was provided by research contract EY-76-S-02-2502 between the Department of Energy and the State University College at Buffalo.

9

Application of Size-Metabolism Allometry to Therapsids and Dinosaurs

M. E. Baur and Randall R. Friedl

Abstract

Many physiological parameters of present-day animals obey allometric laws; they vary systematically with size within suitably chosen taxonomic groups. Presumably this held for ancient animals as well. We show that the assumption that it did furnishes a tool for the study of paleontological problems; we explore in particular the use of allometric relations between animal metabolic rates and total body sizes. A survey of size-metabolism allometry is given in the introduction. We then consider two particular groups of extinct animals, the therapsids - Permo-Triassic precursors of the mammals - and the dinosaurs. We show that the carnivorous therapsids exhibited a long-term pattern of size decrease throughout their evolution and argue that small size was a key feature in the development of the mammalian level of organization. The dinosaurs on the other hand exhibited a tendency toward giantism; we suggest that the contrast in evolutionary strategies between the two groups reflects basic differences in size-metabolism relationships. We next develop a quantitative framework for this suggestion, introducing as our fundamental assumption the hypothesis that selective pressure tends to minimize the mean animal activity rate. The condition of balance between energy input and usage for individual animals yields an algebraic equation for this rate. Application of the criterion of minimization then leads to the conclusion that mammals have always been under pressure toward small size while for dinosaurs there was an optimum size, with body length in the range 3-4 meters. Our formulation sets upper limits to the size ranges available to animals evolving within given phyletic ground plans; for both mammals and dinosaurs these limits are in accord with observation. A mammalian lower size limit of the right magnitude is also predicted. Turning to the question of endothermy, we argue that the mammalian body form was dictated by a need to maintain high body temperature, whereas that of dinosaurs was not well suited to this purpose; moreover, great size probably did not favor high body temperature in any but the largest dinosaurs. It there- fore seems unlikely that the dinosaurs as a group developed any great measure of endothermy. Mammalian endothermy pro- bably resulted from a need to maintain body temperature while size was decreasing in the evolving therapsids. The general "mammalian" tendency toward small size is inadequate to ac- count for this decrease. We suggest that a specific environ- mental factor - a gradual decrease in ambient O_2 pressure - was responsible. To support this proposal, we develop a quantitative model for the dependence of <u>maximal</u> activity rate on O_2 pressure and body size. According to this model, the drop in pressure required to account for the overall size decrease in the therapsid-mammal lineage was about 70 mmHg.

Introduction: Allometric Principles

The possibility that fossil material can be made to yield information on the physiologies of ancient vertebrates has attracted much recent attention. Attempts in this direc- tion include studies of dinosaur metabolism through examina- tion of bone histology (Ricqlès 1974, Bakker 1975a) and of brain evolution as indicated by developments in skull mor- phology (Jerison 1976, Olson 1976, Hopson 1977). Such work assumes a close parallel between the functions of structures preserved in the fossils and those of similar structures in existing animals. This assumption is open to question, and the conclusions reached have not always won universal accep- tance. Nevertheless it is clearly of importance for paleon- tological research that physiological principles continue to be applied to the interpretation of the fossil record. To this end one must utilize properties which can be determined from skeletal material and which bear a reasonably unambig- uous physiological significance. In this work, we present a study along these lines in which the property of interest is an especially simple one: animal body size.

Body dimensions and proportions tend to be correlated with physiological parameters of living animals according to simple empirical equations called allometric relations. Such equations represent the scaling of some parameter with size for a selected group of animals. The most commonly employed index of whole body size is the animal mass M^*, and an allo- metric relation between some parameter X and M is an equation

$$X = a \, M^b. \tag{1}$$

---

[*]A table of symbols is included as an Appendix.

In eq. (1) the <u>allometric exponent</u> b must be a dimensionless number. However, if X has dimensions other than M^b, the <u>allometric coefficient</u> a must be accorded dimensions in order to render the overall equation dimensionally consistent. The usual practice is to specify the units of M and X, and report the coefficient a as a number (as in Bartholomew 1977) with units only implicit. In the present article we shall follow this practice, with all units taken to be those appropriate to the SI system, as summarized by Bartholomew (1977, Ch. 3). It must be noted that the exponent b is permitted to be positive or negative. We shall always give it as a decimal number, usually not equal to an integer or common fraction. Failure to appreciate the flexibility with which a and b can be assigned has tended to retard progress in the use of allometric techniques; in this connection we recommend the thorough critique by Stahl (1967).

We hope that the remarks above give some feeling for the wide applicability of allometric principles to physiology. Here we limit ourselves to one specific class of allometric relationship, that in which the physiological parameter X is the rate of energy metabolism. This quantity has the dimensions of power = energy/time. We shall employ the symbol R for it in what follows. A large amount of research on living vertebrates has demonstrated the validity of eq. (1) with $X \equiv R$ over several orders of magnitude in M (Kleiber 1932, 1961; Benedict 1938; Lasiewski and Dawson 1967; Dawson and Hulbert 1970; Bennett and Dawson 1976). In formulating this relationship, attention must of course be paid to the metabolic state of the animals being examined. For endotherms (mammals and birds), correlation is usually sought between M and the <u>basal metabolic rate</u>, that for the animal at rest in its <u>thermal neutral zone</u> (Bartholomew 1977, Chs. 3 and 8). The latter is that range of environmental temperature around the animal core body temperature for which energy consumption is a minimum, i.e., for which the production of heat by basal processes in the animal is sufficient to balance heat loss to the environment. For endotherms outside the thermal neutral zone, the metabolic level rises above the basal level, and this effect may in particular be responsible for the reported tendency (Pearson 1948) of some very small mammals (shrews) to deviate from the overall mammalian metabolic allometry (Tracy 1977). The data for mammals indicate an allometric dependence of basal metabolic rate on M with exponent b = 0.75, while the best current value for birds is 0.72.

For other groups of vertebrates the situation is more complex. Before proceeding to consider them, we must carefully define terms. It has been conventional to group fish, amphibians and reptiles together as poikilotherms (animals whose temperature conforms to that of their environment) in contrast to the birds and mammals, regarded as endotherms (animals controlling their temperature at a near constant level independent of the environment by internal heat production). Such a division into temperature conformers and temperature regulators is oversimplified. Most "poikilotherms" control their body temperature behaviorally, if left free to do so, and have well defined temperature preferenda (Bartholomew 1977, Ch. 8). Some have as well at least a limited ability to increase metabolic heat production to compensate for heat loss to the environment. Finally, large animals will be able to maintain a core body temperature higher than the environment simply because of a small body surface to volume ratio, as has been shown in a model calculation for large reptiles (Spotila et. al. 1973). Therefore most "poikilotherms" are in reality homoiothermic (maintaining constant internal temperature) to a degree. Accordingly, we distinguish between the active homoiotherms (birds and mammals) for which internal heat generation is the dominant factor in maintaining a nearly constant core body temperature and the more or less passive partial homoiotherms for which greater variation in core temperature is permissible and for which internal heat generation is but one, usually but not always, minor, factor in temperature maintenance. We retain the term endotherm for active homoiotherms; however we shall avoid the ambiguous "poikilotherm".

Reptiles do not of course possess a thermal neutral zone or basal metabolic rate in the sense employed for endotherms. Some do possess a plateau of body temperatures around the temperature preferendum, over which their metabolic rate is essentially constant; but if their core body temperature falls below the preferendum or preferred plateau, this metabolic rate characteristically decreases, in contrast to the situation for endotherms exposed to external temperatures outside the thermal neutral zone. In view of the difficulty of measuring core body temperature accurately, and the variability of the latter, the standard metabolism for reptiles is usually defined as that of the animal at rest at a given external temperature. From their compendium of data, Bennett and Dawson (1976) find allometric coefficients b = 0.80 (20°C) and b = 0.77 (30°C) for all living reptiles as a group, close to those for the endotherms. A similar slight decrease in b in passing from 20°C to 30°C is reported for snakes as a group, but not for lizards. Bennett and Dawson do not consider the decrease to be statistically significant. The determinations of b values by Bennett and Dawson are dominated by data for small species; 35 out of 44 data points in their analysis of reptiles at 30°C are for animals with body mass less than 1 kg. Analysis of only large reptile data gives smaller $\underline{b}$'s; Templeton (1970) found b = 0.65 for large lizards at 37°C. We have carried out a standard linear regression analysis of the 30°C metabolism-body mass data for reptiles with mass greater than 1 kg given by Bennett and Dawson (9 species) and find b = 0.68. It is natural in physiological research to seek organizing principles having as great a generality as possible, and the hypothesis that all terrestrial vertebrates conform to a single $\underline{b}$ value, near 0.75, has an especially appealing simplicity. Indeed, some workers in the field accept this hypothesis as probably correct, and there have been ingenious attempts to prove that a value of 0.75 for $\underline{b}$ must hold for all terrestrial organisms (McMahon 1973). These have not been generally accepted however, and in our opinion the allometric relation (1) is best considered merely an empirical curve fit. Therefore there is no justification, apart from the quality of the fit to available data, for the assertion that a single unique value of $\underline{b}$ applies to all vertebrate groups. We believe that the available data does not rule out values of $\underline{b}$ differing from the empirical "three-quarters" rule, and in particular that a value close to the venerable 0.67 (Kleiber 1932) may be applicable to large reptiles operating with internal temperatures near their preferenda (usually in the range 30–40°C).

From the standpoint of metabolism-size allometry, the most evident distinction between endotherms and the other vertebrate classes is in the coefficient $\underline{a}$, which is typically an order of magnitude greater for endotherms than for reptiles. A large value for $\underline{a}$ means high internal heat production by the animal even in its resting state, and it is thus appropriate to use the value of $\underline{a}$ as an index for endothermicity. Evolutionary progress toward the endothermic state may, therefore, be appropriately studied by centering attention on the consequences for a group of animals of a progressive increase in this index.

The metabolism of an animal is usually above the basal or standard level, of course. Bartholomew (1977, Ch. 3) defines the total energy metabolism to include, besides the basal rate: cost of thermoregulation if the animal is an endotherm outside its thermal neutral zone; specific dynamic action (energy cost of digestion); cost of activity; and cost of production (growth and reproduction). We shall regard the specific dynamic action as equivalent to a reduction in the net energy yield of food not depending in any regular way on body size as such; we shall omit consideration of the cost of production, recognizing that this may restrict the

utility and generality of our results. The energy cost of
activity, and its dependence on size, will be taken up later.
The energy cost of thermoregulation is difficult to treat
quantitatively, and here we must resort to severe oversimpli-
fication of a complex subject. We shall assume that behavioral thermoregulation (as in reptiles) has negligible
energy cost, and only consider compensation by internal heat
production of heat loss by conductance to an ambient environment at low temperature (T_a) from an animal at high core
body temperature (T_b). Following Bartholomew (1977, Ch. 8)
we assume that outside the thermal neutral zone, this internal heat production by active homeotherms can be represented
as

$$R_h = \text{Rate of heat production} = CM(T_b - T_a) \equiv CM\Delta T, \quad (2)$$

where C is the animal thermal conductance per unit mass. C
implicitly contains all active and passive mechanisms by
which the animal can modify its surface properties and it is
also subject to variation as a function of animal activity
level. In order to avoid an excessively unwieldy formulation
with many uncertain parameters, we shall merely adopt for C
the empirical allometric relation reported by Bartholomew
for mammals and birds:

$$C = a_c M^{-0.5}. \quad (3)$$

With the techniques of allometry in the context of
animal metabolic rates in hand, we now consider how they may
be of use in the study of two important extinct assemblages.

Therapsids and Dinosaurs

It seems reasonable to suppose that the metabolism of
ancient vertebrate groups scaled allometrically with size at
least to the same extent as does that of living groups. This
hypothesis is central to our work. How can we bring it to
bear on problems in paleontology? We remarked above that the
advance towards endothermy in advanced vertebrates can be
formulated in terms of a gradual increase in the coefficient
a. During the late Paleozoic and early Mesozoic, the fossil
record reveals a complex pattern in which the Therapsida, or
mammal-like reptiles, radiated and diversified into a wide
variety of both herbivorous and carnivorous forms, only to be
replaced as dominant terrestrial vertebrates in the middle
and late Triassic by an assemblage of reptilian groups whose
most prominent members were the dinosaurs. This assemblage
in turn vanished at the close of the Cretaceous, to be sup-
planted by the mammalian descendants of the therapsids. The
problem of the acquisition of endothermy in these various
lineages has been considered by investigators attempting to

understand these events, and it has in particular been suggested that the long dominance of the dinosaurs may in part have been due to acquisition of some measure of endothermy (Bakker 1975a). Early endothermy in the therapsids has been postulated as well (Olson 1959, 1976; Hopson 1973; Ricqlès 1974). We have no direct way to test these proposals; but the existence of a correlation between metabolic rate and body size suggests that patterns in the latter might be made to yield information on the former.

In stating this, we must recognize that size is a notoriously labile property at low taxonomic rank, whereas metabolic rates as expressed by allometric relations are conservative; $\underline{a}$ is reasonably constant at least at the family level in modern vertebrates, while $\underline{b}$ is probably best considered an order property. Within evolving phyletic lines of low taxonomic rank, we therefore expect size change to occur within the framework of an established metabolic pattern. In lines of higher rank (order or higher) in contrast, we suggest that overall size shifts may be indicative of changes in this pattern, and that in making comparisons between classes, subclasses or orders, it may be reasonable to interpret differences in size range in terms of metabolic differences. Caution in the use of this approach is needed, since it is well established (Rensch 1948, Newell 1949) that long-lived vertebrate (and invertebrate) lineages typically exhibit a pattern of phyletic increase in size over time ("Cope's Rule"), a phenomenon unlikely to be associated with metabolic shifts in general. To explain it, some workers have invoked ecological factors (for example Moynihan (1971)); on the other hand, Stanley (1973) has argued that size increase in successful lineages is a consequence of statistical drift during diversification from small stem forms. Either or both of these arguments are no doubt valid in many cases, but it seems to us that neither is adequate to account for all aspects of the size patterns of dinosaurs and of therapsids. To be sure, some early thecodont precursors of the dinosaurs were relatively small, but it appears that a statistical distribution of sizes around a preferred body length of several meters was established quite soon in dinosaur evolution, with little subsequent overall shift. The real issue is: why was the preferred size of dinosaurs so large, compared, say, with that of early (and modern) mammals? Turning to the therapsids, the herbivorous lineages indeed tended to increase in size with time, but as has frequently been remarked (Olson 1971) the carnivores appear to have diminished in size. We have performed a quantitative study of these trends which we shall present in detail elsewhere; we give an overview of the results here.

The situation is summarized in Figure 1. As an index of

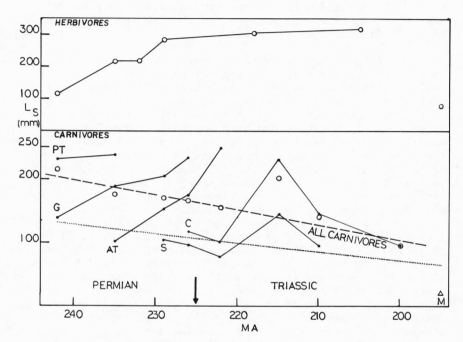

Fig. 1. Size trends in the Therapsida. L$_S$ is skull length,
tip of snout to base of squamosal. Time in MA approximate;
vertical arrow marks boundary between Permian and Triassic.
Circles: mean skull length for all species assigned to the
major assemblages. Isolated herbivore circle: Oligokyphus;
triangle M: the early mammal Morganucodon. Individual carnivore groups designated as: PT, primitive Therocephalia; AT,
advanced Therocephalia; G, Gorgonopsia; S, Scaloposauria; C,
Cynodontia. Dashed line: linear fit to carnivore mean skull
length excluding Cynognathus zone data. Dotted line: linear
fit to mean size at first appearance of carnivore group.

whole body size we have used the skull length L_S (tip of snout to base of squamosal). Whole body lengths are not known for enough therapsids to define an adequate statistical sample, but these animals are on the whole sufficiently uniform in morphology so that skull length probably gives an adequate indication of comparative body length in most cases. In those species for which skull and body dimensions are both accurately known, body length is typically 4-5 times that of the skull as defined above. The correlation with geological time of the stratigraphic zones of the most important source of therapsid fossils, the Karroo formation of South Africa, has not yet been settled; therefore the times given in Figure 1 are approximate. We have grouped the data for the carnivorous therapsids (bottom portion of Figure 1) according to the Karroo zone designations as follows: Tapinocephalus zone, 242 MA; Endothiodon zone, 235 MA; low and middle Cistecephalus zone lumped at 229 MA; upper Cistecephalus (uppermost Permian), 226 MA; Lystrosaurus zone (basal Triassic), 222 MA; Cynognathus zone, 215 MA. The data for the late therapsids is divided into middle Triassic, 210 MA, and late Triassic, 200 MA. The boundary between the Permian and Triassic, indicated by the vertical arrow in Figure 1, is taken at 225 MA. For further discussion of Karroo stratigraphy in the context of the therapsid record, the reader is referred to Boonstra (1971). We have lumped the herbivore data (top portion of Figure 1) for the Lystrosaurus and Cynognathus zones, and for the middle and late Triassic. The circles in Figure 1 give the mean skull lengths of all species assigned to the given zones. No attempt has been made to weight the data for frequency of occurrence. The means are based on a total of approximately 600 pieces of literature data, about 60% for herbivores and 40% for carnivores. We have excluded data on fossils known or suspected to be those of juveniles.

No data have been included for the most primitive group of therapsids, the Dinocephalia. In the first place, the only source of well preserved fossils of these animals sufficient in number to support statistical analysis is the Tapinocephalus zone, so it is impossible to say with precision anything about their size trend with time. Secondly, they seem to have been well off the main line of therapsid evolution. Inclusion of data on these large animals would increase the average sizes of both herbivores and carnivores in the Tapinocephalus zone, but would not materially alter the overall aspect of the plots.

The mean skull lengths for the carnivores have been fit with a straight line, the dashed line in Figure 1, by linear regression analysis (correlation coefficient -0.98) excluding

the point for the Cynognathus zone. The Cynognathus zone
carnivore data is dominated by the single cynodont genus for
which the zone is named, and most of the species referred to
this genus are large forms. However there is considerable
uncertainty as to how many such species there are; Hopson
and Kitching (1972) suggest that all the known Cynognathus
fossils may be of a single species. In view of this uncertainty, the point for the Cynognathus zone carnivores must be
considered as unreliable.

Means over species are given in Figure 1 for individual
carnivore groups labelled as follows: PT = primitive Therocephalia, G = Gorgonopsia, AT = advanced Therocephalia,
C = Cynodontia, S = Scaloposauria. This terminology is based
on Boonstra (1972), in whose taxonomy these groups hold order
status; they stand in approximate correspondence to the infraorders defined by Romer (1966). More properly we should
say that the groups for which we give data are the carnivorous families within these infraorders or orders; the
Gorgonopsia and Cyndontia contain herbivorous branches. The
dotted line for the carnivores in Figure 1 is the linear regression fit (correlation coefficient -0.61) for the average
size at first appearance of each of the carnivore groups,
excluding the primitive Therocephalia. The point denoted by
a triangle labelled M on the carnivore plot and placed at the
Triassic-Jurassic boundary at 195 MA is that for the earliest
known mammal, Morganucodon (Crompton and Jenkins 1973). The
isolated point on the herbivore plot at 195 MA is that for
the remnant herbivorous cynodont genus Oligokyphus.

Several conclusions can be drawn from these data. The
size decrease of the carnivorous therapsids is a statistically significant phenomenon. Moreover it extended over the
entire late Permian-Triassic in fairly regular fashion, except perhaps for the Cynognathus zone. Since the average
linear dimension of the carnivores diminished by almost 50%
in this interval, their average body mass must have fallen
to 50-20% of its value for the earliest lineages. The early
therapsid herbivores had average body sizes on the same order
as, or smaller than, those of the contemporary therapsid
carnivores but the late herbivores had body masses on the
average at least an order of magnitude greater than those of
the late carnivores. It seems inconceivable that the late
carnivores can have preyed on many of the adult late herbivores with any effectiveness, although perhaps juveniles
could have been taken.

We note further that the earlier individual carnivore
infraorders exhibit monotonic size increase with time from
appearance until extinction, whereas the scaloposaurians

and cynodonts tend to decline in size except for the
Cynognathus zone. Thus for the Permian and basal Triassic
we have a situation in which Cope's Rule-like size increase
at the infraorder level coexists with size shrinkage in the
composite. One conceivable explanation for the decrease in
overall mean size might be that evolutionary drift (Stanley
1973) produced expansion of the therapsid size range to encompass smaller forms. This can be ruled out, however, since
further analysis of the carnivore data for each zone reveals
a downward shift of the entire size spectrum; though it is
not evident from Figure 1, not only the mean and minimum but
also the maximum carnivore sizes tended to decrease with
time, the width of the spectral distribution about the mean
remaining approximately constant.

Olson (1975) has argued that the main sequence of
therapsid evolution ran through "upland" forms which provided periodic replenishment of the "lowland" fauna on which
the fossil record is mainly based. If this hypothesis is
accepted, we must interpret the overall trend as reflecting
diminishing sizes in the largely unknown "upland" stem
lineage. Evidently this lineage was under some form of
selection pressure to reduce size, a pressure which, under
lowland conditions, may have been somewhat reduced or super-
ceded by other pressures favoring the size increase seen in
the individual "lowland" infraorders. "Upland" carnivore
stocks might have been undergoing coevolution to smaller
size with a group of herbivore prey animals; but the pattern
among "lowland" herbivores, when analyzed in detail, does not
suggest replenishment by successively smaller "upland" stocks.
The later Permian and Triassic seems to have been a time of
increasing warmth and dryness, so heat stress might have been
an increasingly severe problem for some therapsids, making a
decrease in size with its consequent increase in surface to
volume ratio adaptive for them. Why this should have affected "upland" forms in particular is not evident, however.
Ecological stress arising from competition by non-therapsid
reptiles for the medium to large carnivore role seems also an
insufficient explanation, since the only plausible competitors, the thecodonts, did not become prominent until the
middle Triassic, by which time the carnivorous therapsids had
dwindled to a few, mostly small, remnant forms.

The position of the data point for Morganucodon in
Figure 1 makes it clear that the very small size characteristic of early mammals represented the extreme culmination of
a long established trend. It will certainly not do to dis-
miss this small size as merely an example of the tendency of
early members of successful lineages to be smaller than their
descendants (Stanley 1973); the evolutionary process which

produced <u>Morganucodon</u> apparently contained a marked and on-going reduction in size as an essential ingredient. To put this in another way, attainment of the mammalian level of organization under the conditions of the Permo-Triassic appears to have been linked with a severe reduction in size, and small size has, in a sense, remained characteristic of mammals subsequently. It seems unlikely that a mean taken over all species of mammal present at any given time since the appearance of <u>Morganucodon</u> would give a result as large as the figure of about 1 meter for the mean body length of early carnivorous therapsids.

In this connection we must mention the recent work of McNab (1978), which in some ways parallels our own. McNab has examined the trend to small size in the therapsids, though without noting the intricate fashion in which overall carnivore size decrease is interlinked with individual in-fraordinal increase. McNab also reaches the conclusion that decrease in size was closely coupled with progress toward mammalian status, in particular toward endothermy, and sug-gests, in effect, that the decrease in size with time evident in the data for the cynodonts and scaloposaurians in Figure 1 correlated with the acquisition of endothermy in these lineages. His proposed scenario is as follows: early nonendothermic therapsids acquired a commitment to constant high body temperature as passive homoiotherms, with large body size and possibly a coating of fur or other modifica-tion of the integument as a mechanism to minimize heat loss. Then as size diminished and surface to volume ratio increas-ed, acquisition of endothermy became essential; it was necessary for cynodonts and scaloposaurians to switch from passive to active homoiothermic status as they became smal-ler. As causative agents for the size reduction in these two groups, McNab introduces presumed ecological stress factors, having to do with a change in the food base, compe-tition with other forms and so forth. It is difficult to see how this accounts for the overall long-term downward size trend, however.

During the later Mesozoic the diminutive mammals co-existed with the much larger dinosaurs. The separation of ecological role between these two groups seems to have been nearly complete. During the Mesozoic there were reptiles as small as the early mammals; the latter were evidently able to compete effectively with them, but did not challenge the dinosaurs for large carnivore status. On the other hand, the dinosaurs showed no tendency to develop very small forms. We must conclude that some fundamental difference in physio-logy guaranteed to the mammals a measure of dominance as small carnivores and insectivores, while making it advanta-

geous to the dinosaurs to maintain large size. We turn now
to detailed consideration of this issue, in the context of
a simple allometric model relating metabolic rate and activity.

A Model for Animal Viability

We shall attempt to formulate our model with the maximum degree of simplicity. In so doing we run the risk of
omitting important factors, but the framework which we present is flexible and easily capable of elaboration if required. We seek a basic animal viability parameter, reflecting the conditions under which it functions and its own
metabolic state, and whose variation affects its survival
chances in a predictable way. We propose that this parameter
be taken as the <u>mean animal activity rate</u>, for which we shall
employ the symbol f_a. Following Bartholomew (1977, Ch. 3),
we choose to regard an animal in purely mechanistic terms as
a collector of chemical (free) energy, whose fundamental task
is the search for and exploitation of energy resources.
These resources must obviously be sufficient <u>at least</u> to repay the costs of the search and provide free energy to be
expended in maintaining its biochemical integrity; the rate
of energy usage for the latter is assumed to be given by the
basal (for endotherms) or standard (for nonendotherms) metabolic rate. As previously stated we ignore the costs of
production, whose inclusion we believe would not greatly
alter the predictions of the model. For a given environment,
the amount of energy collected by an animal can be increased
by increasing its activity rate; presumably the mean rate
which must be maintained is set by the balance between the
energy needs of the animal and the resources available to it.
<u>We now offer as a key element in the formulation of the model</u>
<u>the hypothesis that it is selectively advantageous for an</u>
<u>animal to have as small a value of f_a as possible.</u> That is,
evolutionary pressure will always work to reduce f_a. Certainly the larger that f_a is, i.e., the more that the animal
is "on the go", the greater is its risk of suffering death by
predation or accident and the smaller is its margin for increasing its activity to deal with short-term resource fluctuations. Increase in f_a also presumably renders it less
well able to attend to reproduction and care of juveniles.
One can perhaps envision special circumstances in which it
might be fortuitously advantageous for a given individual or
small group of animals to have a high f_a temporarily, but we
can find no support for the position that high activity rate
<u>as such</u> would ever have systematically positive survival
value. We emphasize however that the hypothesis is unproven
and we do not claim it to be beyond question or challenge.

The idea that activity rates should be as small as possible may offend against certain anthropomorphic preju- dices; it is in a sense the reverse of the Puritan "work ethic". On the other hand, we note that it is precisely the drive to reduce human physical activity through the develop- ment of mechanical devices which has been responsible for technological progress. In a more serious vein it might be objected that many groups of animals have very high activity levels. If the criterion of minimal activity rate is mean- ingful, how could active forms, for example birds and mammals, have come into being at all? We believe that the answer to this is that long-term changes in the physical environment and in the ecological setting in which a given phyletic group of animals exists may well impose on the group an increase in activity rate, <u>but that evolutionary change will act in such a way as to minimize this increase</u>.

We have left open the question of the averaging proce- dure by which mean activity rate is to be defined. The time interval for the averaging should be long enough to sample all the usual fluctuations in resource base to which the animal is subject as the result of seasonal climatic varia- tion. Probably therefore an annual average is indicated; it seems to us unnecessary here to make the details more expli- cit than that.

The most obvious quantity to use for f_a would be the mean animal speed of travel, $\bar{v}$. However, a little thought shows that this quantity as it stands is not suitable, for it contains the animal linear dimension, L, as an implicit factor. A large animal moving a few body lengths may have a larger speed than a small animal moving many body lengths in the same time interval, but its activity rate is less. Clearly we must scale the speed to the animal size in order to obtain a parameter which can be meaningfully employed to compare animals of different sizes. Therefore we shall de- fine f_a by

$$f_a \equiv \bar{v}/L. \tag{4}$$

Note that eq. (4) does <u>not</u> imply that $\bar{v}$ is proportional to L. With this definition, f_a has units (time)$^{-1}$, so it is di- mensionally a frequency; it is to be interpreted physically as the mean number of body lengths travelled per unit time.

Our task now is to put the preceding discussion into mathematical terms by expressing in the form of an equation the requirement of balance between energy collected by an animal and that expended by it. Both the energy collected and that expended will depend on animal size and to represent this dependence we shall use allometric relations; the result will be a "viability equation", giving f_a as a function of animal size, the allometric parameters for its metabolic rate, and the quality, in the sense of energy resource availability, of its environment.

Body size usually enters into allometric relations as the animal mass M, but as we have seen the proper definition of f_a necessarily introduces the animal linear dimension L. Therefore we must resort to the somewhat unconventional practice of expressing all equations in terms of L rather than M. To convert from M to body volume V = M/density is straightforward, assuming that body density can always be taken as that of water, 1000 kg m^{-3}. One might expect to have

$$V = \alpha \, L^3, \tag{5}$$

a simple scaling of volume with the cube of linear dimension. For mammals it is customary to assume that L(in cm) = 3 M(in gm)$^{.33}$ (Bartholomew 1977, Ch. 3, p. 99), which when converted to SI units is L(in m) = 0.3 M(in kg)$^{.33}$. Taking the density as given above then gives L(in m) = 3 V(in m^3)$^{.33}$ or α = 1/27. In reality the matter is not so simple. McMahon (1973) has argued that linear dimensions (limb and trunk length) of animals should scale as M$^{.25}$ and this seems to be supported by data on large domestic mammals (Brody 1945); Brody's data correspond in our terms to a relation V (in m^3) = 0.007 L(in m)$^{4.3}$. On the other hand, primate data quoted by McMahon suggests V $\propto$ L$^{3.6}$. Evidently we should use instead of eq. (5) the more general formula

$$V = \alpha_\beta L^\beta. \tag{6}$$

with β greater than 3.5 and perhaps as large as 4.3 for mammals. The situation for dinosaurs is different. The weights of a number of dinosaur species have been estimated by Colbert (1962) and we have fit volumes derived from his data to body length using eq. (6); we find that for bipedal dinosaurs (Allosaurus, Tyrannosaurus, Camptosaurus, Iguanodon, Corythosaurus and Anatosaurus) α_β = 0.005 and β = 2.75; for quadrupedal forms (Brontosaurus, Diplodocus, Brachiosaurus, Stegosaurus, Palaeoscincus, Styracosaurus and Triceratops), α_β =0.005 and β = 2.78. Thus not only do the dinosaurs fail to conform to McMahon's theoretical arguments, but their exponent β appears to be even less than the "classical" value of 3.

The mean rate of energy collection by an animal, R_{coll}, will be taken as the product of the search distance covered per unit time, $\bar{v} = f_a L$, the areal density of energy in the search region, d, and a parameter σ which we shall term the cross section for energy location and capture. The areal density d is the fundamental environmental quality parameter in our approach. Usually it can be equated with the density in J m^{-2} of energy from plant or animal material present on a steady-state basis in the search region, but it is possible that under certain circumstances energy input may be limited not by the availability of organic nutrients but by that of the oxygen required for aerobic metabolism. In the case that oxygen uptake is limiting, d is to be interpreted as O_2 partial pressure. The interpretation of σ is less simple. In the case of limited O_2 availability it will depend on the areal dimensions of the lung and respiratory tract and through them on animal size. For food collection σ must also depend on size, but it is difficult to define this dependence. The simplest situation to deal with would be that of a hypothetical "random grubber", an animal exclusively dependent on short-range stimuli, sweeping the ground from side to side as it moves along a meandering track. The capture region of this animate vacuum-cleaner clearly will depend on the sweep length, which would be expected to scale as linear dimension L. An animal provided with long-range sensory capabilities – vision and hearing – can pursue purposeful motion toward distant food sources and more effectively harvest the available energy. This will certainly increase σ, but it seems to us that it will not change the size dependence of this quantity. While we admit to considerable uncertainty on this important point, we shall in what follows always take for σ

$$\sigma = \sigma_0 L, \tag{7}$$

where σ_0 is size-independent and dimensionless.

We have then

$$R_{coll} = (f_a L)(d)(\sigma_0 L) = f_a L^2 \sigma_0 d, \tag{8}$$

which must be balanced by the mean total energy expenditure, R_{ex}. The latter is composed of three terms; the basal resting metabolic rate R_r, the mean activity metabolic rate R_a, and, for endotherms, the mean rate of heat production R_h given by eqs. (2) and (3). It is well established that the activity metabolic rate of terrestrial vertebrates depends linearly on speed of movement and allometrically on M (Taylor et. al. 1970; Fedak et. al. 1974; Tucker 1975; Bennett and Dawson 1976). The same relation should hold for the mean activity rate as a function of mean speed, so we write

$$R_a = (f_a L)(a_a M^{b_a}), \tag{9}$$

where a_a and b_a are the allometric coefficient and exponent for activity metabolism. For quadrupedal mammals Taylor et. al. (1970) find $b_a = 0.60$ and $a_a = 8.46$ when R_a is expressed in $cm^3 O_2$ (time)$^{-1}$, $f_a L$ in km (time)$^{-1}$ and M in gm. We shall explicitly demonstrate the conversion of these units to SI units, and the consequent change in the numerical value of a_a for this case:

$$\frac{R_a(J\ s^{-1})}{20.1(J\ cm^3 O_2{}^{-1})} =$$

$$= 8.46\ [\ \frac{f_a(s^{-1})\ L\ (m)}{1000\ (m\ km^{-1})}\ ][M(kg)\ 1000\ (gm\ kg^{-1})]^{0.60}$$

or

$$R_a(J\ sec^{-1}) = 10.7\ f_a(s^{-1})L(m)\ [M(kg)]^{0.60}. \tag{10}$$

Thus $a_a = 10.7$ for SI units. Converting from M to V,

$$R_a(J\ s^{-1}) = 10.7\ f_a(s^{-1})\ L(m)\ [V(m^3)\ 1000\ kg\ m^{-3}]^{0.60}$$

$$= 675\ f_a(s^{-1})\ L(m)\ [V(m^3)]^{0.60}. \tag{11}$$

Finally we convert from V to L as size variable:

mammals: $\qquad R_a = 675\ f_a LV^{0.60} = 675\ f_a L[\alpha_\beta L^\beta]^{0.60} =$

$$= 675\ f_a \alpha_\beta{}^{0.60} L^{1+0.60\beta} \tag{12a}$$

To make our equations more compact, we introduce $a_{aL} \equiv 675\ \alpha_\beta{}^{0.60}$ and $b_{aL} \equiv 1 + 0.60\beta$, so that

$$R_a = f_a a_{aL}{}^{b_{aL}}.$$

Exactly the same procedure is followed for all other animal groups, and we shall omit explicit calculation.

For lizards performing submaximal activity Bakker (1972) found $b_a = 0.67$ and $a_a = 5.2$ for the same choice of units as Taylor et. al. Conversion gives

<u>lizards</u>: $R_a = 1.05 \times 10^3 \, f_a \alpha_\beta^{0.67} L^{1+0.67\beta} =$

$$= f_a a_{aL} L^{b_{aL}}. \tag{12b}$$

Also using the same units as Taylor et. al. (1970), Fedak et. al. (1974) found for running birds $b_a = 0.80$ and $a_a = 2.4$. Conversion gives

<u>running birds</u>: $R_a = 3.0 \times 10^3 \, f_a \alpha_\beta^{0.80} L^{1+0.80\beta} =$

$$= f_a a_{aL} L^{b_{aL}}. \tag{12c}$$

In addition, Fedak et. al. (1974) found for all bipedal animals as a group $b_a = 0.76$ and $a_a = 12$, which converts to

<u>all bipeds</u>: $R_a = 2.3 \times 10^3 \, f_a \alpha_\beta^{0.76} L^{1+0.76\beta} =$

$$= f_a a_{aL} L^{b_{aL}}. \tag{12d}$$

We have of course no data for the dinosaurs or therapsids; but it is reasonable to suppose that activity metabolic parameters for therapsids were similar to those for modern quadrupedal mammals, that those for bipedal dinosaurs were similar to those for modern running birds and that those for quadrupedal dinosaurs were similar to those for modern lizards. Alternatively one might take the group of all modern bipeds as a model for bipedal dinosaurs, but the close phylogenetic relationship between birds and bipedal dinosaurs appears to make our choice the natural one.

In the case of the basal metabolic rate, Kleiber (1961) reports for placental mammals $b_r = 0.75$ and $a_r = 70.0$ with R in kcal day^{-1} and M in kg. For marsupial mammals b_r is nearly the same but a_r is reported as 48.6 (Bartholomew 1977, Ch. 3). Converting units,

$$\frac{R_r (J \ s^{-1}) 8.64 \times 10^4 (s \ day^{-1})}{4.19 \times 10^3 \ (J \ kcal^{-1})} = 70.0 \ [M(kg)]^{0.75}$$

or

$$R_r (J \ s^{-1}) = 3.39 \ [M(kg)]^{0.75}. \tag{13}$$

Changing to L-dependence precisely as previously,

<u>placental mammals</u>: $R_r(J\ s^{-1}) = 602\ \alpha_\beta^{0.75}[L(m)]^{0.75\beta} =$

$$= a_{rL}L^{b_{rL}}. \tag{14a}$$

For small reptiles at 30°C, the various data given by Bennett and Dawson (1976) suggest use of the values $b_r = 0.8$ and $a_r = 0.26$ for resting metabolism when R_r is in $cm^3O_2\ hr^{-1}$ and M is in gm. Conversion gives

<u>small reptiles</u>: $R_r(J\ s^{-1}) = 90\ \alpha_\beta^{0.8}[L(m)]^{0.8\beta} =$

$$= a_{rL}L^{b_{rL}}. \tag{14b}$$

For large reptiles at 30°C on the other hand, our analysis of data in Bennett and Dawson (1976) gives $b_r = 0.68$ and $a_r = 0.52$, which converts to

<u>large reptiles</u>: $R_r(J\ s^{-1}) = 35\ \alpha_\beta^{0.68}[L(m)]^{0.68\beta} =$

$$a_{rL}L^{b_{rL}}. \tag{14c}$$

We shall use the values of a_{rL} and b_{rL} for modern mammals as a guide to the situation of the therapsids, and those for large reptiles as indicative of the dinosaurs.

Finally, we require the value of the coefficient in the allometric relation for heat production, eq. (3). According to Bartholomew (1977, Ch. 8), a_c for placental mammals is 0.031 when M is in kg and C in $cm^3O_2gm^{-1}hr^{-1}°C^{-1}$. Conversion of units then gives for R_h, eq. (2),

<u>placental mammals</u>: $R_h(J\ s^{-1}) = 5.4\ \alpha_\beta^{0.5}[L(m)]^{0.5\beta}\Delta T(°C) =$

$$= a_{cL}L^{b_{cL}}\Delta T; \tag{15}$$

a_{cL} for marsupial mammals is about 20% greater than that for placentals.

We are now in position to apply the condition of balance, $R_{coll} = R_{ex}$. Combining eqs. (8), (12), (14) and (15) gives

$$f_a L^2 \sigma_0 d = f_a a_{aL}L^{b_{aL}} + a_{rL}L^{b_{rL}} + a_{cL}L^{b_{cL}}\Delta T. \tag{16}$$

In writing eq. (16) in this form, we must note the fact that animal activity raises the basal or resting metabolism contribution to total energy expenditure (Fedak et. al. 1974) by 50-70%. This can be taken into account by increasing a_{rL} by this amount. Now we rearrange eq. (16):

$$f_a = \frac{a_{rL}L^{b_{rL}} + a_{cL}L^{b_{cL}}\Delta T}{L^2\sigma_0 d - a_{aL}L^{b_{aL}}} , \qquad (17)$$

with the term in ΔT only present for endotherms operating outside their thermal neutral zone. Several points emerge at once. Increase in $\sigma_0 d$, either through an improvement in the food base or in capture ability by the animal, will diminish f_a and increase viability. This is scarcely surprising of course. A trend toward endothermy, that is an increase in a_{rL}, with no other compensating changes in the quantities in eq. (17) increases f_a and diminishes viability. The effect of variation in L on f_a is more complex, and depends critically on the values of the allometric exponents. Let us consider first the case of mammals and by implication therapsids, assuming that β is approximately 4 as argued by McMahon (1973). Then from eq. (12a) b_{aL} = 1 + 0.60 x 4 = 3.4; from eq. (14a) b_{rL} = 0.75 x 4 = 3.0, and from eq. (15) b_{cL} = 0.5 x 4 = 2.0. Substituting these values into eq. (17) and clearing common terms yields

$$f_a(\text{mammals and therapsids(?)}) = \frac{a_{rL}L + a_{cL}\Delta T}{\sigma_0 d - a_{aL}L^{1.4}} \qquad (18)$$

This result predicts that for mammal-like animals, increase in L is <u>always</u> disadvantageous if no other changes occur; there will always be selective pressure on them to decrease size, although for sufficiently small L the temperature term in the numerator of eq. (18) will dominate and the advantage of further size reduction will diminish. To gain some feeling for the size range in which this might occur for modern mammals we can perform a simple calculation. From eq. (14a) with β = 4 and α_β = 0.016, a compromise between the value of 1/27 implied by eq. (5) and that of .007 from Brody (1945), we have a_{rL} = 27 or, with a 50% "activity" augmentation, a_{rL} = 40. From eq. (15) a_{cL} = 0.7. Conceivably the average temperature deviation from the thermal neutral zone experienced by a small mammal in temperate zones might be as great as 20°C. The "thermal" term in the numerator of eq. (18) will dominate the "basal" term, removing the pressure to reduce size, if it is approximately an order of magnitude greater. To what value of L does this correspond? We set

$$(40)\, L = (1/10)(0.7)(20),$$

$$L = 0.03 \text{ m.}$$

We would therefore expect the smallest mammals to be about 3 cm in length, in approximate correspondence with observation. This does not represent an absolute physiological limit on their size in the present theory, but is merely an indication of the size range in which selective pressure in the direction of size decrease ceases to operate.

For small reptiles, the relations previously given (eqs. (12b) and (14b)) together with the guess that $\beta = 3$ may be reasonable for them yields

$$f_a(\text{small reptiles}) = \frac{a_{rL} L^{0.4}}{\sigma_0 d - a_{aL} L}, \tag{19}$$

predicting that some degree of selective pressure toward small size is present no matter what the value of L is.

These results may seem surprising in view of the frequently stated observation that small animals tend to have higher weight-specific energy consumption than large ones. But the point is that absolute efficiency in energy use does not directly increase fitness; the critical factor here is the ease with which energy can be gathered, and this favors small mammals and, apparently, small reptiles insofar as the latter possess the allometric exponents which lead to eq. (19). How, then, can large mammals, or large lizards, come into existence? The key to this in terms of our model is the factor $\sigma_0 d$ in the denominator of eq. (18) or (19). If an animal can, by increasing its size, move into an underutilized ecological niche, it may well augment $\sigma_0 d$ sufficiently to produce a net decrease in f_a. Something of this sort presumably occurred in the Paleocene, after the demise of the dominant large Mesozoic reptiles, when the great radiation and increase in size of the mammals began. The relative paucity of large lizards, especially of carnivores, at the present time may be mainly a reflection of their relative inefficiency in competing with mammals and birds for food resources, that is of a low σ_0; this suggestion has been made in a somewhat different context by Wilson and Lee (1974). The only lizards which have been able to generate large carnivores, beginning in the late Cretaceous (mosasaurs) and continuing to the present (monitor lizards) are the varanids. These animals possess an aerobic scope unusually high for reptiles (Bartholomew 1977, Ch. 8), and it is presumably this which makes them sufficiently able predators to maintain a large size.

Why Were Dinosaurs Large?

The fundamental viability relation, eq. (17), sets an unequivocal upper limit upon the size which an animal can have, so long as $b_{aL} > 2$, which appears always to be the case. If L increases to the point at which $a_{aL}L^{b_{aL}}$ approaches $L^2\sigma_0 d$, the denominator on the right hand side of the equation becomes small and f_a diverges; the animal is too large to be able to gather enough food to survive, no matter how sustained its search. Obviously no species can ever have quite reached this limit, but it should give a rough indication of the upper end of the size scale accessible to animals evolving within a given phyletic ground plan with a fixed allometric exponent b_{aL}. In the case of quadrupedal mammals, we are uncertain of the precise value of the latter and the best we can hope to do is to fix a range within which the upper limit lies. One end of the range is set by the exponent from Brody's data, $b_{aL} = 1 + 0.60 \times 4.3 = 3.58$ and $a_{aL} = 675 \times (0.007)^{0.60} = 34.4$; the other by the conventional choice $\beta = 3$ (Bartholomew 1977, Ch. 8), giving $b_{aL} = 1 + 0.60 \times 3 = 2.80$ and $a_{aL} = 675 \times (1/27)^{0.60} = 93.4$. We must also have a value for $\sigma_0 d$, the density of energy collected. The work of Odum (1971, Ch. 3) on moderately large present-day herbivorous mammals (deer) suggests a figure of about 1000 J m^{-2} for each individual in a small herd. Then the maximum possible L for the Brody choice of α_β and β satisfies

$$L^2_{max} \times 1000 = 34.4 \times L^{3.58}_{max}$$

$$L^{1.58}_{max} = 1000/34.4 = 29.1$$

$$L_{max} = 8.4 \text{ m},$$

While for the conventional choice we have

$$L^2_{max} \times 1000 = 93.4 \times L^{3.58}_{max}$$

$$L^{0.80}_{max} = 1000/93.4 = 10.7$$

$$L_{max} = 19.4 \text{ m}.$$

The largest known land mammal, <u>Baluchitherium</u> of the Oligocene, had a length of approximately 11 meters (Osborn 1923) which falls between the two calculated values. The latter

are clearly of the right order. One might wonder about
marine animals. For them a calculation is not possible
since there are no reliable estimates of $\sigma_0 d$ available, but
since a_{aL} for swimmers is only about 1/10 of the value for
quadrupedal walkers (Bartholomew 1977, Ch. 3), L_{max} for them
could be several times larger than the numbers given above.
The formalism can accomodate the existence of whales.

What then was the situation for the dinosaurs? We must
consider quadrupedal and bipedal forms separately. For
bipeds, using the "big bird" model and $\beta = 2.75$ as suggested
by the work of Colbert (1962), we have $b_{aL} = 1 + 0.80 \times 2.75 = 3.2$ and $a_{aL} = 3000 \times (0.005)^{0.80} = 43$. If the biped could
harvest about as much food energy per unit area as does a
large herbivorous mammal, then

$$L_{max}^{2} \times 1000 = 43 \times L_{max}^{3.2}$$

$$L_{max} = 14 \text{ m},$$

a figure in reasonable correspondence with the dimensions of
<u>Tyrannosaurus</u>. Admittedly the food density figure is of
dubious applicability to the case of a carnosaur. For a
quadrupedal dinosaur $\beta = 2.78$. With the "lizard" parameters
(eq. (12b)), we have $b_{aL} = 1 + 0.67 \times 2.78 = 2.86$ and
$a_{aL} = 1050 \times (0.005)^{0.67} = 30$. Again taking 1000 J m^{-2} for
the food energy per unit area,

$$L_{max}^{2} \times 1000 = 30 \times L_{max}^{2.86}$$

$$L_{max} = 59 \text{ m}.$$

This figure is about double the actual maximum size observed
for the largest saurischian herbivores. Although the uncertainties in the model preclude a firm conclusion, this discrepancy might suggest that the estimate of food energy har-
vested is too large by about a factor of 2, and that a
<u>Brachiosaurus</u> or <u>Diplodocus</u> in fact obtained only about half
as much energy per unit area of feeding ground as does a deer.
It appears unlikely that the vegetation in the swampy areas
thought to have been favored by these creatures could have
been less abundant than that in the habitàt of modern ungulates. Perhaps the large herbivorous dinosaurs utilized
nonaerobic (glycolytic) metabolism to a greater extent than
do mammals, as is the case with some modern reptiles; the
energy yield from glycolysis is only 10% of that from aerobic
metabolism (Bartholomew 1977). Alternatively the dinosaurs
may not have had as efficient a digestive mechanism as do

present day mammalian herbivores. It is also possible that
the maximum size of the largest dinosaurs was set not by
metabolic factors but instead by a limit on the ability of
limbs to support great weight.

Perhaps the most striking difference between the dinosaurs and the therapsids or mammals appears if we write the
analogue of eq. (18) for a (quadrupedal) dinosaur. Assuming
eq. (14c) to apply, we have b_{rL} = 0.68 β = 0.68 x 2.78 = 1.89.
As before, b_{aL} = 2.86 and a_{aL} = 30. Then, if no temperature
term need be included, eq. (17) takes the form

$$f_a = \frac{a_{rL}L^{1.89}}{L^2\sigma_0 d - 30L^{2.86}} = \frac{a_{rL}}{L^{0.11}\sigma_0 d - 30L^{0.97}}, \quad (20)$$

which differs from eqs. (18) and (19) in the crucial feature
that an <u>increase</u> in L will produce a <u>decrease</u> in f_a (enhanced viability), as long as L is less than the <u>optimum</u>
value L_{op} which maximizes the denominator. This maximum is
easily found by setting the derivative of the denominator
with respect to L equal to zero:

$$(0.11)\sigma_0 d \ L_{op}^{-0.89} = (0.97)30L_{op}^{-0.03}$$

$$L_{op}^{0.89} = \frac{(0.11)\sigma_0 d}{29} \ .$$

If $\sigma_0 d$ is again taken equal to 1000, L_{op} = 4.7 m. If we reduce $\sigma_0 d$ to the value needed to fit the observed maximum size
of herbivorous saurischians, L_{op} is lowered to 2.4 m.
Similar calculations, which we shall not give in detail here,
indicate that the optimum size for bipedal dinosaurs was in
the range 3 to 4 m. These numbers are in quite respectable
agreement with the sizes most commonly encountered in dinosaurs. According to the model, then, "small" dinosaur
species - these with linear dimension less than 3 m or so -
should have been under selective pressure to grow larger;
hence a successful dinosaurian challenge of the mammals for
the role of diminutive insectivore would have been just as
unlikely as a mammalian incursion into the dinosaurian size
realm. It is interesting to consider briefly the reason for
this dinosaurian growth imperative. In mathematical terms
it results from the small value of the exponent b_{rL} in the
allometric relation for the dinosaurian resting metabolic
rate; this means physically that the resting rate of dinosaurs rose slowly with increasing body mass, so that the
mass-specific metabolic rate decreased more rapidly with size
in dinosaurs than in mammals. Thus a small dinosaur had a

disproportionately high metabolic rate; by growing larger, it could improve its energy harvest at relatively low additional metabolic cost. This is exactly the argument frequently employed to account for the supposed metabolic superiority of large mammals over small ones. It is curious that while it is spurious in this connection, at least insofar as our model is valid, it may well have held for the dinosaurs.

Our model suggests that an essential factor in producing the large sizes of the dinosaurs was the smallness of the geometrical parameters α_β and β which critically influence the allometric exponents b_{rL} and b_{aL} and the coefficient a_{aL}. Small α_β and β mean a slender body; though their great bulk makes it hard to think of the dinosaurs in such terms, their bodies were graceful and elongated compared with those of most ancient (and present) mammals. The large values of α_β and β for mammals correspond to the rather compact, block-like body form which has been a persistent mammalian characteristic. That such a form should have become fixed very early in the lineage leading to mammals is easily explained if one accepts the hypothesis that maintenance of a high, stable body temperature was always of great importance in this lineage; a compact body with the smallest possible surface area is the optimal form for heat retention. One may wonder what it was that imposed this need for homoiothermy on the precursors of the mammals. The most evident interpretation is a biochemical one; that these animals became committed very early to an almost exclusive reliance on aerobic metabolism with its requirement of high body temperature for efficient function; while in contrast other reptilian groups retained a considerable dependence upon glycolytic metabolism, with its weak temperature dependence, as an energy source (Bartholomew 1977, Ch. 8).

It is evident that the considerations presented above bear strongly on the problem of endothermy and we now turn to a discussion of this issue.

Endothermy in Therapsids and Dinosaurs

The question as to whether the dinosaurs, or some of them, were true endotherms is currently a subject of spirited debate. An approach like ours cannot furnish an unambiguous resolution of this question, if for no other reason than that our conclusions depend critically on the numerical values of certain allometric exponents, quantities which cannot be known with certainty for extinct animals. However we believe that our analysis places the issue of endothermy in a new perspective.

We have suggested above that the requirement of homoiothermy imposed a compact body form upon the therapsids and
their mammalian descendants. Through its influence on the
allometric exponents b_{rL} and b_{aL} this body form was a factor
in the general selection pressure toward small size which we
claim has operated throughout therapsid-mammal evolution.
However, it also plays a role in setting the lower limit to
mammalian size previously discussed, for it helps to guarantee that loss of body heat to the environment will on the
whole be relatively greater for small mammals than for large
ones. This argument is familiar, but is it worthwhile to
recast it here in terms of L rather than M as size variable.
The "three-quarters law" for the dependence of basal metabolic rate on M in present-day mammals, together with
McMahon's (1973) relation $M \propto L^4$, implies that basal metabolic rate varies as L^3. On the other hand, mammals lose heat
at a rate varying approximately as L^2 (cf. the discussion
preceding eq. (18) above). The ratio of heat production associated with basal processes to heat loss through the body
surface thus varies as L (a result consistent with the reported tendency of the width of the thermal neutral zone to
vary as $M^{0.23}$ (Bartholomew 1977, Ch. 8), if McMahon's morphological arguments are accepted). Some of the complexity
of the situation is revealed, however, by noting that the
scaling of mammalian heat loss with size as L^2 is not the
same as a scaling with body area. The latter, following
McMahon (1973), is the product of length times girth, whereas body volume is length times (girth)^2. Assuming that volume scales as M and M as L^4, it follows that girth scales as
$L^{1.5}$ and body area as $L^{2.5}$ in mammals. We suggest that the
failure of heat loss to scale with area may be due to the
fact that limbs, which contribute a larger fraction of
total body area in large mammals then in small, have a relatively small heat loss compared with the head and trunk.
This seems to be a characteristic of endotherms (Bartholomew
1977, Ch. 8), and hence may not have held for the therapsids,
at least the more primitive ones. For a homoiothermic but
not yet endothermic therapsid, the rate of heat loss might
therefore have scaled more or less as body area, that is as
$L^{2.5}$ or so; but even so, the ratio of heat production to
heat loss through the body surface would still have increased
with size, tending to preclude the emergence of very small
varieties. It seems reasonable to conclude that the full
advantages of small size for efficient energy collection
and utilization could be realized in the therapsid-mammal
line only after the acquisition of a measure of endothermy
sufficient to maintain internal body temperatures in small
forms.

The situation for the dinosaurs may have been different

in a number of respects. According to our model, their body form helped to dictate their tendency toward large size by making b_{rL} less than 2. But if their resting metabolic rate indeed scaled as $L^{1.8}$ or $L^{1.9}$, it is likely that large size was of limited effectiveness for promoting passive homoio-thermy in their case. To see this, note that if the dino-saurs' mass and volume indeed scaled as $L^{2.8}$ or so, then by the arguments previously applied to the mammals, their girths scaled as $L^{0.9}$ and their body area as $L^{1.9}$. If their heat loss scaled with body area, therefore, their ratio of resting metabolic rate to rate of heat loss tended to dimin-ish, or at most held approximately constant, as size increas-ed. Insofar as only resting heat production is considered, large dinosaurs would then have been no better able to main-tain constant high body temperature then were small ones and the conclusion of Spotila et al. (1973) that large dinosaurs must have been effective homoiotherms in virtue of their size is by no means certain. We must however consider the alter-native possibility that the dinosaurs resembled mammals in having a rate of heat loss increasing with size less strong-ly than the body area. The explanation of this phenomenon offered above scarcely seems applicable to dinosaurs unless one regards them, too, as having been strongly homoiothermic. But the dinosaurian body form was poorly suited to passive homoiothermy and it is hard to see how a commitment to high body temperatures could have evolved in such animals unless it appeared very early, prior to adoption of the character-istic elongate body form already apparent in the thecodonts. Such early homoiothermy would probably imply that the theco-donts and dinosaurs were endothermic to a degree, for just as the transition to small size in the therapsid-mammal line must have demanded endothermy for maintenance of body tem-perature, so might have the development of a slender body in a homoiothermic thecodont stem lineage. This possibility cannot be dismissed out of hand; a capacity for endothermy must have been present in the thecodont-dinosaur lineage since it gave rise to birds (Romer 1966, Bakker 1975a). On balance, however, we believe it unlikely that the dinosaurs as a group were endothermic or even strongly homoiothermic. As far as is known, in the thecodont-derived lineage only the birds acquired a pelage, a feature present at least vesti-gially in all present-day endotherms. Moreover endothermic dinosaurs would presumably have had a ratio of metabolic heat production to heat loss which increased with size, rendering applicable the arguments of Spotila et. al. (1973); in par-ticular, the very large forms, if endothermic, would probably have run a severe risk of overheating.

It should be noted that considerable heat generation is associated with activity (Bartholomew 1977, Ch. 3); even if the dinosaurs were nonendothermic and had a resting heat production to heat loss ratio more or less independent of size, their activity-related heat production apparently scaled roughly as $L^{2.9}$ (cf. the discussion preceding eq. (20)) and hence probably produced somewhat higher body temperatures in larger forms than smaller, other things being equal.

In summary, we suggest that the therapsid–mammal lineage and the dinosaurs represented divergent strategies for the collection and utilization of energy; one opting for a slender body with its opportunities for high locomotor efficiency, the other for a compact body with high, stable temperatures and a capacity for sustained activity. Each was highly successful, in the range of body sizes appropriate to the fundamental choice of physiology. In what appears to have been an evolutionary tour de force one group, the birds, found a middle way, developing endothermy without entirely relinquishing their thecodont-derived body form.

We turn now to consideration of the detailed implications of the data shown in Figure 1. The primitive carnivorous therapsid infraorders increased in size, counter to the overall trend. It may be that this represented in part an adaptation to cooler ambient temperatures, for homoiotherms evolving in cold climates often tend to increase in size and the data for the earlier therapsids is based mainly upon the fossil record of South Africa, a region believed to have been at high latitudes during the Permo-Triassic (Gilbert Smith et. al. 1973). Perhaps Olson's "upland" stem lineage was native to regions at lower latitude; if so, Figure 1 may record successive colonizations by groups coming from warmer areas and adapting to lower temperatures in their new surroundings. Adaptation by increase in size would be especially likely in a passive homoiotherm; therefore we propose, as has McNab (1978), that the Gorgonopsia and Therocephalia, although homoiothermic, were nonendotherms. The contemporaneous stability or slight decrease in body size in the Scaloposauria and Cynodontia might mean that these advanced therapsids had already evolved toward endothermy and possessed a thermal neutral zone which they could extend by mechanisms - a pelage, for example - not involving size increase. Their short-term size increase in the Cynognathus zone - if genuine - may have represented a drift in the sense of Stanley (1973) toward occupancy of niches left vacant by the demise of the primitive therapsids.

In any case, we are left with an unsolved problem. The acquisition of endothermy is expensive; in our terms, the increase in $\underline{a_{rL}}$ which constitutes the transition to an endothermic state must always increase f_a, other things being equal. While an animal line might evolve more efficient hunters or grazers with increased energy harvesting capabilities by developing an increment of endothermy, this increase could not offset the metabolic expense involved in general or all lineages would have become endothermic. We claim that endothermy can appear only if it partially compensates an increase in f_a imposed by some change in the ecological or environmental setting, and we regard therapsid endothermy as having been an adaptive response to such an external stress. Considering the costs involved the stress must have been profound; certainly the dwindling in diversity and numbers revealed in the therapsid fossil record of the Triassic gives ample supporting evidence for its severity.

A worldwide cooling trend could hardly have been the source of the stress, for it would presumably have been dealt with by adaptive size increase, as proposed above to account for the size trends in the primitive therapsid infraorders. More plausible is the argument of McNab (1978), that size decrease itself was primary and the acquisition of endothermy a concomitant of it. What factor can have acted to promote this decrease? Certainly the general tendency toward small size which we claim is inherent in the therapsid-mammal ground plan cannot be invoked; a decrease in L accompanied by an increase in a_{rL} sufficient to maintain body temperatures would, according to eq. (18), confer no advantage in the sense of reducing f_a, except perhaps marginally for large animals. McNab's (1978) proposal that ecological competition was responsible is also inadequate, for size reduction was a general feature of carnivorous therapsid evolution, by no means limited to the Triassic when competition with the thecodonts could first have become significant. It has been suggested (McAlester 1970, Tappan 1974) that ambient O_2 decreased during the Permo-Triassic; this could have produced a stress favoring a trend to small size of the sort which occurred, as we shall now show.

Oxygen Stress and the Therapsids

We are primarily interested in the carnivorous therapsids; it was this group which exhibited the size decrease which we seek to interpret. These animals must have been able to sustain high activity rates for short periods during capture and killing maneuvers; were some factor to have reduced these maximal activity rates, the deleterious effect on viability through reduction of the term $\sigma_0 d$ in eq. (18) would surely have been severe. So far we have considered only the mean activity rate f_a; but a formulation for the maximal activity rate, f_{max} can be given along similar lines. In the short term, the availability of food is not physiolog-

ically limiting but that of oxygen is, if the animal has a
high degree of dependence on aerobic metabolism. A mammal
engaged in violent activity acquires an oxygen debt, but this
is quickly made up. Let us assume that for such activity,
the energy expenditure must be equal to the free energy
equivalent of inspired oxygen. The rigorous and detailed
calculation of oxygen extraction from inspired air is a complex matter (Otis 1964), but we shall restrict ourselves to a
simple formulation similar to that of Welch and Tracy (1977),
and take oxygen extraction per unit time as proportional to
the difference between the partial pressure of oxygen in the
lung P_{LO_2}, and the steady-state venous pressure P_{vO_2}; for
mammals P_{LO_2} is typically $0.6 P_{O_2}$, where P_{O_2} is the ambient partial pressure of oxygen. The proportionality factor
is the product of breathing frequency, lung/blood transport
coefficient and lung surface area, and the last of these,
like the basal metabolic rate, scales as $M^{0.75}$ in modern
mammals (Stahl 1967, Tenney and Tenney 1970). Lumping all
proportionality factors into a single respiratory constant
γ_r, we then have

$$\begin{array}{l}\text{amount of oxygen extracted} \\ \text{from inspired air per unit time}\end{array} = \gamma_r (0.6 P_{O_2} - P_{vO_2}) M^{0.75}. \quad (21)$$

As a model for therapsids, it is probably appropriate to select the echidna, for which considerable respiratory data are
available (Parer and Metcalfe 1967a, 1967b). According to
Parer and Metcalfe (1967b), the rate of oxygen extraction
by resting echidnas with mean body mass = 2.6 kg and
P_{vO_2} = 26.5 mmHg is 3.0 cm^3 STPD kg^{-1} min^{-1}. Their animals
were breathing approximately 10 times per minute; in mammals
the respiration rate under conditions of maximal activity
rises to about 100 times per minute. As an approximation,
therefore, we suppose that a reasonable figure to use for an
echidna in maximal activity is 30 cm^3 STPD kg^{-1} min^{-1}. Then
taking M in kg, pressures in mmHg and amount of oxygen ex-
tracted in cm^3 STPD min^{-1}, with P_{O_2} = 159 mmHg, we have
γ_r = 0.6. This figure must be converted for use in SI units
with L rather than M as size variable, and with the energy
equivalent of the amount of inspired oxygen rather than the
amount itself as dependent variable. We omit details; the
result based on our previously used "compromise" values
α_β = 0.016 and β = 4 for mammals, is

$$\begin{array}{l}R(J\ s^{-1})\ \text{(rate of energy extraction} \\ \text{from inspired air)}\end{array}$$

$$= 1.5\ [0.6 P_{O_2} - P_{vO_2}\ (mmHg)][L(m)]^3. \quad (22)$$

Now the equation governing f_{max}, assuming it to be oxygen limited, is

$$f_{max} a_{aL} L^{b_{aL}} + a_{rL} L^{b_{rL}} = 1.5 \ (0.6 \ P_{O_2} - P_{vO_2}) \ L^3,$$

or, rearranging and inserting the coefficients $a_{rL} = 27$ and $a_{aL} = 56$, obtained using the "compromise" α_β and β, and the exponents $b_{rL} = 4$ and $b_{aL} = 3.4$,

$$f_{max} = \frac{1.5 \ (0.6 \ P_{O_2} - P_{vO_2}) - 27}{56 \ L^{0.4}} \qquad (23)$$

We have not augmented a_{rL} to account for the activity effect (Fedak et. al. 1974), to compensate for the fact that the echidna basal metabolic rate is considerably lower than that of placental mammals. For the latter, it should be noted, the rate of oxygen extraction from air per unit mass is about four times as great as that of the echidna (Parer and Metcalfe 1967b), so that augmenting a_{rL} and inserting a higher, placental mammal value for P_{vO_2} (40 mmHg) would be offset by an increase in the coefficient of the pressure factor in eq. (23). The maximum activity rate predicted for the echidna by eq. (23) is about 2 body lengths per second, in reasonable agreement with observation (Griffiths 1968), and indeed most mammals have maximum activity rates in the range 2–4 body lengths per second.

The important point to note for our present purposes is that a decrease in ambient oxygen partial pressure is predicted to decrease f_{max} proportionately, but that this can be offset by a decrease in size; the dependence of L on ambient oxygen pressure, if f_{max} is to be maintained is a rather strong one:

$$L \propto (0.6 \ P_{O_2} - P_{vO_2})^{2.5} \ (\text{constant } f_{max}).$$

Thus a reduction in ambient oxygen partial pressure of 10% below the present level would demand a reduction in L by about a half in order to compensate.

The earliest mammals had a body length only about 1/10 that of typical carnivorous therapsids of the Permian. If this decrease were to be associated entirely with the proposed oxygen depletion mechanism, then the inferred drop in ambient oxygen partial pressure would have been quite enormous; if the original P_{O_2} had been like that of the present,

159 mmHg, then the required decrease would have produced a final value in Triassic time of about 90 mmHg. It must however be remembered that the time span was considerable, about 40 million years.

Conclusion

In summary, the main theme which emerges from our analysis is that of a commitment to homoiothermy acquired very early in the therapsid-mammal lineage, probably as a result of a strong dependence on aerobic metabolism. In the earlier members of the lineage, the imperative toward temperature maintenance was primarily expressed through a compact body form. This body form in turn contributed to a general selective pressure in favor of small size which we claim has been operative throughout therapsid-mammal evolution. We do not attribute the extreme size decrease which occurred in the course of the therapsid-mammal transition to this pressure, but rather to a specific environmental stress - a gradual decrease in atmospheric O_2 levels acting throughout the Permo-Triassic - which imposed a small body size on carnivorous therapsids and made endothermy adaptive as a secondary consequence. In contrast to the therapsids, the thecodont-dinosaur lineage early developed a body form which we argue reached its optimum metabolic efficiency in rather large animals and permitted giantism on a scale not possible for land mammals. There seems to be no compelling reason to postulate endothermy in the dinosaurs as a group, and their domination of the large animal role during the Mesozoic can be adequately explained without it.

These ideas are, no doubt, provocative in some ways. They do possess the virtue of being grounded in a concrete, if oversimplified, model capable of yielding quantitative results. Our reasoning admittedly contains tenuous elements and many of the numerical quantities employed in our calculations are uncertain; nevertheless it seems to us that those of our quantitative conclusions for which comparison with fossil data is possible are sufficiently in accord with reality for our conceptual framework to be taken seriously. We believe that it places many of the problems of Paleozoic and Mesozoic paleontology in a new and useful perspective.

Acknowledgment

The authors are grateful to E. C. Olson, J. W. Schopf and R. D. K. Thomas for their advice, encouragement and criticism, which have been invaluable to us in the preparation of this work.

Appendix: Table of Symbols

Symbol	Quantity Denoted	Units
	allometric coefficients:	implicit
a	general allometric coefficient	
a_c	thermal conductance-body mass	
a_{cL}	thermal conductance-body length	
a_r	basal or standard metabolic rate-body mass	
a_{rL}	basal or standard metabolic rate-body length	
a_a	activity metabolic rate-body mass	
a_{aL}	activity metabolic rate-body length	
	allometric exponents:	none
b	general allometric exponent	
b_c	thermal conductance-body mass	
b_{cL}	thermal conductance-body length	
b_r	basal or standard metabolic rate-body mass	
b_{rL}	basal or standard metabolic rate-body length	
b_a	activity metabolic rate-body mass	
b_{aL}	activity metabolic rate-body length	
	metabolic and energy rates:	$J\ s^{-1}$
R	general metabolic or energy rate	
R_h	mean rate of heat production for body temperature maintenance by endotherm outside thermal neutral zone	
R_{coll}	mean rate of energy collection	
R_{ex}	mean rate of total energy expenditure	
R_r	basal or standard metabolic rate	
R_a	mean activity metabolic rate	
	thermal parameters:	
C	animal thermal conductance to environment per unit mass	implicit
T_a	ambient temperature	°C
T_b	animal deep body temperature	°C
ΔT	$T_b - T_a$	°C

Appendix: Table of Symbols (continued).

Symbol	Quantity Denoted	Units
body parameters:		
L	body length	m
L_S	skull length	mm
		(in Figure 1)
L_{op}	optimum body length	m
L_{max}	maximum body length	m
M	body mass (but denotes <u>Morganucodon</u> in Figure 1)	kg
V	body volume	m^3
α	proportionality factor in "classical" length-volume relation: $\alpha \equiv VL^{-3}$	implicit
α_β	proportionality factor in generalized length-volume relation: $\alpha_\beta \equiv VL^{-\beta}$	implicit
β	exponent of length in generalized length-volume relation: $V \propto L^\beta$	none
other quantities:		
d	energy resource density	$J\ m^{-2}$
f_a	mean activity rate	s^{-1}
f_{max}	maximal activity rate	s^{-1}
$\overline{v}$	mean speed of travel	$m\ s^{-1}$
σ	cross section for energy location and capture	m
σ_0	σL^{-1}	none
γ_r	respiratory constant	implicit
P_{LO_2}	lung partial pressure of oxygen	mmHg
P_{vO_2}	venous partial pressure of oxygen	mmHg
P_{O_2}	ambient partial pressure of oxygen	mmHg
X	arbitrary allometrically scaling parameter	

10

Relative Brain Size in Dinosaurs

Implications for Dinosaurian Endothermy

James A. Hopson

Abstract

Because vertebrate brain size varies in proportion to the 2/3 power of body size, the huge dinosaurs
appear to have been extraordinarily small-brained creatures.
However, Jerison (1969, 1973) has argued that when the
allometric relationship is taken into account, dinosaurs are
seen to have possessed brains of expected reptilian size.
My recent analyses of relative brain sizes among dinosaurs,
reviewed and extended here, indicate a clear correlation
between the degree of encephalization and inferred locomotor
speed, agility, and overall activity. Sauropods have by
far the smallest brains, ankylosaurs and stegosaurs have
relatively small brains, and ceratopsians have brains of
intermediate size, while large ornithopods (Iguanodon and
hadrosaurs) and theropods have the largest brains.
Calculation of an "encephalization quotient" (EQ, the
ratio of measured brain size to "expected" brain size for
a standard archosaur of the same body size) indicates that
all dinosaurs except coelurosaurs had relative brain sizes
within the range of living reptiles. Coelurosaurs,
however, had EQ values within the lower part of the
mammalian-avian range. Following a suggestion of Bauchot
(1978), that allometric scaling of brain weight to the 2/3
power of body weight produces overestimates of expected
brain weight for very large vertebrates, I recalculate EQ
for dinosaurs using Bauchot's "corrected" body weights. For
the larger dinosaurs, this procedure raises EQ two- to
three-fold, bringing the large ornithopods and carnosaurs
into the range of the most encephalized living reptiles.
This is also the EQ range of cynodont therapsids, advanced
mammal-like reptiles of the Triassic which are generally
believed to have been partially endothermic. Living
endothermic vertebrates (mammals and birds) possess brains
which are, on average, about ten times larger than those of
living ectotherms (fishes, amphibians, and reptiles),
suggesting a link between activity levels, intensity of

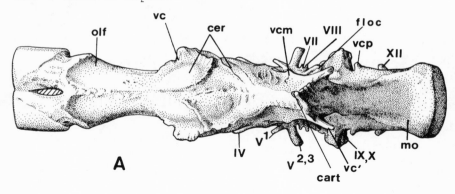

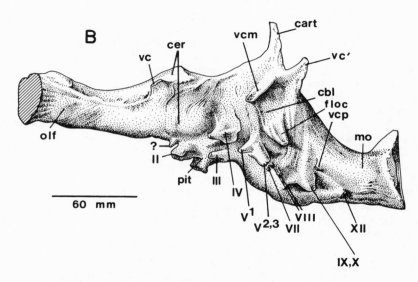

Figure 1. The endocast of Tyrannosaurus rex (redrawn from Osborn 1912). A. Dorsal view. B. Lateral view. Abbreviations: cart, filling of the space for the cartilaginous portion of the supraoccipital; cbl, cerebellar region; cer, cerebrum; floc, flocculus; mo, medulla oblongata; olf, olfactory bulb; pit, proximal portion of the pituitary fossa; vc, minor vascular canal; vc', branch of the longitudinal sinus; vcm, middle cerebral vein; vcp, diverticulum of longitudinal sinus; II, optic nerve; III, oculomotor nerve; IV, trochlear nerve; V^1, ophthalmic branch of the trigeminal nerve; $V^{2,3}$, maxillary and mandibular branches of the trigeminal nerve; VII, facial nerve; VIII, auditory nerve; IX, X, foramen for the glossopharyngeal and vagus nerves; XII, hypoglossal nerve; ?, unidentified process.

metabolism, and relative brain size. The evidence of
relative brain size, combined with the bone histological
evidence of Ricqlès (1974), suggests that most dinosaurs
were intermediate in their metabolic rates between living
reptiles and mammals. Only the coelurosaurs may possibly
have been as metabolically active as living endotherms.
I support Feduccia's (1973) contention: the brains of
reptilian size found in most dinosaurs indicate that Bakker's
claim of mammalian-level endothermy in all dinosaurs cannot
be accepted.

Research reported here was supported in part by National
Science Foundation Research Grants BMS 75-01159 and
DEB 77-25339.

Introduction

The prevailing conception of dinosaurs as small-
brained, slow-witted creatures originated one hundred years
ago with the first description, by O. C. Marsh (1878), of
an internal cast of the brain cavity in the skull of a
dinosaur.

On the basis of the endocranial cast of the sauropod
Morosaurus (now Camarasaurus), Marsh declared that this
dinosaur had possessed a brain which was smaller, in
proportion to the animal's size, than that of any other
known vertebrate. Shortly thereafter, however, Marsh (1880)
described the endocast of Stegosaurus ungulatus, recognizing
a new candidate for the bearer of "the smallest brain".
This conclusion was based on the observation that the
"brain-cast" of a young alligator was about one tenth of
the size of that of Stegosaurus, whereas the dinosaur was
overall about 1000 times larger than the alligator. Hence,
the ratio of brain to body size in Stegosaurus was some
100 times less than that of an alligator! Marsh was aware
that small animals in general have proportionately larger
brains than do large animals, admitting that "this
comparison gives, of course, only approximate results".
Nevertheless, he repeatedly cited the small relative brain
sizes of the gigantic Mesozoic reptiles in support of his
"general law of brain growth". This "law" asserted that
the brains of mammals, over the course of the Tertiary,
and of birds and reptiles from the Jurassic to the present
day show progressive increase in size (Marsh 1886, pp.
58-59).

Most writers following Marsh have likewise dwelt on
the small sizes of dinosaur brains in relation to the
enormous bulk of their bodies. Certainly, when simple

ratios of inferred brain and body weights are compared
between dinosaurs and living reptiles, the dinosaurs
invariably suffer in the comparison. The inadequacy of the
dinosaur brain is one of the best-known "facts" of both the
popular and technical literature of paleontology. This
tiny, supposedly inadaptable brain has been cited as an
important factor in the extinction of the dinosaurs (cf.
Swinton 1970, p. 278), an idea repeated countless times in
popular accounts.

Edinger (1961) severely attacked the proclivity of
paleontologists to equate the small size of dinosaur brains
with maladaptation and, more generally, to attribute great
biological significance to relative brain size. She
pointed out that in living snakes, for example, the brain
of a large python "is an infinitesimal part of the body"
while "the smaller a snake, the larger its relative brain
size". Yet she supposed that the differences in relative
size among their brains mean nothing to the snakes
themselves. In other words, the brains of snakes are
functionally equivalent, irrespective of their sizes in
relation to the body, and the same must undoubtedly have
been true of dinosaurs. Furthermore, Edinger (1961, p. 74)
perceptively noted that, as the dinosaurs had lasted for
over 100 million years, "does it not follow that they were
very well served by their, indeed, relatively tiny brains?"

Like Marsh, and many later paleontologists, Edinger
implicitly recognized the negative allometric relationship
between brain size and body size in vertebrates: larger
vertebrates tend to have relatively smaller brains than do
smaller-bodied members of the same broad taxa. Yet among
vertebrates of comparable body size, it is also observed
that absolute brain size may show a great deal of variation.
The problem, then, is to distinguish between the component
of difference in brain size that is attributable to
difference in body size and that which may reflect a
differential capacity for processing information. As
pointed out by Jerison (1973, p. 41-42), brain size can
only be used as a measure of what we may call "intelligence"
if we can isolate these factors. Jerison has developed
quantitative methods, discussed below, for the comparative
study of the degree of encephalization in vertebrates.
Similar methods have also been developed by Bauchot (1972)
and his colleagues (Bauchot et al. 1976, 1977; Platel 1974,
1975).

Jerison (1969, 1973) analyzed the allometry of brain
size among dinosaurs, concluding that once the effect of
their large body sizes was discounted they could be seen

to have had brains of typically reptilian size. Hence, his
main inference was that dinosaurs fit the common pattern
for "lower" vertebrates (bony fishes, amphibians, reptiles),
which possess a well-defined and characteristic range of
information-processing capabilities. Only in birds and
mammals, the so-called "higher" vertebrates, has a different
relation between brain and body size evolved, resulting in
approximately a ten-fold increase in average brain size
over that of the "lower" vertebrates.

Jerison's data and analysis of dinosaur brain sizes
have been brought to bear on the current controversy over
whether dinosaurs were endotherms or ectotherms. Feduccia
(1973),disputing Bakker's (1971) claim that dinosaurs were
as endothermic as living mammals and birds, pointed out
the great disparity in relative brain size between dinosaurs
and these extant endotherms. He argued that "the greatly
increased motor and sensory control, which would be
prerequisite for Bakker's presumed greatly increased
dinosaurian activity, is not to be deduced from the dinosaur
brain"(Feduccia 1973, p. 168). Dodson (1974) and Bakker
(1974, 1975a) have replied that some dinosaurs (e.g.
certain coelurosaurs) did indeed possess brains within the
mammalian-avian size range, but for the great majority of
dinosaurs Feduccia's observation stands.

I made a further study (Hopson 1977) of relative
brain size in dinosaurs and concluded that the different
subgroups show characteristic levels of encephalization,
which are correlated with activity levels inferred from
the functional interpretation of skeletal morphology.
I inferred from relative brain sizes that most dinosaurs
were less active than living mammals and birds and that
their metabolic rates were below those of living endotherms.
Possible exceptions were the coelurosaurian theropods, some
of which had brains within the size range of those of
comparably sized living endotherms (see also Russell 1969,
1972).

Recently, Bauchot (1978) has suggested that the
allometric scaling of brain weight to the two-thirds power
of body weight, which closely fits the empirical data for
small and medium-sized vertebrates, does not hold for
very large vertebrates, which have smaller brains than
predicted by this relationship. He proposes a correction
factor to linearize the data over all body sizes, which
brings the brain/body relations of large vertebrates more
into line with the expectations derived from behavioral
observations (Bauchot 1978, p. 11). Application of
Bauchot's correction factor to the brain and body size

data for dinosaurs serves to increase the degree of
encephalization of all taxa, in some cases to a substantial
degree. This has implications for the relation of relative
brain size to possible endothermic metabolism in these
giant reptiles.

   In this paper I shall briefly review the treatments
of relative brain size in dinosaurs presented by Jerison
(1969, 1973) and myself (Hopson 1977). I shall then
reassess the same and additional data, using Bauchot's
"corrected" body weights for large vertebrates. Evidence
from other groups of fossil tetrapods will be considered
in a reevaluation of the following arguments, first
presented by Feduccia (1973) and later supported by me
(Hopson 1977): (1) a consistent relationship exists
between activity level, intensity of metabolism, and
relative brain size; (2) on the basis of the relative
sizes of their brains, most dinosaurs were not as
endothermic as are living mammals and birds.

The Study of Relative Brain Size
in Fossil Vertebrates

   It is now generally recognized that large vertebrates
tend to have smaller brains in proportion to body size
than do small vertebrates. Yet it has long been clear
that a rat with a brain to body weight ratio of almost
1/100 is not more intelligent than a horse with a brain/
body weight ratio of 1/1000. As pointed out by Gould
(1975b, p. 245), "any assessment of cephalization must
take absolute body size into account; it must compare
actual brain size with expected brain size for animals
of that body size."

   Jerison (1969, 1970, 1973) has devised a method
which compensates for the effect of body size, allowing
independent comparisons of brain size to be made among
species and higher taxa. A logarithmic plot of brain/body
weight data for a large series of living vertebrates
shows two separate clusters of points, a lower one for
bony fishes, amphibians, and reptiles, a higher one for
birds and mammals. The principal axis of each cluster
is a line of best fit with a slope of approximately 2/3.
Hence, the relationship of brain size (weight or volume)
to body size for a large series of distantly-related
species is represented by the allometric equation:

$$E = k.P^{2/3} \tag{1}$$

where E is brain size, P is body size, and k is a constant

equal to the value of E when P = 1. The higher the value of k, the larger the brain at any given body size.

Levels of encephalization among members of a group are determined by comparing the measured brain size of a given animal with the "predicted" brain size expected for an animal of the same body size, based on the data for the group as a whole. An "encephalization quotient" (EQ) is calculated from the equation:

$$EQ = E_i/E_e \qquad (2)$$

where E_i is the measured brain size and E_e is the expected brain size as determined from Equation 1.

A plot of brain size against body size for a large sample of living mammals yields a cluster of points with a principal axis such that k = 0.12 (Jerison 1973; see Fig. 4). In the following comparisons of encephalization among reptiles, birds, and mammals, the standard against which all species, living and fossil, will be compared is the expected brain size for an "average" mammal of the same body size, determined by the equation:

$$E_e = 0.12 \ P^{2/3} \qquad (3)$$

For comparisons within the Reptilia, I shall use a "typical" archosaur standard, established by passing a line of slope 2/3 through the center of a cluster of points for three living crocodilians (see Fig. 2). For this line, k = 0.005.

The display and comparison of clusters of data points can be simplified by the enclosure of points for individual taxonomic groups within minimum convex polygons. These are polygons of minimum areas, defined by lines joining outlying data points, with no internal angles greater than 180 degrees (Jerison 1969; 1973). Such polygons, enclosing data points for various groups of living vertebrates, can be used as a basis for the interpretation of data for fossil vertebrates. Encephalization quotients for fossil vertebrates can be calculated using EQ values predicted from living groups as standards.

Brain sizes of extinct vertebrates can be determined from their endocasts. Those of mammals and birds provide nearly exact replicas of their brains, because in these groups the brain fills the cranial cavity almost completely. The brains of reptiles generally do not fill the cranial cavity; consequently the endocast does not accurately

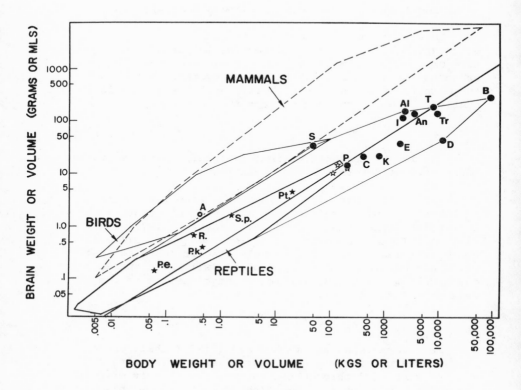

Figure 2. Brain/body size relations in dinosaurs, pterosaurs and the Jurassic bird Archaeopteryx superimposed on minimum convex polygons for living reptiles, birds, and mammals. Scale is log-log. The line with slope 2/3 passes through the approximate center of points for living crocodilians (open stars). Data and key to abbreviations for dinosaurs (closed circles) are presented in Table 1. Data on pterosaurs is from Jerison (1973), on Archaeopteryx from Hopson (1977). Figure reproduced, with permission, from the Annual Review of Ecology and Systematics, Volume 8. c 1977 by Annual Reviews Inc. New data for the endocast of Brachiosaurus (Table 1) indicates that the point for this genus should lie the same distance below the line of slope 2/3 as that for Diplodocus. Abbreviations: PTEROSAURS (solid stars) - P.e., Pterodactylus elegans; P.k., Pterodactylus kochi; Pt. Pteranodon sp.; R., Rhamphorhynchus; S.p., "Scaphognathus" purdoni. BIRD (starred circle) - A, Archaeopteryx.

mirror the size and shape of the brain (Fig. 1). In
fossil reptiles it is therefore necessary to represent
brain size as some fraction of the total volume of the
endocast. Jerison (1969, 1973) used half the volume of
the endocast to represent brain volume in dinosaurs and
therapsids, since the brain fills approximately half the
cranial cavity in the living reptiles Sphenodon and
Iguana. He noted, however, that the fraction of the cranial
cavity of dinosaurs occupied by the brain is itself likely
to have been a negative function of body size (Jerison
1973, p. 144), decreasing with increasing body size. If
this were so, as Gould (1975) rightly pointed out, the
size of the brain in increasingly larger dinosaurs would
tend to be systematically over-estimated. My studies
(Hopson 1977, in press) of the endocasts of living and
fossil archosaurs suggest that the relationship between
brain and endocast sizes, as a function of body size, is
quite variable across a broad taxonomic spectrum. The
endocasts of large dinosaurs may reflect the form of the
brain in as much detail as do those of much smaller living
crocodilians. It is doubtful that the brain ever occupies
less than about 60 percent of the cranial cavity in
larger crocodilians. Since their endocasts are usually
as "brainlike" as those of large crocodiles, I consider
this to be a reasonable (although undemonstrable) minimum
limit for fossil archosaurs. Nevertheless, except where
noted, I have used Jerison's estimate of 50 percent as a
minimum in my analyses of dinosaur brain size.

Estimates of the body sizes of fossil vertebrates
are usually determined from scale models (e.g., Colbert
1962) or from equations, derived empirically from living
species, which relate body weight to body length (Jerison
1973). Like Jerison, I have relied mainly on Colbert's
(1962) estimates of dinosaur body weights, although I
acknowledge that in some cases (but not in all) these
estimates are probably too high. Bakker (1975a, b)
provides independently-determined estimates for several
of the same genera. For some, such as Diplodocus and
Stegosaurus, his body weights are greater than Colbert's;
for others, notably Brachiosaurus, they are less. The
estimates of body size utilized in this study are listed
in Table 1.

Relative Brain Size in Dinosaurs

Comparisons Among Dinosaurs

Brain and body size data for at least one member of
each suborder within the Saurischia and Ornithischia

TABLE 1.   Estimated brain volume (E_i), body volume (P), and Encephalization Quotient (EQ) for 12 genera of dinosaurs. Brain volume is equal to half the endocast volume except in the case of the sauropods and the coelurosaur (see text). EQ is determined with reference to an archosaur standard (equation 4).   Except where noted, brain volumes are from Jerison (1973) and body volumes from Colbert (1962). Letters in parentheses following each name refer to the abbreviations in Figure 2.

	E_i (ml)	P (tons)	EQ
CARNOSAURIA:			
Allosaurus (Al)	168	2.3	1.90
Tyrannosaurus (T)	202	7.7	1.04
COELUROSAURIA:			
Stenonychosaurus (S)	37[a]	.045[c]	5.80
SAUROPODA:			
Brachiosaurus (B)	174[a]	87.0	0.17
Diplodocus (D)	47[a]	11.7	0.18
ORNITHOPODA:			
Anatosaurus (An)	150	3.4	1.30
Camptosaurus (C)	23	0.4	0.83
Iguanodon (I)	125	2.1[d]	1.50
ANKYLOSAURIA:			
Euoplocephalus (E)	41[a]	1.9[e]	0.52
STEGOSAURIA:			
Kentrosaurus (K)	24[a]	0.78[d]	0.56
CERATOPSIA:			
Protoceratops (P)	15[a]	0.2	0.88
Triceratops (Tr)	150[b]	9.4	0.67

[a] Original determinations.
[b] From Lull (1933).
[c] From Russell (1969).
[d] Calculated using Colbert's values for larger related taxa.
[e] From Bakker (1975b).

are presented in Table 1. These data are also plotted
in Figure 2, superimposed on minimum convex polygons
for living reptiles, birds, and mammals. Brain size has
been taken as half the size of the endocast, except in
the case of the sauropods. The endocasts of sauropods
are anteroposteriorly compressed and transversely
widened; their shapes suggest that the brain may have been
closely confined within the cranial cavity. I have therefore utilized the size of the entire endocast (excluding
the cast of the large dorsal fontanelle which is present
in most sauropods) to represent brain volume. Note that
the values for brain volumes of the sauropods listed in
Table 1 are much lower than those given by Jerison (1973,
Table 7.1). This difference reflects the fact that I
have excluded those portions of the endocast which represent
spaces external to the cranial cavity proper.

Brain size for the coelurosaur <u>Stenonychosaurus</u> is
based on a partial endocast, with the remainder of the
brain modeled on that of a crocodilian. Control on its
overall proportions is provided by the braincase of the
closely-related <u>Saurornithoides</u> (Barsbold 1974). The
forebrain of this and other coelurosaurs shows evidence
of having filled the cranial cavity and of having been
atypically large, compared with other reptiles (Hopson
1977, in press). The relative brain size of
<u>Stenonychosaurus</u> was within the range of those of living
birds (Fig. 2), as was independently determined by
Russell (1969).

Dinosaur encephalization quotients are also listed
in Table 1. The ranges in EQ recorded for the individual
suborders of dinosaurs (with the saurischian suborder
Theropoda further subdivided into the infraorders
Carnosauria and Coelurosauria) are displayed in Figure 3.
The reference line here (EQ=1.0) is determined by the
equation:

$$E = .005 \ P^{2/3} \tag{4}$$

which is based upon the brain/body size relations of living
crocodilians. This standard is used because crocodilians
are the closest living reptilian relatives of dinosaurs.

The EQ values of dinosaurs show a poor correlation
with body size, except for the subgroups with the lowest
and highest values. I have argued that the ranking of
dinosaurs in order of increasing EQ likewise ranks them
in order of increasing locomotor speed and agility, as
inferred from skeletal structure (Hopson 1977). There is

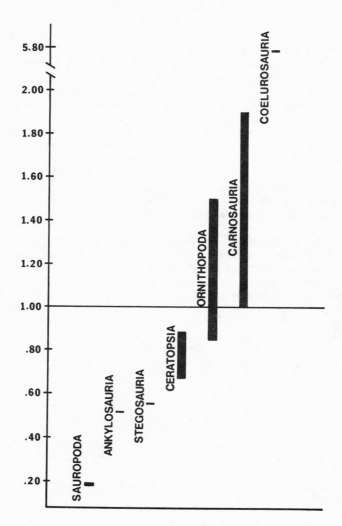

Figure 3. Encephalization Quotients (EQ) for the suborders of dinosaurs (infraorders Carnosauria and Coelurosauria in the suborder Theropoda), calculated with reference to the line with the equation $E = .005 \ P^{2/3}$ in Figure 2. Living crocodilians lie at 1.00. Note the break in the scale between 2.00 and 5.80. Modified from Hopson (1977). Reproduced, with permission, from the Annual Review of Ecology and Systematics, Volume 8. © 1977 by Annual Reviews Inc.

also a correlation between EQ and prior conclusions (my own and those of other paleontologists) about the degree of behavioral complexity that was probably characteristic of each subgroup of dinosaurs. The significance of these behavioral correlations with relative brain size cannot, of course, be tested independently. However, these interpretations gain support from comparable correlations between degrees of encephalization and specialization for particular ways of life among living species in several major vertebrate groups (e.g. lizards, Platel 1974, 1975; elasmobranchs, Bauchot et al. 1976, Northcutt 1977; teleosts, Bauchot et al. 1977; mammals, Jerison 1973).

The behavioral factors which I interpret as having had a significant influence on relative brain size in dinosaurs are: carnivorous/herbivorous feeding habits, bipedalism/quadrupedalism (and associated differences in locomotor speed and agility), active/passive mechanisms of defense against predators (and the relative importance of detecting predators at a distance), as well as the possible use of the forelimbs as grasping organs and the development of more or less complex social behavior.

Sauropods were very large to gigantic quadrupedal herbivores, with limb proportions much like those of elephants, but generally much larger. It is reasonable to believe that their enormous body weights limited them to slow locomotor speeds (Alexander 1971, 1976). The very low EQ values (0.17 - 0.18) of sauropods were probably also importantly affected by their enormous body sizes, comparable to those of all but the largest living species of whales. The influence of large size beyond that taken into account in the scaling of EQ is discussed below.

The armored ankylosaurs and plated stegosaurs had low EQ values (0.52 - 0.56) which are correlated, I believe, with the possession of armor and tails armed with effective weapons. Their limb proportions indicate slow speeds, suggesting that the defensive armor and tail weapons were their principal means of coping with predators. It is possible that a keen awareness of the environment was not as essential to members of either group as it would have been to an unarmed herbivore which relied on early detection and speedy flight to escape.

The large quadrupedal ceratopsians, whose great heads were armed with long forwardly-directed horns, relied on active defensive strategies, both in warding off predators and in intraspecific combat (Farlow and Dodson 1975).

Although I doubt that ceratopsians galloped in the manner advocated by Bakker (1967, 1971), I believe they were capable of faster locomotor speeds and greater agility of movement than were the ankylosaurs and stegosaurs. Their larger brains appear to be correlated with their greater activity.

Encephalization in the larger bipedal ornithopods was comparable to that of the large predatory carnosaurs. Endocasts indicate that the forebrains of hadrosaurs and of Iguanodon were extremely large for dinosaurs. These large herbivores lacked defensive weapons and would have had to rely on acute senses and relatively fast running speeds to escape from carnivores. Further, the interpretation of the cranial crests of hadrosaurs as visual and acoustic display structures, used in intraspecific social interaction, suggests that these dinosaurs engaged in complex patterns of social behavior.

The theropods were all carnivorous and average brain size was greatest in this group of dinosaurs. They were the only obligate bipeds among the dinosaurs, with their forelimbs thus freed to become adapted as grasping organs. Correlated with the habitual bipedalism of theropods is the presence only in this group of a large floccular lobe on the cerebellar region of the endocast (Fig. 1). An enlarged flocculus (concerned with balance) is found elsewhere among the amniotes only in mammals, birds, therapsids, and pterosaurs. These are all known, or presumed, to be very active, partially- to fully-erect terrestrial or aerial vertebrates. The large carnosaurs such as Tyrannosaurus had small forelimbs, of limited use in the capture and killing of prey. Their EQ values, high for dinosaurs, were still within the range of those of living reptiles, broadly overlapping the EQ range of the large ornithopods. The small theropods of the infraorder Coelurosauria, on the other hand, had by far the largest brains in relation to their body sizes of any reptiles described to date. The EQ of Stenonychosaurus (for which EQ = 5.8 is a minimum value, since at 45 kg the body weight is undoubtedly an overestimate; Bakker 1975b) lay well outside the range of living reptiles and within the range of living birds. Relative brain size has not been determined for other coelurosaurs, but the large size of the endocast (or of the cranial cavity) has been noted in the closely-related Saurornithoides (personal observation), ornithomimids (Russell 1972), Oviraptor (Osmolska 1976), and Dromaeosaurus (Colbert and Russell 1969).

Factors which I believe resulted in selection for very large brain sizes in coelurosaurs were their predaceous feeding habits (with relatively small, fast-moving vertebrates as their principal prey), extremely fast running speeds and great agility of movement (Ostrom 1969), and the evolution of grasping hands, which in some species were associated with binocular vision (Russell 1969). I suggest that selection acted upon the central nervous systems of these active hunters to improve the coordination between rapid movements of the hands and visual information about the spatial position of small rapidly-moving prey.

The evidence provided by dinosaurs supports the hypothesis that the degree of encephalization among vertebrates is related to the demands of particular ecological niches. This idea has been advanced by Jerison (1973) and by Bauchot and his co-workers for a variety of vertebrate groups. From this point of view, larger and more complex brains evolved as adaptations for coping with the information-processing requirements of specific ways of life.

Comparisons With Other Vertebrates

In order to compare values of EQ for dinosaurs with those of other groups of vertebrates, I have recalculated them using the "average" mammal (Equation 3) as a standard of comparison. These values are presented in Table 2. The highest value, EQ = 0.24 for Stenonychosaurus, lies within the range of those found in living birds and mammals. The other values, extending from a low of 0.007 for the two sauropods to a high of 0.078 for Allosaurus, all lie well within the range of living reptiles. These data would seem to suggest that activity levels of dinosaurs were comparable to those of living reptiles. However, before conclusions are drawn on the relationship between EQ and activity levels in dinosaurs, an attempt should be made to correct for the residual effect of large body size on relative brain size, which may possibly have been substantial.

Bauchot (1978) has suggested that application of the standard allometric equation, using a slope of 2/3 to calculate expected brain sizes, yields values of EQ that are too low for large vertebrates. They are, in fact, much lower than would be expected from knowledge of the behavior of large species as compared with that of their smaller relatives. For instance, the relative brain sizes of large whales are comparable to those of the most primitive insectivores, among the least encephalized of

TABLE 2. Encephalization Quotients (EQ) for 12 genera of
dinosaurs recalculated using the "average" mammal (equation
3) as the standard of comparison. To remove the residual
effect of large body size, EQ values recalculated using
"corrected" body weights as determined by Bauchot (1978)
are also presented.

	EQ (Mammal standard)	"Corrected" EQ
CARNOSAURIA:		
Allosaurus	.078	.146
Tyrannosaurus	.042	.100
COELUROSAURIA:		
Stenonychosaurus	.240	.250
SAUROPODA:		
Brachiosaurus	.007	.070
Diplodocus	.007	.022
ORNITHOPODA:		
Anatosaurus	.054	.120
Camptosaurus	.034	.045
Iguanodon	.060	.100
ANKYLOSAURIA:		
Euoplocephalus	.020	.032
STEGOSAURIA:		
Kentrosaurus	.028	.033
CERATOPSIA:		
Protoceratops	.036	.045
Triceratops	.027	.075

living mammals; yet in their behavior, the large whales
would not be expected to differ greatly from the smaller
whales and porpoises, which are among the most
encephalized of mammals. Bauchot has sought to correct for
this discrepancy between the degree of encephalization
measured by EQ and the observed complexity of behavior
(whence the inferred level of intelligence) in large
mammals. He introduced a correction factor for brain:body
weight determinations "that modifies as little as possible
the values for species of average or small body weight but
corrects progressively for species of high body weight"
(Bauchot 1978, p. 4). He determined "corrected" body
weights by applying the equation for a hyperbolic tangent
to data for artiodactyles of a wide range of body sizes.
Generalizing from these data, he derived a table of
"corrected" body weights, running from .1 gram to 100 metric
tons.

I have substituted these "corrected" body weights in
Equation 3, to determine "corrected" EQ values for the
dinosaurs; these are presented in Table 2. It can be
seen that for the larger dinosaurs, excluding the enormous
Brachiosaurus, EQ values increase two- to three-fold, as
a result of this correction. However, for the most part
the ranking of the various suborders does not differ from
that shown by the uncorrected values. Brachiosaurus, with
an estimated weight of about 80 tons (Colbert 1962), shows
a ten-fold increase in EQ when the "corrected" weight is
utilized. This elevates its EQ into the ceratopsian range.
Bauchot (1978, p. 7) notes that at very large body weights,
his curve finally begins to decrease; thus, the function
"becomes invalid at a value for body weight almost equal
to the largest body weights known." As the smaller
sauropod, Diplodocus, with an uncorrected body weight of
about 12 tons, continues to be the least encephalized of
dinosaurs, it is likely that the spectacular increase in
the corrected EQ of Brachiosaurus may be primarily due to
an unrealistically low, overcorrected body weight.

Among the more encephalized of the non-coelurosaurian
dinosaurs, such as carnosaurs and advanced ornithopods,
EQ is approximately doubled by the correction factor,
raising these taxa to the level of the most encephalized
reptiles. The implications of these data for the possibility of endothermy in at least some dinosaurs are
discussed in the next section.

Relative Brain Size and
Endothermy in Vertebrates

I have suggested that endothermic vertebrates must
have larger brains than ectothermic vertebrates (Hopson
1977) because: (1) the much greater maintenance energy
requirements of living endotherms require more intense
activity over more extended periods of time than is
necessary for ectotherms; and (2) increased levels of
activity have led to selection for more complex perceptual
abilities and precise sensorimotor control mechanisms,
requiring larger brains. It follows that the order of
magnitude increase in rates of energy consumption seen in
avian- and mammalian-level endotherms, over those which
presumably characterized their ectothermic ancestors, would
require the evolution of brains as large and complex as
those of living birds and mammals.

My previous analysis of relative brain size in
dinosaurs (Hopson 1977) led me to conclude that most
dinosaurs were less active than modern endotherms,
suggesting that their metabolic rates and total energy
budgets were lower than those of modern birds and mammals.
Only coelurosaurs, with EQ in the avian range, were
possibly as endothermic as are living birds and mammals.

As a partial test of the hypothesis that there is a
causal relationship between the energetic demands of
endothermy and increased encephalization, it must be shown
that: (1) a clear separation exists between the EQ ranges
of living ectotherms and endotherms, as well as those of
fossil species which, on the basis of taxonomic and other
criteria, fall unequivocally into one category or the other;
and (2) fossil species which are reasonably considered to
have been partly or incipiently endothermic should exhibit
brain/body weight ratios which plot close to or within
the space which separates the polygons of undoubted
ectotherms and endotherms, in Figure 2. All living birds
and mammals are undoubted endotherms, as almost certainly
were all post-Jurassic fossil members of these groups. The
status of Archaeopteryx has been the subject of disagreement
and very little information is available about Triassic
and Jurassic mammals. Unequivocal ectothermic tetrapods
include all living and fossil amphibians and all living
reptiles, as well as the extinct members of the surviving
reptilian orders. At present we must consider the metabolic
levels of the extinct orders of archosaurs and marine
reptiles to be uncertain.

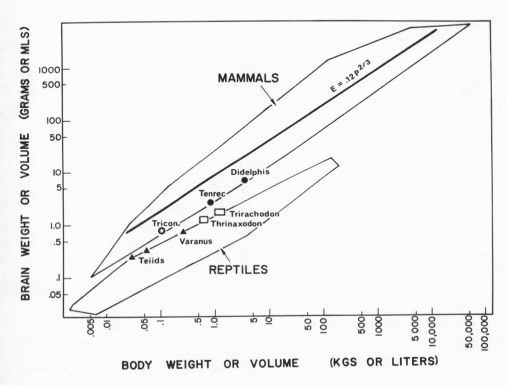

Figure 4. Brain/body size relations in the cynodont therapsids Thrinaxodon and Trirachodon (open rectangles) superimposed on minimum convex polygons for living reptiles and mammals. Points for two of the least encephalized living mammals and the most encephalized living reptiles, plus the late Jurassic mammal Triconodon, are included for comparison. Scale is log-log. Line with slope 2/3 is the approximate central axis of the mammal polygon, as determined by Jerison (1973). Mammal data from Jerison (1973); reptile (lizard) data from Platel (1974, 1975).

There is no overlap in brain/body weight, between the minimum convex polygon for living reptiles and those of living birds and mammals (see Fig. 2). There is a slight overlap in EQ between the most encephalized reptiles (small teiid lizards) and the least encephalized bird (the large ostrich), but application of Bauchot's correction factor to these data effects a separation. Fossil birds and mammals, at least from the Early Cretaceous onward, may be expected to have been as fully endothermic as the most primitive living members of these groups; their values of EQ ought therefore to be distinctly higher than those of living ectotherms. Jerison's (1973) analysis of relative brain size in the Late Jurassic mammal Triconodon indicates that this genus had an EQ within the range of living mammals (Fig. 4). No data are available for Cretaceous mammals, but Jerison (1973) calculated EQ for a number of archaic ungulates of the Paleocene and Eocene. In many of these taxa, Jerison's EQ is below 0.20, reaching as low as 0.11 for a species of Coryphodon.

The highest values of EQ for living lizards are listed in Table 3 (data from Platel 1974, 1975). Clearly there is a substantial overlap between these values and Jerison's results for early Tertiary mammals. However, Radinsky (1978) has reanalyzed the brain/body size data for early Tertiary mammals, concluding that, with one exception (Titanoides, EQ = .19 to .24), EQ is above 0.20 in all archaic ungulates. This is at the upper limit of the reptilian range (Ameiva sp., EQ = 0.21), but it should be noted that these lizards have body weights of 50 g or less, whereas the early Tertiary mammals under consideration had body weights estimated from 10 to over 1000 kg. Again, Bauchot's (1978) analysis suggests that this overlap is a result of differences in size not resolved by the use of EQ.

Cynodont therapsids (advanced mammal-like reptiles) and Archaeopteryx (the earliest known bird) are among those extinct groups which, because of their phylogenetic proximity to living endotherms and their possession of anatomical characters believed to be related to the possession of endothermy, can reasonably be expected to have been partially endothermic. Jerison (1973) presented an analysis of relative brain size in three therapsid genera, the cynodonts Thrinaxodon and Diademodon and the dicynodont Lystrosaurus. His points for brain/body size relations showed a spread from the upper to the lower border of the reptile polygon; he therefore concluded that therapsids "were reptilian and not mammalian with respect to the evolution of their brains" (Jerison 1973, p. 154). This

TABLE 3. Brain weight (E_i), body weight (P), and
Encephalization Quotient (EQ) of two cynodont therapsid
species and the three most encephalized species of living
lizards studied by Platel (1974, 1975). EQ is determined
with reference to a mammalian standard (equation 3).
Maximum and minimum values are presented for the brain and
body weight estimates of the cynodonts.

	E_i (g)	P (g)	EQ
CYNODONT THERAPSIDS:			
Thrinaxodon liorhinus	1.1-1.4	550-700	.12-.17
Trirachodon kannemeyeri	1.5-1.9	1000-1500	.09-.15
LIVING LIZARDS			
TEIIDAE:			
Ameiva sp.	0.23	27.1	.21
Callopistes trimaculatus	0.32	50.3	.19
VARANIDAE:			
Varanus griseus	0.72	254.2	.15

view is disputed on the basis of many details of brain
structure by Olson (1976), who sees the increasing development of mammalian characteristics in the brains of evolving
therapsid lineages. My own analysis of the brain sizes of
two cynodont species (Table 3) differs from that of Jerison
in that I take 80-100% of the endocast volume to represent
the volume of the brain, because the surface modeling of
the cast indicates that the cranial cavity was very closely
molded to the brain. Body weights were determined from
body lengths, using an equation relating weight to length
in living Carnivora (Radinsky 1978). The body weights
so determined are very close to those used by Jerison;
both maximum and minimum values were used in my analysis.

The brain/body weight values for the cynodonts
Thrinaxodon and Trirachodon plot on or slightly above the
upper border of the reptilian polygon (Fig. 4). An
independent analysis of brain/body size relations in
cynodonts by Dr. Juan C. Quiroga (pers. comm.) corroborates
these results. Therefore, it is safe to conclude that
relative brain size in cynodont therapsids was intermediate
between those of living ectothermic reptiles and endothermic mammals. These data provide the best available
evidence in support of the proposed correlation between
EQ and the degree of endothermic metabolism.

Jerison (1973) analyzed relative brain size in
Archaeopteryx and determined that it fell slightly above
the reptile polygon, but still well below the range of
living birds. My reanalysis of Archaeopteryx (Hopson
1977) indicates that this protobird falls just within the
polygons of living endotherms (Fig. 2). With EQ = 0.26,
Archaeopteryx lies within the range of living birds.

Pterosaurs were probably at least partially endothermic, being active flyers with an insulatory coat
(Wellnhofer 1977). Unfortunately, the information available
for pterosaurs is the least reliable for any of the groups
so far considered. Jerison (1973) analyzed relative brain
size in five pterosaur species, but he expressed reservations about the brain size estimates of all but one,
Scaphognathus (= Parapsicephalus) purdoni. The EQ
determined for this species is 0.11, relatively high for
a reptile, although still within the reptilian range. All
of the points for pterosaurs lie within the upper half of
the reptile polygon (Fig. 2), but only two lie close to
the upper border. These data cannot be considered either
to support or contradict the suggested correlation between
EQ and degree of endothermy. A new analysis of brain/body
size relations in pterosaurs, based upon brain size

determinations from actual specimens, rather than published
drawings, and on body size estimates made from scale models
(as suggested by Jerison 1973, p. 170), is much to be
desired.

Making allowance for the effects on EQ of large body
size and variation in body proportions, the evidence
indicates that fully-endothermic tetrapods show a substantial increase in relative brain size over that seen in
ectothermic tetrapods. Where reliable data exist, it can
be shown that partially endothermic fossil taxa (cynodont
therapsids, Archaeopteryx) lie at or above the levels of
the most encephalized of living ectotherms (see Figs. 2
and 4). Among the dinosaurs, only the coelurosaur
Stenonychosaurus, with a "corrected" EQ = 0.25, falls
unequivocally within the range of living endotherms. The
carnosaurs and large ornithopods, with "corrected" EQ
values ranging from 0.10 to 0.146, lie within the range of
the most encephalized living reptiles and the cynodont
therapsids. All other dinosaurs lie well below this level
(EQ from 0.02 to 0.075).

I interpret the significance of relative brain size in
dinosaurs as follows: if the brain required by a vertebrate
is primarily a function of its total level of activity and
therefore reflects its total energy budget, then
coelurosaurs appear to have been metabolically as active as
living birds and mammals, carnosaurs and large ornithopods
appear to have been less active but nevertheless
significantly more so than typical living reptiles, and
other dinosaurs appear to have been comparable to living
reptiles in their rates of metabolic activity. On the
other hand, evidence from bone histology (Ricqlès, 1974,
this volume) suggests continuous rapid growth rates in all
dinosaurs, which in turn suggest elevated metabolic rates
compared with those of living reptiles. These contradictory results lead me to believe that all dinosaurs were
metabolically more active than are living reptiles and
that, in conjunction with the thermal inertia of their
great bulk, they were all endotherms of a sort. However,
every elevated metabolism need not be comparable to those
of living birds and mammals, as Ricqlès (1974) points out.

On the evidence of relative brain size, it is
unlikely that dinosaurs could have maintained the high
levels of activity and continuous high rates of energy
expenditure that are characteristic of avian and mammalian
endotherms. Therefore, I conclude that dinosaurs, with
the possible exception of the coelurosaurs, were
intermediate in their metabolic level between living

reptiles on the one hand and living endotherms on the other. My analysis does not support the view, consistently maintained by Bakker in numerous publications, that dinosaurs were as metabolically active as living mammals and birds.

11

An Alternative to Dinosaur Endothermy

The Happy Wanderers

Nicholas Hotton III

Abstract

The characteristically large size of dinosaurs obscures the distinction between ectothermy and endothermy, for which most criteria are size-dependent. Predator/prey ratios are not discriminative because ectothermic and endothermic metabolic rates converge with increasing size. Bone histology, to the extent that it reflects thermal physiology, means only that dinosaurs were different from living reptiles, not that they were similar to mammals. Water conservation and locomotor refinement were more important than thermal strategy to dinosaur success. Endothermy was only the means by which mammals avoided competition with dinosaurs. The role of size distinguishes dinosaur evolution from that of known endotherms. Large size reflects reduced rates of heat transfer, and erect posture reflects heat production through activity, in combination styled "dinosaur-grade inertial homoiothermy" Hatchlings were large enough to be incipient inertial homoiotherms, or became so after one or two seasons' growth. Small dinosaurs could hibernate or aestivate. Distribution, vagility, and seasonal climates indicate seasonal migration, which was probably integral to thermal strategy as well as to feeding and reproduction. Given world-wide temperature decline, the difference in thermal strategies between dinosaurs and contemporary terrestrial tetrapods may have determined the extinction of one and survival of the rest.

Statement of the problem

Dinosaurs are reptiles distinguished by a fundamentally birdlike morphology, erect posture, and large adult size. They were generally terrestrial, and more active than the

conventional stereotype of reptiles. All of these features
except size are foreshadowed in the radiation of thecodonts
during the Early and Middle Triassic. Dinosaurs arose from
thecodont ancestors near the end of the Middle Triassic,
coincident with the decline of the previously-dominant
therapsid reptiles. By the Late Triassic they had become
the dominant terrestrial tetrapods of moderate and large
size, a position they maintained for the following
140,000,000 years (Ostrom this volume). Extinction was
relatively sudden, and dinosaurs had evidently been extinct
for some time before mammals began to enter large-tetrapod
niches.

Dinosaur thermoregulation is usually treated in terms
of thermal constancy due to large size, as by Wieland
(1942); Colbert, Cowles, and Bogert (1946); Colbert
(1951); Hotton (1963); Heath (1968); Spotila, Lommen,
Bakken, and Gates (1973); and McNab and Auffenberg (1976).
Less commonly, it is said to involve a degree of automatic
endothermy, as by Schuh (1951); Russell (1965); Ostrom
(1969, this volume); Ricqlès (1969, 1974, 1976, this
volume); and Bakker (1971, 1972, 1975a, b, this volume).
Bakker's current thesis, that all dinosaurs were
endothermic, homoiothermic analogues of living birds and
mammals, is broader, more eclectic, and presented in greater
detail than any other. It is also more extreme than most,
and despite its thought-provoking scope is incomplete, both
as to premises and as to formulation of the problem. For
all of these reasons, a critical summary of Bakker's
synthesis provides an appropriate point of departure for the
development of an alternative model.

Bakker's argument proceeds from two premises. One,
unstated, is reflected in his treatment of ectothermy and
endothermy as though they were the sole, mutually exclusive
alternatives of thermal strategy (Bakker 1975a, b; non
Bakker 1971). The other is his contention that the
dominance of endotherms in living and fossil faunas
indicates an intrinsic competitive advantage of endothermy
over ectothermy. The problem, he says, lies in the failure
of mammals, as endotherms, to rise to dominance when the
therapsids declined, and in their long subordination to
dinosaurs (Bakker 1975a). From his premises he argues that
the success of dinosaurs is paradoxical if they are
regarded as merely "good reptiles" on the model of living
lizards, but is readily explained if they were in fact
automatic endotherms on the model of living mammals.

Ectothermy and endothermy appear to be mutually exclusive opposites only when conventional contrasts between them are emphasized at the expense of overlap and variation (Table 1). They look more like the extremes of a graded, if incomplete, series when due account is taken of overlap and variation in living amniotes (e.g.: Bennett 1973a, b; Crompton, Taylor, and Jagger 1978; McNab 1978). The claim that endothermy is intrinsically advantageous accounts neither for the coexistence of small ectotherms and endotherms in modern deserts and rain-forests, nor for the existence of living ectotherms adapted to feed on endotherms (Feduccia 1973). Together, Bakker's premises limit thermal strategies to unrealistically simple roles in the interactions among extinct tetrapods, and foreclose the possibility that dinosaur size reflects a strategy that was neither ectothermic nor endothermic by conventional definition.

The incompleteness of Bakker's argument is illustrated by his formulation of the problem as a paradox. Like all paradoxes, this one arises as a consequence of asking the wrong question, essentially: "How could the dinosaurs have gained dominance over mammals and maintained it for 140,000,000 years unless they, too, were automatic endotherms?" This formulation discounts an historical answer, and therewith much relevant data, for the relationship between dinosaurs and Mesozoic mammals has its roots in the well-documented displacement of therapsids by dinosaur lineages during the Triassic.

A functional argument for dinosaur endothermy is advanced on the basis of metabolic cost (Bakker 1975a,b): endotherms need an order of magnitude more food than ectotherms, in order to supply the fuel that is burned physiologically to maintain a constantly high body temperature. This requirement is said to be reflected in predator/prey ratios of about 3% in dinosaur faunas, which are comparable to those of living mammals and in marked contrast to the 40% to 50% predator/prey ratios of living and fossil ectotherms. The histological patterns of dinosaur bone (Ricqlès this volume) are said to indicate rates of growth, and of resorption and redeposition of inorganic salts, comparable to those of mammals rather than of ectotherms, reflecting the faster turnover of calcium carbonate and phosphate at higher and more constant metabolic rates. Erect posture (= vertical orientation of the femur, sensu Charig 1972), is supposed to imply levels of activity and endurance more nearly compatible with the physiology of living endotherms than of living ectotherms

Table 1. Thermal strategies of living tetrapods. For
sources see text, and figures as indicated.

Components	Contrasts	
	Ectothermy	Endothermy
Body temperature	High level maintained only during activity. Fluctuates with ambient temperature when animal is inactive (poikilo-thermic).	High level maintained irrespective of activity. Constant, independent of ambient temperature (homoio-thermic).
Chief source of heat	Environmental, controlled by behavior.	Metabolic, controlled by physiological means. ("automatic").
Aerobic metabolism (standard metabolism) $M_{std} = ccO_2/gh$	"Low."	About 6 times as high as in ectothermy.
Thermal conductance	High, no insulative integument; in small forms facilitates heat uptake but prevents retention of internal heat.	Low because of hair, feathers, or subcutane-ous fat; helps con-serve internal heat.
Metabolic scope	Narrow, most ecto-therms more dependent on anaerobic path-ways during activity.	From 4 to 10 times as broad as most ecto-therms; endothermic active metabolism chiefly aerobic.

Table 1. (continued)

Overlapping or Common Features

Optimum close to lethal levels. More nearly constant in large ectotherms than in small. Inconstant in young birds and mammals and in hibernating adult mammals.

Behavior vital to both for heat dumping; endotherms also use behavior for absorption of environmental heat.

Highest in viscera and CNS. Difference proportional to concentration of mitochondria. Control mediated in midbrain by comparable structures. Response to fever-producers similar (Kluger 1978). Declines with size increase (Fig. 2). Can be shut off: bats, sloths, and hibernating mammals function at intervals as ectotherms.

Declines with increase in size; overlaps in larger ectotherms and endotherms (Fig. 3).

Difference declines with size increase, may reflect difference in mitochondrial concentration, as does M_{std}. Varanid condition obscures contrast between ectotherms and endotherms: much broader than in other ectotherms, perhaps in part because of more elaborate lung structure and pulmonary circulation.

(Bakker 1971). These criteria, being of necessity defined
by reference to living tetrapods, apply primarily to small
animals. Since they are strongly affected by increasing
size, they are poorly definitive when applied to animals as
large as dinosaurs.

The most direct evidence on which dinosaurs can be
interpreted consists of their distinctive history, size,
and locomotor structure. Concentration on these features
shows, first, that dinosaurs and their ancestors enjoyed
many advantages over their respective contemporaries that
were independent of a putative endothermy; second, that much
of the evidence for automatic endothermy in dinosaurs is
equivocal; and third, that alternative thermal strategies
and life-styles available to dinosaurs may well have been
as exotic as their body form, the like of which no man has
ever seen.

Triassic interactions: dinosaurs vs therapsids

Thecodonts and dinosaurs probably contributed heavily
to the decline and extinction of therapsid reptiles during
the Triassic. They could do this because of two adaptations
that were highly advantageous in the increasingly arid
environments of the time: they were more effective water
conservers than therapsids, and they were more vagile. It
was not necessary that members of dinosaur lineages also be
automatic endotherms, for as Bakker (1971) notes, the
therapsids were characterized by extremely conservative
locomotor systems, and few of them had advanced very far
toward the endothermy of their mammalian descendants.
Bakker's later contention that therapsids had been "fully
endothermic" since the beginning of their dominance in the
Late Permian (Bakker 1975a) is not well-founded. If
endothermy played a role in Triassic competition, it was
probably as the factor which saved the emerging mammals
from the extinction that overtook the rest of the
therapsids.

Water conservation in living vertebrates is a function
of nitrogen excretion. Mammals excrete nitrogen almost
exclusively as urea, which requires flushing with copious
quantities of water, while birds and reptiles excrete it
primarily as uric acid, which is evacuated as a slurry
(e.g. birds) or as a nearly dry pellet (e.g. lizards) and
involves little loss of water. The primitive condition,
utilized by nearly all vertebrates except birds and
reptiles, is excretion of urea or ammonia or some

combination of the two (amphibians excrete ammonia during larval life, urea after metamorphosis). The derived condition, excretion of uric acid, probably arose not much later than the Early Permian, as indicated by its presence in turtles and Sphenodon.

Urea and ammonia excretion are also associated with an aquatic habit, and considerable adaptive variation is reflected in their employment: crocodilians excrete ammonia as well as uric acid, and some turtles alternate between urea and uric acid, depending on the dryness of their environment (Schmidt-Nielsen 1975). The converse is true only for two desert-dwelling amphibians that have shifted to uric acid production (Schmidt-Nielsen 1975). It is not true of desert-dwelling mammals, which save water only by the less effective expedient of concentrating urine to the limited extent allowed by the urea-excreting process.

Dinosaurs, having arisen among the ancestors of living reptiles and having given rise to birds (Ostrom 1976), are bracketed between the two groups to which excretion of uric acid is restricted, and it is therefore probable that they also excreted uric acid and were water conservers. Therapsids, on the other hand, represent a stock that was independent of other reptilian lineages since the Early Pennsylvanian, presumably prior to the origin of the uric acid process. As they include the direct ancestors of mammals, which even today are limited to an apparently primitive mode of nitrogen excretion, the most parsimonious interpretation is that therapsids were like the mammals, water-prodigal excretors of urea.

Locomotor mechanisms were more advanced in the Late Permian and Early Triassic ancestors of dinosaurs than in therapsids. Heleosaurus is an eosuchian satisfactory as an ancestor to Euparkeria (Carroll 1976), which in turn is a good candidate for ancestry of the Saurischia, though not of the Ornithischia (Ewer 1965). These small animals resembled living bipedal lizards in details of the hip joint, in limb proportions, and in body form, and were probably facultative bipeds; both approached the erect posture and parasagittal limb motion of dinosaurs. All therapsids were obligatory quadrupeds, generally with more or less sprawling, wide-track gaits reminiscent of pelycosaurs.

The combination of a water-prodigal mode of nitrogen excretion with archaic locomotor mechanisms suggests that most therapsids did not live far from permanent water, and that their dominance of the Late Permian and Early Triassic

faunas was restricted to riparian and other well-watered
environments. The bulk of terrestrial environments would
have remained open to such tetrapods as the immediate
ancestors of dinosaurs, which possessed the requisite
water-conserving and locomotor abilities to exploit them.
The earliest terrestrial thecodonts may have been insect-
eaters which followed their prey (also water-conservers)
into progressively drier environments, in a Triassic
continuation of the process suggested by Olson (1976) for
Permian tetrapods.

The characteristic dinosaurian refinements of locomotion, erect posture and (in many forms) obligatory
bipedality, apparently evolved in more open upland environments, as dinosaurs at first diversified well away from
competition with most therapsids. Gorgonopsians were the
only therapsids to approach erect posture and parasagittal
limb motion, and may have represented an attempt by
therapsids to penetrate such an environment. Their
extinction at the end of the Permian, well before the
decline of less vagile therapsid stocks, may have foreshadowed the ultimate failure of therapsids in direct
competition with dinosaurs.

Toward the end of the Middle Triassic dinosaurs had
begun to emerge from the environments in which they had
originated, or perhaps were carried along by the expansion
of the environments themselves, as arid climates became
more widespread. In any case, they were able to compete
successfully with therapsids wherever they came into extensive contact with them. By this time, dinosaurs had gained
an edge in size as well as in water conservation and
locomotion.

With these advantages, dinosaurs did not need
endothermy, for the evidence of gross morphology suggests
that therapsids did not become automatically endothermic
until the end of the Triassic. From the end of the Early
Permian their progress in this direction was erratic as well
as gradual. Olson (1944) identified 24 characters evolving
toward mammalian states of expression, but at very different
rates in diverging therapsid lineages, with much
parallelism. He suggested that this parallelism reflected
adaptation to a common selective factor, for which he
postulated a physiological change, incipient homoiothermy,
that coincided with the origin of therapsids (Olson 1959).
In its evolution, morphology must have exerted reciprocal
effects on the physiological novelty to which it was
adapted, so that the latter evolved with a comparable

variability of rates in different lineages. The combined states of morphological characters must therefore indicate the quality and variation of thermoregulatory advance.

On this basis, thermoregulation in therapsids as a whole was extremely variable, which is consistent, given its proximity to its origin, with the thermoregulatory variability of living mammals. It was also of relatively low grade, which contradicts the contention that therapsids had been "fully endothermic" from the time of their origin (Bakker 1975a, b). Bakker's argument is based on the appearance, in the earliest therapsids, of vascularized cortical bone similar in complexity and diversity of histologic pattern to that of mammals (Ricqles 1976). This argument cannot deal with the potential variability of therapsid thermoregulation, because the variation of bone histology in mammals does not correspond to known endo-thermic alternatives, but rather to difference in age, body size, and modes of locomotion (Currey 1962; Bouvier 1977). Without an evaluation of variability, it cannot be said that therapsid bone histology reflects thermoregulation like that of mammals, but only thermoregulation different from that of pelycosaurs. This requires a more conservative inter-pretation of therapsid bone histology, perhaps as an indicator of the beginning of advanced thermoregulation (Olson 1976), which in any case is more nearly consistent with other lines of evidence.

Therapsid thermal strategy was not sufficiently advanced to pose a problem of competition to any of a broad spectrum of animals which were ectothermic by the criterion of bone histology. Parieasaurs, procolophonids, and a variety of early diapsids flourished in some degree of competition with therapsid faunas during the Late Permian. Throughout the Triassic, aquatic thecodonts were probably major predators of therapsids in the riparian environments the latter had dominated since the beginning of the Late Permian. Rhynchosaurs, which became larger and more common during the Middle Triassic when they evolved an herbivorous habit, radiated at the expense of large, herbivorous, dicynodont therapsids. Some of the early terrestrial thecodonts, which according to Bakker (1975a) were ectothermic, may also have been involved, if only peripherially, in some kind of interaction with therapsids.

It is only among very advanced therapsids of the Late Triassic that the majority of gross morphological characters approach mammalian levels of expression. These animals, unlike other therapsids, were probably approaching

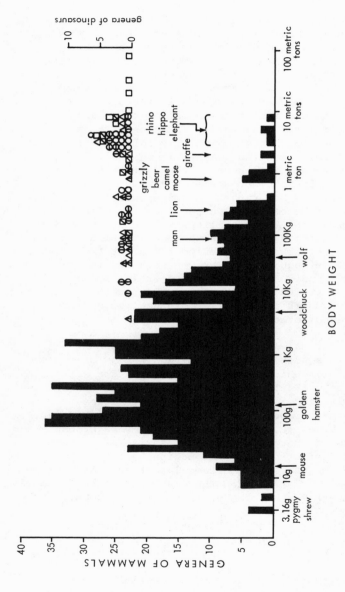

Figure 1. Size distribution (body weight), mammals and dinosaurs. Mammalian data from Walker and Paradiso (1975). Dinosaur data from: Bidar, DeMay, et Thomel (1972); Bonaparte (1976); Colbert (1962, 1963, 1970); Galton (1970a, b); Gilmore (1920); Haughton (1924); Lull (1933); Lull and Wright (1942); Osborn (1924); Osborn and Mook (1921); Ostrom (1969); Raath (1969, 1970, 1972); Santa Luca, Crompton, and Charig (1976); Thulborn (1972). Symbols: □, sauropods; ☒, prosauropods; △, carnosaurs; ▲, coelurosaurs; ○, hadrosaurs; ⏀, iguanodonts and Stegosaurus; ⏀, ceratopsians.

mammalian automatic endothermy, for they were distinguished
not only by advanced character states, but also by small
size (cf. Hopson 1973; Crompton, Taylor, and Jagger 1978).
They were survivors of the Triassic sorting-out of
therapsid lineages, which Olson (1944) compares with a
filter which passed only the most mammal-like forms; some
of them were ancestral to later Mesozoic and Tertiary
mammals. Since the sorting-out seems largely the work of
thecodonts and dinosaurs, it is probable that ancestral
mammals survived primarily because their small size and
endothermy admitted them to niches that were inaccessible
to dinosaurs.

As automatic endothermy was the strategy by which the
earliest mammals escaped the dinosaurian predation and
competition that had overwhelmed their forebears, so it
remained for the next 140,000,000 years. Mammals survived
that interval, not in spite of the dinosaurs, but because
ecological interaction between them and dinosaurs was
minimal. This negates Bakker's postulate of competitive
suppression of Mesozoic mammals by dinosaurs. It looks as
though the requirements of endothermy (Hopson 1973;
Crompton, Taylor, and Jagger 1978; McNab 1978) were more
important than potential competition with dinosaurs in
keeping mammals small during the Mesozoic. This
possibility, and the failure of dinosaurs to penetrate
small-tetrapod niches, suggest that thermal strategies of
dinosaurs were different from those of mammals.

Size, metabolic rates, and predator/prey ratios

Adult sizes attained by more than half of the
dinosaurs (Fig. 1) equal or exceed those of the 2% of
extant mammalian genera of largest individual size. The
smallest known dinosaur, with a live weight of about 4 kg,
was larger than 70% of living mammals. Since this specimen,
and others of comparable size, are the remains of juveniles,
it is possible that the minimum adult weight of dinosaurs
was closer to 10 kg (Bakker 1971), which is larger than 80%
of living mammals.

Size-dependent metabolic rates provide the connection
whereby endothermy of dinosaurs is inferred from fossil
predator/prey ratios comparable to those of the generally
smaller mammals (Bakker 1975a, b). A necessary assumption
is that food requirements are so strongly determined by
metabolic rates that their regressions are the same. A
second assumption, made by Bakker (e.g. 1975a) but rejected

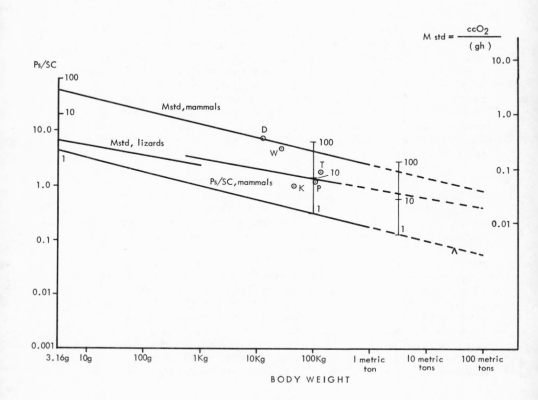

Figure 2. Regressions of standard metabolism, M_{std}, on body
weight for ectotherms (lizards) and endotherms (mammals),
plotted against regression of secondary productivity, Ps/SC
on body weight for mammals. Regressions of predator M_{std}
are assumed to indicate scaling of food requirements as well
as oxygen consumption, with size increase. All regressions
are in the form log Y = log a + b log X: log Y = log (M_{std}
of ectothermic or endothermic predators), or log (Ps/Sc of
potential prey); log X = log (body weight in grams); log a =
Y-intercept; b = slope of regression = rate of decline of
M_{std} or Ps/SC, with increasing size. General procedure
from Bakker (1975a). Parameters of regressions from the
following sources: mammal M_{std}, Schmidt-Nielsen (1975);
"small lizard" M_{std}, Bennett and Dawson (1976); "large
lizard" M_{std}, McNab and Auffenberg (1976); Ps/SC, Farlow
(1976). Values for specified predators based on raw data
on food consumption provided by W. Auffenberg (oral comm.
1978): D, Cape wild dog; W, wolf; T, tiger; P, puma;
K, Komodo monitor.

here, is that the regressions of metabolic rates on body weight for ectotherms and endotherms do not converge. Slopes are equal and the lines parallel, so that metabolic differences, and therefore differences in food requirements, remain the same irrespective of size.

This assumption is unacceptable because its rationale (Hemmingsen 1960) is not appropriate to the problem at hand. Hemmingsen examined metabolic similarity across broad boundaries, but rejected potential differences between relatively limited taxonomic groups. He noted that the slope of the combined regressions of an enormous variety of organisms was the same in ectothermic as in endothermic organisms, the lines differing only in y-intercept. Because of its apparent universality, he regarded this slope as a biological constant, speculating that it was related to requirements of respiration. A more recent attempt to explain the slope as a universal value involves structural constraints of size on biological proportions, and hence on metabolic rates (McMahon 1973). Hemmingsen reported small deviations from this slope in most of the organisms he studied, but dismissed them as statistically insignificant, due to faulty procedure, or temporary effects of unusual circumstances in ontogeny or microevolution.

However, it is probable that deviations are not fortuitous in principle, but rather reflect a measure of adaptive leeway within the constraints emphasized by Hemmingsen and McMahon. McNab (1974), for example, demonstrates that slopes change consistently in a variety of small predatory mammals, values being dependent on whether the animals are larger or smaller than the characteristic size of the groups to which they belong. He concludes that the slope is sensitive to immediate biological demands. In lizards, slopes of the regression of metabolic rates on body weight appear in general to be less steep than the well-documented value of -0.25 for mammals; the most consistent value for lizards tested at 37° C is about -0.18 (Fig. 2, standard metabolism, M_{std} = ccO_2/gh; Bennett and Dawson 1976; see legend for other sources).

Accordingly, the regression of ectothermic M_{std} on body weight converges moderately toward that of endothermic M_{std}. Otherwise, the following model is intended to conform as closely as possible to the procedure of Bakker (1975a). Food requirements of predators are met in nature by the secondary productivity (Ps) of potential prey animals. Secondary productivity is the rate of increase in

biomass, by growth and reproduction, necessary to maintain
a constant population, or standing crop (SC), of prey
animals in the face of predation and other causes of
mortality, assuming an ecological steady state. It is
conventionally expressed as a percentage of the prey
standing crop (Ps/SC). Predator/prey ratios, by definition
percentages of the prey standing crop, reflect the
proportionate biomass of predators that can be supported by
a given prey population. The distance between the M_{std}
lines of lizards and mammals (Fig. 2), determined by the
marked difference in metabolic rates of those animals,
theoretically represents the difference between ectothermic
and endothermic predators in food requirements. The Ps/SC
line is plotted below the line of M_{std} for ectothermic
predators; it is so positioned at the ordinate, that the
vertical distance to a point on either M_{std} line is
proportionate to the theoretical prey biomass needed to
support one unit of predator biomass, of which the
reciprocal is the predator/prey ratio. The value of this
vertical distance is selected so that predator/prey ratios
conform to the specification of Bakker (1975a) at the
smallest body weights: at that point, predator/prey
ratios are 50% for ectotherms and 2% for endotherms
(Table 2).

At the smallest body weights (3.16 g), the graph
indicates that endotherms require over an order of magnitude more food (about 24 times more) than ectotherms,
having been set up to conform to Bakker's views regarding
the disparity in food requirements (Bakker 1975a, b). But,
with converging regression lines, the predicted food
requirement of an endothermic predator the size of a large
Komodo monitor (100 kg) is no more than 6 times that of an
ectothermic predator, well within an order of magnitude.
At the modal size of dinosaurs (3.16 metric tons), the
food requirement of an endotherm is less than 4.5 times
that of an ectotherm (Table 2). Predator/prey ratios,
which change in concert with these values, are now 8% for
ectotherms and 2% for endotherms, a distinction which is
probably too small to be detected in fossil data.

The values upon which this conclusion is based are no
more than the crudest of approximations, but their trend is
conservative when compared with biomass data for monitor
lizards on the island of Komodo, generously provided by
Walter Auffenberg (oral comm. 1978). These data (Table 3)
yield predator/prey ratios that are indistinguishable from
those of endothermic predators. Ratios range from 0.8% to
2.96%, depending on whether the potential prey taken into

Table 2. Food requirements estimated from Figure 2: procedure adapted from Bakker (1975a), see text. Column I: prey biomass necessary to support a single unit of predator biomass, assuming ecological steady state. Column II: endotherm values of Col. I expressed as multiples of ectotherm values. Column III: predator/prey ratios, reciprocals of values in Col. I, or predator biomass that can be supported by a given biomass of prey SC. Values for specified forms, i.e. Komodo monitor, Cape wild dog, wolf, puma, and tiger, from raw data on food consumption provided by W. Auffenberg (oral comm. 1978).

Body weight	I — Biomass of prey SC necessary to support 1 unit biomass of predator.		II — Data from Col. I, endo./ecto.	III — Predator/prey ratio	
	Ecto.	Endo.		Ecto.	Endo.
3.16 g	2.02	47.59	23.58	.50	.02
45.00 kg	8.22	49.72	6.02	.12	.02
Cape wild dog, 18 kg		54.75	13.49		.02
Wolf, 27 kg		45.96	11.32		.02
Monitor, 45 kg	4.06			.25	
Puma, 105 kg		7.65	1.88		.13
Tiger, 136 kg		14.49	3.57		.07
100.00 kg	8.98	51.59	5.75	.10	.02
3.16 tons	12.75	56.72	4.45	.08	.02

Table 3. Biomass of Komodo monitor lizards, <u>Varanus</u> <u>komodoensis</u>, and potential prey, Island of Komodo. Data from Auffenberg (oral comm. 1978).

	Est. mean biomass/km^2 (kg)	Potential prey	Biomass, monitor/prey
Deer	1205		
Boar	1236		
		All	.008
Green jungle fowl	40		
		Ungulates, birds	.030
Freycinet's megapode	4		
Komodo monitor	75	Rodents, locusts, birds	.011
Rodents	2125		
Locusts	4604		

account are large (chiefly artiodactyls), small (chiefly rodents and locusts), or inclusive.

Food consumption data for five predators including a 45 kg Komodo Monitor, also provided by Dr. Auffenberg, are compared with the predator/prey ratios predicted by the converging regressions of Figure 2. Values for canids fall comfortably on the endotherm regression, and the value for the monitor is not too far below the ectotherm line, but the placement of the felid values on the ectotherm line calls into question the basic assumption of strict dependence of food requirement on metabolic rate. The discrepancy between dogs and cats suggests that the food consumption data reflect feeding strategy more closely than they do standard metabolism (J. F. Eisenberg, oral comm. 1978). The difference in this case would be between cursorial and stalking hunters. The correspondence between cats and the monitor recalls the old reference to Komodo "dragons" as ecological counterparts of tigers on islands where the latter are absent. Both tigers and monitors are stalking hunters, and their food requirements appear to be similar despite the difference in thermal strategies.

The convergence of ectothermic and endothermic metabolic rates with increase in size, and field data for moderately large living ectotherms, indicate that predator/prey ratios of large animals are bound to be low, regardless of thermal strategy. The position of big cats, relative to canids on the one hand and Komodo monitors on the other, further undermines the significance of predator-prey ratios in the assessment of thermal strategy. The low ratios that Bakker (1975a, b) reports for dinosaur faunas are as consistent with large size and stalking habit as with endothermy, and are therefore discriminative of none.

Thermal conductance, metabolic rates and dinosaur inertial homoiothermy

The effect of increasing size on A-V ratios (surface area relative to volume) tends to depress thermal conductance from the body core to the external environment ($C = ccO_2/gh$ °C at midpoint of a $20°$ C gradient; Bartholomew and Tucker 1963), although conductance can also be modified independently of changes in size. Since A-V ratios decline more rapidly than metabolic rates as animals become larger, a size may theoretically be reached at which heat is lost no more quickly than it can be replenished from persistently low rates of metabolism. For this reason, dinosaurs probably had no need of increased metabolic rates to go far

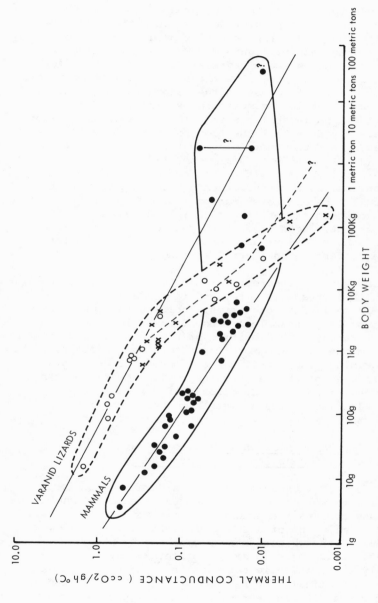

Figure 3. Changes in thermal conductance with increasing size, reptiles and mammals. Modified slightly from McNab and Auffenberg (1976). Symbols: ○, varanid lizards; X, other reptiles, including crocodilians, tortoises, snakes, and iguanid lizards; ●, mammals. The second break in slope of the reptile line, at about 30 kg body weight, is based on the contention (McNab and Auffenberg 1976) that thermal conductance of reptiles larger than 30 kg is "with much doubt" about 2.5 times the value expected (but not realized) in mammals of comparable weight.

toward escaping the dependence on external sources of heat
which is characteristic of living ectotherms.

A strategy based on these relationships is styled
inertial homoiothermy by McNab and Auffenberg (1976). It
is confirmed by the modification of thermal conductance in
living ectotherms (Fig. 3), as a physiological response to
the more directly physical effect of size on A-V ratios.
In ectotherms of up to 3 kg body weight, thermal conductance declines with increasing size as the -0.37 power of
body weight (McNab and Auffenberg 1976), close enough to
-0.33 to be largely the effect of declining A-V ratios.
Thermal conductance is being kept as high as possible as
size increases, in order to facilitate quick absorption of
external heat. But, because A-V ratios continue to depress
rates of heat transfer with increasing size, an ectotherm
lineage must make a choice at a body weight of about 3 kg:
it can stop getting larger, or it can explore the potential
of thermal constancy. At this point, the rate of decline
of thermal conductance increases rather abruptly from the
-0.37 to the -1.03 power of body weight, as though the
effect of surface area had been removed from the equation.
Conservation of body heat is now being reinforced by the
reduction of conductance below the rate controlled by A-V
ratios. A body weight of about 3 kg marks the beginning of
a transition from a thermal strategy dominated by rapid
absorption of external heat to one dominated by thermal
inertia. McNab and Auffenberg (1976) ascribe the steeper
decline in rates of heat transfer in larger ectotherms
partly to thick, insulating integuments, such as those of
turtles and crocodiles. However, non-armored forms,
including large snakes and lizards, also fall on the steep
portion of the regression, which suggests that in these
animals conductance is reduced by modification of
peripheral circulatory patterns and/or reflexes.

The response of endotherms to the effect of increasing
size on A-V ratios is almost a mirror image of that of
ectotherms (Fig. 3). At small body sizes thermal conductance declines as the -0.51 power of body weight (McNab and
Auffenberg 1976), considerably steeper than the rate
dictated by changing A-V ratios. Conductance is held
below the level controlled by A-V ratios by an insulating
pelage, without which the high production of internal heat
would be prohibitively expensive for small animals. But as
rates of heat transfer decline with increasing size, loss
must eventually become slower than internal production, and
a problem of heat disposal arises. Hence at about 10 kg,
the slope of the regression become effectively zero, as

means are found to counteract the effect of declining A-V
ratios and maintain conductance at a constant level. It
appears that if such means had not been found, the high
production of internal heat would have kept mammals from
getting bigger than about 10 kg. As it is, not more than
about 20% of mammals have done so (Fig. 1). The spread of
data points suggests that those which broke through this
barrier did so by a variety of adaptive expedients, and not
by a potential that was characteristic of very many mammals.

Thus ectotherms increase the rate of decline of
thermal conductance with increasing size, while endotherms
bring it to a halt. Ectotherms have obviously found
advantage in the heat-conserving potential of large size.
It was probably pursuit of this advantage, by the simple
expedient of continuing to become larger, that led the
dinosaurs to their characteristic size. Endotherms, on the
other hand, have apparently found the problem of dumping
excess heat so severe as to prevent all but about 2% of
mammals from attaining the modal size of dinosaurs.

With increasing size, resting metabolism of ectotherms
becomes progressively more important as a source of
endogenous heat, according to the convergence of the
ectotherm regression on the endotherm regression (Fig. 2).
The concomittant but independent decline of thermal
conductance would enhance the thermal resemblance between
large ectotherms and endotherms. Does this mean that
large dinosaurs had become endothermic, at least within
certain environmental limits, simply because of their
increase in size? By Bakker's definition of endothermy it
does not: the thermal strategy illustrated by these data is
basically ectothermic, because it involves no increase in
the rate of resting metabolism over what is considered
ectothermic in small living forms. Both the question and
the answer, however, emphasize the equivocality that
appears when the concepts of ectothermy and endothermy,
defined primarily by reference to small living animals, are
applied to extinct animals as big as dinosaurs.

Internal sources of heat have been identified or
inferred in a variety of living ectotherms. McNab and
Auffenberg (1976) demonstrate muscular activity as such a
source of heat in Komodo monitor lizards, which maintain
body temperatures from 0.5 to 5.0 $^{\circ}$C above the ambient,
depending on size (6.7 to 35 kg), during the coolest hours
of the night. The nighttime differential was found to be
consistently greater for muscle than for cloacal temperature in an individual of 12 kg body weight. Johnson,

Voigt, and Smith (1978) report than an alligator weighing 49.9 kg heated up in 39.9% of the time it took to cool down, in a range of ambient temperatures from 15° to 35° C, and imply that fine control of peripheral circulation does not account entirely for the magnitude of the difference between heating and cooling rates. In the agamid lizard <u>Amphibolurus</u> <u>barbatus</u> and four species of Australian varanids, heating is also faster than cooling (Bartholomew and Tucker 1963, 1964). In the agamid, heating is accompanied by a marked increase in heart rate, while in the varanids it is not. The difference suggests that in agamids acceleration of heating is mediated primarily through control of peripheral circulation, whereas in varanids it may include a larger component of endogenous heat.

The increasing significance of internal sources of heat in progressively larger ectotherms is illustrated by the slower decline of standard metabolism, M_{std}, and submaximal active metabolism, M, relative to thermal conductance, C (Fig. 4). The points $B_{M_{std}}$ and B_M, at which the regressions of M_{std} and M intersect with that of C, mark the body weights at which internal heat production is theoretically equal to heat loss. At sizes smaller than $B_{M_{std}}$ and B_M, heat is lost faster than it is generated (heat balance negative), while at larger sizes it is generated faster than it is lost (heat balance positive). These relationships entail a differential between body and ambient temperatures of 10° C, because of the basis for estimating thermal conductance (Bartholomew and Tucker 1963). Values of ectothermic heat gain (Table 4) are simply read from the plot of Figure 4; they are given empirical meaning by expressing them as multiples of mammalian M_{std} (Table 4), for which heat balance is positive throughout the size range of mammals.

At body sizes below 50 g (B_M, Fig. 4), heat balance of both M and M_{std} are negative and reptiles are necessarily heliothermic or thigmothermic. With increasing size, heat balance of reptilian M becomes positive and approaches mammalian M_{std}, attaining parity at about 4 kg (Table 4), the estimated weight of the smallest known dinosaurs. At this size, the heat gain of reptilian M is sufficient to raise body temperature about 3° C/h. Such reptiles cannot, of course, maintain constant body temperature, for the heat balance of M_{std} is still negative, and constant activity is impractical. However, since 3 or 4 kg is also the body weight at which the reptilian decline of thermal conductance

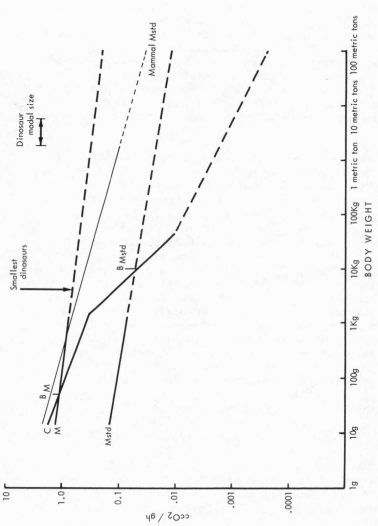

Figure 4. Heat balance in ectotherms, based on reptilian active metabolism, M, and standard metabolism, Mstd, as measures of internal heat production, and thermal conductance, C, as measure of heat loss. The standard for comparison is mammalian standard metabolism (mammal Mstd). Equations: reptilian M (slope -0.12 at 30° C) derived from data in Bakker (1975b); reptilian Mstd (slope -0.17 at 30° C) from Bennett and Dawson (1976); reptilian C simplified from Fig. 3, this paper, from McNab and Auffenberg (1976); mammalian Mstd (slope -0.25 at thermoneutrality) derived from data in Taylor, Schmidt-Nielsen, and Raab (1970).

accelerates (Fig. 3), it probably reflects the smallest size at which inertial homoiothermy is feasible. At 10 kg, the size of the smallest adult dinosaurs, the heat gain of reptilian M is about one-third greater than mammalian M_{std} (Table 4), and that of reptilian M_{std} has just become positive (Fig. 4).

At 100 kg, the maximum size of Komodo monitors and high in the size range of living reptiles, the heat gain of reptilian M is twice mammalian M_{std} (Table 4); heat gain of reptilian M_{std} is 13% of mammalian M_{std}. Galapagos tortoises in this size range maintain deep body temperatures more than 5° C above ambient during the night (Mackay 1964). In their case the differential may be due mostly to very low conductance afforded by the thick shell, but the data from other large reptiles suggest some component due to endogenous heat production. The fact that these tortoises are not fully homoiothermic indicates either that their M_{std} is so low (MacNab and Auffenberg 1976) that its heat gain is less than 13% of mammalian M_{std}, or that this heat gain is not adequate to maintain homoiothermy in their thermal environment, and their level of activity does not compensate for the deficiency. The more active Komodo monitors of comparable size may perhaps maintain higher M_{std}, and hence higher nighttime differentials, but these data are not available for really large specimens.

At the modal size of dinosaurs, reptilian M yields a heat gain from 3.0 to 3.6 times mammalian M_{std}, while reptilian M_{std} yields from 20% to 25% of mammalian M_{std}. Dinosaurs of modal size evidently could maintain temperature differentials comparable in constancy to those of mammals, by being active for less than one-third of the time. Their 7-hour day would have contravened union standards, since it entailed a 7-day week, but these animals could relax without going into torpor because their M_{std} in most circumstances produced heat faster than it could be dissipated passively. Such animals could have engaged in activity as continuous, if not as intense, as that of mammals, without the expense of automatic endothermy and with far less tendency to overheat. But, while they were probably effective high-temperature homoiotherms, they had not raised levels of M_{std}. The heat generated by their resting metabolism allowed considerably less leeway than mammalian M_{std}, so all but the largest dinosaurs retained an appreciably greater dependence on environmental temperatures than do mammals.

Table 4. Heat gain (positive heat balance) in reptiles: rates of active metabolism (M) and resting metabolism (M_{std}), relative to thermal conductance (C). Heat gains based on the regressions in Figure 4 are, respectively, M - C and M_{std} - C. They are compared with mammalian heat output as multiples of mammalian M_{std}. For further explanation see text.

Landmarks	Body weight	Reptilian heat gain (ccO_2/gh)		Reptilian heat gain expressed as multiple of mammalian M_{std}	
		M - C	M_{std} - C	M - C	M_{std} - C
B_M	50 g	0		0	
Smallest dinosaur	4.00 kg	.56		1.09	
$B_{M_{std}}$	8.91 kg		0		0
Smallest adult dinosaur	10.00 kg	.56	.01	1.33	.01
Komodo monitor	100.00 kg	.46	.03	2.04	.13
Low side, dinosaur modal size	1.78 tons	.33	.02	3.08	.19
High side, dinosaur modal size	5.62 tons	.29	.02	3.65	.25

Constantly high body temperatures tend to prolong the time that animals can remain active. The amount of energy available to fuel this activity is reflected by metabolic scope, or the range between resting and active metabolic rates, which therefore determines the effectiveness with which high body temperatures are exploited. In most living ectotherms, metabolic scope is narrow: active metabolism is heavily dependent on anaerobic pathways, endurance in maximum effort is limited, and repayment of oxygen debt is slow. These limitations restrict duration of activity independently of the effect of temperature, and so dilute the potential advantage of constantly high body temperature. Moreover, metabolic scope (treated as aerobic scope, the augmentation of oxygen consumption above resting levels during maximal activity; Bennett 1972b) may itself be temperature-dependent; in many reptiles it decreases with increasing body temperature over the normal temperature range of activity. For these reasons, Bakker (1975a, b) argues that if dinosaurs had been ectothermic, their metabolic scope would have been too narrow for them to utilize the high body temperatures afforded solely by large size.

Narrow metabolic scope, however, is not a universal correlate of ectothermy. In varanid lizards (Bennett 1972b) aerobic scope increases with increase in body temperature, over the normal temperature range of activity; at mammalian body temperatures it approaches the aerobic scope of mammals. Varanids utilize aerobic pathways for active metabolism; they incur oxygen debt no faster than birds and mammals and repay it nearly as quickly. Their endurance in intense activity, which is probably a consequence of aerobic active metabolism, is also remarkable: an animal that can kill and eat its own weight in wild boar in 17 minutes (Auffenberg 1972) without becoming exhausted has put in a performance that is impressive by any standard. Varanids thus appear to have much greater potential than other living reptiles to take advantage of high and constant body temperatures, and it is perhaps no mere coincidence that they have gone further than other families of lizards in the direction of inertial homoiothermy.

The varanid data suggest that it is broad aerobic scope, not endothermy, that is critical for sustained activity, and provide an ectothermic model for dinosaur thermal strategy which is quite as satisfactory as the mammalian model. If the aerobic scope of dinosaurs were comparable to that of living varanids, sustained activity need not have required the prior establishment of high body

temperature. Instead, the two were reciprocally dependent
factors in the evolution of dinosaur thermal strategy.
Starting from an inertial homoiothermy like that of Komodo
monitors (McNab and Auffenberg 1976), the level of activity
that could be supported by broad metabolic scope at high
temperatures would, in turn, have provided an internal
source of heat for the maintenance of body temperatures,
reinforced by the reduction of heat loss that accompanied
increasing size. Inertial homoiothermy made possible the
eventual appearance of erect posture; the enhanced activity
implicit in erect posture then contributed to its refinement
into "dinosaur-grade inertial homoiothermy".

The smallest adult dinosaurs, at about 10 kg body
weight, were big enough that thermal inertia would predominate over rapid absorption of external heat in their
control of body temperature. Being erect, they were
sufficiently active to compensate for heat loss most of the
time. Faced with seasonal depression of ambient temperatures beyond their capacity to accomodate, they were small
enough that a variety of environmental features offered
potential cover, and they were probably quite capable of
hibernating (cf. Thulborn 1978).

Many juvenile dinosaurs, as noted, were smaller than
10 kg, but the evidence of egg-laying includes the
possibility that the majority were large enough at hatching
to function as incipient inertial homoiotherms. All
dinosaurs probably hatched from eggs, as do their closest
living relatives, the birds and crocodilians. The
physiological evidence that crocodilians never evolved
viviparity (Packard, Tracy, and Roth 1977), which also
applies to birds, can readily be extended to include
dinosaurs, because the eggs of all three groups are very
similar. The largest amniote eggs on record are estimated
to have weighed about 9 kg and 7 kg; they are respectively,
the eggs of the elephant bird, Aepyornis, adult weight
about 500 kg, and those imputed to a sauropod about the
size of Diplodocus, adult weight about 10 tons. The
pelvic openings of a range of dinosaurs from a 2-ton
Antrodemus to Diplodocus are of a size to transmit comfortably objects in the size range of the largest amniote eggs.
The uniformity of inferred egg size in a wide variety of
adult body sizes suggests that these eggs approach the
ultimate size limit of amniote eggs, a limit imposed,
perhaps, by the demands of metabolism on surface area for
respiration. Weights in the range of 7 to 9 kg are therefore taken as maximum hatchling size for dinosaurs. If
Antrodemus, at an adult weight of 2 tons, produced a.

hatchling weighing from 7 to 9 kg, so did about half of all dinosaurs (Fig. 1). This means that a good deal more than half, perhaps two-thirds, of all dinosaur hatchlings were larger than the minimal size for inertial homoiothermy.

The remaining one-third, which were smaller than 4 or 5 kg, probably managed well enough as poikilotherms, but even the smallest may have graduated to inertial homoio-thermy by the end of their first season. Bakker (1971) noted that in Protoceratops, the size ratio of hatchling (0.5 kg) to adult (500 kg) is about 10 times that of crocodilians, which led him to suggest that dinosaurs, being endotherms, had evolved large hatchling size to com-pensate for their lack of insulation. However, Protoceratops is much closer to ectotherms than to endotherms in this respect, for its hatchling-to-adult size ratio is only about 1/18 that of Aepyornis. An animal that hatched at a body weight of 0.5 kg had to increase its weight but tenfold to enter the threshold of thermal inertia; such a growth rate is well within the first-year capacity of alligator hatchlings under favorable conditions (Coulson, Coulson, and Hernandez 1973). Like adult dinosaurs of small body size, juveniles could hibernate through adverse seasons, if necessary, and second-season growth rates, enhanced by increasing thermal stability, would have seen them well on their way to adult thermal strategies.

The young of larger dinosaurs had a long way to grow before they approached the size of their parents, but being already at the threshold of inertial homoiothermy at hatching, they would attain a measure of adult thermal control with the rapid growth of their first season. Thus in spite of the disparity in size between young and adult of the larger species, it does not seem likely that there was a long interregnum between the incipient inertial homoiothermy of the hatchling and the attainment of definitive dinosaur-grade inertial homoiothermy. The behavioral differences between hatchling and adult dinosaurs, imposed by differences in thermal control, would have been no more profound than those in living reptiles which are dictated by differences in food and sources of protection.

Relationships between thermal and locomotor strategies

The origin of dinosaurs records an interaction between size increase and locomotor specialization that probably

reflects the evolution of dinosaur-grade inertial homoiothermy. Many details of dinosaurian locomotor systems
indicate that dinosaur activity, while more intense and
continuous than that of reptiles of sprawling gait, was
less feverish than that which Bakker (1971, 1975a) proposes.

The trend toward increasing size that culminated with
the dinosaurs began no later than the Late Permian, and had
been paralleled in a variety of other reptilian lineages
since the origin of reptiles in the Early Pennsylvanian.
The pervasiveness of these trends suggests that many
different kinds of reptiles, including pelycosaurs and
early therapsids, were discovering the uses of thermal
inertia. The ancestry of lizards, in which small size and
heliothermy or thigmothermy appear to have predominated,
may represent a consistent exception to the common tendency.
Two genera of pelycosaurs, Edaphosaurus and Dimetrodon,
apparently aimed for the best of both worlds. They evolved
dorsal fins, the allometric growth of which maintained
large surface areas, and hence the advantage of heliothermy,
even as the animals in question pursued the advantages of
body bulk of up to 200 kg or so.

Dinosaur evolution looks as though size increase and
locomotor refinement reinforced one another in a positive
feed-back system that led to dinosaur-grade inertial
homoiothermy. Among the thecodonts, moderate rates of size
increase were accompanied by trends toward parasagittal
limb motion and erect posture, which were probably adaptations for vagility that had become feasible as thermal
inertia increased. Perfection of erect posture marked the
transitions to true dinosaurs, and was followed by further
rapid size increase to 1000 kg and more. Erect posture
implies more continuous activity, which would have meant
more continuous heat production in the earliest dinosaurs;
more continuous heat production would further facilitate
continuous activity and therewith vagility. This in turn
promoted further increase in size, reinforcing thermal
inertia, until an optimum was attained at which heat loss
could be compensated, under most circumstances, by heat
generated by muscular activity. As this mode of temperature
regulation became more finely tuned, metabolic and
behavioral changes would have precluded most dinosaurs from
reentering the small-tetrapod niches of their more remote
ancestors.

No such features, relating thermal strategy to size
increase and activity, are evident in the early evolution
of mammals. The earliest mammals were all very small, and

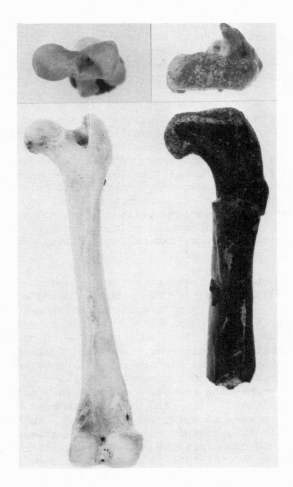

Fig. 5. Proximal articulation of right femur. Left, mammal (domestic dog); right, dinosaur (small Jurassic theropod cf. <u>Coelurus</u>, USNM 256583). Top, proximal aspect; bottom, posterior aspect. For scale, length of dog femur is exactly 11 cm.

not readily distinguishable from their immediate ancestors
in size, gait, or limb structure. They were probably
already functional endotherms at their first appearance,
albeit at lower body temperatures than they later achieved
(Crompton, Taylor, and Jagger 1978). Erect limb posture
comparable to that which is characteristic of all
dinosaurs has never been universal among mammals, first
appearing only when mammals evolved cursorial and graviportal adaptations, some 140,000,000 years after their
origin.

Erect posture opens a new range of locomotor
possibilities with respect to duration and intensity of
activity. One of its costs, however, is the possibility of
lateral instability of the limb, with its attendant hazard
of injury to foot, ankle, or shank because of excessive
shear. Erect posture therefore requires not only that limb
motion be restricted to a parasagittal plane, but also that
some means of transverse adjustment of footfall be retained
to accomodate to irregularities of the ground, which are a
primary cause of momentary lateral instability and therefore of shear injury.

Dinosaurs met the requirement of parasagittal limb
motion by modifying the hip joint, but in doing so they
restricted its capability of transverse adjustment of
footfall. The femoral component of the hip is cylindrical
(Fig. 5) and fits deeply into an acetabulum of up to 1.5
times its diameter. Because of its cylindrical shape, the
femoral component of the joint allows the femur very little
transverse deviation from a parasagittal plane of travel,
is fully congruent with the acetabular surface only during
strict parasagittal motion, and quickly becomes incongruent
as the femur is rotated about its long axis. In consequence, the hip is extremely stable during parasagittal
motion, but such capability as dinosaurs have for transverse adjustment of footfall is confined to rotation of the
femur, which is itself limited by decreasing stability of
the joint.

The hip joint of mammals is profoundly different from
that of dinosaurs (Table 5). The femoral component is a
well-defined spherical or ellipsoidal head (Fig. 5), which
forms a ball-joint with the close-fitting, shallow
acetabulum. The surfaces of the ball-joint are fully
congruent, and the joint correspondingly stable, throughout
an enormous range of transverse deviation of the femur from
a parasagittal plane of motion, and a comparable range of
rotation about its long axis. Mammals, unlike dinosaurs,

Table 5. Anatomical comparison of hip joints. Dinosaur genera examined: Anatosaurus, Antrodemus, Brachyceratops, Camarasaurus, Camptosaurus, Ceratosaurus, Diplodocus, Gorgosaurus, Ornithomimus, Stegosaurus, Thescelosaurus, Triceratops.

Characters	Mammals	Dinosaurs
A. Marked angulation of articular end of femur relative to axis of shaft, a concomitant of erect posture.	Reduced in gravigrades as acetabulum is reoriented.	No change with increasing size.
B. Shape of femoral component.	Spheroidal or ellipsoidal head joined to femoral shaft by non-articular neck.	Cylindroid; no head-and-neck. Region of mammalian neck is articular surface.
C. Acetabulum.	Shallow, non-fenestrate, fits closely about head of femur.	Deep, fenestrate, ca 1.5 times diam. of femoral component.
D. Reinforcement of iliac rim of acetabulum.	Thickened all around in gravigrades; anterodorsal thickness especially marked in bounding forms, e.g. kangaroo, deer.	Posterodorsal reinforcement opposed to lateral face of femoral articulation in all dinosaurs.
E. Stressing of ilium.	Anterodorsal: slants up and forward; sacrum stouter in front.	Posterodorsal: corrugations run up and back; sacrum stouter in back.
F. Orientation of acetabulum.	Lateroventral in gravigrades, lateral in others.	Lateral in all.

depend almost exclusively on muscles and ligaments to
confine the femur to a parasagittal plane of travel.

These differences reflect the radically different
adaptive histories of dinosaurs and mammals. The cylindrical dinosaurian form of the femoral component first
appeared in animals of modest size, indicating an origin
more closely related to the establishment of parasagittal
travel of the femur, as a prerequisite of erect posture,
than to support of weight. The joint was, however,
preadapted for weight-bearing. The ball-joint hip, by
contrast, probably arose in relation to the very small
sizes of the earliest mammals. Well-suited by its range of
motions to progress over irregular surfaces, it would have
been particularly useful to mammals so small that almost
any natural surface was very irregular. To such animals,
erect posture is of secondary significance, but the ball-
joint hip is retained even in the cursorial and large
mammals which evolved later, to which erect posture is
essential. Mammals have capitalized on the capability of
the ball-joint for quick adjustments of footfall, to evolve
the fast cursorial locomotion of horses and camels, not to
mention the acrobatics of dik-diks and mountain goats.
Without comparable flexibility of the hip articulation,
dinosaurs could not have attained comparable cursoriality.
Small dinosaurs may have been disproportionately more
agile than large ones, if instability of the hip imposed
less rigid constraints on animals of lighter weight, but
the structure of the dinosaur hip joint would have
precluded the speed and flexibility of mammals.

The condition of bone surfaces underlying the
articular cartilages also supports the view that dinosaurs
were less intensely active than mammals. These surfaces
are rough in dinosaurs weighing less than 30 or 40 kg, as
they are in living crocodilians, lizards and turtles. In
dinosaurs weighing more than about 50 kg, the roughness is
exaggerated to a distinctively coarse rugosity, which is
most fully developed in the joints subject to the greatest
weight and friction, and in the largest animals. Cartilages are thicker in living reptiles than in birds and
mammals, and in dinosaurs their thickness was probably
proportionate to rugosity. In larger dinosaurs, and
particularly in sauropods, stegosaurs, and ceratopsians,
articular cartilages must have been very thick indeed. In
birds and mammals, the bone surfaces are smoothly polished,
irrespective of position or of body size, and the articular
cartilages are no more than thin veneers. The thinness of
this cartilage is probably adaptive to the stresses

generated by the fast acceleration of which these animals
are capable, for although cartilage has considerable
compressive strength, its tensile strength is negligible.
The thicker the cap, the more likely it is to fail by shear
during acceleration. The thick articular cartilages of
dinosaurs would have been satisfactory as weight-bearing
structures, especially when reinforced by the rugosity of
the underlying bone, but they probably could not tolerate
accelerations comparable to those of which birds and mammals
are capable.

Other aspects of limb structure confirm the evidence
from the joints that dinosaurs were not particularly fast
runners. The shortness of the dorsal articular surface of
the femur, illustrated by a coelurosaur cf. Coelurus (Fig.
5, B) but also observed in carnosaurs, sauropods,
stegosaurs, hadrosaurs, and ceratopsians, would have
limited travel from an anterior position 50° or 60° off
vertical to a posterior position at the vertical or a little
behind it. This is consistent with the range advocated by
Charig (1972) on the basis of muscle attachments. In
ornithomimids, the femoral abductors and adductors are
poorly developed, while the protractors and retractors are
so oriented as to function most effectively in a parasagittal plane (Russell 1972). Russell views this pattern
as limiting maneuverability but not speed. However,
since muscle position is consistent with the constraints
suggested by hip morphology, it may reflect limited speed
as well as limited maneuverability. In Dromiceiomimus the
protractors and retractors are inserted lower on the femur
than in Struthio, in direct proportion to the overall
length of the hind limb (Russell 1972). Russell concludes
that work output of the hind limb was similar and that
speeds were comparable in these animals. However, femoral
length is a larger component of stride length in dinosaurs
than in birds, because the dinosaur femur is more nearly
vertical; the lower insertion of muscles in dinosaurs
indicates slower motion of the femur, resulting in a lower
stride frequency and consequently a slower speed. The
acetabular rim of dinosaurs is reinforced posteriorly
(Fig. 6) and the ilium is stressed to the rear, along a
line from the back of the acetabulum to the stouter
posterior end of the sacrum. This is the exact reverse of
the condition of patently cursorial mammals, in which the
acetabular rim is reinforced anteriorly, and the ilium
stressed from the front of the acetabulum to the stouter
anterior end of the sacrum. Stressing in dinosaurs is
oriented to receive the strain transmitted through the
protracted limb as the animal puts its weight on it at each

Figure 6.   Left ilium, **Antrodemus**, USNM 4734, length 64.3 cm.

step, while stressing in cursorial mammals is oriented to receive the strain generated by the hind limbs against the inertia of the body, as the animal accelerates from a standing start. Such a contrast negates the interpretation of dinosaurs as cursorial animals.

Dinosaurs appear to have been primarily walkers, not runners. The earliest forms were faster and more agile than most of their contemporaries, simply by virtue of their erect posture, which must have conferred an immediate advantage in competition. However, the long-term adaptive value of dinosaur limb structure was for vagility, not speed, a potential that was most fully realized as dinosaurs became larger. Increasing size is in itself a simple means of increasing vagility, but it may in turn require vagility, because of the potential large animals have for damage to the environment (Béland and Russell 1978). With erect posture, any lengthening of the limb increases the length of stride, and with it the amount of ground covered for a given expenditure of energy. The entire limb may be lengthened, as in the columnar elongation of the sauropod limb, or the distal segment alone, as in the presumed cursorial struthiomimids (Russell 1972) and <u>Hypsilophodon</u> (Galton 1974). The first adaptation, though primarily graviportal, serves to increase vagility. The second serves to enhance walking as well as running ability: since the chief force in propulsion is exerted on the femur, the shank and foot play a more nearly passive role, and differential lengthening of the shank and foot is therefore a simple way to increase stride length. If speed is to be increased, the femur is shortened, its musculature is strengthened, and the frequency of femoral swing is increased, but these adaptations have not as yet been described in dinosaurs.

Implications of dinosaur-grade inertial homoiothermy

Dinosaurs, like mammals, enlarged their capacity for continuous activity by reducing their dependence on the physical environment as a source of body heat. They did so, however, at low cost, by a system of heat conservation that shaped life-styles which were very different from those conditioned by the high-cost, heat-generating system of mammals. Locomotor mechanisms and size illustrate a fundamental difference: the activity of dinosaurs was more sedate than that of mammals. The basic strategy of dinosaurs in general was "slow and steady", and what it lacked in mammalian élan, it made up in economy.

Seasonal migration as a general aspect of life is consistent with the characteristic vagility of dinosaurs. Vagility was no doubt more than adequate to the seasonal migration imputed to the Late Triassic prosauropod Plateosaurus (von Huene 1928), which appears to have traversed a belt of coastal desert on its annual trek back and forth between regions of winter and summer rainfall. Von Huene's line of argument, somewhat modified and supplemented by additional data, applies to most dinosaurs as well as to Plateosaurus, and includes movements dominated by seasonal changes in light and temperature as well as those dictated by seasonal changes in available water.

All large dinosaurs, herbivores and predators alike, would have had to be wanderers in order to gather enough food to keep themselves going, even at modest rates of ectothermic metabolism. Dinosaurs were well-suited by their water conservation to the wet/dry seasonal migration proposed by von Huene, and in addition may have incorporated temperature-related migration into their thermal strategy. First, the continuous, if leisurely, activity demanded by a wandering habit would provide a reliable source of internal heat. Second, following temperature gradients was a means of maintaining the most nearly optimal thermal environments, since dinosaur tolerance of thermal fluctuation was restricted by a relatively narrow margin of heat output from resting metabolism. Such a practice is qualitatively no different from the microclimatic adjustments of small living ectotherms, but when pursued on a scale appropriate to dinosaurian size, and effectiveness of day-to-day inertial homoiothermy, it would have measured space by degrees of latitude and time by seasons.

Seasonal climates were sufficiently widespread and persistent during the Mesozoic, as indicated by growth rings in fossil wood, that they may be expected to have influenced the adaptive evolution of dinosaurs. They were characteristic of the Triassic at high paleolatitudes in South Africa and at low paleolatitudes in North America. They were evidently restricted to very high paleolatitudes during the Jurassic, but were more marked as far south as 55° N paleolatitude in the Late Cretaceous.

Temperature and light-dominated, long-range, seasonal migration of dinosaurs is readily modelled from the elements present in the Late Cretaceous paleogeography (Smith, Briden, and Drewry 1973) and paleontology of western North America. Poleward-declining temperature gradients are suggested by oxygen isotope analysis of marine invertebrate fossils (Lowenstam and Epstein 1959; Lowenstam 1964). Dinosaur fossils are known from 70° N (Yukon Territory; Rouse and Srivastava 1973) to 20° N (Honduras, USNM 181339); both the Yukon (R. C. Fox, oral comm. 1978) and the Honduras material consist of hadrosaurs. Dinosaur remains are abundant and diverse at 60° N (Dinosaur Provincial Park, Alberta, Canada), where they are associated with fossil wood showing clear seasonal growth rings (Dodson 1971). Dodson interprets the Late Cretaceous climate of 60° N as warm temperate, comparable to the present-day Gulf Coast of the U. S. Today, the climate at New Orleans includes the expectation of frost at any time during December and January (Westerman and Bacheller 1977). This is also a reasonable expectation for the northern Late Cretaceous climate. At the winter solstice at 60° N, the amount of daylight would approach the present-day value of four hours, to the extent that the Late Cretaceous tilt of the Earth's axis approximates its present-day angle with respect to the orbital plane. Despite the climatic equability over much of the Earth, winters at 60° N would have been cold as well as dark, and conditions at 70° N, with weeks of winter darkness, would have been still more severe. Dinosaurs could probably accomodate to momentarily low temperatures by stepping up their activity, but without an insulative integument they could not have adapted to protracted freezing conditions. It is therefore inferred that few if any dinosaurs lived from 60° to 70° N during the winter, and that the fossils at those latitudes reflect summer occupancy only. The factor which assured the dinosaurs' annual return to high latitudes was probably the enormous productivity (Dodson 1971; Béland and Russell 1978) of the northern summer, generated by the increase of daylight to upwards of 20 hours at the solstice.

Dinosaur migration is envisioned as having begun with random drift in the course of everyday foraging, over distances commensurate with size, locomotor ability, and continuous activity. In the early spring, a northward bias would be introduced into foraging drift, because increasing duration of daylight, rising temperatures, and increasing primary productivity all acted to expand available range to the north. After the spring equinox, northward movement is likely to have accelerated with the northward-rolling wave of vernal productivity of the flora, and with the faster increase of day length to the north. As with many birds, the climax of spring migration may have been reproduction, survival of hatchlings being enhanced by the high productivity of the short summer season at high latitudes. The return trip was probably cued primarily by decline of daylight and northern productivity, but if declining ambient temperatures stimulated activity as a means of maintaining body temperature, they too would have played a part in getting the fall migration under way.

The distances dinosaurs would have had to travel are great, but assuming parallel displacement of the majority of the population, no animal would have had to cover more than 30° of latitude, about 2000 miles. With four to six months to complete the trip each way, they would need to have averaged from 12 to 17 miles per day. Given a daily average of 12 hours' activity, this represents speeds about half those of the slowest dinosaurs (sauropods) reported by Alexander (1976) on the basis of trackways. Sauropod speeds were uniform irrespective of size, which confirms the view that the trackways were left by a herd. The taxonomically diverse and unassociated bipedal dinosaurs were moving consistently about twice as fast as the sauropods, except for one of moderate size in a hurry and another dawdling (Alexander 1976). These speeds may have been somewhat greater than foraging speeds appropriate to the time and place, for the mudflats and river margins where trackways were preserved were probably not the places where dinosaurs foraged. Foraging speeds are envisioned as variable with season and with local conditions. If, as seems likely, their mean was greater than half the values estimated by Alexander, they would have been more than adequate to get dinosaurs from winter to summer range and back in a year's time.

Distance of migration probably corresponded roughly to size and the range of daily foraging, large animals travelling farther than smaller ones, but this rule must have had many exceptions. On the one hand, ankylosaurs of any size simply were not built for long-distance travel. On the other hand, many dinosaurs may have migrated distances far greater than their size would indicate, if, because of relatively small body weight, they were subject to less rigid mechanical constraints on locomotion. It would have been their potential for more intense activity, rather than their size, that permitted such animals to travel long distances. This category might have included not only obligate bipeds of small adult size, but also, in large migrant species, the young that hatched in the far north. The latter, however, probably had two choices: those which grew fast enough in their first season could accompany their adult congeners on the southward trek, and

those which didn't were small enough to hibernate through
their first winter. The dinosaurs of smallest adult size
may not have migrated at all. Their vagility was restricted
by the distance-limiting effect of small size itself, com-
pounded by the size-dependency of inertial homoiothermy,
and they never outgrew the capacity of their environment to
provide cover for hibernation.

"There is grandeur in this view" of migration as an
integral feature of dinosaur life, the great animals
surging northward and southward with the seasons like a
living tide. In its great distance, and in the likelihood
that it was timed by visual cues, this migration less
resembles the limited movement of a few specialized mammals
than it does the extensive migrations of living birds.
This may be no coincidence, in view of the close
phylogenetic relationship between dinosaurs and birds
(Ostrom 1976).

Despite the similarity between dinosaurs and birds in
structure, and in the pattern of migration suggested here,
it is doubtful that the thermal strategy of dinosaurs had
much to do with the origin of endothermy in birds. If
Archaeopteryx is a sound indication, the first birds were
smaller as adults than most dinosaurs were as hatchlings.
The size gap between dinosaurs and Archaeopteryx is
reminiscent of the size gap between therapsids and the
first mammals, and like it may mark the splitting-off of
endothermic derivatives from a non-endothermic parent
lineage. The archosaurian lineage manifests a single
morphological feature that can be unequivocally related to
endothermy, and that feature, feathers, is restricted to
Archaeopteryx. There is no evidence that dinosaurs had an
insulative coat such as that postulated by Bakker (1975a);
known dinosaur integuments show a cover of non-insulative
scales. The first feathers, therefore, were apparently
where we see them, in the first birds. The first birds,
being furthest removed from dinosaur-grade inertial
homoiothermy because of their small size, were the only
members of the line to become endothermic.

They were also the only members of the dinosaur-bird
line to survive the environmental changes at the end of the
Cretaceous, which presumably involved a decline of ambient
temperatures (Russell 1965; Norris 1976; Roy and Russell
1976; Van Valen and Sloan 1977). If dinosaurs had been
endothermic, some of them should also have survived. If
none were insulated, large forms should have survived, at
least for a time, and perhaps only in isolated refugia.

If small dinosaurs were insulated, they should have
survived in diversity comparable to that of surviving birds
and mammals. None did, and the survival of ectotherms as
well as endotherms across the Cretaceous-Tertiary transition further reinforces the view that there were great
differences in thermal physiology between dinosaurs and
living tetrapods.

The strategy of thermal stability by virtue of large
size, documented empirically by Colbert, Cowles, and
Bogert (1946) and elaborated by Spotila, Lommen, Bakken,
and Gates (1973) and McNab and Auffenberg (1976), is here
examined in detail as it was probably manifest in
dinosaurs. Its sharp contrast with mammalian endothermy is
emphasized by the profound differences between dinosaurs
and mammals in structure, life-style, history, and fate.
However, its chief adaptive value, constant high body
temperatures, is evidently the same as that of mammalian
endothermy. In consequence, dinosaur-grade inertial
homoiothermy mimics the major effects which Bakker (1971,
1972, 1975a, b, this volume) treats as unequivocal indication of endothermy in dinosaurs. Dinosaur food requirements would be higher per unit body weight than those of
living poikilothermic ectotherms, in proportion to the
expense of more continuous activity. This would reinforce
the effect of converging metabolic rates with increasing
size, further obscuring the contrast between predator/prey
ratios of large ectotherms and endotherms. Physiological
effects of continuously high body temperatures on bone
deposition and resorption would reinforce the effects of
mechanical stress and activity imposed by the size and
habits of dinosaurs. This must be expected to duplicate
the patterns of bone vascularity which Ricqlès (1976)
ascribes to gross features of thermal physiology, but which
Bakker (1972) claims are exclusively a consequence of
endothermy. Finally, long-distance migration, the
presumptive dinosaurian method for avoiding extreme
ambient temperatures, resulted in the scattering of
dinosaur remains across as broad a geographic range as any
endotherm ever attained.

12

Dinosaur Heresy—
Dinosaur Renaissance

Why We Need Endothermic Archosaurs for a Comprehensive Theory of Bioenergetic Evolution

Robert T. Bakker

Abstract

Large land vertebrates cannot easily escape direct
interactions with predators and competitors by climbing or digging. In direct interactions natural selection
should favor those animals which have the highest levels of
physiological performance. Minimizing the fluctuation of
tissue temperature maximizes the performance of the digestive,
musculoskeletal and central nervous systems. The "Good
Reptile" model for dinosaur biology states that: 1) in a
tropical climate a large reptile with relatively low metabolic heat production can minimize body temperature fluctuations nearly as well as a mammal of the same size with a
relatively high heat production; 2) dinosaurs were successful
because they were very large and lived in tropical habitats.
However, for the last 65 million years, nearly all large
tropical land vertebrates have been mammals, not reptiles.
The few large land reptiles which have coexisted with large
mammals have special refuges from predation: land tortoises
have effective armour; giant snakes have cryptic appearance
and locomotion. Large aquatic reptiles use water as a
refuge from predatory mammals and have always been diverse in
the tropics. Even in the Early Paleocene, when all mammals
were on a very primitive grade of locomotor anatomy and brain
size, mammals, not reptiles, were the predominant tropical
large land vertebrates. Dinosaurs suppressed the evolution of
large mammals for 145 million years; mammals did not begin to
evolve into the size range and feeding types represented by
dinosaurs until after the dinosaurs had become extinct.
Therefore, in all land habitats primitive mammals were
superior to typical reptiles in the context of large size,
and dinosaurs were superior to primitive mammals. Despite
published comments to the contrary, patterns of bone histology

and predator/prey ratios clearly identify vertebrates with
high heat production in most cases. Therapsids (mammal-like
reptiles) probably were the first land vertebrates to
use high heat production for temperature regulation; the
radiation of therapsids suppressed the evolution of large
land reptiles with low metabolism. Dinosaurs probably had
higher and more continuous levels of heat production than
therapsids; the radiation of thecodonts and dinosaurs
replaced that of therapsids. We need endothermic dinosaurs:
evolutionary theory demands them; the empirical data confirm
that they existed.

Introduction

Field Boots, Fossils and Theories

     The joys of paleontology are discovery, puzzlement, and
evolutionary theory. Dinosaur paleontology is richly
supplied with all three. I know of no more exhilarating
feeling than field fever—that special electricity generated
when geological maps are spread out to mark spots for prospecting, the trucks are loaded with picks, awls, plaster and
glue, and we count the days until we can set off for Como
Bluff, or the Freezeout Hills, or any other spot in Wyoming
where people are few, water is scarce, but fossil bones are
abundant.

     The first dinosaur discoveries galvanized scientific
and popular imagination—the idea of a lizard-like reptile
larger than a rhinoceros expanded the concept of the
Reptilia and proved that the Mesozoic World had a spectacular
fauna of extinct land vertebrates profoundly different from
that of the present day. Acute puzzlement, the most heuristic
of scientific mental states, has followed dinosaurs all
through the history of their discovery, description, and
interpretation. How would a rhino-sized lizard function?
Could a forty-ton brontosaur, five times heavier than an
adult African Elephant, support its great bulk on land? How
could such immense beasts feed themselves? Would a simple,
two-chambered heart be powerful enough to pump blood from the
chest of a Brachiosaurus to its head, twenty-five feet above?

     These questions are the product of our curiosity, as we
muse about how a dinosaur, or part of a dinosaur, might have
functioned as a biological machine. Such questions are provocative and intellectually productive. My ultimate
conceptual goal is to use the fossil record to generate and
test hypotheses about what controls the direction and rate
of evolution. I enjoy discussions about the anatomical or
physiological adaptations of dinosaurs, but I want to put
dinosaurs in an evolutionary context of predators and
competitors, plants and herbivores, evolving at different

rates in a shifting global mosaic of climatic belts and
habitats. I believe that we cannot understand dinosaur
biology without a broad comparative approach which can
extract ecologic and evolutionary data from the entire
history of land vertebrates, from the first amphibians
of the Devonian to the mammal-dominated megafauna of today's
tropical forests and plains. Likewise, I believe that we
cannot generate a rigorous theory about the long-term
evolutionary processes which affect all large land vertebrates without understanding dinosaurs.

Body Size and the Rules of the Ecologic Game

I am attracted to large land vertebrates, such as dinosaurs, mammoths, coryphodonts, and giant therapsids, because
the pattern of biotic interactions among large species should
be less varied and the evolutionary directions should be
simpler and more predictable than among small species. A
squirrel or an agamid lizard in a tropical woodland plays the
game of predation and competition in a complex three-dimensional
matrix. If they are threatened by an unfavorable biotic
encounter, these animals have refuges from direct interactions in burrows, crevices, and holes in the floral
architecture. But with increasing body size, the abundance
and variety of such refuges decreases. Few holes are large
enough to hide an adult bear; fewer still, a rhinoceros.
Increasing body size also suppresses the three-dimensionality
of the locomotor repertoire. In animals with similar shape,
body weight increases in proportion to the cube of the linear
dimension. But, the strength of limb muscles increases as the
cross section of the muscle, and their power output as the 3/4
power of body weight. The efficiency of climbing does not
change with body size. About the same amount of metabolic
energy and muscular strength is needed by a lion as by a
squirrel to raise each gram of body weight one meter up a
tree. Thus the maximum speed of climbing decreases with
increasing weight. Few mammals or reptiles over 100 kg body
weight regularly use climbing as a refuge from competitors and
predators. Similarly, it becomes increasingly difficult to
dig burrows big enough to hide in, as body size becomes
larger. For very large land vertebrates the entire geometry
of movement and interaction becomes severely limited to one
environmental plane, the ground. For these species escape
from predation or dangerous competitors depends far more
upon adaptations for speed and strength than for small
species.

I would expect that the evolutionary results of interactions among large land vertebrates would include consistent,
directional changes in anatomy and physiology to increase
the capacity for vigorous pursuit and subduing of prey and
for rapid escape from predators and competitors.

Large species have few refuges from unfavorable physical conditions. A burrow or hollow tree may guarantee survival to a small mammal or lizard through the coldest part of the winter in the cold temperate zone, or through the harshest part of the dry season in the tropics. Such refuges also provide short-term protection from the extremes of daily climatic fluctuation. Desert iguanas can remain in their burrows during the night and throughout cloudy days, emerging only when the combination of air temperature and solar radiation permits them to operate on the ground surface at close to their preferred body temperature. Desert rodents and night lizards take a complementary approach, confining their activity to the time between dusk and dawn, avoiding the heat and water stress of midday. The effects of physical and biotic factors in the environment are rarely completely separate. For any one species physical factors define the limits of the climate space. This climate space may be defined as the range of geography, microhabitat, season, and time of day which permits the animal to maintain a body temperature and water balance which are favorable for foraging, reproduction, and other activities. The presence of different predators and competitors may force this one species to restrict its activity to a small fraction of its climate space defined by physical factors. A hypothetical desert lizard may be able to forage for food at any body temperature between 25 and 35°C, but it might be able to escape predation from a roadrunner only when the body temperature is between 32 and 35°C. Since large species have few refuges from physical conditions, I would expect that long-term evolutionary trends towards increased capacity for physiological homeostasis would be more characteristic of large species than of small species.

Body Size and Paleoecological Resolution

Because of the effects of size on movement and microhabitat choice, the reconstruction of ecological interactions among fossil vertebrates is far easier for large species than for small species. Attempting paleoecological reconstructions from samples of small vertebrates often is a frustrating experience. Even if a lizard jaw and a mammal tooth are found side by side in the same sediment, there is no assurance that the populations represented by these individual specimens interacted in life. The lizard species may have been of a fossorial type, while the co-existing mammal was an arboreal species, so that the two populations could have been separated vertically by forty meters. But if a large hyaena is preserved among antelope the probability that the two species did interact is quite high.

* * * * * * * * *

My plan for this paper is as follows. First I will describe the sequence of major groups of land vertebrates, emphasizing the successive adaptive radiations of primitive reptiles, mammal-like reptiles, thecodonts, dinosaurs, and mammals. Next I will review briefly the data on body size, abundance, and species diversity for the important land vertebrate groups in different habitats and at different geological times. These data show that large vertebrates with high metabolism are superior in biotic interactions to large vertebrates with low metabolism, even in the tropics. In the next section I will outline some hypotheses relating to the advantage of a high, constant body temperature, thereby showing why high internal heat production is necessary for thermoregulation in large tropical species. I will use the fossil record to tease apart the evolutionary roles of brain size, locomotion, and heat production, developing a general hypothesis that the key adaptation which permitted the adaptive radiation of large Early Cenozoic mammals was high heat production. Finally I will review the empirical evidence for metabolic rates in therapsids, thecodonts and dinosaurs. This review will show that the close similarity between dinosaurs and large mammals in bone histology and predator/prey ratios cannot be dismissed as merely the result of large body size, but rather must be interpreted as direct evidence of high rates of metabolism in all dinosaurs.

Sequence and Pattern in Tetrapod Evolution

Figures 1 through 6 represent a bestiary for the large tetrapods which are important in discussions of the ecological context of bioenergetic evolution. Each figure shows genera which are found in one, thin stratigraphic interval in one biogeographic province. The genera were chosen to represent the families which make up most of the preserved sample of large tetrapods. The drawings were made from carefully constructed plans, based on complete or nearly complete skeletons, which were used to make three-dimensional models. The models were employed to calculate body weights by immersion in water. Displacement was measured and weight calculated assuming a specific gravity of 0.9. Top and side views are given in the figures, because the adaptive configuration of head and body cannot be expressed by a side view alone.

The entire fossil history of large tetrapods can be divided into five successive units, based on evolutionary rates, evidence for bioenergetic adaptations, and adaptive radiations.

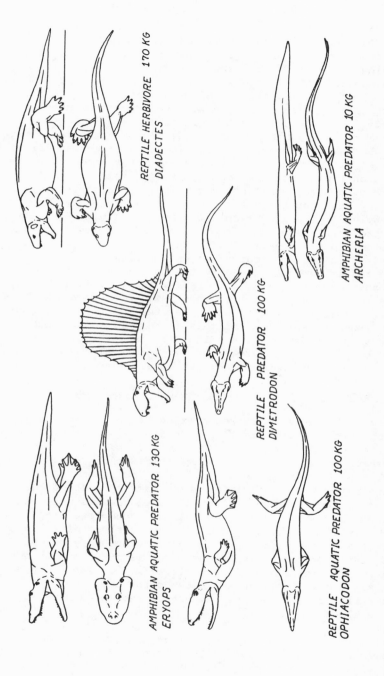

FIGURE 1. A bestiary for the Early Permian, about 260 million years b.p. All of these restorations, and those which follow, were drawn from studies of complete or nearly complete skeletons. The weight given is for a large adult. Nearly all workers agree that all Early Permian vertebrates had low resting metabolic rates.

Age of Primitive Reptiles and Amphibians, Devonian-Early Permian (Figure 1)

The earliest known tetrapods are the ichthyostegid amphibians from the latest Devonian, about 350 million years b.p. Quite a variety of both large and small aquatic amphibian predators are known from the Carboniferous, 345 to 280 million years b.p.; less common and diverse are some amphibian families which seem to have been terrestrial as adults. Reptiles first appear in the Late Carboniferous, about 260 million years b.p. In the Early Permian occur the first well known tetrapod faunas which had clearly defined terrestrial predators capable of killing and dismembering prey as large as or larger than themselves. The predators are the sphenacodonts, a family of pelycosaurian reptiles; Dimetrodon, a genus with a tall sail formed by elongated vertebral spines, is the best known genus. Sphenacodont teeth are like steak-knives—laterally flattened blades with sharply keeled edges fore and aft bearing fine serrations. With this dentition, sphenacodonts could cut up large prey items into chunks small enough to swallow. Nearly all the other terrestrial and aquatic predators, reptile and amphibian, have dentitions composed of simple, conical teeth, without cutting edges, adapted for piercing and crushing prey which was swallowed whole. Ophiacodon, an aquatic pelycosaur, has teeth of delicate proportions and must have taken relatively small prey; the massive, alligator-like jaws and teeth of the common aquatic amphibian Eryops suggest that this genus took a wider variety of prey items. Elongated, eel-like aquatic amphibians were common in swamps (Archeria). Diversity among these aquatic predators was high, but rarely does the fossil sample from one stratigraphic level and one environment yield more than one common large herbivore. The terrestrial herbivorous reptile Diadectes is common in a few local samples; the pelycosaur Edaphosaurus is an aquatic herbivore, very common in swamp deposits. In the late Early Permian the caseids, herbivorous pelycosaurs adapted for digging tubers, are very common in sediments representing semiarid environments. But in any one environment, usually one genus and species contributes most of the large herbivore specimens.

Nearly all authors have agreed that all of these early amphibians and reptiles were typical ectotherms with a resting metabolic heat production no higher than that of a living reptile or amphibian of the same weight and body temperature.

The Kazanian Revolution: Therapsid Takeover (Figure 2)

In the early Late Permian, the Kazanian Stage, the first therapsids, direct descendents from sphenacodonts, appeared

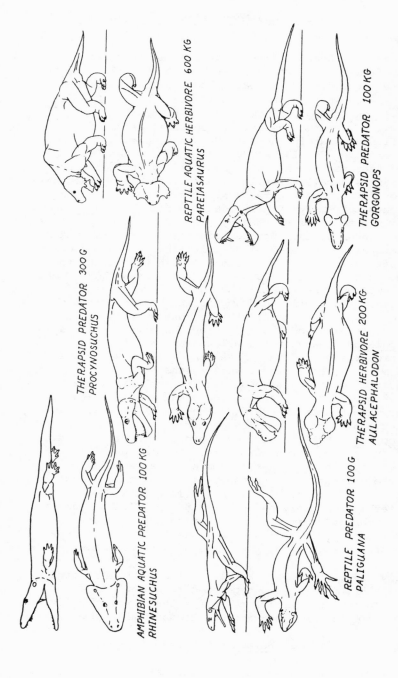

THERAPSID PREDATOR 300 G
PROCYNOSUCHUS

REPTILE AQUATIC HERBIVORE 600 KG
PAREIASAURUS

AMPHIBIAN AQUATIC PREDATOR 100 KG
RHINESUCHUS

THERAPSID PREDATOR 100 KG
GORGONOPS

THERAPSID HERBIVORE 200 KG
AULACEPHALODON

REPTILE PREDATOR 100 G
PALIGUANA

FIGURE 2. A bestiary for the middle Late Permian, about 245 million years b.p. Early therapsids dominate the terrestrial roles. Data from predator/prey ratios and from bone histology strongly suggest that these therapsids had metabolic rates intermediate between those of a typical reptile and a modern mammal of the same size.

and immediately produced a spectacular adaptive radiation, far exceeding the evolutionary rates of diversification seen in the preceding Early Permian faunas. In the first therapsid faunas from South Africa (the <u>Tapinocephalus</u> Zone) at least six genera representing four families of large terrestrial predator can be found in one small geographical area. Terrestrial herbivore diversity is as high or higher than in most faunas of large Cenozoic mammals; at least four families and six genera of herbivores with adult weights of 100 kg or more are common and widespread. The initial burst of therapsid diversification also produced a half dozen families of small terrestrial predators, omnivores, and herbivores. Structural divergence is so great among these early therapsids that all authorities recognize at least five taxonomic categories of the rank of suborder or order. Only a short time was required for this blossoming of adaptive types— perhaps as little as five million years, probably no more than ten million. Thus the radiation of large therapsids was probably as rapid as that of large mammals in the Early Cenozoic.

Very few of the families of terrestrial amphibians and reptiles from the Early Permian survived into the Kazanian. Most of the large semiaquatic predators, such as the eryopids, which hunted at the water surface or along the shore, also disappeared. The big aquatic amphibian predators found with therapsids in the Late Permian are flat-headed, flat-bodied types adapted for a relatively sedentary, benthic style of predation (<u>Rhinesuchus</u> in Figure 2). One group of non-therapsid reptiles did produce a limited radiation of big herbivores, the pareiasaurs. However, in the <u>Tapinocephalus</u> Zone, where pareiasaurs reach their maximum relative abundance and diversity, the mode of preservation strongly suggests that they were swamp-dwelling herbivores which could use water as a refuge from predation by therapsids.

Henceforth I shall use the term "Good Reptile" for those tetrapods which traditionally are classified within the Reptilia and which seem to have the same general level of bioenergetic adaptations as have the living lizards, snakes, crocodilians and turtles, with a relatively low metabolic rate at rest and no mechanism for increasing heat production during cold stress without exercise. This usage excludes those fossil groups for which there is evidence of higher levels of thermo-regulatory heat production, the therapsids, thecodonts, flying reptiles, and dinosaurs. For the sake of brevity, in the figure labels the term "Reptile" is used only for the "Good Reptiles."

Although fully terrestrial Good Reptiles are rare or

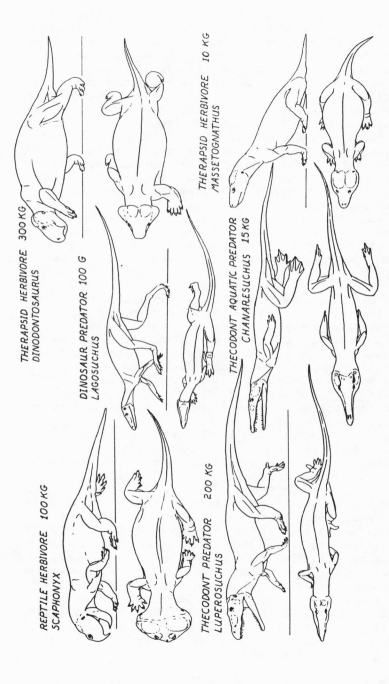

REPTILE HERBIVORE 100 KG
SCAPHONYX

THERAPSID HERBIVORE 300 KG
DINODONTOSAURUS

DINOSAUR PREDATOR 100 G
LAGOSUCHUS

THERAPSID HERBIVORE 10 KG
MASSETOGNATHUS

THECODONT PREDATOR 200 KG
LUPEROSUCHUS

THECODONT AQUATIC PREDATOR 15 KG
CHANARESUCHUS

FIGURE 3. A bestiary for the early Late Triassic, about 210 million years b.p. A mixed fauna of therapsids, thecodonts, Good Reptiles, and the first dinosaur, Lagosuchus. Bone histology and predator/prey ratios in thecodonts are like those of therapsids, suggesting a similar, intermediate level of metabolism.

absent in the early therapsid faunas, a variety of small
families do occur, including the first lizards (Paliguana
in Figure 2).

At present we cannot be certain that the radiation of
big therapsid predators and herbivores caused the extinction
of the characteristic Early Permian semiaquatic and terrestrial reptiles and amphibians. Well preserved therapsids
have not been found with the Early Permian families, and it
is possible that these families became extinct before the
beginning of the therapsid radiation. However, the therapsids
definitely appear to have had some basic advantage in direct
biotic interactions with other tetrapods, because no other
group produced many large terrestrial species.

Early and Middle Triassic: Mixed Thecodont and Therapsid
    Faunas (Figure 3)

The Intensity of Competition Among Large Predators. All
of the large terrestrial predators capable of killing and
dismembering prey as large as or larger than themselves in
the Late Permian were therapsids. I believe that both
exploitative and interference competition are especially
intense in the context of this trophic role. Interference
competition results from direct biotic confrontation between
competitors; for example, male lions frequently are observed
driving away hyaenas and stealing their kills. Exploitative
competition occurs when one competitor deprives another of a
limiting resource by harvesting the resource. The two categories overlap. In one area of Africa, lions may harvest
zebra more rapidly than do hyaenas, but part of this superiority
in exploitation of resources may be the result of lions in-
timidating hyaenas and chasing them away from the best hunting
grounds (Schaller 1972). Interference competition overlaps
with predation. Hyaenas sometimes kill and eat lions; leop-
ards prey heavily upon jackals. Predators which feed on
large prey items are harvesting a coarse-grained resource,
one with a high concentration of calories and protein. Since
the payoff to the winner in energy and protein is large, such
coarse-grained resources should encourage big predators to
employ direct confrontation, threats, and theft of carcasses.
The intensity of interference competition among large terrestrial predators should be further increased by the limited
locomotor repertoire of big land vertebrates; only a very few
large predators can protect their kills by dragging the
carcasses into trees or caves. Recent field work among the
extant large mammals of East Africa does in fact show that
sympatric large predators harass their interspecific and
intraspecific competitors almost continuously (Schaller 1972).
Within the context of large land predators, natural selection

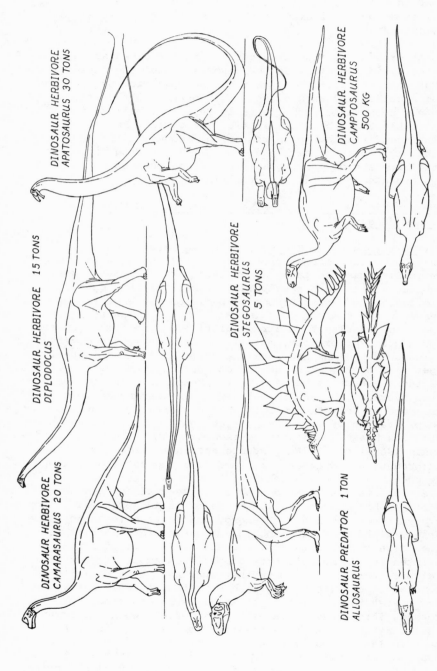

DINOSAUR HERBIVORE
CAMARASAURUS 20 TONS

DINOSAUR HERBIVORE 15 TONS
DIPLODOCUS

DINOSAUR HERBIVORE
APATOSAURUS 30 TONS

DINOSAUR HERBIVORE
STEGOSAURUS
5 TONS

DINOSAUR HERBIVORE
CAMPTOSAURUS
500 KG

DINOSAUR PREDATOR 1 TON
ALLOSAURUS

FIGURE 4. A bestiary for the Late Jurassic, about 140 million years b.p. The Golden Age of Giants: a fauna rich in sauropod dinosaurs.

should favor adaptations for increasing the speed and power
of the predator, the quickness of prey capture, the rapidity
of carcass dismemberment, and the ability to repel carcass
pirates on one hand, and to be an effective carcass pirate
on the other. The complete domination by therapsids of the
large predator role is a powerful testimony to the basic
superiority of therapsids in direct biotic interactions with
all non-therapsids.

   <u>Competitive Replacement of Therapsids by Thecodonts</u>.
The therapsid monopoly on the large predator role was broken
in a series of steps by the adaptive radiation of thecodonts
in the Early and Mid-Triassic. The earliest thecodonts
(prolacertids) probably were semiaquatic predators, and a
series of thecodont families exploited freshwater resources
throughout the Triassic (proterosuchids; chanaresuchids;
phytosaurs). In the Late Permian, predatory therapsids
reached adult weights of 400 kg or more (gorgonopsids and
anteosaurids). In the Mid-Early Triassic the largest terrestrial predators were thecodonts (erythrosuchids and raui-
suchids; up to 600 kg or more); the largest contemporary
therapsid predator weighed less than 100 kg (cynognathids).
By the late Mid-Triassic the largest therapsid predator
weighed only about 30 kg (belesodontid), and the small
therapsid predators were fewer and less diverse than the
small thecodont predators. This paleontologic pattern of
replacement of therapsids by thecodonts, first in the largest
size categories, then progressively in the smaller size
ranges, strongly suggests that thecodonts possessed a general
superiority to therapsids in direct biotic interactions.

   Only one family of thecodonts seems to have been omnivorous or herbivorous: the armored aetosaurs, weighing up to
200 kg, were common in the Middle and Late Triassic. The
common, diverse large herbivores in the Early and Mid-Triassic
were still therapsids. Only one family of large terrestrial
"Good Reptiles" existed during this interval, the grotesque
herbivorous rhynchosaurs (<u>Scaphonyx</u> in Figure 3). Much more
taxonomic variety existed among small terrestrial groups:
several families of lizards and other "Good Reptiles" were
common. Flat-bodied, benthic amphibian predators existed
through the end of the Triassic, but the more active, surface-
swimming amphibians were extinct by Mid-Triassic time, quite
possibly because of predation and competition from thecodonts.

<u>The Age of Dinosaurs, Late Triassic through Late Cretaceous</u>,
   (<u>Figures 4 & 5</u>)

   <u>Origin of Dinosaurs</u>. Bakker and Galton (1974) and
Bonaparte (1975, 1976) independently came to the conclusion

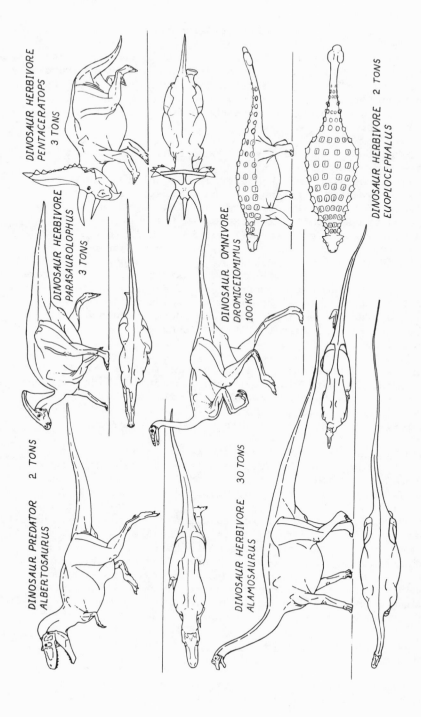

DINOSAUR PREDATOR   2 TONS
ALBERTOSAURUS

DINOSAUR HERBIVORE
PARASAUROLOPHUS
3 TONS

DINOSAUR HERBIVORE
PENTACERATOPS
3 TONS

DINOSAUR OMNIVORE
DROMICEIOMIMUS
100 KG

DINOSAUR HERBIVORE   2 TONS
EUOPLOCEPHALUS

DINOSAUR HERBIVORE   30 TONS
ALAMOSAURUS

FIGURE 5. A bestiary for the Late Cretaceous, about 70 million years b.p., shortly before the total extinction of dinosaurs and the end of the Mesozoic Era.

that Lagosuchus (Figure 3), a small, elegantly long-limbed
predator of the late Mid-Triassic, was very close to the
common ancestry of all dinosaurs. Bonaparte retained
Lagosuchus in the Thecodontia, as part of a "horizontal"
classification; Bakker and Galton preferred a "vertical"
classification which identified Lagosuchus as a very primitive
dinosaur. A vigorous debate is in progress about the phyletic
relationships between the two orders of dinosaurs recognized
in traditional classification, the Saurischia and the
Ornithischia. I am reviewing this dispute in another place,
and will state simply here that careful study of the skull in
some very primitive dinosaurs (Anchisaurus and early ornithischians) reinforces my belief that Lagosuchus and all the
dinosaurs should be recognized as a clade distinct from all
the well known thecodont groups of the Triassic. Lagosuchus
appeared at a busy time in land vertebrate history when small
carnivorous therapsids were still common and a bewildering
variety of thecodonts occupied most of the roles of terrestrial predators. In faunas only slightly younger than those
with Lagosuchus occur the first large dinosaurs, the carnivorous staurikosaurs, of up to 30 kg live weight. Even larger
predatory dinosaurs, the herrerasaurs, weighing up to 100 kg,
appear in the next faunal level. Thecodont predators remain
more common and diverse than dinosaurs through most of the
Late Triassic, but by the Triassic-Jurassic boundary, at about
200 million years b.p., carnivorous dinosaurs had completely
replaced thecodonts. The adaptive radiations of herbivorous
dinosaurs began in the early Late Triassic; by late Late
Triassic time nearly all large herbivores were dinosaurs.

The most advanced of the Triassic therapsids (cynodonts
such as Massetognathus in Figure 3) were very close to
primitive mammals in most details of the skull and skeleton.
The gradual replacement of both carnivorous thecodonts and
herbivorous therapsids by Triassic dinosaurs is striking
evidence of a basic superiority of dinosaurs.

Origin of Mammals. Very mammal-like cynodont therapsids
occur with Lagosuchus, and the first undoubted mammal is from
the latest Triassic. All the Triassic and earliest Jurassic
mammals were minute predators and omnivores, of 10 to 100 g
adult weight. At several sites these early mammals are
found with a diverse assemblage of small lizards, sphenodontids, and other "Good Reptiles."

Jurassic Dinosaurs: The Golden Age of Giants (Figure 4).
The Triassic radiation of early dinosaur herbivores and carnivores was replaced by the sauropod-stegosaur-allosaur faunas
of the later Jurassic, the most spectacular land megafauna
ever to appear. Average adult body size of the very diverse

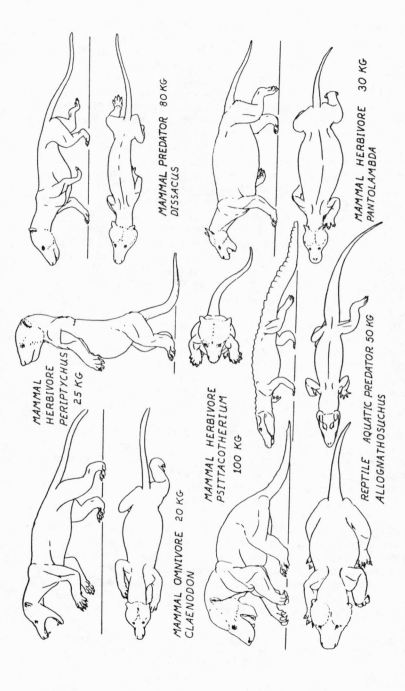

FIGURE 6. A bestiary for the Mid-Paleocene, about 60 million years b.p. The adaptive radiation of large mammals had begun, but nearly all species were still plantigrade (flatfooted), short-legged, and equipped with relatively tiny brains.

sauropod dinosaurs was at least 20 tons; five genera can be found in one quarry at one stratigraphic level. The fresh-water tetrapod predators included a variety of crocodilians, turtles and small frogs and salamanders.

Cretaceous Dinosaurs, Marsupials and Placental Mammals (Figure 5). The Cretaceous was the third Age of Dinosaurs. Sauropods remained common locally in semiarid environments, while new groups of ornithischians (duckbills, horned dino-saurs, ankylosaurs) dominated the large herbivore role in most habitats, especially those with high rainfall. By the Late Cretaceous the radiations of modern families of turtles, crocodilians, lizards, frogs and salamanders had begun. All of the Jurassic and Cretaceous mammals were small, most under 100 g live weight. Only a few reached 1 kg, but the mammal faunas were varied, and morphologic rates of evolution, especially in teeth and jaws, were high. The common ancestor of marsupials and placental mammals must have existed in the Early Cretaceous. Marsupials were already diverse, as small omnivores and predators, in the Late Cretaceous; the adaptive radiation of the Cenozoic families of placentals began in the latest Cretaceous.

Experimental Paleoecology: The Dinosaur Exclusion Cage and the Radiation of Cenozoic Mammals (Figure 6)

Mammals Replace Dinosaurs: A Noncompetitive Transition. All dinosaurs, except that clade commonly known as birds, became extinct rather suddenly at the end of the Cretaceous. The term "suddenly" has different meanings to different stu-dents of dinosaur extinction; to some it means over a period of several million years (Bakker 1977); to others it means a cataclysmic weekend of exploding supernovae. For discussions of dinosaur bioenergetic adaptations the important property of the dinosaur extinction is not suddenness, but rather the noncompetitive nature of the replacement of dinosaurs by mammals. As I have just described, the adaptive radiation of thecodonts seems to have displaced that of therapsids in a series of steps, and the initial radiation of dinosaurs seems to have had a similar effect upon thecodonts near the end of the Triassic. The replacement of dinosaurs by mammals does not conform to this pattern. The radiation of Cenozoic mammals did not begin to produce species which had body sizes and trophic roles overlapping those of Cretaceous dinosaurs until after the dinosaurs had already become extinct.

Periodically the notion is expressed that the Late Cretaceous mammals were partly to blame for the dinosaur extinction through egg predation or competition. The idea is appealing: the small but clever mammals, after over a hundred

million years of oppression, finally overthrew the brawny but
brainless dinosaurs as rulers of the land ecosystem. But
this bit of mammal chauvinist propaganda can be disproved, I
believe, quite thoroughly.

The feeding adaptations of Late Cretaceous dinosaurs show
that they were exploiting a variety of plant species, growth
forms, and plant organs, including plant tissue very high in
fiber.   Sauropod teeth show severe tooth-food-tooth wear,
suggesting that these dinosaurs were cropping abrasive and
tough plant tissue, such as conifer branchlets; the neck and
limbs and tail of sauropods gave them an enormous vertical
range for browsing. The most diverse herbivorous groups, the
ceratopsids and duckbills, had complex, self-sharpening, and
continuously growing batteries of cheek teeth which maintained
throughout life a very long occlusal area with a long, sharp
cutting edge and a shredding surface composed of a mosaic of
enamel and dentine. These cutting and shredding mechanisms
are analogous to the high crowned and continuously growing
cheek teeth of the most specialized mammalian grazers and
browsers, such as the Late Cenozoic horses, antelope and
rhinos.   Duckbill dinosaurs must have ground and shredded
very resistant plant parts; the vertical occlusal planes
of horned dinosaurs must have been used to chop extremely
tough fibers. Other Late Cretaceous dinosaurian
herbivores had similar but less complex dental adaptations
(protoceratopsids, hypsilophodonts).

The most specialized Cretaceous mammalian herbivores
were the multituberculates, a varied group with biting or
gnawing incisors and cutting and shredding cheek teeth. Multituberculates may have competed with some dinosaurs; the two
groups coexisted from the Mid-Jurassic until the Late Cretaceous, but multituberculates suffered declines in relative
abundance and diversity at the end of the Cretaceous. The
latest Cretaceous radiation of placental mammals did produce
a cluster of families which expanded in numbers and diversity
throughout the Early Cenozoic, but none of these families
seems to have been adapted for exploiting high fiber or
extremely tough plant tissue. The taeniodonts (<u>Psittacotherium</u>
in Figure 6) had powerful digging claws and teeth, adaptations for harvesting roots and tubers. The periptychids
(<u>Periptychus</u>) resembled the living lesser pandas in their
massive chopping and crushing premolars and powerful, deep
mandibles; periptychids probably cut and crushed hard plant
food but could not shred high fiber leaves or stems. Early
phenacodont, arctocyonid (<u>Claenodon</u>) and hyopsodont condy-
larths had cheek teeth combining features seen in living
species of lemurs, raccoons and pigs, and must have been
omnivores taking a wide range of relatively high protein, high

calorie, low fiber food: insects, small vertebrates, nuts, fruit, but certainly not tough leaves or stems. The Late Cretaceous representatives of all these groups were very small, none larger than a squirrel. These Cretaceous mammalian herbivores must have competed with dinosaurs no more than the living species of tropical, South American opossums, raccoons and squirrel monkeys compete with bison, llamas, pronghorns and deer.

Many species of vertebrate egg predators exist today, including lizards, birds and mammals, yet, except for humans, none of these seem to be important agents of extinction of the egg-layers. It is not known that all dinosaurs laid eggs; the huge pelvic canals of sauropods and some other groups suggest that the young were born alive at a relatively large size. Finally, dinosaurs and a considerable array of potential egg robbers, lizards, sphenodontids, and many families of mammals coexisted from the Late Triassic through the Creta- ceous, and there is no reason to suppose that egg predation suddenly became more intense when the dinosaurs suffered their Götterdammerung.

The Dinosaur Exclusion Cage and the Release of Mammalian Evolutionary Hyperspace. The most delightful aspect of the fossil record is that it can be read as a series of grand experiments in ecological manipulation. Experimental manipu- lation has become a powerful tool in field ecology. A typical, hypothetical experiment might be set up as follows: the dis- tributions of various epifaunal mollusks are mapped along depth transects across a rocky intertidal habitat; cages are built over test areas to exclude predatory starfish; if the ranges of certain mollusk species, not found with starfish in control areas, now expand into the caged areas, we have strong evidence that the depth ranges of these species are controlled by biotic interaction with the predators. The fundamental niche is a useful term for the total potential range of resources which would be exploited by a species in the absence of competition and predation; the realized niche is the range of resources exploited with any given set of predators and competitors. In a larger sense, we could say that the fundamental niche suite of a clade of high taxonomic rank, such as the Class Mammalia, is the total range of resources which would be exploited in an adaptive radiation free from interference from any other adaptive radiation. Thus the fundamental niche suite is a hypothetical evolutionary hyperspace mapped out by the distribution of all possible body sizes, trophic roles, and habitats. I am interested to know whether dinosaurs were mammal-like endo- therms or not, but what I am really after is a general theory relating bioenergetic adaptations among coevolving groups

to the realized niche suite, the observed evolutionary
hyperspace of the great clades of vertebrates.

The events at the end of the Cretaceous built a dinosaur-
exclusion cage over the terrestrial ecosystem. For the first
time in 145 million years, all of the groups of small land
vertebrates, lizards, mammals, and others were free from
interactions with dinosaurs. How did the realized evolutionary hyperspace of the Class Mammalia change? Immediately
after the dinosaur extinction, major evolutionary increases
in body size occurred for the first time among mammals. By
the time of the Puercan faunal stage, only a few million years
after the dinosaur extinction, several lines of mammals,
including taeniodonts, periptychids, arctocyonids, and
predatory mesonychids, had produced species with body weights
of 20 and even 50 kg (Matthew 1937). A few million years
later mammals surpassed the 100 kg mark (taenidonts and
large species of pantolambdids). The first one-ton land
mammals were the uintatheres of the Mid-Eocene, about 18
million years after the end of the Cretaceous.

Most of the big Early Cenozoic mammals can be traced
back into the Cretaceous to ancestors which probably used
trees as a refuge from predation. Primitive arctocyonids,
the ancestors of the many condylarth groups, have adaptations
of the limbs for walking and running over a wide range of
three-dimensional substrates: the toes are long, with ball-
in-socket interphalangeal joints; the claws are laterally
compressed and curved; the feet are plantigrade with five
spreading digits, and the joint between the astragulus and
the tibia-fibula is very mobile, permitting a great variety
of foot postures. A few of the large Early Cenozoic mammals
(e.g. Claenodon in Figure 6) retained this generalized and
flexible locomotor system, but most show marked adaptations
for restricting activity to the ground: the toes are short,
with hinge-like interphalangeal joints; claws are modified
into hoofs; and the ankle joint restricts movement to one
plane of flexion-extension (periptychids, pantodonts such as
Pantolambda, predatory mesonychids such as Dissacus).

Thus the dinosaur-exclusion cage permitted an undeniably
spectacular increase in the dimensions of the mammalian
evolutionary hyperspace. It is hard to resist the conclusion
that for 145 million years the presence of dinosaurs had
suppressed the evolution of large mammals, especially large,
fully terrestrial, non-arboreal mammals.

Why the "Good Reptile" Model Fails

"...we have no reason to believe that a constant

body temperature characterized a dinosaur any more
than a modern crocodile, although such ideas have
been advanced. That their activity, which implies
increased metabolism, raised the bodily temperature
during the time of such activity, it is, I think,
safe to assume,—an analogy is seen in the tuna
among bony fishes today,—but that they possessed
a mechanism for the maintenance of a constant body
temperature irrespective of external conditions,
as with birds and mammals, is sustained by no
evidence thus far offered. With such bulk as the
greater of the dinosaurs possessed, with its relatively small radiating surface, which increases
with the square of the diameter while the bulk
increases with the cube, the retention of heat
accompanying muscular activity would probably be
somewhat prolonged."
            Richard Swann Lull, Professor of Paleontology at
            Yale University, 1924, p. 225-226

Were he alive today, Professor Lull probably would have
been asked to participate in this symposium. His sober,
succinct appraisal of the nature of dinosaurian bioenergetics
would be an excellent summary of what I believe is still the
majority opinion. Lull's words have a surprisingly modern
ring. He seems to have had all of the conceptual pieces of
the "Good Reptile" model: the surface-area to volume law gave
dinosaurs heat-saving advantages; dinosaur heat production
and thermoregulation at rest were probably like that of
today's large reptiles, and the only mechanism for increasing
heat production which dinosaurs probably employed was
vigorous exercise like that of tuna. Also, in the same
work quoted, Lull emphasized the tropical climates of
dinosaurian habitats and the lack of severe cold stress.

Body Size in Tropical Dinosaurs and Mammals

The body size of dinosaurs has attracted attention,
speculation, and theorizing ever since their initial discovery.
In this section I shall review some quantitative aspects of
body size in tropical fossil and extant tetrapods to show that
dinosaurs were not so very different from mammals in the adaptive radiation of size, and that the "Good Reptile" model
proposed by Lull and more recent writers fails because it predicts that in the tropics the adaptive radiation of large
terrestrial reptiles should be as successful as that of large
terrestrial mammals, something which has never occurred.

Body Size in Dinosaurs and Fossil Mammals

Hotton, in this symposium, has argued that the dinosaur

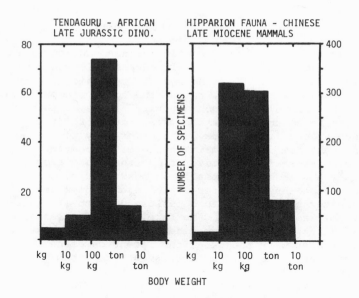

FIGURE 7. Size-frequency distributions for a Jurassic
sauropod fauna (Tendaguru, East Africa) and for a Late
Miocene mammal fauna from China. Mammal data calculated
from the tables in Kurtén (1952).

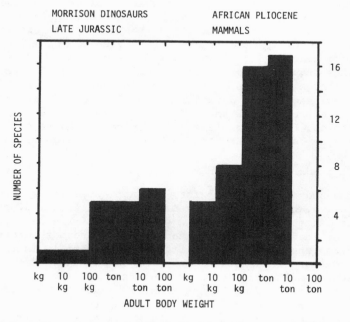

FIGURE 8. Size-frequency distribution for species in a
Jurassic sauropod fauna (Morrison Formation, western United
States) and for the Pliocene mammal faunas of East Africa.
Mammal data from Maglio and Cooke (1978).

adaptive radiation was fundamentally different from that of mammals because small dinosaur species were few and most dinosaur species were large to gigantic. Hotton, I believe, has overstated this contrast because he uses only living mammal species for comparison; today's mammalian fauna is impoverished in large species, a state of affairs which we may well blame on the efficient hunting techniques of our Pleistocene ancestors. In Figure 7, I have plotted the size-frequency data for all individual dinosaur specimens, juvenile and adult, from the fabulous Tendaguru Fauna, an African Late Jurassic sample dominated by giant sauropods. Note that although several dinosaur species exceeded ten tons adult weight, the modal size class is the 100 kg to 1 ton interval. The Late Jurassic sauropod-stegosaur fauna was the result of 60 million years of evolution from ancestors of much more modest size in the Late Triassic. The number and diversity of large land mammals increased steadily from the Early Cenozoic through the Pliocene, also a time span of about 60 million years. Figure 7 shows the size frequency distribution of all individual specimens from the Late Miocene mammal fauna of the Chinese Hipparion Zone. Note that although no mammals exceeded 10 tons, mammals in the 100 kg to 1 ton class were very common. The Pliocene was undeniably the Age of Giants for land mammals; dozens of genera of proboscideans, rhinos, giraffids, hippos, sloths, and armored edentates exceeded a ton in weight. Figure 8 gives the distribution of adult weights for all African Pliocene mammal species, compiled from a recent symposium, and for all dinosaur species from the Late Jurassic Morrison Formation, a complex sedimentary unit deposited in a variety of environments in the continental Western Interior of the U.S. over a time interval of several million years. The geographic area, time interval and range of habitats sampled in the Morrison are roughly comparable with those of the African Pliocene. Again, the maximum adult weight of dinosaurs exceeded that of the mammals, but the number of species of mammals between 1 ton and 10 tons is two or three times that of the dinosaurs. A few of the largest sloths and elephants in the Late Cenozoic probably did exceed 10 tons in weight.

Given enough time, any adaptive radiation of land tetrapods will probably produce a high diversity of species exceeding 1 ton, because natural selection in fully terrestrial species generally seems to favor size increase as a mechanism to deal with dangerous prey, predators, and competitors.

Figure 9 shows the size-frequency distribution for all known tetrapod species in the latest Cretaceous faunas of the Western Interior, from Montana to Texas. Sauropods were rare and few dinosaurs exceeded 10 tons; this pattern is repeated

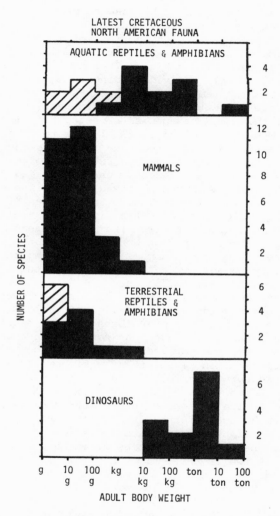

FIGURE 9. Body sizes for species in the late Late
Cretaceous faunas of North America, from Montana to Texas.
Data mostly from Clemens (1963) and Estes (1964) and the
sources cited therein. Amphibians are distinguished by
the hatched pattern.

in nearly all Cretaceous dinosaur samples. The size-frequency distribution for all dinosaur species of all ages, except sauropods, resembles the upper part of the distribution for Pliocene mammals, with the highest frequencies in the 100 kg to 1 ton and 1 ton to 10 ton intervals. I suspect that the large adult size of sauropods is an element in their adaptation for feeding high among the canopies of Mesozoic conifers, and not a thermoregulatory device.

Why No Small Dinosaurs?

A very few carnivorous dinosaurs may have been adult at a few kilograms (Ostrom 1978), but, except for Lagosuchus, I know of no well preserved adult dinosaur which was as small as 100 g. The scarcity of tiny dinosaurs had been made part of the "Good Reptile" model; dinosaur success depended upon the surface area/volume advantages of large size. But there is an alternative explanation. Among living mammals, species in the 10 g to 100 g interval have the highest frequency, for in this range occur most rodents, bats and insectivores. Small terrestrial mammals usually have a varied locomotor repertoire, including some digging and climbing, because the world of the small tetrapod is full of significant relative topographic relief, even if the species is not arboreal. The limb anatomy of small lizards and mammals usually permits a wide range of postures, and the hip joint permits movement outward (abduction-adduction of the femur as well as fore and aft (protraction-retraction) movement. The limb movements of ungulate mammals, such as pigs, deer, antelope, horses, and rhinos, are much less complex; the hip joint severely restricts femur movement to protraction-retraction, with little abduction-adduction. The restricted movement at the hip in ungulates is part of a suite of adaptations for concentrating the limb stroke in a vertical plane, increasing running speed on relatively flat terrain. The ungulate-type of joint system constricts the locomotor repertoire; most ungulates do not climb or dig or use holes for refuges (warthogs hiding in aardvark burrows constitute one exception). The size frequency distribution of ungulate species reflects this limitation. Very few species are smaller than 10 kg (mouse deer, some duikers). Dinosaur hip structure is analogous to that of ungulates in possessing two sets of joint surfaces, a femoral ball which fits deeply into the hip socket, and an external rim on the femur which articulates with the posterior edge of the hip socket. This double articulation severely limits abduction-adduction, and must have limited the locomotion of most dinosaurs to flat, horizontal surfaces. Hotton (this volume) also calls attention to the double articulation in dinosaurs. Thus the size distribution of the adaptive radiation of dinosaurs should resemble that of ungulate mammals, not that of all mammal species. Small dinosaur species are rare for the same reasons that most fossil and living ungulates are over 10 kg adult weight. All through the Jurassic and Cretaceous, the small terrestrial tetrapods were members of groups which retained a flexible and varied pattern of joint movements, mostly lizards and mammals (Figure 9). The therapsids never lost this primitive locomotor flexibility, and thus the therapsid radiations included a rich variety of small species (Keyser 1973, and references cited therein).

Refuges for Large Good Reptiles

There are four ecological-morphological categories in which large Good Reptiles have done well in the presence of large mammals. But these four exceptions seem to prove the rule that large non-marine reptiles cannot cope with large mammal predators and competitors.

Freshwater Aquatic Habitats. The evolutionary dominance of big terrestrial mammals during the Cenozoic ended at the water's edge. In all tropical and subtropical habitats most of the species and individuals in the large aquatic tetrapod category were not mammals but reptiles: turtles, snakes, lizards, and especially crocodilians. Crocodilians are direct descendents of early thecodonts, but bone histology data strongly suggest that all fossil aquatic crocodilians had a Good Reptile grade of physiological adaptation, like that of living species. Although physiological adaptations are diverse among living reptiles, all species studied differ from nearly all mammal species in having a much lower resting metabolism and in tolerating much larger fluctuations in body temperature without incurring tissue damage. Low minimum metabolic requirements give reptiles the ability to stay submerged far longer than mammals of the same weight; tolerance of body temperature fluctuations permits reptiles to stay submerged without the need of the thick dermal insulation seen in diving mammals. Thus Good Reptiles can escape mammalian predators by using water as a refuge. Individual packages of freshwater habitats, rivers, streams, lakes, are small and ephemeral compared to the oceans. The low energy requirements of reptiles enable them to maintain populations in these local habitats where the productivity may be too low or fluctuate too widely to support mammal species of the same body weight. The adaptive radiation of large marine mammals is impressive, but very few freshwater aquatic mammals have exceeded 10 kg, and some of these, such as the hippos, are herbivores which feed mostly on land.

Serpentine Shape and Locomotion. The great constrictors, boas and pythons, are outstanding exceptions to the rule that

mammals have monopolized the role of large terrestrial predatory tetrapod for the last 65 million years. First appearing in the Cretaceous, constrictors are represented today by
20 or so species larger than 20 kg (Table 1). The largest
snakes kill and swallow deer, monkeys and occasionally small
adult <u>Homo sapiens</u> (Minton and Minton 1973). Serpentine form
and locomotion confer unique advantages on a Good Reptile:
even the largest snakes climb well; a hole with a relatively
small diameter can serve as a refuge for a large snake; very
cryptic locomotion permits the snakes to stalk and ambush
mammalian prey and escape detection by mammalian predators.

    <u>Heavy Bony Armor</u>. Large freshwater aquatic turtles have
been common since the Jurassic. Large, fully terrestrial
turtles (true tortoises) appeared in the Middle Eocene and
were common in many tropical and subtropical habitats thereafter. In the Late Miocene, Pliocene and Pleistocene, truly
giant tortoises, from 100 to 1000 kg adult weight, rivaling
contemporary rhinos in size, were widespread in Asia, Africa
and North America (Holman 1976, 1971). These Late Cenozoic
giant tortoises are found in faunas with diverse large
mammal predators and herbivores and are examples of the past
being the key to understanding the present, not <u>vice versa</u>.
Today giant tortoises are restricted to a few oceanic islands
where no native mammalian competitors or predators exist, and
we might be tempted to conclude that tortoises cannot evolve
large size in the presence of a varied mammal fauna.
Extinction of giant tortoises on the continents was a Pleistocene event; human hunting is the most probable cause. The
success of the adaptive radiation of big tortoises probably
reflects the efficacy of their mobile refuges from predation; the highly domed shells of adult tortoises repel most
mammalian predators.

    <u>Islands</u>. Terrestrial reptiles should be capable of
greater oceanic dispersal than land mammals of the same
weight, because the reptiles can survive a much longer time
without food or water. Since their energy requirements are
lower, reptiles should be able to maintain populations on
islands too small for mammals of the same weight. Thus
reptiles should be better colonizers of small islands.
Remote islands may serve as evolutionary refuges as long as
mammal predators and competitors cannot establish populations.
Although giant tortoises were widespread on the continents,
large terrestrial lizards did not evolve in the presence of
large mammals except in Australia. However, on the Isle of
Komodo, in the absence of any endemic mammalian large predators, a giant monitor lizard has evolved to fill the role of
top carnivore. The Komodo Dragon preys upon large mammals,
deer, monkeys, small domestic ungulates, thus proving that

Table 1. Numbers of species, in relation to body size and habitat, of living mammals, reptiles and amphibians (except marine and flying species).

	Total Species	Aquatic Spp.	Aquatic Spp. ≥20 kg	Terrestrial Spp.	Terres. Spp. ≥20kg
MAMMALS	3100	100	3	3000	197
REPTILES					
Sphenodonts	1	0	0	1	0
Turtles	210	181	4	29	4
Lizards	2839	20	2	2819	2
Snakes	1945	200	1	1745	10
Crocodilians	20	20	20	0	0
AMPHIBIANS					
Salamanders	316	160	0	156	0
Frogs	2600	1500	0	1100	0
Apodans	150	12	0	138	0

Data from Walker (1968) and Porter (1972) for species numbers in various families; Minton and Minton (1973) supplied some data on size; I have generated more data using regressions for weight as a function of head and body length. Aquatic species are those which, as adults, spend most of their time in the water or at the water's edge and use water as a refuge from predation. The estimates of numbers of aquatic species are mine.

Good Reptiles besides snakes can cope with endothermic prey. The Komodo Dragon is a favorite model of those who prefer a Good Reptile physiology for hypothetical dinosaurs (Auffenberg 1976; McNab 1978). But we should remember that the Komodo Dragon might be a Red Herring; after all, this great hunting lizard exists only on a few tiny islands where it is free of any threat from large mammalian predators. Large, terrestrial predatory lizards did not suppress the evolution of large mammals on the continents. Large dinosaurs did.

Body Size Distribution in the Evolutionary Hyperspace

Figures 10-12 are what I call "guild-grams", maps showing how the adaptive radiations of the major tetrapod groups filled out the categories of ecological guilds defined by body size, trophic position, and habitat. The tone patterns used in the figures reflect my hypotheses about bioenergetic grades. Good Reptiles and amphibians are black; intermediate-level endotherms are shown in a parallel-line pattern; endotherms with resting heat production as high as in a typical mammal of the same weight are shown in white. The data for Figures 10-12 were gathered during an extensive survey of most of the Permian and Mesozoic collections in North America and Africa, supplemented by a review of published faunal lists for other continents and other ages (Bakker 1975b, 1977, and in press).

Success of Dinosaurs and Thecodonts Caused by Uric Acid?

Hotton (this volume) has made the interesting suggestion that dinosaurs and thecodonts had an advantage over therapsids because the former groups used uric acid in nitrogen excretion, as do most extant Reptilia, while the therapsids used urea, as do most modern mammals. Use of uric acid certainly does permit reduction of water loss without major remodeling of the kidneys, and should be an advantage in an adaptive radiation in arid habitats. However, Hotton's hypothesis fails to explain why in modern deserts most of the large species (adult weight above 20 kg) are mammals, not reptiles, and why in all habitats, arid and well-watered, the Late Permian therapsids were the dominant large land vertebrates.

Good Reptiles in Tropical Lowlands

The Good Reptile model for dinosaurs, as expressed recently by Spotila et al. (1973), McNab (1978), Auffenberg (1976) and others predicts that the advantage of high heat production disappears in the context of large body size and tropical climate. But many of the well known Cenozoic faunas represent tropical habitats. Most of

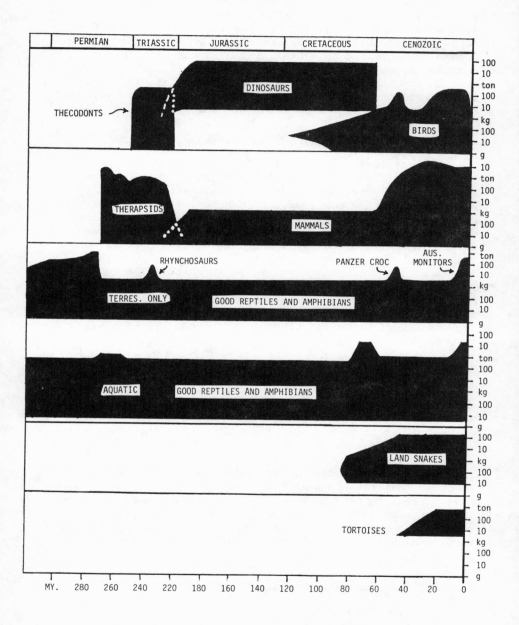

FIGURE 10 (facing page). Body size and evolution in land
vertebrates. In this and all other figures the term
"reptile" is used for all amniote vertebrates except
therapsids, mammals, thecodonts, pterosaurs, dinosaurs
and birds. For each vertebrate group the black area shows
the range of adult weights of all species known through
geologic time. Adult weight is shown on the vertical axis,
on a logarithmic scale. The reptiles and amphibians are
broken down into four categories: tortoises; snakes; fully
terrestrial species except tortoises and snakes; and
freshwater aquatic species. Note the following patterns:
1) sudden drop in maximum size of land reptiles and
amphibians when therapsids appeared; 2) thecodonts partially
replaced therapsids in the Triassic; 3) dinosaurs replaced
thecodonts and therapsids; 4) mammals remained small as long
as dinosaurs existed; 5) except for tortoises, snakes, and a
few lizards and land crocodilians, terrestrial reptiles and
amphibians have been limited to small size since the first
appearance of therapsids.

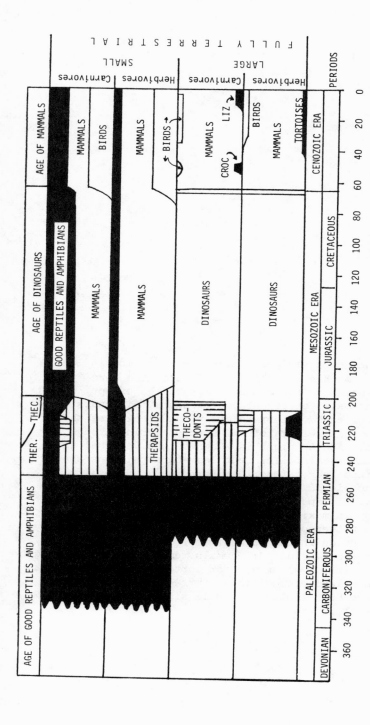

FIGURE 11. Size and feeding types in fully terrestrial land vertebrates. In this and other figures, "large" means an adult weight of 20 kg or more. For each size and feeding category, the patterns show the proportion of the total number of known species contributed by the various groups of land vertebrates. Reptiles and amphibians are shown in black. Thecodonts and therapsids are shown by ruled patterns, the therapsids by horizontal lines, the thecodonts by vertical lines.

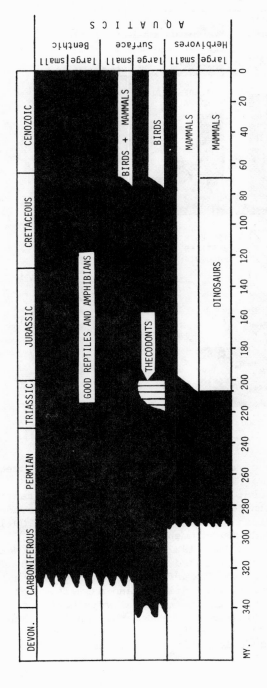

FIGURE 12. Size and feeding types in freshwater aquatic tetrapods. Patterns and symbols as in the previous figure. Benthic species are those which move and feed primarily on the bottom; surface species are those which actively pursue prey at or near the surface. Some therapsids may have been aquatic, but none show obvious swimming adaptations. Dinosaurs probably supplied all the semi-aquatic herbivores in the Jurassic and Cretaceous, but none of the known groups seem specialized for this role. Note that reptiles and amphibians, shown in black, continue to make up a significant part of the aquatic fauna up to the present day.

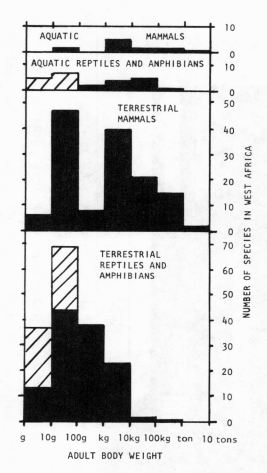

FIGURE 13. Numbers of reptile, amphibian and mammal species
in a modern equatorial lowland habitat. Bats excluded.
Amphibians are hatched; reptiles in black. The habitat is
the West African rain-forest and adjacent woodland savannahs,
sampled by the American Museum Congo Expedition of 1909-1915.
Species lists and body measurements from Noble (1924),
Schmidt (1919, 1923), Allen (1922-1925), Hatt (1940), Walker
(1968). Body weights calculated from body lengths and
regressions of body weight as a function of body length for
frogs, lizards, turtles, crocodilians and mammals. Note that
mammals monopolize the large terrestrial vertebrate categories although the minimum air temperature in these habitats
rarely falls below 20°C. The only terrestrial reptile with
an adult weight of over 10 kg is one species of python.

the Paleocene and Eocene mammal faunas occur with fossil plants or large aquatic crocodilians and turtles, indicating a warm, frost-free climate. Without doubt the mammal faunas of the later Cenozoic in East Africa, India and Java lived in a tropical setting. In all these Cenozoic faunas, nearly all large land vertebrates are mammals; the few large reptiles are tortoises and snakes.

If the Good Reptile model is correct, then the ideal habitat today for an adaptive radiation of large terrestrial reptiles would be the lowland forest, swamps and open woodland of equatorial West Africa, where air temperature rarely falls below 20°C. Figure 13 shows a census of the amphibian, reptile and mammal species collected by the magnificent American Museum Congo Expedition of 1909-1915. The so-called "Lower Tetrapods" dominate in species number in most categories here; the total number of species of reptiles exceeds that of mammals, excluding bats (about 190 versus 140). The number of genera and families is also higher for the herpetofauna; the terrestrial reptile and amphibian species outnumber the terrestrial mammals by three to one; nearly all the aquatic species are reptiles and amphibians. None of the aquatic mammals approaches the size of the Congo crocodilians, but there is one category where mammal dominance is clear. About 35 species of terrestrial mammal exceed 10 kg; only three terrestrial reptiles reach this weight, all snakes. About 15 terrestrial mammal species exceed 100 kg; only one terrestrial reptile does, a python.

This census is quite typical of lowland tropical habitats. It is true that in the tropics terrestrial reptiles and amphibians often outnumber mammals, but mammals retain their nearly complete monopoly in the large-body size roles (Table 1). The Congo census is quite similar in pattern to that of the Late Cretaceous shown in Figure 9, except that the large terrestrial category is filled by dinosaurs in the Cretaceous.

Fatal Non Sequitor of the Model of Spotila et al.

Spotila and his colleagues (Spotila et al. 1973) have presented an elegant mathematical model for thermoregulation in a tropical, three-ton Good Reptile, and have applied this model to dinosaurs. I admire the precision of their hypothesis, but I believe their model has some errors of natural history and one fatal non sequitor, as shown by the following quotations from Spotila et al. (1973):

> "The present dominance of mammals and birds clearly demonstrates the numerous advantages that result from the ability to maintain a constant, relatively high body temperature..." (p. 391).

"As long as a warm equable climate prevailed, there would have been little selection pressure (in dinosaurs) for a high metabolic rate for thermoregulation, since some of the advantages of homeothermy would be achieved without altering reptilian metabolism." .... (p. 400).
"There is no need to postulate any but reptilian physiological characteristics to these giants for thermoregulatory purposes, because their large size alone could have provided the basic thermoregulatory strategy required to ensure their success for over 100 million years." (p. 400).

It is unclear what sort of dominance Spotila et al. ascribe to living birds and mammals. Although some of my colleagues accuse me of being a "mammal chauvinist," I am quite happy to point out that the total number of species of amphibian and reptile today equals or exceeds the number of bird and mammal species (8000-9000 altogether), and the total number of non-flying species of bird and mammal is less than half that of the lower tetrapods. The dominance of mammals is obvious only in the category of large terrestrial species; today this category has only just over 200 species (Table 1). I should emphasize that all my arguments about bioenergetic evolution in large land vertebrates are concentrated on this category, which probably has contained only one-twentieth or less of all tetrapod species at any one time in geological history. The living Reptilia and Amphibia are very successful, diverse groups which dominate mammals in species number in many habitats (Figure 13; Table 1).

The fatal non sequitor in the argument of Spotila et al. occurs when they jump from stating that a large tropical Good Reptile would have <u>some</u> of the advantages of homeothermy, to assuming that natural selection would not favor evolution of high metabolism in a large tropical animal. The graphs presented by these authors show clearly that even in the tropics the body temperature of the three-ton reptile fluctuates more widely from season to season than would that of a mammal. Spotila et al. assume, but do not prove, that the difference between the thermoregulatory performance of the big tropical reptile and that of a mammal of the same size is not significant. Spotila et al. fail to explain why large tropical mammals have the same high heat production as their temperate zone and arctic relatives of the same weight (Taylor et al. 1973, Brody 1945, Kleiber 1961, Bakker 1975b). Why do large tropical cattle, camels, rhinos and elephants have resting heat productions four to seven times higher than that calculated for reptiles of the same weight, if no advantage is purchased by this energy expenditure? The high resting heat production of tropical mammals would seem to be a monumental waste if we accept the conclusions of Spotila et al. Spotila et al. assert, but do not prove, that large size alone is enough to win success in an adaptive radiation of tropical land vertebrates. Their model fails to explain why so few large land reptiles have evolved in the presence of large mammals. Since the model cannot explain the success of large tropical mammals, the model cannot explain the success of dinosaurs and their dominance over mammals.

Spotila et al. (1973) argue as if all dinosaurs were large. But the dinosaurs which probably interacted most frequently with Mesozoic mammals were the small predators such as Compsognathus and Ornitholestes, with adult weights of 5-10 kg, and small juveniles of predatory species with larger adult weights. The Good Reptile model certainly does not explain why dinosaurs, adults of small species and small juveniles of larger species make up nearly all of the specimens of land vertebrates with body weights of 5-50 kg throughout the Jurassic and Cretaceous.

Limits of Herpetophilia

I am an admitted herpetophiliac. When I read Kipling's Rikki-tikki-tavi, I root for the snakes. My herpetological friends sometimes get the impression from my arguments on the importance of endothermy in biotic interactions that I think there is something disreputable or immoral in being a reptile with a low metabolic rate. It is not so. Extant reptiles and amphibians show an extraordinary range of physiological adaptations which make the stereotyped bioenergetics of advanced mammals seem rather unimaginative. Having a low resting metabolic rate provides a powerful advantage in many habitats and habits, since low energy budgets should permit greater specialization of food choice in time and space. Reptiles and amphibians probably have outnumbered mammals in the tropics all through the Cenozoic, as they do today. Good Reptiles and amphibians almost certainly outnumbered dinosaurs in the Mesozoic. There are only 200 or so land mammal species over 20 kg adult weight today, and much of this limited diversity is the result of the present dispersal of the continental masses, caused by seafloor spreading in the Cenozoic, which encourages endemicity. The continents were close together during the Mesozoic, and the total number of dinosaur species at any one time was probably as low as 30 or 40. The contemporary herpetofaunas were probably richer. As I edit this text for the last time, lines at gasoline stations are growing and Western civilization is beginning to realize that its energy-consuming life style must change. At such a time, the energy-efficient lizards and salamanders seem to be admirable models of bioenergetic thrift. Most advanced mammals have a compulsive approach to temperature regulation; they insist on producing metabolic heat at prodigious levels to keep the body's internal environment at a very high and nearly constant temperature. Rather than fighting the environment with high heat expenditure, reptiles and amphibians substitute clever patterns of posture, movement, microhabitat choice and cardiovascular responses to take advantage of the thermal diversity in the environment. There is more Zen in this approach. If the environment does not offer the requisite combinations of heat sources and heat sinks, most reptiles and amphibians can remain safe in their refuges for much longer periods than can mammals, which survive only a short time without feeding.

But there are limits to herpetophilia. The Good Reptile model states that the thermoregulation of a large reptile in the tropics is not inferior to that of a mammal with high heat production. This statement is a bioenergetic hypothesis, but its truth can be tested through its ecological and evolutionary corollaries. If the Good Reptile model is true, then the basic thermoregulatory strategy of big reptiles is far more efficient than that of mammals in the tropics, and the adaptive radiation of large reptiles should exceed that of large mammals in the tropics. The recent advocates of the model, especially Spotila, Auffenberg, and McNab, have, I believe, overlooked this point. The distribution of body sizes in living and fossil tropical faunas shows distinct, non-random patterns; these patterns suggest an evolutionary process: natural selection favors high heat production in large land vertebrates in all habitats.

Adaptive Value of Thermoregulation

The mathematical models of Spotila et al. show that a large tropical Good Reptile thermoregulates quite well; certainly a three-ton hypothetical tropical lizard would never be in danger of fatally low body temperatures; the maximum daily fluctuations in body temperature usually would be only a few degrees, and the total seasonal variation in average daily body temperature would be only 8 degrees or so (Spotila et al. 1973). But the high heat production of a typical large mammal would purchase an even better thermoregulatory performance; the total seasonal variation in average daily body temperature in a large tropical bovid, camel or elephant is only a degree or so (Schmidt Nielson 1964) as long as water is freely available. Most large placental mammals maintain a relatively high body temperature, 37-38°C, higher than that of Spotila's hypothetical three-ton lizard for most of the year. The dominance of big

mammals in the tropics suggests that the difference in
performance between large mammals and large reptiles is very
significant. In this section I will develop some ideas which
indicate that fluctuations in body temperature might be
extremely important in determining the winner during a long
term evolutionary interaction between two adaptive radiations.

Experiments In Vitro and In Vivo

Living lizards show a diversity of body temperature
adaptations. Species which forage in shaded habitats or at
night prefer relatively low body temperatures, 20-30°C;
species which are active in bright, sunny microhabitats,
especially in deserts, prefer much higher body temperatures,
35-43°C. Most species studied in the field show some
combination of physiological and behavioural temperature
regulation. During the hours of active foraging, mating,
defending territories, and digestion, the lizards will
shift from one microhabitat to another, seeking heat sources
(such as warmed substrates or perches exposed to the sun),
or heat sinks (such as cool substrates, shaded
perches or burrows), so as to maintain the preferred
temperature. For many desert species with high preferred
temperatures, this shifting of microhabitats is a
marvelously efficient thermal choreography which can keep
body temperatures within a few degrees of the preferred set
point for hours at a time. The lizards usually increase
the efficiency of microhabitat shifts by changing the heat
flow properties of the skin. When increased heat flow from
the environment is needed, blood circulation to the skin
increases, posture is adjusted, and the lizard may change its
skin color to maximize absorption of thermal energy;
when overheating is a danger, blood flow to the skin is
reduced, and skin absorptivity is minimized.

The differences in preferred body temperatures among
lizard species have permitted several elegant experiments in
the laboratory (Figure 14). In four North American species,
with preferred body temperatures ranging from about 30° for
the alligator lizard, Gerrhonotus, to about 40° for the desert
iguana, Dipsosaurus, Licht (1964) measured the changes in
activity of one very important enzyme, ATPase, as the enzyme
temperature changed. The maximum activity for each species
occurred at about the same temperature as that preferred by
the living lizard. A few years later, Licht et al. (1969)
measured the change in maximum muscle tension developed by limb
muscles as the temperature of the muscle changed. Again, for each
species the best performance occurred at about the preferred
body temperature observed in the living lizards in the field
and laboratory. Many fish species also show marked body

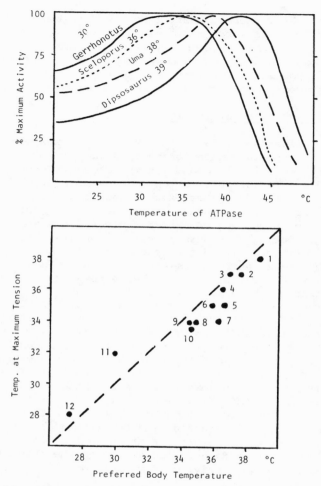

FIGURE 14.   Maximum physiological output and body temperature in lizards.

<u>Above</u>: Activity of ATPase as a function of the temperature of the ATPase solution in four species of lizard.   The preferred body temperature for each species is indicated on the curves. Note the correspondence of maximum activity with preferred temperature.   (Redrawn from Licht 1964).

<u>Below</u>: Relation between preferred body temperature and the temperature at which skeletal muscle generates maximum tension in each species.   1 - <u>Dipsosaurus</u>; 2 - <u>Uma</u>; 3 - <u>Physignathus</u>; 4 - <u>Amphibolurus</u>; 5 - <u>Amphibolurus</u>; 6 - <u>Diplodactylus</u>; 7 - <u>Sceloporus</u>; 8 - <u>Egernia</u>; 9 - <u>Gehyra</u>; 10 - <u>Eumeces</u>; 11 - <u>Gerrhonotus</u>; 12 - <u>Phyllurus</u>.   Dashed line has a slope of 1.   (Redrawn from Licht, Dawson and Shoemaker 1969).

temperature preferences; feeding experiments show that the digestion rate falls rapidly as the body temperature is depressed below the preferred set point (Figure 15). These experiments strongly suggest that minimizing fluctuations in body temperature is a powerful adaptation for maximizing the performance of all body tissues.

Growth Rates of Individuals and Populations

Natural selection works not only on adaptations for direct biotic encounters between predators, prey and competitors, but also on the subtler aspects of life-history strategies: the growth rate, age at first reproduction and litter size. Since most mammals should be able to reduce fluctuations in body temperature to narrower limits than can reptiles and amphibians of the same weight, we might predict that, everything else being equal, mammals should grow more rapidly than reptiles in the field. This prediction is tested in Figure 16 where generation interval is plotted as a function of weight at first reproduction in females. In mammals, the time elapsed from fertilization of the egg and creation of a female embryo until the first reproduction of that female increases with increasing body weight. This elapsed time, the generation interval, is as low as 50 days for small rodents, and six or seven thousand days for elephants. Primates and bats have exceptionally long generation intervals, probably because they suffer relatively little predation. For the other land mammals the scatter of points in Figure 16 can be contained neatly within two lines with slopes of 0.25. Thus mammal generation intervals increase in proportion to the 0.25 power of body weight. The metabolic rate per gram per hour decreases in proportion to body weight to the 0.25 power. These two relations combine to yield an intriguing result: the total metabolism per gram is about the same over one generation interval for large and small land mammals.

The data for reptile and amphibian generation interval and weight at first reproduction are far more scattered (Figure 16). Most reptiles and amphibians in the field do grow far more slowly than mammals of comparable weight at sexual maturity. The great Aldabra giant tortoise reaches first breeding at about 20 kg, about the weight of a female German shepherd, and requires from 20 to 40 years to reach this weight. The Nile crocodile requires 10 to 20 years to reach first breeding weight of about 50 kg. Some of these slow growth rates in the field may be the result of very high population densities and intense intraspecific competition, but I suspect that much of the data results from the fluctuating body temperatures and efficiencies of the reptiles.

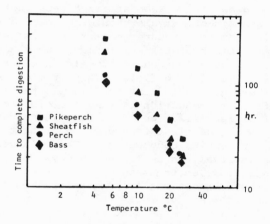

FIGURE 15.   Rate of digestion in relation to body temperature
in predatory fish.   On the y axis is the time in hours to
total digestion of one weight-standardized meal.   On the x
axis is body temperature.   (Data from Molnar, Tamassy, and
Tolg 1972).

The spectacular improvement in growth rates of reptiles raised under ideal conditions of temperature and food in captivity suggests that reptiles are not genetically inferior to mammals in maximum growth potential. Bustard (1968) reports that large crocodilians raised on hide farms in the tropics reach breeding weight in about five years, one-third or one-fourth the time for wild individuals. Similar striking improvements occur in the great sea turtles in turtle farms. Jackson et al. (1976) raised gopher tortoises to breeding weight, about a kilogram, in three years; in the field most specimens require fifteen or eighteen years to reach that weight. Most of the life-history information for living reptiles and amphibians comes from temperate climates. In some of the small tropical species growth rates and generation intervals are well within the range of mammals of the same weight (Figure 16). The large tropical reptiles (tortoises and crocodilians) have relatively long generation intervals in the field.

Is a High Body Temperature Advantageous?

A large placental mammal maintaining a body temperature of 37°C would have a body temperature higher than that of Spotila's hypothetical three-ton Good Reptile, even in the tropics. It has been suggested that higher body temperatures permit higher maximum work output from muscles and other tissues (Hill 1970 and references cited therein). Within any one species, the metabolic rates of the whole animal and most isolated enzyme systems do increase with increasing temperature, up until the preferred body temperature is reached. The factor by which metabolic rate increases with a temperature increase of 10°C is the "Q_{10}"; most observed Q_{10}'s are between 2.0 and 2.7. It has been argued that a mammal at 37°C body temperature would have an enormous advantage over a lower tetrapod at 17°C: the work output per unit weight of muscle would be four times greater in the mammal (Hill 1970). However, the interspecific Q_{10} effect does not necessarily have the same magnitude as the intraspecific Q_{10} effect. In fact, a colleague of mine, a physiologist, has suggested that the maximum output per unit weight in all species may be essentailly the same, if we measure output at the preferred body temperature for each species. Certainly, species with low preferred temperatures, such as Sphenodon and many temperate zone salamanders, can forage for food at body temperatures far below the minimum necessary for coordinated muscular activity in species with very high preferred body temperatures. Sphenodon and salamanders of the genus Desmognathus can stalk, capture and digest food at body temperatures of 10°C; desert iguanas and monitor lizards do not respond to food at

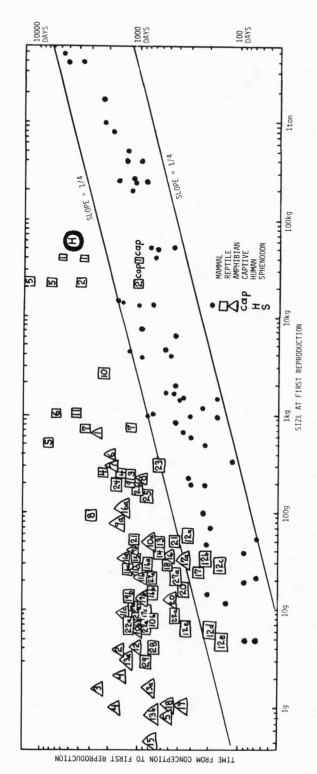

FIGURE 16. Growth rates in amphibians (triangles), reptiles (squares) and mammals (dots). Time from conception to first reproduction in females plotted on the y axis; weight of female at first conception on the x axis. Accelerated growth in captive specimens indicated by CAP. Mammal points from Walker (1968); primates and bats excluded. Human values indicated by H. Note that the mammal points are contained between two parallel lines with a slope of 0.25. Data for reptiles and amphibians from Healy (1975), Tinkle (1973), Pianka and Parker (1975), Taber et al. (1975), Andrews (1976), Bruce (1975), Bauman and Metter (1977), Clark, (1976), Ernst (1975), Smyth and Smyth (1974), Jameson, (1974), Coulson et al. (1973), Dixon and Staton (1976), Jackson et al. (1976), Ernst et al. (1973), Goldberg (1972), Goldberg and Bezy (1974), Clark (1975), Graham and Doyle (1977), Simmons (1975), and Porter (1972).

FIGURE 16. (continued)

REPTILES SQUARES

Crocodilians

1 Crocodilus niloticus
2 Alligator mississippiensis

Turtles

3 Kinosternum subrubrum
4 Terrapene ornata
5 Geochelone gigantea
6 Gopherus agassizi
7 Pseudemys scripta
8 Clemmys guttata
9 Sternothaerus odoratus
10 Trionyx japonicus
11 Emydoidea blandingii

Lizards

12a Anolis gundlachi
12b Anolis frenatus
12c Anolis garmani
12d Anolis acutus
12e Anolis carolinensis
13 Sceloporus woodi
14 Morethia boulengeri
15 Moloch horridus
16a Phrynosoma solare
16b Phrynosoma platyrhinos

(Lizards cont.)

17 Mabuya buettneri
18 Cnemidophorus sexlineatus
19a Xantusia vigilis
19b Xantusia riversiana
20 Menetia greyii
21 Crotaphytus collaris
22a Eumeces fasciatus
22b Eumeces septentrionalis
23 Gerrhonotus multicarinatus

Serpents

24 Elaphe obsoleta
25 Crotalus viridis
26 Natrix sipedon
27a Thamnophis sirtalis
27b Thamnophis proximus
28 Tropidoclonium lineatum
29 Storeria occipitomaculata

AMPHIBIANS TRIANGLES

Salamanders

1 Cryptobranchus alleganiensis
2 Bolitoglossa rostrata
3 Notophthalmus viridescens
4 Pseudotriton montanus
5 Eurycea neotenes

(Salamanders cont.)

6 Necturus maculosus
7 Amphiuma tridactylum
8 Pleurodeles waltl
9a Salamandra salamandra
9b Salamandra atra
10a Ambystoma jeffersonianum
10b Ambystoma macrodactylum
11a Triturus cristatus
11b Triturus alpestris
11c Triturus vulgaris
12 Leurognathus marmoratus
13a Plethodon glutinosus
13b Plethodon cinereus
14 Ensatina eschscholtzi
15 Desmognathus aeneus

Frogs and Toads

16a Rana catesbeiana
16b Rana pipiens
16c Rana clamitans
17a Bufo valliceps
17b Bufo canorus
17c Bufo hemiophrys
18 Acris gryllus
19 Syrrhophus marnocki
20 Leptodactylus macrosternum

FIGURE 17. Two alternative models for dinosaur thermo-regulation.

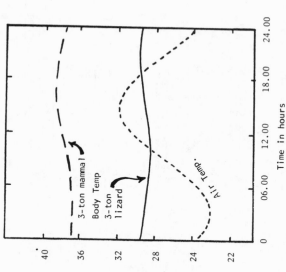
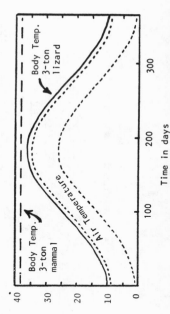

(Above) Air temperature (small dashes) and body temperature (solid line) of a 3-ton hypothetical lizard with Mstd one-fourth that of a mammal of the same weight and body tempera-ture. These two lines were calculated by Spotila et al. (1973) from a mathematical model for body temperature in a giant reptile, using climatic data for a subtropical habitat. The body temperature of a 3-ton typical mammal in the same habitat is shown in long dashes. The graph represents one full 24 hour cycle in the warm season and assumes that neither animal is short of water. Note that both the "Good Reptile" and the mammal have stable body temperatures, but that of the mammal is 8° to 10°C higher.

(Below) Seasonal fluctuation of air temperatures, daily minimum and maximum, and the body temperatures of the hypo-thetical 3-ton lizard-like reptile and the 3-ton advanced mammal. Air and giant reptile temperatures calculated by Spotila et al. (1973).

such temperatures (observations on captive specimens at
Harvard). Nevertheless there is some suggestion that a high
preferred body temperature may increase the maximum physiological output, although with an interspecific Q_{10} far lower
than two. The fastest running speeds observed among lizards
occur in species with high preferred temperatures (Belkin
1961, Bakker 1975b). For any given body weight, the highest
sustained (aerobic) metabolism measured in lizards during
exercise also occurs in species with high preferred body
temperatures (Bakker 1975b; Bennett and Dawson 1976). In
direct, vigorous interactions among predators and competitors
natural selection may favor the higher preferred body temperatures. But I must emphasize that for most species of lower
tetrapod the observed preferred body temperature seems to fit
the behavioral context of microhabitat choice in time and
space; a low preferred temperature is an advantage to a
lizard which forages at night or in deeply shaded microhabitats and which has refuges from predators and competitors
with much higher body temperatures. Selection for high body
temperatures should be most severe among large, fully
terrestrial tetrapods with few refuges.

Physiological Output: Three-Ton Good Reptile versus Three-Ton Mammal

In Figures 17-19 I have used Spotila's mathematical
model for a three-ton Good Reptile and the experimental data
on changes in enzyme activity to estimate the physiological
advantage a three-ton mammal might possess. Spotila used
climate data from southern Florida, a subtropical region
(Figure 17). In Figure 18 I have redrawn Spotila's curves
for average daily body temperature of the three-ton reptile
for the warmest 120 days of the year, an interval when
air temperature does not fall below 20°C. The air temperature
fluctuations during this interval are about the same as
those during the entire year in the equatorial lowlands
of the Congo Basin. Thus Figure 18 shows the body
temperature responses of the hypothetical big Good Reptile
in a fully tropical climate like that generally ascribed to
the Jurassic and Cretaceous habitats of dinosaurs. Figure
18 also shows how much higher or lower the body temperature of the hypothetical reptile would be than the
preferred body temperature, if the preferred body temperature is 30°C and if the preferred body temperature is
36.5°C. Spotila's model shows that at any given season
daily fluctuations in body temperature in the reptile would
be only a degree or so, no larger than the daily fluctuations in most mammals (Figure 17). However, even during
the warmest 120 days, the average daily body temperature
of the reptile rises gradually from about 30°C to 36.5°C, and

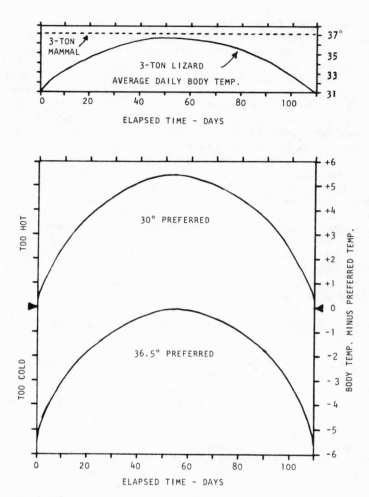

FIGURE 18.   Limits of mass homeothermy.

(Above)   Comparison of temperature homeostasis in a 3-ton
mammal and a 3-ton lizard during the warmest 120 days in
southern Florida.   Lizard body temperature taken from the
mathematical model of Spotila et al. (1973); see Figure 17.
Note that the mammal average daily temperature shows little
seasonal fluctuation.

(Below)   The difference between body temperature and preferred
body temperature in two hypothetical 3-ton lizards during
this 120 day interval.   On the Y-axis is shown the difference
between body temperature and preferred body temperature.   One
lizard has a preferred temperature of 30°C, and the other of
36.5°C.

then falls back to 30°C (Figure 18). The average daily
body temperature of a large placental mammal would remain
at about 37°C all through this interval. In Figure 19,
I have used the curves from Figure 14 to calculate the
activity of ATPase at the body temperature of the
hypothetical three-ton reptile during the 120 day interval
if the preferred temperature is 30°C and if it is 36.5°C.
Thus Figure 19 shows the loss in physiological output
caused by the difference between preferred and actual body
temperature.

If the preferred temperature is 30°C, then the hypothetical reptile would suffer a 10% drop in enzyme activity
during the warmest part of the year. If the preferred
temperature is 36.5°C, the loss would be a maximum of 20% at
the coolest parts of the cycle (Figure 19).

I believe that Figure 19 shows the correct order of
magnitude for the likely seasonal reduction in maximum
output in big tropical reptiles. Gradual acclimatization
from season to season might reduce this loss, but there
are no published data suggesting that acclimatization
can change preferred body temperature as much as
4°C. The percentage of maximum ATPase activity in the big
hypothetical reptiles in Figure 19 was calculated from
the curves in Figure 14 for species of Gerrhonotus and
Sceloporus, animals with adult weights under 100 g.
But there is no reason to believe that the shape of the
curve of % maximum output as a function of body temperature would change significantly with increased body
size. The maximum difference between preferred body
temperature and actual body temperature in Figure 18 is
about 5°C. If we assume a Q_{10} of 2.0, then the change in
metabolic rate for a five degree change in temperature
would be 40%, an estimate which is probably too high.

Would this 10-20% seasonal drop in maximum output
explain the long-term evolutionary dominance of big terrestrial mammals over big reptiles in the tropics? I have kept
two species of monitor lizards in the lab, Varanus niloticus
and V. exanthematicus. In thermal gradients the individuals
exhibited preferred body temperatures of from 36.5 to 38°C.
All individuals could stalk, kill and digest live mammalian
prey at body temperatures from 30 to 40°C. The theoretical
three-ton reptiles in Figures 17-19 probably could function
in a similarly adequate way all through the year. The
central tenet of the Good Reptile model for dinosaur thermoregulation is that a big tropical Good Reptile would
perform adequately, with which I agree. However, except perhaps on small, remote islands, dinosaurs, mammals and Good

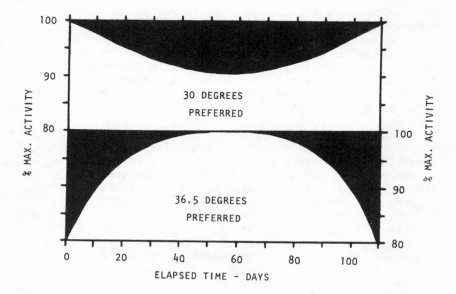

FIGURE 19.   Loss of physiological output in a 3-ton lizard in the tropics.   Same environmental conditions as in Figures 17 and 18.   The percent of maximum activity of ATPase has been calculated from the body temperature of the lizard and its deviation from the preferred temperature, given by Figure 18, together with the temperature activity relations of ATPase shown in Figure 14.   Two hypothetical lizards are shown: one with a preferred temperature of 36.5°C, and one with a preferred temperature of 30°C.

Reptiles have not evolved in isolation from each other; the adaptive radiation of dinosaurs was accompanied by a complex adaptive radiation of mammals; the radiations of the modern groups of reptiles and mammals occurred in the same habitats all through the Cenozoic. A three-ton Good Reptile would take from 20 to 100 years to reach sexual maturity. After a weight of 100 kg is reached, this Good Reptile would have few refuges from interactions with mammals. If the Good Reptile has one interaction with a potentially dangerous mammalian predator or competitor each year at the season when the reptile's maximum physiological output is reduced by 10-20%, the probability becomes quite significant that the reptile will at some time during its life engage in an interaction with a mammal which will cause the reptile's death or at least reduce its reproductive success. If we imagine a mosaic of populations of big land reptiles and big mammals interacting through thousands of generations of evo-lutionary time, then we can see that the net long-term advan-tage of the mammals may well suppress the adaptive radiation of the reptiles. The concept of natural selection implies a choice; if the long-term evolutionary choice is between an adequate system and one which is 10-20% better than adequate, evolutionary theory predicts that the slightly better system will displace the adequate system. The most important prin-ciple of the genetic theory of evolution outlined by Fisher, Haldane and Wright, forty years ago, was that very small differences in fitness would be sufficient to drive evolu-tionary change in populations. Similarly, small differences in the value of adaptations for direct biotic interactions with predators and competitors may well be sufficient to cause the suppression of one adaptive radiation by another.

Occasional Thermal Disasters in the Tropics

Low heat production and a low surface-area to volume ratio would confer another possible advantage upon a hypo-thetical giant tropical reptile. If a thermal disaster did lower the body temperature by ten or fifteen degrees, a great deal of time would be required to regain the preferred body temperature. A prolonged rainy season could reduce the body temperature of Spotila's three-ton Good Reptile from 35°C to 20°C. Precipitation would continue to evaporate as long as skin temperature is above air temperature, with 550 calories of heat dissipated with each gram of water evaporated. The continuously renewed film of rainwater would also remove heat by conduction and convection. Few if any living reptiles and amphibians can increase heat production without exercise to cope with cold stress. In contrast, most mammals have not only a high resting heat production but also some capacity to increase heat production through shivering

or non-shivering thermogenesis (Jansky 1973). The total
thermoregulatory heat production of a mammal shivering at
maximum capacity is quite prodigious, fifteen to thirty times
the resting heat production of a reptile of the same weight
at the same body temperature (Jansky 1973, Bakker 1975b).
Thus most mammals can maintain a high body temperature through
far more severe thermal crises than can a Good Reptile.

To raise one gram of tissue 1°C requires about 0.8
calories of heat. If the metabolism in reptiles scales
according to Kleiber's Law (Kleiber 1961, see the discussion
which follows below), then the heat production at a body
temperature of 20°C would be about 1.0 calories per gram per
hour in a three-gram lizard, and about 0.031 calories per
gram per hour in the three-ton Good Reptile. If all the
metabolic heat could be stored, then the three-gram reptile
could raise its body temperature from 20 to 35°C in about
twelve hours; the three-ton reptile would require about
fifteen days. Increasing body size decreases the surface
area to body weight ratio, an advantage in conserving body
heat when the body temperature is above air temperature, but
a disadvantage when the animal must use external heat sources
to raise body temperature above air temperature. If body
shape remained constant, surface area per unit weight would
decrease in proportion to the 0.33 power of weight.
McMahon (1973, 1975) has shown that in closely related
species shape does not stay constant with increasing adult
size, but rather the bodies and limbs tend to get relatively
shorter and stockier, with lengths increasing in proportion
to the 2/3 power of diameters. Hence surface area per unit
body weight decreases in proportion to about the 0.36 power
of weight. A three-ton Good Reptile has about .008 times as
much surface area per unit weight as a three-gram Good
Reptile. If the time required to raise body temperature a
certain number of degrees depended only on the surface area
per unit weight, then the three-ton reptile would need over
a hundred times longer period of heating than would the
three-gram lizard. If the three-gram lizard required ten
minutes to raise the body temperature by 15°C, then the
three-ton reptile would require about three and one-half
days.

A big terrestrial reptile operating at a body temperature from 10 to 15°C below its preferred body temperature
would be unable to cope with a big mammal predator operating
at its preferred body temperature. Even if such a thermal
disaster occurred only once in every generation interval,
the presence of big mammalian predators with high
thermoregulatory heat production would probably suppress the
adaptive radiation of big Good Reptiles.

The Scaling of Thermoregulatory Heat Production

An analysis of the fossil evidence for the evolution of thermoregulation requires a review of some of the quantitative aspects of heat production among extant tetrapods.

Automatic Endotherms

Evolutionary theory owes much to empirical rules, those statistical generalizations which come from measuring some adaptation through a wide range of body weights, or climate types, or feeding roles. The single most important empirical rule is the famous "mouse to elephant curve," the relation between metabolism and body weight in mammals. Max Kleiber showed that the metabolism of mammals, measured in the standard state, i.e. with the animal completely at rest, but awake, not expending any energy for digestion or any other activity, could be expressed by the equation:

$$M_{std} = 17(W)^{-0.25}$$

where M_{std} is standard metabolism in calories per gram per hour, and W is body weight in grams (see Kleiber 1961 for a historical review). This relation, quite appropriately known as Kleiber's Law, is based on measurements on advanced placental mammals with body temperatures of about 37°C. Some mammal species regulate at 30°C or lower, but their M_{std} obeys Kleiber's Law if we correct the observed metabolic rate by applying the standard Q_{10} factor (Dawson 1973). Birds have higher body temperatures than mammals but conform to Kleiber, if the Q_{10} correction is applied. Standard metabolism can be thought of as a minimum alert idling speed for the metabolic machinery. Several dozen species of mammals and birds have special adaptations to permit metabolism to fall far below the usual M_{std} during hibernation and other forms of torpor. Hummingbirds and bats show daily cycles of torpor; the egg-laying spiny anteater will drop off into torpor when exposed to severe food shortage (Augee et al. 1966). Daily or seasonal torpor is the rule rather than the exception in living reptiles and amphibians in the temperate zones, since their body temperatures fluctuate much more frequently and widely than those of mammals and birds. But the torpor of birds and mammals is a more sophisticated adaptation than that of reptiles and amphibians, because birds and mammals can bring their body temperatures back up to alert levels with metabolic heat production. A ground squirrel coming out of hibernation produces massive amounts of heat through shivering. Torpid lizards or frogs must wait until the environmental heat sources are adequate for bringing body temperatures back up to the preferred set point.

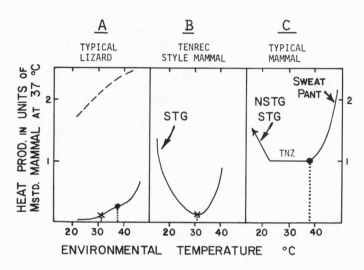

FIGURE 20. Idealized metabolic responses to environmental temperature: A - lizard-like ectotherm; B - tenrec-like mammal; C - advanced mammal or bird. Metabolic heat production is given in units of the standard metabolism of the advanced mammal. For a given body temperature and body weight the advanced mammal M_{std} is about four times that of the lizard or tenrec. Heat production at an environmental temperature of 37°C is indicated by a dot; at 32°C by an X. The solid line in each case gives the heat production of M_{std} plus thermoregulatory responses; exercise heat production is assumed to be nil. Maximum sustained (aerobic) heat production during exercise in the lizard is indicated by a dashed line. Abbreviations: NSTG - non-shivering thermogenesis; STG - shivering; TNZ - thermoneutral zone.

Except for those special cases of controlled torpor, most living birds and mammals produce much more heat than a reptile or amphibian of comparable size. Indeed, birds and mammals are unique among all known organisms in possessing such high levels of metabolism when completely at rest. I have called birds and mammals "automatic endotherms" because the high heat production of M_{std} requires no muscle contractions, no postural adjustments, no special activity of any sort. Bird and mammal M_{std} is produced by all body cells, possibly as part of the sodium-pump mechanism at the cell membrane (Jansky 1973, Edelman and Ismail-Beigi 1971).

High, constant M_{std} is the core of mammal and bird thermoregulation. At first glance, automatic endotherms seem very wasteful of heat energy. Over a wide range of environmental temperatures automatic endotherms can keep their body temperatures constant with the heat production of M_{std} alone, without shivering or non-shivering thermogenesis. This range of environmental temperatures, in which a constant body temperature is maintained with only M_{std}, is known as the "thermoneutral zone," TNZ (Figure 20). In the TNZ the automatic endotherm regulates the heat loss from body to environment by controlling blood circulation to the skin and changing the orientation of fur or feathers to modify the insulating properties of the pelage. Automatic endotherms in their TNZ are analogous to a house where room temperature is kept constant by keeping the furnace on a very high, constant level and varying heat loss to the outside by opening and closing windows. It would seem far less wasteful of metabolic energy to maintain as low a heat loss as possible, and to change the heat production to keep body temperature constant in a fluctuating environment. The ecologic advantage of automatic endothermy is probably the quickness of thermoregulatory response when the bird or mammal moves from one microhabitat to another. If a wolf trots from a sunny field into deep forest shade, the skin circulation changes instantly, the fur is fluffed by cutaneous muscles, and body temperature remains constant. To change metabolic heat production would require hormonal intervention and a considerable time lag.

Kleiber's Law is astonishingly stable from the Equator to the Poles. An arctic fox has the same M_{std} as a coyote of the same weight in Death Valley. The two canines differ in the insulation value of the fur, not in metabolism (Scholander et al. 1950).

Does Kleiber's Law Work for Reptiles?

Bennett and Dawson (1976) have reviewed heat production

in reptiles and have shown that M_{std} decreases in proportion
to a constant power of body weight; hence the standard allometric equation can be used: $M = bW^a$ where M is heat production per gram per hour, W is weight and a and b are constants.
Bennett and Dawson and other workers have calculated the exponent, a, for separate groups of reptiles (turtles, lizards,
snakes) and for all reptiles together after applying the Q_{10}
correction where necessary. The values for a vary widely,
from about -0.38 to -0.18. If the absolute value of the exponent in reptiles is significantly smaller than -0.25, then
the heat production per unit weight in reptiles decreases less
rapidly with increasing weight than in mammals, and at some
large weight the M_{std} of a reptile would be the same as that
of a mammal. If true, this convergence of allometric relations
would mean that the functional difference between Good Reptiles and automatic endotherms gradually decreases with increasing weight. Hotton and Farlow discuss this possibility
elsewhere in this volume. However, I believe that there are
very good reasons to suspect that the value of a in reptiles
is not significantly different from that in mammals. The 95%
confidence interval for a in reptiles usually includes -0.25,
or values very close to it (Bennett and Dawson 1976). We do
not yet have enough data on M_{std} from very large extant reptiles to be certain that their a is significantly different
from the value in the Kleiber equation for placental mammals.
Hemmingsen (1960) reviewed heat production at rest in an
enormous range of ectothermic invertebrates and vertebrates,
from unicellular protists to tortoises, and found that the
exponent calculated for all species combined was not significantly different from the Kleiber exponent of -0.25.
McMahon (1973, 1975) has developed an attractive general
theory for the control of metabolism by scaling factors; he
predicts that for all terrestrial tetrapods the scaling exponent should be -0.25. It may well turn out that the
scatter in the data on metabolism in extant reptiles will
always be too great to prove that the difference between the
exponents calculated for reptiles and mammals is in fact
significant. If so, the observations of Hemmingsen and the
theoretical predictions of McMahon become important arguments
for accepting the Kleiber exponent for all tetrapods. The
fossil record offers an empirical test of theories of bioenergetic scaling; as I shall describe below, predator/prey
ratios are controlled by metabolic rates, and predator/prey
ratios for very large extinct Good Reptiles suggest that heat
production decreased with increasing rate according to the
Kleiber scaling exponent.

Special Cases: Brooding Pythons; Hot-Blooded Tuna; Endothermic Moths

Unlike birds and mammals, most reptiles do not increase

metabolic heat production when environmental temperature
drops below the level necessary for maintaining the preferred
body temperature; in general the living Reptilia do not
shiver and do not have non-shivering thermogenetic
mechanisms. Female pythons do display a shivering-like
adaptation for keeping the egg temperature above substrate
temperature (Hutchinson et al. 1966). Some large fish have a
high rate of sustained swimming and use the heat of exercise
to maintain a tissue temperature far above that of their
environment (Carey and Teal 1956, 1969). Fast flying insects,
such as the hawkmoths, use the immense heat output of flight
muscles to elevate body temperatures (Bartholomew and Epting
1975). In these fish and insects heat loss during exercise
is reduced; in the fish the arrangement of blood flow
restricts the heat lost through the fins and surface layers
of muscle; the moths have heavy insulation over the flight
muscle compartment. Some workers have suggested that large,
active lizards use exercise heat for thermoregulation, and
the body temperature of big monitor lizards does rise a bit
during prolonged struggling (Bartholomew and Tucker 1964).
The automatic endothermy of birds and mammals is unique
because the high heat production of M_{std} requires no exercise.
An exercise endotherm like the hawkmoth is a part-time endotherm; its body temperature quickly falls back down to lower
levels after the exercise ends.

Tenrecs: Mammals with Fluctuating Endothermy

Tenrecs, moonrats, hedgehogs and a few other small,
structurally primitive extant mammals have intriguing thermoregulatory adaptations which combine features of Good Reptiles and automatic endotherms. Resting, alert tenrecs have
very low heat production, not significantly higher than that
of a reptile of the same weight (Crompton, Taylor and Jagger
1978). As long as the body temperature remains near the
preferred level, this low heat production is maintained. But
moonrats, tenrecs and hedgehogs do shiver to increase heat
production in cold stress; they probably have non-shivering
thermogenetic mechanisms, and they have the typical automatic-
endotherm type of torpor which includes the capacity for
self-arousal through high heat production (Dawson 1972, 1973;
E. Gould pers. comm. 1979). Tenrecs seem to be the ideally
efficient endotherms—they elevate heat production only when
the body temperature begins to fall below the preferred level
or when coming out of torpor (Figure 20); they do not have
the high, continuous heat production of typical placental
mammals and birds. The tenrec style of fluctuating endothermy may have been present in therapsids and some Mesozoic
mammals, as I shall discuss below.

408   Robert T. Bakker

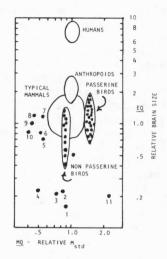

FIGURE 21. Relative brain weight compared with relative
metabolic rate in extant birds and mammals. The encephalization quotient, EQ, is the observed size of the brain
divided by the size of the brain in an average living mammal
of the same body weight, calculated by Jerison's (1973)
equation $B = 0.12(W)^{.67}$. The metabolic quotient, MQ, is the
observed M_{std} (corrected to $37°C$) divided by the M_{std} of a
typical placental mammal of the same body weight, calculated
from Kleiber's equation $M_{std} = 17(W)^{-0.25}$. Thus for each
species plotted here, brain size and M_{std} are expressed
relative to the brain size and M_{std} of an advanced mammal of
the same body weight. Note that there is no correlation
between relative M_{std} and relative brain size. Hence, there
is no evidence for a close evolutionary link between relative
brain size and metabolic rate. EQ determined from data in
Crile and Quiring (1940); MQ determined from data in Dawson
(1973) and Calder and King (1974). 1 - shrew, Sorex minutus;
2 - oppossum, Didelphis marsupialis; 3 - hedgehog, Erinaceus
europaeus; 4 - Malagasy insectivore, Tenrec ecaudatus;
5 - armadillo, Dasypus novemcinctus; 6 - sloth, Choloepus
hoffmanni; 7 - anteater, Tamandua tetradactyla; 8 - duckbilled
platypus, Ornithorhynchus anatinus; 9 - spiny anteater,
Tachyglossus aculeatus; 10 - sloth, Bradypus griseus;
11 - ostrich, Struthio camelus.

Teasing Apart the Evolutionary Consequences of Heat Production, Brain Size and Locomotion

In an earlier section I suggested several reasons why high thermoregulatory heat production might be an important direct advantage for large tropical mammals. It is also possible that high heat production is an indirect advantage. Most large placental mammals differ from reptiles of the same size in having much larger brains and more prolonged intervals of vigorous locomotor activity. It could be argued that the high heat production of mammals is not a great advantage per se, but rather is somehow linked to the capacity for high levels of exercise metabolism and to the proper functioning of the complex central nervous system. The fossil record can be used to test these notions.

Relative Brain Size: Reptile versus Mammal

For a given body weight, the brain size in most mammals is 5 to 20 times larger than that of most extant reptiles. Most of this difference in brain size is caused by the enlargement of the neocortex in mammals, the center for the "higher" neurophysiological functions of information processing, integration, and decision-making. It is generally assumed that the enlarged, convoluted neocortex gives mammals a greater capacity for learning and behavioural complexity, a reasonable hypothesis which has not yet been tested rigorously in experiments. Many tetrapods, including lizards, birds and mammals, have special adaptations to regulate brain temperature within narrower limits than other tissues, and it is not unreasonable to suppose that the high heat production of mammals is a necessary precondition for the evolution of an enlarged neocortex.

Jerison (1973) has shown that in a series of mammal species of the same general evolutionary grade, brain weight increases as the 0.67 power of body weight. Jerison argues that this scaling relation maintains a constant capacity for processing information. Whether or not this last proposition is true, the scaling relation certainly is useful for comparing relative brain size in a great variety of tetrapods. Jerison uses a measure called the EQ to compare brain-size grades. EQ is the observed brain size in any species divided by the brain size of the average placental mammal of the same body weight. By definition the average placental mammal today has an EQ of one. Primates have above average EQ's, 4 to 7 for apes and humans. Some structurally primitive placentals and marsupials have EQ's from 0.2 to 0.4 (Figure 21). Most extant reptile species have EQ's less than 0.1 as adults. Jerison developed his theory of brain size evolution by comparing EQ data for adult specimens only. Such selectivity is reasonable for mammals and birds, because the juveniles do not begin to forage independently until they reach nearly adult size. But in most reptiles the period of parental care is short or nonexistent, and juveniles begin to interact independently with other animals soon after hatching. Any theory of the evolutionary interaction between mammals and reptiles must incorporate EQ data from juvenile reptiles. One published brain weight/body weight data point does exist for a hatchling alligator (Crile and Quirling 1940); the calculated EQ is 0.22, higher than that of ostriches and several species of structurally primitive mammals.

It is often asserted that the coevolution of metabolism and brain size is very tight and that small brains are always accompanied by low metabolism, large brains by high metabolism. After giving my dinosaur lecture, on a number of occasions, I have been assaulted from the audience by the statement that dinosaurs could not have had high metabolic rates because they did not have brains as large as those of mammals of the same weight. It has been suggested (Hopson 1977) that some of the dinosaurs with relatively large heads and large braincases, such as the predatory tyrannosaurs, had higher metabolic rates than the dinosaurs with relatively small heads and braincases, such as the stegosaurs and sauropods. It is true that extant reptiles have lower metabolic rates and smaller EQ's than do mammals of the same weight. However, for any given weight there is a wide range of EQ and metabolic rates among living automatic endotherms.

In Figure 21 I have compared EQ in living birds and mammals with a parameter I call MQ, the metabolic quotient. The metabolic quotient is the observed M_{std} of a typical placental mammal of the same weight and is calculated by the formula

$MQ = \dfrac{M_{std}37}{17(W)^{-.25}}$. The $M_{std}37$ is the observed M_{std} for the

species, corrected to 37°C, with the assumption that $Q_{10} = 2$, when necessary. When $MQ = 1$, the M_{std} at 37°C is that predicted by the Kleiber equation for typical advanced placental mammals. Figure 21 shows that there is no significant correlation between MQ and EQ among living mammals and birds. Humans have an EQ averaging about 7.5 and an MQ of about 1; other anthropoid primates have an EQ of 2 to 4; for several marsupials, EQ is as low as 0.2. Yet in none of these mammals is MQ significantly different from 1. Passerine birds have significantly larger MQ's than mammals but do not differ significantly from them in EQ. A number of generalized insectivorous mammals (5 to 10 in Figure 21) have significantly lower MQ's than typical placental mammals

but do not differ from them in EQ. The ostrich has a very
low EQ but an MQ of 1. The total range of MQ in living
mammals and birds is from about 0.4 to 2.1; the range of EQ
is from about .18 to 10.0. With the exception of the big-
brained modern humans, the pattern of EQ shown in Figure 21
has been rather constant for the last 10 or 15 million years.
Thus, the modern ranges of EQ for birds, apes, ungulates,
carnivores and insectivores had evolved by 10 to 15 million
years ago (Radinsky 1978). Human EQ has increased relatively
rapidly in the last 7 million years. The lack of correlation
between MQ and EQ in mammals and birds shows that the
coevolution of brain size and metabolic rate is not tight at
all. Clearly the adequacy of brain size for any species
cannot be predicted from EQ alone. Ostriches and shrews
seem to be doing quite well despite their low EQ scores.

Exercise Metabolism and Locomotor Style

The maximum level of sustained exercise is controlled by
the capacity of the heart-lung system for delivering oxygen
and sources of aerobic energy to the muscles. In most
advanced, large placental and marsupial mammals, the maximum
aerobic exercise metabolism is 20 to 30 times the M_{std}
(Bakker 1975a). In reptiles the maximum aerobic capacity is
usually 6 to 15 times M_{std} (Bakker 1975b, Bennett and Dawson
1976). Since the mammal M_{std} is much higher than that of
reptiles of the same weight, the aerobic exercise capacity of
these mammals is 5 to 25 times greater than that of reptiles
of comparable size. This striking difference in exercise
physiology is reflected in anatomy: compared to reptiles,
mammals usually have lungs which are much more highly subdivided and hearts and major blood vessels which have thicker
walls. Powered flight requires a high level of sustained
exercise. Two groups of automatic endotherms, birds and
bats, have evolved powered flight, but no Good Reptiles have
done so. The locomotor style of most reptiles consists of
short bursts of activity, powered by anaerobic metabolism,
and more prolonged intervals of slow foraging. In general,
the capacity for bursts of anaerobic metabolism seems to be
about equal in Good Reptiles and in advanced mammals (Bakker
1975b).

The locomotor style of large, advanced mammals shows
longer intervals of moderate to high exercise levels; the
high energy budgets of automatic endotherms demand more
intense patterns of foraging than those seen in reptiles.
Locomotor anatomy shows the influence of the contrast in
behavioural style. In large lizards, crocodilians and
turtles, the sprawling or semi-erect gait (Bakker 1971)
provides for short sprints at moderately high speeds as well

as for digging, climbing and moving over uneven terrain. In
most large, fully terrestrial mammals the limbs are adapted
for a fully erect gait, which provides a narrow trackway for
maximizing running speed over flat, level topography.

Experiments: Brains-Legs-Heat Production Combinations

Ideally, to tease apart the evolutionary consequences of
EQ, locomotion, and thermoregulation, we would construct a
series of long-term evolutionary experiments to analyze the
adaptive radiations of different grades of mammals as they
evolve in the presence of modern types of reptiles. One such
experiment would be to stock an empty continent with a
variety of small, modern reptiles and a few families of very
primitive mammals which have a low EQ, a low capacity for
exercise metabolism, but a high M_{std}. We would follow the
adaptive radiation of both mammals and reptiles and keep
score by calculating the percent of the total number of big
terrestrial species contributed by mammals and by reptiles.
Then we could repeat the experiment, this time with mammals
with a low EQ and high M_{std} and high exercise metabolism,
repeating the experiment until all possible combinations of
adaptive levels had been tried. One of the most extraordinarily exciting properties of the vertebrate fossil
record is that it does provide just this type of experiment.

What Was the Grade of Mesozoic and Cenozoic Mammals?
The dental and skeletal anatomy of the primitive placental
and marsupial mammals at the Cretaceous-Cenozoic boundary
resembles that of didelphids and dasyurids among living
marsupials and tenrecs, hedgehogs, moonrats, and generalized
mustelid carnivores among living placentals. Crompton,
Taylor and Jagger (1978) argue that the primitive mammals of
the Mesozoic had a low M_{std} like that of extant tenrecs.
Their hypothesis is plausible but we should note that many
very primitive living marsupials have an MQ just as high as
that of advanced placentals (Dawson 1973). Furthermore,
the living monotreme mammals (platypus and spiny anteater)
have high MQ's (Figure 21), and monotremes represent a basic
grade of skeletal anatomy far more ancient than that of marsupials and placentals. The monotremes are frozen at a Late
Triassic level of postcranial organization; the placental-
marsupial grade is no older than Early Cretaceous. The
hypothesis of Crompton, Taylor and Jagger requires that a
high M_{std} evolved independently in monotremes, marsupials
and placentals. Certainly it is equally plausible that the
Triassic common ancestor of all living mammals had acquired
a high M_{std}, and that the low resting metabolism of tenrec-
like placentals is a secondary adaptation to cope with the
problems of being a highly carnivorous small mammal. Perhaps
it is significant that bats, the most diverse group of small

predatory mammals, have evolved daily torpor to reduce the total amount of animal prey needed per unit time. Crompton, Taylor and Jagger call tenrecs "mammals with reptilian energetics," but I think that this label is misleading. Although they have a reptilian-grade MQ, tenrec-like Insectivora do have the typically mammalian capacity for arousal from torpor by increased heat production and can increase heat production when alert and exposed to cold stress.

Biogeographic Experiments. During most of the Cenozoic Era, South America and Australia have been island continents, separated from other major land masses by oceanic barriers which, until very recently, prohibited the dispersal of most large land vertebrates. North America and Eurasia, on the other hand, were connected intermittently throughout the era. When the dinosaurs became extinct, suddenly at the end of the Cretaceous, no large land vertebrate remained. On all continents, possibly excepting Antarctica, were a variety of primitive mammals and modern families of lizards, crocodilians, and turtles. All these groups had the opportunity to produce an adaptive radiation of big land tetrapods, to replace the dinosaurs.

Evolutionary rates among Cenozoic mammals seem to correlate with the continental area. On all the continents evolutionary trends among most large, fully terrestrial mammals were towards higher EQ and increased specialization for fast locomotion for pursuit of prey or flight from predators. The evolutionary rates of change in EQ and locomotor anatomy are notably higher on the North American-Eurasian landmass than in either South America or Australia. The influence of area on evolutionary rate is especially marked among large predators. The most specialized, long-snouted, running predator produced in Australia was the marsupial wolf, the thyacine, which first appeared in Middle to Late Miocene time, about 12 million years ago. The limbs and brain of the marsupial wolf represent an evolutionary grade equivalent to that of Early Eocene long-snouted, running predators in North America and Eurasia (genus <u>Pachyaena</u> of the extinct family Mesonychidae) about 47 million years ago. The Mid-Eocene running predators of the Holarctic Realm were decidedly more advanced than the Miocene marsupial wolves. By the Middle or Late Miocene, Eurasia had produced several varieties of hyaenas which were as advanced as living species and far more specialized than contemporaneous Australian predators. In South America, the endemic mammal predators were also marsupials, the borhyaenids and thyeacosmilids. The most specialized South American endemic predators were the sabre-toothed thylacosmilids of the Pliocene, of about 5 million years b.p., which had limbs and brains representing a structural grade equivalent to that of Oligocene sabre-

toothed predators of Holarctica about 35 million years b.p.;
thus the Pliocene Holarctic sabretooths were far more advanced in brain and limbs. The consequences of this contrast
in evolutionary rates can be seen from the faunal changes
that occurred when Australia and South America imported
Holarctic predators. When the dingo, a wolf-like feral dog,
arrived in Australia from Asia a few thousand years ago, the
marsupial wolf immediately disappeared from the mainland and
became restricted to Tasmania. When wolves, pumas, jaguars,
and advanced sabre-tooth cats arrived in South America about
3 million years ago, the big marsupial predators vanished
quickly and completely.

Since large mammal predators evolved more slowly on the
island continents, we might predict that Good Reptiles would
be more successful in producing adaptive radiations of big
land species in Australia and South America during the
Cenozoic than in Holarctica. This prediction is correct.
Australia did not have native giant tortoises, but giant
terrestrial turtles did evolve from an endemic group, the
Meiolaniidae (Owen 1880, 1886). Today, Australia has a much
higher diversity of terrestrial predatory lizards than any
other land mass; Australian monitor lizards fill many of the
roles elsewhere occupied by mammals: canids, felids, mustelids and viverrids (Pianka 1969). The largest extant terrestrial monitor lizard in Australia is the perentie (Varanus
giganteus), reaching adult weights of 40 kg. It may be that
the desert habitat of much of Central Australia gives lizards
a special advantage in coping with mammals; high air temperatures and abundant solar radiation should permit the lizards
to maintain high, fairly constant body temperatures more
easily than can species in more heavily vegetated habitats
with higher rainfall. The ratio of the number of lizard
species to the number of mammal species does increase from
woodland habitats to semiarid and arid habitats (Kiester
1971, Simpson 1964); this increase is especially obvious
among lizards with high preferred body temperatures. During
the Late Cenozoic the diversity of Australian predatory
lizards was even greater than today. Giant hunting monitors
of the genus Megalania reached lengths of four meters and
estimated weights of 200 to 500 kg, larger than any of the
contemporaneous marsupial predators (Owen 1859, 1884).

South America did not produce large terrestrial lizard
predators in the Cenozoic, but did have a long-lived family
of crocodilians, the sebecosuchids, land predators, 50 to 200
kg in adult weight, which were widespread up until the Late
Miocene (Langston 1956). It is hard to resist the conclusion
that the lower grade of mammalian predators in South America
and Australia permitted the unusual success of terrestrial
crocodilians and lizards. Nevertheless, the marsupial

predators in South America greatly outnumbered the hunting
crocodilians in most habitats sampled by the fossil record.
Moreover, during the Oligocene, Miocene and Pliocene the
largest land predators in South America were neither mammals
nor reptiles, but rather another group of automatic endotherms, the flightless phororhacoid birds. In Australia, the
diversity and abundance of marsupial predators certainly was
greater than that of the large monitors, and the mammal
predators were more widespread geographically. In both South
America and Australia mammals produced most of the large
herbivores. Thus even in the island continents, the adaptive
radiation of large terrestrial Reptilia was still a minority
component; automatic endotherms dominated the megafauna.

The Early Cenozoic Experiment: Best Chance for Good
Reptiles. The Middle and Late Cenozoic mammals of South
America and Australia represent an intermediate grade of
organization, more advanced in general adaptations than the
primitive Insectivora, such as the tenrecs and moonrats, but
more primitive than the typical modern placentals. In the
Paleocene all of the placental and marsupial mammals on all
the continents were on a very primitive structural level.
Jerison (1973) estimates that the EQ of Paleocene mammals on
all the continents was no greater than that of the Mesozoic
Mammalia, about 0.15 to 0.25. The beginning of the enlargement of the neocortex seen in later Cenozoic mammals occurred
10 million years afterwards, in the Early Eocene. An EQ in
the 0.15 to 0.25 range is only slightly greater than that of
an adult gila monster (Heloderma), an extant predatory lizard
of the American Southwest (Crile and Quirling 1940) and is not
significantly larger than that of young crocodilians. The
locomotor anatomy of the Early Paleocene mammals was very
generalized; the joints were adapted for a semierect gait;
the feet were plantigrade (flatfooted, with metatarsus and
metacarpus placed along the ground); the elbows and knees
were strongly everted during the propulsive stroke; the
shoulder, hip, knee, and elbow were sharply flexed; and the
toes were long, flexible, and spreading. Among living
mammals the closest approach to this archaic organization is
found among the plantigrade mustelids, including the
wolverine, pine marten, and otters. These early Paleocene
mammals certainly could climb well, but they were not more
specialized for fast terrestrial locomotion than are monitor
lizards and perhaps less so than the crocodilians.

During most of the Early and Mid-Paleocene frost-free
climates spread much further north than at present. This was
the ideal opportunity for the Good Reptiles to produce a
major adaptive radiation of large land species; the mammals
were only slightly superior in relative brain size and
complexity, and roughly equal in locomotor grade. The only

Table 2. Evolutionary Experiments. Abbreviations: $\underline{M1}$, $\underline{M2}$, $\underline{M3}$ grades of mammals; GR Good Reptiles; $\underline{A}$ amphibians; $\underline{D}$ dinosaurs; $\underline{T}$, thecodonts; $\underline{Tr}$ therapsids.

	Biogeography	Time	Habitat	Body Size	Trophic Roles	How New Grades Were Introduced	Results
1	Australia	9000-3000 B.P.	Terres.	Large	Pred.	Biogeog. mix.	M3>>M2 =0
2	Australia	Late Cenoz.	Terres.	Large	Pred.	Evol. in place	M2 >GR >>0
3	So. America	Pleistocene	Terres.	Large	Pred.	Biogeog. mix.	M3>>M2 =0
4	So. America	Late Cenoz.	Terres.	Large	Pred.	Evol. in place	M2 >GR >0
5	Holarctica	Eocene	Terres.	Large	All	Evol. in place	M2 >M1 >0
6	Holarctica	Miocene	Terres.	Large	All	Evol. in place	M3 >M1 =0
7	Holarctica	Pal.-Eoc.	Terres.	Large	Pred.	Evol. in place	M1 >GR >0
8	Everywhere	Cenozoic	Terres.	Small	All	Evol. in place	A+GR >M1-3>>0
9	Everywhere	Cenozoic	Aquatic	All	Pred.	Evol. in place	A+GR>>M1-3 >0
10	Everywhere	Jur.-Cret.	Terres.	Large	All	Evol. in place	D>>M1 =0
11	Everywhere	Jur.-Cret.	Terres.	Small	All	Evol. in place	M1∿GR>> D =0
12	Everywhere	Jur.-Cret.	Aquatic	All	All	Evol. in place	A+GR>> D >0
13	Everywhere	Triassic	Terres.	Large	Pred.	Evol. in place	D+T >>Tr =0
14	Everywhere	M-Late Trias.	Terres.	Large	Herb.	Evol. in place	Tr >D∿T >0
15	Everywhere	Late Perm.Trias.	Aquatic	All	All	Evol. in place	A+GR>>T >Tr >0
16	Everywhere	Late Perm.	Terres.	Large	All	Evol. in place	Tr>>GR >0
17	Everywhere	Late Perm.	Terres.	Small	All	Evol. in place	Tr >GR >0

general adaptive advantage the mammals possessed was a capacity for high thermoregulatory heat production; the Early Paleocene mammals almost certainly were equipped with shivering and non-shivering thermogenetic mechanisms, and probably many of them had a high M_{std} and controlled torpor. But the adaptive radiation of large, terrestrial Good Reptiles in the Paleocene was puny. The only reptiles to challenge the dominance of Early Cenozoic mammals were the pristichampsids, or panzer crocodiles, which were predators up to 200 kg in adult weight, armored with a complete flexible body curiass of bony plates, and armed with steak-knife-like teeth reminiscent of those of Dimetrodon, thecodonts and theropod dinosaurs (Langston 1975). The toes of panzer crocodiles ended, not in claws as is usual among aquatic crocodilians, but rather in stout hooves. Panzer crocodiles are not uncommon in local faunas in the Mid-Eocene of North America and Europe, and have been reported from fragmentary material from the Paleocene. Unquestionably, the panzer crocodiles represent the most advanced, large fully terrestrial Good Reptiles known from anywhere and any geologic age. Yet, the most common and diverse big land predators of the Paleocene were mammals, the primitive mesonychids such as Dissacus (Figure 6). Even in the swampy woodlands of the Mid-Eocene of Wyoming, where panzer crocodiles reached their greatest relative abundance, they were outnumbered by big mammalian predators at least twenty to one.

Conclusion: Even Without Specialized Limbs and Brains, High Heat Production Is an Irresistible Advantage for a Big Tropical Land Tetrapod

The experiments in biogeography and evolution recorded by the fossils of the various Cenozoic continents do indicate that large brains and specialized locomotion are important advantages for large land tetrapods. However, the extremely limited adaptive radiation of Good Reptiles which occurred in the Paleocene, within the context of very primitive mammal faunas, strongly suggests that high thermoregulatory heat production alone was a sufficient advantage to guarantee the immediate dominance of mammals and the suppression of evolution of large reptiles. The mammals of the earliest Paleocene were not fundamentally more advanced than those of the Cretaceous. It is highly unlikely that the suppression of the evolution of large mammals all through the Jurassic and Cretaceous could have been accomplished by any group of Good Reptiles without high thermoregulatory heat production. The dinosaurs were responsible for this suppression.

Summary of the Fossil Record of Evolutionary Experiments

Table 2 summarizes the natural experiments which

occurred when adaptive radiations of differing grades
interacted. Adaptive radiations come into contact in two
ways: they may evolve separately in different biogeographical
provinces, as did the South American and Holarctic mammal
faunas, and then suddenly mix when oceanic barriers are
bridged; or they may evolve together within the same province
as did the Eurasian mammals and Good Reptiles. Change in
grade can occur after biogeographical mixing, such as the
replacement of marsupial wolves by dingos, or during evolution of lineages in one province, such as the gradual
replacement of primitive mammals by intermediate-grade mammals
in the Eocene of Holarctica. Mammals are subdivided into
three grades in Table 2: M1—the very primitive mammals, with
low EQ like that of the primitive extant Insectivora, and
very generalized locomotion like that of Early Paleocene
mammals; M2—the mammals with limbs of intermediate grade and
EQ's like those of Eocene-Oligocene species in North America
and Eurasia or the Late Cenozoic predators of Australia and
South America; M3—the typical advanced placental grade, with
EQ averaging 1.0 and limbs highly specialized for fast
terrestrial locomotion. The habitat, body size, and trophic
roles represented in the experiment are indicated. The
results column indicates the relative sizes of the adaptive
radiations of the interacting grades, in terms of the number
of species present within the habitat/body-size/trophic role
category. For example, after the entry of the dingo, an M3
mammal, into Australia (experiment 1), the marsupial wolf, an
M2 mammal, became extinct and its contribution to the species
number in the predator category falls to zero. In experiment
8, which took place on all continents during the Cenozoic,
mammals of all grades produced many terrestrial species, and
the reptiles and amphibians produced even more species than
the mammals. Several general patterns are apparent: the
greatest diversity of grades occurs in the small terrestrial
category, where mammals of all sorts are mixed with large
numbers of terrestrial salamanders, frogs, apodans, lizards
and snakes. The greatest number of species of non-flying
tetrapods also occurs in the small terrestrial category
(Table 1). The aquatic categories have always been dominated
by the lower tetrapods. Progressive evolution, the replacement of a lower grade by a higher grade, is best shown in the
large terrestrial categories: in Holarctica, M2 mammals
replaced M1 mammals during the Eocene and Oligocene, and M3
mammals replaced M2 mammals in the Miocene; whenever M3
predators were introduced to a continent with endemic M2
predators, the M2 predators quickly became extinct. Within
the context of large terrestrial tetrapods, we can make the
general statement that the evolutionary interaction of
adaptive radiations would occur according to the following
inequalities: $M3 > M2 > M1 > GR > 0$. These patterns confirm
the general hypothesis that within large land vertebrate

systems evolutionary trends should be relatively simple and concentrated towards increasing the ability of the animal to cope with direct interactions with predators and competitors.

Fossil Calorimeters: Some Things Which Don't Work Well

A number of methods of estimating metabolic grade in fossil tetrapods have been suggested by different authors. In this section I shall evaluate some widely used methods which do not work very well.

Relative Head Size

It has been asserted that the sauropods and other dinosaurs with relatively small heads could not have had high energy budgets because their mouths would have been too small to process food at the required rate. It is true that sauropods, prosauropods and stegosaurs have heads which seem, at first sight, absurdly small compared to those of elephants, rhinos and other large herbivorous animals. But it is unrealistic and unfair to compare relative head size in these dinsosaurs to that of mammals because the dinosaur heads were used only for cropping food, not for mastication, while the mammal heads not only crop fodder but also grind and shred it in large, complex batteries of cheek teeth. Sauropod teeth were limited to the front of the jaws and often show severe food-to-tooth wear, suggesting that they were used to chop and break off resistent branches. However, sauropod teeth did not form a complex grinding-shredding battery like that of mammals. The leaves and branches cropped by the anterior dentition probably were swallowed and passed on to be crushed in a muscular gizzard-like device. Skeletons representing several types of herbivorous dinosaurs (sauropods, prosauropods, psittacosaurs) have been found with concentrated masses of polished pebbles in the anterior stomach region of the rib cage. In some of these specimens (prosauropods from the Forest Sandstone) the polished pebbles represent rock types not found in the surrounding sediment; the animal must have procured its gizzard stones from areas which were many kilometers away. Similar bundles of gizzard stones have been found in the rib cages of the moas, extinct New Zealand giant herbivorous ground birds (Buick 1931). Moas have relatively tiny heads and small beaks without complex grinding areas; clearly the head was used only for cropping food. In contrast, most herbivorous mammals crop food with the incisors and/or prehensile lips and pass the food back to the cheek teeth where it is shredded and ground by massive dental batteries powered by relatively huge jaw muscles. Cheek teeth and the jaw muscles for their use account for most of the bulk in herbivorous mammal heads; the anterior cropping part of the skull in these mammals is no larger than that of a sauropod of the same weight. Paul (1979) has developed a scaling analysis of mouth width as a function of body size in herbivorous tetrapods and has found that sauropods have mouths as wide or wider for their weights than herbivorous mammals or birds. At a distance, an elephant with an outstretched trunk has a silhouette like that of a sauropod—the trunk has the proportions of the sauropod neck, and the trunk tip resembles the small head of the sauropods. Elephants lack anterior cropping teeth; cropping is performed by pulling leaves and branches with the end of the trunk. Since the trunk is adequate to crop food for the energy budgets of an elephant, it is not unreasonable to suppose that the mouth size of sauropods was not a limiting factor in food processing.

Small heads did not characterize all herbivorous dinosaurs. The ceratopsids (horned dinosaurs), protoceratopsids, hadrosaurs (duckbills) and a variety of other ornithischian families had heads as large as or larger than those of herbivorous mammals of the same weight. Most of these groups had complex dental batteries and large jaw muscles.

Insulation

Half a century ago, Lull (1924) argued that dinosaurs could not have been "warm blooded" because the skin impressions which had just been discovered around the skeletons of duckbills and ceratopsids showed no evidence of an insulating cover of either hair or feathers. Skin impressions devoid of any insulation are also known from sauropods and other large species. But the relation between insulation, body size, and climate is not simple. The skin of many living large tropical mammals has little or no hairy insulation. The black, white, and Indian rhinos, most populations of both species of elephants, the pigmy hippo, and the Nile hippo are naked, or nearly so. The absence of epidermal insulation certainly does not prove that a tropical tetrapod of large size had low heat production. Large size, tropical habitat and high heat production may require a naked skin. As I have suggested in an earlier section, a high M_{std} quite probably confers a significant advantage in preventing the body temperature from falling below optimum. However, the low surface area to body weight ratio makes heat loss during exercise an increasingly difficult problem for large tropical tetrapods. If surface area per unit weight decreases in proportion to $W^{0.36}$ or $W^{0.35}$ and maximum sustained exercise heat production decreases in proportion to $W^{0.25}$, then the heat production per unit surface area increases in proportion to $W^{0.11}$ or $W^{0.10}$. A three-ton tetrapod would have a heat production per unit surface area about five times greater than that of a three-gram species. A naked skin may be necessary for dumping heat during prolonged exercise in a

hot climate, especially during daylight activity in habitats
with little shade.

Well preserved skin impressions from relatively small
dinosaurs are not yet known. Ostrom (1978) has redescribed a
specimen of the very small theropod Compsognathus, about the
size of a small chicken. Ostrom claims that the absence of
impressions of hair or feathers in this specimen proves that
the skin in life was naked. I am not persuaded by this
argument. The specimen in question comes from the famous
Late Jurassic lithographic limestones of Germany. Hundreds
of superbly preserved pterosaur (flying reptile) skeletons
are known from these beds, but only a very few show good skin
impressions. Fewer still show the impressions of hair-like
filaments on the wings. But Sharov (1971) has described very
similar pterosaurs preserved in shales which show clearly a
very dense covering of hair-like pelage all over the body.
The absence of pelage impressions in most of the pterosaur
specimens no more proves that pelage was absent in life than
the absence of skin impressions in most specimens proves that
skin was not present in life. Well preserved skin impressions
are rare in the lithographic limestones, and the Compsognathus
specimen provides no evidence for or against epidermal insulation. It is probably correct to say that if large, robust
primary and secondary feathers had been present on the little
dinosaur, they would have had a higher probability of being
recorded in the sediment than a hair-like or down-like
insulation. Thus the Compsognathus specimen does suggest
that wings were absent.

Feather-like structures have been reported from small,
thecodont-like tetrapods from the Triassic (Sharov 1970), and
it is possible that pelage is very ancient in the Archosauria.
Ostrom (1977) has argued at length that the original function
of wing feathers was not flight but rather to increase the
effectiveness of the forelimbs for apprehending small prey.
At one time, accepting this idea, I illustrated Archaeopteryx
as a terrestrial predator, using its outstretched wings
as an insect net (Bakker 1975a). Since that time I have had
the opportunity to dissect the forelimb of a nestling Hoatzin,
an extant bird of the Amazon Basin which, as a juvenile, has
two free, claw-tipped fingers on each wing. The proportions
of the wing bones, the mechanical properties of the joints,
and the processes for the claw flexor muscles are strikingly
similar to those of Archaeopteryx. Hoatzin nestlings use
their forelimbs to climb in the foliage near the nest. I
have little doubt that Archaeopteryx could climb very well
using both the forelimbs and the hindfeet, which had long,
backwardly-oriented inner toes. Fedducia and Tordoff (1979)
have pointed out that the wing feathers of Archaeopteryx have
the asymmetry characteristic of feathers in flying birds.

The most plausible interpretation of <u>Archaeopteryx</u> is that it was a specialized, climbing predator which could glide and achieve at least some powered flight. The question of the origin of feathers for flight may then be quite distinct from the question of the presence of insulating pelage in thecodonts and small dinosaurs. A filamentous pelage, like that in pterosaurs, may have been present in the small, terrestrial theropods which were the ancestors of birds, and the origin of large feathers may have occurred as an adaptation for gliding and flight in a small arboreal theropod which already had acquired long forelimbs for precise, quadrupedal climbing.

Biogeography and Latitudinal Temperature Gradients

In the present world the mean winter temperature decreases rapidly with increasing latitude. The poleward temperature gradient restricts the distribution of large reptiles and amphibians, because these ectotherms must find secure refuges for hibernation. Not only must ectotherms have refuges from the danger of suffering fatally low body temperatures, but also they must seek shelter when body temperature is still far above the critical thermal minimum but enough below the preferred level so that the animal is vulnerable to mammalian or avian predators. Large reptiles today are restricted mostly to latitudes of 30°C or less; small species, which can find refuges more easily, are found at much higher latitudes, as far north as Alberta in North America. Large aquatic species may have higher limits than those of terrestrial types, because the muddy bottoms of ponds and streams provide freeze-proof refuges. The snapping turtle occurs in Massachusetts, where it hibernates in pond bottoms below the ice cover, and reaches adult weights an order of magnitude greater than that of the terrestrial turtles. Marine reptiles may have even higher latitudinal limits. The great leatherback sea turtle, weighing up to several hundred kilograms, occasionally occurs off the New England states. Warm oceanic currents and the use of exercise heat production for thermoregulation probably give the sea turtles their ability to extend their distribution to higher latitudes than can land tortoises of the same weight.

It is tempting to use poleward distributions of fossil tetrapods as indicators of thermoregulation, but biothermal paleobiogeography is a frustratingly complex discipline. The distribution of fossil plants, especially in Siberia (Bakker 1975b and references cited therein) strongly suggests that tropical and subtropical terrestrial habitats extended to much higher latitudes in the Middle and Late Mesozoic and Early Cenozoic than at present; the maximum extent of frost-free climate probably occurred in the Middle or Late Jurassic. Cretaceous dinosaurs have been reported from northern

Canada and Alaska, but the local climate may have been mild
and such occurrences do not constitute irrefutable evidence
of high heat production.

The paleogeography of the Late Permian and Triassic
offers more hope for unambiguous biothermal interpretation.
During the Carboniferous and Early Permian the southern parts
of the southern continents, Australia, Antarctica, India,
South Africa, and South America, suffered massive continental
glaciation. All of these now separate continental masses at
that time constituted Gondwanaland, the southern part of the
single great world continent of Pangaea. By the early Late
Permian, when the initial, spectacular bursts of therapsid
evolution occurred, the southern glaciers had disappeared in
most areas. However, glaciers remained in Tasmania and at
the northern edge of the Eurasian subcontinent, in northeast
Siberia (Bakker 1975a). Early therapsid faunas are well
known from European Russia, near the Late Permian Equator,
where the fossils are found in sediments indicating a very
hot, arid climate, and in South Africa and Rhodesia-Zimbabwe,
between 58° and 65° South paleolatitude. Almost certainly
the minimum winter temperature was far lower in South Africa
than in Russia. Large aquatic amphibians are very common and
diverse at the Russian Late Permian sites, sometimes making
up the bulk of local fossil vertebrate samples. In South
Africa big amphibians are very rare and are outnumbered by
therapsids by a factor of about one hundred to one. It is
quite probable that populations of big amphibians spread
southward to southern Africa only intermittently, during
intervals when the winters were unusually mild. The low
abundance and diversity of the African amphibian faunas
certainly suggests some sort of thermal restrictions. For
any given latitude, land habitats near the ocean can enjoy
more temperate climates than inland habitats, because of the
moderating effects of heat transport by ocean currents. In
the latest Permian and Triassic, aquatic amphibians and
reptiles were still far less common and diverse in southern
South Africa and South America than in North America and
Europe, where most sites lay within 30° of the paleoequator.
The South American and South African faunas lived within the
great southern heartland of the Gondwana continent, far from
any open ocean circulation, and shielded on several sides by
active mountain ranges. Yearly temperature fluctuations
probably were far more severe than in habitats at the same
latitude but closer to seaways, as in Tasmania and eastern
Australia. The eastern Australian tetrapod faunas of the
Triassic are strikingly different from those of South Africa
and South America: big aquatic amphibians are very diverse
and abundant. These patterns suggest that therapsids were
far less limited by cool temperatures than are typical
reptiles and amphibians.

Working Fossil Calorimeters: Bone Histology

There are two methods of calculating heat production in
fossil tetrapods which work very well: bone histology and
predator/prey analysis. The data now available for both
methods are so comprehensive and unambiguous that I am confi-
dent that the patterns will withstand all rigorous statistical
tests and the onslaughts of subjective doubt and incredulity.

Review of Published Data and Opinions

Scattered references to thin sections of fossil bone
exist even in the nineteenth century literature, but the
first comprehensive survey was undertaken by Enlow and Brown
(1956, 1957, 1958). These authors reviewed all of the published data and added original observations on dozens of
species. Their conclusions about the two mammal-like reptiles
studied were quite unambiguous:

About Kannemeyeria: "These plexiform tissues closely
resemble the plexiform bone of many living artiodactyls and
of certain dinosaurs...." (Enlow and Brown 1957, p. 206).

About Dinodontosaurus: "...the rib...like the bones of
many modern mammals, is composed of well-developed, dense
Haversian tissue." (Enlow and Brown 1957, p. 206).

Their conclusions about a wide range of dinosaur bony tissue
were similar:

"The bone tissues of the saurischian dinosaurs, together
with the ornithischians are distinctive among all recent and
fossil reptiles. In structure the bone of these extinct
animals is similar to, if not identical with, the bone tissue
of many living mammals, including man." (Enlow and Brown
1957, p. 200).

"Most of the extinct reptilian groups had dense, heavily-
laminated bone with well-developed endosteal or irregular
Haversian tissue. Only the saurischian and ornithischian
dinosaurs and certain therapsids possessed dense Haversian
tissue." (Enlow and Brown 1958, p. 226).

Enlow and Brown found that the range of tissue types in dinosaurs and therapsids was indistinguishable from that of
modern mammals and quite thoroughly different from the range
seen in other fossil and living reptiles.

In 1962, Currey presented a detailed, quantitative study
of the density of vascularization in a very primitive dinosaur, a prosauropod, and a mammal-like reptile. Enlow and

Brown had concentrated their attention on the secondary
tissues, especially on the bone deposited in long spindles of
concentric laminae (Haversian systems) which fills in spaces
eroded into the cortex of bone as the tissue is remodeled.
Currey emphasized the geometry of the blood vessels contained
in the primary bone, the tissue laid down at the peripheral,
periosteal boundary, as the bone grows in circumference.
Like Enlow and Brown before him, Currey found that dinosaur
and therapsid bone was organized like that of living mammals,
not like that of typical reptiles:

"The vascularization of the dinosaur bone is compared
quantitatively with that of recent mammals and reptiles. The
amount of vascularization is much greater than in recent
reptiles, and is of the same order as, but rather more than,
in recent mammals. It is argued that this may indicate
physiological specialization in the dinosaurs." (Currey 1962,
p. 238).

Currey found the same type of densely vascularized
primary tissue, which he named laminar bone, in the therapsid
<u>Dinodontosaurus</u>:

Finally, over the last decade, Ricqlès (1968-1978) has
assembled a monumental body of data on the paleohistory of
bone, including analysis of new thin sections representing
hundreds of specimens and scores of species of reptile,
amphibian, therapsid, dinosaur, and thecodont. Ricqlès has
added a new dimension to bone analysis. He has studied the
occurrence of Haversian systems and the pattern of vascularization in primary bone, as had Enlow and Brown, and Currey,
but also he has found distinctions between mammals and
primitive reptiles in the fabric of bone crystals as they are
deposited in primary bone. He likewise concludes that the
range of tissue types in therapsids and dinosaurs is the same
as that in living mammals of comparable body sizes and quite
different from that of other "lower tetrapod" groups.

Most of the published studies of bone histology group
specimens in taxonomic categories. I have been interested in
what I call "histofaunas": the bone micro-structures of fossil
vertebrates which are found preserved together at the same
locality and in the same thin stratum of rock, representing
one environment. At the Johns Hopkins University we have
data for three histofaunas: Late Jurassic (dinosaurs, turtles,
crocodilians, fish); early Mid-Paleocene (fish, turtles,
crocodilians, very primitive placental mammals); and Mid-
Oligocene (large tortoises, lizards, mammals). In each one
of these histofaunas we observe the same clear-cut distinctions between dinosaurs and mammals on the one hand, and
fish and typical reptiles on the other.

Several critics have argued that the correlation between bone histology and physiological grade is not proven, some citing a short paper by Bouvier (1977). Bouvier claimed that dinosaur bone is not fundamentally different from that of other lower tetrapods, because scattered Haversian systems do occur in a wide range of primitive fossil reptiles. But Bouvier has misrepresented the case: Enlow and Brown, Currey and Ricqlès have shown that dinosaurs and therapsids differed from typical reptiles in possessing densely spaced Haversian systems, and densely spaced vascular patterns in primary bone. No one has claimed that some Haversian systems do not occur in typical and even primitive reptiles. At the same time, all the published descriptions agree in showing that densely packed secondary Haversian systems are extremely rare in "lower tetrapods" except for therapsids and dinosaurs.

The dismissal by various authors of the histological evidence linking therapsids and dinosaurs to mammals takes no account of the enormous amount of data and analysis now available. Some of those who have expressed doubt about the correlation between physiology and histology cite only one or two short review papers in English by Ricqlès. I would challenge any and all who remain unbelievers to spend some time with the many splendid photomicrographs, drawings and detailed discussions in the major series of papers in French by Ricqlès. The documentation is irresistible.

Body Size and Bone Histology

Authors who are inclined to reject high heat production in therapsids and dinosaurs because they accept the "Good Reptile" model of Spotila et al. (McNab 1978; McNab and Auffenberg 1976) are also inclined to see the mammal-like bone histology of therapsids and dinosaurs as merely reflecting the great size of these animals. For example: "De Ricqlès (1974) has an interesting discussion of the significance of Haversian canals in the structure of bone.... It seems perfectly clear that de Ricqlès is describing a condition in which Haversian substitution is correlated with thermal constancy (i.e., homoiothermy) and not with endothermy. This conclusion would explain why Haversian substitution is not characteristic of small endotherms.... This interpretation may also explain why dinosaurs had many secondary osteons: they were inertial homoiotherms." (McNab 1978, pp. 16-17).

McNab makes several errors of interpretation. First, most of the published work of Ricqlès is on primary bone tissue and vascularization, not on Haversian systems. Second, McNab accepts as proven the hypothesis that in the tropics, a big reptile with low M_{std} would maintain a constant body

temperature just as effectively as would a mammal of the same
weight. Spotila et al. (1973) did not prove this; they
showed that some of the advantages of homeothermy were
available to the hypothetical three-ton reptile, not all of
the advantages. Third, McNab assumes that all the therapsids
and dinosaurs which show mammal-like bone histology were big
enough to practice "inertial homeothermy."

The numbers of genera with mammal-like and non-mammal-
like bone histologies, according to body weight classes and
major taxonomic categories, are shown in Figure 22. The body
weight for each extinct genus was calculated by determining
the size of the bone sectioned and then by using regressions
for body weight as a function of limb bone size. These
regressions have been developed in my lab over the last four
years from a series of scale models of extinct vertebrates,
built from drawings of reconstructed skeletons. The category
of "mammal-like bone histology" was defined as the total range
of bone microstructure, both primary and secondary, which is
present in mammals and which has never been found in any non-
marine reptile. As Ricqlès points out, some of the large
marine reptiles do have histological features suggestive of
mammals. The category of "non-mammal-like bone histology"
was defined as the total range of types seen in non-marine
reptiles and amphibians. Figure 22 shows that it is quite
incorrect to assume that bone histology is simply a function
of size. Except for the big marine reptiles, very large
tetrapods which are not mammals or therapsids or dinosaurs
do not show mammal-like bone histology. The bone histology
of a giant tortoise (estimated weight, 100 kg) from the
Oligocene of North America shows structures like that of a
small tortoise; the structure of a huge fossil tortoise (1000
kg) of late Cenozoic age from India also shows non-mammalian
types of histology. All of the primitive big tetrapods from
the Early Permian of Texas show non-mammal-like bone, although
the climate was hot year around, as the Permian equator
passed close to the area. The huge Late Permian pareiasaurs
from South Africa and Europe show features of bone deposition
which are non-mammalian, and yet these reptiles, which are
not closely related to either therapsids or dinosaurs,
reached weights of one ton or more.

Many of the therapsids and dinosaurs which show mammal-
like bone are smaller than 100 kg. Ricqlès presents data for
therapsids with mammal-like bone with body weights as small
as 5 kg (Notosallasia, several small gorgonopsians, and
dicynodonts). Living and fossil turtles and crocodilians in
this weight range do not show mammal-like bone histology,
even if the sample comes from the tropics (Peabody 1956). At
Johns Hopkins we have thin sections of a very small, herbivorous dinosaur from the Late Jurassic (?Laosaurus), with an

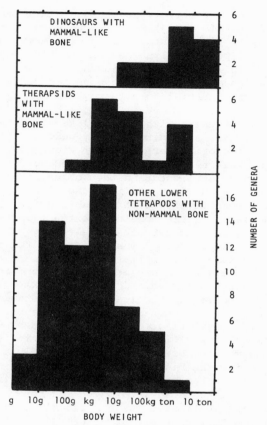

FIGURE 22. Bone histology and body size. For each genus
studied by Enlow and Brown (1956, 1957, 1958), Currey (1962),
Ricqlès (1968-1977), and the Johns Hopkins Histofauna
project, body weight was calculated from regressions for body
weight as a function of limb bone size. Note that many dinosaurs and therapsids weighing less than 100 kg have mammal-
like bone histology, while many primitive lower tetrapods
have non-mammalian bone histology at body weights up to
1000 kg. The mammal-like bone histology of therapsids and
dinosaurs cannot be explained on the basis of body size alone.
Mammal-like bone histology includes the following tissue
types: fibro-lamellar primary bone with some randomly
oriented fibers; fibro-lamellar bone with extensive secondary
Haversian reconstruction; and cortical bone composed entirely
of densely packed Haversian systems.

estimated body weight of 20 kg; the bone histology is like
that of many therapsids and mammals of the same size, not
like that of a crocodilian or turtle of the same weight from
the same fossil site. Samples from an Early Cretaceous small
carnivorous dinosaur (?<u>Deinonychus</u>) are similar.

There are very small (under a kilogram) mammals and
mammal-like reptiles which do not fall into the "mammal-like
bone histology" categories. Many small rodents have rather
simple bone microstructures, compared to larger species. But
the lower size limit for mammal-like bone is very much lower
than McNab assumes. Rabbits and hares, with adult weights as
low as 3 kg, still have a complex bone histology rather like
that of antelope and deer (Enlow and Brown 1958). If we
compare very small therapsids with primitive reptiles of the
same weight, the therapsids still have more complex bone
histology than the primitive reptiles. Ricqlès gives data on
<u>Oligokyphus</u>, a tiny therapsid, of only about 100 g adult
weight; the cortical bone is less complex than in 5 kg
therapsids, but still has an abundance of primary vascular
canals. The cortical bone of 100 g lizards is nearly always
totally devoid of vascularization (Enlow and Brown 1957).

There can be no ambiguity. The bone histology of dinosaurs and therapsids, down to a weight of 100 g, is like that
of mammals of the same size, and more complex than that of
typical reptiles and amphibians. Even in the tropics, very
large non-marine turtles, crocodilians, and primitive Permian
reptiles do not develop mammal-like bone histology.

Interpretation of Bone Histology

Ricqlès (1968-1978) argues that differences in primary
bone structure are explained by differences in growth rate.
He states that most reptiles grow more slowly and more intermittently than mammals of the same weight. The generation
intervals plotted in Figure 16 show that Ricqlès is correct;
even in the tropics, reptiles and amphibians on the average
grow more slowly than mammals of the same weight. When
mammal bones grow rapidly, a spongy matrix of randomly
oriented collagen fibers is formed; bone mineral is deposited
in this matrix and the resulting bone is called fibro-
lamellar by Ricqlès. Holes in the collagen matrix, occupied
by vascular spaces, are filled up by bone deposited more
slowly in concentric lamellae; in each lamella the fibers
tend to be parallel, not random, and the fiber orientation
changes from lamella to lamella. Fibro-lamellar bone is very
common in subadult therapsids and dinosaurs, suggesting
mammal-like patterns of growth.

The density of vascularization certainly reflects

metabolic activity in some way. Since the total energy budget of a mammal is about ten times higher than in a reptile of the same weight (Bakker 1975b), the total blood flow should be much higher in the mammal. Perhaps the higher density of primary blood vessels in mammals simply reflects the greater vascular needs of all mammal tissue.

In humans, growth is very slow compared to that of most non-primate mammals of the same weight. Cortical bone is first deposited as a random fibro-lamellar matrix, but soon spindle-shaped holes are eroded in the matrix and filled up with concentric lamellae which form Haversian systems. Adult human long bones have cortices made up mostly by secondary Haversian systems which are in a continuous process of erosion and redeposition. Haversian systems usually become much more common with age in all types of tetrapods; thus an increasing abundance of Haversian systems reflects a slowing down of growth. Adult dinosaurs, therapsids, and mammals show much greater densities of secondary Haversian systems than do adults of other tetrapods in the same weight, indicating similar growth patterns in these groups.

Growth Rest Lines

Ricqlès argues that distinct growth-rest lines, marking the temporary cessation of bone accretion, should be much more common in tetrapods with low metabolism than in those with high metabolism. Growth lines do occasionally appear in the bone of extant mammals, particularly those from temperate habitats with severe winters (Klevezal 1956; Ricqlès 1975). However, growth-rest lines are far more common in reptiles, even in the tropics and in large species (Peabody 1956; Ricqlès 1968-77).

Johnston (1979) has recently announced the discovery of growth-rest lines in the teeth of Late Cretaceous dinosaurs from Alberta. He asserts that his discovery proves that dinosaurs were not endothermic, but he does not discuss the apparent discrepancy between his conclusion and those drawn in all the major works on bone histology. In fact, Johnston's discovery provides evidence neither for nor against dinosaur endothermy, because growth-rest lines are known from the teeth of a variety of mammals, including several species from the tropics (Spinage 1973). Strong seasonal fluctuations in the availability of food and water can induce growth-rest lines in automatic endotherms; in the tropical mammals cited by Spinage (1973) growth lines in the teeth are almost certainly correlated with dry seasons which occur once or twice each year. Seasonal variations in productivity exist in tropical and temperate marine ecosystems, and growth-rest lines are used regularly in fisheries management for

constructing life tables. The great inland sea of the Late
Cretaceous of North America probably had seasonal fluctuations
in productivity. Nearly a hundred years ago, Marsh (1880)
described and figured sections through the teeth of the great
flightless diving bird of the Cretaceous, <u>Hesperornis</u>. Very
distinct growth-rest lines, like those of contemporaneous
terrestrial dinosaurs, are present. The growth lines
reported by Johnston were probably induced by dry seasons.
The presence of mummified dinosaur carcasses in the Late
Cretaceous sediments of Alberta suggests that prolonged intervals of dry weather did occur. Johnston found no growth-rest
lines in mammals from the Late Cretaceous but all of the
species examined were tiny, with adult weights of 10 to 500 g.
The adult dental tissue of these small mammals was probably
formed in a few weeks or months and would not record seasonal
cessation in growth.

Fossil Calorimetry: Predator/Prey Ratios

Golley's Law

The notion of using predator/prey relations to gauge
heat production in fossil vertebrates first occurred to me
after reading Golley's (1968) excellent review of secondary
productivity and efficiency among living animals. Secondary
productivity is the caloric value of all the new tissue
added by a population through growth and reproduction. If
the population is in an energetic steady-state, the energy
value of this new tissue balances the energy value of all the
individuals which are lost through mortality. The secondary
productivity of prey, usually expressed as biomass or calories
per year, is the maximum amount of food energy available to
predators dependent upon those prey species. Since most
predators will consume carcasses of other predators, the
maximum food available per year to a population of pure carnivores is the secondary productivity of all the prey species
plus that of the predators themselves. Assimilation is
defined as the amount of energy contained in the food
ingested minus the loss through regurgitation and defecation.
Most carnivores have very high digestive efficiencies;
predatory spiders, lizards, mammals and birds assimilate 90%
or more of the energy contained in ingested prey, so little
of the carcass energy is wasted (Bakker 1975b; Golley 1968).

Golley (1968) showed that the ratio of secondary productivity to assimilation, which I call productivity
efficiency, is much higher in ectothermic invertebrates and
lizards than in mammals and birds (Figures 23, 24). In ectotherms, productivity efficiency ranges from 10% to 60%; in
mammals and birds, it ranges from 0.5% to 8%. Thus mammals
and birds pay a high price for their elevated heat

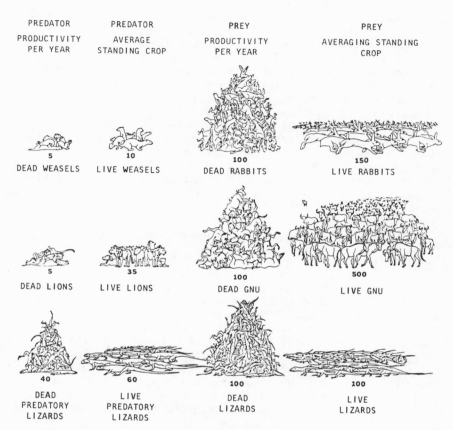

PREDATOR PRODUCTIVITY PER YEAR	PREDATOR AVERAGE STANDING CROP	PREY PRODUCTIVITY PER YEAR	PREY AVERAGING STANDING CROP
5 DEAD WEASELS	10 LIVE WEASELS	100 DEAD RABBITS	150 LIVE RABBITS
5 DEAD LIONS	35 LIVE LIONS	100 DEAD GNU	500 LIVE GNU
40 DEAD PREDATORY LIZARDS	60 LIVE PREDATORY LIZARDS	100 DEAD LIZARDS	100 LIVE LIZARDS

FIGURE 23. The efficiency of converting ingested prey into growth and reproduction in predatory mammals and lizards. Each horizontal row shows one idealized predator-prey system. The live animals represent the average population size during the year (standing crop). The pile of dead animals represents the total number of carcasses produced by all types of mortality during the year (productivity). For simplicity it is assumed that the average body weight of predator and prey is the same within each system. The predator population represents the maximum predator standing crop which could be supported if the predators consumed all of the prey carcasses. Note that the ratio of predator carcasses to prey carcasses is about the same in large and small mammals, and the ratio in lizards is an order of magnitude larger.

production; they are very inefficient in converting assimilated energy into growth. Efficiency can be increased in
captivity: laboratory populations of mice have productivity
efficiencies of up to 15% or 20% (Myrcha 1975); chickens
raised in a controlled environment with high protein food,
hormone supplements to accelerate growth, and little or no
exercise can achieve productivity efficiencies up to 40% or
60%, which is as high as wild populations of ectotherms
(Brody 1945; Kleiber 1956). However, wild populations of
mammals and birds never come close to these high efficiencies.

Fossil Productivity Efficiency

Most of the time, the processes of fossilization sample
the production of carcasses in an area; thus the relative
abundances of the fossils reflect the rates of secondary
productivity of the various species. In nearly all of the
fossil samples I have examined, primitive tetrapods of the
Early Permian, mammal-like reptiles, dinosaurs and Cenozoic
mammals, the preservation indicates that the bones accumulated over a period of several months to several years;
animals died, predators chewed up the remains, dismembered
and scattered skeletons, and the agents of weathering cracked
and decayed the bone surfaces. These chewed and weathered
samples may have been covered with fine-grained sediment as
they lay on a floodplain or they may have been washed into a
river channel during a flood and buried with coarser deposits.
This type of preservation provides us with a fossil calori-
meter. If the predators and prey died in the same depositional area, and fossilization was not strongly biased against
one or the other, then the biomass and energy represented by
all the preserved carcasses reflect the rates of secondary
productivity of predators and prey. The predator carcasses
represent predator productivity, and the sum of the carcasses
of predators and prey represents the maximum amount of energy
available to the predator. The ratio of the energy value of
carcasses of predators to that of predators and prey should
be about equal to the productivity efficiency of the predator.

Sometimes a fossil assemblage provides a sample of the
standing crop, of all the populations that were living
together in one area at one time. A severe drought followed
by flooding may have killed most of the large mammals in one
area and covered the carcasses with sediment. However, as
long as fossilization is not strongly biased for or against
predators, for any given community, the calculated biomass of
any predator divided by the biomass of the predator and its
prey should be about the same, whether a sample represents
secondary productivity or standing crop. I have discussed at
length why predator/prey ratios of biomass and energy should
be about the same in productivity samples and standing crop

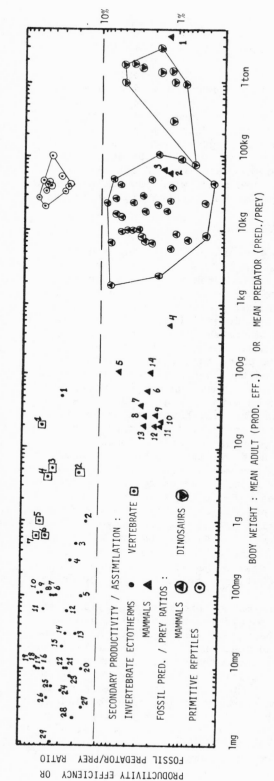

FIGURE 24. Productivity efficiency and body size. Efficiency is expressed as the caloric value of all new tissue added during a year (secondary productivity) divided by the total amount of energy assimilated by the population during the year. Note that all productivity efficiencies in mammals are below 10%, and all those for ectotherms, both vertebrate and invertebrate, are above 10%. In steady-state populations the caloric value of all carcasses produced in a year is equal to the value of secondary productivity. Thus fossil predator/prey ratios represent productivity efficiencies. Fossil ratios from Bakker (in press). Other data from the following sources: Invertebrates – Englemann 1966; Golley 1968; Wiegert, 1965; Van Hook 1971; Moulder and Reichle 1972; Mann 1965; Hughes 1970; Edgar 1971; Teal 1957; Varley 1970. Ectothermic vertebrates – Golley 1968; Fitzpatrick 1971; Burton and Likens 1975; Kitchell and Windel 1972; Dutton et al. 1975; Mueller 1970. Mammals – Golley 1968; Buechner and Golley 1967; Davis and Golley 1963; Fleharty and Choate 1973; Golley 1960; Grodzinski 1966; Grodzinski et al. 1969; Montgomery 1975; Odum et al. 1962.

FIGURE 24. (continued)

Invertebrates

1. Modiolus
2. Littorina
3. Lycosa
4. Lycosa
5. Orthoptera
6. orthoptera
7. orthoptera
8. orthoptera
9. orthoptera
10. Orthoptera
11. Pyrrhosoma nymphula (dragonfly)
12. Trichoptera
13. Isopod
14. Asellus
15. Lycosa lugubrix
16. Bivalves
17. Hemiptera
18. Hemiptera
19. Hemiptera
20. Midges
21. Midges
22. Tubifix
23. Mites
24. Gastropods
25. Hidryta - wasp larva
26. Hemiptera
27. Amphipods
28. Hidryta - wasp adult
29. Pelodera - nematode

Vertebrate Ectotherms

1. Sceloporus olivaceous
2. Sceloporus graciosus
3. Uta stansburiana
4. Anolis carolinensis
5. Desmognathus ochrophaeus
6. Plethodon cinereus
7. Plethodon cinereus

Mammals

1. Loxodonta africana
2. Odocoileus virginianus
3. Adenota kob
4. Sciurus carolinensis
5. Sigmodon hispidus
6. Mustela frenata
7. Microtus pennsylvanicus
8. Apodemus flavicollis
9. Microtus oeconomys
10. Microtus agrestis
11. Clethrionomys rutilus
12. Peromyscus polionotus
13. Chlethrionomys glareolus
14. Sigmodon hispidus
15. Tamiasciurus hudsonicus
16. Ground squirrels
17. Glaucomys sabrinus
18. Microtus subterraneus

samples from the same community (Bakker 1975b). Charig and
Horsfield (1975) have argued that productivity ratios would
not be reliable indicators of standing crop ratios because
the mortality per unit standing crop in a predator might be
an order of magnitude different from that of the prey. However, they offer no example from extant large vertebrate communities. In the terrestrial large-mammal faunas of Africa
and India the productivity per unit standing crop of predators
usually does not differ by more than a factor of two from
that of the prey species (Bakker 1975b).

Body Size Effects

     Figures 23 and 24 illustrate some of the possible effects
of body size on productivity ratios and standing crop ratios.
Max Kleiber (1961) stated that the productivity efficiency in
mammals does not change with increasing body weight; a ton of
grain produces the same amount of meat whether it is fed to a
herd of cattle or a hutch of rabbits. Data from field studies
of wild mammal populations confirm Kleiber's rule of constant
efficiency (Figure 24; Bakker 1975b). Thus if we sample
productivity, as illustrated in Figure 23, we should get about
the same predator/prey ratio for weasels as we get for lions.
For small ectotherms the productivity efficiency is much
higher, as illustrated in the lizard system in Figure 23.
However, few data exist on productivity efficiency in large
extant reptiles. If the difference between the metabolism of
reptiles and mammals gradually decreases with increasing
weight, then we might expect the difference in productivity
efficiencies to follow suit. It is possible that productivity
efficiency slowly decreases with increasing weight in reptiles, and that the difference between the productivity
ratios of mammals and ectotherms tends to disappear at very
large sizes. Farlow and Hotton discuss this possibility
elsewhere in this volume. This possibility can be tested
with data from very large fossil reptiles.

     If we sample standing crop, not productivity, the
predator/prey ratio will always be a function of the relative
sizes of the predators and prey. Since both the productivity
per unit standing crop in prey and the prey consumption per
unit standing crop in predators will decrease with increasing
weight, a very small predator feeding on very large prey
(weasels hunting gnu in Figure 23) will maintain a much lower
standing crop predator/prey ratio than a very large predator
feeding on very small prey (lions preying on rabbits in
Figure 23). The majority of large mammal predators (adult
weight > 20 kg) get most of their prey from animals which do
not differ by more than a factor of five or ten in body
weight from themselves (Bakker 1975b; Schaller 1972). To get
a ten-fold increase in standing crop predator/prey ratio in

mammals, the body size of the predator would have to be
increased by a factor of 10,000 relative to that of the prey.
Thus the standing crop ratios should not be affected seriously
by body weight.

Caveats and Taphonomic Homogeneity

Fossil predator/prey ratios are constructed by the
following procedure: 1) calculate the proportion of individuals contributed by each species to the total sample;
2) calculate the body weight of each species, if only adults
are present, or of each age class of each species if many
juveniles are present; 3) use the data from steps 1 and 2 to
calculate the proportion of the total biomass contributed by
each species; 4) identify all the predators by means of a
functional analysis of teeth and jaws; 5) calculate the total
proportion of the biomass sample contributed by all the
predators. The result is the predator/prey ratio, which I
usually express as a percentage. It should be noted that
what is being calculated is the proportion of the total preserved biomass contributed by predators; thus the ratio
expresses the biomass of the predators divided by the total
biomass of all species, predators included. All predators
are assumed to be cannibals, and the total "prey" biomass is
simply the total biomass. It has been suggested that cannibalism among predators may distort predator/prey ratios in
curious ways, but in fact the methodology used here avoids
these problems.

A great deal of thoughtful discussion among paleo-
ecologists has been focused on the calculation of the "minimum number of individuals" represented by vertebrate samples.
The object is to determine the smallest number of animals
which theoretically could supply all the skeletal parts
preserved. If a sample of specimens of a very long-tailed
beast includes thirty isolated vertebrae from the middle of
the tail, six left and three right lower jaws, the minimum
number of individuals is six. In fact, if tooth wear is
examined carefully, it may be possible to state that the six
left and three right jaws came from a minimum of eight individuals, if two of the right jaws have teeth that are much
more worn than any of those in the left jaws. For the purpose of predator/prey analysis, minimum numbers of individuals do not necessarily provide the most reliable data.
What we want is the most unbiased estimate of the proportion
of the sample made up by predators. This proportion is best
estimated by making a census of some skeletal part which
occurs in the same number in the predator skeleton and in the
prey skeleton, which has about the same size, robustness,
resistance to the effects of scavengers and weathering, and
is easily identifiable. In Early Permian samples, the

relative size of the skull varies enormously: both Eryops
and Edaphosaurus reached lengths of two meters or more and
weights of over 100 kg, but Eryops had a huge, alligator-like
head, solidly constructed and very resistant to all biological
and physical agents of destruction, while the edaphosaurs had
minute, delicate heads which were less than one-tenth as
bulky as those of Eryops of the same weight. Counting heads
in this case would introduce a bias in favor of Eryops. However, the two genera have femora and humeri of about the same
size relative to the rest of the skeleton; counting these
long bones would produce a much less biased census. For all
Early Permian faunas I have used femora and humeri for a
census; for the mammal-like reptiles, all of which have
relatively large, massive heads, I have used a count of
snouts; thecodont samples are small, so I have used either
snouts or long bones, whichever category had a larger sample
size; for all dinosaur samples I used femora, because the
predators usually had small humeri; for most of the mammal
samples, I used published minimum numbers of individuals,
usually based on dentition. Each of the samples used for
predator/prey analysis came from one closely integrated set
of depositional environments, from one small geographical
area (usually a small part of a structural basin), and from
one thin stratigraphic interval. Details for each sample are
given elsewhere (Bakker, in press).

Testing the Faithfulness of the Fossil Record

Taphonomic Atheists and Taphonomic Agnostics. Many, but
by no means all paleontologists express considerable lack of
confidence in vertebrate fossil assemblages as reliable
quantitative records. Some workers, the taphonomic atheists,
are absolutely convinced that patterns of mortality among big
land vertebrates are so unpredictable in time and space that
the fossils cannot possibly preserve predator/prey ratios
which faithfully reflect ecological relationships. Other
workers, the taphonomic agnostics, admit that there might be
a meaningful pattern in the accumulation of carcasses in one
environment, but believe that the processes of destruction by
scavengers, weathering, and the dispersal of bones by running
water are so complex and unpredictable that the fossil sample
has been scrambled beyond hope of meaningful analysis. I
subscribe to neither philosophy. Taphonomic processes can be
studied and various forms of bias can be clearly identified
(Shotwell 1955; Voorhies 1969; Behrensmeyer 1975). In many
terrestrial depositional environments, such as floodplains,
where large areas receive a blanket of sediment at one time,
predator carcasses are probably preserved in the same micro-
stratigraphic unit as the carcasses of their prey.

The Cenozoic Mammal Test. I have found that argument

with taphonomic agnostics and atheists is rarely productive;
the issue of the faithfulness of the fossil record will not
be settled by a priori assertions about its bias or lack of
bias. The best test is provided by the fossil record of
Cenozoic mammals. Many large samples of big predators and
their prey have been carefully excavated, described and analyzed. Most of the Late Cenozoic predators belong to families
which are still with us, such as dogs, cats, and hyaenas, so
it is safe to assume that these advanced types were automatic
endotherms. In Figure 25 I have made four tests of bias for
Cenozoic predator/prey ratios. 1) Early Cenozoic predator/
prey ratios, where the predators belonged to extinct families,
are compared to Late Cenozoic ratios. There is no significant
difference between the distributions of ratios in these two
groups; predator/prey ratios have remained relatively constant throughout the last 60 million years. 2) Samples from
coarse-grained sediment, deposited by high energy streams and
rivers, are compared to those from fine-grained sediment laid
down in more tranquil environments on floodplains, lake
margins, and estuaries. There is no significant difference
between the ratios in these two groups; current energy does
not cause either winnowing out or concentration of predators.
3) The samples are divided into two groups according to the
concentration of specimens; in one group are those sites
where dozens or hundreds of individuals are found in one small
area, packed into a thin layer or lens of sediment; in the
other group are samples composed of more scattered finds of
single specimens and small groups of specimens distributed
over a large part of one depositional basin. There is no
significant difference in the ratios between these two
groups. 4) The samples are divided into two groups, with
partial skeletons and whole bones in one group, fragmentary
jaws and isolated teeth in the other. Again, no significant
difference exists between these groups.

Figure 25 gives, without exaggeration, a quite splendid
vindication of the faithfulness of fossils. In each group,
for each test, there is a fair amount of variance; most of
the observed variance in mammal predator/prey ratios could be
the result of sample size. In many samples no more than ten
specimens constitute the predator proportion of the biomass,
so random sampling effects would produce a high variance
even if the samples all came from the same living community.
But there is no evidence whatever for a systematic bias
induced by the principal components of the fossilization
process: transport, fragmentation and concentration or
dispersal.

Body Size Effects in Cenozoic Mammals. In Figure 24,
productivity efficiencies for extant vertebrates and fossil
predator/prey ratios are plotted together as functions of

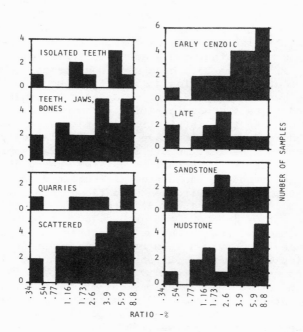

FIGURE 25. The effect of different types of preservation upon Cenozoic mammal predator/prey ratios. The ratio is given on a logarithmic scale, with class intervals separated by a factor of 1.5. Upper Right: Cenozoic faunas divided into early (Paleocene through Oligocene) and late (Miocene through Pliocene). Lower Right: Faunas divided into two groups according to the grain size of the sediment. Upper Left: Faunas divided according to the completeness of preservation of individual specimens. Lower Left: Faunas divided according to the concentration of fossils. In all four of these comparisons, no significant difference exists between the mean predator/prey ratios.

body weight. For the living animals, body weight is the
average adult body weight. For the fossils, body weight is
the average weight of all individuals in the predator sample.
There is no significant correlation between mean predator
weight and predator/prey ratio in Cenozoic mammals, or in any
other fossil group. In Figure 26, fossil predator/prey
ratios are plotted against the relative weight of the prey,
calculated by dividing the average weight of all individuals
in the prey sample (all individuals which are not predators)
by the average weight of all individuals in the predator
sample. A significant negative correlation is observed: as
the relative weight of the prey increases, the predator/prey
ratio decreases (slope = -0.34; r = .51). This result can be
viewed in two ways. If the predator/prey ratios reflect
standing crop, not productivity, then we would expect the
predator/prey ratio to decrease as the average size of the
prey increases relative to that of the predators. However,
for most of these sites, the chewed condition of the bones
and the nature of the sediments strongly indicate that the
carcasses accumulated gradually by the usual day-to-day
causes of mortality. Thus the ratios should record productivity. If this is so, the negative correlation may be
explained by the bias of fossilization and discovery against
smaller skeletons. Skeletons of prey ten times heavier than
their predators may be expected to have survived scavengers,
weathering before burial, and weathering after fossilization
much better than the predator skeletons. A prospecting
paleontologist would be more likely to overlook such predator
remains than those of the prey.

   Predator Traps. In any discussion of predator/prey
ratios, the La Brea tar-pits of downtown Los Angeles immediately come to mind. The tar-pit sample is heavily biased
toward carnivores, which predominate in this assemblage.
Quite probably the struggles of the first animals to become
mired in the asphalt-soaked sand attracted predators, which
themselves became mired and attracted more predators, and so
on. The skeletons at La Brea are usually very well preserved,
concentrated in rich pockets, and show few marks of chewing,
but they have become disarticulated by convective movements
within the tar-soaked sand. Similar taphonomic modes are
displayed at a series of predator-rich sites widely scattered
through the stratigraphic column, from the Early Permian
onwards (Bakker, in press). All these predator-rich sites
share the following features: 1) the skeletons are very well
preserved, with delicate processes intact; 2) chew marks and
other evidence of predator activity are few; 3) the skeletons
are usually disarticulated, but most of the elements of
single individuals may be found within a small area; 4) the
sediment is poorly-sorted mud, predominantly fine-grained, or
a tar-sand, or a carbonate mud; 5) the predator remains are

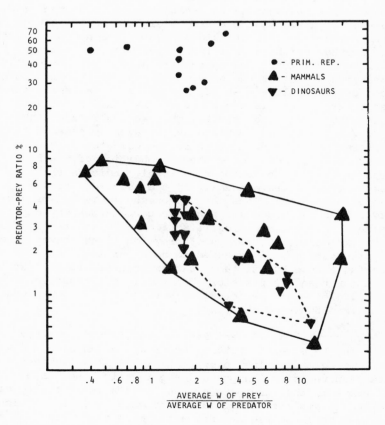

FIGURE 26. Size bias and predator/prey ratios. The predator/
prey ratio shows a significant decrease as the average size
of the predators decreases relative to the average size of
their prey.

highly concentrated. In all cases the sediment seems to have been very viscous as the carcasses accumulated in it. Probably each of these sites represents some sort of trap which mired predators as they came to feed on individuals already caught in the muck.

Excluding the predator traps, the mean Cenozoic predator/prey ratio is 3.36% (Table 3). The mean productivity efficiency for living mammals is about 2.2%, which is not significantly different from the mean predator/prey ratio from the fossil mammals (Figure 24). Here again is encouraging evidence of the faithfulness of the fossil record; predator/prey ratios do seem to reflect productivity ratios. Variation in the predator/prey ratios from fossils is much higher than that of the productivity efficiency data (Figure 24). Nevertheless, the entire range of values for productivity efficiency and fossil predator/prey ratios in mammals is below 10%; the entire range of productivity ratios for all extant ectotherms, invertebrates and vertebrates, is above 10% (Figure 24).

Predator/prey Ratios and Standing Crop Ratios: A Discrepancy. Schaller (1972) noted that in the big game parks of Africa the ratio of the big-predator standing crop to that of the big herbivores is about 1%. Schaller's 1% rule seems to hold for most large-mammal systems in the tropics (Bakker 1975b, and in press; Farlow 1976). Very few of the well studied large-mammal systems have a standing crop or predator/prey productivity ratio much greater than 1%. The Cenozoic fossil ratios are significantly higher. Why? Farlow (1976) and Russell and Béland (1978) have assumed that the low standing crop ratios in the game parks represent typical values for large-mammal systems. Yet many of the fossil faunas with ratios of 4% to 6% are based on large samples and there is no reason to suspect strong bias in preservation or in collection of fossils (Bakker, in press). Moreover, the highest fossil mammal ratios come from faunas where the average predator was about as heavy as the average prey species, so size bias should be minimal. I believe that we must accept this overwhelming evidence and conclude that, on the average, the productivity efficiency of predators was higher, and perhaps predator standing crops were relatively higher, during the Cenozoic than they are today in game parks. There is no physiological reason why a large-mammal predator population in the wild could not achieve a productivity efficiency of 4% to 6%; such high values have been reported for a variety of small mammals, both predators and herbivores. Captive large-mammal predators can achieve productivity efficiencies close to 10% (Bakker 1975b). Perhaps we should ask, not why the Cenozoic ratios are so high, but rather why efficiency is so low among living big-mammal predator populations.

Table 3. Statistical tests of predator/prey data.

Group	Symbol	Number of Samples	Mean Ratio %	S.D.	Mean arcsin √ratio in radians	S.D. arcsin √ratio in radians
WITHOUT PREDATOR TRAPS						
Living Mammals		5	0.82	0.42		
Fossil Mammals	m	32	3.36	2.45	0.1727	0.0689
Dinosaurs	d	11	2.09	1.37	0.1384	0.0464
Therapsids	tr	5	10.07	1.08	0.3329	0.0178
Thecodonts	t	5	11.22	5.68	0.3337	0.0894
Sphenacodonts	s	12	44.7	13.42	0.7298	0.1380
WITH PREDATOR TRAPS						
Fossil Mammals	M	34	5.02	9.03	0.1958	0.1318
Dinosaurs	D	12	5.33	11.31	0.1848	0.1666
Therapsids	TR	6	24.1	32.8	0.4885	0.3813
Thecodonts	T	6	21.0	24.5	0.4430	0.2800
Sphenacodonts	S	16	56.0	23.8	0.8674	0.2810

MODEL I ANOVA – WITHOUT PREDATOR TRAPS – arcsin √ratio transformation

Null Hypothesis	F	Probability
$\mu s = \mu(m + d + tr + t)$	93.0	$P < 0.01$
$\mu(tr + t) = \mu(m + d)$	7.77	$P < 0.01$
$\mu m = \mu d$	0.32	$P > 0.10$
WITH PREDATOR TRAPS		
$\mu S = (M + D + TR + T)$	68.9	$P < 0.01$
$\mu(TR + T) = \mu(M + D)$	10.7	$P < 0.01$
$\mu M = \mu D$	0.423	$P > 0.05$

A very plausible explanation for the low predator frequency in today's big game parks exists. In most of the
Cenozoic fossil mammal samples a great diversity of predators
occurs, including species capable of killing the largest prey
species. Several of these predator types, such as the sabre-
toothed cats and paleofelids, and gigantic running predators
like the big mesonychids of the Eocene or the even bigger
hyaenaelurids of the Late Cenozoic, have no living counterparts. Human hunting over the last 2 million years was
probably the chief agent in the reduction of predator diversity, as well as the cause of the general decline in large
mammals of all sorts. Modern game parks are relatively tiny
areas of habitat, rarely free from human interference. It
comes as no surprize that predator efficiency is low in these
small, disjunct areas, populated by predators whose diversity
is much reduced in comparison with Cenozoic faunas. In this
case the present is not the key to the past, because of the
profound effects of human activity on the present. If the
game parks of Africa were ten times as large, with the diversity of big predators we see in the Late Cenozoic, including
species which could regularly kill elephants and rhinos, I
strongly suspect that we would see predator/prey ratios in
the 4% to 6% range.

Correction for Collector's Bias

In a preliminary analysis of predator/prey ratios in
Late Cretaceous faunas, I accepted the suggestion of other
workers that collectors had been biased in favor of the
usually rare carnivores (Bakker 1972). However, in a comprehensive review of predator/prey ratios in sixty fossil communities (Bakker, in press) I have abandoned all attempts at
correcting suspected human bias. The data summarized here
are abstracted from that study.

Ratios in Early Permian Tetrapods

Nearly all writers have agreed that the reptiles and
amphibians of the Early Permian were typical ectotherms, with
no means of generating additional heat for thermoregulation.
Studies of bone histology support this view. One would expect very high predator/prey ratios, and in fact the average
for these communities is between 45% and 56% (Table 3,
Figures 26, 27). These high values are within the range of
productivity efficiencies seen among extant ectotherms
(Figure 24).

Significance of Aquatic Prey. As described above, "prey"
biomass is simply all of the carcass biomass available to
predators, including the carcasses of the predators them-

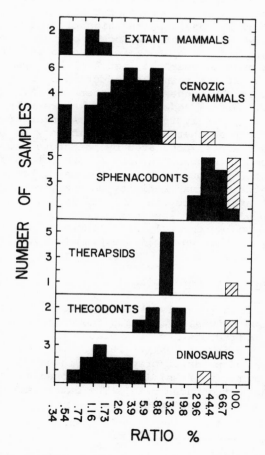

FIGURE 27.   Frequency of occurrence of predator/prey ratios for various groups, plotted on a semi-logarithmic scale. Hatched boxes represent inferred "predator traps," localities where predators dominate in small, highly concentrated masses of nearly completely disarticulated bones, with delicate elements well preserved in a matrix deposited as tar sand or sticky mud.

selves. The only predators capable of killing and
dismembering large prey in the Early Permian were the sphenacodonts, Dimetrodon and its kin (Figure 1). The teeth of
sphenacodonts were laterally compressed blades with serrated
edges, well designed for killing large tetrapod prey. It has
been suggested that Dimetrodon preyed heavily upon freshwater
sharks and other fish. Certainly, sphenacodonts may have
caught fish trapped in shallow pools, as do bears and even
jaguars in the tropical rain-forests today. Yet the very tall
sail along the back of Dimetrodon would have made diving and
swimming underwater nearly impossible, and the short jaws and
blade-like teeth are marks of a predator upon tetrapods, not
a piscivore. However, in most of the Early Permian samples,
most of the carcass biomass is contributed by reptiles and
amphibians with semiaquatic habits: the ophiacodont pelycosaurs and eryopid amphibians. Tooth marks in the bones of
these semiaquatic types match the tooth shape of sphenacodonts; there can be no doubt that they were sphenacodont prey.
It is not unusual for land predators to feed extensively on
semiaquatic prey in the tropics. Living semiaquatic fish-
eaters, the turtles and crocodilians, come on shore to bask
in the sun and to prey upon small terrestrial animals.
Jaguars and other big cats have been observed to hunt crocodilians in South America, India, and Africa (Bakker and Meyer,
in prep.). At several sites in the Mid-Paleocene Torrejon
Zone of New Mexico, field crews from Johns Hopkins found
abundant disarticulated alligator remains, with tooth marks
of mammalian predators, preserved in floodplain sediments.
Evidently a predator, probably a big species of Dissacus
(Figure 6), had been killing alligators, dragging their carcasses onto the floodplain and chewing them to pieces. In
all the predator/prey analyses presented in this paper, all
tetrapod prey, including semiaquatic species, are included.
At the one Mid-Paleocene site just mentioned, alligators make
up one-half of the prey biomass.

    At a few Early Permian sites, as in the Arroyo Formation
around Coffee Creek and Crooked Creek, Texas, large land
herbivores do contribute most of the prey carcass biomass.
At these sites the predator/prey ratio is from 35% to 60%,
not significantly different from those areas where semiaquatic prey were the most important food species.

    Hotton (this volume) claims that energy budgets in large
Komodo Dragons are much higher than would be predicted from
Kleiber's Law and that predator/prey ratios are much lower
than those calculated for Early Permian faunas. I am not at
all persuaded that the very small populations of Komodo
Dragons, restricted to a few tiny islands and suffering some
interference from human activity, are good models for the

assessment of energy consumption in large Good Reptiles.
Moreover, to be comparable to the Early Permian samples,
data on Komodo Dragon habitats would have to be gathered by
counting carcasses of dragons and all prey species accumulated
within the same small area over a period of ten years or more.
This has not been done.

Body Size and Kleiber's Rule of Constant Efficiency.
The large average size of many Dimetrodon samples enables us
to test the hypothesis that productivity efficiency does not
change with increasing weight. As shown in Figure 24, productivity efficiency data for extant species are available
for body weights from a few milligrams to a few hundred grams;
no significant change occurs over this weight range.
Dimetrodon predator/prey ratios represent productivity
efficiencies for body weights approaching 100 kg. The
Dimetrodon ratios are not significantly different from the
productivity efficiencies of extant invertebrates.

Therapsids and Thecodonts

Predator/prey ratios for therapsids and thecodonts
average about 10% (Table 3), suggesting an intermediate
level of heat production. One possible model is that
therapsids and thecodonts had metabolic rates like those of
tenrecs: low M_{std} when the environment was mild; increased
heat production only during cold stress.

Dinosaurs

The mean and variance of dinosaur predator/prey ratios
are not significantly different from those of fossil mammals
(Table 3, Figures 24, 27). Dinosaur ratios are higher than
standing crop ratios for today's big-game parks; Russell and
Béland (this volume) have interpreted this discrepancy as
indicating ectothermy in Cretaceous dinosaurs. However, the
ratios for Late Cretaceous dinosaurs range from 2% to 6%, not
significantly different from the Cenozoic fossil mammal
ratios but very significantly less than the productivity
ratios of extant ectotherms and the predator/prey ratios of
the Early Permian communities. The dinosaur ratios show the
same negative correlation with the relative size of their
prey as was found in fossil mammals (Figure 26). No significant correlation exists between dinosaur ratios and the
average weight of the individual predators (Figure 24).

The statistical comparisons in Figures 24, 26 and Table
3 are thoroughly unambiguous. Dinosaur predator/prey ratios
are indistinguishable from those of fossil Cenozoic mammals,
and this equivalence cannot be dismissed as merely the result
of large size in the dinosaurs.

Running Speed and Locomotor Repertoire

Flaws in the Traditional Model

Coombs (1978) has recently presented a useful summary of traditional ideas about adaptations for running in large land vertebrates, especially dinosaurs. These arguments have several serious flaws of observation and logic. Today, the largest land mammals, elephants with weights greater than 3 tons, are slow, ambling animals, so it might be concluded that high running speeds are unlikely in large dinosaurs of any sort. This conclusion is based on the erroneous application of the uniformitarian principle to phenomena, the results of processes, rather than to natural laws or processes themselves. The fact that extant elephants do not gallop does not prove that evolutionary processes cannot produce a 7-ton galloping tetrapod. The recent discovery of flying reptiles with wing-spans of nearly 20 meters shows that the distribution of size among extant species of an adaptive type does not necessarily indicate the extreme limits of evolutionary modification. We need rigorous biomechanical models to evaluate adaptations in large extinct vertebrates.

A second error of traditional notions lies in the assertion that running speed in tetrapods is predicted by the relative lengths of the lower limb segments. This argument states that the fastest running species have the highest tibia/femur and metatarsal/femur ratios. Within some closely related groups of species this relation does hold: for example, cheetahs are faster and have relatively larger lower limb segments than jaguars. But to compare relative lengths of lower segments in two groups with very different basic locomotor anatomies can be misleading. In birds, the femur moves little in running over flat surfaces; in most mammals the femur moves through a large arc. Ostriches have a much higher tibia/femur ratio than do cheetahs, but cheetahs run much faster. In general, ungulate mammals have much higher tibia/femur ratios than do carnivorous mammals of the same speed and weight.

McMahon's Model

In Figures 28 to 30, I have attempted to compare limb strengths in large quadrupedal dinosaurs with those of living mammals. These comparisons are, I believe, valid despite general differences in locomotor pattern (Bakker and Paul, in prep.). Figure 28 shows the sum of the squares of the minimum circumferences of the humerus and femur, plotted against body weight. Limb strength is commonly thought of as being proportional to the cross-section area, and hence to the square of the linear dimension. This is not the case, as

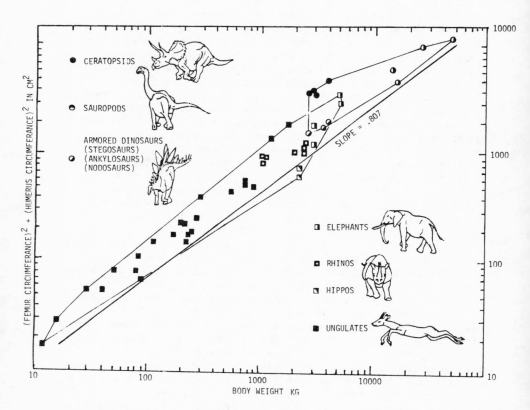

FIGURE 28.   Limb strength in dinosaurs and mammals.   The sum
of the squares of the circumferences of the humerus and
femur is given as a function of body weight.   Slope is given
for mammals, excluding elephants and hippos.

McMahon (1973) has shown; nevertheless, an interesting
relationship appears in Figure 28, which provides a valid
empirical comparison. A linear regression of the data for
ungulate mammals, except elephants and rhinos, has a slope of
0.807. The extant rhinos reach adult weights of 2 or 3 tons;
all can gallop at full speed, using a gait which has a suspended phase when all four feet are off the ground at once.
Extant hippos gallop rarely, if at all, but can trot, a gait
which also involves a suspended phase. Extant elephants
never use a suspended phase; the fastest gait is a running
walk. Hippos have smaller sums of squares of circumference
than rhinos of the same weight, consistent with the higher
speeds in rhinos. The sums of squares of circumference in
dinosaurs are as great or greater for their body weights than
those of mammals. These data will be discussed at length
elsewhere.

McMahon's theory of elastic scaling is illustrated in
Figure 29. McMahon points out that limbs are not simple,
weight-bearing columns, resisting only compressive forces,
but rather, dynamic supports which must have elastic properties to resist bending and breaking. In Figure 29, two
hypothetical mammals are drawn to scale with the following
assumptions: 1) the maximum thrust delivered by the limb to
the ground is a constant multiple of body weight; 2) the
angle at which the limb strikes the ground is constant;
3) the modulus of elasticity of the bone material is constant.
McMahon's model predicts that if these conditions are met,
the width or circumference of the limbs should scale in
proportion to the 3/2 power of the length, to maintain a
constant safety factor. The two animals in Figure 29 are
drawn to match this prediction; the length/diameter ratio of
the foreleg in the small species is 4; in the large species
it is 2. The body weights differ by a factor of 25.6.

McMahon's theory is applied to mammals and dinosaurs in
Figure 30. Femur circumference is plotted as a function of
length. The data for ungulate mammals, excluding elephants,
fall within a narrow band between two lines with a slope of
3/2. Elephants, the only extant large ungulates which do not
trot or gallop, fall below this band; they have weaker limbs
for their weights than other ungulates. The giant, extinct,
elephant-like baluchithere rhinos are likewise weak-limbed
and probably did not trot or gallop. The sauropods and
armored dinosaurs are as strong as elephants and baluchi-
theres. There is no question about the ability of sauropods
to walk on land; they had the same safety factor as elephants
and probably could sustain a running walk. The horned dinosaurs, the ceratopsids, have extraordinarily thick limbs
relative to limb length. <u>Triceratops</u> was as large as most
elephants, but had much stronger limbs for its weight. All

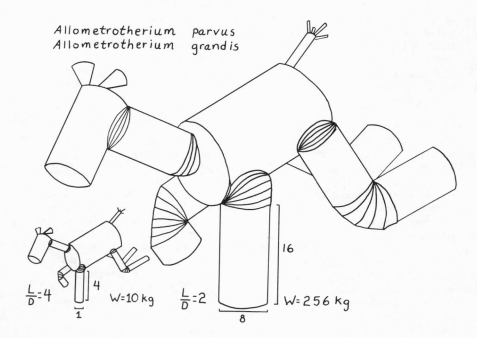

Allometrotherium parvus
Allometrotherium grandis

$\frac{L}{D}=4$ 4   W=10 kg $\frac{L}{D}=2$ 16   W=256 kg   8   1

FIGURE 29.   McMahon's theory of scaling.   Two hypothetical mammals are shown with the same strength to resist bending. The lengths of the limbs and body segments scale as the 2/3 power of the diameters.

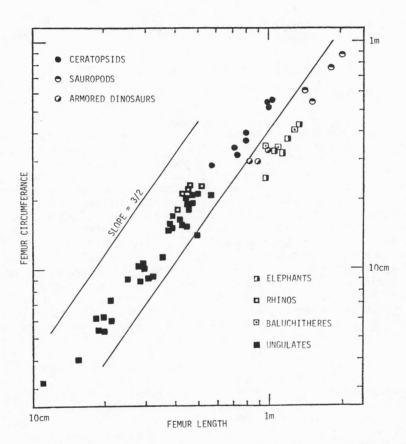

FIGURE 30. Femur circumference plotted against femur length for dinosaurs and mammals.

of the data for ceratopsids suggest that their limbs were scaled for a maximum thrust as high relative to body weight as that of living rhinos. Ceratopsids probably had a gait which included a suspended phase.

Thus the adaptive radiation of dinosaurs produced an array of locomotor types, including species which were much larger than the largest extant rhino and were strong enough for rhino-like locomotion.

Energy Budgets and Evolutionary Rates

Family Longevity

One might predict that the high energy budgets of automatic endotherms would increase the tempo of their evolution. Although the automatic endotherm is superior to the ectotherm in most types of direct biotic confrontation, the endotherm will starve to death or die of thirst in a fraction of the time that may pass before an ectotherm will expire. Since the intensity of foraging activity is much higher, the frequency of encounters among endotherms is probably much greater than among ectotherms. The extinction rate of local populations of endotherms should be greater than that of ectotherms, and extinction provides the opportunity for the spread of new species. More rapid growth of individuals and populations further intensifies resource consumption, which should make competition far more consistently severe among automatic endotherms than among ectotherms. Finally, high resource consumption may increase the number of small populations and encourage allopatric speciation.

In Figure 31, I have plotted the longevities of families of land mammals and ectothermic tetrapods which have survived to the present day. Only groups with good fossil records were included; bats and families which probably originated in in Africa and Australia, where the Early Cenozoic record is poor, were excluded. The longevity of Cenozoic mammal families is about one-half that of Cenozoic Good Reptiles and amphibians. Sources for these longevities are given elsewhere (Bakker 1977). The longevities of genera and species of Good Reptile and amphibian also seem to be significantly greater than those of mammals. Many extant crocodilian and turtle genera appeared in the Early Cenozoic; few mammal genera extend back into the Miocene. This contrast in the rate of family turnover is not an artifact of taxonomic practice, but rather reflects profound differences in the rate of total morphological change. The reptiles of the Paleocene and Eocene, as a whole, are far more similar in morphology to their living relatives than are the Paleocene and Eocene mammals to theirs.

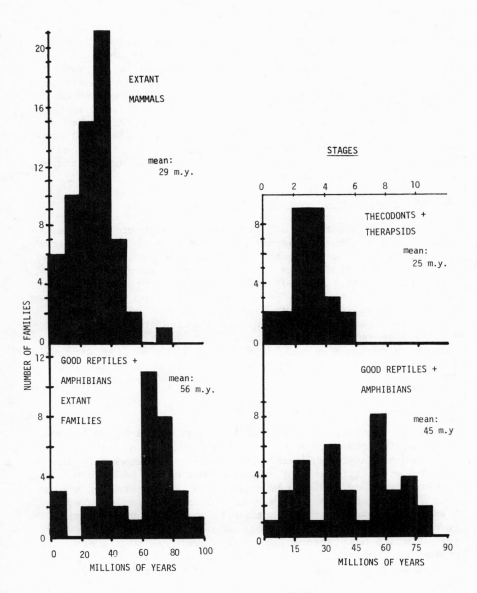

FIGURE 31. Longevity of taxonomic families.

The fossil record of dinosaur faunas sampled so far is too incomplete to permit the calculation of similar family longevity data. However, the primitive reptiles and amphibians and therapsid-thecodont faunas of the Permo-Triassic are very well sampled by rich collections. In Figure 31, family longevity of therapsids and thecodonts is compared with that of amphibians and Good Reptiles during the interval from Late Carboniferous to earliest Jurassic. Sources of data are given in Bakker (1977). Longevity is given in units of geological stages and in millions of years, with the average stage lasting 7.5 million years. The average longevity of the therapsid and thecodont families is about half that of the amphibians and Good Reptiles. The higher turnover rate suggests higher energy budgets.

Vulnerability to Mass Extinction

Although superior in direct biotic encounters with ectotherms, automatic endotherms are vulnerable to perturbations of the physical environment. Sudden, mass extinctions among large land tetrapods seem to be restricted to groups with mammal-like bone histology and low predator/prey ratios (Bakker 1977). The best known mass extinction of vertebrates is the terminal Cretaceous event, which snuffed out the dinosaurs. Large crocodilians and turtles showed little or no response to this catastrophe. Less well known mass extinctions struck therapsids, thecodonts and earlier dinosaur faunas in the late Permian, Triassic and Jurassic (Bakker 1977).

Diversity Among Large Herbivores

One might expect that the diversity of large herbivores would become greater in an adaptive radiation of automatic endotherms than among Good Reptiles, for two reasons. The rate of speciation should be higher among the endotherms, and the evolution of herbivores rather than carnivores should be encouraged by the very high energy demands of endothermy. A switch from animal to plant food increases the potential food supply by about two orders of magnitude. Today few reptiles are herbivorous; probably about 90% to 95% are predators throughout their lives. In contrast, the majority of mammal species get most of their protein and energy directly from plants.

There are fossil communities in which all of the large herbivores are Good Reptiles. In Table 4, the diversity of large herbivores in these faunas is expressed by the minimum number of genera which contribute 96% of the specimens with a live weight of 20 kg or more. These Good Reptile faunas are made up of families which had long histories of evolution as

herbivores, yet the diversity at any one place and time is
surprisingly low. In most cases a single genus (usually a
single species) contributes 96% or more of the known specimens. The diversity of large mammal herbivores was usually
much higher throughout the Cenozoic (Bakker, in press).
Table 4 also gives the large-herbivore diversity for the best
known therapsid and dinosaur faunas. In some of these
samples one or two genera contribute nearly all the specimens,
but in most three to six genera are needed to account for 96%.
The increase in herbivore diversity is obvious, even in the
earliest therapsid faunas from South Africa, where a complex
therapsid community lived on floodplains adjacent to swamps
which accommodated a low-diversity pareiasaur community.

Thus the evolutionary tempo, reflected in the rate of
extinction and speciation, the long-term rate of morphological change, and the rate of diversification of large
herbivores, was significantly higher in those tetrapod groups
which probably had high energy budgets.

Summary

Paleontology has been an emphatically empirical science.
The empirical data now available which bear in one way or
another on vertebrate bioenergetics fall into an unambiguous
pattern: dinosaurs are statistically indistinguishable from
fossil mammals, while thecodonts and therapsids are intermediate between Good Reptiles and these two groups.

Evolutionary Hyperspace

Cenozoic fossil mammals and their living descendants
occupy an evolutionary hyperspace with very characteristic
dimensions: in all habitats, even equatorial rain-forests,
mammals dominate the roles of large land predator, omnivore
and herbivore; reptiles and amphibians outnumber mammals in
small terrestrial roles and dominate mammals in the freshwater aquatic system. The dinosaur hyperspace was similar:
they monopolized the large terrestrial roles during the
Jurassic and Cretaceous, while the terrestrial amphibians,
Good Reptiles and mammals were restricted to small body sizes.

Locomotor Repertoire and Body Size

The hyperspace of dinosaurs was more restricted than
that of the Cenozoic Mammalia, because the limb anatomy of
dinosaurs limited their locomotion to walking and running
over flat surfaces; digging and climbing adaptations were
rare. Dinosaur hyperspace thus resembled that of Cenozoic
ungulate mammals and terrestrial carnivores. Limited

Table 4.   Diversity of large herbivores in fossil tetrapod
faunas.   The column on the right (#) gives the minimum
number of genera which make up 96% of specimens of herbivores
weighing 20 kg or more.

Local Fauna	Herbivore Types	#
GOOD REPTILES		
Briar Creek, Admiral Fm. Early Permian, Texas	edaphosaurs	1
Geraldine, Belle Plains Fm. Early Permian, Texas	edaphosaurs	1
Crooked Creek Area, Arroyo Fm. Early Permian, Texas	diadectids	1
Red Mudstones, Hennesey Fm. Early Permian, Texas	caseids	1
San Angelo - Flower Pot Fm. Early Late Permian, Texas	caseids	2
North Dvina River, Zone IV Late Permian, Russia	pareiasaurs	1
Blue Mudstones, Tap. Zone Late Permian, So. Africa	pareiasaurs	1
THERAPSIDS		
Variegated Mudstone, Tap. Zone Late Permian, So. Africa	deinocephalians	5
Variegated Mudstone, Dapto. Zone Late Permian, So. Africa	dicynodonts	4
Variegated Mudstone, Kiste. Zone Late Permian, So. Africa	dicynodonts	3
Variegated Mudstone, Lyst. Zone Early Triassic, So. Africa	dicynodonts	1

Table 4. (continued)

Local Fauna	Herbivore Types	#
DINOSAURS		
Lufeng Beds Late Triassic, China	prosauropods	1
Tendaguru Late Jurassic, East Africa	sauropods stegosaurs ornithopods	6
Limestone Facies, Morrison Fm. Late Jurassic, North America	sauropods stegosaurs ornithopods	5
Mudstone Facies, Morrison Fm. Late Jurassic, North America	sauropods stegosaurs ornithopods	6
Sandstone Facies, Morrison Fm. Late Jurassic, North America	sauropods stegosaurs ornithopods	6
Sandstone Facies, Cloverly Fm. Early Cretaceous, North America	ornithopods ankylosaurs sauropods	3
Mudstone Facies, Cloverly Fm. Early Cretaceous, North America	ornithopods ankylosaurs	2
Upper Wealden Fm. Early Cretaceous, England	ornithopods ankylosaurs sauropods	4
Old Man Fm. Late Cretaceous, North America	ornithopods ceratopsids ankylosaurs	5
Lance Fm. Late Cretaceous, North America	ceratopsids ornithopods	3
Hell Creek Fm. Late Cretaceous, North America	ceratopsids ornithopods ankylosaurs	3

locomotor patterns inhibit the evolution of small species because small species usually must climb or dig.

Insulation and Habitat

Among extant tropical mammals, large species often lack dense pelage, and naked skin is common. Most dinosaur habitats were tropical, and all skin impressions from big species are naked. Hair-like or feather-like insulation was present in pterosaurs and small, primitive thecodonts; both groups are related to dinosaurs, and insulation in small dinosaur species is quite possible.

Bone Histology

In Cenozoic fossil mammals and their recent descendants, bone histology for any given body size is more complex than that of reptiles and amphibians: primary vascularization is denser; vascularization patterns are more regular; if Haversian systems appear, they are more numerous for any given ontogenetic stage. Dinosaur bone histological types show the same differences as these mammalian types from those of typical Good Reptiles.

Predator/Prey Ratios

Among Cenozoic fossil mammals predator/prey ratios average 3% to 5%. Ratios for modern large mammals are significantly lower, averaging 1% or less. The higher ratios of fossil communities probably should not be ascribed to the supposed biases of the fossil record. Rather, the low diversity of present-day carnivores is presumably due to the small size of game parks where the modern predators have been studied, and long-term disturbance of their habitats by humans during the last 2 million years. The Cenozoic ratios are probably better indicators of typical mammalian predator efficiency than are the ratios from game parks.

Limb Strength

Large modern mammals can be divided into two groups: those which use a suspended phase in locomotion, as in a trot or gallop; and those which never have all four feet off the ground at once. Rhinos belong to the first group, elephants to the second. Large dinosaurs also fall into two groups: sauropods and stegosaurs had limbs as strong for their body weights as those of elephants; horned dinosaurs had limbs as strong for their body weights as do rhinos.

Dinosaur Endothermy Cannot Be Swept Under the Allometric Rug

For at least fifty years, the evidence for high heat

production in dinosaurs has been dismissed as merely the consequence of immense body size. Yet the range of adult body size in Cenozoic ungulates and terrestrial predators is very similar to that of dinosaurs; the diversity of mammals in the one to ten ton range in the Late Cenozoic was as high as or higher than that of dinosaurs. The only strikingly unique feature of dinosaur size distribution is the great size of the sauropods, most of which exceeded 20 tons in body weight. Nevertheless, the size of the food-cropping apparatus in sauropods is large enough to supply the energy needs of an automatic endotherm of such a weight. The bone histology of dinosaurs of all sizes differs notably from that of Good Reptiles of the same weights. Statistical tests show that predator/prey ratios do not change significantly with increasing body size. The strength of dinosaur limbs is as great as that of mammals of the same weight. In bone histology, predator/prey ratios, and limb strength, small dinosaurs resemble small modern mammals, large dinosaurs resemble large mammals, and both dinosaurs and mammals differ in a consistent way from Good Reptiles in the same size class.

Thecodonts and Therapsids Are Intermediate Types

The dominant large tetrapods of the Late Permian and Triassic, the therapsids and thecodonts, are intermediate in their predator/prey ratios and limb anatomy between Good Reptiles and Cenozoic mammals. At any given body size, the bone histology of most therapsids and thecodonts is like that of mammals.

Evolutionary Concepts

The empirical patterns seen in the fossil record are powerful tools for constructing and testing evolutionary hypotheses. The goal of the study of adaptations should be to explain the range and limits of the evolutionary hyperspace. Why do the species of extant reptiles and amphibians outnumber those of non-flying mammals? Why do reptiles dominate as aquatic freshwater predators? Why are so few reptiles herbivorous? Why do mammals dominate in the roles of large land tetrapods, even in the tropics? It has been postulated that the high heat production of modern mammals gives them an irresistible advantage, even in the tropics, in direct interactions with typical reptiles and amphibians. A corollary of this hypothesis is that high heat production provides a lesser advantage to a small land tetrapod and a distinct disadvantage in a freshwater aquatic species. This hypothesis is not limited to any particular taxonomic group or geological age. Rather, if correct, it should apply to the long-term evolutionary interaction of any adaptive radiations of automatic endotherms and ectotherms.

The fossil record confirms the hypothesis. The first
tetrapod group showing evidence of high heat production, the
therapsids, quickly gave rise to dominant large land animals.
Dinosaurs appear to represent a higher level of endothermy,
and they replaced the therapsid-thecodont dynasties. The
entire fossil history of large land vertebrates shows the
progressive nature of evolution among large land tetrapods.
Intense, direct biotic interactions have driven adaptive
trends towards more complete optimization of performance of
muscle, heart, lungs and brains. Dinosaurs appear to have
reached a level of performance in thermoregulation and locomotion comparable with that of many Late Cenozoic mammals.
Some of the smaller predatory dinosuars seem to have acquired
brains of a size and complexity equal to those of modern
ground birds of the same weights. As reinterpreted, the
Mesozoic "Age of Dinosaurs" ceases to be an anomalous period
of evolutionary divergence ruled by giant Good Reptiles.
Rather, the success of dinosaurs becomes part of an unre-
versed, coherent progression, leading from the first land
tetrapods of the Devonian to the grand complex of modern
mammals.

Bibliography

ADAMS, P. A. and J. E. HEATH. 1964. Temperature regulation in the sphinx moth, Celerio lineata. Nature,
Lond. 201: 20-22.
ADOLPH, E. F. 1951. Some differences in responses to
low temperatures between warm-blooded and cold-blooded
vertebrates. Amer. J. Physiol. 166: 92-103.
ALEKSIUK, M. 1976. Reptilian hibernation: evidence of
adaptive strategies in Thamnophis sirtalis parietalis.
Copeia 1976: 170-178.
_____. 1977. Cold-induced aggregative behavior in the
red-sided garter snake (Thamnophis sirtalis parietalis).
Herpetologica 33: 98-101.
ALEXANDER, C. E. and W. G. WHITFORD. 1968. Energy
requirements of Uta stansburyiana. Copeia 1968:
678-683.
ALEXANDER, R. M. 1971 Size and shape. Inst. Biol.,
Studies in Biology 29. E. Arnold, London. 59 p.
_____. 1976. Estimates of speeds of dinosaurs.
Nature, Lond. 261: 129-130.
ALLEN, J. A. 1922-1925. I. The American Museum Congo
Expedition Collection of Insectivora. II. Sciuridae,
Anomaluridae and Idiuridae. III. Carnivora.
IV. Primates. Bull. Amer. Mus. Nat. Hist. 47: 1-524.
ALTMAN, P. L. and D. S. DITTMER. 1968. Metabolism.
Fed. Amer. Soc. for Experimental Biology, Committee on
Biological Handbooks, Bethesda, Maryland. 737 p.
_____. 1973. Biology data book, Second Edition,
Vol. 2. Fed. Amer. Soc. for Experimental Biology,
Committee on Biological Handbooks, Bethesda, Maryland.
1432 p.
AMPRINO, R. 1947. La structure du tissu osseux envisagée
comme expression de différences dans la vitesse de
l'accroissement. Archives de Biologie 58: 315-330.
_____. 1967. Bone histophysiology. Guy's Hospital
Report 116(2): 51-69.

ANTHONY, J. 1961. Encéphale morphologie encéphalique
et moulages endocraniens. In: J. Piveteau (ed.),
Traité de paléontologie 6(1): 436-458.

ARISTOTLE. 1968. Parts of Animals, with an English
translation by A. L. Peck. Harvard Univ. Press,
Cambridge, Mass.

ARUTYUNYAN, G. S., M. D. MASHKOUSKII and L. F. ROSHCHINA.
1964. Pharmacological properties of melatonin.
Federation Proc. 23: 1330-1332.

ASPLUND, K. K. 1970. Metabolic scope and body temperatures of whiptail lizards (Cnemidophorus).
Herpetologica 26: 403-411.

AUFFENBERG, W. 1971. Report on a study of the Komodo
dragon. Animal Kingdom 73: 18-23.

_____. 1972. Komodo dragons. Natural History
81(4): 52-59.

AUGEE, M. L. 1976. Heat tolerance in monotremes.
J. Thermal Biol. 1: 181-184.

AUGEE, M. L., E. H. M. EALEY and H. SPENCER. 1970.
Biotelemetric studies of temperature regulation and
torpor in the echidna, Tachyglossus aculeatus.
J. Mammalogy 51: 561-570.

AVERY, R. A. 1971. Estimates of food consumption by
the lizard Lacerta vivipara Jacquin. J. Anim. Ecol.
40: 351-365.

_____. 1976. Thermoregulation, metabolism and social
behavior in Lacertidae. In: A. d'A. Bellairs and
C. B. Cox (eds.), Morphology and biology of reptiles.
Linn. Soc. Lond., Symp. 3: 245-259. Academic Press,
London.

AXELROD, D. I. and H. P. BAILEY. 1968. Cretaceous
dionsaur extinction. Evolution 22: 595-611.

BAKER, M. A. 1972. Influence of the carotid rete on brain
temperature in cats exposed to hot environments.
J. Physiol. 220: 711-728.

_____ and L. W. CHAPMAN. 1977. Rapid brain cooling in
exercising dogs. Science 195: 781-783.

_____ and J. N. HAYWARD. 1968. The influence of the
nasal mucosa and the carotid rete upon hypothalamic
temperature in sheep. J. Physiol. 198: 561-579.

BAKKEN, G. S. 1976. A heat transfer analysis of animals:
unifying concepts and the application of metabolism
data to field ecology. J. Theoret. Biol. 60: 337-348.

_____ and D. M. GATES. 1975. Heat transfer analysis
of animals: some implications for field ecology,
physiology and evolution. In: D. M. Gates and
R. B. Schmerl (eds.), Perspectives of biophysical
ecology, pp. 255-290. Springer-Verlag, New York.

BAKKER, R. T. 1968. The superiority of dinosaurs.
Discovery, Peabody Mus., Yale 3(1): 11-22.

_____. 1971. Dinosaur physiology and the origin of mammals. Evolution 25: 636-658.

_____. 1972a. Anatomical and ecological evidence of endothermy in dinosaurs. Nature, Lond. 238: 81-85.

_____. 1972b. Locomotor energetics of lizards and mammals compared. Physiologist 15: 278.

_____. 1974. Dinosaur bio-energetics - a reply to Bennett and Dalzell, and Feduccia. Evolution 28: 497-503.

_____. 1975a. Dinosaur renaissance. Sci. American 232(4, April): 58-78.

_____. 1975b. Experimental and fossil evidence for the evolution of tetrapod bioenergetics. In: D. M. Gates and R. B. Schmerl (eds.), Perspectives of biophysical ecology, pp. 365-399. Springer-Verlag, New York.

_____. Ms. Dinosaurs and bioenergetic evolution: quantitative test of the predator/prey model.

_____ and P. M. GALTON. 1974. Dinosaur monophyly and a new class of vertebrates. Nature, Lond. 248: 168-172.

BARBAULT, R. 1971. Recherches ecologiques dans la savane de Lamto (Côte d'Ivoire): production annuelle des populations naturelles du lézard Mabuya buttneri Matschie). Terre Vie 118: 203-217.

BARBER, B. J. and E. C. CRAWFORD. 1977. A stochastic dual-limit hypothesis for behavioral thermoregulation in lizards. Physiol. Zool. 50: 53-60.

BARNETT, S. A. and L. E. MOUNT. 1967. Resistance to cold in mammals. In: A. H. Rose, (ed.), Thermobiology, pp. 411-477. Academic Press, New York.

BARRETT, G. W. 1969. Bioenergetics of a captive least shrew, Cryptotis parva. J. Mammalogy 50: 629-630.

BARSBOLD, R. 1974. Results of the Polish-Mongolian Palaeontological Expedictions. V. Saurornithoididae, a new family of small theropod dinosaurs from Central Asia and North America. Palaeontol. Polonica 30: 5-22.

BARTHOLOMEW, G. A. 1972. Body temperature and energy metabolism. In: M. S. Gordon et al., Animal physiology: principles and adaptations, 2nd edition, pp. 298-368. Macmillan, New York.

_____. 1977. Energy metabolism. Body temperature and energy metabolism. In: M. S. Gordon et al., Animal physiology: principles and adaptations, 3rd edition, pp. 57-110 and 364-449. Macmillan, New York.

_____ and T. M. CASEY. 1977. Endothermy during terrestrial activity in large beetles. Science 195: 882-883.

_____ and R. J. EPTING. 1975. Rates of post-flight cooling in sphinx moths. In: D. M. Gates and R. B. Schmerl (eds.), Perspectives of biophysical ecology, pp. 405-416. Springer-Verlag, New York.

_____ and B. HEINRICH. 1973. A field study of flight temperatures in moths in relation to body weight and wing loading. J. Exp. Biol. 58: 123-135.

_____ and B. HEINRICH. 1978. Endothermy in African dung beetles during flight, ball making, and ball rolling. J. Exp. Biol. 73: 65-83.

_____ and R. C. LASIEWSKI. 1965. Heating and cooling rates, heart rate and simulated diving in the Galapagos marine iguana. Comp. Biochem. Physiol. 16: 573-582.

_____ and V. A. TUCKER. 1963. Control of changes in body temperature, metabolism, and circulation by the agamid lizard Amphibolurus barbatus. Physiol. Zool. 36: 199-218.

_____ and V. A. TUCKER. 1964. Size, body temperature, thermal conductance, oxygen consumption, and heart rate in Australian varanid lizards. Physiol. Zool. 37: 341-354.

BARTLETT, P. N. and D. M. GATES. 1967. The energy budget of a lizard on a tree trunk. Ecology 48: 315-322.

BAUCHOT, R. 1972. Encéphalisation et phylogenie. C. R. hebd. Seanc. Acad. Sci. Paris D 275: 441-443.

_____. 1978. Encéphalization in vertebrates: a new mode of calculation for allometry coefficients and isoponderal indices. Brain Behav. Evol. 15: 1-18.

_____, M. L. BAUCHOT, R. PLATEL and J. M. RIDET. 1977. Brains of Hawaiian tropical fishes: brain size and evolution. Copeia 1977: 42-46.

_____, R. PLATEL and J. M. RIDET. 1976. Brain-body weight relationships in Selachii. Copeia 1976: 305-310.

BEHRENSMEYER, A. K. 1975. The taphonomy and palaeoecology of Plio-Pleistocene vertebrate assemblages east of Lake Rudolf, Kenya. Bull. Mus. Comp. Zool., Harvard 146(10): 473-578.

BÉLAND, P. and D. A. RUSSELL. 1978. Palaeoecology of Dinosaur Provincial Park (Cretaceous), Alberta, interpreted from the distribution of articulated vertebrate remains. Can. J. Earth Sci. 15: 1012-1024.

BÉLANGER, L. F. 1977. Osteocytic osteolysis in a Cretaceous reptile. Rev. Can. Biol. 35: 71-73.

BELKIN, D. A. 1961. The running speed of the lizards Dipsosaurus dorsalis and Callisaurus draconoides. Copeia 1961: 223-224.

BENEDICT, F. G. 1932. The physiology of large reptiles. Carnegie Inst. Wash. Publ. 425: 1-539.

_____. 1936. The physiology of the elephant. Carnegie Inst. Wash. Publ. 474: 1-302.

_____. 1938. Vital energetics. Carnegie Inst. Wash. Publ. 503: 1-215.

BENNETT, A. F.   1972a.   The effect of activity on oxygen consumption, oxygen debt, and heart rate in the lizards, Varanus gouldii and Sauromalus hispidus. J. Comp. Physiol. 79: 259-280.

_____ . 1972b.   A comparison of activities of metabolic enzymes in lizards and rats. Comp. Biochem. Physiol. 42B: 637-647.

_____ . 1973a.   Ventilation in two species of lizards during rest and activity. Comp. Biochem. Physiol. 46A: 653-671

_____ . 1973b.   Blood physiology and oxygen transport during activity in two lizards, Varanus gouldii and Sauromalus hispidus. Comp. Biochem. Physiol. 46A: 673-690.

_____ . 1974.   A final word. Evolution 28: 503.

_____ . 1978.   Activity metabolism of the lower vertebrates. Ann. Rev. Physiol. 40: 447-469.

_____ and B. DALZELL. 1973.   Dinosaur physiology: a critique. Evolution 27: 170-174.

_____ and W. R. DAWSON. 1976.   Metabolism. In: C. Gans and W. R. Dawson (eds.), Biology of the Reptilia 5: 127-223. Academic Press, New York.

_____ and P. LICHT. 1972.   Anaerobic metabolism during activity in lizards. J. Comp. Physiol. 81: 277-288

_____ and K. A. NAGY. 1977.   Energy expenditures in free-ranging lizards. Ecology 58: 697-700.

BIDAR, A., L. DeMAY, and G. THOMEL. 1972. Compsognathus corallestris, nouvelle espèce de dinosaurien théropode du Portlandien de Canjuers. (Sud-est de la France). Ann. Mus. Hist. Nat., Nice. 1(1): 1-34.

BINKLEY, S. A. 1974.   Pineal and melatonin: circadian rhythms and body temperatures of sparrows. In: L. E. Scheving, F. Halberg and J. E. Pauly (eds.), Chronobiology, pp. 582-585. Symp. Internat. Soc. Chronobiology, Univ. Arkansas, Little Rock, 1971. Igaku Shoin Ltd., Tokyo.

_____ , E. KLUTH and M. MENAKER. 1971.   Pineal function in sparrows: circadian rhythms and body temperature. Science 174: 311-314.

BIRD, R. T. 1941.   A dinosaur walks into the museum. Natural History 47: 75-81.

_____ . 1944.   Did Brontosaurus ever walk on land? Natural History 53: 61-67.

BIRKEBAK, R. C. 1966.   Heat transfer in biological systems. Intern. Rev. Gen. Expt. Zool. 2: 269-344.

BLIGH, J. 1973.   Temperature regulation in mammals and other vertebrates. North-Holland Res. Monogr., Frontiers Biol. 30. American Elsevier, New York. 436 p.

_____ and K. G. JOHNSON. 1973. Glossary of terms for thermal physiology. J. Applied Physiol. 35: 941-961.

BLOCK, J. A. 1974. Hand-rearing seven-banded armadillos at the National Zoological Park, Washington. Zool. Soc. Lond., Internat. Zoo Yearbook 14: 210-211.

BOBEK, B. 1971. Influence of population density upon rodent production in a deciduous forest. Ann. Zool. Fenn. 8: 137-144.

BOGERT, C. M. 1953. Body temperatures of the tuatara under natural conditions. Zoologica 38: 63-64.

_____. 1959. How reptiles regulate their body temperature. Sci. American 200(4, April): 105-120.

BONAPARTE, J. 1975. Neuvos materiales de Lagosuchus talampayensis Romer (Thecodontia-Pseudosuchia) y su significado en el origen de los Saurischia; Chanarense inferior, Triasico Medio de Argentina. Acta Geol. Lilloana 13(1): 1-85.

_____. 1976. Pisanosaurus mertii Casamiquela and the origin of the Ornithischia. J. Paleont. 50: 808-820.

BONIS, L. de, M. O. LEBEAU and A. de Ricqlès. 1972. Étude de la répartition des types de tissus osseux chez les vertébrés tétrapodes au moyen de l'analyse factorielle des correspondances. C. R. hebd. Séanc. Acad. Sci. Paris D 274: 3084-3087

BOONSTRA, L. D. 1971. The early therapsids. Ann. S. Afr. Mus. 59: 17-46.

_____. 1972. Discard the names Theriodontia and Anomodontia: a new classification of the therapsids. Ann. S. Afr. Mus. 59: 315-338.

BOURN, D. and M. J. COE. 1978. The size, structure and distribution of the giant tortoise population of Aldabra. Phil. Trans. Roy. Soc. Lond. (B) 282: 139-175.

BOUVIER, M. 1977. Dinosaur Haversian bone and endothermy. Evolution 31: 449-450.

BOWEN, R. 1966. Paleotemperature analysis. Elsevier, New York. 265 p.

BOWLER, P. J. 1976. Fossils and Progress. Paleontology and the idea of progressive evolution in the Nineteenth Century. Science History Publ., New York. 191 p.

BRAMBILLA, G. 1972. Primi dati morfometrici sulle lacune ossee di vertebrati fossili: Kritosaurus notabilis (Lambe). Atti Soc. Ital. Sci. Nat. Mus. Civ. Stor. Nat., Milano 113: 313-327.

BRAMWELL, C. D. and P. B. FELLGETT. 1973. Thermal regulation in sail lizards. Nature, Lond. 242: 203-205.

BRATTSTROM, B. H. 1963. A preliminary review of the thermal requirements of amphibians. Ecology 44: 238-255.

_____. 1965. Body temperatures of reptiles. Amer. Midl. Nat. 73: 376-422.

_____. 1968. Heat retention by large Australian monitor lizards, Varanus varius. Amer. Zool. 8: 766.

_____. 1972. Temperature changes in heat producting plants. Bull. So. Calif. Acad. Sci. 71: 54-55.

_____. 1974. The evolution of reptilian social behavior. Amer. Zool. 14: 35-49.

_____, A. J. STABILE, F. R. LAUIERS, and D. POPE. 1963. Body temperature of Indian elephants. J. Mammalogy 44: 282.

BRIDEN, J. C., G. E. DREWRY and A. G. SMITH. 1974. Phanerozoic equal-area world maps. Jour. Geol. 82: 555-574.

BRINK, A. S. 1955. Note on a very tiny specimen of Thrinaxodon liorhinus. Palaeont. Africana 3: 73-76.

_____. 1956. Speculation on some advanced characteristics in the higher mammal-like reptiles. Palaeont. Africana 4: 77-96.

_____. 1963. The taxonomic position of the Synapsida. S. Afr. J. Sci. 59: 153-159.

BRODY, S. 1945. Bioenergetics and growth. With special reference to the efficiency complex in domestic animals. Reinhold Publ. Corp., New York. 1023 p. Reprinted (1964): Hafner Publ. Co., Darien, Connecticut.

BROILI, F. 1922. Ueber den feineren Bau der "vernöcherten Sehnen" (= verknöcherten Muskeln) von Trachodon. Anat. Anz. 55: 465-75.

BROWN, B. 1917. A complete skeleton of the horned dinosaur Monoclonius, and description of a second skeleton showing skin impressions. Bull. Amer. Mus. Nat. Hist. 37: 281-306.

BRUNER, H. L. 1907. On the cephalic veins and sinuses of reptiles, with a description of a mechanism for raising venous blood pressure in the head. Amer. J. Anat. 7: 1-117.

BUECHNER, H. K. and F. B. GOLLEY. 1967. Preliminary estimation of energy flow in Uganda kob (Adenota kob thomasi Neumann). In: K. Petrusewicz (ed.), Secondary productivity in terrestrial ecosystems; principles and methods, pp. 243-254. Proc. IBP Meeting, Jablonna, Poland, 1966. Państwowe Wydawn. Naukwowe, Warszawa.

BUCKNER, C. H. 1964. Metabolism, food capacity and feeding behavior in four species of shrews. Can. J. Zool. 42: 259-279.

BURGHARDT, G. M. 1977. Of iguanas and dinosaurs: social behavior and communication in neonate reptiles. Amer. Zool. 17: 177-190.

BURT, W. M. and R. P. GROSSENHEIDER. 1952. A field guide to the mammals. Houghton Mifflin, Boston. 284 p.

BURTON, T. M. and G. E. LIKENS. 1975a. Energy flow and nutrient cycling in salamander populations in the

Hubbard Brook Experimental Forest, New Hampshire.
Ecology 56: 1068-1080.

_____. 1975b. Salamander populations and biomass in
the Hubbard Brook Experimental Forest, New Hampshire.
Copeia 1975: 541-546.

BUSTARD, H. R. 1967. Activity cycle and thermoregulation
in the Australian gecko Gehyra variegata. Copeia
1967: 753-758.

CALDER, W. A. and J. R. KING. 1974. Thermal and caloric
relations of birds. In: D. Farner and J. R. King (eds.),
Avian biology 4: 259-293. Academic Press, New York.

CAMP, C. L. 1930. A study of phytosaurs with descriptions
of new material from western North America. Mem. Univ.
California 10: 1-174.

_____. 1942. California mosasaurs. Mem. Univ.
California 13: 1-68.

_____. 1956. Triassic dicynodont reptiles.
2. Triassic dicynodonts compared. Mem. Univ.
California 13: 305-348.

CAMPBELL, J. G. 1966. A dinosaur bone lesion resembling
avian osteopetrosis and some remarks on the mode of
development of the lesion. J. roy. microsc. Soc.
85: 163-174.

CAREY, F. G. 1973. Fishes with warm bodies. Sci.
American 228(2, Feb.): 36-44.

_____ and K. D. LAWSON. 1973. Temperature regulation
in free-swimming bluefin tuna. Comp. Biochem. Physiol.
44A: 375-392.

_____ and J. M. Teal. 1966. Heat conservation in tuna
fish muscle. Proc. Nat. Acad. Sci. USA 56: 1464-1469.

_____ and J. M. TEAL. 1969a. Regulation of body
temperature by the bluefin tuna. Comp. Biochem. Physiol.
28: 205-213.

_____ and J. M. TEAL. 1969b. Mako and porbeagle: warm
bodied sharks. Comp. Biochem. Physiol. 28: 199-204.

CARLISLE, H. J. 1969. Effect of preoptic and anterior
hypothalamic lesions on behavioral thermoregulation in
the cold. J. Comp. Physiol. Psychol. 69: 391-402.

CARROLL, R. L. 1976. Eosuchians and the origin of
archosaurs. In: C. S. Churcher (ed.), Essays on
palaeontology in honour of Loris Shano Russell,
pp. 58-79. Royal Ontario Mus. Life Sci., Misc. Publ.,
Toronto.

CASE, T. J. 1978. Speculations on the growth rate and
reproduction of some dinosaurs. Paleobiology 4: 320-328.

CASTANET, J. 1978. Les marques de croissance osseuse comme
indicateurs de l'age chez les lézards. Acta zool.,
Stockholm 59: 35-48.

_____, F. J. MEUNIER and A. de RICQLÈS. 1977.
L'enregistrement de la croissance cyclique par le tissu

osseux chez les vertébrés poikilothermes: données
comparatives et essai de synthèse. Bull. Biol. Fr.
et Belgique 61: 183-202.

CHARIG, A. J. 1972. The evolution of the archosaur pelvis
and hind limb: an explanation in functional terms.
In: K. A. Joysey and T. S. Kemp (eds.), Studies in
vertebrate evolution: essays presented to Dr. F. R.
Parrington, FRS, pp. 121-155. Winchester Press, New
York.

_____. 1976. "Dinosaur monophyly and a new class of
vertebrates": a critical review. In: A. d'A. Bellairs
and C. B. Cox (eds.), Morphology and biology of reptiles.
Linn. Soc. Lond., Symp. 3: 65-104. Academic Press,
London.

_____ and B. HORSFIELD. 1975. Before the Ark. British
Broadcasting Corporation, London. 160 p.

CHATTERJEE, S. 1978. A primitive parasuchid (phytosaur)
reptile from the Upper Triassic Maleri Formation of
India. Palaeontology 21: 83-127.

CHEW, R. M. and A. E. CHEW. 1970. Energy relationships
of the mammals of a desert shrub (Larrea tridentata)
community. Ecol. Monogr. 40: 1-21.

CLEMENS, W. 1963. Fossil mammals of the type Lance
Formation, Wyoming. Part I. Introduction and Multi-
tuberculata. Univ. California Publ. Geol. Sci.
48: 1-105.

CLOUDSLEY-THOMPSON, J. L. 1971. The temperature and water
relations of reptiles. Merrow Technical Library,
Watford, England. 159 p.

_____ and D. K. BUTT. 1977. Thermal balance in the
tortoise and its relevance to dinosaur extinction.
Brit. J. Herpetology 5: 641-647.

COE, M. J., D. H. CUMMING and J. PHILLIPSON. 1976.
Biomass and production of large African herbivores in
relation to rainfall and primary production.
Oecologia 22: 341-354.

COGBURN, L. A., P. C. HARRISON and D. E. BROWN. 1976.
Scotophase-dependent thermoregulatory dysfunction in
pinealectomized chickens. Proc. Soc. exp. Biol. Med.
153: 197-201.

COLBERT, E. H. 1951. Environment of adaptation of certain
dinosaurs. Biol. Rev. 26: 265-284.

_____. 1958. Morphology and behavior. In: A. Roe and
G. G. Simpson (eds.), Behavior and Evolution, pp. 27-47.
Yale Univ. Press, New Haven.

_____. 1961. Dinosaurs, their discovery and their
world. E. P. Dutton, New York. 300 p.

_____. 1962. The weights of dinosaurs. Amer. Mus.
Novitates 2076: 1-16.

_____. 1963. Fossils of the Connecticut Valley. The age of dinosaurs begins. Bull. Connecticut geol. nat. Hist. Survey 96: 1-31.

_____. 1970. A saurischian dinosaur from the Triassic of Brazil. Amer. Mus. Novitates 2405: 1-39.

_____, R. B. COWLES and C. M. BOGERT. 1946. Temperature tolerances in the American alligator and their bearing on the habits, evolution and extinction of the dinosaurs. Bull. Amer. Mus. Nat. Hist. 86: 327-373.

_____, R. B. COWLES, and C. M. BOGERT. 1947. Rates of temperature increase in dinosaurs. Copeia 1947: 141-142.

_____ and D. A. RUSSELL. 1969. The small Cretaceous dinosaur Dromaeosaurus. Amer. Mus. Novitates 2380: 1-49.

COLLIN, J. P. 1971. Differentitation and regression of the cells of the sensory line in the epiphysis cerebri. In: G. E. W. Wolstenholme and J. Knight (eds.), The pineal gland, pp. 79-125. Ciba Foundation Symp., Churchill Livingstone, Edinburgh.

COOMBS, W. P. 1975. Sauropod habits and habitats. Palaeogeogr. Palaeoclimatol. Palaeoecol. 17: 1-33.

_____. 1978. Theoretical aspects of cursorial adaptations in dinosaurs. Quart. Rev. Biol. 53: 393-418.

COOPER, K. E. 1966. Temperature regulation and the hypothalamus. Brit. Med. Bull. 22: 238-242.

COPE, E. D. 1870. On the hypothesis of evolution: physical and metaphysical. Lippincott's Magazine, Philadelphia. Reprinted in: E. D. Cope, 1887, The origin of the fittest, pp. 128-172. Macmillan, New York.

COTT, H. B. 1961. Scientific results of an enquiry into the ecology and economic status of the Nile crocodile (Crocodilus niloticus) in Uganda and Northern Rhodesia. Trans. zool. Soc. Lond. 29: 211-356.

COULSON, T. D., R. A. COULSON and T. HERNANDEZ. 1973. Some observations on the growth of captive alligators. Zoologica 58: 47-52.

COWLES, R. B. 1940. Additional implications of reptilian sensitivity to high temperatures. Amer. Nat. 74: 542-561.

_____. 1946. Fur and feathers: a response to falling temperature: Science 103: 74-75.

_____. 1962. Semantics in biothermal studies. Science 135: 670.

_____ and C. BOGERT. 1944. A preliminary study of the thermal requirements of desert reptiles. Bull. Amer. Mus. Nat. Hist. 83: 265-296.

_____ and C. M. BOGERT. 1947. Untitled. In: "Comments by Readers", Science 105: 282.

COX, A., R. R. DOELL and G. B. DALRYMPLE. 1963. Geomagnetic polarity epochs and Pleistocene geochronometry. Nature, Lond. 198: 1049-1051.

_____. 1964. Reversals of the earth's magnetic field. Science 144: 1537-1543.

CRAIGHEAD, J. J. and F. C. CRAIGHEAD. 1956. Hawks, owls and wildlife. The Stackpole Co., Harrisburg, Pennsylvania.

CRAWFORD, E. C. 1972. Brain and body temperatures in a panting lizard. Science 177: 431-433.

CRILE, G. and D. P. QUIRING. 1940. A record of the body weight and certain organ and gland weights of 3690 animals. Ohio J. Sci. 40: 219-259.

CROMPTON, A. W. 1968. The enigma of the evolution of mammals. Optima (Anglo-American Corp.) 18: 137-151.

_____ and F. A. JENKINS. 1973. Mammals from reptiles: a review of mammalian origins. Ann. Rev. Earth Planetary Sci. 1: 131-155.

_____ and P. PARKER. 1978. Evolution of the mammalian masticatory apparatus. Amer. Sci. 66: 192-201.

_____, C. R. TAYLOR and J. A. JAGGER. 1978. Evolution of homeothermy in mammals. Nature 272: 333-336.

CROWCROFT, P. 1957. The life of the shrew. Max Reinhardt, London. 166 p.

CUELLO, A. C. and J. H. TRAMEZZANI. 1969. The epiphysis cerebri of the Weddell Seal: its remarkable size and glandular pattern. Gen. Comp. Endocrinol. 12: 154-164.

CURREY, J. D. 1962. The histology of the bone of a prosauropod dinosaur. Palaeontology 5: 238-246.

CURRY-LINDAHL, K. 1957. Behavior of the tropical rock lizard Agama cyanogaster (Ruppel) in hot environments. Ann. Soc. Roy. Zool. Belg. 87: 45-74.

DASMANN, R. F. and A. S. MOSSMAN. 1962. Abundance and population structure of wild ungulates in some areas of Southern Rhodesia. J. Wildl. Manage. 26: 262-268.

DAVIDSON, F. D., J. P. LEHMAN, P. TAQUET and R. W. G. WYCKOFF. 1978. Analyse des proteines de vertébrés fossiles devoniens et crétacés du Sahara. C. R. hebd. Séanc. Acad. Sci. Paris (D): (in press).

DAVIS, D. E. and F. B. GOLLEY. 1963. Principles in mammalogy. Reinhold Publ., New York. 335 p.

DAWSON, T. J. 1972. Primitive mammals and patterns in the evolution of thermoregulation. In: J. Bligh and R. E. Moore (eds.), Essays on temperature regulation, pp. 1-18. North Holland Publ., Amsterdam.

_____. 1973. "Primitive" mammals. In: G. C. Whittow (ed.), Comparative physiology of thermoregulation 3: 1-46. Academic Press, New York.

DAWSON, W. R. 1975. On the physiological significance of the preferred body temperature of reptiles. In: D. M. Gates and R. B. Schmerl (eds.), Perspectives of biophysical ecology, pp. 443-473. Springer-Verlag, New York.

_____ and G. A. BARTHOLOMEW. 1958. Metabolic and cardiac responses to temperature in the lizard (Dipsosaurus dorsalis). Physiol. Zool. 31: 100-111.

_____ and J. W. HUDSON. 1970. Birds. In: G. C. Whittow (ed.), Comparative physiology of thermoregulation 1: 223-310. Academic Press, New York.

_____ and A. J. HULBERT. 1970. Standard metabolism, body temperature and surface areas of Australian marsupials. Amer. J. Physiol. 218: 1233-1238.

_____ and C. R. TAYLOR. 1973. Energetic cost of locomotion in kangaroos. Nature 246: 313-314.

DENDY, A. 1899. On the development of the parietal eye and adjacent organs in Sphenodon (Hatteria). Quart. J. Microscop. Sci. 42: 111-153.

_____. 1911. On the structure, development and morphological interpretation of pineal organs and adjacent parts of the brain in the tuatara (Sphenodon punctatus). Phil. Trans. Roy. Soc. Lond. B 201: 227-331.

DESMOND, A. J. 1975. The hot-blooded dinosaurs. Blond and Briggs, London. 238 p.

_____. 1977. The hot-blooded dinosaurs. Reprinted, with a postscript added. Warner Books, New York.

DeWITT, C. B. 1967. Precision of thermoregulation and its relation to environmental factors in the desert iguana, Dipsosaurus dorsalis. Physiol. Zool. 40: 49-66.

_____. 1971. Postural mechanisms in the behavioral thermoregulation of a desert lizard, Dipsosaurus dorsalis. J. Physiologie 63: 242-245.

DIETZ, R. S. 1961. Continent and ocean basin evolution by spreading of the sea floor. Nature, Lond. 190: 854-857.

_____. 1962. Ocean-basin evolution by sea-floor spreading. In: G. A. Macdonald and H. Kuno (eds.), The crust of the Pacific Basin. Amer. Geophys. Union, Monogr. 6: 11-12.

DODSON, P. 1971. Sedimentology and taphonomy of the Oldman Formation (Campanian), Dinosaur Provincial Park, Alberta (Canada). Palaeogeogr. Palaeoclimatol. Palaeoecol. 10: 21-74.

_____. 1974. Dinosaurs as dinosaurs. Evolution 28: 494-497.

DOLLO, L. 1886. Note sur les ligaments ossifiés des dinosauriens de Bernissart. Archives de Biologie 7: 249-264.

DORF, E. 1970. Paleobotanical evidence of Mesozoic and Cenozoic climatic changes. North. Am. Paleont. Convention, Chicago, 1969. Proc. D: 323-346.

DOUGLAS, R. G. and S. M. SAVIN. 1973. Oxygen and carbon isotope analyses of Cretaceous and Tertiary Foraminifera from the central north Pacific. In: E. L. Winterer, J. I. Ewing, et al. (eds.), Initial Rep. Deep Sea Drilling Project 17: 591-605. U. S. Govt. Printing Office, Washington, D.C.

DOUGLAS-HAMILTON, I. and O. DOUGLAS-HAMILTON. 1975. Among the elephants. Collins, London. 285 p.

EAKIN, R. M. 1964. Development of the third eye in the lizard, Sceloporus occidentalis. Rev. Suisse Zool. 71: 267-285.

_____. 1973. The third eye. Univ. California Press, Berkeley. 157 p.

EATON, T. H. 1960. The aquatic origin of tetrapods. Trans. Kansas Acad. Sci. 63: 115-120.

EDELMAN, I. S. and F. ISMAIL-BEIGI. 1972. Role of ion transport in thyroid calorigenesis. In: R. E. Smith et al. (eds.), Bioenergetics, pp. 67-70. Proc. Internat. Symp. on Environmental Physiology, Dublin, 1971. Publ. by Fed. Amer. Soc. Expt. Biol., Bethesda, Maryland.

EDGAR, W. D. 1971. Aspects of the ecological energetics of the wolf spider Pardosa (Lycosa) lugubris (Walckenaer). Oecologia, Berlin 7: 136-154.

EDINGER, T. 1942. The pituitary body in giant animals, fossil and living: a survey and a suggestion. Quart. Rev. Biol. 17: 31-45.

_____. 1955. The size of parietal foramen and organ in reptiles. A rectification. Bull. Mus. comp. Zool., Harv. 114: 1-34.

_____. 1956. Paired pineal organs. In: J. A. Kappers (ed.), Progress in neurobiology. Proc. First Internat. Meeting Neurobiol., pp. 12-19. Elsevier, Amsterdam and New York.

EGGELING, H. von 1938. Allgemeines über den Aufbau knöcherner Skeletteile. In: L. Bolk, E. Goppert, E. Kallius and W. Lubosch (eds.), Handbuch der vergleichenden Anatomie der Wirbeltiere 5: 275-304. Urban und Schwarzenberg, Berlin.

ELDER, W. H. and D. H. ROGERS. 1975. Body temperature in the African elephant as related to ambient temperature. Mammalia 39: 395-399.

EMILIANI, C. 1954. Temperature of Pacific bottom waters and polar superficial waters during the Tertiary. Science 119: 853-855.

ENGBRETSON, G. A. and V. H. HUTCHISON. 1976. Parietal-ectomy and thermal selection in the lizard Sceloporus magister. J. Exp. Zool. 198: 29-38.

ENGBRETSON, G. and C. M. LENT. 1976. Parietal eye of the
lizard: neuronal photoresponses and feedback from the
pineal gland. Proc. Nat. Acad. Sci. 73: 654-657.

ENGLEMANN, M. D. 1966. Energetics, terrestrial field
studies, and animal productivity. In: J. B. Cragg
(ed.), Advances in ecological research 3: 73-115.
Academic Press, New York.

ENLOW, D. H. 1962. Functions of the Haversian systems.
Amer. Jour. Anatomy 110: 268-306.

_____. 1963. Principles of bone remodeling.
Charles C. Thomas, Springfield, Illinois. 131 p.

_____. 1966. An evaluation of the use of bone
histology in forensic medicine and anthropology. In:
F. G. Evans (ed.), Studies on the anatomy and function
of bone and joints, pp. 93-112. Springer-Verlag,
Berlin and New York.

_____. 1969. The bone of reptiles. In: C. Gans and
A. d'A. Bellairs (eds.), Biology of the Reptilia
1: 45-80. Academic Press, New York.

_____ and S. O. Brown. 1956. A comparative histological study of fossil and Recent bone tissues. Part I.
Texas Jour. Sci. 8: 405-443.

_____ and S. O. BROWN. 1957. A comparative histological study of fossil and Recent bone tissues. Part II.
Texas Jour. Sci. 9: 186-214.

_____ and S. O. BROWN. 1958. A comparative histological study of fossil and Recent bone tissues. Part III.
Texas Jour. Sci. 10: 187-230.

EPSTEIN, S., R. BUCHSBAUM, H. LOWENSTAM and H. C. UREY.
1951. Carbonate-water isotopic temperature scale.
Bull. Geol. Soc. Amer. 62: 417-426.

ESTES, R. 1964. Fossil vertebrates from the Late
Cretaceous Lance Formation, eastern Wyoming. Univ.
California Publ. Geol. Sci. 49: 1-180.

EWER, R. F. 1965. The anatomy of the thecodont reptile
Euparkeria capensis Broom. Phil. Trans. Roy. Soc. Lond.
B 248: 379-435.

FARLOW, J. O. 1976. A consideration of the trophic
dynamics of a Late Cretaceous large-dinosaur community
(Oldman Formation). Ecology 57: 841-857.

_____. 1976b. Speculations about the diet and
foraging behavior of large carnivorous dinosaurs.
Amer. Midl. Nat. 95: 186-190.

_____. 1976c. Tables of feeding rate and productivity
data for terrestrial vertebrates. Privately circulated
appendix to Farlow (1976a).

_____ and P. DODSON. 1975. The behavioral significance
of frill and horn morphology in ceratopsian dinosaurs.
Evolution 29: 353-361.

_____, C. V. Thompson, and D. E. Rosner. 1976. Plates of the dinosaur Stegosaurus: forced convection heat loss fins? Science 192: 1123-1125.

FEDAK, M. A., B. PINSHOW and K. SCHMIDT-NIELSEN. 1974. Energy cost of bipedal running. Amer. J. Physiol. 227: 1038-1044.

FEDUCCIA, A. 1973. Dinosaurs as reptiles. Evolution 27: 166-169.

_____. 1974. Endothermy, dinosaurs and Archaeopteryx. Evolution 28: 503-504.

_____ and H. B. TORDOFF. 1979. Feathers of Archaeopteryx: asymmetric vanes indicate aerodynamic function. Science 203: 1021-1022.

FITZPATRICK, L. C. 1973. Energy allocation in the Allegheny Mountain salamander, Desmognathus ochrophaeus. Ecol. Monogr. 43: 43-58.

FLEHARTY, E. D. and J. R. CHOATE. 1973. Bioenergetic strategies of the cotton rat, Sigmodon hispidus. J. Mammalogy 54: 680-692.

FOX, L. R. 1975. Cannibalism in natural populations. Ann. Rev. Ecol. Syst. 6: 87-106.

FRAIR, W., R. G. ACKMAN and N. MROSOVSKY. 1972. Body temperature of Dermochelys coriacea: warm turtle from cold water. Science 177: 791-793.

FREELAND, W. J. and D. H. JANSEN. 1974. Strategies in herbivory by mammals: the role of plant secondary compounds. Amer. Nat. 108: 269-289.

GAFFNEY, E. S. 1977. An endocranial cast of the side-necked turtle, Bothremys, with a new reconstruction of the palate. Amer. Mus. Novitates 2639: 1-12.

GALTON, P. M. 1970. The posture of hadrosaurian dinosaurs. J. Paleont. 44: 464-473.

_____. 1974a. Notes on Thescelosaurus, a conservative ornithopod dinosaur from the Upper Cretaceous of North America, with comments on ornithopod classification. J. Paleont. 48: 1048-1067.

_____. 1974b. The ornithischian dinosaur Hypsilophodon from the Wealden of the Isle of Wight. Bull. Br. Mus. Nat. Hist. (Geol.) 25: 1-52.

GANS, C. 1970. Strategy and sequence in the evolution of the external gas exchangers of ectothermal vertebrates. Forma et Functio 3: 61-104.

GASTON, S. and M. MENAKER. 1968. Pineal function: the biological clock in the sparrow? Science 160: 1125-1127.

GATES, D. M. 1968. Physical environment. In: E. S. E. Hafez (ed.), Adaptation of domestic animals, pp. 46-60. Lea and Febiger, Philadelphia.

GILMORE, C. W. 1919. A new restoration of Triceratops, with notes on the osteology of the genus. Proc. U. S. Natl. Mus. 55: 97-112.

_____. 1920. Osteology of the carnivorous Dinosauria in the United States National Museum, with special reference to the genera Antrodemus (Allosaurus) and Ceratosaurus. Bull. U. S. Natl. Mus. 110: 1-159.

GIRARDIER, L. 1977. The regulation of the biological furnace of warm blooded animals. Experientia (Basel) 33: 1121-1262.

GLADSTONE, R. J. and C. P. G. WAKELEY. 1940. The pineal organ. Williams and Wilkins, London and Baltimore. 528 p.

GLASER, R. 1958. Increase in locomotor activity following shielding of the parietal eye in night lizards. Science 128: 1577-1578.

GOLLEY, F. B. 1960. Energy dynamics of a food chain of an old-field community. Ecol. Monogr. 30: 187-206.

_____. 1967. Methods of measuring secondary productivity in terrestrial vertebrate populations. In: K. Petrusewicz (ed.), Secondary productivity of terrestrial ecosystems; principles and methods, pp. 99-124. Proc. IBP Meeting, Jablonna, Poland, 1966. Państwowe Wydawn. Naukwowe, Warszawa.

_____. 1968. Secondary productivity in terrestrial communities. Amer. Zool. 8: 53-59.

GORDON, M. S. (ed.). 1977. Animal physiology, third edition. Macmillan, New York. 699 p.

GOSZ, J. R., R. T. HOLMES, G. E. LIKENS and F. H. BORMANN. 1978. The flow of energy in a forest ecosystem. Sci. American 238(3, March): 92-102.

GOULD, S. J. 1966. Allometry and size in ontogeny and phylogeny. Biol. Rev. 41: 587-640.

_____. 1975a. Review: Evolution of the brain and intelligence, by Harry J. Jerison. Paleobiology 1: 125-128.

_____. 1975b. Allometry in primates, with emphasis on scaling and the evolution of the brain. In: F. Szalay (ed.), Approaches to primate paleobiology. Contrib. Primat. 5: 244-292. Karger, Basel.

GRAHAM, J. B. 1975. Heat exchange in yellowfin tuna, Thannus albacares, skipjack tuna, Katsuwonus pelamis, and the adaptive significance of elevated body temperatures in scombrid fishes. Fishery Bulletin 73: 219-229.

GREENBERG, N. 1976. Thermoregulatory aspects of behavior in the blue spiny lizard Sceloporus cyanogenys (Sauria, Iguanidae). Behavior 59: 1-21.

_____. 1978. Ethological considerations in the experimental study of lizard behavior. In: N. Greenberg and P. D. MacLean (eds.), Behavior and neurology of lizards, pp. 203-224. Nat. Inst. Mental Health, Rockville, Maryland.

GREER, A. E., J. D. LAZELL and R. M. WRIGHT. 1973.
Anatomical evidence for a counter-current heat
exchanger in the leatherback turtle, (Dermochelys
coriacea). Nature 244: 181.

GREGORY, J. T. 1962. The genera of phytosaurs.
Amer. J. Sci. 260: 652-690.

GREGORY, W. K. 1951. Evolution emerging: a survey of
changing patterns from primeval life to man. Macmillan,
New York. 2 vols., 736 p. and 1013 p.

GRIFFITHS, M. 1968. Echidnas. Pergamon Press, Oxford.
282 p.

GRODZINSKI. W. 1966. Bioenergetics of small mammals from
Alaskan taiga forest. Lynx (Prague) 6: 51-55.

_____, B. BOBEK, A. DROZDZ and A. GORECKI. 1969.
Energy flow through small rodent populations in a beech
forest. In: K. Petrusewicz and L. Ryszkowski (eds.),
Energy flow through small mammal populations, pp. 291-
298. Proc. IBP Meeting, Oxford, England, 1968.
Państwowe Wydawn. Naukwowe, Warszawa.

GROSS, W. 1934. Die Typen des mikroskopischen
Knochenbaues bei fossilen Stegocephalen und Reptilien.
Z. Anat. 103: 731-764.

GRUBB, P. 1971. The growth, ecology, and population
structure of giant tortoises on Aldabra. Phil. Trans.
roy. Soc. Lond. B 260: 327-372.

GUNDY, G. C. 1974. The evolutionary history and
comparative morphology of the pineal complex in
Lacertilia. Ph.D. dissertation, Univ. Pittsburgh, 168 p.

_____, C. L. RALPH and G. Z. WURST. 1975. Parietal
eyes in lizards: zoogeographical correlates. Science
190: 671-673.

_____ and G. Z. WURST. 1976a. The occurrence of
parietal eyes in recent Lacertilia (Reptilia).
J. Herpetology 10: 113-121.

_____ and G. Z. WURST. 1976b. Parietal eye-pineal
morphology in lizards and its physiological
implications. Anat. Rec. 185: 419-431.

HAFEZ, E. S. E. 1964. Behavioral thermoregulation in
mammals and birds. A review. Int. J. Biometeorol.
7: 231-239.

HALSTEAD, L. B. 1975. The evolution and ecology of the
dinosaurs. Peter Lowe, London. 116 p.

_____. 1976. Dinosaur teleology. Nature, Lond.
260: 559-560.

_____ and J. R. MERCER. 1968. Histology of dinosaur
bone. In: 16th Symposium Vert. Palaeont. and Compar.
Anat., Reading. Reading, England, 2 p., 4 figs.

_____ and J. MIDDLETON. 1972. Bare bones: an
exploration in art and science. Oliver and Boyd,
Edinburgh. 119 p.

HAMASAKI, D. I. and D. J. EDER. 1977. Adaptive radiation of the pineal system. In: F. Crescitelli (ed.), The visual system in vertebrates, pp. 498-548. H. Autrum et al. (eds.), Handbook of sensory physiology 8(5). Springer-Verlag, New York.

HAMMEL, H. T. 1976. On the origin of endothermy in mammals. Israel J. Med. Sci. 12: 905-915.

_____, F. T. CALDWELL and R. M. ABRAMS. 1967. Regulation of body temperature in the blue-tongued lizard. Science 156: 1260-1262.

HANITSCH, R. 1888. On the pineal eye of the young and adult Anguis fragilis. Proc. Liverpool Biol. Soc. 3: 87-95.

HANKS, J. and J. E. A. McINTOSH. 1972. Population dynamics of the African elephant (Loxodonta africana). J. Zool., Lond. 169: 29-38.

HANSSON, L. 1971. Estimates of the productivity of small mammals in a south Swedish spruce plantation. Ann. Zool. Fenn. 8: 118-126.

HARRIS, V. A. 1964. The life of the rainbow lizard. Hutchinson, London. 174 p.

HATCHER, J. T. 1903. Osteology of Haplocanthosaurus with description of a new species, and remarks on the probable habits of the Sauropoda and the age and origin of the Atlantosaurus bed. Mem. Carnegie Mus. 2: 1-72.

HATT, R. T. 1940. Lagomorpha and Rodentia other than Sciuridae, Anomaluridae and Idiuridae, collected by the American Museum Congo Expedition. Bull. Amer. Mus. Nat. Hist. 76: 456-604.

HAUGHTON, S. H. 1924. The fauna and stratigraphy of the Stromberg Series. Ann. S. Afr. Mus. 12: 323-497.

HEANEY, L. R. 1978. Island area and body size of insular mammals: evidence from the tri-colored squirrel (Callosciurus prevosti) of southwest Asia. Evolution 32: 29-44.

HEATH, J. E. 1964a. Head-body temperature differences in horned lizards. Physiol. Zool. 37: 273-279.

_____. 1964b. Reptilian thermoregulation: evaluation of field studies. Science 146: 784-785.

_____. 1965. Temperature regulation and diurnal activity in horned lizards. Univ. Cal. Publ. Zool. 64(3): 97-136).

_____. 1966. Venous shunts in the cephalic sinuses of horned lizards. Physiol. Zool. 39: 30-35.

_____. 1968. The origins of thermoregulation. In: E. T. Drake (ed.), Evolution and environment, pp. 259-278. Yale Univ. Press, New Haven.

_____. 1970. Behavioral regulation of body temperature in poikilotherms. Physiologist 13: 399-410.

_____, E. GASDORF and R. G. NORTHCUTT. 1968. The effect of thermal stimulation of anterior hypothalamus on blood pressure in the turtle. Comp. Biochem. Physiol. 26: 509-518.

HEATWOLE, H., B. T. FIRTH and G. J. W. WEBB. 1973. Panting thresholds, I. Some methodological and internal influences on the panting threshold of an agamid, Amphibolurus muricatus. Comp. Biochem. Physiol. 46A: 799-826.

HEINRICH, B. 1974a. Thermoregulation in bumblebees: I. Brood incubation by Bombus vosneasenskii Queens. J. Comp. Physiol. 88: 129-140.

_____. 1974b. Thermoregulation in endothermic insects. Science 185: 747-756.

_____. 1977. Why have some animals evolved to regulate a high body temperature? Amer. Nat. 111: 623-640.

_____ and T. M. CASEY. 1978. Heat transfer in dragonflies: 'fliers' and 'perchers'. J. Exp. Biol. 74: 17-36.

HEINTZ, N. 1963. Dinosaur footprints and polar wandering. Årbok Norsk. Polarinst. 1962: 35-43.

HELLER, H. C. and D. M. GATES. 1971. Altitudinal zonation of chipmunks (Eutamias): energy budgets. Ecology 52: 424-433.

HEMMINGSEN, A. M. 1960. Energy metabolism as related to body size and respiratory surfaces, and its evolution. Rept. Steno Memorial Hospital Nordisk insulinlab 9(2): 1-110. C. Hamburgers bogtrykkeri, Copenhagen.

HESS, H. H. 1962. History of the ocean basins. In: A. E. J. Engel, H. L. James and B. F. Leonard (eds.), Petrologic studies: a volume to honor A. F. Buddington, pp. 599-620. Geol. Soc. America, Boulder, Colorado.

HILEY, P. 1975. How the elephant keeps its cool. Natural History 84: 34-40.

HILL, A. V. 1956. The design of muscles. British Med. Bull. 12: 165-166.

_____. 1970. First and last experiments in muscle mechanics. Cambridge Univ. Press, Cambridge, England. 141 p.

HIRST, S. M. 1975. Ungulate-habitat relationships in a South African woodland/savanna ecosystem. Wildlife Monogr. 44: 1-60.

HOCHACHKA, P. W. 1973. Basic strategies and mechanisms of enzyme adaptation to temperature. In: W. Wieser (ed.), Effects of temperature on ectothermic organisms, pp. 69-81. Springer-Verlag, New York.

HOCK, R. J. 1951. The metabolic rates and body temperatures of bats. Biol. Bull. 101: 289-299.

HOHNKE, L. A. 1973. Haemodynamics in the Sauropoda. Nature, Lond. 244: 309-310.

HOLLAND, W. J.   1906.   The osteology of Diplodocus Marsh.
Mem. Carnegie Mus.   2(6): 225-278.
_____.   1924.   The skull of Diplodocus.   Mem. Carnegie
Mus.   9: 379-403.
HOLMAN, J. A.   1970.   Herpetofauna of the Wood Mountain
Formation (Upper Miocene) of Saskatchewan.   Can. J.
Earth Sci.   7: 1317-1325.
_____.   1971.   Climatic significance of giant tortoises
from the Wood Mountain Formation (Upper Miocene) of
Saskatchewan.   Can. J. Earth Sci.   8: 1148-1151.
_____.   1976.   Cenozoic herpetofaunas of Saskatchewan.
In: C. S. Churcher (ed.), Essays on palaeontology in
honour of Loris Shano Russell, pp. 80-92.   Royal Ontario
Mus. Life Sci., Misc. Publ., Toronto.
HOLMES, E. B.   1975.   A reconsideration of the phylogeny
of the tetrapod heart.   J. Morph.   147: 209-228.
HOPSON, J. A.   1964.   The braincase of an advanced mammal-
like reptile Bienotherium.   Peabody Mus. Yale Univ.,
Postilla   87: 1-30.
_____.   1973.   Endothermy, small size, and the origin
of mammalian reproduction.   Amer. Nat.   107: 446-452.
_____.   1976.   Hot-, cold-, or lukewarm-blooded
dinosaurs?   Review of The hot-blooded dinosaurs: a
revolution in paleontology, by A. J. Desmond.
Paleobiology   2: 271-275.
_____.   1977.   Relative brain size and behavior in
archosaurian reptiles.   Ann. Rev. Ecol. Syst.
8: 429-448.
_____.   In press.   Paleoneurology.   In: C. Gans,
R. G. Northcutt and P. S. Ulinski (eds.), Biology of
the Reptilia   9, Neurology A.   Academic Press, London.
_____ and J. W. KITCHLING.   1972.   A revised classification of cynodonts (Reptilia: Therapsida).   Palaeont.
Africana   14: 71-85.
HOTTON, N.   1963.   Dinosaurs.   Pyramid Press, New York.
192 p.
_____.   1974.   A new dicynodont (Reptilia, Therapsida)
from Cynognathus zone deposits of South Africa.
Ann. S. Afr. Mus.   64: 157-165.
HUDSON, J. W.   1965.   Temperature regulation and torpidity
in the pygmy mouse, Baiomys taylori.   Physiol. Zool.
38: 243-254.
HUENE, F. von   1911.   Beiträge zur Kenntnis und Beurteilung
der Parasuchier.   Geol. paläont. Abhandl. Jena (n.F.)
10: 65-121.
_____.   1914.   Beiträge zur Geschichte der Archosaurier.
Geol. paläont. Abhandl. Jena. (n.F.)   13: 1-53.
_____.   1926.   Vollständige Osteologie eines
Plateosauriden aus dem Schwäbischen Keuper.   Geol.
paläont. Abhandl. Jena (n.F.)   15: 1-43.

_____. 1928. Lebensbild des Saurischier-Vorkommens im obersten Keuper von Trossingen im Württemberg. Palaeobiologica 1: 103-116.

HUEY, R. B. and M. SLATKIN. 1976. Cost and benefits of lizard thermoregulation. Quart. Rev. Biol. 51: 363-384.

HUGHES, B. 1963. The earliest archosaurian reptiles. S. Afr. J. Sci. 59: 221-241.

HUGHES, R. N. 1970. An energy budget for a tidal-flat population of the bivalve Scrobicularia plana (Da Costa). J. Anim. Ecol. 39: 357-381.

HUTCHINSON, V. H., H. G. DOWLING and A. VINEGAR. 1966. Thermoregulation in a brooding female Indian Python, Python molurus bivittatus. Science 151: 694-696.

HUTCHINSON, V. H. and R. J. KOSH. 1974. Thermoregulatory function of the parietal eye in the lizard, Anolis carolinensis. Oecologia 16: 173-177.

HUXLEY, T. H. 1868. On the animals which are most nearly intermediate between birds and reptiles. Ann. Mag. Nat. Hist. 2: 66-75.

_____. 1870. Contributions to the anatomy and taxonomy of the Dinosauria. Quart. J. geol. Soc. Lond. 26: 1-51.

IRVING, L. 1966. Adaptations to cold. Sci. American 214(1, Jan.): 94-101.

ISACKS, B., J. OLIVER and L. R. SYKES. 1968. Seismology and the new global tectonics. Jour. Geophys. Res. 73: 5855-5899.

JACKSON, C. G., J. A. TROTTER, T. H. TROTTER and M. W. TROTTER. 1976. Accelerated growth rate and early maturity in Gopherus agassizi (Reptilia: Testudines). Herpetologica 32: 139-145.

JANSKY, L. 1965. Adaptability of heat production mechanisms in homeotherms. Acta. Univ. Carol. Biol. 1: 1-91.

_____. 1973. Non-shivering thermogenesis and its thermoregulatory significance. Biol. Rev. 48: 85-132.

JEPSEN, G. L. 1964. Riddles of the terrible lizards. Amer. Scient. 52: 227-246.

JERISON, H. J. 1969. Brain evolution and dinosaur brains. Amer. Nat. 103: 575-588.

_____. 1970. Brain evolution: new light on old principles. Science 170: 1224-1225.

_____. 1973. Evolution of the brain and intelligence. Academic Press, New York. 482 p.

_____. 1976. Principles of the evolution of the brain and behavior. In: R. B. Masterson, W. Hodos and H. J. Jerison (eds.), Evolution, brain and behavior: persistent problems, pp. 23-45. Lawrence Erlbaum Assoc., Publ., Hillsdale, New Jersey.

JOHANSEN, K. 1962. Evolution of temperature regulation
in mammals. In: J. P. Hannon and E. Viereck (eds.),
Comparative physiology of temperature regulation,
pp. 73-131. Arctic Aeromedical Laboratory, Fort
Wainwright, Alaska.

JOHN, T. M., S. ITOH and J. C. GEORGE. 1978. On the role
of the pineal in thermoregulation in the pigeon.
Hormone Research 9: 41-56.

JOHNSON, C. R., W. G. VOIGT and E. N. SMITH. 1978.
Thermoregulation in crocodilians. III. Thermal
preferenda, voluntary maxima, and heating and cooling
rates in the American alligator, Alligator
mississippiensis. Zool. J. Linn. Soc. Lond. 62: 179-188.

JOHNSTON, P. A. 1979. Growth rings in dinosaur teeth.
Nature, Lond. 278: 635-636.

JORDAN, P. A., D. B. BOTKIN and M. L. WOLFE. 1971.
Biomass dynamics in a moose population. Ecology
52: 147-152.

JÜRGENS, U. 1974. The hypothalamus and behavioural
patterns. In: D. F. Swaab and J. P. Schade (eds.),
Integrative hypothalamic activity, pp. 445-463.
Elsevier, Amsterdam.

KAHL, M. P. 1963. Thermoregulation in the wood stork,
with special reference to the role of the legs.
Physiol. Zool. 36: 141-151.

KEITH, M. L. and J. N. WEBER. 1964. Carbon and oxygen
isotopic composition of selected limestones and fossils.
Geochim. Cosmochim. Acta. 28: 1787-1816.

KEYSER, A. W. 1973. A preliminary study of the type area
of the Cistecephalus Zone of the Beaufort Series, and a
revision of the anomodont family Cistecephalidae.
S. Afr. Geol. Surv., Mem. 62: 1-71.

KIESTER, A. R. 1971. Species density of North American
amphibians and reptiles. Syst. Zool. 20: 127-137.

KING, J. R. 1974. Seasonal allocation of time and energy
resources in birds. In: R. A. Paynter (ed.), Avian
energetics. Nuttall Ornithology Club Publ. 15: 4-70.

_____ and D. S. FARNER. 1961. Energy metabolism,
thermoregulation and body temperature. In:
A. J. Marshall (ed.), Biology and comparative physiology
of birds, pp. 215-288. Academic Press, New York.

KITCHELL, J. F. 1969. Thermophilic and thermophobic
responses of snakes in a thermal gradient. Copeia
1969: 189-191.

_____ and J. T. WINDELL. 1972. Energy budget for the
lizard, Anolis carolinensis. Physiol. Zool. 45: 178-188.

KLEIBER, M. 1932. Body size and metabolism. Hilgardia
6: 315-353.

_____. 1961. The fire of life; an introduction to
animal energetics. John Wiley, New York. 454 p.

KLEVEZAL, G. A. and S. E. KLEINENBERG. 1967. <u>Age</u>
<u>determination</u> <u>of</u> <u>mammals</u> <u>from</u> <u>layered</u> <u>structures</u> <u>in</u>
<u>teeth</u> <u>and</u> <u>bone</u>. (In Russian). Nauka, Moscow. English
transl. by J. Salkind (1969), Israel Program for
Scientific Translations, Jerusalem, 128 p.

KLUGER, M. J. 1978. The evolution and adaptive value of
fever. <u>Amer</u>. <u>Scient</u>. <u>66</u>: 38-43.

KNUTSON, R. M. 1974. Heat production and temperature
regulation in eastern skunk cabbage. <u>Science</u>
<u>186</u>: 746-747.

KURTÉN, B. 1952. The Chinese <u>Hipparion</u> fauna.
A quantitative survey with comments on the ecology of
the machairodonts and hyaenids and the taxonomy of the
gazelles. <u>Soc</u>. <u>Scient</u>. <u>Fennica</u>, <u>Commentat</u>. <u>Biol</u>.
<u>13</u>(4): 1-82.

LANGSTON, W. 1956. The Sebecosuchia: cosmopolitan
crocodilians? <u>Amer</u>. <u>J</u>. <u>Sci</u>. <u>254</u>: 605-614.

_____. 1975. Ziphodont crocodiles: <u>Pristichampsus</u>
<u>vorax</u> (Troxell), new combination, from the Eocene of
North America. <u>Fieldiana</u>, <u>Geology</u> <u>33</u>: 291-314.

LaPOINTE, J. L. 1966. Investigation of the function of
the parietal eye in relation to locomotor activity
cycles in the lizard, <u>Xantusia</u> <u>vigilis</u>. Ph.D.
dissertation, Univ. California, Berkeley, 96 p.

LAPPARENT, A. F. de 1947. Les dinosauriens du Crétacé
supérieur du Midi de la France. <u>Mém</u>. <u>Soc</u>. <u>géol</u>. <u>Fr</u>.
(<u>n.s.</u>) <u>26</u>(56): 1-54.

_____. 1960. Les dinosauriens du "Continental
intercalaire" du Sahara central. <u>Mém</u>. <u>Soc</u>. <u>géol</u>. <u>Fr</u>.
(<u>n.s.</u>) <u>39</u>(88A): 1-57.

_____. 1962. Footprints of dinosaurs in the Lower
Cretaceous of Vestspitsbergen-Svalbard. <u>Årbok</u> <u>Norsk</u>.
<u>Polarinst</u>. <u>1960</u>: 14-21.

LASIEWSKI, R. C. 1963. Oxygen consumption of torpid,
resting, active and flying hummingbirds. <u>Physiol</u>. <u>Zool</u>.
<u>36</u>: 122-140.

_____ and W. R. DAWSON. 1967. A reexamination of the
relation between standard metabolic rate and body
weight in birds. <u>Condor</u> <u>69</u>: 13-23.

LAWSON, D. A. 1975. Pterosaurs from the latest Cretaceous
of West Texas: discovery of the largest flying creature.
<u>Science</u> <u>187</u>: 947-948.

LAWTON, R. 1977. Taphonomy of the dinosaur quarry,
Dinosaur National Monument. <u>Univ</u>. <u>Wyoming</u> <u>Contrib</u>.
<u>Geol</u>. <u>15</u>: 119-126.

LEOPOLD, A. 1933. <u>Game</u> <u>management</u>. C. Scribner's,
New York. 481 p.

LEVY, I. L. 1973. Effects of pinealectomy and melatonin
injections at different seasons on ovarian activity in
the lizard <u>Anolis</u> <u>carolinensis</u>. <u>J</u>. <u>Exp</u>. <u>Zool</u>.
<u>185</u>: 169-174.

LICHT, P. 1964. The temperature dependence of myosinadenosine-triphosphatase and alkaline phosphatase in lizards. Comp. Biochem. Physiol. 12: 333-340.

_____, W. R. DAWSON and V. H. SHOEMAKER. 1969. Thermal adjustments in cardiac and skeletal muscles of lizards. Z. vergl. Physiol. 65: 1-14.

_____, W. R. DAWSON, V. H. SHOEMAKER and A. R. MAIN. 1966. Observations on the thermal relations of western Australian lizards. Copeia 1966: 97-110.

_____ and W. R. MOBERLY. 1965. Thermal requirements for embryonic development in the tropical lizard Iguana iguana. Copeia 1965: 515-517.

LIPTON, J. M. 1968. Effects of preoptic lesions on heat escape responding and colonic temperature in the rat. Physiol. Behav. 3: 165-169.

LOWE-McCONNELL, R. H. 1975. Fish communities in tropical freshwaters: their distribution, ecology and evolution. Longmans, London and New York. 337 p.

LOWENSTAM, H. A. 1964. Paleotemperatures of the Permian and Cretaceous Periods. In: A. E. M. Nairn (ed.), Problems of paleoclimatology, pp. 227-248. Wiley-Interscience, New York.

_____ and S. EPSTEIN. 1959. Cretaceous paleo-temperatures as determined by the oxygen isotope method, their relations to, and the nature of rudistid reefs. In: El Sistema Cretacico 1: 65-76. 20th Internat. Geol. Congress, Mexico City.

LULL, R. S. 1924. Dinosaurian climatic response. In: M. R. Thorpe (ed.), Organic adaptation to environment, pp. 225-279. Yale Univ. Press, New Haven, Connecticut.

_____. 1933. A revision of the Ceratopsia or horned dinosaurs. Mem. Peabody Mus. Nat. Hist. Yale 3(3): 1-135.

_____ and N. E. WRIGHT. 1942. Hadrosaurian dinosaurs of North America. Geol. Soc. Amer., Spec. Paper 40: 1-242.

MACKAY, R. S. 1964. Galapagos tortoise and marine iguana deep body temperatures measured by radio telemetry. Nature, Lond. 204: 355-358.

MADSEN, J. H. 1976. Allosaurus fragilis: a revised osteology. Utah Geol. Min. Surv. Bull. 109: 1-163.

MAGLIO, V. J. and H. B. S. COOKE (eds.), 1978. Evolution of African mammals. Harvard Univ. Press., Cambridge, Massachusetts. 642 p.

MANN, K. H. 1976. Production on the bottom of the sea. In: D. H. Cushing and J. J. Walsh (eds.), The ecology of the seas, pp. 225-250. W. B. Saunders, Philadelphia.

MANTELL, G. A. 1850a. On the Pelorosaurus, an undescribed gigantic terrestrial reptile, whose remains are associated with those of the Iguanodon and other saurians in the strata of Tilgate Forest, in Sussex. Phil. Trans. roy. Soc. Lond. 140: 379-390.

_____. 1850b. On a dorsal dermal spine of the Hylaeosaurus recently discovered in the strata of Tilgate Forest. Phil. Trans. roy. Soc. Lond. 140: 391-392.

MARCHANT, R. and W. L. NICHOLAS. 1974. An energy budget for the free-living nematode Pelodera (Rhabditidae). Oecologia, Berlin 16: 237-252.

MARGARIA, R. 1972. The sources of muscular energy. Sci. American 226(3,March): 84-91).

MARSH, O. C. 1878. Principal characters of American Jurassic dinosaurs. Part I. Amer. J. Sci. 116: 411-416.

_____. 1880a. Principal characters of American Jurassic dinosaurs. Part III. Amer. J. Sci. 119: 253-259.

_____. 1880b. Odontornithes: a monograph of the extinct toothed birds of North America. Rept. U. S. Geol. Explor. 40th Parallel 7: 1-201.

_____. 1886. Dinocerata. U. S. Geol. Surv., Monogr. 10: 1-243.

MATTHEW, W. D. 1937. Paleocene faunas of the San Juan Basin, New Mexico. Trans. Amer. Phil. Soc., n.s. 30: 1-510.

MAY, M. L. 1976. Thermoregulation and adaptation to temperature in dragonflies (Odonata: Anisoptera). Ecol. Monogr. 46: 1-32.

MAYR, E. 1963. Animal species and evolution. Harvard Univ. Press, Cambridge, Massachusetts. 797 p.

_____. 1970. Populations, species, and evolution. Harvard Univ. Press, Cambridge, Massachusetts. 453 p.

MAYR, F. X. 1973. Ein neuer Archaeopteryx-Fund. Paleont. Zeitschr. 47: 17-24.

McALESTER, A. L. 1970. Animal extinctions, oxygen consumption and atmospheric history. J. Paleont. 44: 405-409.

McGINNIS, S. M. and L. L. DICKSON. 1967. Thermoregulation in the desert iguana, Dipsosaurus dorsalis. Science 156: 1757-1759.

McLEAN, D. M. 1978. A terminal Mesozoic "greenhouse": lessons from the past. Science 201: 401-406.

McMAHON, T. 1973. Size and shape in biology. Science 179: 1201-1204.

_____. 1975. Allometry and biomechanics: limb bones in adult ungulates. Amer. Nat. 109: 547-563.

McNAB, B. K. 1969. The economics of temperature regulation in neotropical bats. Comp. Biochem. Physiol. 31: 227-268.

_____. 1970. Body weight and the energetics of temperature regulation. J. Exp. Biol. 53: 329-348.

_____. 1971. On the ecological significance of Bergmann's Rule. Ecology 52: 845-854.

_____. 1974. The energetics of endotherms. Ohio J. Sci. 74: 370-380.

_____. 1978. The evolution of endothermy in the phylogeny of mammals. Amer. Nat. 112: 1-21.

_____ and W. AUFFENBERG. 1976. The effect of large body size on the temperature regulation of the Komodo dragon, Varanus komodoensis. Comp. Biochem. Physiol. 55A: 345-350.

MECH, L. D. 1977. Wolf-pack buffer zones as prey reservoirs. Science 198: 320-321.

MEINERTZHAGEN, R. 1938. Some weights and measurements of large mammals. Proc. zool. Soc. Lond., ser. A 108: 433-439.

MENHINICK, E. F. 1967. Structure, stability and energy flow in plants and arthropods in a Sericea lespedeza stand. Ecol. Monogr. 37: 255-272.

MERRITT, D. A. 1972. Edentate immobilization at Lincoln Park Zoo, Chicago. Zool. Soc. Lond., Internat. Zoo Yearbook 12: 218-220.

_____. 1974. A further note on the immobilization of sloths. Zool. Soc. Lond., Internat. Zoo Yearbook 14: 160-161.

MINTON, S. A. and M. R. MINTON. 1973. Giant reptiles. Charles Scribner's, New York. 345 p.

MOBERLY, W. R. 1968. The metabolic responses of the common iguana, Iguana iguana, to activity under restraint. Comp. Biochem. Physiol. 27: 1-20.

MONTGOMERY, S. D., J. B. WHELAN and H. S. MOSBY. 1975. Bioenergetics of a woodlot gray squirrel population. J. Wildl. Manage. 39: 709-717.

MOODIE, R. L. 1921. Status of our knowledge of Mesozoic pathology. Bull. Geol. Soc. Amer. 32: 321-326.

_____. 1923. Paleopathology. Univ. Illinois Press, Urbana. 567 p.

_____. 1926. Studies in paleopathology. XIII. The elements of the Haversian system in normal and patho-logical structures among fossil vertebrates. Biol. Gen. 2: 63-95.

_____. 1928. The histological nature of ossified tend-ons found in dinosaurs. Amer. Mus. Novitates 311: 1-15.

MORGAREIDGE, K. R. and F. N. WHITE. 1969. Cutaneous vascular changes during heating and cooling in the Galapagos marine iguana. Nature, Lond. 223: 587-591.

MORRIS, P. A. 1970. A method for determining absolute age in the hedgehog. J. Zool., Lond. 161: 277-281.

MORRISON, P. R., M. PIERCE and F. A. RYSER. 1957. Food consumption and body weight in the masked and short-tail shrews. Amer. Midl. Nat. 57: 493-500.

MOULDER, B. C. and D. E. REICHLE. 1972. Significance of spider predation in the energy dynamics of forest-floor arthropod communities. Ecol. Monogr. 42: 473-498.

MOYNIHAN, M. 1971. Successes and failures of tropical mammals and birds. Amer. Nat. 105: 371-383.

MROSOVSKY, N. and P. C. H. PRITCHARD. 1971. Body temperatures of Dermochelys coriacea and other sea turtles. Copeia 1971: 624-631.

MUELLER, C. F. 1970. Energy utilization in the lizards Sceloporus graciosus and S. occidentalis. J. Herpetology 4: 131-134.

MUTH, A. 1977. Thermoregulatory postures and orientation to the sun: a mechanistic evaluation for the zebra-tailed lizard, Callisaurus draconoides. Copeia 1977: 710-720.

MYRCHA, A. 1975. Bioenergetics of an experimental population and individual laboratory mice. Acta Theriol. 20: 175-226.

MYRES, B. C. and H. M. EELS. 1968. Thermal aggregation in Boa constrictor. Herpetologica 24: 61-66.

NEILL, W. H. and E. D. STEVENS; F. G. CAREY and K. D. LAWSON; N. MROSOVSKY and W. FRAIR. 1974. Thermal inertia versus thermoregulation in "warm" turtles and tunas. Science 184: 1008-1010.

NEILL, W. T. 1971. The last of the ruling reptiles; alligators, crocodiles and their kin. Columbia Univ. Press, New York. 486 p.

NEWELL, N. D. 1949. Phyletic size increase, an important trend illustrated by fossil invertebrates. Evolution 3: 103-123.

NEWTON, E. T. 1888. On the skull, brain, and auditory organ of a new species of pterosaurian (Scaphognathus purdoni), from the Upper Lias near Whitby, Yorkshire. Phil. Trans. roy. Soc. Lond. B 179: 503-537.

NOBLE, G. K. 1924. Contributions to the herpetology of the Belgian Congo based on the collection of the American Museum Congo Expedition, 1909-1915. Part III. Amphibia. Bull. Amer. Mus. Nat. Hist. 49: 147-347.

NOPCSA, Fr. von and E. HEIDSIECK. 1933. On the histology of the ribs in immature and half-grown trachodont dinosaurs. Proc. zool. Soc. Lond. 1: 221-226.

_____. 1934. Über eine pachyostotische Rippe aus der Kreide Rügens. Acta zool., Stockholm 15: 431-455.

NORRIS, G. 1976. Phytoplankton changes near the Cretaceous-Tertiary boundary. Syllogeus, Nat. Mus. nat. Sci. Canada 12: 51-57.

NORRIS, K. S. 1967. Color adaptation in desert reptiles and its thermal relationships. In: W. W. Milstead (ed.), Lizard ecology: a symposium, pp. 162-229. Univ. Missouri Press.

_____ and J. L. KAVENAU. 1966. The burrowing of the western shovel-nosed snake, Chionactis occipitalis Hallowell, and the undersand environment. Copeia 1966: 650-664.

NORTHCUTT, R. G. 1977. Elasmobranch central nervous system organization and its possible evolutionary significance. Amer. Zool. 17: 411-429.

ODUM, E. P. 1971. Fundamentals of ecology, third edition. W. B. Saunders, Philadelphia. 574 p.

_____, C. E. CONNELL and L. B. DAVENPORT. 1962. Population energy flow of three primary consumer components of old-field ecosystems. Ecology 43: 88-96.

ODUM, H. T. and E. P. ODUM. 1955. Trophic structure and productivity on Eniwetok Atoll. Ecol. Monogr. 25: 291-320.

OHMART, R. D. and R. C. LASIEWSKI. 1971. Roadrunners: energy conservation by hypothermia and absorption of sunlight. Science 172: 67-69.

OHTAISHI, N., N. HACHIYA and Y. SHIBATA. 1976. Age determination of the hare from annual layers in the mandibular bone. Acta Theriologica 21: 168-171.

OLSON, E. C. 1944. Origin of mammals based upon the cranial morphology of the therapsid suborders. Geol. Soc. Amer., Spec. Pap. 55: 1-136.

_____. 1959. The evolution of mammalian characters. Evolution 13: 344-353.

_____. 1962. Late Permian terrestrial vertebrates, U. S. A. and U. S. S. R. Trans. Am. Phil. Soc. 52: 1-244.

_____. 1966. Community evolution and the origin of mammals. Ecology 47: 291-302.

_____. 1971. Vertebrate paleozoology. Wiley-Interscience, New York. 839 p.

_____. 1974. On the source of the therapsids. Ann. S. Afr. Mus. 64: 27-46.

_____. 1975. Permo-Carboniferous paleoecology and morphotypic series. Amer. Zool. 15: 371-389.

_____. 1976a. Rates of evolution of the nervous system and behavior. In: R. B. Masterton, W. Hodos and H. J. Jerison (eds.), Evolution, brain and behavior: persistent problems, pp. 47-77. Lawrence Erlbaum Assoc., Publ., Hillsdale, New Jersey.

_____. 1976b. The exploitation of land by early tetrapods. In: A. d'A. Bellairs and C. B. Cox (eds.), Morphology and biology of reptiles. Linn. Soc. Lond., Symp. 3: 1-30. Academic Press, London.

_____ and P. P. VAUGHN. 1970. The changes of terrestrial vertebrates and climates during the Permian of North America. Forma et Functio 3: 113-138.

OSBORN, H. F.   1912. Crania of Tyrannosaurus and
   Allosaurus. Mem. Amer. Mus. Nat. Hist. (n.s.)
   1(1): 1-30.
_____. 1917. Skeletal adaptations of Ornitholestes,
   Struthiomimus, Tyrannosaurus. Bull. Amer. Mus. Nat.
   Hist. 35: 733-771.
_____. 1923. The extinct giant rhinoceros
   Baluchitherium of western and central Asia. Natural
   History 23: 209-228.
_____. 1924. Psittacosaurus and Protiguanodon: two
   Lower Cretaceous iguanodonts from Mongolia. Amer. Mus.
   Novitates 127: 1-16.
_____ and C. C. MOOK. 1921. Camarasaurus, Amphicoelias,
   and other sauropods of Cope. Mem. Amer. Mus. Nat. Hist.,
   n.s. 3: 247-387.
OSMÓLSKA, H. 1976. New light on the skull anatomy and
   systemic position of Oviraptor. Nature, Lond.
   262: 683-684.
OSTROM, J. H. 1961. Cranial morphology of the
   hadrosaurian dinosaurs of North America. Bull. Amer.
   Mus. Nat. Hist. 122: 33-186.
_____. 1964. A reconsideration of the paleoecology
   of hadrosaurian dinosaurs. Amer. J. Sci. 262: 975-997.
_____. 1966. Functional morphology and evolution of
   the ceratopsian dinosaurs. Evolution 20: 290-308.
_____. 1969. Osteology of Deinonychus antirrhopus,
   an unusual theropod from the lower Cretaceous of
   Montana. Bull. Peabody Mus. Nat. Hist. Yale 30: 1-165.
_____. 1970. Terrestrial vertebrates as indicators of
   Mesozoic climates. North Am. Paleont. Convention,
   Chicago, 1969. Proc. D: 347-376.
_____. 1972. Were some dinosaurs gregarious?
   Palaeogeogr. Palaeoclimatol. Palaeoecol. 11: 287-301.
_____. 1973. The ancestry of birds. Nature, Lond.
   242: 136.
_____. 1974a. Archaeopteryx and the origin of flight.
   Quart. Rev. Biol. 49: 27-47.
_____. 1974b. Reply to "Dinosaurs as reptiles".
   Evolution 28: 491-493.
_____. 1975a. The origin of birds. Ann. Rev. Earth
   Planet. Sci. 3: 55-77.
_____. 1975b. On the origin of Archaeopteryx and the
   ancestry of birds. Centre Nat. Recherche Scient.
   218: 519-532.
_____. 1976. Archaeopteryx and the origin of birds.
   Biol. Jour. Linn. Soc. Lond. 8: 91-182.
_____. 1978a. A new look at dinosaurs. National
   Geographic 154(2): 152-185.
_____. 1978b. The osteology of Compsognathus longpipes
   Wagner. Zitteliana, Abh. Bayerischen Staat. f. Paläont.
   Hist. Geol. 4: 73-118.

OTIS, A. B.   1964.   Quantitative relationships in steady-
state gas exchange. In: W. O. Fenn and H. Rahn (eds.),
Handbook of physiology, section 3, Respiration
1: 681-698. American Physiol. Soc., Washington, D.C.
OWEN, R.   1842.   Report on British fossil reptiles. Part II.
British Ass. adv. Sci., Rept. 11th meeting, Plymouth,
1841, p. 60-204.
_____.   1859a.   Monograph of the fossil Reptilia of the
Wealden and Purbeck formations. Suppl. II. Crocodilia
(Streptospondylus, etc. Wealden). Monogr. Palaeontogr.
Soc. Lond. 11: 20-44.
_____.   1859b.   On the orders of fossil and recent
Reptilia, and their distribution in time. British Ass.
adv. Sci., Rept. 29th meeting, p. 153-166.
_____.   1859c.   Description of some remains of a
gigantic land-lizard (Megalania (Varanus) prisca Ow.)
from Australia. Phil. Trans. roy. Soc. Lond.
149: 43-48.
_____.   1881.   Description of some remains of the
gigantic land-lizard Megalania prisca (Owen) from
Australia. Phil. Trans. roy. Soc. Lond. 171: 1037-1050.
_____.   1884.   Evidence of a large extinct lizard
(Notiosaurus dentatus Owen) from Pleistocene deposits,
New South Wales, Australia. Phil. Trans. roy. Soc.
Lond. 175: 249-251.
_____.   1886a.   Description of fossil remains of two
species of a megalanian genus (Meiolania) from "Lord
Howe's Island". Phil. Trans. roy. Soc. Lond.
177: 471-480.
_____.   1886b.   Description of fossil remains,
including foot-bones, of Megalania prisca. Phil. Trans.
roy. Soc. Lond. 177: 327-330.
OWENS, D. W. and C. L. RALPH.   1978.   The pineal paraphyseal
complex of sea turtles. I. Light microscopic description.
J. Morphology 158: 169-180.
PACKARD, G. C.   1966.   The influence of ambient temperature
and aridity on modes of reproduction and excretion of
amniote vertebrates. Amer. Nat. 100: 667-682.
_____ and M. J. PACKARD.   1972.   Photic exposure of the
lizard Callisaurus draconoides following shielding of
the parietal eye. Copeia 1972: 695-701.
_____, C. R. TRACY and J. J. ROTH.   1977.   The physio-
logical ecology of reptilian eggs and embryos and the
evolution of viviparity within the class Reptilia.
Biol. Rev. 52: 71-105.
PARER, J. T. and J. METCALFE.   1967a.   Respiratory studies
of monotremes II. Blood of the echidna (Tachyglossus
setosus). Respir. Physiol. 3: 143-150.
_____.   1967b.   Respiratory studies of monotremes III.
Blood gas transport and hemodynamics in the

unanesthetized echidna. Respir. Physiol. 3: 151-159.

PASCAL, M. and J. CASTANET. 1978. Méthodes de détermination de l'âge chez le chat Haret des Îles Kerguelen. Terre et Vie 32: 529-555.

PAUL, G. 1979. Saurpod energetics: mouth size and feeding rates. Nature, Lond. (in press).

PAWLICKI, R. 1975. Studies of the fossil dinosaur bone in the scanning electron microscope. Z. mikrosk. anat. Forsch. (Leipzig) 89: 393-398.

_____. 1976. Preparation of fossil bone specimens for scanning electron microscopy. Stain. Technol. 51: 147-152.

_____. 1977. Histochemical reactions for mucopolysaccharides in the dinosaur bone. Studies on Epon- and metacrylate-embedded semithin sections as well as on isolated osteocytes and ground sections of bone. Acta histochem. 58: 75-78.

_____. 1978. Morphological differentiation of the fossil dinosaur bone cell. Light transmission, electron and scanning electron microscopic studies. Acta Anatomica 100: 411-418.

_____, A. KORBEL and H. KUBIAK. 1966. Cells, collagen fibrils and vessels in dinosaur bone. Nature, Lond. 211: 655-657.

PEABODY, F. E. 1958. A Kansas drouth recorded in growth zones of a bullsnake. Copeia 1958: 91-94.

_____. 1961. Annual growth zones in living and fossil vertebrates. J. Morph. 108: 11-62.

PEARSON, O. P. 1948. Metabolism of small mammals, with remarks on the lower limit of mammalian size. Science 108: 44.

_____. 1954. Habits of the lizard, Liolaemus multiformis multiformis, at high altitudes in southern Peru. Copeia 1954: 111-116.

_____. 1960. Torpidity in birds. Bull. Mus. Comp. Zool., Harvard 124: 93-103.

_____ and D. F. BRADFORD. 1976. Thermoregulation of lizards and toads at high altitudes in Peru. Copeia 1976: 155-170.

PETERSEN, H. 1930. Die Organe des Skelettsystems. In: W. H. W. von Möllendorf (ed.), Handbuch der mikroskopischen Anatomie des Menschen, v. II(2), p. 521-676. Springer, Berlin.

PIANKA, E. R. 1969. Habitat specificity, speciation, and species density in Australian desert lizards. Ecology 50: 498-502.

PIENAAR, U. de V. 1969. Predator-prey relationships among the larger mammals of the Kruger National Park. Koedoe 12: 108-176.

PLATEL, R. 1974. Poids encéphalique et indice
d'encéphalisation chez les reptiles sauriens.
Zool. Anz. 192: 332-382.
_____. 1975. Nouvelles données sur l'encéphalisation
des reptiles squamates. Z. Zool. Syst. Evolutionsforsch.
13: 161-184.

POOLEY, A. C. 1969. The burrowing behavior of crocodiles.
Lammergeyer 10: 60-63.

PORTER, K. 1972. Herpetology. W. B. Saunders,
Philadelphia. 524 p.

PORTER, W. P. and D. M. GATES. 1969. Thermodynamic
equilibria of animals with environment. Ecol. Monogr.
39: 227-244.

PORTER, W. P. and C. R. TRACY. 1974. Modeling the effects
of temperature changes on the ecology of the garter
snake and leopard frog. In: J. W. Gibbons and
R. R. Sharitz (eds.), Thermal ecology, pp. 594-609.
U. S. Atomic Energy Commission, Conf. 730505.

POUGH, F. H. 1969. The morphology of undersand
respiration in reptiles. Herpetologica 25: 216-223.
_____. 1973. Lizard energetics and diet. Ecology
54: 837-844.

PRITCHARD, J. J. 1956. General anatomy and histology of
bone. In G. H. Bourne (ed.), The biochemistry and
physiology of bone, pp. 1-25. Academic Press, London
and New York.

PROSSER, C. L. and F. A. BROWN. 1962. Comparative animal
physiology. W. B. Saunders, Philadelphia. 688 p.

QUAY, W. B. 1978. Quantitative morphology and environmental responses of the pineal gland in the collared
lemming (Dicrostonyx groenlandicus). Amer. J. Anat.
153: 545-562.

QUEKETT, J. T. 1855. Descriptive and illustrated
catalogue of the histological series contained in the
Museum of the Royal College of Surgeons. II. Structure
of the skeleton of vertebrate animals. London. 248 p.
_____. 1869. On the intimate structure of bone as
composing the skeleton in the four great classes of
animals, etc. Trans. Microscop. Soc. Lond. 2: 46-58.

RAATH, M. A. 1969. A new coelurosaurian dinosaur from
the Forest Sandstone of Rhodesia. Arnoldia 4(28): 1-25.
_____. 1970. A new Upper Karroo dinosaur fossil
locality on the lower Angwa River, Sipolilo District,
Rhodesia. Arnoldia 4(35): 1-10.
_____. 1972. Fossil vertebrate studies in Rhodesia:
a new dinosaur (Reptilia: Saurischia) from the Trias-
Jurassic boundary. Arnoldia 5(30): 1-37.

RADINSKY, L. B. 1978. Evolution of brain size in carnivores and ungulates. Amer. Nat. 112: 815-831.

RALPH, C. L. 1975a. The pineal complex: a retrospective view. In: E. J. W. Barrington (ed.), Trends in comparative endocrinology. Amer. Zool. 15(Suppl. 1): 105-116.

_____. 1975b. The pineal gland and geographical distribution of animals. Int. J. Biometeor. 19: 289-303.

_____, B. T. FIRTH and J. S. TURNER. 1979. The role of the pineal body in ectotherm thermoregulation. Amer. Zool. 19: 273-293.

RAND, A. S. 1968. A nesting aggregation of iguanas. Copeia 1968: 552-561.

REGAL, P. J. 1966. Thermophilic response following feeding in certain reptiles. Copeia 1966: 588-590.

_____. 1967. Voluntary hypothermia in reptiles. Science 155: 1551-1553.

_____. 1975. The evolutionary origin of feathers. Quart. Rev. Biol. 50: 35-66.

_____. 1978. Behavioral differences between reptiles and mammals: an analysis of activity and mental capabilities. In: N. Greenberg and P. D. MacLean (eds.), Behavior and neurology of lizards, pp. 183-202. N.I.M.H. Publ., Rockville, Maryland.

REISZ, R. R. 1977. Petrolacosaurus, the oldest known diapsid reptile. Science 196: 1091-1093.

REITER, R. J. 1977. The Pineal. Ann. Research Rev. 2. Eden Press, Montreal. 184 p.

RENSCH, B. 1948. Histological changes correlated with evolutionary changes of body size. Evolution 2: 218-230.

RICHARDS, S. A. 1970. The biology and comparative physiology of thermal panting. Biol. Rev. 45: 223-264.

RICKLEFS, R. E. 1973. Ecology. Chiron Press, Newton, Mass. and Portland, Oregon. 861 p.

RICQLÈS, A. J. de 1968a. Quelques observations paléohistologiques sur le dinosaurien sauropode Bothriospondylus. Ann. Univ. Madagascar 6: 157-209.

_____. 1968b. Recherches paléohistologiques sur les os longs des tétrapodes. I. Origine du tissue osseux plexiforme des dinosaurien sauropodes. Ann. Paléont. (Vertébrés) 54: 133-145.

_____. 1969. L'histologie osseuse envisagée comme indicateur de la physiologie thermique chez les tétrapodes fossiles. C. R. hebd. Séanc. Acad. Sci. Paris D 268: 782-785.

_____. 1972. Vers une histoire de la physiologie thermique: les données histologiques et leur interprétation fonctionelle. C. R. hebd. Séanc. Acad. Sci. Paris D 275: 1745-1749.

_____. 1974. Evolution of endothermy: histological evidence. Evolutionary Theory 1: 51-80.

_____. 1975. Recherches paléohistologiques sur les os longs des tétrapodes. VII. Sur la classification, la signification fonctionelle et l'histoire des tissus osseux des tétrapodes. Première partie: structures. Ann. Paléont. (Vertébrés) 61: 51-129.

_____. 1976. On bone histology of fossil and living reptiles, with comments on its functional and evolutionary significance. In: A. d'A. Bellairs and C. B. Cox (eds.), Morphology and biology of reptiles, Linn. Soc. Lond., Symp. 3: 123-150. Academic Press, London.

_____. 1976b. Recherches paléohistologiques sur les os longs des tétrapodes. VII. Idem. Deuxième partie: fonctions. Ann. Paléont. (Vertébrés) 62: 71-126.

_____. 1977a. Recherches paléohistologiques sur les os longs des tétrapodes. VII. Idem. Deuxième partie: fonctions (suite). Ann. Paléont. (Vertébrés) 63: 33-56.

_____. 1977b. Recherches paléohistologiques sur les os longs des tétrapodes. VII. Idem. Deuxième partie: fonctions (suite et fin). Ann. Paléont. (Vertébrés) 63: 133-160.

_____. 1978a. Recherches paléohistologiques sur les os longs des tétrapodes. VII. Idem. Troisième partie: évolution. Ann. Paléont. (Vertébrés) 64: 85-111.

_____. 1978b. Recherches paléohistologiques sur les os longs des tétrapodes. VII. Idem. Troisième partie: évolution (fin). Ann. Paléont. (Vertébrés) 64: 153-176.

ROBERTS, W. W., R. D. MOONEY and J. R. MARTIN. 1974. Thermoregulatory behaviors of laboratory rodents. J. Comp. Physiol. Psychol. 86: 693-699.

RODBARD, S. 1949. On the dorsal sail of Dimetrodon. Copeia 1949: 244.

_____, F. SAMSON and D. FERGUSON. 1950. Thermosensitivity of the turtle brain as manifest by blood pressure changes. Amer. J. Physiol. 160: 402-408.

ROMER, A. S. 1927. Notes on the Permo-Carboniferous reptile Dimetrodon. J. Geol. 35: 673-689.

_____. 1948. Relative growth in pelycosaurian reptiles. In: A. L. DuToit (ed.), Robert Broom commemorative volume, pp. 45-55. Spec. Publ. Roy. Soc. So. Africa.

_____. 1958. Phylogeny and behavior with special reference to vertebrate evolution. In: A. Roe and G. G. Simpson (eds.), Behavior and evolution, pp. 48-75. Yale Univ. Press, New Haven.

_____. 1966. Vertebrate paleontology, third edition. Univ. Chicago Press, Chicago. 468 p.

_____. 1968. Notes and comments on vertebrate paleontology. Chicago Univ. Press, Chicago. 304 p.

ROTH, J. J. and C. L. RALPH. 1976a. Body temperature of the lizard Anolis carolinensis: effect of parietalectomy. J. Exp. Zool. 198: 17-28.

_____. 1976b. Thermal and photic preferences in intact and parietalectomized Anolis carolinensis. Behav. Biol. 19: 341-348.

ROUSE, G. E. and S. K. SRIVASTAVA. 1972. Palynological zonation of Cretaceous and Early Tertiary rocks of the Bonnet Plume Formation, northeastern Yukon, Canada. Can. J. Earth Sci. 9: 1163-1179.

ROY, J. R. and D. A. RUSSELL. 1976. Introduction: Cretaceous-Tertiary extinctions and possible terrestrial and extraterrestrial causes. Syllogeus, Nat. Mus. nat. Sci. Canada 12: 5-9.

RUDWICK, M. J. S. 1964. The inference of function from structure in fossils. Brit. J. Phil. Sci. 15: 27-40.

RUSSELL, D. A. 1967. A census of dinosaur specimens collected in western Canada. Natl. Mus. Can., Nat. Hist. Pap. 36: 1-13.

_____. 1969. A new specimen of Stenonychosaurus from the Oldman Formation (Cretaceous) of Alberta. Can. J. Earth Sci. 6: 595-612.

_____. 1970a. A skeletal reconstruction of Leptoceratops gracilis from the upper Edmonton Formation (Cretaceous) of Alberta. Can. J. Earth Sci. 7: 181-184.

_____. 1970b. Tyrannosaurs from the Late Cretaceous of Western Canada. Nat. Mus. Canada, Publ. Paleont. 1: 1-34.

_____. 1972. Ostrich dinosaurs from the Late Cretaceous of western Canada. Can. J. Earth Sci. 9: 375-402.

_____. 1973. The environments of Canadian dinosaurs. Canad. Geog. Jour. 87: 4-11.

_____. 1976. The biotic crisis at the end of the Cretaceous Period. Syllogeus, Nat. Mus. nat. Sci. Canada 12: 11-23.

_____ and P. BELAND. 1976. Running dinosaurs. Nature, Lond. 264: 486.

RUSSELL, L. S. 1965. Body temperature of dinosaurs and its relationships to their extinction. J. Paleont. 39: 497-501.

SACHS, R. 1967. Live-weights and body measurements of Serengeti game animals. E. Afr. Wildl. J. 5: 24-36.

SANTA LUCA, A. P., A. W. CROMPTON, and A. J. CHARIG. 1976. A complete skeleton of the Late Triassic ornithischian Heterodontosaurus tucki. Nature, Lond. 264: 324-328.

SATINOFF, E. 1974. Neural control of thermoregulatory responses. In: L. V. DiCara (ed.), Limbic and autonomic systems research, pp. 41-83. Plenum Press, New York.

_____. 1978. Neural organization and evolution of thermal regulation in mammals. Science 201: 16-22.

SCHALL, J. J. 1977. Thermal ecology of five sympatric
    species of Cnemidophorus (Sauria: Teiidae).
    Herpetologica 33: 261-272.
SCHALLER, G. B. 1967. The deer and the tiger. Univ.
    Chicago Press, Chicago. 370 p.
_____. 1968. Hunting behaviour of the cheetah in the
    Serengeti National Park, Tanzania. East Afr. Wildl. J.
    6: 95-100.
SCHMIDT. K. P. 1919. Contributions to the herpetology
    of the Belgian Congo based on the collection of the
    American Museum Congo Expedition, 1909-1915. Part I.
    Turtles, crocodiles, lizards and chamaeleons.
    Bull. Amer. Mus. Nat. Hist. 39: 385-602.
_____. 1923. Contributions to the herpetology of the
    Belgian Congo based on the collection of the American
    Congo Expedition, 1909-1915. Part II. Snakes.
    Bull. Amer. Mus. Nat. Hist. 49: 1-146.
SCHMIDT-NIELSEN, K. 1964. Desert animals; physiological
    problems of heat and water. Oxford Univ. Press,
    Oxford. 277 p.
_____. 1975. Animal physiology; adaptation and
    environment. Cambridge Univ. Press, New York. 699 p.
_____, T. J. DAWSON and E. C. CRAWFORD. 1966.
    Temperature regulation in the echidna (Tachyglossus
    aculeatus). J. Cell. Physiol. 67: 63-72.
SCHOLANDER, P. F. 1955. Evolution of climatic adaptations
    in homeotherms. Evolution 9: 15-26.
_____. 1967. Mammalian hibernation. In: K. C. Fisher
    et al. (eds.), Mammalian hibernation III, pp. 97-109.
    Proc. Internat. Symp. on natural mammalian hibernation,
    Toronto, 1965. American Elsevier, New York.
SCHUH, F. 1951. Das Warmblüterproblem in der Paläontologie.
    Paläont. Z. 24: 194-200.
SEITZ, A. L. 1907. Vergleichenden Studien über den
    mikroskopischen Knochenbau fossiler und rezenter
    Reptilien. Nova Acta abh. Kaiser Leop. Carol. Deutsch.
    Akad. Naturforsch. 37: 230-370.
SEYMOUR, R. S. 1976. Dinosaurs, endothermy and blood
    pressure. Nature, Lond. 262: 207-208.
SHACKLETON, N. J. and J. P. KENNETT. 1975. Paleotempera-
    ture history of the Cenozoic and the initiation of
    Antarctic glaciation: oxygen and carbon isotope
    analyses in DSDP sites 277, 279 and 281. In:
    J. P. Kennett, R. E. Houtz, et al. (eds.), Initial Rep.
    Deep Sea Drilling Project 29: 743-755.
SHAROV, A. G. 1970. An unusual reptile from the Lower
    Triassic of Fergana. (In Russian). Paleont. Zh.
    1: 127-130.

_____. 1971. New flying reptiles from the Mesozoic deposits of Kazakhstan and Kirgizia. (In Russian). Trudy. Paleont. Inst. Akad. Nauk S.S.S.R. 130: 104-113.

SHOTWELL, J. A. 1955. An approach to the paleoecology of mammals. Ecology 36: 327-337.

SIKES, S. K. 1971. The natural history of the African elephant. Weidenfeld and Nicolson, London. 397 p.

SIMPSON, G. G. 1964. Species density of North American Recent mammals. Syst. Zool. 13: 57-73.

SLOAN, R. E. 1970. Cretaceous and Paleocene terrestrial communities of western North America. North Am. Paleont. Convention, Chicago, 1969. Proc. E: 427-453.

SMITH, A. G., J. C. BRIDEN and G. E. DREWRY. 1973. Phanerozoic world maps. In: N. F. Hughes (ed.), Organisms and continents through time. Palaeont. Ass., Spec. Pap. Palaeont. 12: 1-42.

SONDAAR, P. Y. 1977. Insularity and its effect on mammalian evolution. In: M. K. Hecht, P. C. Goody and B. M. Hecht (eds.), Major patterns in vertebrate evolution, pp. 671-707. Plenum Press, New York.

SOUTH, F. E., J. P. HANNON, J. R. WILLIS, E. T. PENGELLEY and N. R. ALPERT (eds.). 1972. Hibernation and hypothermia, perspectives and challenges. Symp. held at Snow-Mass-at-Aspen, Colorado, 1971. Elsevier, Amsterdam and New York. 765 p.

SPAETH, C., J. HOEFS and U. VETTER. 1971. Some aspects of isotopic composition of belemnites and related paleotemperatures. Bull. Geol. Soc. Amer. 82: 3139-3150.

SPINAGE, C. A. 1973. A review of the age determination of mammals by means of teeth, with especial reference to Africa. E. Afr. Wildl. J. 11: 165-187.

SPOTILA, J. R. and D. M. GATES. 1975. Body size, insulation, and optimum body temperature of homeotherms. In: D. M. Gates and R. B. Schmerl (eds.), Perspectives of biophysical ecology, pp. 291-301. Springer-Verlag, New York.

SPOTILA, J. R., P. W. LOMMEN, G. S. BAKKEN and D. M. GATES. 1973. A mathematical model for body temperatures of large reptiles: implications for dinosaur ecology. Amer. Nat. 107: 391-404.

SPOTILA, J. R., O. H. SOULE and D. M. GATES. 1972. Biophysical ecology of the alligator - heat energy budgets and climate spaces. Ecology 53: 1094-1102.

SPOTILA, J. R., K. M. TERPIN and P. DODSON. 1977. Mouth gaping as an effective thermoregulatory device in alligators. Nature 265: 235-236.

SPRUNT, A. and H. S. ZIM. 1961. Gamebirds: a guide to North American species and their habits. Golden Press, New York. 160 p.

STAHL, W. R.   1967.   Scaling of respiratory variables in mammals. J. Appl. Physiol. 22: 453-460.

STANLEY, S. M.   1973. An explanation for Cope's rule. Evolution 27: 1-26.

STEBBINS, R. C.   1958. An experimental study of the "third eye" of the tuatara. Copeia 1958: 183-190.

————. 1960. Effects of the pinealectomy in the western fence lizard, Sceloporus occidentalis. Copeia 1960: 276-283.

————. 1963. Activity changes in the striped plateau lizard, with evidence on influence of the parietal eye. Copeia 1963: 681-691.

————. 1970. The effect of pinealectomy on testicular activity and exposure to light in the desert night lizard (Xantusia vigilis). Copeia 1970: 261-270.

———— and N. W. COHEN.   1973. The effect of parietalectomy on the thyroid and gonads in free-living western fence lizards, Sceloporus occidentalis. Copeia 1973: 662-668.

———— and R. M. EAKIN.   1958. The role of the "third eye" in reptilian behavior. Amer. Mus. Novitates 1870: 1-40.

STERNBERG, C. M.   1932. A new fossil crocodile from Saskatchewan. Canadian Field-Nat. 46: 128-133.

STEVENS, E. D.   1973. The evolution of endothermy. J. Theoret. Biol. 38: 597-611.

STEYN, W.   1961. Some epithalambic organs, the subcommissural organ, and their possible relation to vertebrate emergence on dry land. S. Afr. J. Sci. 57: 283.

STONES, R. C. and J. E. WIEBERS.   1965. A review of temperature regulation in bats (Chiroptera). Amer. Midl. Nat. 74: 155-177.

STREL'NIKOV, I. D.   1944. Importance of solar radiation in the ecology of high mountain reptiles. Zool. Zh. S.S.S.R. 23: 250-257.

————. 1959. On thermoregulation among living reptiles and on likely thermal regimes among Mesozoic reptiles. (In Russian). In: Problems in paleobiology and biostratigraphy, Proc. 2nd Session Sov. Paleont. Soc., pp. 129-144.

STUDNICKA, F. K.   1905. Die Parietalorgane. In: A. Oppel (ed.), Lehrbuch der vergleichenden mikroskopischen Anatomie der Wirbelthiere, part 5. Fischer, Jena.

SWAN, H.   1974. Thermoregulation and bioenergetics: patterns for vertebrate survival. American Elsevier, New York.   430 p.

SWINTON, W. E. 1936. Notes on the osteology of Hypsilophodon, and on the family Hypsilophodontidae. Proc. Zool. Soc. Lond. 1936: 555-578.

_____. 1958. Dinosaur brains. New Scientist 4: 707-709.

_____. 1970. The dinosaurs. Wiley-Interscience, New York. 331 p.

TABER, C. A., R. F. WILKINSON and M. S. TOPPING. 1975. Age and growth of Hellbenders in the Niangua River, Missouri. Copeia 1975: 633-639.

TAPPAN, H. 1974. Molecular oxygen and evolution. In: O. Hayaishi (ed.), Molecular oxygen in biology: topics in molecular oxygen research, pp. 81-135. North-Holland Publ., Dordrecht, Holland.

TARTARINOV, L. 1967. Development of a system of labial (vibrissial) blood vessels and nerves in the theriodonts. Paleont. Jour. (transl. of Paleont. Zh. Akad. Nauk SSSR) 1: 3-17.

TAYLOR, C. R. 1966. The vascularity and possible thermoregulatory function of the horns in goats. Physiol. Zool. 39: 127-139.

_____. 1970a. Strategies of temperature regulation: effect on evaporation in East African ungulates. Amer. J. Physiol. 219: 1131-1135.

_____. 1970b. Dehydration and heat: effect on temperature regulation of East African ungulates. Amer. J. Physiol. 219: 1136-1139.

_____, R. DMI'EL, M. FADAK and K. SCHMIDT-NIELSEN. 1971. Energetic cost of running and heat balance in a large bird, the rhea. Amer. J. Physiol. 221: 597-601.

_____ and V. J. ROWNTREE. 1973a. Running on two or four legs: which consumes more energy? Science 179: 186-187.

_____ and V. J. ROWNTREE. 1973b. Temperature regulation and heat balance in running cheetahs: a strategy for sprinters? Amer. J. Physiol. 224: 848-851.

_____, K. SCHMIDT-NIELSEN and J. L. RAAB. 1970. Scaling of energetic cost of running to body size in mammals. Amer. J. Physiol. 219: 1104-1107.

TEMPLETON, J. R. 1960. Respiration and water loss at the higher temperatures in the desert iguana, Dipsosaurus dorsalis. Physiol. Zool. 33: 136-145.

_____. 1970. Reptiles. In: G. C. Whittow (ed.), Comparative physiology of thermoregulation 1: 167-221. Academic Press, New York.

TENNEY, S. M. and J. B. TENNEY. 1970. Quantitative morphology of cold-blooded lungs: Amphibia and Reptilia. Resp. Physiol. 9: 197-215.

TERPIN, K. M. 1976. Thermoregulatory adaptations and heat energy budget analyses of the American alligator, Alligator mississippiensis. M.A. dissertation, State Univ. Coll. Buffalo, New York, 57 p.

_____, P. DODSON and J. R. SPOTILA. 1978. Ketamine hydrochloried as an effective anesthetic for alligators. Copeia 1978: 147-148.

THULBORN, R. A. 1972. The postcranial skeleton of the Triassic ornithischian dinosaur Fabrosaurus australis. Palaeontology 15: 29-60.

_____. 1973. Thermoregulation in dinosaurs. Nature, Lond. 245: 51-52.

_____. 1978. Aestivation among ornithopod dinosaurs of the African Trias. Lethaia 11: 185-198.

TILNEY, F. and L. F. WARREN. 1919. The morphology and evolutional significance of the pineal body. Amer. Anat. Mem. 9: 1-258.

TRACY, C. R. 1976. Tyrannosaurs: evidence for endothermy? Amer. Nat. 110: 1105-1106.

_____. 1977. Minimum size of mammalian homeotherms: role of the thermal environment. Science 198: 1034-1035.

TREMTER, D. J. 1976. Herbivore production. In: D. H. Cushing and J. J. Walsh (eds.), The ecology of the seas, pp. 186-225. W. B. Saunders, Philadelphia.

TUCKER, V. A. 1970. Energetics of locomotion. Comp. Biochem. Physiol. 34: 841-846.

_____. 1975. The energetic cost of moving about. Amer. Scient. 63: 413-419.

TURNER, F. B., P. A. MEDICA and B. W. KOWALEWSKY. 1976. Energy utilization by a desert lizard (Uta stansburiana). U. S. Internat. Biol. Progr., Monogr. 1: 1-57. Utah State Univ. Press.

UNDERWOOD, H. 1977. Circadian organization in lizards: the role of the pineal organ. Science 195: 587-589.

UREY, H. C., H. A. LOWENSTAM, S. EPSTEIN and C. R. McKINNEY. 1951. Measurement of paleotemperatures and temperatures of the Upper Cretaceous of England, Denmark and the southeastern United States. Bull. Geol. Soc. Amer. 62: 399-416.

VAN HOOK, R. I. 1971. Energy and nutrient dynamics of spider and orthopteran populations in a grassland ecosystem. Ecol. Monogr. 41: 1-26.

VAN MIEROP, L. H. S. and S. M. BARNARD. 1976. Thermoregulation in a brooding female python, Molurus bivattatus (Serpentes: Boidae). Copeia 1976: 398-401.

VAN SOEST, R. W. M. and W. L. VAN UTRECHT. 1971. The layered structure of bones of birds as a possible indication of age. Bijdragen Dierkunde 41: 61-66.

VAN VALEN, L. and R. E. SLOAN. 1977. Ecology and the extinction of the dinosaurs. Evolutionary Theory 2: 37-64.

VAN ZOEREN, J. G. and E. M. STRICKLER. 1977. Effects of preoptic, lateral hypothalamic, or dopamine-depleting lesions on behavioral thermoregulation in rats exposed to the cold. J. Comp. Physiol. Psychol. 91: 989-999.

VARLEY, G. C. 1970. The concept of energy flow applied to a woodland community. In A. Watson (ed.), Animal populations in relation to their food resources, pp. 389-405. Blackwell Sci. Publ., Oxford and Edinburgh.

VINE, F. J. 1966. Spreading of the ocean floor; new evidence. Science 154: 1405-1415.

_____ and D. H. MATTHEWS. 1963. Magnetic anomalies over oceanic ridges. Nature, Lond. 199: 947-949.

VINEGAR, A., V. H. HUTCHISON and H. G. DOWLING. 1970. Metabolism, energetics, and thermoregulation during brooding of snakes of the genus Python (Reptilia, Bordae). Zoologica 55(2): 19-48.

VOORHIES, M. R. 1969. Taphonomy and population dynamics of an Early Pliocene vertebrate fauna, Knox County, Nebraska. Univ. Wyoming Contrib. Geol., Spec. Paper 1: 69 p.

WALKER, A. D. 1977. Evolution of the pelvis in birds and dinosaurs. In: S. M. Andrews, R. S. Miles and A. D. Walker (eds.), Problems in vertebrate evolution, Linn. Soc. Lond., Symp. 4: 319-358. Academic Press, London.

WALKER, E. P. and J. L. PARADISO (eds.). 1975. Mammals of the world, third edition. Johns Hopkins Univ. Press, Baltimore 2 vols., 1500 p.

WEATHERS, W. W. 1970. Physiological thermoregulation in the lizard Dipsosaurus dorsalis. Copeia 1970: 549-557.

_____ and K. R. MORGAREIDGE. 1971. Cutaneous vascular responses to temperature changes in the spiny-tailed iguana, Ctenosauria hemilopha. Copeia 1971: 548-551.

WEBB, G. and HEATWOLE, H. 1971. Patterns of heat distribution within the bodies of some Australian pythons. Copeia 1971: 209-220.

WEBB, G., C. R. JOHNSON and B. T. FIRTH. 1972. Heat-body temperature differences in lizards. Physiol. Zool. 45: 130-142.

WEIDENREICH, F. 1930. Das Knochengewebe. In: W. H. W. von Möllendorf (ed.), Handbuch der mikroskopischen Anatomie des Menschen, v. II(2), p. 391-520. Springer, Berlin.

WEINTRAUB, J. D. 1968. Winter behavior of the granite spiny lizard, Sceloporus orcutti Stejeneger. Copeia 1968: 708-712.

WEISS, B. and V. G. LATIES. 1961. Behavioral thermoregulation. Science 133: 1338-1344.

WELCH, W. R. and C. R. TRACY. 1977. Respiratory water loss: a predictive model. J. Theor. Biol. 65: 253-265.

WELLES, S. P. 1943. Elasmosaurid plesiosaurs with description of new material from California and Colorado. Mem. Univ. California 13: 125-254.

WELLNHOFER, P. 1977. Die Pterosaurier. Naturwissenschaften 65: 23-29.

WELTY, J. C. 1962. The life of birds. W. B. Saunders, Philadelphia. 546 p.

WHEELER, P. E. 1978. Elaborate CNS cooling structures in large dinosaurs. Nature, Lond. 275: 441-443.

WHITE, F. N. 1956. Circulation in the reptilian heart (Caiman sclerops). Anat. Rec. 125: 417-431.

_____. 1959. Circulation in the reptilian heart (Squamata). Anat. Rec. 135: 129-134.

_____. 1968. Functional anatomy of the heart of reptiles. Amer. Zool. 8: 211-219.

_____. 1969. Redistribution of cardiac output in the diving alligator. Copeia 1969: 567-570.

_____. 1970. Central vascular shunts and their control in reptiles. Federation Proceedings 29: 1149-1153.

_____. 1976. Circulation. In: C. Gans and W. R. Dawson (eds.), Biology of the Reptilia 5: 275-334. Academic Press, New York.

WHITE, T. E. 1953. A method of calculating the dietary percentage of various food utilized by aboriginal peoples. Amer. Antiquity 18: 396-398.

WHITTOW, G. C. 1966. Terminology in thermoregulation. Physiologist 9: 358-360.

_____ (ed.). 1970-73. Comparative physiology of thermoregulation. Academic Press, London and New York. 3 vols.

WIEGERT, R. G. 1964. Population energetics of meadow spittlebugs (Philaenus spumerius L.) as affected by migration and habitat. Ecol. Monogr. 34: 217-241.

_____. 1965. Energy dynamics of the grasshopper populations in old field and alfalfa field ecosystems. Oikos 16: 161-176.

_____ and F. C. EVANS. 1967. Investigation of secondary productivity of grasslands. In: K. Petrusewicz (ed.), Secondary productivity in terrestrial ecosystems; principles and methods, pp. 499-518. Proc. IBP Meeting, Jablonna, Poland, 1966. Państwowe Wydawn. Naukwose, Warszawa.

WIELAND, G. R. 1942. Too hot for the dinosaur! Science 96: 359.

WILBER, C. G. 1964. Animals in aquatic environments. In: D. B. Dill, E. F. Adolph and C. G. Wilber (eds.), Handbook of physiology: adaptation to the environment, pp. 661-682. Amer. Physiological Soc., Washington. D.C.

WILHOFT, D. C. 1958. The effect of temperature on thyroid histology and survival in the lizard, Scleroporus occidentalis. Copeia 1958: 265-276.

WILSON, K. J. and A. K. LEE. 1974. Energy expenditure of a large herbivorous lizard. Copeia 1974: 338-348.

WINDLEY, B. F. 1977. The evolving continents. John Wiley, New York. 371 p.

WITHERS, P. C. 1977. Respiration, metabolism, and heat exchange of euthermic and torpid poorwills and hummingbirds. Physiol. Zool. 50: 43-52.

WOLEDGE, R. C. 1968. The energetics of tortoise muscle. J. Physiol. 197: 685-707.

WOODBURY, A. M. and R. HARDY. 1948. Studies of the desert tortoise, Gopherus agassizi. Ecol. Monogr. 18: 145-200.

WRIGHT, B. S. 1960. Predation on big game in East Africa. J. Wildlife Manage. 24: 1-15.

WYCKOFF, R. W. G. 1971. Trace elements and organic constituents in fossil bones and teeth. North Am. Paleont. Convention, Chicago, 1969. Proc. K: 1514-1524.

_____. 1972. The biochemistry of animal fossils. Scientechnica, Bristol, England. 152 p.

YOUNG, F. N. and J. R. ZIMMERMAN. 1956. Variations in the temperature in small aquatic situations. Ecology 37: 609-611.

YOUNG, J. Z. 1962. The life of vertebrates, second edition. Oxford Univ. Press, New York. 820 p.

ZANGERL, R. 1960. The vertebrate fauna of the Selma Formation of Alabama. Part 5. An advanced chelonid sea turtle. Field Mus. Nat. Hist., Fieldiana Geol. Mem. 3: 285-312.

ZHUKOV, Ye. K. 1965. Evolution of physiological mechanisms of tonus in the vertebrates. In: J. W. S. Pringle (ed.), Essays on physiological evolution, pp. 339-349. Pergamon Press, Oxford.

Index

Italic page numbers indicate figures; page numbers followed
by "t" indicate tables.